A Probus Guide to World Markets

THE EUROPEAN OPTIONS AND FUTURES MARKETS

An Overview
and Analysis
for Money Managers
and Traders

Edited by Stuart K. McLean
Storebrand International

THE EUROPEAN BOND COMMISSION
A Standing Commission of the European
Federation of Financial Analyst Societies

PROBUS PUBLISHING COMPANY
Chicago, Illinois

Library of Congress Cataloging in Publication Data Available

ISBN 1-55738-119-4

Printed in the United States of America

2   3   4   5   6   7   8   9   0

Table of Contents

The Futures and Options Markets in Austria   67

The Futures and Options Markets in Belgium   81

Belgian Futures and Options Exchange "BELFOX"   84

The Futures and Options Markets in Denmark 101

Marché des Options Négociables de Paris
MONEP   208

The Organiastion de Marchés Financiers "OMF" -Now Renamed France Matif Automatique "FMA" 225

The Futures and Options Markets in Germany (Deutsche Terminbörse) 239

The Futures Market in Ireland   281

The Futures and Options Markets in Italy   309

The Futures and Options Markets in the Netherlands   315

Agricultural Futures Market Amsterdam (Nederlandse Liquidatiekas) - "NLK KAS"   388

The Futures and Options Markets in Norway   393

The Forwards, Futures and Options Markets in Spain   415

The Forward Market   418

The Futures & Options Markets in Sweden   449

The Futures and Options Markets
in Switzerland   491

The Futures and Options Markets in the United Kingdom   525

The International Petroleum Exchange of London Ltd. ("IPE")   587

The London International Financial Futures Exchange ("LIFFE")   667

The London Metal Exchange ("LME")   737

The London Traded Options Market   791

The London Clearing House
a division of The International Commodities
Clearing House "ICCH"   861

Taxation of Futures and Options in the
United Kingdom   873

Preface

The vigorous growth of world financial markets in recent years has been paralleled by a growing awareness of the need to diversify investments on an international scale. This international diversification raises specific problems within the European context. The juxtaposition of Latin and Anglo-Saxon origins and the historically grounded differences of each country's regulatory system, have led to a fragmenting of our continent into a variety of markets, each with its own characteristics.

The aim of the **European Federation of Financial Analysts Societies "EFFAS"**, which numbers 9,000 analysts from sixteen national societies, is to reduce these country-specific differences, rendering markets as uniform as possible so that they can be approached as a single entity. For this goal of unification to be achieved, it is essential that the difference and similarities are clearly established at the outset. The Bond Commission has undertaken this task in the fourth edition of the Guide to the European Bond Markets and this the first edition of the Guide to the European Futures and Options Markets.

This high quality reference document could not have been realized without the generous contributions of a number of experts. I would like to thank them wholeheartedly for providing us with what is unquestionably an indispensable work. We hope that the considerable time and effort entailed in collecting the information for this reference work will advance "EFFAS" in its path towards a single uniform market and that, by identifying the differences existing in Europe's financial markets, it will contribute to eliminating them.

From the investor point of view, we hope that this progressive move towards unification will be reflected in increasingly homogeneous and liquid markets in Europe. The road is a long one and there is still much left to do, bond and futures markets are not the only ones in need of uniformity.

Our aim will have been achieved if the information contained in these pages help the reader improve the quality of his fund management and give him a wider knowledge of the investment opportunities offered by our European markets.

Jean-Guy de Wael

Chairman of the European Federation of Financial Analysts Societies.

Introduction to the European Futures and Options Markets

Stuart K. McLean

At the first meeting of the European Bond Commission after the publication of the fourth edition of "The Guide to the European Bond Markets", the members thoughts turned to our next major project. Normally, we would have begun to write the next edition of the Guide. Hopefully, it would be completed by the next European Federation of Financial Analyst Societies (EFFAS)'s Congress in Stockholm in June 1990. However, many of the members thought that the shelf life of the fourth edition would probably be longer than two years and that we should consider another project. Because many of us were being called upon to apply our numerical analytical skills to evaluate options, whether embedded in securities or naked as in warrants and the derivative markets, it seemed obvious that futures and options should be covered. We were also well aware of their role in the risk management systems that were being set up to protect the trading and capital market positions.

Anyway, there were unlikely to be many changes by 1990 to justify many changes to the text in the Guide. How wrong we experts were!!! Shortly after publication, Norway and Sweden removed restrictions on overseas investors buying domestic bonds. They also removed exchange control restrictions. Interest rates fell as domestic investors tried to anticipate overseas interest. At the same time, Swedish investors were allowed to diversify overseas. Other European countries such as Italy and Spain continued to liberate and expand their markets. Overseas investors took advantage of the major changes in the economies of Europe and invested in many countries previously reserved for the domestic investors. Nowadays, the impact of overseas investors' expectations can be such as to induce major effects on that economy. The United Kingdom, having indicated that it would link Sterling to the Deutschemark at DM 3.00, saw tremendous inflows of funds as the overseas investors considered the U.K. to be a high yielding Deutschemark market. As funds continued to invest in the U.K. domestic market or take advantage of the high yields in the money markets interest rates fell with Bank Rates as low as 7.5 per cent. This encouraged the public to take out very large loans, available from the recently liberated credit institutions and fuelled the tremendous rise in property prices and a spending boom. This resulted in the need to clamp down on the economy as inflation began to soar to eventually over 10 per cent. Interest rates rose to over 15 per cent and the famous Chancellor Lawson lost his position in the cabinet. Sterling rose briefly to DM 3.20 and then fell to below DM 2.80 before rallying.

The announcement of the changes in Eastern Europe caused far more than a rejoicing at the easing of political tensions in Europe. The realization of the probability that the Democratic and Federal Republics of

Germany could be united caused considerable concern. As this event became more a question of time, the mighty Deutschemark and the much envied West German economy became threatened. How would this unification be paid for, what would be the fate of the East German currency and the social consequences? The Deutschemark interest rates were seen as the base of all European rates and many countries interest rates were benchmarked from them. During 1990, these relationships began to change.

The Iraq crisis, also at the time of writing threatens the world security markets. The price of oil is steadily rising to over US$40 and the costs of the military deployments will have to be found. These factors alone without war are having an impact on the economies of Europe and their relationships with other parts of the world.

All these factors underline the value of this publication. For in recent years, having seen one of the longest bull markets in bonds, many institutional investors are appreciating the value of risk management and control while many commodity producers appreciate the value of insuring future prices. There has also been a substantial growth in security houses' and banks' in-house arbitrage teams, whose function is to generate profits from the anomalies in pricing within markets. While the relative valuations within a market are usually small, by using derivative products, interest rate and currency swaps even greater opportunities with far greater profits present themselves. This is mainly because few players are able to encompass several markets at once. Finally, investors today are under pressure to perform. While one can be concerned that in order to attract funds undue risk may be undertaken to produce that extra performance, the futures and options markets enable the risk to be contained yet the potential to be realized. No doubt, in future, these products will be in everyday use and therefore a full appreciation of what is available is essential.

We have written this book with the intention of providing the reader with not only a list of contracts but a real insight into the markets. By drawing on individuals who operate in each market and country, we are able to make the reader aware of those factors that are important to the players in that market. It is all too easy as an outsider to apply one's own analysis and interpretations and find one has missed a vital point and lost a lot of money. We hope that the details and analysis we have provided will assist the reader in feeling able to operate in these markets and attract them to markets that they may have not appreciated before.

There is no doubt that the markets in Europe are developing rapidly. While writing this book several new markets, the OTB in Austria, OML in

London and BELFOX in Belgium have been finalized and the DTB in Germany and ROEFFEX in the Netherlands have started to operate. The contracts on many exchanges have also been altered or even cancelled, due to lack of interest or severe competition from other exchanges. Several contracts have been refined to make them more attractive to investors by broadening their international appeal, for example by changing the actual terms of the contract such as quality of the underlying asset or delivery/expiry dates. Therefore, this guide will have to be updated every few months to be correct. That is not our purpose. We believe that by understanding markets, their backgrounds and essential factors, the reader will be more confident in working in these markets.

The European Federation of Financial Analyst Societies (EFFAS)

Each country in Europe has a domestic Investment Analyst Society. Their role is to raise the standard of analysis within the investment community and to provide a professional body to look after the interests of its members. To widen their scope across the whole of Europe, they are all members of EFFAS. By providing members to the Board, various Standing Committees and the Organisation Committee of the Congress, each domestic society is able to contribute to and learn from each other. By this means the standards within Europe are improving all the time.

EFFAS has a number of permanent Standing Commissions whose role is to look at specific projects and work to bring together the views of each country and produce a unified approach. These commissions cover Accounting, the Equity Markets, the Bond Markets and Training.

In 1990, Finland, Greece and Luxembourg joined EFFAS and we look forward to working with their members.

The European Bond Commission

The full and correct title of the European Bond Commission is "The European Federation of Financial Analyst Societies' Standing Commission for Convertibles and Bonds". However, this has been shortened to its current name for simplicity. The Commission was originally created to analyze convertibles. We can trace our present structure to the mid 1970s when, under the Chairmanship of Stewart Millman, the main focus was turned to encompass the whole of the domestic markets. More recently, we have been involved in the euro-markets and the futures and options markets. Several members of the Commission also have important roles in the development of their own markets, not only through their day to day position within their companies but also in a wider sense providing advice and information in terms of structure, regulation and future development to the authorities. Originally, the membership was a number of enthusiastic researchers drawn principally from Belgium, France, the Netherlands, Sweden, the United Kingdom and West Germany. Over the following years, this group expanded to include Austria, Denmark, Ireland, Italy, Norway, Spain and Switzerland with very recent introductions from Portugal. In the beginning, each country was usually represented by an individual, but, today, each country has a domestic Commission from whom representatives are drawn to attend the main Commission's meetings. The members are drawn from the research departments of the major banks and security houses as well as major institutions in each country, with each country sending two representatives (normally the same ones) to the meetings which are held in January, May and September of each year.

The aims of the Commission are:-

- **to standardize the methods of analysis of bonds across the markets**

- **to provide information to market participants**

- **to act as an exchange of information to encourage the promotion of international participation in those markets.**

To this end, the Commission has produced a number of publications, the most important of which is "The Guide to the European Bond Markets". The fourth edition was published by Probus Publishing. In the past, limited financial resources meant that the early editions were cheaply and primitively produced. However, with the aid of sponsorship from several European institutions, this edition was issued as a hard-bound book. Another publication has been the International Glossary, which provides not only a Glossary in English, but also furnishes the reader with the equivalents in French, German, Spanish, Italian and Norwegian. The members have not only generated a number of papers which can be found in a variety of publications, but also, have worked with various authorities to establish common standards including the calculation of yields and margins on floating rate notes. The EFFAS Bond Indices calculated by Datastream provide a number of indices for the European markets back to 31st December 1984. They cover all the major markets of Europe. (For further details, see the Guide to the European Bond Markets and/or Datastream.)

Book Format

Europe is a diversity of nationalities, languages and cultures. As a traveller moves from one country to another, he changes his expectations and ways of interacting. The investor should do the same but seldom does. Lack of information often leads to individuals assuming that what works in one country will work in another. This assumption can and often will be an expensive mistake.

This publication is a compilation of a large number of authors' work from different European countries. There are inevitable problems when trying to impose a rigid format on contributors describing very different markets in different stages of evolution. Each author has therefore been allowed to emphasize those points which are of domestic importance within a basic structural framework which is outlined below. In some cases, access to statistics has been very difficult and what may be crucial to one market is incidental to another. The extent and detail of each section necessarily differs widely between each chapter.

We have asked each author to write using the following sections:-

Introduction

Organization of the Market

History of Market

Overview of Products

Detailed Contract Specifications

Taxation

Regulation

Quote Vendors

Sources of Information

There follows a short description of each section:

Introduction

> This provides an overview of the market. It covers a historical perspective and discusses the evolution of the exchange and important factors. In many cases, these factors include major changes to the regulatory environment and taxation.

Organization of the Market

> This section is very wide and comprehensive. It provides lot of information on the exchanges with many practical details such as:
>
> > **Membership**
> >
> > **Types of Members**
> >
> > **Members' Names**
> >
> > **Board of Directors**
> >
> > **Management**
> >
> > **Regulations**
> >
> > **Transaction Costs**
> >
> > **Education**
> >
> > **Address**

Detailed Contract Specifications

> This section provides detailed information and data (where possible) on each of the contracts. It is usually organized into the following order:
>
> > **Interest Rates**
> >
> > **Equities**
> >
> > **Commodities**
>
> with the following sub-divisions
>
> > **Underlying Asset eg Notional 10% 7-10 Year Government Bond**
> >
> > **Contract Type ie Future then Option**
>
> The contract details provided are:

Overview:

This provides a general overview of the specific contract with comments on features of importance such as activity, liquidity and historical development.

Contract Type:

FOR OPTIONS ONLY: Whether American or European calls and/or puts.

Contract Size:

This gives the smallest contract unit.

Delivery/Expiry Months:

This indicates which months are available for contracts. We have used the convention of using **Delivery** for those contracts with physical delivery of the underlying asset and **Expiry** for cash settlement.

Delivery/Expiry Day:

This is the day of the delivery/expiry month when the contract terminates.

Last Trading Day:

This is the last trading day of the contract.

Quotation:

This is the format for pricing the contract.

Minimum Price Movement:

This is the smallest price change that can occur and is shown both as a quotation (tick size) and in cash terms (value).

Trading Hours:

This is the time when transactions can take place on the exchange. It is usually shown in local time. If several periods per day are used, each is shown separately.

Initial Margin:

This is the initial margin or deposit required when opening a position per contract. However, this amount does change from day to day on some exchanges, especially for option contracts which depend on the volatility of the contract at that time. A further example is the oil contracts on IPE which are higher at the time of writing due to the exaggerated volatility and uncertainty due to the Iraq Crisis. In more normal times, these figures would be lower. Several exchanges such as OM operate sophisticated margining systems.

Price Limit:

This is the maximum price limit movement allowed before trading is stopped (sometimes for the rest of the day or sometimes for a short period). During this time, additional variation margin is called for. Several exchanges have no formal system, yet reserve the right to halt trading and call for further margins if the market conditions require it.

Contract Standard:

This indicates the type of settlement on the contract, **physical delivery** or **cash settlement**. When there is physical delivery, details of acceptable assets are provided.

Exchange Delivery Settlement Price:

This is the price on which contracts are settled and/or margins are calculated. Details are usually given of when and how this price is derived.

Reuters Pages and Telerate Pages:

These are the page numbers on which information for the contract are displayed. It should be noted that several other quote vendors also provide this service and the reader should refer to the Quote Vendors section at the end of each chapter for details.

Data and Graphs:

The authors and editor have tried very hard to provide the reader with as much data as possible in order to allow them to evaluate the value of each contract. This has been done, for the most part by the use of four graphs. However, the reader will notice that we have been unable to provide data for all the contracts and for the same time periods. When the book was first suggested, it was expected that it would be published in May 1990. Therefore, the timetable forced us to adopt a data period of June to December, 1989. As the year went on, the major changes in Europe and the Iraq Crisis put everyone under tremendous pressure from their day to day work. Therefore, the publication date was delayed and the data period was changed to January to June 1990. Unfortunately, we also suffered major problems in collecting data. In some cases, data was just not available. In some cases, the data was available - but only in hard copy (sometimes with one data item per day per page). This necessitated the authors and the editor to transcribe to computer form, enforcing a major delay. Finally, even if the data was available it could be in a computer format that required ingenuity to convert it to Lotus format for an IBM computer for the book. In some cases, such were the problems that the data period of June to December 1989 was retained. The reader should appreciate that data in some cases is just not available to the public. We have even heard of one exchange that produces large quantities of data daily, without a historical database capacity, having to ask another exchange for historic data for its own publications. Therefore, we ask for understanding and appreciation of the very hard work done by everyone to provide the data shown.

Daily Volume:

This is the number of contracts traded that day.

Open Interest:

This is the number of contracts still not exercised or completed.

Liquidity:

This is a measure of the liquidity of the contract by using the formula:

LIQUIDITY = VOLUME / OPEN INTEREST

It is possible to convert our measure to the number of days required to turnover all the open positions in that contract e.g.

0.25 equates to 4 days

1.00 equates to 1 day and so on.

Therefore, the reader should appreciate that the higher the number, the more liquidity the contract. A figure below 0.10 indicates 10 business days which is two weeks.

Graph of Liquidity Equivalent

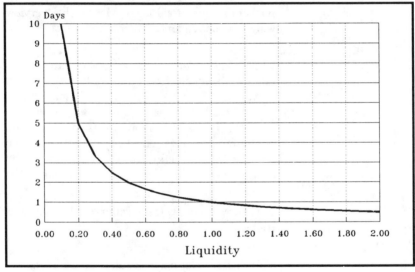

Price/Yield History:

Where possible we have shown the price/yield for both the future and the underlying asset. By comparing this graph with those of daily volume and implied volatility/repo rate, the reader can derive an insight into the quality of the contract and what is happening. Prices of options have not been provided as it is of little value. The implied volatility is a much better indicator.

Implied Repo Rate (for Futures Contracts):

This shows the rate of interest that the contract implicitly has which can be compared with the actual money market rates for that contract. Where there are large differences, arbitrage opportunities exist.

Implied Volatility (for Options Contracts):

This is a measure of value for options and can be compared to the historical volatility of the underlying asset.

Other graphs:

Where the author believes it is valuable to show further data we have done so. Usually the overview will draw the readers attention to this fact.

Regulation

The regulation of the exchange is of vital importance to the investor. Since derivative markets can be volatile, the rules that govern the market and safeguard all participants must be known to reassure the investor that his transaction will be honoured. This may have been covered by some authors in the section on Organization of the Market.

Taxation:

This section covers the taxation of the contracts traded.

Quote Vendors:

This section gives details of all data providers.

Sources of Reference:

This section provides sources of information that will be valuable to operators in this market. It covers both the contracts and their underlying assets.

The Authors

The authors of each section are major practitioners in their markets. A real understanding of how the market operates and the factors that affect it are essential for the investor. Therefore, by asking these authors to contribute, we hope we are able to provide a more practical approach than an "academic" one.

Acknowledgements

In order to produce this publication a veritable army of participants have made their contributions. I wish to personally thank the following for their help, patience and the vast amount of work.

The EFFAS Board

> for their support in allowing us to follow our previous publication with this one.

The Sponsors

> for their financial support which enabled us to complete this publication in this form.

Probus Publishing (especially Michael Jeffers)

> for their support and patience as we changed the deadline due to market events.

I wish to also thank the following and give them a special mention.

The Authors and their assistants

> for their hard work. They must be congratulated for completing the work with all the pressures of their everyday work in this volatile time. They have been especially patient and responsive as I made demands for changes, further information and to keep to the deadline.

The Ventura Helpline at Xerox in San Diego,
especially Suzanne and Ralph.

> for their help in sorting out the problems I encountered due to my ignorance or the glitch when I converted to Version 3. I must also thank the company for their excellent product that allowed me to produce this publication to such a high quality.

My wife Anna

who provided me with the space to complete the task and kept the children out of the study when I was working. Her support and understanding were tremendous. On the bad days, she kept me going.

This product was produced using the following software on an IBM AT with lots of extras:

Lotus 123 Version 2.2

Harvard Graphics 2.13

Wordperfect Version 5.1

Ventura Publisher Version 3 with Professional Extension.

The Sponsors

Our thanks goes to the following sponsors:

Full Sponsors

Deutsche Bank

Dresdner Bank

Grupo Ahorro Corporación

KAS Clearing

MATIF SA

OM of Sweden

Unibors of Denmark

Supported by

Caisse des Dépots et Consignations of France

Christiania Bank of Norway

Creditanstalt of Austria

Datastream of the United Kingdom

Die Erste of Austria

DnB Securities of Norway

Fondsfinans a.s of Norway

Girozentrale Vienna of Austria

Landerbank of Austria

Norsk Opsjonsmarked - NOM AS of Norway

Oesterreichische Kontrollbank AG of Austria

OM Ibérica of Spain

Pierson Heldring Pierson of the Netherlands

Pre Fonds a.s of Norway

Profilo

Raiffeisen Zentralbank Österreich Aktiengesellschaft of Austria

Finally, I have now completed my period as Chairman of the European Bond Commission. During this period, we will have produced three major publications. I would like to thank all the members for their support and hard work.

The Demise of ROEFEX

Since completion of this book, but just before we sent it to the publisher, we have been advised that ROEFEX has decided to close. This came as no surprise since volumes have been very small inspite of the Iraq Crisis. This underlines the strength of the International Petroleum Exchange in London.

The Finnish Futures & Options Markets

Having completed this book, our new Finnish member asked if we could include a chapter on the Finnish markets. Because recent changes to the legislation allowed international investors to participate in the markets and in recognition of her hard work (she only took two weeks), we felt it was best to delay the book that extra week. We added the chapter at the end because everything else was complete, page numbered and indexed. We hope this does not cause too much inconvenience.

WARNING

The editor and authors have made every effort to ensure that the information in this book is correct. However, they can not be responsible for any errors that may occur. Therefore, please check fully before proceeding with any transactions.

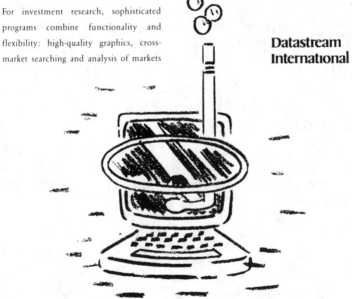

An Overview of the European Futures & Options Markets

Richard Komarnicki

This book is about the Futures and Options Markets in Europe which are a significant part of the worldwide Futures and Options Markets.

The most common way to measure the activity and importance of exchanges is to use daily volumes as a "common denominator". This is accepted by most market observers and participants, although we all know that figures are not necessary comparable. For instance, one Long Gilt (U.K. Government bond) contract has an underlying value of GBP 50,000 with is quite in line (using very roughly one pound for ten French francs) with the nominal value of the French Notional Bond Contract; FRF 500,000. At the same time, the Bund (German Government Bond) contract quoted on LIFFE has a nominal value of DEM 250,000 which is over GBP 80,000 and FRF 800,000.

Options on stocks can also be looked at: depending on the exchange, one option gives the buyer the right to buy (or sell) 5, 10, 50, 100, 400 or even 1,000 stocks; and even if all exchanges used the standard of 100 stocks per contract, there would still be discrepancies: in the U.K., the market price of one stock is a few pounds; in France, hundreds or even thousands of French francs; in Switzerland, very many stocks have prices in excess of 1,000 Swiss francs. Nevertheless, exchanges have roughly taken that situation into consideration and for instances, one unit is:

1,000 shares in the U.K.

100 shares in France

5 shares in Switzerland.

World Futures & Options Markets

The following table shows an alphabetic list of all futures and options exchanges in the world:

Exchange	Ctry	Full Name
AMEX	USA	American Stock Exchange (New York)
ATA	NL	Agricultural Futures Market (Amsterdam)
AUS	AUS	Australian Stock Exchange (Sydney)
BELFOX	B	Belgian Futures & Options Exchange (Brussels)
BFE	UK	Baltic Futures Exchange (London)

BM&F	BR	Sao Paulo Mercantile & Futures Exchange
BOVESPA	BR	Sao Paulo Stock Exchange
BSE	B	Brussels Stock Exchange
BVRJ	BR	Rio de Janeiro Stock Exchange
CBOE	USA	Chicago Board Options Exchange
CBOT	USA	Chicago Board of Trade
CME	USA	Chicago Mercantile Exchange
COMEX	USA	Commodity Exchange (New York)
CSCE	USA	Coffee Sugar and Cocoa Exchange (New York)
DTB	D	Deutsche Termin Börse (Frankfurt)
EOE	NL	European Options Exchange (Amsterdam)
FINEX	USA	Financial Instruments Exchange
FOM	SF	Finnish Options Market (Helsinki)
FOX	UK	London Futures & Options Exchange
FTA	NL	Financial Futures Market (Amsterdam)
FUTOP	DK	Futures & Options Exchange (Copenhagen)
GAR	DK	Garantifonden (Copenhagen)
IFOX	IRL	Irish Futures & Options Exchange (Dublin)
IPE	UK	International Petroleum Exchange (London)
LIFFE	UK	London International Financial Futures Exchange
LME	UK	London Metal Exchange

LTOM	UK	London Traded Options Market
MATIF	F	Marché A Terme International de France (Paris)
ME	CDN	Montréal Exchange
MEFF	E	Mercado de Futuros Financieros (Barcelona)
MONEP	F	Marché des Options NEgociables de Paris
NYCE	USA	New York Cotton Exchange
NYFE	USA	New York Futures Exchange
NYMEX	USA	New York Mercantile Exchange
NYSE	USA	New York Stock Exchange
NZFOE	NZ	New Zealand Futures & Options Exchange
OM	S	Stockholm Options Market
OMF	F	Organisation de Marchés Financiers (Paris)
OMI	E	OM Ibérica (Madrid)
OSA	JPN	Osaka Securities Exchange
PHLX	USA	Philadelphia Stock Exchange
PSE	USA	Pacific Stock Exchange (San Francisco)
ROEFFEX	NL	Rotterdam Energy Futures Exchange
SFE	AUS	Sydney Futures Exchange
SIMEX	SNG	Singapore Mercantile Exchange
SOFE	S	Sweden's Options & Financial Futures Exchange
SOFFEX	CH	Swiss Options and Futures Exchange (Zurich)

TFE	CDN	Toronto Futures Exchange
TIFFE	JPN	Tokyo International Financial Futures Exchange
TOB	AU	Österreichische Termin und Optionsbörse (Vienna)
TSE	CDN	Toronto Stock Exchange
VSE	CDN	Vancouver Stock Exchange
WCE	CDN	Winnipeg Commodity Exchange

World Futures & Options Markets Trading Volumes

The following table shows, for each exchange, the average daily volume traded in the first half of 1990 and in the first half of 1989 and the rate of growth.

Exchange	Total 1990	Total 1989	Growth
AMEX	172,165	193,704	-11.1%
ATA	691	530	+30.4%
AUS	38,765	47,495	-18.04%
BELFOX	N/A	N/A	N/A
BFE	830	926	-10.4%
BM&F	23,987	50,433	-52.4%
BOVESPA	2,955	130,969	-97.7%
BSE	2	10	-80.0%
BVRJ	N/A	64936	N/A
CBOE	519,617	481,040	+8.0%
CBOT	635,582	543,374	+17.0%

CME	402,054	411,955	-2.4%
COMEX	83,343	75,012	+11.1%
CSCE	56,485	44,165	+27.9%
DTB	24,801	N/A	N/A
EOE	41,476	52,718	-21.3%
FINEX	3,858	5,323	-27.5%
FOM	3,140	3953	-20.6%
FOX	20,757	16,868	+23.1%
FTA	1,842	1,481	+24.4%
GAR	2,224	1,141	+94.9%
IFOX	197	128	+53.9%
IPE	20,033	14,682	+36.4%
LIFFE	142,358	96,173	+48.0%
LME	47,092	39,702	+18.6%
LTOM	33,334	37,712	-11.6%
MATIF	117,421	102,370	+14.7%
ME	6,191	5,958	+3.9%
MEFF	654	N/A	N/A
MONEP	17,854	14,636	+22.0%
NYCE	9,479	9,972	-4.9%
NYFE	7,024	7,014	+0.1%

NYMEX	167,142	151528	+10.3%
NYSE	12,238	16,635	-26.4%
NZFOE	1,879	1,902	-1.2%
OM	29,195	32,418	-9.9%
OMF	172	333	-48.3%
OSA	79,816	67,335	+18.5%
PHLX	89,233	90,832	-1.8%
PSE	56,359	70,798	-20.4%
ROEFFEX	70	75	-6.7%
SFE	48,135	46,683	+3.1%
SIMEX	20,046	24,689	-18.8%
SOFE	N/A	2	N/A
SOFFEX	31,578	24,172	+30.6%
TFE	174	137	+27.0%
TIFFE	91,028	186,637	-51.2%
TSE	9,790	11,516	-15.0%
VSE	1,427	2,136	-33.2%
WCE	5,079	5,953	-14.7%
TOTALS	3,079,572	3,188,161	-3.4%

Notes:

DTB	The Deutsche Terminbörse opened Jan 26, 1990
IFOX	Opened May 1989
ME	The Montréal Exchange started trading futures Sept 15, 1989
MEFF	The Mercado de Futuros Financieros started trading March 15, 1990
N/A	Not Applicable: no trading during period
OMF	OMF incorporated in MATIF end April 1990 under the name FMA (France MATIF Automatique)
OSA	Trading in Nikkei 225 options started June 12, 1989
ROEFFEX	Opened October 31, 1989
TIFFE	Trading in TOPIX options started Oct 20, 1989
TSE	Includes option volume of the TFE
TYO	Trading in TOPIX options started Oct 20, 1989

World Futures & Options Markets Trading Volumes (in descending order)

The table below shows the same information but the exchanges are sorted by decreasing 1990 volumes.

Exchange	Total 1990	Total 1989	Growth
CBOT	635,582	543,374	+17.0%
CBOE	519,617	481,040	+8.0%
CME	402,054	411,955	-2.4%
AMEX	172,165	193,704	-11.1%
NYMEX	167,142	151,528	+10.3%
LIFFE	142,358	96,173	+48.0%
MATIF	117,421	102,370	+14.7%

TIFFE	91,028	186,637	-51.2%
PHLX	89,233	90,832	-1.8%
COMEX	83,343	75,012	+11.1%
OSA	79,816	67,335	+18.5%
CSCE	56,485	44,165	+27.9%
PSE	56,359	70,798	-20.4%
SFE	48,135	46,683	+3.1%
LME	47,092	39,702	+18.6%
EOE	41,476	52,718	-21.3%
AUS	38,765	47,495	-18.4%
LTOM	33,334	37,712	-11.6%
SOFFEX	31,578	24,172	+30.6%
OM	29,195	32,418	-9.9%
DTB	24,801	N/A	N/A
BM&F	23,987	50,433	-52.4%
FOX	20,757	16,868	+23.1%
SIMEX	20,046	24,689	-18.8%
IPE	20,033	14,682	+36.4%
MONEP	17,854	14,636	+22.0%
NYSE	12,238	16,635	-26.4%
TSE	9,790	11,516	-15.0%

NYCE	9,479	9,972	-4.9%
NYFE	7,024	7,014	+0.1%
ME	6,191	5,958	+3.9%
WCE	5,079	5,953	-14.7%
FINEX	3,858	5,323	-27.5%
FOM	3,140	3,953	-27.5%
BOVESPA	2,955	130,969	-97.7%
GAR	2,224	1,141	+94.9%
NZFOE	1,879	1,902	-1.2%
FTA	1,842	1,481	+24.4%
VSE	1,427	2,136	-33.2%
BFE	830	926	-10.4%
ATA	691	530	+30.4%
MEFF	654	N/A	N/A
IFOX	197	128	+53.9%
TFE	174	137	+27.0%
OMF	172	333	-48.3%
ROEFFEX	70	75	-6.7%
BSE	2	10	-80.0%
BVRJ	N/A	64,936	N/A
SOFE	N/A	2	N/A

TOTALS	3,079,572	3,188,161	-3.4%

LIFFE and MATIF are the 6th. and 7th. largest exchange in the world, the five largest ones being American. In terms of countries, the U.K. and France are the 2nd. and 3rd. in the world before Japan.

The Proportions of World Markets

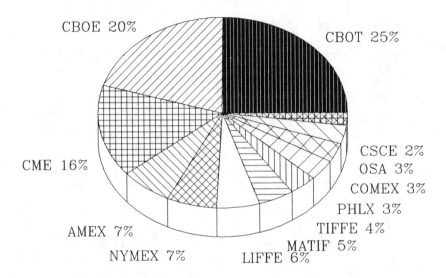

This pie-chart illustrates the previous table: the first exchange in the world (the CBOT) accounts for more than 20 per cent of the world trading volume. American markets represent more than 60 per cent of activity in the world.

Trading Volumes of Leading Exchanges

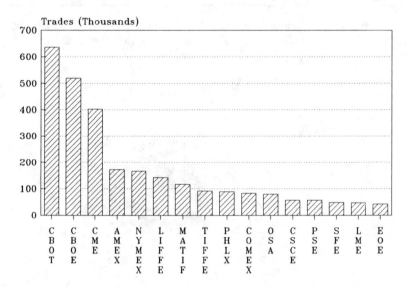

This graph shows the "Top 16" exchanges in the world by decreasing order of daily traded volume.

Exchange	Total 1990	Total 1989	Growth
LIFFE	142,358	96,173	+ 48.0%
MATIF	117,421	102,370	+ 14.7%
LME	47,092	39,702	+ 18.6%
EOE	41,476	52,718	-21.3%
LTOM	33,334	37,712	-11.6%
SOFFEX	31,578	24,172	+ 30.6%
OM	29,195	32,418	-9.9%
DTB	24,801	N/A	N/A

FOX	20,757	16,868	+23.1%
IPE	20,033	14,682	+36.4%
MONEP	17,854	14,636	+22.0%
FOM	3,140	3,953	-27.5%
GAR	2,224	1,141	+94.9%
FTA	1,842	1,481	+24.4%
BFE	830	926	-10.4%
ATA	691	530	+30.4%
MEFF	654	N/A	N/A
IFOX	197	128	+53.9%
OMF	172	333	-48.3%
ROEFFEX	70	75	-6.7%
BSE	2	10	-80.0%
SOFE	N/A	2	N/A
TOTALS	535,721	440,030	+21.7%

This table shows only volumes traded in the European exchanges. The top two are LIFFE and MATIF and the 1990/1989 comparison illustrates quite well the competition between the two. It is also interesting to see that with 535,721 lots traded in 1990, European exchanges accounted for 17.4 per cent of the worldwide volume (figures for 1989 are 440,030 and 13.8 per cent), and that while over the year world volume has been decreasing by 3.4 per cent, European volume has been **INCREASING** by 21.7 per cent.

Trading Volumes of Leading European Exchanges

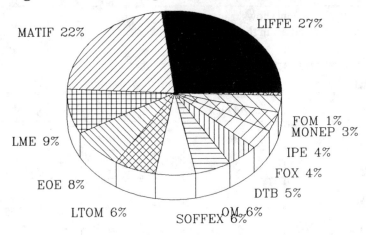

This pie-chart shows how much LIFFE and MATIF account for almost half of the European traded volume.

Trading Volumes of ALL European Exchanges

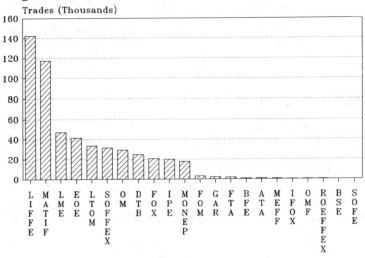

This bar chart shows traded volume of ALL European exchanges in the first half of 1990.

Trading Volumes of Leading European Exchanges

The bar chart below shows traded volume of leading European exchanges
(LIFFE to MONEP) in the first half of 1990.

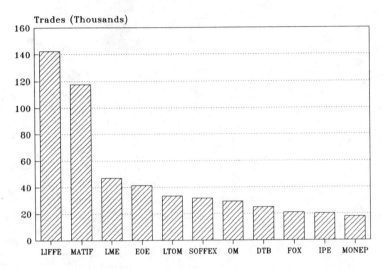

Trades (Thousands)

The four tables below show the evolution of futures and options
volume, separately, for each exchange in the world, exchanges being sorted
by descending volume of activity in the first half of 1990.

Futures: All World Markets

Exchange	Total 1990	Total 1989	Growth
CBOT	500,225	441,344	13.3%
CME	333,996	343,001	-2.6%
NYMEX	143,626	126,670	13.4%
LIFFE	127,921	87,586	46.1%
MATIF	86,105	74,222	16.0%

TIFFE	81,681	88,564	-7.8%
COMEX	72,747	64,813	12.2%
LME	45,218	38,677	16.9%
OSA	45,148	21,429	110.7%
SFE	42,507	41,073	3.5%
CSCE	42,472	35,501	19.6%
SIMEX	19,932	24,633	-19.1%
FOX	19,467	16,257	19.7%
IPE	19,101	14,305	33.5%
NYCE	7,999	8,197	-2.4%
NYFE	6,912	6,845	1.0%
WCE	5,079	5,953	-14.7%
FINEX	3,819	5,302	-28.0%
ME	3,440	1,170	194.0%
BM&F	2,526	21,613	-88.3%
GAR	1,931	981	96.8%
FTA	1,842	1,481	24.4%
NZFOE	1,822	1,771	2.9%
BFE	791	925	-14.5%
ATA	691	530	30.4%
MEFF	654	NA	NA

FOM	220	275	-20.0%
IFOX	197	128	53.9%
TFE	174	137	27.0%
OMF	172	333	-48.3%
OM	85	1	8,400.0%
ROEFFEX	70	75	-6.7%
TOTALS	1,618,570	1,473,792	9.8%

Futures: All European Markets

Exchange	Total 1990	Total 1989	Growth
LIFFE	127,921	87,586	+46.1%
MATIF	86,105	74,222	+16.0%
LME	45,218	38,677	+16.9%
FOX	19,467	16,257	+19.7%
IPE	19,101	14,305	+33.5%
GAR	1,931	981	+96.8%
FTA	1,842	1,481	+24.4%
BFE	791	925	-14.5%
ATA	691	530	+30.4%
MEFF	654	N/A	N/A
FOM	220	275	-20.0%

IFOX	197	128	+ 53.9%
OMF	172	333	-48.3%
OM	85	1	+ 8,400.0%
ROEFFEX	70	75	-6.7%
TOTALS	304,465	235,776	+ 29.1%

It is interesting to see that while Futures volume in the world have increased by around 10 per cent year-on-year, European Futures have increased by almost 30 per cent.

Options: All World Markets

Exchange	Total 1990	Total 1989	Growth
CBOE	519,617	481,040	+ 8.0%
AMEX	172,165	193,704	-11.1%
CBOT	135,357	102,030	+ 32.7%
PHLX	89,233	90,832	-1.8%
CME	68,058	68,954	-1.3%
PSE	56,359	70,798	-20.4%
EOE	41,476	52,718	-21.3%
AUS	38,765	47,495	-18.4%
OSA	34,668	45,906	-24.5%
LTOM	33,334	37,712	-11.6%
SOFFEX	31,578	24,172	+ 30.6%

MATIF	31,316	28,148	+11.3%
OM	29,110	32,417	-10.2%
DTB	24,801	N/A	N/A
NYMEX	23,516	24,858	-5.4%
BM&F	21,461	28,820	-25.5%
MONEP	17,854	14,636	+22.0%
LIFFE	14,437	8,587	+68.1%
CSCE	14,013	8,664	+61.7%
NYSE	12,238	16,635	-26.4%
COMEX	10,596	10,199	+3.9%
TSE	9,790	11,516	-15.0%
TIFFE	9,347	98,073	-90.5%
SFE	5,628	5,610	+0.3%
BOVESPA	2,955	130,969	-97.7%
FOM	2,920	3,678	-20.6%
ME	2,751	4,788	-42.5%
LME	1,874	1,025	+82.8%
NYCE	1,480	1,775	-16.6%
VSE	1,427	2,136	-33.2%
FOX	1,290	611	+111.1%
IPE	932	377	+147.2%

GAR	293	160	+ 83.1%
SIMEX	114	56	+ 103.6%
NYFE	112	169	-33.7%
NZFOE	57	131	-56.5%
FINEX	39	21	+ 85.7%
BFE	39	1	+ 3,800.0%
BSE	2	10	-80.0%
BVRJ	N/A	64,936	N/A
SOFE	N/A	2	N/A
TOTALS	1,461,002	1,714,369	-14.78%

Options: All European Markets

Exchange	Total 1990	Total 1989	Growth
EOE	41,476	52,718	-21.3%
LTOM	33,334	37,712	-11.6%
SOFFEX	31,578	24,172	+ 30.6%
MATIF	31,316	28,148	+ 11.3%
OM	29,110	32,417	-10.2%
DTB	24,801	N/A	N/A
MONEP	17,854	14,636	+ 22.0%
LIFFE	14,437	8,587	+ 68.1%

FOM	2,920	3,678	-20.6%
LME	1,874	1,025	+82.8%
FOX	1,290	611	+111.1%
IPE	932	377	+147.2%
GAR	293	160	+83.1%
BFE	39	1	+3,800.0%
BSE	2	10	-80.0%
SOFE	N/A	2	N/A
TOTALS	231,256	204,254	+13.22%

While world options volume has been **DECREASING** by 15 per cent year-on-year, European options volume has been **INCREASING** by 13 per cent, a nice figure but lower than the increase in futures volume.

One can also note that while the EOE in Amsterdam is the first options exchange in Europe by volume in the first half of 1990, the first european country in Europe is the United Kingdom (51,906 lots between LTOM, LIFFE, LME, LondonFOX, IPE and BFE), narrowly followed by France (49,170 lots for MATIF and MONEP), well above Amsterdam and Zurich. The latter two are smaller countries which would have the best "per capita" ratio and which in absolute terms are ahead of Germany.... but the Deutsche Termin Börse is a very recent market.

It is also interesting to see that market organization in the different countries in the world is diverse:

- there can be a single exchange or numerous ones

- exchanges may be public (i.e. the Stock Exchange of many countries, if not, in Europe, or private (U.S. exchanges are generally privately owned organizations)

- very commonly, futures and options are traded in different exchanges, although it is not always the case: generally, equity options are traded on the Stock Exchanges and interest rate

futures are traded on independent exchanges which can also trade options on interest rate futures.

Another important point is that, in essence, Futures and Options markets are different: although both are "zero sum games", in Futures markets all participants can be called equal. In Options markets, options buyers have to pay a determined amount of money and can expect unlimited profits, while options writers earn a determined premium and have an unlimited loss risk.

Volatility in the markets in 1990 has been higher than in 1989. This has resulted in higher prices for options (a way to measure the dearness of options is to check the implied volatility of the underlying asset), as well as a relative downturn in options volume as opposed to an upturn in futures volume.

Another study which would have been interesting to be carried out is to see, inside each exchange and inside each contract, the call/put ratio (i.e. how many call options are written versus how many puts). We know that some people may say that this ratio is of no interest because the buyer of a put, for instance, who simultaneously buys the stock finds himself as a synthetic call buyer and therefore can sell a call so he does not take any market risk and simply "builds a synthetic short-term investment". Full statistics on such detailed data are not necessarily available in every country and if available, could lead to thousands of papers of comprehensive (but drowning) data.

We hope that the reader of this book will find sufficient insight into the European Futures & Options markets and those who may need to obtain further information can apply directly to the exchanges (generally, contacts and their addresses are listed) or to the members of the European Bond Commission who have been very glad to put this piece of work altogether.

Summary Table of Futures and Option Contracts

Notes:

1: This table has been compiled from a large number of sources. The author believes that it is as correct as possible. However, even throughout the writing of this book contracts are being added and withdrawn. Therefore, readers are asked to check before using the data.

2: For North America, only two Exchanges (**NA1 & NA2**) are shown. It is possible that more than one North American Exchange may trade a particular contract but only two will be shown eg. Sterling/US Dollar is traded on Chicago Mercantile Exchange (**CME**), Midamerica Commodity Exchange (**MCE**) and Philadelphia Stock Exchange (**PHS**)

3: For Far East (**FE**) only one Exchange is shown. It is possible that more than one Far East Exchange may trade a particular contract but only one will be shown.

Summary Table of Future & Option Contracts

Futures

Interest Rates

Contract (Futures)	Au§	Be§	Den	Fr.	Ir.	It.	Ned	Nor	Sp.	Swe	Swi	UK	WG	NA1	NA2	FE
Australian 90 day Bank Bills																SFE
Australian 10yr Government Bonds																SFE
Belgian Government Bonds		OTC														
Canadian Treasury Bills														TFE		
Canadian Treasury Bonds														TFE		
Danish Bullet Bonds			FUT													
Danish Mortgage Bonds			FUT													
E.C.U. 3 Months												LIF				
E.C.U. Long Bonds				MAT												
French 90 day Treasury Bills				MAT												
French PIBOR 3 Months				MAT												
French 4 year BTANs				OMF												

Summary Table of Future & Option Contracts

Contract (Futures)	Au§	Be§	Den	Fr.	Ir.	It.	Ned	Nor	Sp.	Swe	Swi	UK	WG	NAI	NA2	FE
French 7-10yr. Government Bonds				MAT												
German Euromark 3 Months												LIF				
German Government Bonds												LIF	DTB			
Irish DIBOR 3 Months					IFX											
Irish Long Government Bonds					IFX											
Japanese Government Bonds												LIF		CBT		
Japanese 10yr. Government Bonds																TSE
Japanese 20yr. Government Bonds																TSE
New Zealand 90 day Bank Bills																NZF
New Zealand Dollars 3 Months																NZF
New Zealand Treasury Notes																NZF
Nederland 7% Notional Bond							FTA									
Norwegian 3 Months								FRA								
Norwegian 6 Months								FRA								
Norwegian 12 Months								FRA								
Spanish 3yr. Government Bonds									MEF							

Summary Table of Future & Option Contracts

Contract (Futures)	Aug§	Be§	Den	Fr.	Ir.	It	Ned	Nor	Sp.	Swe	Swi	UK	WG	NA1	NA2	FE
Swedish Long Government Bonds										OM						
U.K. Sterling 3 Months												LIF				
U.K. Long Government Bonds												LIF				
U.S. 30 day Interest Rate														CBT		
U.S. Eurodollar 3 Months												LIF		CME		SFE
U.S. Treasury Bills														CME	MCE	
U.S. 2yr. Government Notes														CBT	MCE	
U.S. 5yr. Government Notes														CBT	MCE	
U.S. 5yr. Treasury Note(FYTR)														NYC		
U.S. 10yr. Government Notes														CBT	MCE	
U.S.(Long) Government Bonds												LIF		CBT	MCE	SFE

Bond Index

Contract (Futures)	Aug§	Be§	Den	Fr.	Ir.	It	Ned	Nor	Sp.	Swe	Swi	UK	WG	NA1	NA2	FE
Nederland Bond Index							FTA									
U.S.Corporate Bonds														COM		
U.S.Municipal Bonds														CBT		

Summary Table of Future & Option Contracts

Contract (Futures)	Au§	Be§	Den	Fr.	Ir.	It.	Ned	Nor	Sp.	Swe	Swi	UK	WG	NA1	NA2	FE
Currencies																
Australian $/U.S.$														CME	PHS	
Canadian $/U.S.$														CME	PHS	
Deutschemark/U.S.$										OM				CME	PHS	SIM
E.C.U./U.S.$														NYC	PHS	
French Franc/U.S.$														CME	PHS	
Japanese Yen/U.S.$														CME	PHS	SIM
N.Z. Dollars/U.S.$																NZF
Swedish Krone/U.S.$										OM						
Swiss Franc/U.S.$														CME	PHS	
U.K. Sterling/U.S.$														CME	PHS	SIM
U.S. Dollar Index														NYC		
Equities																
Individual Equities																

Summary Table of Future & Option Contracts

Contract (Futures)	Au§	Be§	Den	Fr.	Ir.	It.	Ned	Nor	Sp.	Swe	Swi	UK	WG	NA1	NA2	FE
Norwegian Stocks										OM		OML				
Swedish Stocks												OML				
Equity Index																
Australian All-Ordinaries																SFE
Canadian TSE-35														TFE		
Danish KFX			FUT													
French CAC-40				MAT												
German DAX													DTB			
Hong Kong Hang Seng																HKF
Irish ISEQ					IFX											
Japanese Nikkei 225																OSE
Japanese St. Futures 50																OSE
Japanese TOPIX																TSE
New Zealand Barclays (BSI)																NZF
Nederland EOE							FTA									

Summary Table of Future & Option Contracts

Contract (Futures)	Auš	Beš	Den	Fr.	Ir.	It.	Ned	Nor	Sp.	Swe	Swi	UK	WG	NA1	NA2	FE
Swedish OM										OM						
Swiss SMI											SOF					
U.K. FT-SE 100												LIF				
U.S. Major Market														CBT		
U.S. Mini Value Line														KCB		
U.S. National OTC														PHS		
U.S. NYSE Composite														NYF		
U.S. Russell 3,000														NYF		
U.S. Russell 2,000														NYF		
U.S. S & P 500														CME		
U.S. Value Line														KCB		
Commodities																
Softs																
Barley (Alberta)														WCE		
Barley (domestic)														WCE		

Summary Table of Future & Option Contracts

Contract (Futures)	Au§	Be§	Den	Fr.	Ir.	It.	Ned	Nor	Sp.	Swe	Swi	UK	WG	NA1	NA2	FE
Barley (EEC)												BFE				
Coffee (Robusta)												FOX				MIF
Coffee (C)														CSC		
Cocoa												FOX		CSC		KLC
Copra																MIF
Corn														CBT	MCE	
Corn Syrup (High fructose)														MGE		
Cotton														NYC		
Cotton CRCE														MCE		
Flaxseed														WCE		
Grain Sorghum (No 2)														KCB		
Oats														CBT	MGE	
Oats (domestic)														WCE		
Orange Juice														NYC		
Palm Oil (Crude)																KLC
Potatoes				MAT			NLK					BFE				

Summary Table of Future & Option Contracts

Contract (Futures)	Aug	Beg	Den	Fr.	Ir.	It.	Ned	Nor	Sp.	Swe	Swi	UK	WG	NA1	NA2	FE
Random Lumber														CME		
Rapseed/Canola														WCE		
Rice CRCE														MCE		
Rubber												FOX				
Rubber (SMR 20)																KLC
Rye														WCE		
Soyabeans														CBT	MCE	HKF
Soyabean Cattle Cake				MAT												
Soyabean Oil														CBT		
Soyabean Meal												BFE		CBT	MCE	
Soyabean Meal (Hi Pro)												BFE				
Sugar																HKF
Sugar (No 6 Raw)												FOX				MIF
Sugar (No 5 White)				MAT								FOX		CSC		
Sugar (No 11)														CSC		
Sugar (No 14)														CSC		

Summary Table of Future & Option Contracts

Contract (Futures)	Auß	Beß	Den	Fr.	Ir.	It.	Ned	Nor	Sp.	Swe	Swi	UK	WG	NA1	NA2	FE
Wheat														CBT	MCE	
Wheat (domestic)														WCE		
Wheat (Hard Red Spring)														MGE		
Wheat (Red No 2)														KCB		
Wheat (White)														MGE		
Wheat (EEC)												BFE				
Wool																SFE
CRB Futures Index														NYF		
Freight Rates																
BIFFEX Rate Index												BFE				
Livestock																
Feeder Cattle														CME		
Live Cattle														CME	MCE	SFE
Live Hogs							NLK					BFE		CME	MCE	
Pork Bellies														CME		

Summary Table of Future & Option Contracts

Metals

Contract (Futures)	Auß	Beß	Den	Fr.	Ir.	It.	Ned	Nor	Sp.	Swe	Swi	UK	WG	NA1	NA2	FE
Aluminium												LME		COM		
Copper												LME		COM		
Gold (33.2troz)														MCE		
Gold (100troz)														CBT	COM	SFE
Gold (1 kilo)														CBT		
Lead												LME				
Nickel												LME				
Palladium														NYM		
Platinum (25troz)														MCE		
Platinum (50troz)														NYM		
Silver (1,000troz)														CBT	MCE	
Silver (5,000troz)														CBT	COM	
Tin												LME				KLC
Zinc												LME				

Summary Table of Future & Option Contracts

Contract (Futures/Options)	Au§	Be§	Den	Fr.	Ir.	It.	Ned	Nor	Sp.	Swe	Swi	UK	WG	NA1	NA2	FE
MGMI Metal Index												FOX				
Oil																
Brent Crude							ROE					IPE				
Dubai Crude												IPE				
Fuel Oil (High Sulphur)																SIM
Gas Oil							ROE					IPE				
Heating Oil (No 2)														NYM		
Heavy Fuel							ROE					IPE				
Propane														NYM		
Unleaded Gasoline														NYM		
WTI Crude														NYM		
Options																
Interest Rates																
Australian 90 day Bank Bills																SFE

Summary Table of Future & Option Contracts

Contract (Options)	Au§	Be§	Den	Fr.	Ir.	It.	Ned	Nor	Sp.	Swe	Swi	UK	WG	NAI	NA2	FE
Australian 10yr. Government Bonds																SFE
Canadian Bankers Accept.														ME		
Canadian Treasury Bonds (25/-)														ME		
Canadian Treasury Bonds (100/-)														TFE		
Danish Mortgage Bonds			FUT													
Danish Bullet Bonds			FUT													
French 7-10yr. Government Bonds				MAT												
French PIBOR 3 Months				MAT												
German Euromarks 3 Months				MAT								LIF				
German Government Bonds												LIF				
Japanese Government Bonds														CBT		
Nederland Indiv.Long Bonds							EOE									
Nederland Long Government Bonds							EOE									
New Zealand Dollars 3 Months																NZF
New Zealand Treasury Notes (GSO)																NZF
Spanish 3yr. Government Bonds									OMI							

Summary Table of Future & Option Contracts

Contract (Options)	Aug	Beg	Den	Fr.	Ir.	It.	Ned	Nor	Sp.	Swe	Swi	UK	WG	NA1	NA2	FE
Spanish 12.5% 1992									OMI							
Swedish Long Government Bonds										OM						
U.K. Sterling 3 Months												LIF				
U.K. Long Government Bonds												LIF				
U.S. Eurodollars 3 Months												LIF		CME		SIM
U.S. 5yr. Government Notes														CBT	CBO	
U.S. 5yr Treasury Notes (FYTR)														NYC		
U.S. 10yr. Government Notes														CBT	CBO	
U.S.(Long) Government Bond												LIF		CBT	CBO	
Bond Indexes																
Nederland Bond Index							EOE									
U.S.Municipal Bond Index														CBT		
Currencies																
Australian $/U.S.$														PHS		

Summary Table of Future & Option Contracts

Contract (Options)	Au§	Be§	Den	Fr.	Ir.	It.	Ned	Nor	Sp.	Swe	Swi	UK	WG	NA1	NA2	FE
Canadian $/U.S.$														CME	PHS	
Deutschemark/U.S.$										OM				CME	PHS	SIM
E.C.U./U.S.$													PHS			
French Francs/U.S.$													PHS			
Japanese Yen/U.S.$														CME	PHS	SIM
Swedish Krone/U.S.$										OM						
Swiss Franc/U.S.$														CME	PHS	
U.K. Sterling/Guilders							EOE									
U.K. Sterling/U.S.$														CME	PHS	
U.S.$/Guilders							EOE									
U.S.$/Guilders (Jumbo)							EOE									
U.S. Dollar Index													NYC			
Equities																
Individual Equities																
Austrian	OTC															

Summary Table of Future & Option Contracts

Contract (Options)	Auß	Beş	Den	Fr.	Ir.	It.	Ned	Nor	Sp.	Swe	Swi	UK	WG	NA1	NA2	FE
Australian																AOE
Belgium		OTC														
French				MON												
German													DTB			
Italian						OTC										
Nederlands							EOE									
Norwegian									NOM			OML				
Swedish										OM		OML				
Swiss											SOF					
United Kingdom												LOM				
United States 1														AME	CBO	
United States 2														NYS	PHS	
Equity Indexes																
Austrian EKA-Stock	OTC															
Australian All-Ordinaires																SFE

Summary Table of Future & Option Contracts

Contract (Options)	Au§	Be§	Den	Fr.	Ir.	It.	Ned	Nor	Sp.	Swe	Swi	UK	WG	NA1	NA2	FE
Canadian TSE-35														TFE		
Danish KFX			FUT													
French CAC-40				MAT												
French OMF-50				OMF												
International Market														AME		
Japanese TOPIX														CBT		
New Zealand Barclays (BSO)																NZF
Nederlands EOE							EOE									
Swedish OM										OM						
Swiss SMI											SOF					
U.S. Computer Stocks														AME		
U.S. FNCI Stock														PAS		
U.S. Gold/Silver Stocks														PHS		
U.S. Institutional Stocks														AME		
U.S. Major Market														AME		
U.S. National OTC														PHS		

Summary Table of Future & Option Contracts

Contract (Options)	Aug	Beg	Den	Fr.	Ir.	It.	Ned	Nor	Sp.	Swe	Swi	UK	WG	NA1	NA2	FE
U.S. NYSE Composite														NYF	NYS	
U.S. Oil Stocks														AME		
U.S. S & P 100 (OEX)														CBO		
U.S. S & P 500 (SPX)														CBO		
U.S. S & P 500 (NSX)														CBO		
U.S. S & P 500 (SPL)														CBO		
U.S. S & P 500														CME		
U.S. Utility Stocks														PHS		
U.S. Value Line Composite														PHS		

Commodities

Softs

	Aug	Beg	Den	Fr.	Ir.	It.	Ned	Nor	Sp.	Swe	Swi	UK	WG	NA1	NA2	FE
Barley (EEC)												BFE				
Cocoa												FOX		CSC		
Coffee (C)														CSC		
Coffee (Robusta)												FOX				

Summary Table of Future & Option Contracts

Contract (Options)	Au§	Be§	Den	Fr.	Ir.	It.	Ned	Nor	Sp.	Swe	Swi	UK	WG	NA1	NA2	FE
Corn														CBT		
Cotton														NYC		
Orange Juice														NYC		
Potatoes												BFE				
Random Lumber														CME		
Rubber												FOX				
Soyabeans														CBT	MCE	
Soyabean Meal												BFE		CBT		
Soyabean Meal (HiPro)												BFE				
Soyabean Oil														CBT		
Sugar (No.11)														CSC		
Sugar (Raw)												FOX				
Sugar (White)				MAT								FOX				
Wheat														CBT	MCE	
Wheat (EEC)												BFE				
Wheat (Hard Red Spring)														MGE		

Summary Table of Future & Option Contracts

Contract (Options)	Au§	Be§	Den	Fr.	Ir.	It.	Ned	Nor	Sp.	Swe	Swi	UK	WG	NA1	NA2	FE
Wheat (Red No 2)														KCB		
CRB Futures Index														NYF		
Livestock																
Feeder Cattle														CME		
Live Cattle														CME		
Live Hogs														CME		
Pork Bellies														CME		
Metals																
Aluminium												LME				
Copper												LME		COM		
Gold (10troz)							EOE							ME	VSE	
Gold (33.2troz)														MCE		
Gold (100troz)														COM		AOE

Summary Table of Future & Option Contracts

Contract (Options)	Au§	Be§	Den	Fr.	Ir.	It.	Ned	Nor	Sp.	Swe	Swi	UK	WG	NA1	NA2	FE
Lead												LME				
Nickel												LME				
Platinum (10troz)														ME	VSE	
Silver (100troz)														TFE		
Silver (1,000troz)							EOE							CBT	VSE	AOE
Silver (5,000troz)														COM		
Zinc												LME				
MGMI Metal Index												FOX				
Oil																
Brent Crude												IPE				
Gas Oil												IPE				
Heating Oil														NYM		
Heavy Fuel												IPE				
Unleaded Gasoline														NYM		
WTI Crude														NYM		

Summary Table of Future & Option Contracts

Key to the Summary Table

§ The Austrian and Belgian Futures and Options Exchanges have not at the time of writing confirmed the exact contracts to be traded on the Exchanges.

AME	American Stock Exchange ("AME")
AOM	Australian Options Market ("AOM")
BEL	Belgian Futures & Options Exchange ("BELFOX")
BFE	Baltic Futures Exchange ("BFE")
CBT	Chicago Board of Trade ("CBOT")
CBO	Chicago Board Options Exchange ("CBOE")
CME	Chicago Mercantile Exchange ("CME")
CSC	Coffee, Sugar & Cocoa Exchange ("CS&CE")
COM	Comex (COMEX")
DTB	Deutsche Terminbörse ("DTB")
EOE	European Options Exchange ("EOE")
FOX	London Futures & Options Exchange ("LondonFOX")
FRA	Forward Agreements ("FRA" & "FR")
FTA	Financial Futures Exchange ("FTA")
FUT	Guarantee Fund for Danish Options & Futures ("FUTOP")
HKF	Hong Kong Futures Exchange ("HKFE")
IFX	Irish Futures & Options Exchange ("IFOX")

Summary Table of Future & Option Contracts

IPE	International Petroleum Exchange ("IPE")
KBT	Kansas City Board of Trade ("KCBOT")
KLC	Kuala Lumpur Commodity Exchange ("KLCE")
LIF	London International Financial Futures Exchange ("LIFFE")
LME	London Metal Exchange ("LME")
LOM	London Traded Options Market (LTOM")
MAT	Marché a Terme des Instruments Financiers ("MATIF")
MCE	Midamerica Commodity Exchange ("MCE")
ME	Montreal Exchange ("ME")
MEF	Mercado de Futuros Financieros ("MEFF")
MGE	Minneaplois Grain Exchange ("MGE")
MIF	Manila International Futures Exchange ("MIFE")
MON	Marché de Options Négociables de Paris ("MONEP")
NLK	Nederlandse Liquidatiekas ("NLK KAS")
NOM	Norwegian Options Market ("NOM")
NYC	New York Cotton Exchange ("NYCE")
NYF	New York Futures Exchange ("NYFE")
NYM	New York Mercantile Exchange ("NYME")
NYS	New York Stock Exchange (NYSE")
NZF	New Zealand Futures Exchange ("NZFE")

Summary Table of Future & Option Contracts

OM	Optionsmarknad ("OM")
OMF	Organisation de Marchés Financiers ("OMF")
OMI	OM Ibérica ("OM Ibérica)
OML	OM London ("OML")
OSE	Osaka Securities Exchange ("OSE")
OTC	Over-the-Counter Market ("OTC")
PAS	Pacific Stock Exchange ("PACSE")
PHS	Philadelphia Stock Exchange ("PSE")
ROE	Rotterdam Energy Futures Exchange ("ROEFEX")
SFE	Sydney Futures Exchange ("SFE")
SIM	Singapore International Monetary Exchange ("SIMEX")
SOF	Swiss Options & Financial Futures Exchange ("SOFFEX")
TFE	Toronto Futures Exchange ("TFE")
TSE	Tokyo Stock Exchange
VSE	Vancouver Stock Exchange ("VSE")
WCE	Winnipeg Commodity Exchange ("WCE")

The Futures and Options Markets in Austria

Franz Fasching
First Austrian Bank

Andreas Matje
Creditanstalt-Bankverein

&

Erich Obersteiner
Raiffeisen Zentralbank Österreich AG (RZB-Austria)

Introduction

The Vienna Stock Exchange is one of the oldest stock exchanges in the world. After Frankfurt (1585), Amsterdam (1611) and Paris (1724), it was founded in 1771. Structural changes in international financial markets started in the early 1980s effected the Vienna Stock Exchange with a delay of some four years.

An Austrian Options (and Financial Futures) Exchange is being considered and may possibly be established in 1991. This chapter deals with recent developments in Austria's market for shares and the performance of instruments similar to options. Legal prerequisites and the way forward to a Futures and Options Exchange will be described in the final part of this chapter.

Developments of the Austrian Stock Market

Stock Exchange & Overall Turnover

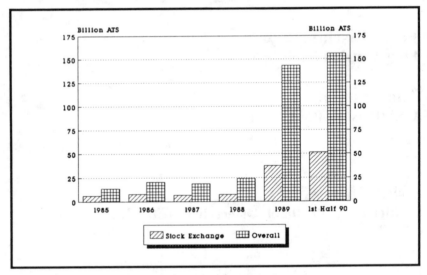

The slump in oil prices and its impacts on the balances of payments of OPEC countries, increasing debts of developing countries, deregulation of financial markets in industrialized countries as well as globalization and securitization all affected the Austrian turnover in stocks.

In 1981, the trading volume of domestic and foreign shares traded on the Stock Exchange amounted to ASch 560 million. After having doubled by 1983 (Asch 1,203 million), this figure started to rise constantly in 1985. This increase was interrupted only briefly by the 19th October 1987 Crash. Eventually, in 1989, the Vienna stock market "exploded" not only in terms of share prices, but also turnover increased by some 500 per cent to Asch 143.2 trillion.

Besides institutional domestic and in increasing numbers foreign investors, many private investors took advantage of this boom. Before 1984, only one per cent of Austria's population owned shares and only four per cent owned any kind of security. These percentages rose to three per cent (shares) and 8 (securities) respectively. This development can be explained by the following:-

- Ending of buying cycles concerning certain durable consumer goods.

- Increasing confidence in price stability because of low inflation rates (therefore purchasing tangible assets is less profitable).

- Considerable real income growth and increasing propensity to save together with a shift away from low interest savings books.

Since 1987, domestic and foreign capital looking for profitable assets could also be invested in participation certificates and in more attractive warrants.

Nominal & Market Value of Stocks
Quoted on the Vienna Exchange

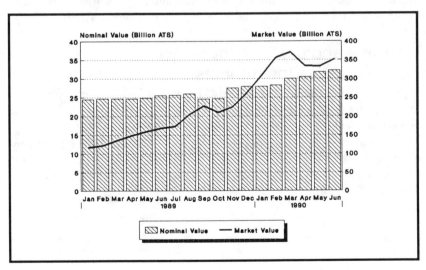

Nominal & Market Value of PCs
Quoted on the Vienna Exchange

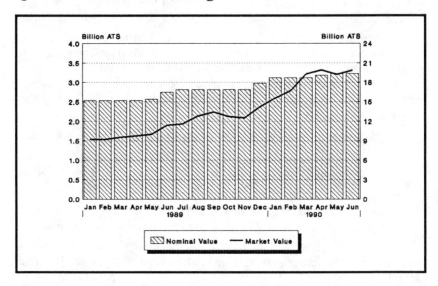

Performances of these assets in 1989 are shown in the charts and tables above. The boom being represented in those figures goes hand in hand with an increasing demand for new investment and hedging instruments. This can also be seen from the demand for warrants and "shorties" being offered at the moment.

Warrants and the Development of
New Derivative Instruments

At the beginning of 1989, only 21 domestic call warrants were listed for official trading on the Vienna Stock Exchange. The market capitalization of these warrants amounted to Asch 1,024 million then.

Following the enormous rise of the Vienna Stock Market, many new stock purchase warrants, mainly in the form of naked warrants, were issued by several banks. By October 1989, the number of listed warrants more than doubled (49 calls and 6 puts).

Nominal & Market Value of Warrants
Traded on the Vienna Exchange

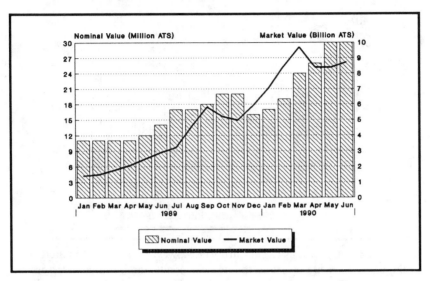

The chart above compares the increase in nominal value (plus 120 per cent) of listed warrants with their increase in market value (plus 410 per cent) for the period January to December 1989. The new issues were met by huge demand from private investors and have been heavily oversubscribed. They were accompanied by a strong increase in prices for the underlying as well as the derivative instruments, thus creating still more demand potential and stronger price increases as speculative investors entered the market. When in summer 1989 the market started to show some saturation, new issues became more sophisticated. The Vienna Stock Exchange saw several new products already known on foreign markets for quite a long time (basket warrants, straddles, puts, "shorties"). The general investing public was slightly overcharged for the flood of new products. Several investors who bought into the rising market did not always understand the sense and the mechanics of these sophisticated products.

Stock Market Turnover

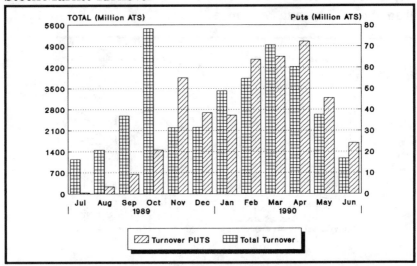

The tremendous rise in turnover, however, indicates the increasing willingness of private investors to buy risky assets. Institutional investors, on the other hand, were in urgent need of instruments to hedge their positions in a market with increasing volatility. The new Stock Exchange Act takes into account both necessities. It also contains certain articles to prevent the private investor from taking inconsiderate action.

Options-like Instruments - "Shorties"

At the moment, no options in the traditional sense are available in Austria. As products grew more sophisticated, however, certain warrants were issued, which show several characteristics of orthodox options. In September 1989, eight warrants were offered for subscription for the same underlying instrument - the EKA-Stock Austria, an investment fund concentrating mainly on Austrian securities. There were four put warrants and four call warrants, respectively, each with four different maturities. As distinguished from conventional options, only one strike-price was offered for each date. After the maturity of the EKA11(89) warrants, a new pair of warrants was issued with an 11/90 maturity.

Calls

Warrant	Strike Price	Exercise Period	Issue Volume ('000s)
EKA 11(89)	1377	12.09.89-24.11.89	120
EKA 02	1377	12.09.89-23.02.90	100
EKA 05	1100	13.06.89-25.05.90	100
EKA 08	1443	12.09.89-31.08.90	100
EKA 11(90)	1453	12.12.89-30.11.90	150

Puts

EKA 11(89)	1209	12.09.89-24.11.89	50
EKA 02	1209	12.09.89-23.02.90	50
EKA 05	1145	12.09.89-25.05.90	50
EKA 08	1145	12.09.89-31.08.90	50
EKA 11(90)	1154	12.12.89-30.11.90	100

EKA-Fund-Austria Warrant 11/89 Price & Premium (1989)

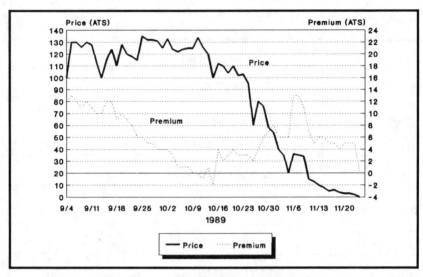

Although the issue volume and the turnover of these new products was not very high as compared to the whole market and taking into consideration that these instruments were rather new to the Austrian private investor, no major market inefficiencies occurred (see above). While the price of the underlying instrument rose considerably, the premium showed an increased downward movement, as the likelihood of further price increases declined. When the tone of the market changed, panic selling drove the premium even negative for a short term. Shortly afterwards the premium rose again, as the bullish sentiment returned and the odds for a rising market increased. Considerations based on Black-Scholes-type models, however, generally indicate an overpriced situation.

Trading Details

Just like most warrants, these options-like instruments - or "shorties" as they are commonly called - are quoted on the Vienna Stock Exchange and are thus governed by the rules and regulations of the Vienna Stock Exchange. In addition to that, they are available in off-floor trading between banks.

Stock Exchange:

Contract Size:	One Investment Fund certificate.
Contract Months:	February May August November.
Trading Hours:	11.00 a.m. to 1.30 p.m. (Central European Time).
Quotation:	Asch for the smallest available unit.
Minimum Trading Lots:	10 units.
Fees:	1.25 per cent of market value.
Settlement Date:	Second Monday following the transaction.

Off-floor Trading:

Trading Hours:	Business hours of banks.
Quotation:	Reuters "FABF" in Asch.
Minimum Trading Lots:	Subject to negotiation (larger volumes).
Fees:	Net Price.
Settlement Date:	Second Monday following the transaction.

REGULATION
Austria's Way to a Financial Futures & Options Exchange

Up to now, a relatively small domestic market for underlying assets, the dominant position of market-making banks and an unfavorable legal situation hindered the establishment of a Futures and Options Market. Concerning the first two problems, we have shown that major changes are occurring. The legal situation has now also changed fundamentally with the new Stock Exchange Act.

New Legal Situation
History

At the beginning of 1989, Austria's Constitutional Court abrogated the Stock Exchange Act of 1875. The old act had as its general purpose, the maintenance of fair and equitable securities markets and the regulation of security exchanges in general, after the crash of the state-run Stock Exchange in 1873. To achieve this, the act provided for a "Chamber of the Stock Exchange" to administer the law.

As the management of the securities (and commodities) trading was in the hands of the Stock Exchange itself, adaptations and supplements to its rules and regulations were made internally and did not need Parliamentary approval. Because there was little legal validity to enforce these internal decisions, Austria's Constitutional Court repealed the provisions of 1875. After 30th November 1989, a new act providing more specific regulations was established. Concerning an "Austrian Options (and Financial Futures) Exchange", the new act's chapters "General Provisions" and "Provisions for Stock Exchanges" are of special interest.

General Provisions

The General Provisions focus on the reduction of governmental influence by liberalization and integration of EEC rules on the one hand and the protection of investors' interests on the other. In respect of a market for options and financial futures the most important changes are:

- **Definition of Stock Exchanges** (par. 1 sect. 2).The new definition includes options and financial futures as trading assets.

- **Options Committee** (par. 6 sect. 2 item 3). If options and financial futures are to be traded, a Stock Exchange Options Committee has to be established to be responsible for official listings, their withdrawal and for fixing trading hours.

● **Trading Regulations** (par. 26 sect. 3). The Council of the Vienna Stock Exchange is responsible for the issuing rules and regulations concerning exchange transactions and for establishing clearing facilities. If correct and reliable clearing is guaranteed, it can also be used by private corporations. Under the new Act, as well as under the old one, it is possible to use computer trading systems. (At the moment, warrants and shares are traded by using **PATS** - Partly Assisted Trading System.)

● **Definition of Stock Exchange Transactions** (par. 27).The new definition of exchange transactions includes transactions effected by using a computer trading system.

●**Estoppels by Judgement referring to Gambling Contracts** (par. 28). The Austrian Civil Code regards gambling and betting debts as generally unenforceable. As options and financial futures contracts contain speculatory aspects, these provisions have so far prevented the establishment of a market for such instruments. Under the new Act, nobody will be allowed to raise any estoppel based on these gambling provisions, if the options or financial futures contract is quoted on any recognized domestic or foreign stock exchange.

Integration of EEC Rules

In summer 1989, Austria applied for membership of the EEC. Since stock and bond markets are becoming increasingly international, many provisions of the new Stock Exchange Act correspond to the relevant EEC Rules. EEC Rules and corresponding Austria provisions are shown in the following "Integration Balance":

EEC Rules and Provisions concerning:	Austrian Stock Exchange Act Corresponding Provisions:
Quotation of Securities (draft as of 3rd March 1982)	paragraphs 64 66 68 70 - 73 82 - 84.

Establishment Control and Dissemination of **Circular Notes** (draft as of 22nd June 1987)	paragraphs 74 - 80
Information to be published **regularly** by corporations quoted on a Stock Exchange (draft as of 15th February 1982)	paragraphs 87 - 90
Information to be published on the occasion of purchasing or selling **major stakes** (draft as of 12th December 1988)	paragraphs 91 - 93

Concerning the forthcoming EEC Rules for Insider Trading being in the pipe-line, the Austrian Ministers of Justice and Finance are requested to prepare a penal statute considering the developments within the EEC.

Further Steps

In order to establish an "Austrian Options and Financial Futures Exchange (TOB: Österreichische Termin und Optionsbörse EDV-Betriebs-system Gesellschaft m.b.H.)", a research commission was founded on 16th November 1989. The members of this study group are:

● Creditanstalt

● Girozentrale

● Länderbank

● Raiffeisen Zentralbank (formerly Genossenschaftliche Zentralbank).

After thorough investigation into possible forms for organizing the market, possible underlying assets, different computerized trading and clearing models and systems (OM, SOFFEX, etc.) an official call for tenders was made in March 1990. The establishment of the Austrian Financial Futures & Options Exchange is intended to be by mid 1991 with the OM system being adopted.

When establishing an Options and Futures Exchange some further provisions will have to be made. These will have to deal with subjects like the obligation to trade options and financial futures exclusively on the Stock Exchange and how customers will be informed of the risks involved in trading these instruments. A way to solve this latter problem could be the so called "information model": before effecting the first transaction customers have to confirm receipt of a standardized information sheet outlining the risks.

SOURCES of REFERENCE

Mitteilungen der Direktoriums der Oesterreichischen Nationalbank (Monthly)

General economic data on Austrian economy and detailed data on bank activity including capital market statistics.

Anleiheninformationen der Oesterreichischen Kontrolbank (Weekly)

Detailed information on each bond quoted on the Vienna Stock Exchange - basic primary and secondary market data including yields (to maturity, to next call and minimum/maximum yields in the case of serial bonds).

Some major banks publish information on the Austrian money and capital markets on a more or less regular basis.

The Futures and Options Markets in Belgium

Chris Van Aeken
Kredietbank

&

Gilbert François
**Belgian Futures & Options Exchange
("BELFOX")**

INTRODUCTION

At the time of writing, Belgium does not have an officially organized Futures and Options Market. Plans to establish such an Exchange, however, are well under way and the opening is expected in the first quarter of 1991.

The enormous and still expanding capacity of global financial markets to cope with growing trading volumes and a large number of new financial instruments is a recognized factor in Belgium. This evolution has been going hand in hand with an increasing volatility in Belgian interest rates. At the same time, as a result of the explosive growth in both the central government budget deficit and the overall level of government debt, Belgian government bond holdings have increased dramatically. Total central government debt at the end of September, 1990 stood at BEF 7,179 billion. More than half of this debt has been financed in the domestic capital markets through the issue of Belgian Government bonds. The trading volume of government and government-guaranteed bonds on the Brussels' Stock Exchange amounted to BEF 185 billion in 1989. No figures are available for block transactions outside the market, but the latter are substantial (and estimated at roughly five times greater than the trading volume on the Exchange).

Government bond futures and options have already become an indispensable part of the fixed rate debt markets. The size of the Belgian bond market, its increasing price volatility and the growing liquidity of the secondary bond market created the need for Belgian government bond futures and options contracts.

In recent years, two initiatives to establish an over-the-counter government bond derivatives market have been taken by major players in the secondary BEF-bond market. In doing so, they hoped to provide institutional and professional investors with efficient hedging instruments that would enable them to protect the market value of their BEF bond holdings and/or to benefit from their specific views on interest rate movements.

Responding to strongly innovative capital markets, a Commission to study the reform and modernization of the Belgian financial market, called "Commission Maystadt" after the Minister of Finance, was put into place in December, 1988. The decisions of this Commission concerning access to the market, reporting, mechanisms of negotiation and security are now being translated into legislation.

In anticipation of this modernization being officially enforced, the Brussels' Stock Exchange introduced at the beginning of 1989, the continuous listing system Computer Assisted Trading System "CATS" for forward market transactions. New regulations concerning disclosure requirements and insider trading also provided new incentives to improve market transparency. As a result, the Brussels' market further consolidated its position as a medium-sized Exchange, ranking eighth among the continental European Stock markets. The current stock market capitalization is BEF 2,677 billion.

Following the remarkable success of option transactions in the Nederlands, the Brussels' Stock Exchange created in 1985 an embryonic call options market. This however did not attract much interest because of legal impediments and its organizational structure. It is due to disappear as soon as the new official market is to be launched.

The New Markets and Products report of the Commission Maystadt advised the Authorities and the financial community of the usefulness and the need for a Belgian Options and Futures market. A specially dedicated Steering Committee has chosen the infrastructure which will allow the launching of this official market in stock options, index contracts and notional bond futures. This official Exchange, called **BELFOX** (Belgian Futures and Options Exchange), is now actively being prepared and promoted by the major Belgian financial institutions, brokerage firms and the Brussels Stock Exchange, under the auspices of the Minister of Finance and the Banking Commission in order to be launched in spring 1991. **BELFOX** will provide Belgium with its first Futures and Options Exchange to confirm its ambitions as a specialized financial centre.

ORGANIZATION OF THE MARKET

As explained before, at this time there is no official Futures and Options Market in Belgium. However, one fixed income over-the-counter contract is traded, and call options are listed on four stocks in the Brussels' Stock Exchange.

Over-the-counter Contracts

In May 1987, the Belgian Brokerage House Peterbroeck, Van Campenhout launched American call and put options on the Belgian Government Bond 9.75 % 14 Feb. 1986-1994 . The nominal value of the options contract was BEF 5,000,000. A standardized cycle of expiration days (the third Friday of the expiry month) was established. Petercam guaranteed bid and offer prices in the option. Despite its relative success during the first months, the market interest remained limited. At the same time, the underlying instrument became illiquid as all market makers gradually withdrew the issue from their trading list. Late 1988, Petercam decided to stop trading the bond option. Instead of changing the underlying bond of the option, they agreed to support the establishment of the official Options and Futures market.

In May 1988, as one of the major players in the BEF-bond market, Kredietbank came forward to take the lead in organizing an over-the-counter debt futures market. Kredietbank strongly believed that this notional bond futures contract on Belgian bonds could develop into a liquid and highly efficient trading and hedging instrument. Liquidity and price efficiency are ensured by Kredietbank's undertaking to act as a professional market maker and administrator for the contract. This initiative can be judged as a relative success and the contract will be the reference for the notional bond future to be traded on the official Options and Futures Exchange.

Call Options on Individual Stocks

As a result of the successful creation of option exchanges worldwide, the Brussels' Stock Exchange started to study the option market in 1976. In April 1985, they created an intentionally limited "open outcry" options market integrated within the Stock Exchange. It is characterized by the requirement of full coverage for option writers to provide the utmost security to the system. Because of legal impediments, only calls were allowed at that time. The market started with calls on five stocks, of which four are still traded at this time with very limited volumes.

Belgian Futures and Options Exchange ("BELFOX")

Resulting from the talks within the Commission Maystadt, the major Belgian financial institutions and the Stock Exchange Commission, representing the brokerage houses, are preparing the creation of an official Options and Futures Market. The market will be a fully integrated, automated Exchange with around 60 members. The London based **ICCH** Financial Markets has been appointed project manager for the full implementation of the Trading, Clearing House and Procedures. Trading in a long term notional bond future, in an stock index option and in options on six stocks will commence in the spring of 1991. Directives concerning trading, clearing and the regulatory framework were formulated by a special Steering Committee.

As the **BELFOX** market does not inherit a "pit trading" background, it stresses conceptual simplicity rather than continuity with past practice. The system designs and the proposed rules and regulations tend to be an elegant synthesis of the theory and practice of existing Futures and Options Markets.

Access to the Exchange is reserved for those establishments accepted by the Exchange Authorities. **BELFOX** is characterized by its "lateral" structure, meaning that each participant is also a "Clearing Member".

ORGANIZATION of the MARKET
Founding Shareholders

Brussels' Stock Exchange Commission
Kredietbank
Generale Bank
Bank Brussels Lambert
Banque Degroof
ASLK-CGER Bank

Board of Directors

R. Vermeiren (President)
     Kredietbank
J. Peterbroeck (Vice President)
     Stock Exchange Commission

M.Bayot	Generale Bank
E. Boyer de la Giroday	Bank Brussels Lambert
A. Philippson	Banque Degroof
J. Leleux	Brokerhouse Leleux
L. De Brabandere	Brussels' Stock Exchange
Ph. Costermans	Brokerhouse Branquart
H. Servais	Brokerhouse Dewaay
P. Henrion	ASLK-CGER Bank

Membership Types

There will be the following capacities of membership:

Public Order Member "POM"

A Public Order Member is entitled to accept orders and to have orders executed by a Broker for his own account or for the account of principals (clients).

Broker

A Broker is entitled to accept orders from Public Order Members and to conclude contracts from them or for his own account on the Electronic Trading System of **BELFOX** or to instruct other Brokers to conclude such contracts.

Market Maker "MM"

A Market Maker is entitled to conclude option and futures contracts solely for his own account and is obliged to make a market in one or more option capacities and/or futures contracts. During trading hours, at all reasonable times, he shall continuously provide Bid and Offer Prices applying to the minimum number of contracts/trading size/specified by **BELFOX**.

BELFOX may set a maximum permitted difference between the Bid and Offer price provided to the Market Maker. Incentives shall be provided to the Market Maker, such as reduced clearing fees or other favourable conditions. Market Makers quotations are public and binding at all times unlike those associated with the **POM**. For admission to the capacity of Market Maker, one must execute a significant proportion of business in options or futures trading. If a Member does not actually exercise the capacity, he will be considered to be in breach of the obligations prescribed in the Rules and Regulations, unless he has the written approval of **BELFOX** Board.

To provide the most reliable safeguards for the market as well as for the Members, **BELFOX** will admit Clearing Members only after having conducted a thorough selection process. The minimum capital requirements defined by the Board and in conformity with the respective EEC directives are as follows:

Public Order Member	10 million BEF
Broker	10 million BEF
Market Maker	50 million BEF

The main functions of the **BELFOX** Clearing House, which is granted controlling powers over its members are:

- to concentrate all the credit and compensation risks on a single establishment (that enjoys a high solvency because of its capital (BEF 500 million) and guarantee fund (BEF 250 million)

- to guarantee the irrevocability and the completion of contracts by the immediate substitution at the time of trading

- to insure and to manage in real time the inherent financial risk.

The risks inherent in those functions are reduced to a minimum through the requirement of an initial margin and through daily variation margin calls to reflect the worst possible price movements.

The clearing system will be able to calculate margins, to control positions and to evaluate risks at client level. The final element of the financial stability of the Clearing House is the real-time risk management at all levels through price variation limits and position limit monitoring.

An automatic trading system with immediate and definitive trade registration will be installed. The open outcry market has indisputable advantages, however, **BELFOX** judged:

- **its break-even point was too high because skilled traders must be retained on the floor**

- **the development of modern technology enabled increasingly accurate trading facilities and trading control in real time.**

Besides the Public Order Book, fixed prices given by market makers will ensure the continuity of quotations. A facility for competitive trading for block orders (i.e. large and/or complex orders), based on an "auction mechanism", will be added to the trading system. The system will support the concept of a second-order derivative market in spreads with a guarantee of simultaneous execution of each leg and the possibility of quoting for such spreads. All components from the automatic trading system, as there is the Public Order Book, the block orders and the underlying stock and bond prices will be available to the trader from the same screen. Because prices and quotes are the basis of business, they will be actively and widely circulated in real time.

Systems

Implementation of the **BELFOX** system solution for trading and clearing on computer hardware from Digital Equipment Corporation (DEC) and software developed by **ICCH** - trading (ATS/2) and clearing (ARCH).

Back Office

Each **BELFOX** member is required to operate a back-office adapted to the requirements as formulated by **BELFOX**. The effective operations of all rules and procedures will be judged on a regular basis by the **BELFOX** audit. **BELFOX** provides members with details and recommendations on various back office system that are available in the market.

Education and Information

The **BELFOX** marketing department, together with **ICCH** Exchange Services, is charged with the promotion of the market. A three-monthly **BELFOX** magazine and brochures on the market and its products are being sent to all interested parties. The accents are put on information and training.

To this end, all participants, as well as the trading room the clearing department are required to take basic and intermediate courses - followed by
examinations. Workshops are also provided to all interested persons and
institutions. Highly reputed foreign institutions (IFT and Euromoney) offer
at the same time advanced training, especially adapted to the **BELFOX** needs
and with a **BELFOX** quality control.

Transaction Costs

Full details on transaction costs will only be available as of the
opening of the market.

Address and Management

General Manager	Mr. Jos Schmitt
Address:	BELFOX
	H. Mausstreet 2
	1000 BRUSSELS
Tel:	(32) 2 509 13 70
Fax:	(32) 2 509 13 95
Auditors:	Ernst and Young, Brussels

OVERVIEW of PRODUCTS

	Futures	Options
Interest Rate Contracts		
Notional Long Term Bond	*	
Equities		
Actual Stocks		*
Stock Index		*

HISTORY of the FUTURES & OPTIONS MARKETS

Date of Launch	Type of Contract	Exchange	Average Monthly Trading Volume
April 1985	Launch of 5 call options	Brussels' Stock Exchange	
May 1987	Options on a long term bond	OTC	
15 May 1988	Launch of notional 5-10 year bond futures contract	OTC	15,000

DETAILED CONTRACT SPECIFICATIONS
Interest Rates
Kredietbank's OTC Long Term 8 percent 5-10 Year Notional Bond Futures Contract

This contract was launched as an over-the-counter future in May 1988 by Kredietbank. It has known a reasonable success with volumes growing all the time and with an increasing number of users, both hedgers and speculators. An average daily volume of 750 lots is traded (March 1990). A substantial part of this volume is generated by foreign investors.

The contract will be the basis of the notional government bond contracts to be traded in the Official Belgian Futures and Options Exchange, which is planned to go live early 1991.

Contract Size:	BEF 2,500,000.
Delivery Months:	March June September December.
Delivery Day:	Last business day of the delivery month.
Last Trading Day:	Two business days prior to expiry.

Quotation:	0.01 per cent of par.
Minimum Price Movement (Tick Size and Value):	0.05 per cent = BEF 1,250.
Exchange:	Over-the-Counter.
Trading Hours:	09.30 a.m. - 16.00 p.m..
Initial Deposit:	5 per cent = BEF 125,000.
Price Limit:	No price limit.
Contract Standard:	Physical or cash settlement (at seller's choice). The underlying bonds are issued by the Belgian treasury or the Road Fund maturing at least 5 years from the expiry date (if callable the first call date must be at least two years from the expiry date).
Exchange Delivery Settlement Price:	The price quoted at 10.00 a.m. on the last trading day.
Reuters Pages:	KBBQ.
Telerate Pages:	3268.

Notes:

- Participants in the market are allowed to act as principals (counterparty) and as agents (intermediary).

- The contract will be integrated into the new official Futures and Options Exchange (BELFOX).

Conversion Factors

Conversion factors are:

BONDS	DEC 90	MAR 91	JUN 91
BELGIUM 8.00 1/96	1.0000	1.0000	n.a.
BELGIUM 7.75 4/96	0.9888	0.9896	0.9899
BELGIUM 7.75 7/96	0.9885	0.9890	0.9900
BELGIUM 8.00 2/97	1.0000	1.0000	1.0000
BELGIUM 8.25 3/97	1.0113	1.0115	1.0105
BELGIUM 8.25 6/99	1.0141	1.0141	1.0140
BELGIUM 8.25 6/97	1.0115	1.0113	1.0115
BELGIUM 10.00 4/96	1.0826	1.0799	1.0761
BELGIUM 10.00 3/97	n.a.	1.0919	1.0881
BELGIUM 10.00 8/00	n.a.	n.a.	1.1255

Trading Dates

The June 1991 is the last OTC contract in which Kredietbank plans to make a market. All contracts with later expiration dates will be traded in BELFOX.

Months	Last Trading Day	First	Last
DEC 90	27/12/90	28/12/90	28/12/90
MAR 91	26/03/91	28/03/91	28/03/91
JUN 91	26/06/91	28/06/91	28/06/91

Price History of September Future (Jan 2, 1990 - Sept 27, 1990)

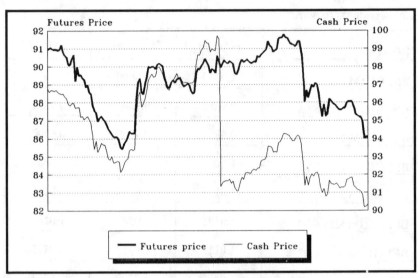

Implied Repo Rate (Jan 2,1990 - Sept 26, 1990)

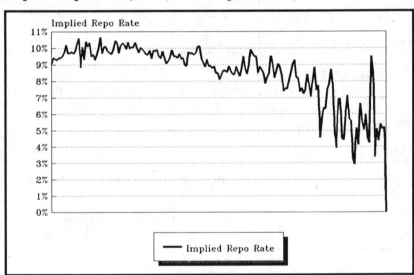

Volume Traded by Type of Client (December 1989)

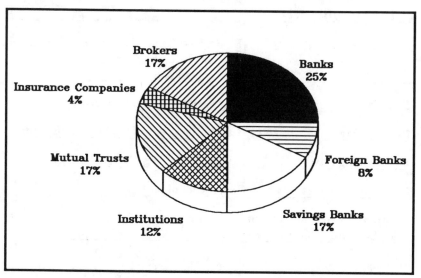

Cheapest to Deliver

On the 15.3.90 with the price of the September contract at 89.15.

	Price	Yield	Conversion Factor
BELGIUM 8.25% 24/03/97	90.000	10.32	1.0115
BELGIUM 8.25% 01/06/99	89.500	10.04	1.0145
BELGIUM 8.25% 23/06/97	89.600	10.34	1.0120

BELFOX Notional 9% 5-10 Year Government Bond Futures Contract

Contract Size:	BEF 2,500,000 nominal value of a notional Belgian Government bond with a coupon 9 per cent coupon.
Delivery Months:	March June September December.
Delivery Day:	Last business day of the Delivery month.
Last Trading Day:	Seven trading days prior to the Delivery day.
Quotation:	In per cent of par value.
Minimum Price Movement (Tick Size and Value):	0.01 per cent = BEF 250.
Trading Hours:	09.00 a.m. - 16.00 p.m.
Initial Margin:	Four per cent of the contract value (or BEF 100,000) and is set by the BELFOX Clearing House.
Price Limit:	No price limit.
Contract Standard:	Physical delivery of deliverable grade bonds issued by the Belgian Treasury maturing at least 5 years and no later than 10 years from the delivery date. If callable the first call date must be at least 2 years from the delivery date and the call should not be "in the money". A provisional list of deliverable bonds is published by BELFOX Clearing House at the launching of a new delivery month and the final list is published a minimum of 10 days before the delivery date.

Exchange Delivery Settlement Price:	
Reuters Pages:	Not known.
Telerate Pages:	Not known.

Delivery Method

On the expiration date, the sellers are required to close outstanding open positions by delivery of bonds against payment. Buyers pay the delivery price on the delivery date and receive the bonds. The invoice price on the delivery date is adjusted for coupon rates different from 9 per cent and for varying maturities by the "conversion factor" system, published by **BELFOX**.

Foreign Exchange Contracts

For the moment no foreign exchange futures or options contracts are listed in Belgium. They may be launched at a later stage in the Official Futures and Options Exchange.

Equities

Individual Stocks Call Option Contracts Traded on the Stock Exchange

The stock options market was opened by the Brussels Stock Exchange in April 1985. Because of legal impediments and organizational problems, the market has never been very successful. There is no volume.

The market will cease to exist from the start of the official Futures and Options Market (**BELFOX**) when six call and put options on Belgian stocks will be launched as well as an option on a Belgian stock index.

Option Style	American calls.
Contract Size:	GBL 50; Petrofina 20; Inco 200 and Stilfontein 1,000.
Delivery Months:	January April July October.
Delivery Day:	Last Thursday of Delivery Month.
Last Trading Day:	Last business day of the Contract Month.

Quotation:	In BEF.
Minimum Price Movement:	BEF 1.
Trading Hours:	09.30 a.m. - 16.00 p.m.
Initial Deposit:	For the writer (seller) only fully covered (ie 100 per cent) transactions are allowed. The buyer only pays the premium.
Price Limit:	No price limit.
Contract Standard:	Physical delivery of the actual stocks.
Exercise Price:	Not known.
Reuters Pages:	Not known.
Telerate Pages:	Not known.

The stocks on which options are available at present are:

● Petrofina

● Groupe Bruxelles Lambert

● Inco

● Stilfontein

Individual Stock Option Contracts to be Traded on BELFOX

BELFOX will start a market in options on six Belgian shares. These have been selected by a dedicated user-group because they respond to the following criteria:

● quoted on the forward market

● capitalization

● volatility

● free float and

● international reputation.

They belong to different sectors.

Option Style:	American calls and puts.
Contract Size:	20 underlying shares.
Delivery Months:	March June September and December.
Delivery Day:	Last Friday of Delivery month.
Last Trading Day:	Delivery day.
Quotation:	In BEF.
Minimum Price Movement:	BEF 1.
Trading Hours:	10.15 a.m. - 16.00 p.m.. Pre-opening 10.00 a.m.
Initial Margin:	To be determined by the **BELFOX** Clearing House.
Price Limit:	No price limit.
Contract Standard:	Physical delivery of the actual stocks.
Exercise Price:	5 price series will be quoted for each stock. One at-the-money and two out-of and in-the-money. For exercise intervals see table below.
Exchange Delivery Settlement Price:	
Reuters Pages:	Not known.
Telerate Pages:	Not known.

Exercise Price Intervals

Price of Underlying	Interval
0 - 899	50
900 - 2,799	100
2,800 - 5,999	200
6,000 - 8,999	400
9,000 and over	500

The stock on which options will be quoted are:

Petrofina	Oil Industry
Solvay	Chemicals
Electrabel	Utilities
Delhaize	Retail
Acec-Union Minière	Steel
Société Générale	Holding Company

Stock Index Options Contracts to be traded on BELFOX

An options contract will be launched on a **BEL-20** Price Index. The exact composition is not finalized yet, but will take into account the following criteria:

- capitalization
- liquidity
- maximum part of one company: 10 per cent
- good tracking of the general index
- a quarterly evaluation of the index.

Option Style:	European calls and puts.
Contract Size:	20 units.
Expiry Months:	One two three and six months. At every expiry day a new three months contract is to be created. At every quarter a new six months contract is to be created.
Expiry Day:	Last Friday of expiry month.
Last Trading Day:	Expiry day.
Quotation:	In BEF.
Minimum Price Movement:	1 BEF.
Trading Hours:	10.15 a.m. - 16.00 p.m.
Initial Margin:	To be determined by the **BELFOX** Clearing House.
Price Limit:	No price limit.
Contract Standard:	Cash settlement.
Exercise Price:	5 contracts per stock will be offered with exercise intervals of BEF 250 if the index is BEF 10,000.
Exchange Delivery Settlement Price:	Not known.
Reuters Pages:	Not known.
Telerate Pages:	Not known.

Metals

There are no futures nor option contracts on metals in Belgium.
They are not envisaged to be launched either.

Commodities

There are no futures nor option contracts on commodities in Belgium.

They are not envisaged to be launched either.

REGULATION

BELFOX is a Coöperative Vennootschap/Société Coopérative domiciled in Brussels, Belgium. The **BELFOX** Market and Clearing House are fully integrated. **BELFOX** is highly self-regulated, concerning its trading and clearing constitution. With respect to the prudential aspects, the Banking and Financial Commission and the Caisse de Garantie/Garantiekas will assume the control.

The Rules and Regulations - with all procedures - are being drafted with the helpful participation of the Banking Commission and the Ministry of Finance & the Ministry of Justice. relevant articles will become Royal decrees within the new Belgian "Big Bang" financial laws.

TAXATION

Stamp Duties

Trading in options and futures is not subject to stamp duties, except in the case of delivery of the underlying security.

Withholding Taxes

Capital gains originated from trading options and futures are not subject to withholding taxes.

Direct Taxes

Profits and losses from trading options and futures of companies are regularly accounted and taxes are levied accordingly.

For further tax information, please contact the **BELFOX** Finance Department.

SOURCES of REFERENCE

For brochures and information on **BELFOX** and its products, please contact the **BELFOX** Marketing Department.

The Futures and Options Markets in Denmark

Jesper Christiansen
and
Soren Lassen
Unibørs Securities

INTRODUCTION

The creation of an options and futures market in Denmark goes back to the summer of 1987 with the establishment of the Guarantee Fund for Danish Options and Futures ("the Fund") by the Danish Central Bank, the Danish Bankers' Association, the Danish Association of Saving Banks and the Confederation of Danish Stockbroking Companies. After one year of preparation, the Danish market for options and futures listed on the Copenhagen Stock Exchange ("CSE") was finally launched in September 1988.

The first options and futures contracts were based on the nine per cent mortgage-credit bonds maturing in 2006. Being the bench mark bonds on the Danish Bond market since 1987, these bonds were a natural choice for the first underlying asset on the Danish Options and Futures market, known as the "FUTOP" market. The name was originally a contraction of FUTures and OPTions. The name later became a registered trade mark for the Danish futures and options exchange. It is only natural that the first products were based on bonds, because the Danish bond market is the ninth largest in the world when measured in terms of bond volume.

During 1989 new contracts have been introduced based on the FUTOP Bond Index, Danish Government Bonds and a new Danish Stock Index, "KFX". The Index name comes from the initials of the Danish words for the Copenhagen Stock Exchange. At the end of 1989 the daily turnover was on an average 2,000 contracts a day. For the KFX futures contracts the turnover in the first months has been as high as 50 per cent of the turnover in the stock market.

During the beginning of 1990, the activity on the Danish Options and Futures market rose dramatically due to higher volatility on the Danish bond market as well as in the international bond and stock markets.

ORGANIZATION of the MARKET

The official marketplace for the Danish options and futures market is the Copenhagen Stock Exchange. CSE operates a decentralized electronic trading system used for trading in stocks, bonds as well as futures and options. All the futures and options contracts on the Exchange have to be registered by the Guarantee Fund for Danish Options and Futures. However, the Fund also registers, clears and settles listed contracts traded outside the Exchange.

This market is rather unique, even by international standards. User-defined trading screens connected to the same electronic trading systems make simultaneously dealing in different underlying assets possible. This ensures the best possible basis for effective pricing as well as consistent pricing between the market for underlying securities, viz options and futures.

The Guarantee Fund for Danish Options and Futures

The Guarantee Fund for Danish Options and Futures was established as a non-profit fund in the summer of 1987. Its principal function is to guarantee the performance of obligations arising from trading in options and futures. If a member goes bankrupt or is excluded from the Guarantee Fund, the Fund will step in and guarantee the obligations of the member. Apart from other futures and options markets, the guarantee of the obligations covers not only the members of the Fund, but also their clients. Consequently, all clients are covered by the guarantee when trading futures and options with a member of the Fund.

The objectives of the Guarantee Fund are:

- to be one of two parties to options and futures contracts admitted for official listing on the Copenhagen Stock Exchange,

- to determine administrative rules for the said securities regarding the issuing, trading and settling of transactions between members and the Fund and between members and their clients,

- to facilitate clearing and settlement of transactions in the securities referred to above, and

- to inform investors about the special nature of the risk associated with investing in the securities traded.

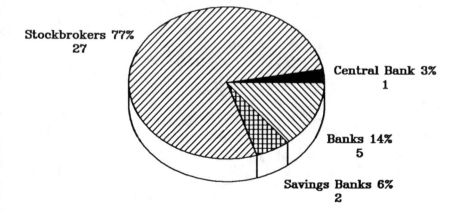

Membership of the Fund

In order to be a member of the Fund, the clearing members have to establish electronic relationship with the Danish Securities Center and also have accounts in the Danish Central Bank. At the end of 1989 the Fund had 35 active affiliated clearing members.

Regulatory Authority

The Regulatory Authority for the Fund is the Danish Supervisory Authority of Financial Affairs. The CSE and the Danish Securities Center as well as all the Fund's clearing members are also under the supervision of the above-mentioned authority. The authority also supervises the underlying markets of the futures and options.

Copenhagen Stock Exchange

	6 Nikolaj Plads
	P.O.Box 1040
	DK-1007 COPENHAGEN K
Tel:	(45) 3393 3366
Telex:	16496 costex dk
Fax:	(45) 3312 8613
Chairman	Sven Caspersen
President	Bent Mebus
Trading hours:	09.00 a.m. - 15.30 p.m..

The Guarantee Fund for Danish Options and Futures

	15 Kompagnistræde
	P.O.Box 2017
	DK-1012 COPENHAGEN K
Tel:	(45) 3393 3311
Telex:	(45) 3393 4480
Chairman	Jens Otto Veile
Chief Executive Officier	Tyge Vorstrup Rasmussen
Opening Hours	10.00 a.m. - 15.40 p.m..

HISTORY of the MARKET

Date of Launch	Type of Contract
22 September 1988	Futures on 9 per cent 2006 Mortgage-credit bonds
22 September 1988	Call options on 9 per cent 2006 Mortgage-credit bonds
04 December 1988	Put options on 9 per cent 2006 Mortgage-credit bonds
23 March 1989	Futures on the **FUTOP** Index
22 September 1989	Futures on Danish Government bonds
07 December 1989	Futures on **KFX** Stock Index
01 July 1990	trading in futures on the **FUTOP** Bond Index was terminated
21 September 1990	Options on futures on the **KFX** Stock Index

OVERVIEW of the PRODUCTS

	Futures	Options	
		on cash	on futures
9 per cent 2006	*	*	
Bullet bond	*		(1)
KFX - Stock Index	*		*

Note (1): options will be launched later.

The products of the Danish **FUTOP** market reflect the underlying market. As the Danish bond market - both by size and by turnover - exceeds the Danish stock market by far, the largest interest for futures and options lies in the products with fixed income based underlying assets.

DETAILED CONTRACT SPECIFICATION
Long Term Interest Rates
9 % 2006 Mortgage-credit Bonds Futures

This futures contract was the first to be listed on the Copenhagen Stock Exchange in September 1988. The underlying asset comprises of the three Danish 9% coupon mortgage-credit bonds maturing in 2006.

As most other Danish mortgage-credit bonds, the three bonds serving as the first underlying asset, are callable, which means that the issuer can redeem the bonds at par value before maturity. In order to counter the problems which will arise if a huge number of bonds are called and the underlying bonds literally disappear, a ceiling has been set for the computed price of the underlying bond at price 105.

Turnover has been growing teadily since the introduction of the market in 1988. However, in periods with low volatility, turnover in the futures market has been very low. In the first half of 1990, the interest rate uncertainty caused by the German reunification boosted turnover. Increase in turnover was also seen as the Danish investors became more interested in the uses of derivatives.

In general, the bond futures contracts track the underlying bond quite well. As liquidity lies mainly in the three months contracts it is only natural that the track performance is best in these contracts.

Major movements in the money market rates are in general well reflected in the bond futures implied repo rate.

Contract Size:	DKK 1,000,000.
Expiry Months:	January April July October. **The expiry date is the first business day of the month** therefore these could be consider as March June September and December as in other Exchanges.
Expiry Day:	The first business day of the expiry month.
Last Trading Day:	The last business day of the month before the expiry date.
Quotation:	Per cent of par.

Minimum Price Movement (Tick Size and Value):	0.05 per cent = DKK 500.
Trading Hours:	09.00 a.m. - 15.30 p.m. by electronic trading.
Initial Margin:	4 per cent = DKK 40,000.
Price Limit:	300 basis points (3 per cent) above or below the last settlement price.
Contract Standard:	Cash settlement.
Exchange Delivery Settlement Price:	The price is fixed as a simple average of the prices on the expiry date for the three Mortgage-credit bonds forming part of the underlying asset as listed on the CSE. The final settlement price is determined on the basis of the trading between 11.00 a.m. and 12.00 a.m.
Reuters Pages:	**DKOA** (General Information) & **UDKF**.
Telerate Pages:	None
Guarantee Fund fee;	DKK 50 per transaction plus DKK 50 per contract.

The underlying securities are;

- 9 per cent 2006 BRFkredit (DKK 7.5 billion)
- 9 per cent 2006 Kreditforeningen Danmark (DKK 16.1 billion)
- 9 per cent 2006 Nykredit (DKK 13.0 billion)

Daily Volume and Open Interest (Jan 2,1990 - Jun 29,1990)

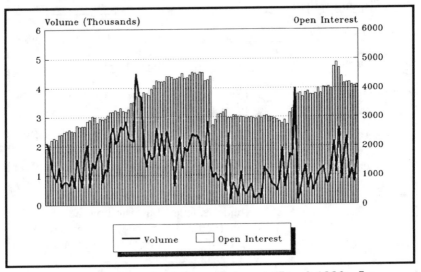

Volume/ Open Interest and Open Interest (Jan 2,1990 - Jun 29,1990)

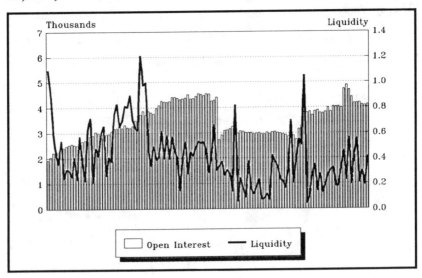

Price/Yield History (Jan 2,1990 - Jun 29,1990)

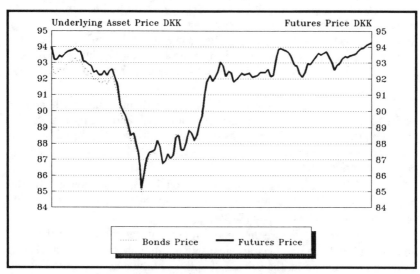

Implied Repo Rate (Jan 2,1990 - Jun 29,1990)

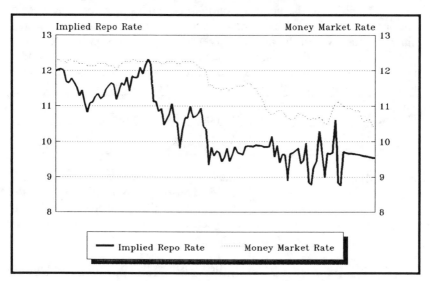

9 per cent 2006 Mortgage-credit Bonds Options

Call options on the 9% 2006 mortgage-credit bonds were launched at the same time as the futures contracts on 22 nd September 1988. As for futures contracts on the 9% 2006 mortgage-credit bond a ceiling has been set for the computed price of the underlying bond at price 105. This rule will have consequences for a number of investment strategies when the price gets close to 105.

All options are of the European type, with automatic settlement at expiry of options with a positive intrinsic value. Call and put options can be traded on three, six, or nine months contracts. However, the liquidity lies in the three months contracts. Option contracts are listed with a limited number of exercise prices.

Options contracts are not exercised by physical delivery of the underlying securities, but by cash settlement of the value of the respective rights and commitments of the parties.

The expiry dates are the same as for the futures contracts on the same underlying bonds. In practice this means, that although the options are based on the underlying bond, the pricing of options in the market is based on the price of the futures contract with the same expiry date as the options.

Turnover in the bond option market is of course very sensitive to movements in the underlying bond market. In periods with only little uncertainty, the turnover in the option market has been even very low. With the rising uncertainty in the spring of 1990, caused by the German reunification, turnover rose sharply. Increase in turnover was also seen as the Danish investors became more interested in the uses of derivatives.

Option Style	European calls and puts.
Contract Size:	DKK 1,000,000.
Expiry Months:	January April July October. **The expiry day is the first business day of the expiry month** therefore this could be considered as March June September December as in other Exchanges.
Expiry Day:	The first business day of the expiry month.

Last Trading Day:	The last business day in the month before the expiry month.
Quotation:	Per cent of par.
Minimum Price Movement (Tick Size and Value):	0.05 per cent = DKK 500.
Trading Hours:	09.00 a.m. - 15.30 p.m. by electronic trading.
Initial Margin:	None for the buyer. for the seller the initial margin ranges from 0 to 4 per cent = DKK 40,000. Maintenance margin is the maximum of the settlement premium or the intrinsic value of the option.
Price Limit:	300 basis point (3 per cent) above or below the settlement price.
Contract Standard:	Cash settlement.
Exercise Price:	2 per cent intervals. A minimum of three prices exist 1 above and 1 below the current price. If prices of the underlying asset moves below the lowest or above the highest exercise price contracts with new exercise prices are opened.
Reuters Pages:	DKOA (general information) & UDKF.
Telerate Pages:	None
Guarantee Fund fees:	DKK 50 per transaction plus DKK 50 per contract.

Daily Volume and Open Interest (Jan 2,1990 - Jun 29,1990)

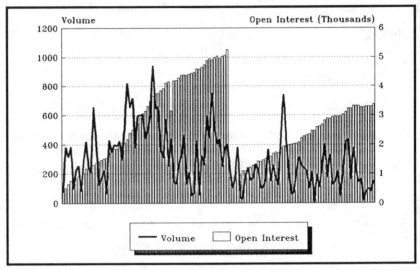

Volume/ Open Interest and Open Interest (Jan 2,1990 - Jun 29,1990)

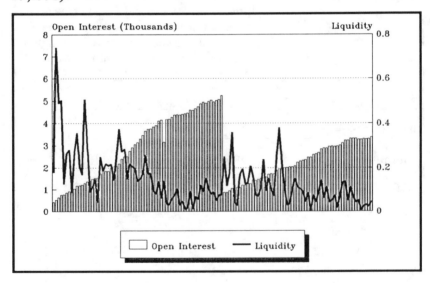

Implied Volatility (Jan 2,1990 -Jun 29,1990)

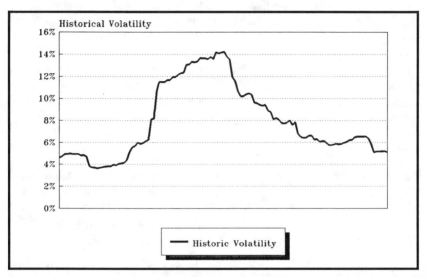

Danish Government Bullet Bonds Futures

Futures on Danish Government bonds were launched 22nd September 1989. This day being the one-year birthday for the official Danish Options and Futures market. Throughout 1989, the Kingdom of Denmark financed its majority of the net borrowing requirement by issuing long-term bullet bonds. As a consequence, the outstanding volume of 9% bullets with maturities ranging from 1994 to 1998 reached a magnitude that made them relevant as underlying assets for futures and options.

The underlying asset is based on a simple average of maximum four Danish Government bonds. For the moment the underlying asset comprises of the three 9 per cent bullet bonds 1996, 1998, and 2000. These series all consist of non-callable bullet bonds issued by the Kingdom of Denmark.

The simplicity of the underlying asset means that the Government bonds forming part of the asset will have to be replaced after a certain period. The replacement of bonds may alter the characteristics of the underlying asset, but will only affect the new term to maturity.

Immediately after the introduction, the Government Bullet futures was a success. Later, however, turnover declined somewhat as the 9 per cent 2006 future totally dominated the bond future market. Turnover has therefore been quite low in the first half of 1990.

The prospects for the Government Bullet future seems better than the history suggests. In the near future the 9 per cent 2006 contract is still expected to overshadow the Bullet contract. Later on, the advantages of the Bullet bond, not being callable, is expected to cause a more liquid market for Government Bullet futures.

Also the Government Bullet futures tracks the underlying bond prices quite well. Not surprisingly, the track performance is best when liquidity is high. The track performance is also affected by the closing of the contracts.

Contract Size:	DKK 1,000,000.
Expiry Months:	January April July October. **The expiry day is the first business day of the month** therefore this could be considered as March June September December as on other Exchanges.
Expiry Day:	The first business day of the expiry month.
Last Trading Day:	The last business day in the month before the expiry months.
Quotation:	Per cent of par.
Minimum Price Movement (Tick Size and Value):	0.05 per cent = DKK 500.
Trading Hours:	09.00 a.m. - 15.30 p.m. by electronic trading.
Initial Deposit:	4 per cent = DKK 40,000.
Price Limit:	300 basis points (3 per cent) above or below the last settlement price.
Contract Standard:	Cash settlement.

Exchange Delivery Settlement Price:	The settlement price is calculated as a simple average of the prices on the expiry date for the Government bonds forming part of the underlying asset as listed on CSE. The final settlement price is determined on the basis of the trading between 11.00 a.m. and 12.00 p.m..
Reuters Pages:	**DKOA** (general information) & **UDKF**.
Telerate Pages:	None
Guarantee fund fee:	DKK 50 per transaction plus DKK 50 per contract.

The underlying assets are:

● 9 per cent Danish Government 1996 (DKK 27.6 billion)

● 9 per cent Danish Government 1998 (DKK 27.4 billion)

● 9 per cent Danish Government 2000 (DKK 15.2 billion)

Daily Volume and Open Interest (Jan 2,1990 - Jun 29,1990)

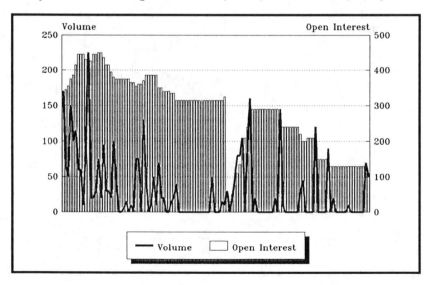

Volume/ Open Interest and Open Interest (Jan 2,1990 - Jun 29,1990)

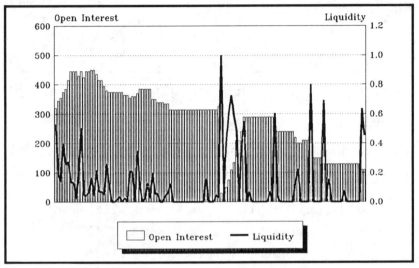

Price/Yield History (Jan 2,1990 - Jun 29,1990)

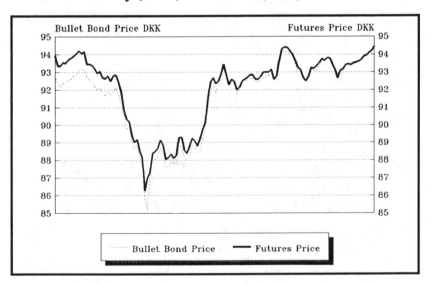

Implied Repo Rate (Jan 2,1990 - Jun 29,1990)

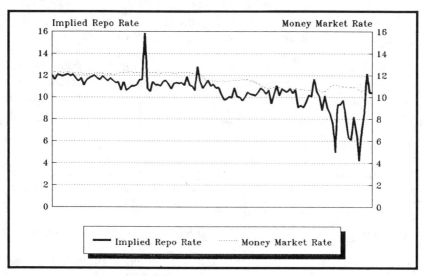

Foreign Exchange

For the moment, there is no official market for futures or options on the foreign exchange markets, and no plans of establishing one have been launched. Some of the large Danish banks trade in the international markets for options and futures on foreign exchange.

Equities

Individual Stocks

At the end of 1989 there was no official market in Denmark for futures and options on individual stocks. No such market is expected to be launched in the near future.

Stock Indices

KFX Stock Index Futures

Trading **KFX** futures contracts started on December 7th 1989. From the very outset the contract turned out to be one of the most traded instruments on the Danish stock market.

The **KFX** index has been constructed as a benchmark for tracking price developments for highly capitalized, high-liquidity stocks listed on the Copenhagen Stock Exchange.

The stocks making up the **KFX** index constitute around 50% of the total capitalized value of stocks listed on the Copenhagen Stock Exchange.

Trading the **KFX** stock index future started on 7th December 1989. Since then, liquidity has increased considerably and the index future is among the most traded items in the stock market. So far, the **KFX** stock index future has not tracked the **KFX** index too well. Thus, a major difference between the futures' implied repo rate and the corresponding money market rate is seen. The difficulties in trading the index' 25 stocks in blocks are the main reason for this difference.

Contract Size:	DKK 100,000.
Expiry Months:	Contrary to the rest of the Danish futures market the **KFX** future expires in March June September and December.
Expiry Day:	The first business day of the expiry month.
Last Trading Day:	The last business day in the month before the expiry months.
Quotation:	Per cent of par.
Minimum Price Movement (Tick Size and Value):	0.05 per cent = DKK 50.
Trading Hours:	09.00 a.m. - 15.30 p.m. by electronic trading.
Initial Deposit:	12 per cent = DKK 12,000.
Price Limit:	900 basis point (9 per cent) above or below the last settlement price.
Contract Standard:	Cash settlement.
Exchange Delivery Settlement Price:	The price is fixed as the official value of the KFX index as calculated by CSE (based July 3)
Reuters Pages:	**DKOA** (general information) & **UDKF**.

Telerate Pages:	None
Guarantee Fund fee:	Dkk 50 per transaction plus DKK 50 per contract.

Composition of the KFX Index

The **KFX** Index is composed solely of Danish equities. In contrast to the Copenhagen Stock Exchange's other indeices, the **KFX** is a pure price index. When the component shares go ex-dividend, this will consequently be reflected in the index. The fall in the price of a component caused by a dividend payment will thus result in a corresponding relative fall in the **KFX**.

The base date for the **KFX** is 3 July 1989. On the basis of the official prices of that day, the index value has been established at 100.00. The index value is established on the basis of a portfolio consisting of the market value of 25 equities. Among the shares that can be included in the **KFX**, 40 shares are selected every three months and these make up the **base portfolio**. These 40 shares are the most liquid shares over the last twelve months as they have been among the 40 most actively traded shares for the highest number of days in terms of market value. Turnover is determined on the basis of inter-broker trading and trading via the Copenhagen Stock Exchange screen-based trading system.

The **active portfolio** is in turn selected among the components of the **base portfolio**. This portfolio is the actual basis for the calculation of the **KFX**. The active portfolio consists of 25 equities with the highest market capitalisation. The potfolio will then form the basis for the calculation of the **KFX** for the three-month period beginning one month after the selection date.

The official calculation of the Index is prepared on an ongoing basis by the Copenhagen Stock Exchange on the basis of all transactions in the match and accept system on the Exchange. The index value is calculated at a fixed interval, so far every five minutes. In conjunction with the index portfolio revision every three months, the index is adjusted to secure that the index value is not affected

KFX active portfolio as at 1 June 1990

	Market Cap DKKm	Weight KFX	Weight CSE Index
Banks			
Den Danske Bank	17,131.8		
Sparekassen Biluben	2,951.8		
Unidanmark A	10,964.3		
Jyske Bank	2,776.7		
Total	33,824.6	22.79%	17.80%
Insurance			
Codan Forsikring	5,781.8		
Total	5,781.8	3.90%	7.50%
Trade and Services			
Ostasiatisk Kompagni (EAC)	5,073.0		
Sophus Berendsen A/S B	3,113.9		
Dansk Luftfartsselskab A	2,791.0		
Total	10,977.9	7.40%	10.80%
Shipping			
D/S 1912 B	10,552.0		
D/S 1912 A	10,530.0		
D/S Svendborg B	10,470.1		
D/S Svendborg A	10,432.8		

J.Lauritzen	3,562.3		
Total	45,547.1	30.69%	20.00%
Industrials			
Danisco	9,513.2		
Novo-Nordisk B	7,705.8		
FLS B	5,600.2		
Carlsberg pr.	3,844.2		
NKT	2,891.2		
Total	29,554.6	19.92%	31.70%
Investement Trusts			
Baltica Holding	10,331.7		
Hafnia Holding B	3,577.9		
Hafnia Holding A	3,197.1		
Topdanmark	3,099.7		
Potagua B	2,505.0		
Total	22,711.3	15.30%	12.20%
GRAND TOTAL	148,397.2	100.00%	100.00%

Daily Volume and Open Interest (Jan 2,1990 - Jun 29,1990)

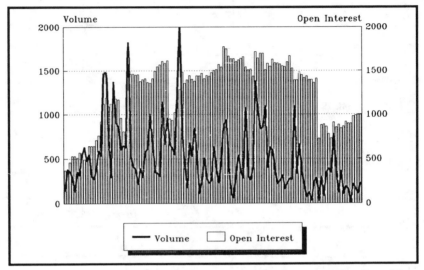

Volume/ Open Interest and Open Interest (Jan 2,1990 - Jun 29, 1990)

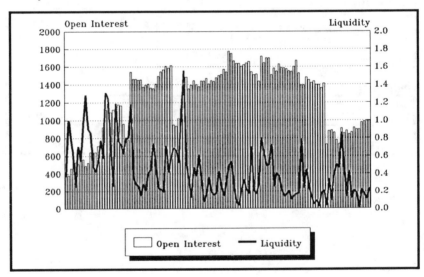

Price/Yield History (Jan 2,1990 - Jun 29,1990)

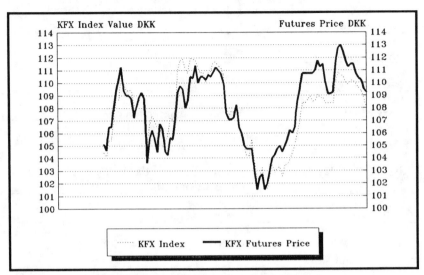

Implied Repo Rate (Jan 2,1990 - Jun 29,1990)

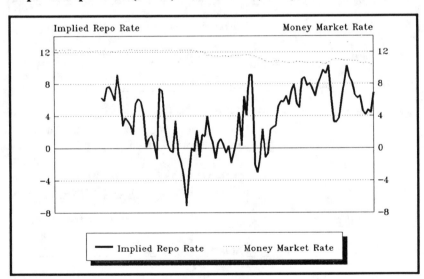

KFX Stock Index Futures Options Contract

On the 21st September 1990, options on the KFX Stock Index Futures will be launched.

Option Style	European calls and puts.
Contract Size:	DKK 100,000.
Expiry Months:	March June September December.
Expiry Day:	The first business day of the expiry month.
Last Trading Day:	The last business day in the month prior to the expiry month.
Quotation:	Per cent of par.
Minimum Price Movement (Tick Size and Value):	DKK0.05 per cent = DKK 50.
Trading Hours:	09.00 a.m. - 15.30 p.m. by electronic trading.
Initial Margin:	12 per cent = DKK 12,000.
Price Limit:	900 basis points (9 per cent).
Contract Standard:	Cash settlement.
Exercise Price:	Exercise intervals of 5 index points. A minimum of three prices exist one above and one below the current level. if the prices of the underlying asset moves below the lowest or above the highest exercise price contracts with new exercise prices are opened.
Reuters Pages:	DKOA (general information) & UDKF.
Telerate Pages:	None
Guarantee Fund fees	DKK 50 per transaction plus DKK 50 per contract.

Metals

At the mid 1990 there was no official market in Denmark for futures and options on metals. Some of the large Danish banks trade in the international markets for futures and options on metals.

Commodities

At the mid 1990 there was no official market in Denmark for futures and options on commodities. Some of the large Danish banks trade in the international markets for futures and options on commodities.

TAXATION

No legislation governing the Danish Tax treatment of options and futures has been adopted to date for domestic private and institutional investors.

However, it is expected that a new tax-law for options and futures will be adopted in 1990.

Since Danish options and futures are exempted from withholding tax this has no direct consequences for foreign investors, except that the liquidity is lower as it would be with a tax legislation for all types of domestic investors.

Over-the-Counter Contracts

A small OTC market exists alongside the official market for non-guaranteed options and futures. The rules of both the Copenhagen Stock Exchange and the Guarantee Fund do not extend to such markets, and contracts of this type are not covered by the Fund's guarantee.

It is not forbidden for members of the Fund to trade OTC contracts although the members have been asked not to trade OTC contracts similar to the official contracts.

SOURCES of INFORMATION

Official material from the Guarantee fund, including prospecta for the various contracts can be obtained from:

Address: The Guarantee Fund of Danish Options and Futures
15 Kompagnistræde
P.O.Box 2017
DK-1012 COPENHAGEN K

Tel: (45) 3393 3311

Fax: (45) 3393 4480

Official price lists are published by the Copenhagen Stock Exchange (Kobenhavns Fondsbors), published daily and monthly can be obtained from:

Address: Copenhagen Stock Exchange
                              6 Nikolaj Plads
                              P.O.Box 1040
                              DK-1007 COPENHAGEN K
Tel: (45) 3393 3366
Fax: (45) 3312 8613

Publications by the Danish Central Bank (Danmarks Nationalbank) in English:

                              Annual Report, published in May/June
                              Quarterly Review, published quarterly February,
                              May, August and November
Address: Havnegade 5
                              DK-1093 COPENHAGEN K
Tel: (45) 141411

Local papers emphazising bond market coverage:

Dagbldet Borsen   Montergade 19
                              DK-1014 COPENHAGEN K
Tel: (45) 157250
Berlingske Tidende   Pilestræde 34
                              DK1147 COPENHAGEN K
Tel: (45) 131012

Reuters Pages covering bond markets:

ANDA onwards

COHA onwards

PRBA onwards

SDA onwards

SUNQ onwards

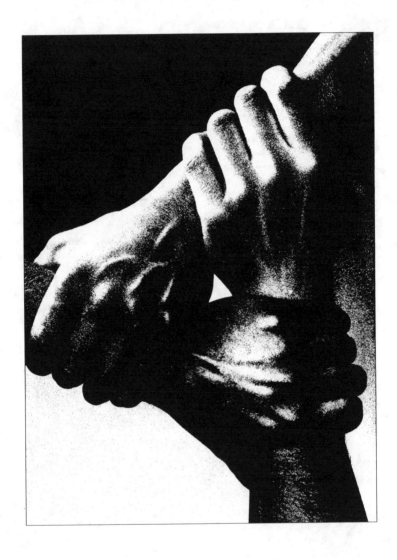

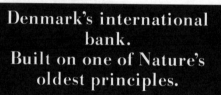

The Futures & Options Markets in France

Richard Komarnicki

Marie-Pierre Gontard
CARDIF

Philippe Willemetz

with assistance from:
MATIF SA
MONEP
OMF/FMA
and
Messrs. Michel Piermay and Pierre Mathoulin
from La Mondiale

INTRODUCTION

The creation of the Futures markets in France can be traced back to 1885, but concerned only commodities. After being closed in 1939 because of World War II, trading has progressively resumed in the different markets; cocoa opened in 1962, white sugar in 1964, Robusta coffee in 1972 and Soya Cattle cakes in 1982.

The **Marché A Terme des Instruments Financiers "MATIF"** was created by law on July 11, 1985, a hundred years almost to the day after the creation of the Bourse de Commerce de Paris (Paris Commodities Exchange). Certainly, the two markets are different in many aspects, but their purpose is the same, that of providing futures contracts enabling the user to hedge himself against price fluctuations.

Indeed, it is true that commodity prices have seen major movements since they began trading, however interest rate and foreign exchange rate fluctuations are a more recent phenomenon, mainly due to the cancellation of the Bretton-Woods agreement in 1971 (or the de-linking of the U.S. Dollar to Gold), the 1973 oil-shock and the change in American monetary policy in 1979. Protection against risks resulting from these fluctuations has become a necessity for all those involved in commodity or financial markets. The first interest rate futures contract opened in Chicago in the late 1970's. Progressively, Exchanges throughout out the world have launched contracts of this type, the major markets being in the USA, the UK, France and Japan.

1987 proved to have been for **MATIF** a testing year. The behaviour of the futures market in this context has been a real success. The October 1987 Crisis has passed without market stability having been put into question, and, furthermore, has witnessed an exceptional development with a trading volume of 12 million contracts for the Notional Bond Future.

Having become the third most important Interest Rate Futures Market worldwide, **MATIF** has been a major contributor to ensuring liquidity in the French Government Debt Market during a particularity stormy economical period. The security and liquidity of the market in 1987 are major examples of what will enable the financial community to fight tomorrow's battles.

At the same time (September 1987), trading in stock options began on the **Marché des Options Négociables de PARIS "MONEP"**, an Exchange of which the only members are Stockbroker firms. It was a difficult beginning because of the October 1987 crisis, but by January 1988, trading volume began to increase sharply from a monthly average of 100,000 contracts in 1987, to 200,000 in 1988 and to over 300,000 in 1989.

At the end of 1988, **Organisation des Marchés Financiers "OMF"**, a third Exchange created by the same organisation who opened **OM** in Stockholm in 1985, started to trade a stock index future (**OMF50**) based on 50 active stocks as well as an option based on this contract. This Exchange, although official, was considered as "private" and a direct competitor to **MATIF**. In response, **MATIF** started to trade its own stock index future, the **CAC40**, on November 8, 1988. After a few months of "cohabitation", the **CAC40** future overwhelmed the **OMF50** future.

The opening, on December 5, 1988, of the third trading floor "**MATIF 3**" has provided traders with a totally progressive trading place under the technical and technological points of views. With more than 16 million contracts traded in 1988 (an increase of 36 per cent year-on-year), **MATIF** confirmed its third rank worldwide. The year 1988 marked the technical maturity of the French Futures Market, while success in the financial field was confirmed by the creation of three new contracts: Options on the Notional Bond Future, 3 Month **PIBOR** Future and the CAC40 Stock Index Future. **MATIF** was in 1989 the first ranked European Futures Market, just ahead of London's LIFFE and worldwide, it ranked just behind Chicago and Tokyo.

As of **MATIF**'s third anniversary, on February 20, 1989, over 33 million contracts had been traded since its introduction. A few months later, in October 1989, 50 million contracts have been traded.

1989 has begun with the appearance of the first Locals, which in French are called NIPs (Négociateurs Individuels de Parquet). This initiative came from the will to strengthen market liquidity and to improve the performance of the Parisian market. During the first half of 1989, a new 4-Year Treasury Note Contract had been launched by **OMF (a necessary complement to the Notional Bond Contract)**, and **MATIF launched an option on the 3-Month Paris Inter Bank Offer Rate "PIBOR"** futures contract. This latter product began trading more than 10,000 lots a day.

More recently, a 3-Month Euro-Deutschemark contract has been launched and the opening of a six to ten year European Currency Unit ("ECU") bond futures contract is imminent, a real sign of the further internationalization of the Market. The opening date for this contract has been set for the 18th October 1990.

ORGANIZATION of the MARKETS

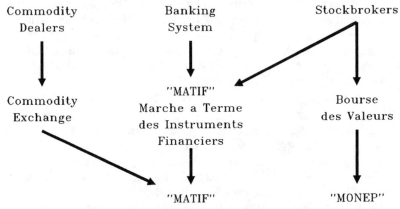

As explained before, there are three different Futures and Options Exchanges in France.

- MATIF (Marché A Terme International de France)

- MONEP (Marché des Options Négociables de Paris)

- OMF (Organisation de Marchés Financiers) - recently changed into the France Matif Automatique FMA

The main reason for this resides in the ancient monopoly of stockbrokers. There had been some concern among the stockbrokers that when MATIF opened membership would no longer be restricted to stockbrokers but would also encompass banks, money market brokers etc..

Therefore, when options on stocks began trading, stockbrokers wanting to maintain a monopoly (which some would say to be theoretical because for a number of years , banks etc, have been allowed to hold shares in stockbroker firms). The **MONEP** was created and only options traded in this market.

At the same time, commodities dealers did not want to be divorced from the changes they were witnessing. So, after some debate, the commodities Exchange merged with the **MATIF** and the name of **MATIF** changed from **Marché A Terme des Instruments Financiers** to **Marché A Terme International de France** (see diagram above). Finally, the **MATIF** is taking a stake in the capital of OMF, the independent electronic Exchange. The name of OMF has been changed from Organisation de Marchés Financiers to France Matif Automatique FMA.

HISTORY of the FUTURES & OPTIONS MARKET

Date of Launch	Type of Contract	Exchange	Traded Volume (Monthly Average)
11 February 1963	Cocoa Futures	MTMP	-
28 May 1964	White sugar Futures	MTMP	22,009
14 December 1972	Robusta Coffee Futures	MTMP (Paris & Le Havre)	204
09 May 1984	Potato Futures (50 mm)	MTMP (Lille)	2,856
09 May 1984	Potato Futures (40 mm)	MTMP (Lille)	42
20 February 1986	Opening of the Notional 7-10 year bond futures market	MATIF	1,218,375
25 June 1986	90 Day Treasury Bill futures Contract	MATIF	No longer traded
End 1986	Trading of options on the Notional 7-10 year bond futures contract on an OTC basis	MATIF	
10 September 1987	Opening of MONEP	MONEP	
10 September 1987	Options on Stocks	MONEP	

16 September 1987	White Sugar Option	MTMP	
October 1987	3 Month **PIBOR** future trades OTC	**MATIF**	
12 November 1987	Potato Future (50mm)	MTMP (Lille)	2,856
31 December 1987	Merging of the Commodities and Financial Futures Markets **MTMP** into one Exchange: Marché à Terme International de France	MATIF	
14 January 1988	Notional 7-10 Year Bond Option Officially listed with **EVEN** strike price eg 98 100 102	MATIF	595,500
21 July 1988	Opening of **OMF**	OMF	
21 July 1988	OMF 50 Stock Index Future	OMF	
19 August 1988	CAC 40 Stock Index Future on **THS**	MATIF	
08 September 1988	3 Month **PIBOR** Future	MATIF	166,563
09 November 1988	OMF 50 Stock Index Future, OMF		
09 November 1988	CAC 40 Stock Index Future in Pit	MATIF	58,083
09 November 1988	CAC 40 Stock Index Option	MONEP	70,000
09 January 1989	Decrease in Tick size from 0.05 to 0.02 - Notional bond contract	MATIF	

14 February 1989	CCIFP becomes MATIF SA	MATIF	
01 March 1989	THS* trading in Notional Bond Option with ODD strike prices	MATIF	595,500
13 March 1989	Notional 7-10 Year Bond Option with ODD strike price in Pit	MATIF	
12 April 1989	THS* trading of 3 Month Eurodeutschemark Future	MATIF	
02 May 1989	3 Month Eurodeutschemark Future in Pit	MATIF	73,791
01 June 1989	BTAN Future	OMF	9,729
01 March 1990	3 Month PIBOR Option in Pit & THS*	MATIF	69,355
05 April 1990	3 Month Eurodeutschemark Option in Pit & THS	MATIF	17,917

Averages per month are based on the volume of the last six months of 1989, or since inception if launched after July 1, 1989.
* THS - Transactions Hors Seance - after hours trading.

OVERVIEW of PRODUCTS

Contracts	Futures	Options	
		on Futures	on Cash
Long/Medium Term Interest Rates			
Actual Long Term Bonds			#
Notional Long Term Bonds	*	*	
Notional Medium Term Notes	*	#	

Actual Medium Term Notes			#
Short Term Interest Rates			
3 Month Treasury Bill	*		
3 Month PIBOR	*	*	
3 Month Eurodeutschemark	*	*	
Currencies			
Foreign Exchange			#
Equities			
Actual Stocks			*
Stock Indices	*		*
Commodities			
Metals			
Potatoes	*		
White Sugar	*	*	
Cocoa	*		
Robusta Coffee	*		
Soya Cattle Cakes	*		

* contracts available at present

contracts traded OTC only

The Marché A Terme International de France "MATIF"

ORGANIZATION of MATIF

The Conseil du Marché a Terme des Instruments Financiers **CMT**, the "Sages' Council", plays a similar role to that of the CFTC in the USA. It, among others, discusses the principles of the functioning of the market, determines the rules, decides on products policy, acts as the regulatory body of the market and plans the future direction of the Exchange. The Board of this Institution consists of senior representatives of institutions involved.

The Chambre de Compensation des Instruments Financiers de Paris "**CCIFP**" is the clearing house. The CCIFP changed its name to "**MATIF SA**" during a special shareholders meeting on February 14, 1989. Its role is to:-

●**ensure market transparency**

●**improve services**

●**improve methods (i.e. calculation of deposits,etc.)**

●**control daily operations**

●**develop the market (research, etc.).**

MATIF SA are advised of and clear all transactions for all trades dealt on the THS in the morning and on the official market **up to** 16.00 p.m. Paris time that day. Trades on the THS in the evening are cleared the next day. It is also a member of Globex which is an electronic quotation system on futures and options. Its aim is not to make the open outcry system or the pit obsolete but to make it possible to trade 24 hours a day and increase liquidity and reduce counterparty risks. The CME is also a member of the Globex quotation system.

Board of Directors at 10.5.1990

M. Gerard Pfauwadel	Chairman
Mme. M. Bourven	C.N.C.A.
M. H. Daru	U.A.P.
M. P. Duverger	Société Generale
M. A. Ferri	Société de Bourse Ferri-Ferri-Germe
M. J.P. Hellebuyck	Groupe AXA
M. D. Hoenn	Paribas
M. J.P. Lefoulon	B.N.P.
M. G. de la Martinière	Société de Bourse Meeschaert-Rouselle
M. C. Prince	Societe de Bourse Schelcher-Prince
M. S. Sayan	A.G.F.
M. J.F. Theodore	Société de Bourses Françaises
M. S. Allain	Commissaire du Governement, Ministry of the Economy, Finance and the Budget
M. R. Raymond	Banque de France

Management

M. Gerald Pfauwadel	Chairman
M. Gilbert Durieux	Director General
M. Jean Sicard	Director of Promotion and Communication

Membership

The main members of the Exchange are:-

● Stockbrokers

● Banks

● Credit Institutions

● Financial Institutions incorporated under Article 99 of the Banking Law

● Joint ventures between the above.

● Négotiateurs Individuels de Parquet "NIPs" - "Locals"

MATIF Membership Types

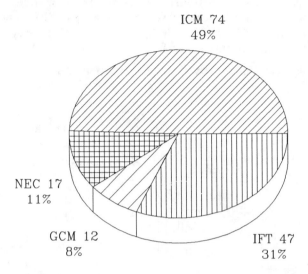

ICM 74
49%

NEC 17
11%

GCM 12
8%

IFT 47
31%

     The graph above illustrates the breakdown of 1989 activity by type of member. In addition, notwithstanding the type of institution members are, they are further divided into four categories. These are:-

- **General Clearing Members "GCM". There are twelve General Clearing Members "GCM" ("Adherents Compensateurs Généraux"). They must have a net worth of at least FRF 750 million. They provide the funds for their own trading, those of their customers and their trading brokers.**

- **The Trader Brokers "NECs" ("Negociateurs - Courtiers") are required to have a net worth of FRF 7.5 million and are named by a General Clearing Member with whom their clients' operations are recorded either anonymously or not. NECs clear their trades through their GCM, have the status of Broker/Trader and are allowed to trade on behalf of their clients.**

- **Independent Clearing Members "ICM" ("Adhérents Compensateurs Individuels") trade for their own account as well as for their clients. They have a minimum net worth of FRF 50 million along with a bank guarantee. There are 74 such firms.**

● Independent Floor Traders IFTs or "Locals" (NIPs - "Négotiateurs Individuels de Parquet") who provide the market with potential buyers and sellers. There are 47 "IFT" at present out of a limit of 50. They are designated by the GCMs or by ICMs with whom an account is opened.

Membership of MATIF by Type of Organisation

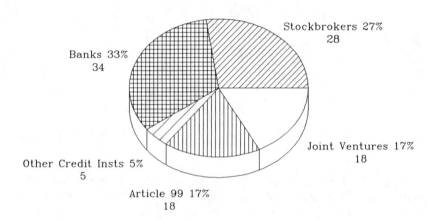

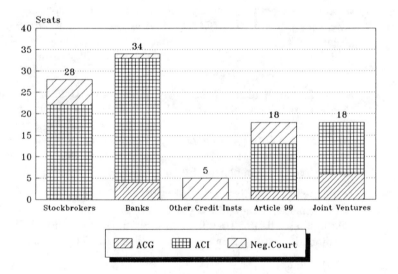

Geographical Distribution of Membership

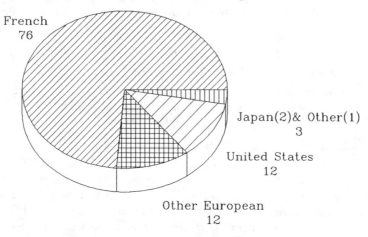

French
76

Japan(2)& Other(1)
3

United States
12

Other European
12

     Out of a total of 103 members of **MATIF**, 27 are subsidiaries of non-French groups or are under non French majority control.

     MATIF SA has designated some members as market makers committed to provide greater liquidity on particular contracts (Notional Options, 3 Month PIBOR and 3 Month Euro-DM Options) by pledging to quote prices on them permanently.

Globex

     Members of MATIF and international broker members of a Globex Partner Exchange, when equipped with a Globex terminal will be able to trade the MATIF futures and options on the Notional Bond and PIBOR contracts starting at the beginning of 1991. International brokers will just need to make a Clearing agreement with a MATIF Clearing member. Electronic trading on Globex will be possible during THS hours when trading in the pit stops. As an example, MATIF members will be able to trade CME's Eurodollar futures and MATIF 3 month PIBOR on the screen.

Margin Requirement for Options

     The margin is calculated by MATIF SA. It is due in the event of a short sale; sale of a call or a put. The Initial margin corresponds to the liquidating of a portfolio at a price determined by the cumulative unfavorable possible changes in the following three parameters:

●Futures contract varying within a range of plus/minus 4 per cent in the case of the 7-10 years notional bond (ie a limit up or down).

●A corrective 20 per cent increase or decrease in implied volatility that also goes against the holders' position.

●Inter-maturity differential of futures prices.

The maximum futures contract price variation is taken into consideration in calculating the theoretical value of the options and the most negative liquidating value gives the initial margin.

MATIF Exchange Fees

The Exchange fee paid by members of MATIF SA is FRF 8.00 + VAT per contract (the same price for a futures or an options contract). For very active members, a re-allowance is given by MATIF SA, reducing the contract exchange fees to FRF 6.00. Locals have an exchange fee of FRF 4.00 per contract. Specialist members chosen by MATIF SA to make markets on specific contracts pay no exchange fee.

Education

Two seminars are organized by MATIF SA.

1.   General and technical information on the MATIF contracts. (Three times two days over three weeks.)

2.   A seminar specifically for the traders in the Pit followed by an examination that all floor traders need to pass (regulation dated December 14, 1989).

Contact: M. Sniter
Tel: (33) 1 40 28 82 82

MATIF offers a variety of publications covering its contracts and their use.

Contact: Mme. Decea
Tel: (33) 1 40 28 82 82

Address: MATIF SA
                176, Rue Montmatre
                75002 PARIS
Tel: (33) 1 40 28 82 82

| Fax: | (33) 1 40 28 80 01 |
| Telex: | 218 362 F |

Brokerage Fees (Commission)

In addition to the Exchange fees, a client who is not a member of MATIF (or MONEP) but the client of a broker must pay the broker a brokerage fee (or commission). This commission is negociable abd can vary between 10 and 100 francs per contract. Brokers who supply clients with research tend to charge a little bit more than the others which is understandable.

OVERVIEW of PRODUCTS

	Futures	Options
Interest Rates		
Notional 10% 7-10 Year Government Bond	*	*
90 Day Treasury Bill	*	
3 month PIBOR	*	*
3 month Eurodeutschemark	*	*
Long Term ECU Bond	*	
Stock Index		
CAC 40 Stock Index	*	
Commodities		
Cocoa	*	
Potatoes 40mm	*	
Potatoes 50mm	*	
White Sugar	*	*
Soya Cattle Cakes	*	

HISTORY of MATIF MARKET

Date of Launch	Type of Contract	Trading Volume (Monthly Average)
20 February 1986	Notional 10% 7-10 Year Bond Future	1,218,375
25 June 1986	90 Day Treasury Bill Future	No longer traded
14 January 1988	Notional 10% 7-10 Year Bond Option	595,500
08 September 1988	3 Month PIBOR Future	166,563
09 November 1988	CAC 40 Stock Index Future	58,083
02 May 1989	3 Month Eurodeutschemark Future	73,791
01 March 1990	3 Month PIBOR Options	69,355
05 April 1990	3 Month Eurodeutschemark Options	17,917

Trading Volume: Averages per month are based on the volume of the last six months of 1989 or since inception if launched after July 1, 1989.

DETAILED CONTRACT SPECIFICATIONS
Interest Rates
Long Term French Government 10.00% 7-10 Year Notional Bond Futures Contract

This contract, the first to be listed on the Exchange, has been trading since February 20, 1986. It was the first Financial Futures contract on the Continent. Its success is due to the interaction of the different financial players interested in the evolution of French long term bond interest rates.

The major users of the contract are fund managers who need to cover or enhance the exposure of their portfolios and increase the performance potential of the funds they manage. Bond traders and syndicate managers in the primary market departments of banks and S.V.T. also need to hedge their bond allotments of new issues. The speculative domestic and international clients are interested in this contract as they only need to place a deposit of 5 per cent of the nominal amount in order to participate in the fluctuations of a volatile market thus creating an important opportunity for capital gain or loss against the initial amount of the deposit. There are many arbitrage opportunities such as cash and carry and reverse cash and carry operations, as well as spread trading between different delivery months of the same contract.

The 10 per cent 7-10 year Notional bond future is the most traded contract on the MATIF. MATIF is the second futures exchange in Europe (by volume) and this contract is also the second most traded. It is the most traded bond contract in Europe.

Over the first six months of 1990, the average daily volume of this contract has been around 60,000 contracts, a figure a little bit lower than that of 1989 because of a sort of stagnation in interest rate levels in France (except for the end of February/beginning of March where price volatility and volumes literally soared). As in any exchange, daily volume figures witness peaks and troughs, for reasons very much understandable as price movements, expectation changes, etc. as well as bank holidays. It is common knowledge that in the last days of May, most of France is on holiday, which is reflected in the statistics.

Open interest in the 7-10 year notional bond futures contract has been remaining at the average level of 80,000 contracts day after day. This figure may be interpreted as rather high (i.e. people hedging portfolios and keeping positions for quite a while) but, if one looks at the liquidity levels, the interpretation is quite different.

As explained before, one defines liquidity as: volume ÷ open interest.

A figure of 0.5, for instance, would indicate that the exchange turns over 50 per cent of the open interest in one single day. The higher the figure, the greater the liquidity. Over the first half of 1990, liquidity on the notional bond contract has averaged around 0.8 or 80 per cent, which is one of the highest figures in the world.

The price history of the futures contract has been staying very much in line with that of the cash market. As usual, when long-term yields are higher than short-term rates, the further the contract, the lower its price compared to the more nearby ones.

As France has experienced inverted rather than flat yield curves, it is no surprise that the prices of the different month contracts have been crossing each other. The difference in price between the futures contracts and a cash price index can be better reflected by the difference between implied repo rates and the cash market rates.

Historical volatility of a futures contract is an interesting statistic in the sense that it can explain at the same time sharp movements in:

a) the volume of futures contracts traded

b) the volume **and the price** of options on the aforesaid futures contract.

Further comments on this particular fact will be made in the paragraphs regarding the options contract.

As everybody knows, it is almost impossible for an implied repo rate to be higher than the interbank money market rate. If such were the case, every banker would borrow money in the market, buy bonds and sell a futures contract and deliver the bonds on expiry. Implied repo rates are generally lower than money market rates.

If they are close to them, many players in the market who do not have access to the money market may find there are opportunities to build synthetic money market rates going through "cash and carry" operations.

If implied repo rates are much lower than money market rates then "reverse repo" operations are available where if one can borrow physical bonds, one sells them "short" and buy simultaneously a futures contract.

Contract Size:	FRF 500,000 nominal value 7-10 Year French Government bond with a notional 10 per cent coupon.
Delivery Months:	March June September December.
Delivery Day:	Last business day of the Delivery Month.
Last Trading Day:	Fourth Bourse business day before the last session of the delivery month.
Quotation:	Per cent FRF 100.
Minimum Price Movement (Tick Size and Value):	0.02 per cent = FRF 100.
Trading Hours:	09.00 a.m. - 16.00 p.m. Trading also takes place **over the counter** from 08.00 a.m. - 08.59 a.m. and 16.00 p.m. - 19.00 p.m. or later if there is demand. These transactions are called **Transactions Hors Seance "THS"**.
Initial Margin:	Until March 8,1990 4.0 per cent. Since then it has been increased to 5.0 per cent = FRF 25,000.
Price Limit:	250 basis points (2.5 per cent) above or below the last settlement price. This was increased from 2.0 per cent on March 8,1990.
Contract Standard:	Physical delivery is made of French Government bonds with maturities of between 7 and 10 years. However any given bond belonging to the underlying basket of deliverables will not be deliverable if its coupon (generally annual) is to be detached within two weeks of the settlement date.

Exchange Delivery Settlement Price:	The settlement price at 16.00 p.m. four bourse business days before the last trading day of the delivery month. The invoice amount is to be calculated with the conversion factor.
Reuters Pages:	MATD and for "THS" MEUN PLUW PUGF
Telerate Pages:	3215

Delivery

In order to illustrate the delivery mechanism, the following OATs are deliverable at the time of writing.

Bonds	Outstanding Nominal FRF m.
OAT 8.500% 25-06-1997	26,268
OAT 9.700% 12-12-1997	27,123
OAT 9.900% 13-12-1997	19,281
OAT 9.500% 25-06-1998	21,908
OAT 8.125% 25-05-1999	28,501
OAT 8.500% 28-03-2000	10,400
OAT 10.00% 27-05-2000	19,828

Conversion Factors

The number of bonds to be delivered is calculated for each period by using the following conversion factors. These factors determine the number of bonds required to equate to a 7-10 Year 10 per cent nominal bond. In reality, a further calculation is required to determine which bond is "Cheapest to Deliver". This takes into account the actual market prices of the bonds.

Bonds	Jun 1990	Sep 1990	Dec 1990	Mar 1991	Jun 1991
OAT 7.5% 07/01	(*1)	(*1)	(*1)	(*1)	0.845394
OAT 8.5% 03/00	0.908470	0.909634	0.911357	(*2)	0.914378
OAT 8.125% 05/99	0.892392	0.893771	0.895694	0.888103	0.900397
OAT 9.5% 06/98	0.973313	0.973046	0.973348	0.974214	(*3)
OAT 9.7% 12/97	0.983580	0.984301	(*3)	(*3)	(*3)
OAT 9.9% 12 /97	0.993736	0.994228	(*3)	(*3)	(*3)

Notes:

(*1) Not yet in the basket (over 10 years to maturity)
(*2) Temporarily out of basket (coupon payment)
(*3) Out of basket (less than 7 years to maturity)

Delivery Dates

Relevant Dates for the Futures Contracts up to June 1991.

Contract Months	Last Trading Day	Delivery Date
March 1990	26-03-1990	30-03-1990
June 1990	25-06-1990	29-06-1990
September 1990	24-09-1990	28-09-1990
December 1990	24-12-1990	31-12-1990

| March 1991 | 25-03-1991 | 29-03-1991 |
| June 1991 | 24-06-1991 | 28-06-1991 |

N.B. Deliveries take place on the last business day of the quarter.

Daily Volume and Open Interest (Jan 2,1990 - Jul 31,1990)

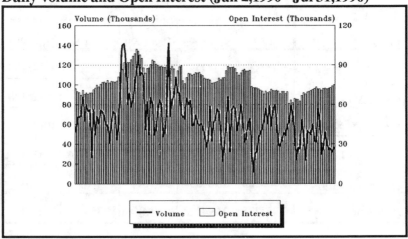

Open Interest and Volume/Open Interest (Liquidity) (Jan 2,1990 -Jul 31,1990)

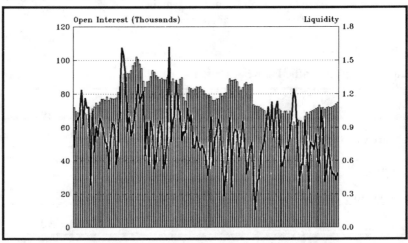

20 Day Moving Average Volumes (Jan 29,1990 - Jul 31,1990)

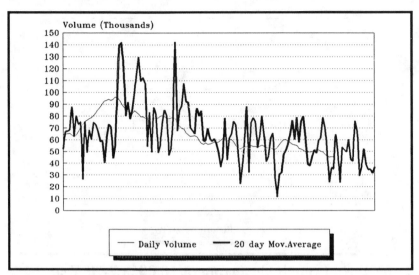

Price History (Jan 2,1990 - Jul 31,1990)

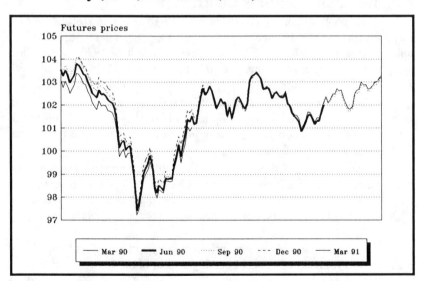

Historical Volatility (Jan 2,1990 - Jul 31,1990)

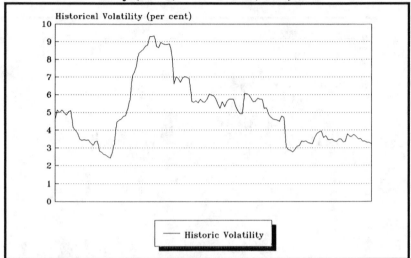

Long Term French Government 10.00% 7-10 Year Notional Bond Options Contract

This options contract on the Notional 7-10 years bond future was first listed on the **MATIF** Exchange on January 14, 1988. There were over 3.5 million options traded in 1988. During the first half of 1989, 3.43 million options were traded, an increase of 107 per cent over the first half of 1988. There were 3,563,263 options traded in the second half of 1989.

The success of this options contract is due to the preference of some investors to be invested in bond options where they have a limited risk exposure and the freedom to exercise or not the options, whereas the futures contracts have unlimited risk.

Daily volume of the options on the 7-10 year notional bond futures has been generally significant over the first half of 1990, although decreasing from an average of 40,000 contracts a day in the first quarter to an average of 20,000 at the end of the second quarter, reflecting the activity of the underlying futures market.

The correlation between options volume and futures volume is very high, options volume averaging about 40 per cent of the futures volume.

It is also interesting to split the options traded volume by month of expiry. This sort of analysis shows, for instance, that before the February peak, the most traded contract was March and that after that peak, the most traded one was June. On the two highest peak days in February, half of the volume was on the March contract, the other half on the June contract. As can be seen, open interest did not increase during these days. The explanation of this upsurge is simply the fact that many participants "rolled up" their positions from the March to the June contract. The peaks in the futures volume may also be explained by this "rolling over" around options positions. As it is known, the options market on the MATIF is lead by market makers who hedge their options positions by positions on futures.

A typical graph of open interest in option positions is quite different from the one on the futures contracts: there are great plunges every three months. This is explained by the fact that, on average, 50 per cent of the open interest in options is out-of-the-money at expiry and that holders of these positions did not close positions because of costs involved so those positions "die" (are abandoned) upon expiry.

The liquidity ratio of options is much lower than the one of the futures: almost ten times smaller. This is explained by the fact that many open interest positions are kept for a long time by market makers because of the role they play. It is also understandable that for one who wants to actively hedge a portfolio (i.e. participate from a favorable movement of the market but limit losses in the other case), options are preferable to futures and therefore relatively expensive - so less liquid.

As usual, the implied volatility of an options contract:

1)is generally higher than the historical volatility of the underlying

2)very often anticipates movements in the price of the underlying.

The MATIF has also witnessed this phenomenon over the months.

Option Type:	American Calls and Puts.
Contract Size:	One FRF 500,000 futures contract on the Notional 7-10 year bond.
Delivery Months:	March June September December.
Delivery Day:	Up to 16.00 p.m. on last day of trading.
Last Trading Day:	The last Friday of the month before the one of the close of trading on the Bond Future.

Quotation:	In percentage of the price of the underlying asset.
Minimum Price Movement (Tick Size and Value):	0.01 per cent = FRF 50.
Trading Hours:	09.05 a.m. - 16.00 p.m.
Initial Margin:	None for the buyer. For the seller it is calculated according to the risk factors used in the official formulae.
Price Limit:	No price limit.
Contract Standard:	Physical delivery of one Notional Bond Future.
Exercise Prices:	FRF1 intervals with 9 option prices - 4 above and 4 below the current exercise price.
Reuters Pages:	**BTRB** and following.
Telerate Pages:	33919

Daily Volume and Open Interest (Jan 2,1990 - Jul 31,1990)

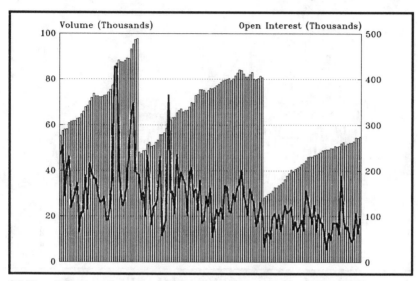

20 Day Moving Average of Options Volume (Jan 29,1990 - Jul 31,1990)

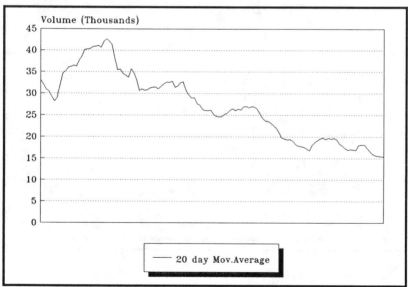

Daily Volume of Futures and Options (Jan 2,1990 - Jul 31,1990)

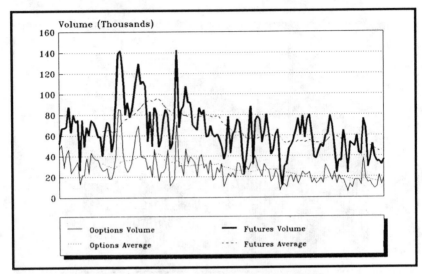

Daily Volume by Expiry (Jan 2,1990 - Jul 31,1990)

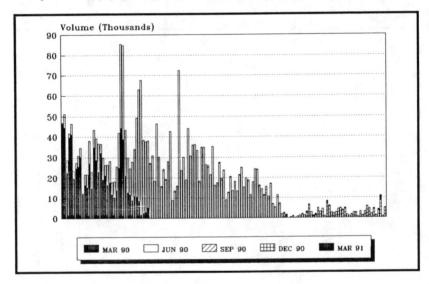

Open Interest and Volume/Open Interest (Liquidity)
(Jan 2,1990 -Jul 31,1990)

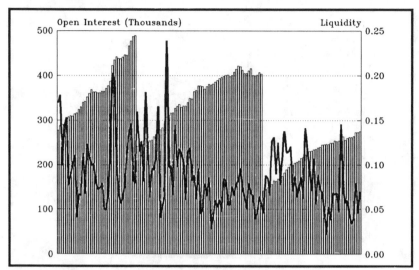

Implied Volatility (Jan 2,1990 - Jul 31,1990)

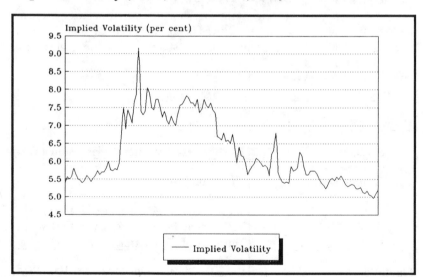

Volatilities of Futures and Options
(Jan 2,1990 - Jul 31,1990)

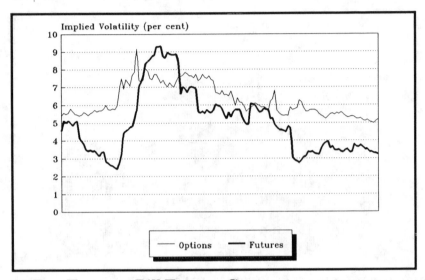

90 Day Treasury Bill Futures Contract

This contract, historically the first short-term contract to be listed on the **MATIF**, has never been very active. It was launched on June 25, 1986. Although still officially in existence, it is almost dead as not one single lot has been traded for months.

Contract Size:	FRF 5,000,000.
Delivery Months:	March June September December.
Delivery Day:	Two business days after the last trading day.
Last Trading Day:	The second Bourse day before the eleventh Thursday of the quarter except if the first day of the quarter is a Thursday then it will be the second Bourse day before the twelfth Thursday of the quarter.
Quotation:	100.00 minus the implicit rate i.e. 100 - 9.25 = 90.75.

Minimum Price Movement (Tick Size and Value):	0.01 per cent = FRF 125.
Trading Hours:	08.30 a.m. - 16.00 p.m.
Initial Margin:	FRF 15,000.
Price Limit:	60 basis points above or below the last settlement price.
Contract Standard:	Physical delivery of 90 day Treasury bills.
Exchange Delivery Settlement Price:	See note below.
Reuters Pages:	MATE

Exchange Delivery Settlement Price

The settlement price of the maturing contract is determined at the close of the last day at 16.00 p.m.. A just issued 13 weeks Treasury Bill or a seasoned Treasury Bill maturing in 13 weeks can be delivered against payment of a sum calculated as follows:

$$Amount\ due = FRF5,000,000 \times (1 - \frac{(100 - SP) \times ND}{36000})$$

where SP = Settlement Price

ND = exact number of days between the delivery day and the maturity of the bill.

i.e. SP = 91.25

ND = 91.

$$= 5,000,000 \times \left\{ 1 \frac{(100 - 91.25) \times 91}{36,000} \right\}$$

$$= 5,000,000 \times \left\{ 1 - \frac{8.75 \times 91}{36,000} \right\}$$

$$= 5,000,000 \times \left\{ 1 - 0.02218 \right\}$$

$$= 5,000,000 \times 0.977882$$

$$= 4,889,409.72$$

There are no graphs for this contract as there were no trades.

Three Month Paris Inter-Bank Offered Rate "PIBOR" Futures Contract

This contract was the third to be listed on the **MATIF** on September 8, 1988, as it became necessary to provide a futures contract with a short term interest rate reference regularly used by the market. In effect, it replaced the 90 day Treasury Bill contract which was launched on June 25, 1986 and had never been a success.

The combined use of the 3 Month PIBOR rate as a money market instrument and an underlying relationship to Treasury Bills and commercial paper has made this contract an immediate success. The use of the contract as a short term hedging tool for Treasury management operations of banks and corporations enhances its liquidity. In fact, this short term monetary product became the most widely used reference for the floating rate bond market by gradually replacing other indexes such as the **TAM**. The average daily volume in December 1989 was 5,984 contracts.

As the open position in the 3 Month PIBOR futures is usually important and greater than the volume of money market transactions in 3 Month PIBOR on the expiry date, the Association Française des Banques "AFB" checks the PIBOR rates at 09.30 a.m., 11.00 a.m. and 12.30 p.m. Paris time. The average of these quotes is the Exchange Delivery Settlement Price quoted. The 3 Month PIBOR can fluctuate widely around 11.00 a.m. on the expiry day.

Although lower than volume in the Notional Bond Futures Contract, volume in the 3 Month PIBOR Futures Contract has been keeping a steady pace during the first half of 1990, averaging more than 8,000 lots daily. Some observers even say that as the underlying value of one contract is FRF 5,000,000 versus FRF 500,000 for a notional bond contract, then volume expressed in terms of underlying value is higher in the PIBOR contract. Other people comment that although the above is true, the price sensitivity to a given change in the market interest rates is 22 times higher in the notional contract than in the PIBOR contract. Which poses the question of how to compare activity in different contracts!

It is very clear from the open interest figures that open interest plunges dramatically on contract maturity dates. This is obviously explained by the fact that many PIBOR contracts are exercised on expiry (contrary to the notional bond contract), and other positions "rolled over".

Liquidity in the PIBOR contract is lower than in the Notional Bond contract: about half the figure. This is explained by the fact that in this contract open positions tend to be kept longer. However, a contract that needs only 3 days to turn over the whole open interest can be indeed be considered as **very** liquid.

The price history of the PIBOR futures contract reflects quite well the evolution of interest rates in the cash market. We started the year with an inverted yield curve i.e. nearby contract higher in yield (and therefore cheaper in price) than the other contracts with an inversion of the trend at the end of February. When price movements are translated into interest rates, the flattening of the yield curve is clearly seen at the end of February and in July.

This is confirmed by the last graph which shows implicit futures yields and cash market rates. One aspect has to be highlighted: the PIBOR contract is based on the **domestic** 3 months forward /futures rates. It is therefore arbitraged by domestic operators against the domestic money-market rates. As foreign investors do not have access to the domestic money markets, they tend to arbitrage the futures contracts against the Euro-French franc 3 month rate. These crossed arbitrages have resulted in a narrowing of the spread between domestic and euro rates.

Contract Size:	FRF 5,000,000.
Delivery Months:	March June September December.
Delivery Day:	Two days after the last settlement day.
Last Trading Day:	11.00 a.m. Second Bourse day preceding the eleventh Thursday of each quarter except if the first day of the quarter is the first Thursday of the quarter. It will then be the second business day before the twelfth Thursday of the quarter. As from June 1991 this will be 11.00 a.m. Paris time two business days before the third Wednesday of the contract month.
Quotation:	100.00 minus the implied rate.
Minimum Price Movement (Tick Size and Value):	0.01 per cent = FRF 125. (1/4 of 0.01% x FRF 5,000,000.)

Trading Hours:	08.30 a.m. - 16.00 p.m.
Initial Margin:	1.2 per cent = FRF 15,000.
Price Limit:	60 basis points above or below the last settlement price.
Contract Standard:	Cash settlement.
Exchange Delivery Settlement Price:	The Association Française des Banques "AFB" checks the PIBOR rates at 09.30 a.m. 11.00 a.m. and 12.30 p.m. - see above.
Reuters Pages:	PIBN.
Telerate Pages:	3216

Daily Volume and Open Interest (Jan 2,1990 - Jul 31,1990)

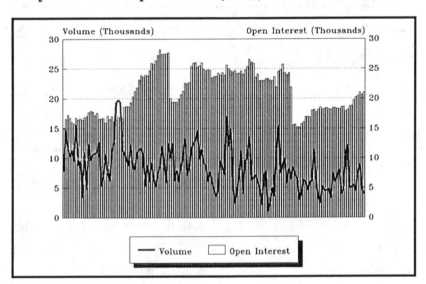

20 Day Moving Average of Futures Volume (Jan 2,1990 - Jul 31,1990)

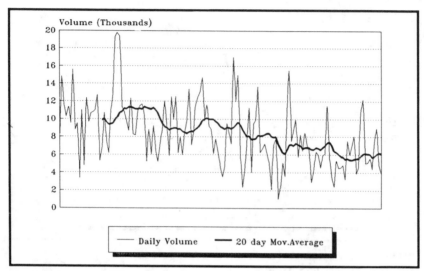

Open Interest and Volume/Open Interest (Liquidity) (Jan 2,1990 -Jul 31,1990)

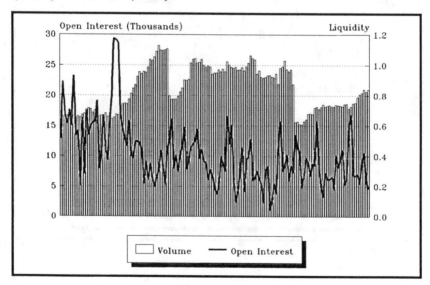

Price History (Jan 2,1990 - Jul 31,1990)

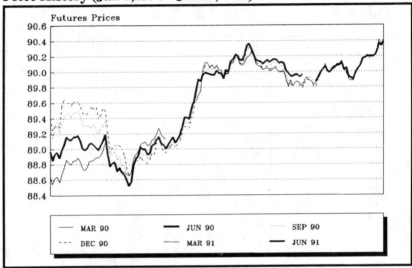

Interest Rate History (converted from prices)
(Jan 2,1990 - Jul 31,1990)

Comparison of Futures Implied Repo Rates and Money Market Rates (Jan 2,1990 - Jul 31,1990)

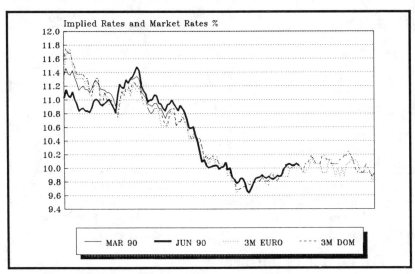

Historical Volatility (Jan 2,1990 - Jul 31,1990)

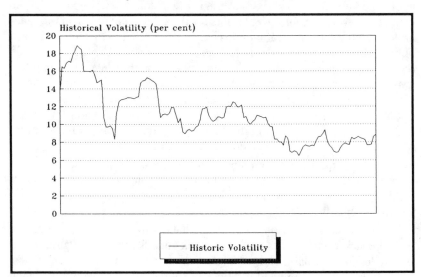

Relevant Dates for MATIF "PIBOR" Futures

Month	Last Trade	Delivery Date
March 1990	13/03/90	15/03/90
June 1990	12/06/90	14/06/90
September 1990	11/09/90	13/09/90
December 1990	11/12/90	13/12/90
March 1991	12/03/91	14/03/91
June 1991	17/06/91	15/06/91

The last day of trading in the 3 month PIBOR futures and options is being changed as from June 1991 so that the last trade date is going to be the same as the 3 month Eurodeutschemark futures and options contract.

Three Month Paris Inter-Bank Offered Rate PIBOR Options Contract

Apart from an exceptional peak in the first days after the contract opened, daily volumes have been averaging 3,000 lots a day, which is 37.5 per cent of the average figure of 8,000 lots for the futures contracts on the same underlying investment, a ratio quite comparable to that of the notional bond option. March 1990 figures were not significant for it was the first month this option ever traded. We witness the same plunge in open interest as in other option contracts. However, the plunge is not so sharp as in other options, which can be explained by the fact that contrary to long bond futures/options, options on 3 month rates are often used to hedge forward/forward positions and therefore open interest in the nearby contract is relatively not as overwhelming as in bond or stock index futures.

The liquidity ratio (volume open interest) of the option on the 3 month PIBOR futures is poorer than the notional long bond, although not by much. This is because open positions in these options are, on average, generally kept longer.

It is very interesting to witness that on the first days the options traded, market participants used as implicit volatility the exact figure of the 20 day historical volatility of the underlying futures contract. Then, as the weeks passed by, the implied volatility of options always stayed at a higher level than the historical volatility of futures, although some sort of correlation between respective volatility movements can be easily observed.

Option Style:	American calls and puts.
Contract Size:	One FRF 5,000,000 3 month PIBOR futures contract.
Delivery Months:	March June September December.
Delivery Day:	Two days after last trading day.
Last Trading Day:	Same as the future.
Quotation:	In percentage points with three decimal points.
Minimum Price Movement (Tick Size and Value):	0.005 per cent = FRF 62.5.
Trading Hours:	08.35 a.m. - 16.00 p.m. and the THS.
Initial Margin:	None for the buyer. For the seller the initial margin is calculated by adding positions held in futures and options and using the risk factors used is the formulae.
Contract Standard:	Physical delivery of a PIBOR futures contract.
Exercise Price:	0.10 per cent intervals.There are 5 options strike prices quoted on either side of the current value of the futures contract.
Reuters Pages:	**PIUA - PIUZ.**
Telerate Pages:	3216

Daily Volume and Open Interest (Mar 1,1990 - Jul 31,1990)

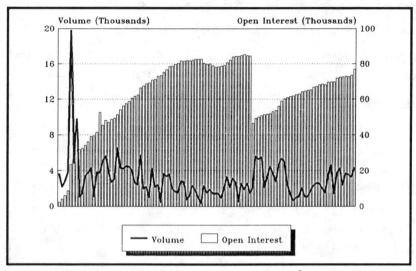

20 Day Moving Average of Options Volume (Mar 1,1990 - Jul 31,1990)

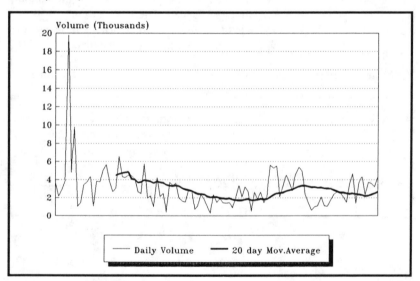

Open Interest and Volume/Open Interest (Liquidity)
(Mar 1,1990 -Jul 31,1990)

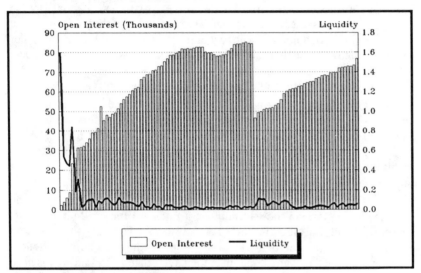

Historical and Implied Volatility (Mar 1,1990 - Jul 31,1990)

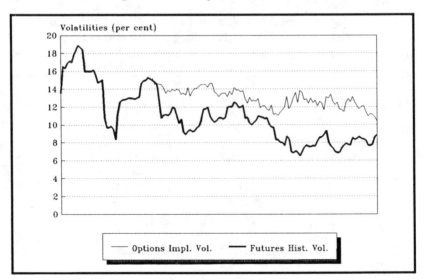

Three Month Eurodeutschemark Futures Contract

Daily volume in this contract has plunged from an average of 3,500 lots a day during the very first months of the year to less than 600 lots in June/July. This was due to the fact that in the beginning of the year the market was driven by market makers, who sort of turned on artificial volume in order to let the figures show that this contract was very active and could compete with London. But, it was artificial and now that we do not have market makers anymore, present figures show the real interest in this contract.

Open interest in this contract has not plunged as much as daily volume: this is because many positions are kept to hedge forward/forward rates and there still is open interest generated by the higher activity of the beginning of the year. The liquidity figures also reflect the turndown of activity in this contract: daily volume represented around 100 per cent of open interest in the beginning and at mid-year fell to 20 per cent.

The prices graph, together with the yield graph, show not only the general rise in German short-term interest rates in February/March and its subsequent fall, but also the fact that before mid-February there was an inverted yield curve and that when rates went up the yield curve flattened, keeping a classical upward slope since then. (Average prices and yields have been obtained by weighting the prices of each contract month by their respective volumes.)

Average historical volatility has itself been very volatile, reflecting very well the uncertainty of the market during the first time of the year, when short-term German rates moved sharply due to the factors we all know: German Unification, Monetary policy, Bundesbank policy, etc.

Contract Size:	DM 1,000,000.
Delivery Months:	March June September December.
Delivery Day:	Third Wednesday of the Delivery month.
Last Trading Day:	11.00 a.m. Paris time. Two London business days before third Wednesday of the Delivery Month.
Quotation:	100.00 minus implied rate.

Minimum Price Movement (Tick Size and Value):	0.01 per cent = DM 25.
Trading Hours:	08.30 a.m. - 16.00 p.m. and **THS**.
Initial Margin:	DM 1,000.
Price Limit:	30 basis points above or below the last settlement price.
Contract Standard:	Cash settlement.
Exchange Delivery Settlement Price:	**MATIF SA** selects 12 banks at random from a panel of 40 first class banks chosen by the Forex France Association active in Eurodeutschemark deposits in nine European cities. It discards the two highest and the two lowest. An arithmetic average of the remaining eight constitutes the settlement price.
Reuters Pages:	MATR and EDMF for THS transactions.
Telerate Pages:	3216 and 20169 for THS transactions and 20168 for open interest.

Daily Volume and Open Interest (Jan 2,1990 - Jul 31,1990)

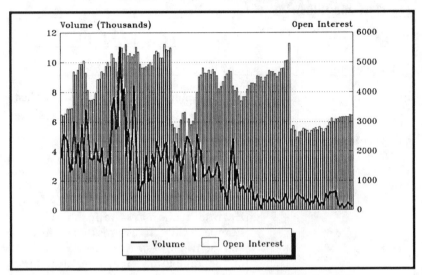

20 Day Moving Average of Futures Volume (Jan 2,1990 - Jul 31,1990)

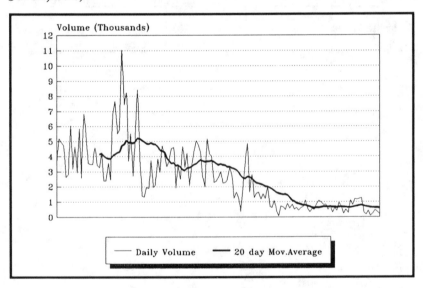

Open Interest and Volume/Open Interest (Liquidity) (Jan 2,1990 -Jul 31,1990)

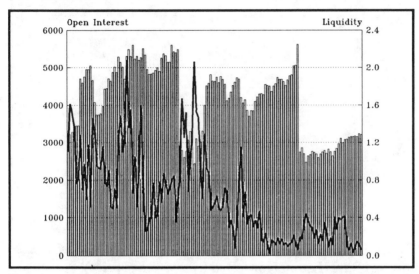

Futures Contract Price Histories (Jan 2,1990 - Jul 31,1990)

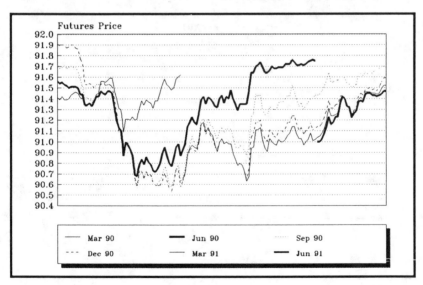

Average Price History (Jan 2,1990 - Jul 31,1990)

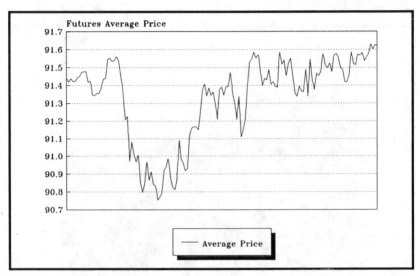

Interest Rate History (converted from average price)
(Jan 2,1990 - Jul 31,1990)

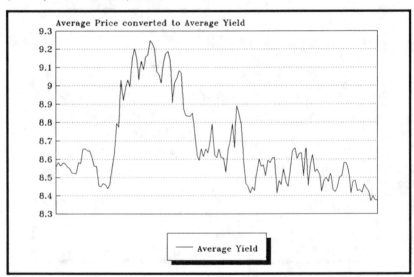

Implied Volatility (Jan 2,1990 - Jul 31,1990)

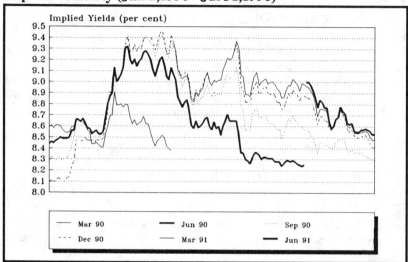

Historical Volatility (Jan 2,1990 - Jul 31,1990)

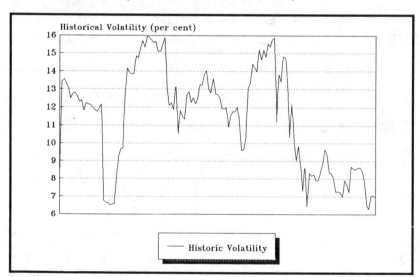

Three Month Eurodeutschemark Options Contract

The volumes of options on the 3 month euro-deutschemark futures have seen erratic figures: the average volume being around 1,000 lots in the first half of the year (one quarter of the volume on the futures in the first quarter to almost the same figure during the second quarter). There were only two occasions when volume traded in one single day exceeded the figure of 3,000 lots: in April and June. On these two days volume was respectively 9,167 and 11,110! No-one could provide an economical explanation. Such volumes may very well have been done by either market makers or financial institutions who "crossed risks" between different accounts. The average futures and options graph shows that not only have these been falling but also show that the fall in options has been slower than in the futures contract, with options volumes even higher than futures in July 1990. Although volumes were falling, open interest has been increasing steadily.

Liquidity in the contract is very poor. The two peaks shown in the graph correspond to the market maker driven transactions in the futures contract.

As usual, the implied volatility of options is higher than the 20 day moving average of futures contract. The graph clearly shows how the options market anticipates price movements (volatility) in the underlying markets (cash and futures).

Option Style	American calls and puts.
Contract Size:	One DM 1,000,000 futures contract.
Delivery Months:	March June September December.
Delivery Day:	Two days after the last trade day.
Last Trading Day:	11.00 a.m. Paris Time. Two London business days before the third Wednesday of the Delivery Month - the same as futures contract.
Quotation:	In percentage points to three decimal places.
Minimum Price Movement (Tick Size and Value):	0.005 per cent = DM 12.5.

Trading Hours:	09.10 a.m. - 15.50 p.m. and **THS**.
Initial Margin:	None for the buyer and for the seller it is calculated according to the risk incurred with the use of the official standard formula.
Price Limit:	See futures contract.
Contract Standard:	Physical delivery of one futures contract.
Exercise Price:	0.10 per cent intervals. There are 5 option contracts listed on either side of the current value.
Reuters Pages:	MATA
Telerate Pages:	39340 - 39358.

Daily Volume and Open Interest (Apr 5,1990 - Jul 31,1990)

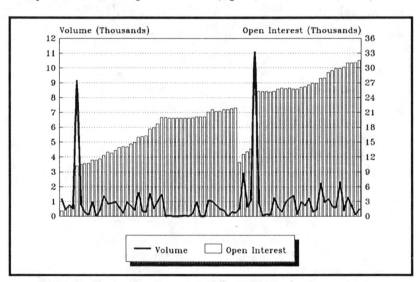

20 Day Moving Average of Options Volume (Apr 5,1990 - Jul 31,1990)

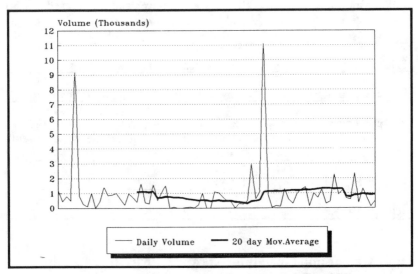

Option and Futures Volumes (Apr 5,1990 - Jul 31,1990)

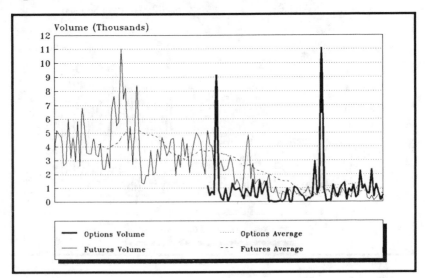

Open Interest and Volume/Open Interest (Liquidity)
(Apr 5,1990 -Jul 31,1990)

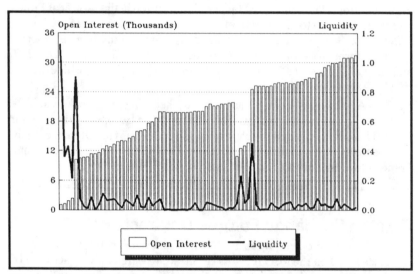

Historical and Implied Volatility (Apr 5,1990 - Jul 31,1990)

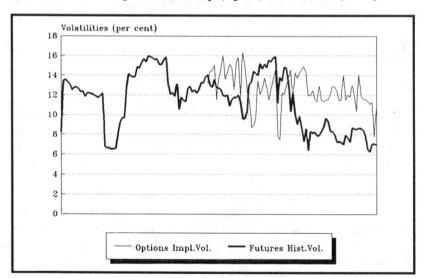

Long Term ECU Bond Futures Contract

MATIF is considering the creation of a long term ECU interest rates future contract. The Minister of Finance is interested in the project as France intends to issue up to 15 per cent of all new French State loans in the form of ECU bonds. The increase in the outstanding amount of this bond is expected quarterly through the opening of a Tap stock, the OAT 8.5 per cent 12/05/1997 and the OAT 9.5% 4/2000. The current amount outstanding is in excess of ECU 1,500 million.

A study has been undertaken to check if other stocks could be delivered i.e. issues by Supranationals and for other European State loans in ECU. There is obviously a problem to be solved in terms of differences in the credit ratings of some of these institutions. For the present, a basket of only French Government ECU denominated bonds will be deliverable.

The opening date of this contract has been set for October 18th, 1990.

Foreign Exchange Futures Contracts

For the moment, there are **NO** foreign exchange futures or options contracts listed on the **MATIF**. **MATIF SA**, well aware of a very active OTC currency option market is considering the creation of a currency option. The expected opening could take place in the near future. Possible contracts are U.S. Dollar/ECU or Yen/ECU.

Equities

CAC 40 Stock Index Futures Contract

This contract is based on the CAC 40 Stock Index (CAC stands for "Compagnie des Agents de Change" - the Stockbrokers Association), calculated from a sample of the 40 main stocks listed on the monthly settlement market "RM" with a basis value of 1,000 on December 31, 1987. These stocks represent around 60 - 65 per cent of the market capitalization and a larger share of the traded volume (around 70 per cent). Quotation is based on an outcry system relayed by an after-hours trading system (**THS**).

Volume traded in this contract has been keeping at a steady pace of around 5,000 lots a day, with peaks occurring at the turn of every month. This is quite natural as stocks included in the CAC 40 Index are all traded on a monthly settlement forward basis in the cash market. As there are contracts for every three consecutive months after the trading day, turnover fluctuates wildly around the expiry date. With daily volume averaging 75 per cent of open interest, the contract is rather liquid and there is no great correlation between daily liquidity and daily prices nor historical volatility.

Price history of the different expiry date contracts has been almost the same; in an environment of uncertainty and with a flat yield curve there is nothing to draw from differences between contract months and although a theoretical implied repo rate could be deducted from the difference between the futures prices and the cash price, it would not be relevant because of transaction costs in the cash market. When considering equities, historical volatility is rather high, around 15-16 per cent which means in ordinary terms, an average fluctuation of more or less 1 per cent every day.

Contract Size:	FRF 200 times the futures quoted index.
Delivery Months:	3 consecutive months and one of the quarterly cycle March June September December.
Delivery Day:	16.00 p.m. last trading day.
Last Trading Day:	Last business day of the month.
Quotation:	Index points to one decimal place i.e. 2123.4.
Minimum Price Movement (Tick Size and Value):	0.1 of an Index point = FRF 20.
Trading Hours:	10.00 a.m. - 17.00 p.m.
Initial Margin:	Standard contract = FRF 30,000 per contract and for a Straddle FRF 12,000.
Price Limit:	120 Index points from the previous clearing price.
Contract Standard:	Cash settlement.
Exchange Delivery Settlement Price:	The first CAC 40 index quotation after 16.00 p.m. on the last trading day.
Reuters Pages:	CACF CSIE CACE.

Telerate Pages:	3215 - 3216.
Exchange Fees:	FRF 8 per contract.

Constitution of the CAC40 Index in Alphabetic Order

Stocks	Weighting %	Stocks	Weighting %
Accor	1.82	Havas	2.34
Air Liquide	3.37	Lafarge	2.15
Arjomari	0.74	Legrand	0.83
Bancaire	1.27	LVMH	6.45
Bouygues	0.99	Lyonnaise des Eaux	1.68
BSN	4.62	Merlin	0.98
Cap Gemini	1.32	Michelin	1.62
Carrefour	2.37	Midi	3.58
Casino	0.65	Nav. Mixte	2.54
CCF	1.17	L'Oréal	2.95
CGE	6.66	Paribas	4.61
CGIP	0.87	Pechelbronn	1.97
Chargeurs	0.83	Pernod Ricard	1.58
Club Mediterranée	0.75	Peugeot	4.67
CFRF	1.45	St Gobain	4.17
Dumez	0.69	St Louis	1.08

Elf Aquitaine	7.59	Sté Générale	3.99
Essilor	0.42	Suez	6.02
Hachette	0.83	Thomson	1.77

Notes:

The total is not exactly 100 per cent because figures for each stock are rounded.

Distribution of the CAC 40 Index Weightings

With this pie chart, it is clear that

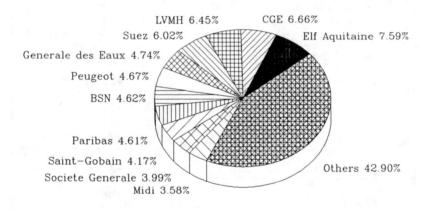

- **more than 25 per cent of the index is accounted for by the first four stocks**

- **around 50 per cent of the index by the first nine.**

But this does not necessarily mean that one could replicate the index by, for instance, having an interest in the first nine stocks only for correlation reasons. This sort of study being beyond the scope of this book, we therefore recommend the interested reader to study the subject more deeply himself.

Constitution of the CAC 40 Index in Descending Weighting Order

STOCK	WEIGHTING %
Elf Aquitaine	7.59
CGE	6.66
LVMH	6.45
Suez	6.02
Générale des Eaux	4.74
Peugeot	4.67
BSN	4.62
Paribas	4.61
Saint-Gobain	4.17
Société Générale	3.99
Midi	3.58
Air Liquide	3.37
L'Oréal	2.95
Nav. Mixte	2.54
Carrefour	2.37

Havas	2.34
Lafarge	2.15
Péchelbronn	1.97
Sanofi	1.85
Accor	1.82
Thomson	1.77
Lyonnaise des Eaux	1.68
Michelin	1.62
Pernod Ricard	1.58
Crédit Foncier de France	1.45
Cap Gemini	1.32
Bancaire	1.27
CCF	1.17
Saint Louis	1.08
Bouygues	0.99
Merlin	0.98
CGIP	0.87
Legrand	0.83
Hachette	0.83
Chargeurs	0.83
Club Méditerranée	0.75

Arjomari	0.74
Dumez	0.69
Casino	0.65
Essilor	0.42
TOTAL	99.98

Daily Volume and Open Interest (Jan 2,1990 - Jul 31,1990)

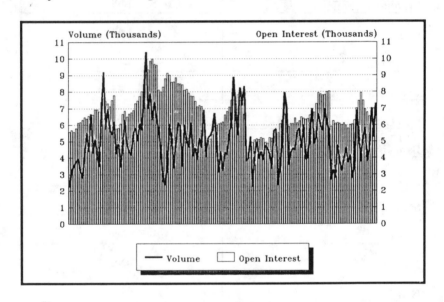

20 Day Moving Average Volume (Jan 29,1990 - Jul 31,1990)

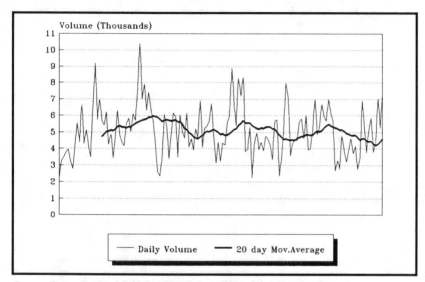

Open Interest and Volume/Open Interest - Liquidity
(Jan 2,1990 - Jul 31,1990)

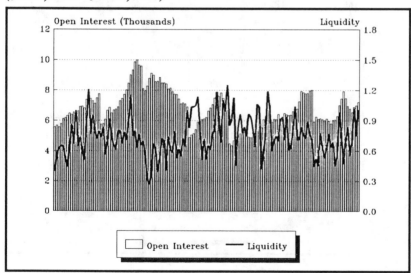

Price History (Jan 2,1990 - Jul 31,1990)

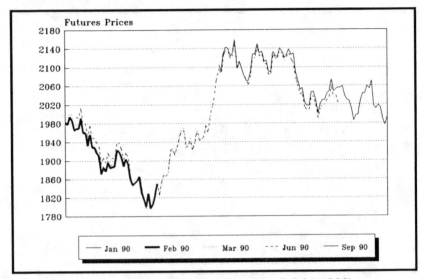

Average Historical Volatility (Jan 2,1990 - Jul 31,1990)

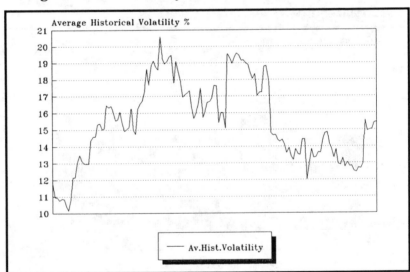

CAC40 Stock Index Option

For details of the Option on the CAC40 see the section on MONEP.

Commodities

Members of the Exchange

In addition to the previous categories of Authorized Brokers (14 members - "Commissaires Agréés") and Sworn Brokers (6 members - "Courtiers Assermentés"), a new trading status was created of Authorized Commodities Traders (2 members - "Negotiateurs Agréés en Marchandises"). The Authorized brokers were given the opportunity of obtaining the status of trader brokers ("Negotiateurs Courtiers") which allows them to trade financial futures as well. As of March 1990, four of them had chosen this possibility and were designated as GCMs ("Compensateurs generaux").

The "Banque Centrale de Compensation" BCC, the Clearing House of the Commodities futures market was purchased by MATIF SA in December 1989 as requested by CMT to regroup all operations under one Exchange and one Clearing House under the supervision of MATIF SA. Hence the revival of the French commodities futures market is directed at white sugar and potatoes futures.

THS operations (after hours trading - "kerb trading" as far as the sugar market is concerned) take place from 19.00 p.m. until 30 minutes after the close of the Coffee, Sugar and Cocoa Exchanges in New York. BCC record these THS transactions.

White Sugar Futures Contract

321,463 contracts of 50 tons of white sugar were recorded by the BCC in 1989, which represents a 9 per cent reduction (i.e. 31,189) compared with 1988. White sugar transactions represent 89 per cent of overall trading on the Commodities Exchange in France. The Open Interest was 13,084 contracts at the end of 1989. Only 1,690 contracts (i.e. less than 1.0 per cent of transactions) were exercised for physical white sugar. The contract can be converted into US dollars if the customer wishes. The initial margin and subsequent margin calls will also be paid in US dollars.

Monthly volume in this contract, which one has to remember represents around 90 per cent of commodities futures volume in France has been staying on an average of a little less than 20,000 lots a day. Open interest has been staying at an average of 17,000 lots which is about half of average monthly trading volume. Positions are kept open for quite reasonable periods. Liquidity is not very high.

The price history of this contract (we were only able to obtain the highest and the lowest data month by month) has been following the price trend of the cash market. It has to be known that at the time of writing, world consumption of sugar exceeds by about 1 per cent world production (therefore inventories are decreasing) and also that the volatility of sugar prices is very high, higher than that of equities.

Average historical volatility of sugar futures is higher than that of equity index futures (more than 1,5 times) and shows that there are great opportunities for gains (and losses) in this market which still has an image of "taboo" because of the scandal in the 1970s. However, the exchange has been working to repair the damage and achieve a more serious and sound market.

Contract Size:	50 metric tons of physical white sugar.
Delivery Months:	March May August October and December upto a total of 16 months including the current month.
Delivery Day:	The last day of the month although delivery can take place anytime during the month.
Last Trading Day:	15th day of the month preceding the contract month (or first business day open before the 15th).
Quotation:	FRF per metric ton.
Minimum Price Movement (Tick Size and Value):	FRF 1 per ton = FRF 50.
Trading Hours:	10.45 a.m. - 13.00 p.m. and 15.00 p.m. - 19.00 p.m. plus **THS**.
Initial Margin:	Between 8 per cent and 12 per cent of the average value of the three closest contract months. FRF 9,000 or US$1,450.

Price Limit:	No price limit on the first day of trading on a new contract and also on the last month of trading of a maturing contract. the price limit otherwise is in the range of 8.5 per cent to 13 per cent of the value of the contract. The limit decreases as the contract value increases.
Contract Standard:	Physical delivery - see below.
Exchange Delivery Settlement Price:	The liquidation price is known at 18.00 p.m. on the last day of trading. The sellers advise MATIF SA and BCC of the delivery arrangements (Day plus 1). MATIF notify the buyers of the delivery information who accept it (Day plus 2).
Reuters Pages:	SUGC.

Delivery and Delivery Grade

Delivery is FOB stowed, trimmed and custom cleared during the delivery month and the following month. The delivery point is in a port approved by the technical committee.

White crystal sugar delivery grade is that of any origin, with maximum polarization of 99.8 degrees and maximum moisture of 0.06 degrees.

Monthly Volume and Open Interest (January - June 1990)

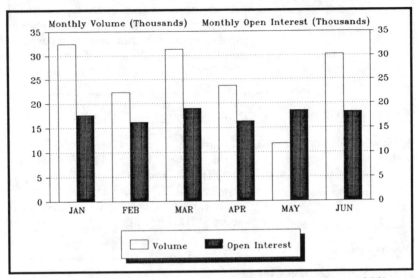

Monthly Open Interest and Liquidity (January - June 1990)

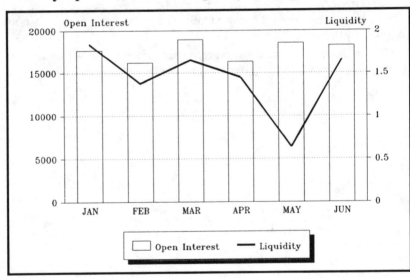

Monthly Maximum and Minimum Prices (January - June 1990)

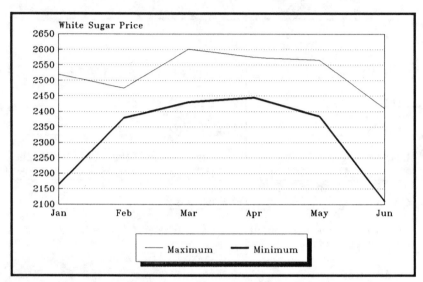

Average Historical Volatility (January - June 1990)

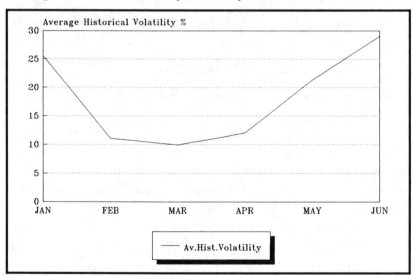

White Sugar Option

Option Style	American.
Contract Size:	One white sugar futures contract.
Delivery Months:	March May August and October.
Delivery Day:	Upto the close of the option.
Last Trading Day:	Last business day of the month before the one closing of the contract.
Quotation:	FRF per ton.
Minimum Price Movement (Tick Size and Value):	FRF 1.0 = FRF 50.
Trading Hours:	10.45 a.m. - 13.30 p.m. and 15.00 p.m. - 17.00 p.m.
Initial Margin:	The buyer pays none. The seller pays the same margin as that for the futures contract.
Price Limit:	No price limit.
Contract Standard:	Physical delivery of a futures contract.
Exercise Price:	Exercise intervals of FRF 100 per ton.

There are two Potato contracts, both listed in Lille. Due to the recent takeover of the Commodities Market by MATIF SA, no statistics were available at the time of press. There is some activity but it is relatively quiet.

The potatoes futures market is the only one in France showing an increase in turnover. 35,376 contracts of the 20 tons were traded in 1989, 8,000 contracts more than the previous year. The Open Interest, 2,527 lots at the beginning of the year was 2,191 lots at the end of the year does not reflect the increase in turnover. Only 73 contracts were exercised for physical delivery.

The 40mm contract, the first one to be listed is almost dying; less than 10 contracts traded in any given month of 1990. On the contrary, the 50mm contract is quite active and traded volumes have remained constant over the years. There are four contract months for the 50mm contract, November, February, April and May. They correspond to the natural cycles and therefore it is quite natural that March and April witness steadier volumes. The open interest graph shows that it decreases in March and April as this is the period when the contracts would be unwound. Therefore, the greatest liquidity is in April: average monthly volume is 5 times the open interest at the end of the month.

Price histories of the futures contract reflect well the situation in the cash market with the peak in April a natural consequence of the supply and demand at that time. It has to be noted that volatility in this soft commodities market is quite high: there are good opportunities but also a certain danger.

Potatoes 40 mm (with a maximum of 12 potatoes per kilo) Futures Contract

Contract Size:	20 tons in bags on pallets.
Delivery Months:	April November.
Delivery Day:	Second business day of the third week of the contract month.
Last Trading Day:	Second Tuesday of the contract month.
Quotation:	FRF per 100 Kilos to two decimal places.
Minimum Price Movement (Tick Size and Value):	FRF 0.25 per 100 Kilos = FRF 50.
Trading Hours:	11.00 a.m. - 12.45 p.m. and 15.00 p.m. - 16.30 p.m.
Initial Margin:	Around 15 per cent of the value of the contract.
Price Limit:	FRF 15 per 100 kilos

| Contract Standard: | Physical delivery of 40mm caliber potatoes with a maximum of 12 tubers per kilo.. |
| Exchange Delivery Settlement Price: | The price at closing on the last trading day. |

Potatoes 50 mm (with a maximum of 8 potatoes per kilo) Futures Contract

Contract Size:	20 tons in bags on pallets.
Delivery Months:	February April May November.
Delivery Day:	Second business day of the third week of the contract month.
Last Trading Day:	Second Tuesday of the contract month.
Quotation:	FRF per 100 Kilos to two decimal places.
Minimum Price Movement (Tick Size and Value):	FRF 0.25 per 100 Kilos = FRF 50.
Trading Hours:	11.00 a.m. - 12.45 p.m. and 15.00 p.m. - 16.30 p.m.
Initial Margin:	Around 15 per cent of the value of the contract.
Price Limit:	FRF 15 per 100 kilos.
Contract Standard:	Physical delivery of 50mm caliber potatoes with a maximum of 12 tubers per kilo..
Exchange Delivery Settlement Price:	The closing price on the last trading day.

Total Volume - First Half of Year (1986 - 1990)

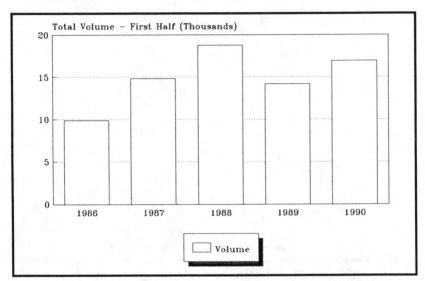

Monthly Volume and Open Interest (January - June 1990)

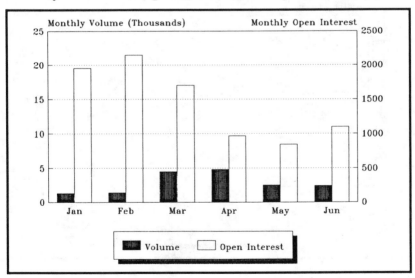

Monthly Open Interest and Liquidity (January - June 1990)

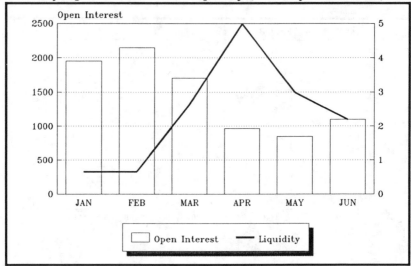

Monthly Maximum and Minimum Prices (January - June 1990)

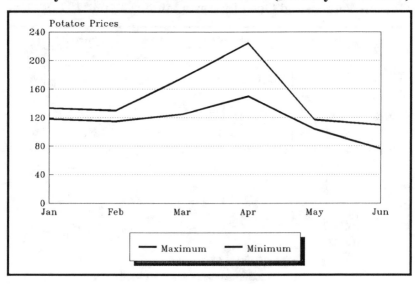

Average Historical Volatility (January - June 1990)

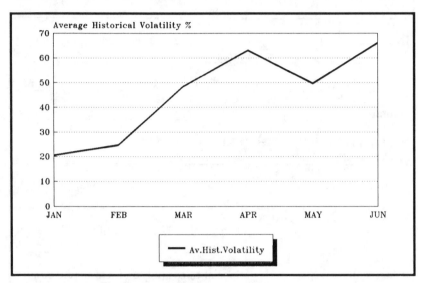

Robusta Coffee Futures Contract

The activity in Robusta coffee traded in Paris and Le Havre with 2,826 lots represents a reduction of 63 per cent against the previous year. 178 contracts were exercised for physical delivery (ie less than 1 per cent of transactions). The Open Interest on December 31, 1989 was 173 contracts.

Activity in this contract has been decreasing quite steeply over the years, due to competition from other exchanges and to lack of interest. Traded volumes during the first half of the 1990 has been quite poor. Open interest remained constant but 200 times 5 metric tons only equals 1,000 tons which is nothing if compared to world production (see London FOX). Liquidity in this contract is poor: an average figure of 0.5 indicates that one needs two months (note these are monthly figures) to turnover the open interest.

Price fluctuations, although significant are not as high as in other contracts. For instance, historical volatility averages 30 per cent (which means price fluctuations of around 2 per cent each day).

Option Style	American.
Contract Size:	5 metric tons in bags.

Delivery Months:	January March May July September November.
Delivery Day:	Up to the last business day of the delivery month.
Last Trading Day:	The last business day of the delivery month.
Quotation:	FRF per 100 kilos - to zero decimal places.
Minimum Price Movement (Tick Size and Value):	FRF 1 = FRF 50.
Trading Hours:	10.15 a.m. - 13.00 p.m. and 15.00 p.m. - 18.30 p.m..
Initial Margin:	8 per cent to 12 per cent of the value of the contract.
Price Limit:	Special rules apply and one should contact the exchange before trading.
Contract Standard:	Physical delivery of coffee - see below.

Delivery and Delivery Grade

Delivery is into authorized warehouses in the delivery ports approved by the technical committee (CIF basis). Robusta coffee of Ivory Coast origin grade 2 is accepted. However, other origins may from time to time be accepted if agreed by the technical committee.

Total Volume - First Half of Year (1986 - 1990)

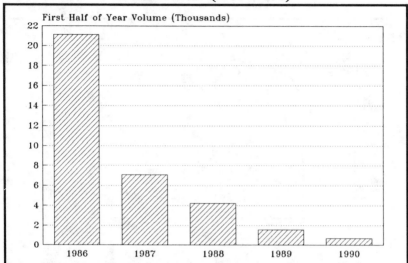

Monthly Volume and Open Interest (January - June 1990)

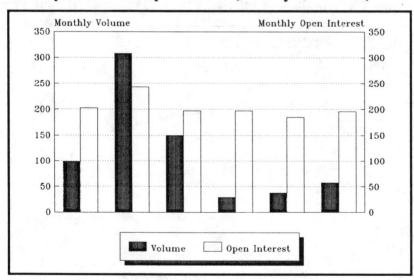

Monthly Open Interest and Liquidity (January - June 1990)

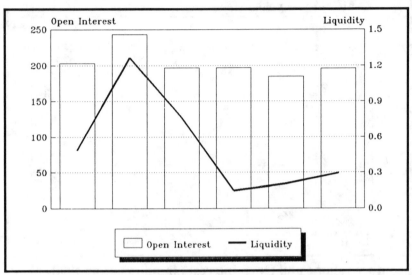

Monthly Maximum and Minimum Prices (January - June 1990)

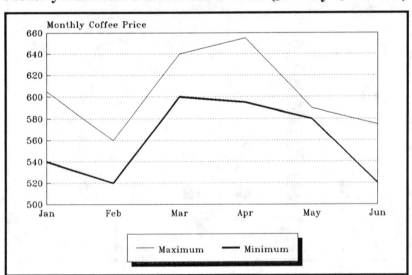

Average Historical Volatility (January - June 1990)

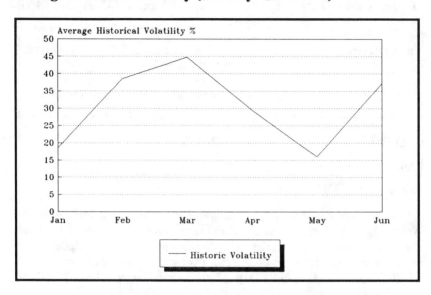

Cocoa Futures Contract

167 contracts were traded in the first two months of 1989 and 121 contracts were exercised for physical delivery. Since November 1989, there has been no transactions with not a single contract traded in 1990.

Contract Size:	10 metric tons in bags.
Delivery Months:	March May July September December.
Delivery Day:	Two days after the last trading day.
Last Trading Day:	13.00 p.m. The last business day of the contract month.
Quotation:	FRF per 100 kilos (no decimal places).
Minimum Price Movement (Tick Size and Value):	FRF 100 = FRF 100.

Trading Hours:	10.30 a.m. - 13.00 p.m. and 15.00 p.m. - 18.30 p.m.
Initial Margin:	Between 8 per cent and 12 per cent of the value of the contract.
Price Limit:	FRF 50 per 100 kilos but special rules may be applied.
Contract Standard:	Physical delivery.
Reuters Pages:	COCK.

Delivery and Delivery Grade

Delivery is into authorized warehouses in the delivery ports of Amsterdam and Dunkerque. The delivery grade is of good fermented maincrop cocoa beans from the Ivory Coast, Togo, Cameroon, Madagascar. In addition, deliveries from Ghana (with correction factors of plus FRF 50 per 100 kilos), Bahia (less FRF 20 per 100 kilos) and Nigeria (less FRF 10 per 100 kilos) may be accepted (CIF basis).

Total Volume - First Half of Year (1986 - 1990)

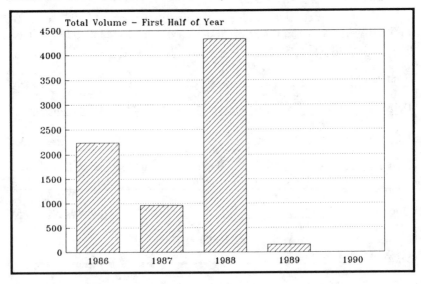

Soya Cattle Cake Futures Contract
A Soya Cattle Cake Futures contract still officially exists but has not traded for quite a long time.

Gold Futures Contracts
The current tax of 7 per cent on all gold transactions in France disrupts the interest in this metal and reduces the liquidity of the market. So without liquidity, there is little value in setting up a futures market, at the moment. A team has been formed by **MATIF** to study ways to solve this problem. Another team at the Minister of Finance is looking at the request by **MATIF** to have the tax abolished.

A tentative opening date for this future contract is 1992. The **MATIF** is also considering other metal futures contracts but is weary of current competition from the U.K. and Germany.

Marché des Options Négociables de Paris
MONEP

INTRODUCTION

Stock and Index options in Paris are traded on the Marché des Options Négociables de Paris "**MONEP**", and are governed by the Paris Bourse regulatory body, the Conseil des Bourses de Valeurs ("**CBV**" or French Stock Exchange Council).

Clearing

Decisions taken by the "**CBV**" are implemented by the Société des Bourses Françaises "**SBF**" which handles day-to-day administration, security, development and promotion for Paris Bourse markets, and ensures that they operate smoothly. In the case of "**MONEP**" stock and index options, the "**SBF**" has delegated full responsibility for technical clearing, general administration, market surveillance and control to its subsidiary Société de Compensation des Marchés Conditionnels "**SCMC**". The "**SBF**" acts as depository and manages cover requirements deposited with it by clearing members. It is also the market's financial guarantor of last resort and steps in if necessary after the "**SBF**" guarantee fund has been called into play to guarantee execution of contracts registered by "**SCMC**".

Members

The sole intermediaries authorized to deal on the "**MONEP**" are the Paris Bourse's 44 members firms. They operate through representatives acting in two distinct and mutually exclusive capacities.

- **As brokers, who trade orders received directly from clients or issued for brokerage houses' own accounts. These orders are executed among brokers, with order book officials at "SCMC", or with market makers.**

- **As market makers, who help to ensure that the market operates smoothly and is sufficiently liquid. In return for full exemption from trading fees in both underlying stocks and in options, market makers must be able to provide a spread of buy/sell prices for each series of classes attributed to them (a class designates all options**

having the same underlying stock), at any time. Within this spread,
they must be able to execute a minimum number of contracts in
accordance with very clearly defined rules.

"SCMC" has also been designated by Bourse member firms as depository
for a P.O.B. or public order book, whose orders are given priority in execution over all others at the same price. Starting at the beginning of 1990,
trading members will enjoy direct access to this decentralized automatic
order book from terminals located in their own trading rooms.

Clearing Members

French brokerage firms enjoy automatic membership of the
"MONEP" clearing structure. After obtaining "SBF" approval and signing an
additional membership agreement with "SCMC", credit institutions and
banks may also opt to join, acquiring a direct linkup with "SCMC" for the
calculation and settlement of their operations and cover requirements.

Trading

Stock and Index options are currently traded on the floor of the Paris
Bourse in continuous open outcry from 10.00 a.m. to 17.00 p.m.. Once the
decentralized computer network created to manage the POB is up and
running (scheduled January 1990), trading members will have two means of
access to the market:

- traditional phoning or routing of orders to their representatives
  on the floor, where these orders can be executed in open outcry
  trading

- for retail orders from clients, through terminal screens in their
  own trading rooms. In this case, orders are keyed into the central
  system of the POB and data is displayed and disseminated to
  users. Such orders are either matched automatically inside the
  book, if that is where the market's best prices are, or routed to
  "SCMC" officials for priority execution on the floor, if better prices
  are available there.

DETAILED CONTRACT SPECIFICATIONS
Individual Stock Options

The Stock Options market was opened by the Paris Bourse on September 10, 1987. This market has steadily grown from 100,000 contracts per month in 1987 to 300,000-400,000 contracts in 1989. Settlement is essentially made in cash because of transaction costs in the underlying stocks. In fact, many open positions are unwound before expiry.

The evaluation of margin calls is based on a Cox-Ross-Rubinstein model. Depending on the investor's position, theoretical premiums are calculated using a volatility decreased or increased by a predetermined amount, currently set at 20 per cent and a fluctuation range of 20 per cent of the underlying stock price. The most negative value is the Initial Margin. Cover is provided by cash, Government bills, notes or bonds or the underlying stocks.

With an average of around 12,000 contracts a day, **MONEP** options are an active market. Calls account for around 80 per cent of volume and puts around 20 per cent. For space reasons, it has not been possible to include the relevant data for every contract, However, as an example, the Call/Put ratio is the highest for:

- **Pechiney (93%) - but only for 5 days history**
- **Suez (85%)**
- **CGE (84%)**

lowest for

- **CMB Packaging (47%) - but only for 5 days history**
- **ACCOR (62%)**
- **Eurotunnel (66%)**

and that the highest volume is on the following stocks:

Name	% of TOTAL Volume
Peugeot	16.87
Thomson	10.53
CGE	9.79

| Elf Aquitaine | 8.89 |
| Suez | 8.19 |

The reader can look up in the previous sections how these companies rank
in the CAC 40 Stock Index: they are amongst the most important and this is
quite natural. As usual in options, open interest falls sharply on expiry
dates but nevertheless stays at a quite reasonable level. Liquidity is poor, as
usual very rarely daily volume does exceed 8 per cent of open interest.

The graph for implied volatility is a classical one with an average of
25 per cent. It has to be noted that most generally implied volatility in puts is
higher than in calls. This is due to two factors:

1.   Market participants tend to use
        - a Black & Scholes model for calls
        - a Cox-Ross-Rubinstein model for puts
        therefore they may not use the same volatility factor.

2.   There are much less put writers than call writers and this
        may be why volatility in puts is higher than in calls (volatility
        is a way of measuring the value of options). Although, the
        implied volatility for each stock is not shown, as an example
        the following can be used as indicators:

● the highest volatilities were (for puts)
        Eurotunnel: 52 per cent (peaking at 72 per cent)
        Thomson: 40 per cent (peaking at 51 per cent)

● the lowest were (for calls)
        ACCOR: 19 per cent (lowest at 12 per cent)
        CGE: 21 per cent (lowest at 13 per cent).

Option Style	American calls and puts on stocks.
Contract Size:	100 shares (except for Eurotunnel and Euro-Disney Land with 500 shares).
Delivery Months:	March June September December.
Delivery Day:	Last business day of contract month.

Last Trading Day:	Day before last business day of contract month.
Quotation:	FF per share i.e. 12.34.
Minimum Price Movement (Tick Size and Value):	FF 0.01 = FF 1 (or FF 5 for Eurotunnel and Euro-Disney Land).
Trading Hours:	10.00 a.m. - 17.00 p.m.
Initial Margin:	See above.
Price Limit:	No price limit.
Contract Standard:	Physical delivery of stocks or cash settlement (on the first day after the last trading day).
Exercise Price:	Exercise prices are set in increments of 10 per cent of stock price rounded down to FF 10,20,40,100 or 200. 5 prices are available: 2 above and 2 below the current price. New contracts are created should the price of the underlying stock change to demand it.
Reuters Pages:	**MOPN FQHL.**
Telerate Pages:	
Commissions and Fees:	Brokerage fees = 2 per cent and the "SCMC" fee is FF 12.50 per contract.

List of Options Contract on Stocks and Reuters Pages

Stock	Launch Date	Reuters	
		Options* Price	Underlying Quote
Lafarge Coppeé	10-09-1987	KKAA - H	LAFP.PA
Paribas	10-09-1987	KJAA - H	PARI.PA
Peugeot	10-09-1987	KMAA - H	PEUP.PA
Thomson CSF	01-10-1987	KGAA - H	TCFP.PA
Elf Aquitaine	08-10-1987	KGAQ - X	ELFP.PA
Compagnie du Midi	15-10-1987	KNAA - H	MCDP.PA
Saint Gobain	22-01-1988	KIAA - H	SGOB.PA
Michelin	22-01-1988	KFAA - H	MICP.PA
Accor	22-04-1988	KJAI - P	ACCP.PA
CGE	22-04-1988	KKAI - P	CGEP.PA
Société Générale	18-07-1988	KMAI - P	SOGN.PA
Eurotunnel	09-05-1989	KNAI - P	EUTL.PA
Perrier	17-07-1989	KFAI - P	PRRR.PA
Suez	17-07-1989	KJAI - P	SUZF.PA
Bouygues	16-10-1989	KRAA - H	BOUY.PA
Pernod Ricard	16-10-1989	KRAI - P	PERP.PA
Havas	18-12-1989	KFAS - X	AGHP.PA
Rhône Poulenc CIP	18-12-1989	KIAI - P	RHON.PA

Cerus	31-01-1990	KKAQ - X	DULE.PA
Euro-Disney Land	31-01-1990	KMAQ - X	EDLP.PA
Pechiney International	25-06-1990	KGAQ - X	PIKG.PA
CMB Packaging	25-06-1990	KIAQ - X	CMBP.PA
Total	21-09-1990	KNAQ - X	TOTF.PA
L'Oréal	21-09-1990	KNBA - H	OREP.PA

*Complete list available on MOPN.

N.B. In France, all options based on one given stock constitute what is known as a "class."

Total Market Statistics

Daily Volume and Open Interest (Jan 2,1990 - Jun 29,1989)

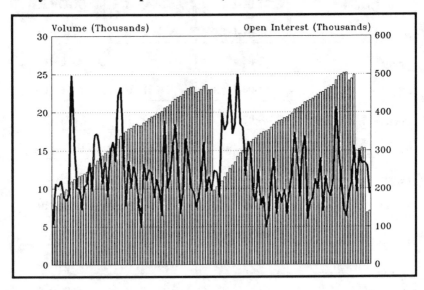

Open Interest and Volume/Open Interest("Liquidity")
(Jan 2,1990 - Jun 29,1989)

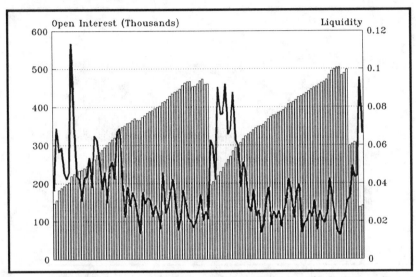

Implied Volatility (Jan 2,1990 - Jun 29,1989)

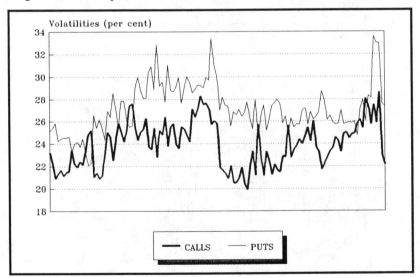

Peugeot
Daily Volume and Open Interest (Jan 2,1990 - Jun 29,1989)

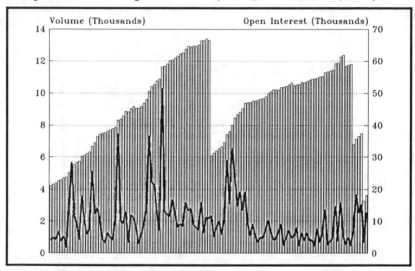

Open Interest and Volume/Open Interest("Liquidity") (Jan 2,1990 - Jun 29,1989)

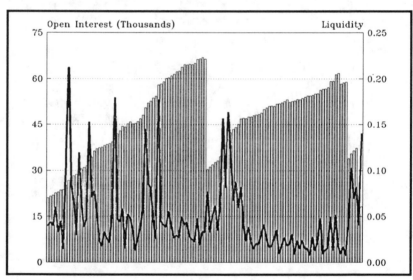

Implied Volatility (Jan 2,1990 - Jun 29,1989)

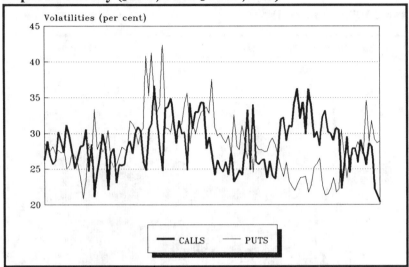

Thomson CSF

Daily Volume and Open Interest (Jan 2,1990 - Jun 29,1989)

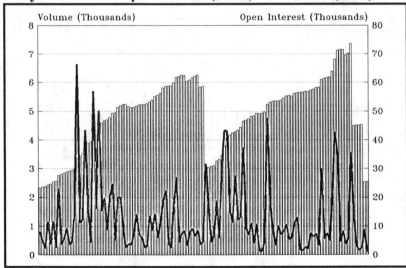

Open Interest and Volume/Open Interest("Liquidity")
(Jan 2,1990 - Jun 29,1989)

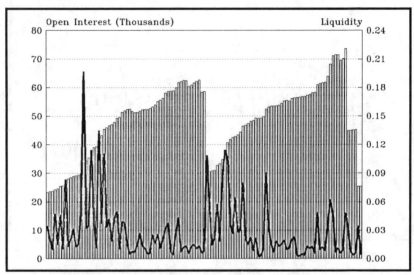

Implied Volatility (Jan 2,1990 - Jun 29,1989)

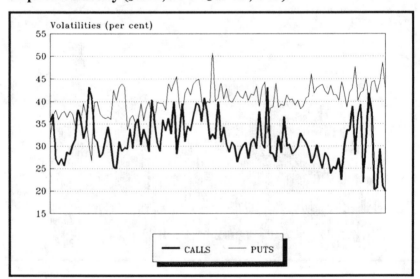

CGE
Daily Volume and Open Interest (Jan 2,1990 - Jun 29,1989)

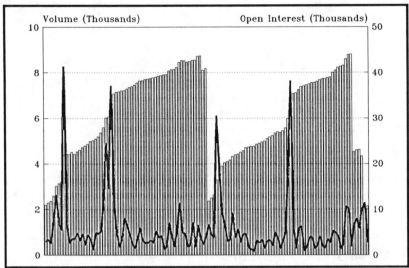

Open Interest and Volume/Open Interest("Liquidity")
(Jan 2,1990 - Jun 29,1989)

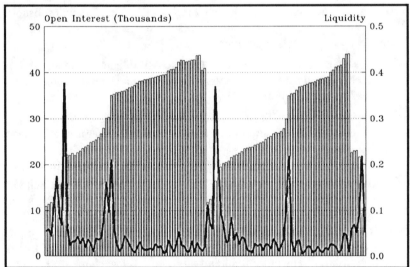

Implied Volatility (Jan 2,1990 - Jun 29,1989)

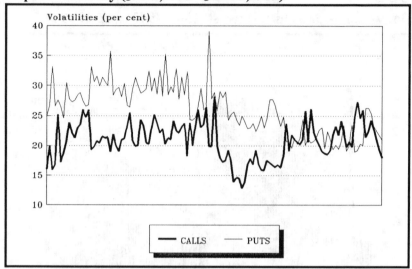

CAC 40 Stock Index Option

Launched by **MONEP** (**SBF** - the Société des Bourses Françaises) at the same time as the CAC40 Future, **"MONEP"** Stock Index options are based on the underlying cash CAC 40 Index (a selection of 40 stocks traded on the Paris Bourse monthly settlement market - RM - Règlement Mensuel). When options are exercised, sellers are selected at random by **"SCMC"**. Margin calls for net sellers (option writers):

- **are calculated with a Cox-Ross-Rubinstein model and a hypothesis of plus or minus 120 points change on the Index and a 20 per cent volatility**

- **are covered with cash, Government bills, notes or bonds (90 per cent of market value) or underlying stocks (80 per cent of market value).**

Slightly more options on the CAC 40 were traded than futures contracts. However, as those who are used to arbitrage, an average delta of 0.5 means that one can arbitrage and/or hedge futures positions by using twice as many options; therefore figures are quite comparable. One interesting point is that while for stock options the Call/Total ratio was around 80 per cent, in this index option it is only (on average) 45 per cent. This means that these options are really more fluid and more liquid. The shape of the open interest graph is quite unusual: expiry dates only occur every 3 months but here we witness severe depressions in the open interest every month. This is due to the fact that many market participants arbitrage/hedge options positions with positions on the monthly settlement cash market. Because of the general interest in an index options contract and because there is also a futures contract based on the same index, liquidity is much higher than on stock options.

The comparison of volatilities on options and futures shows how, as usual, options implied volatility generally exceeds futures historical volatility. As explained before, this is quite understandable and although scientific measures would render a poor correlation factor, the human eye can witness that there is still some sort of correlation. As so often seen, put volatility is higher than call volatility; over the period they were on average respectively 24 per cent and 15 per cent, a lower figure than the average for individual stock options. This should be expected as any basket is less volatile than its components.

Option Style	American calls and puts.
Contract Size:	FF 200 x strike price.
Expiry Months:	Next three consecutive months plus next quarterly month from the March June September December cycle.
Expiry Day:	First day after last trading day of contract month.
Last Trading Day:	Last business day of contract month.
Quotation:	FF per index point i.e. 12.34.
Minimum Price Movement (Tick Size and Value):	FF 0.01 = FF 2 x strike price.
Trading Hours:	10.00 a.m. - 17.00 p.m.
Initial Margin:	None for buyers. See above.
Price Limit:	No price limit.

Contract Standard:	Cash settlement.
Exercise Price:	25 Index point intervals. 5 exercise prices 2 above and 2 below the current strike price.
Reuters Pages:	KQAI - KQAJ.
Commissions and Fees;	2 per cent Brokerage fees and FF 12.5 per contract Commission.

Index Composition

For details of the stocks in the Index, see MATIF the CAC40 Futures Contract.

Daily Volume and Open Interest (Jan 2,1990 - Jun 29,1990)

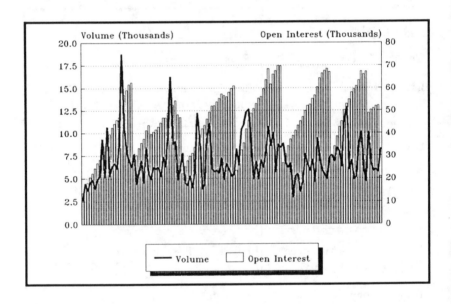

Open Interest and Volume/Open Interest("Liquidity")
(Jan 2,1990 - Jun 29,1989)

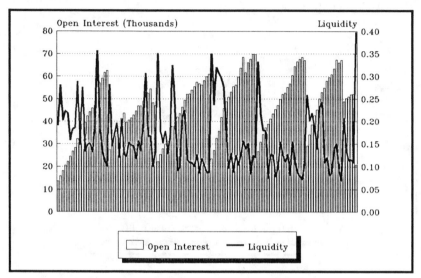

Implied Volatility (Jan 2,1990 - Jun 29,1990)

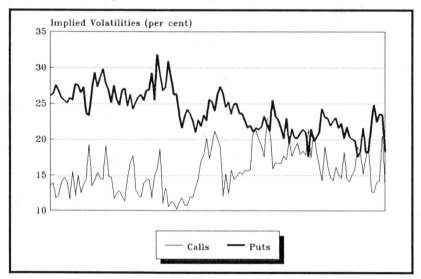

Options Implied and Futures Historic Volatilities (Jan 2,1990 - Jun 29,1990)

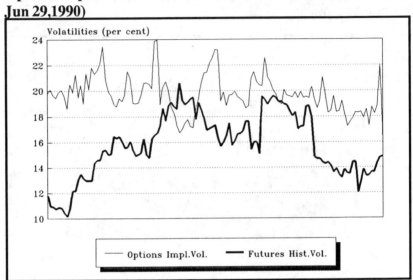

The Organisation de Marchés Financiers "OMF" Now renamed France Matif Automatique "FMA"

INTRODUCTION

The Organisation de Marchés Financiers was a newly created Paris Future and Options Exchange. "OMF" was both an Exchange and a clearing house. As an Official Exchange, it was controlled and regulated by the Futures Market Commission "CMT", the French Securities Commission "COB" and the Ministry of Finance; as a Clearing House it was regulated by the French central bank (Banque de France).

"OMF" featured an integrated state of the art trading and clearing organization that provides market security, efficiency, fairness in execution of trades and liquidity.

Trading in Index futures and options on the "OMF" 50 index started on November 8, 1988. A four year Treasury Note ("BTAN") futures contract was launched June 1, 1989.

In early 1990, 50 of the largest banks, brokerage and trading firms (which account for more than 90 per cent of the total volume traded in Paris on financial futures - including 9 foreign institutions) had joined "OMF" as clearing members. Seven official market makers ensured liquidity. These were:

- Banque Finance Plus
- Banque Nationale de Paris
- Caisse des Dépôts et Consignations
- Crédit Commercial de France
- Crédit Lyonnais
- Meeschaert Rousselle
- Société Générale

One of the distinctive features of the "OMF" Exchange was its computerized trading and clearing system, designed for maximum security. Each member entered bids and offers directly into terminals located in his premises. Where a match was found the deal was automatically executed. Processing for clearing, risk monitoring and back office functions automatically followed. Moreover, Bids and Asks were ranked according to price and time precedence, thus guaranteeing fairness in the execution of trades. Additionally, a clearing member had access to each account's open interest, thus allowing real-time risk management. Finally, a central block order system contributed to transparency.

Providing customers with the best risk management opportunities was "OMF"'s goal. It has been attained by constantly ensuring the highest standards of security, efficiency and fairness on market activities.

Although technically sound, OMF has never been a commercial success. It has been a sort of "laboratory" where new products were tested. For instance, the OMF 50 Stock Index Future was the first one to be traded before the CAC 40 Stock Index Future. As the ideas were good, but financial results were poor, OMF has been taken over by MATIF SA, officially taking the name France Matif Automatique on July 28, 1990.

The new Chairman of FMA is M. Jaques Pfauwadel, the Chairman of MATIF SA, but a separate staff has been retained.

For further information, one should contact:

Contact:	**Daniel Lellouche**
	Armand Abraham
Address:	**F.M.A.**
	52 Avenue des Champs Elysées
	75008 PARIS
	France
Tel:	**(33) 1 42 25 66 25**
Fax:	**(33) 1 42 25 72 45**

DETAILED CONTRACT SPECIFICATIONS
"OMF" 50 Stock Index Futures Contract

This contract launched on November 8, 1989 immediately came under pressure from the rival MATIF contract the CAC40 Stock Index future. As a result, this contract has become inactive.

Contract Size:	FF 500 x index value.
Expiry Months:	One month plus the nest three quarterly contracts from March June September and December.
Expiry Day:	Last business day of the contract month.
Last Trading Day:	Last business day of the contract month.
Quotation:	FF index points
Minimum Price Movement (Tick Size and Value):	0.1 of an index point = FF 50.
Trading Hours:	10.00 a.m. - 17.00 p.m..
Initial Deposit:	11 per cent of index value (2 per cent for spreads).
Price Limit:	Plus or minus 5 per cent of last settlement price.
Contract Standard:	Cash settlement.
Exchange Delivery Settlement Price:	Average of the official quotations during the last hour of the last trading day.
Reuters Pages:	IEFX OXBA-OXBG OXMC OXME OXNE OXNG.
Telerate Pages:	3214.

Composition of "OMF"50 Stock Index

Stocks	Weighting %	Stocks	Weighting %
Accor	1.3	Eurotunnel*	4.1
Air Liquide	3.6	Essilor	0.6
Alcatel*	1.2	Groupe de la Cite*	0.6
Alsthom*	0.9	Havas	1.3
Arjomari	0.74	L'Oreal	2.9
Auxiliaire*	0.5	Lafarge Coppée	2.6
Beghin-Say*	0.9	LVMH	6.2
BNP*	0.5	Metaleurope*	0.3
Bouygues	0.99	Michelin	2.2
BSN	4.62	Moulinex*	0.3
Canal Plus*	1.6	Navigation Mixte	1.2
Carrefour	2.37	Occidental*	0.9
Carnaud*	1.1	Paribas	3.7
Casino	0.65	Pernod Ricard	1.7
CCF	1.17	Peugeot	5.5
CFAO*	0.7	Saint Gobain	4.5
CGE	6.66	Sanofi	1.6
Chargeurs	0.83	Schneider*	1.1

Ciments Francais*	1.2	Source Perrier*	2.0
Cie du Midi	3.1	Suez	3.9
Club Mediterranee	0.75	Société Générale	3.7
CFF	1.45	Thomson CSF	3.4
Dumez	0.69	Total*	1.3
Generale des Eaux	4.74	Valeo*	1.1
Elf Aquitaine	7.59	Vallourec*	0.2

* Indicates not in CAC 40 .

Interest Rates

Four Year BTAN Futures Contract

The 4 year **BTAN** future contract was launched June 1, 1989 by "OMF." As a result of the Government securities reform, the capitalization of **BTAN**s has grown rapidly and trading on the secondary market has been improved with the appointment of 12 market makers ("**SVT**" - Treasury Security Specialists). Designed for hedging those medium term portfolios and arbitraging along the yield curve, the **BTAN** future contract has not reached its expected potential.

The relative lack of success of the **BTAN** futures contract lies behind a relatively illiquid **BTAN** cash market, mainly because until recently institutional investors had no obligation to "mark to market" positions. As from January 1990, "indicative quotations" are given by the Banque de France so that those who want to value positions can do so. However, such an obligation will only be effective in the coming year.

This fact shows very clearly how fragile is the limit between securities and money-market instruments: a limit that in most peoples' mind is going to vanish progressively. Therefore, although activity in this contract is rather low, market authorities have decided to keep it going.

The rather modest volume has been decreasing over the months. Open interest has also been declining. Liquidity in this contract is rather poor: around ten days of the trading are needed to turn open interest over.

Price history of the contract has been quite correctly reflecting interest rate movements in the cash market: a rise up to late February and an easing over the rest of the period reviewed.

Contract Size:	FF 1,000,000
Delivery Months:	March June September and December.
Delivery Day:	Last trading day of the contract month.
Last Trading Day:	Last trading day of the contract month.
Quotation:	In percent of Par to two decimal places.
Minimum Price Movement (Tick Size and Value):	0.02 per cent = FRF 20,000.
Trading Hours:	10.05 a.m. - 16.00 p.m.
Initial Deposit:	5 per cent = FF 50,000 or FF 20,000 for spreads.
Price Limit:	200 basis points (2 per cent).
Contract Standard:	Physical Delivery of French Government Notes **BTAN** with maturities between 3.5 and 5 years.
Exchange Delivery Settlement Price:	The most significant price quoted in the last minutes of trading.
Reuters Pages:	OXBA.

Daily Volume and Open Interest (Jan 2,1990 - Jul 31,1990)

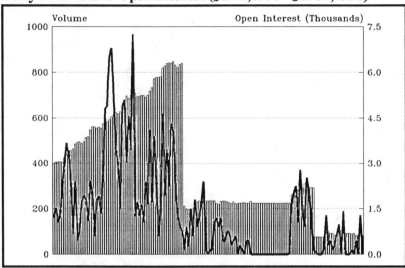

Open Interest and Volume/Open Interest ("Liquidity")
(Jan 2,1990 - Jul 31,1990)

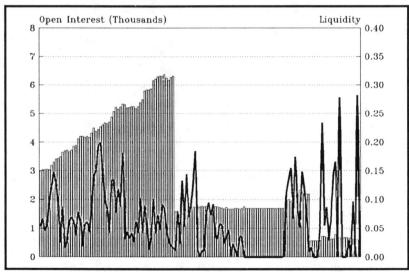

Price History (Jan 2,1990 - Jul 31,1990)

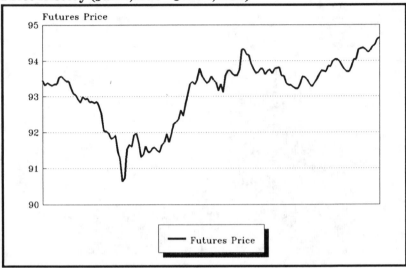

Historical Volatility (Jan 2,1990 - Jul 31,1990)

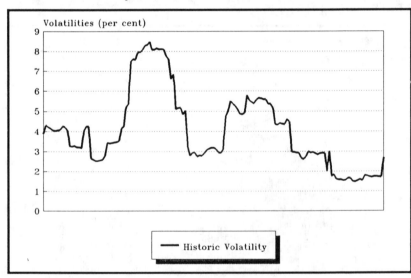

Over-the-Counter Contracts ("OTC")

A certain freedom is allowed in France so far as Over-the-Counter contracts are concerned. It has to be understood that the general policy, as far as Futures and Options contracts are concerned, is that development has to happen in the most natural way, that is, by public demand. For instance, letting OTC contracts on the non-Exchange traded contracts trade such as a new futures contract or a new option on an existing futures contract. Then, if the market is deep enough, the contract may be traded on the official Exchange. (See the development of the PIBOR futures contract and the Option or the Odd-Strike price options on the Notional Futures contract.)

This has not to be confused with the notion of Transactions Hors Séance "THS" -Off Trading Hours trading where, because there is no reason to prevent market participants from trading while the Exchange is closed, it is allowed to trade between institutions in the evening, or at night or even in the early morning, the transactions being "officialized" during the next trading session.

However, whenever an officially Exchange traded contract is involved, it is forbidden to trade on an OTC basis during official Trading Hours. Only when a telephone or power cut happens during official hours does the THS take over.

REGULATION

The regulations that are applied to each market have been discussed in the Organisation of the Market section for each exchange.

TAXATION
Non-Residents

As there is no withholding tax on Futures and Options in France and as Non Residents are not liable to French Tax on Income or Capital Gains, French Futures and Options markets are tax free to Non Residents.

Residents
a) Private Individuals

With the exception of those people whose principal activity is to trade in the Exchange for their own account (i.e. locals) and who are taxed on profits as on income (with the progressive tax rate system), all private individuals are taxed on profits from Futures and Options (whether French or foreign) as follows:

- Profits on Financial Futures and Options (ie Bonds, Stocks and Stock Index) at a flat rate of 16 per cent* (probably to be raised in the coming years)

- Profits on other Futures and Options not referenced to Bonds or Stocks (ie Commodities) are taxed at a flat rate of 32 per cent*.

(*) To these flat rates of 16 and 32 per cent, there has to be added a further special tax of 1 per cent (until December 31,1990) for the Social Security Fund.

b) Corporations

Pension Funds pay no tax at all.

For any other corporation (including Insurance companies), profits and losses on Futures and Options are taxed as regular profit/loss or income. Regular profits and losses as well as income are taxed at the same rate. this rate is at present:

- 42 per cent for distributed profits

- 39 per cent for retained profits. This rate of 39 per cent might be lowered to 37 per cent and then 34 per cent in the next years.

There is a special rate of 19 per cent on profits on securities only if they have been held for more than 2 years and one day. There is therefore only one exception to the general rule: as far as symmetric positions are concerned (physical assets hedged by an opposite position in Futures and Options) profits and losses on hedges have to be taxed in the same fiscal year as the hedged position. Therefore, when profits are claimed as "long term profits taxed at 19 per cent", if they occur on hedged positions the loss on the hedge side has to be declared together. In other words, losses on Futures and Options can be claimed with the ordinary taxable profit only if it is proven that they are not hedging a position which will be taxed at the low long term rate. If this can not be proven in advance (because one does not always know in advance if a cash position is going to be profitable), then when the profit is claimed to be taxed at the low rate the loss on the hedge will be "reintegrated". The low rate of 19 per cent may rise during the next years: many people agree that everything should be taxed at the same rate.

QUOTE VENDORS

Automatic Data Processing
Bloomberg

Bridge Data
CMS
Fininfo
IDM
Knight Ridder Unicom
Reuters
Servisen
Telerate
Dafsa
Garban
GL Services Financiers
Pont Data
Prominofi
Quotron
SDIB
SITB
Tog Europe
Valgest

SOURCES of REFERENCE

All the Exchanges produce a wide range of publications both in English and French. For further information on any contract and their use please contact the Exchanges direct.

Most brokers and banks supply their clients with statistics and research material.

Daily market information can be found in:
specialized newspapers such as
Agefi, La Tribune and Cote Desfossés
general interest newspaper such as
Le Figaro
specialized weekly papers
Les Echos, La Synthèse Financière
specialized magazines
Option Finance, MTF.

THERE'S ONE GOOD WAY
OF FACING ECONOMIC UNCERTAINTY.

EQVATEUR

The Futures and Options Markets in Germany (Deutsche Terminbörse)

Dorothée Nilsson
Deutsche Bank AG, Frankfurt
Futures & Options Group

&

assisted by:
Igor Uszczapowski
Dresdner Bank AG

INTRODUCTION

Following nearly 40 years of little activity in the German futures markets, trading in stock options was introduced in Germany in 1970. Over the next two decades, the system underwent substantial revisions. During the 1980s, strike prices and expiration dates were standardized to facilitate dealing in the secondary market. On April 1, 1986, option trading was extended to include fixed-income securities. These reforms led to an increase in the volume of options traded. However, the traded volume in options still represented less than 10 per cent of the volume of stocks traded at the German stock exchanges (on average 1970-1989 1.35 per cent). Presently, 50 German and 13 foreign stock options are traded. During the last few years fixed-income options were traded rarely on the secondary market.

Previous Difficulties Concerning Forward Trading

Until now, the traditional German options market has been characterized by low liquidity and inefficiency. There have been several reasons for this situation, most of which are of a legal nature.

The German Speculating and Gambling Paragraph ("Differenzeinwand")

Until August 1, 1989, German banks were confronted with major difficulties when private customers dealt in options. Until then a private investor's liability in connection with futures and options trading was treated as a gambling debt. Consequently, the law treated a private investor's liability as uncollectible for the banks.

As a result the banks could rarely make claims against private customers having liabilities in connection with option dealing. In order to insure themselves against this, the banks imposed harsh conditions on private investors trading with futures and options.

Short Positions

In the past it was not possible to close a short position in the secondary market. If the option writer wanted to hedge himself by buying the same option he had written, the law still required that the writer keep the security until the option was exercised or until expiry date.

Capital Investment and Insurance Companies

In the past Capital Investment Companies as well as Insurance Companies have been extremely restricted in their possibilities to use deriva-

tive instruments for hedging purposes. Since March 1st 1990, capital investment companies may invest upto roughly 20 per cent of their fund assets in
futures and options as instruments for hedging purposes. Insurance companies can invest only a small part of their free capital. This restriction keeps
potentially liquidity away from these markets. A revision of the Insurance
Supervision Act (VAG) is planned which will allow to insurance companies
to use futures and options for transactions not related to hedging.

Deutsche Terminbörse (DTB)

A two-part survey was conducted in April 1987, in the first case to
test the feasibility of a German futures and options exchange, and in the
second, to quantify its demand. The study came to the following results:

a)   a new futures and options exchange should be started as
     soon as possible

b)   the exchange should have a fully automated trading and
     clearing system

c)   a market-maker system should be organized to provide
     market liquidity

d)   a clearing house should be integrated as a component of the
     exchange and should be a contractual partner for all trans-
     actions done at the exchange

e)   the hardware of the SOFFEX system developed in Switzer-
     land should serve as the basis of the DTB system.

The goals of the new exchange include the following:

a)   to strengthen the international attractiveness of the German
     financial market

b)   to satisfy the increased demand for derivative instruments
     in DM paper

c)   to offer new instruments for risk management purposes

Stock Exchange Act

In Germany, an exchange is a corporate body, i.e. Public law institution, and subject to the Stock Exchange Act. A new Stock Exchange Act was
passed in June 1989, and has been effective since August 1, 1989. For the DTB
the most important changes were:

a)   Until recently the physical presence of exchange players was
     mandatory during trading. Stock exchange trading has been
     given a broader definition which paved the way to set up the

               DTB as a fully computerized exchange. Dealing in futures and options need not be through an open out-cry system. Instead, trading can be executed via electronic data transmission.

b)   Trading with futures and options has been made accessible to private investors, provided they have been adequately informed of the risks involved in futures and options. The responsibility lies with the investment consultant, such as a bank, to inform the private investor of these risks. For this purpose an "information model" has been created by the Federal Association of German Banks (Bundesverband Deutscher Banken). This information will be supplied through:

- **a "risk information" document which must be signed by the client**

- **a standard product brochure and**

- **individual service.**

Once the client has signed the form, he can conclude futures and options, i.e. he can no longer avoid the responsibility of his actions by resorting to the speculation and gambling law.

Securities Lending and Borrowing

      For certain strategies with futures and options, short sales of the underlying securities are necessary. However, a cash flow can be generated only if the sale is settled. This can be accomplished either by entering into a repurchase/reverse repurchase agreement or by borrowing securities.

      Since securities lending was exempted from Stock Exchange Turnover tax on January 1, 1990, this product is also offered in Germany by larger banks and the Deutscher Kassenverein. A repo market for DM issues does not exist in Germany.

ORGANIZATION of the MARKET

DTB was registered as an exchange in September, 1989. The **DTB** office is located in Frankfurt am Main and subject to legal supervision, i.e. stock exchange supervision, by the Federal State of Hesse. Legal body of the German futures and options exchange is **DTB** GmbH, a private limited company with capital of DM 10 million.

Shareholders

Shareholders are 17 banks, representing a cross-section of the large banks, savings banks, cooperative banks, regional banks and private bankers.

Bankhaus Merck, Fink & Co

Bankhaus B. Metzler Seel. & Co.

Bankhaus M.M. Warburg Brinckmann, Wirtz & Co.

Bayerische Hypotheken- und Wechsel-Bank

Bayerische Vereinsbank AG

Berliner Bank AG

BHF-Bank

Commerzbank AG

Delbrück & Co., Privatbankiers

Deutsche Bank AG

Deutsche Genossenschaftsbank

Deutsche Girozentrale

Deutsche Kommunalbank

Dresdner Bank AG

Georg Hauck & Sohn Bankiers KGaA

Sal. Oppenheimer jr. & Cie.

Trinkaus & Burkhardt KGaA

Vereins- und Westbank AG

The **DTB** GmbH has a Supervisory Board with seven members, drawn from the management boards of the shareholder banks.

Board of Directors

B. von Ribbentrop	Deutsche Bank AG
P. Ertel	Bankers Trust GmbH
W. Chrobok	Bankhauses Gebrüder Bethmann
D. Wolf	Bayerische Vereinsbank AG
Dr. R. Baur	Bayerische Vereinsbank AG
Dr. W. Graebner	Berliner Handels- und Frankfurter Bank
G. Scleif	Berliner Handels- und Frankfurter Bank
Dr. M. Schröder	Bremer Landesbank
D-K. Frowein	Commerzbank AG
W. Otto	Commerzbank AG
Dr. J. Remmers	DG Bank
Dr. R.E. Breuer	Deutsche Bank AG
M. Zass	Deutsche Girozentrale - Deutsche Kommunal-bank
W. Müller	Deutsche Girozentrale - Deutsche Kommunal-bank
G. Eberstadt	Dresdner Bank AG
H. Kramer	Dresdner Bank AG
B. P. Kluge	Frankfurter Sparkasse
G. Roggemann	J.P. Morgan GmbH

Membership

Representing the two main functions of the **DTB**, there are also two types of membership:

- **exchange membership and/or**

- **clearing membership**

The conditions governing exchange membership are:

- **a registered office in Germany**

- **special qualifications in accordance with Section 14 of the Stock Exchange Act, and:**

- **for a non-bank applicant, security of DM 500,000.**

Exchange members are entitled to execute futures and options transactions for their own account (principal account) and for the account of third parties (agent account). A market-maker is also necessarily an exchange member, but only qualifies after fulfilling special qualification requirements laid down in Section 17 of the Stock Exchange Act.

Functions

The **DTB** GmbH fulfills two functions:

a)   it provides the facilities necessary for futures and options trading, at the **DTB**

b)   it guarantees through an integrated clearinghouse the proper settlement of transactions concluded at the **DTB**.

Geographical Independence

As a fully computerized exchange the **DTB** offers equal access to every potential exchange player anywhere in Germany. The floor of the exchange is replaced by the electronic trading system. The result is concentration of trading at one exchange.

Market Transparency

All data and information relevant for trading in futures and options is shown on-line on the **DTB** trading screens. As a result, all players receive comprehensive information at the same time.

Market-Maker System

For option series, the market-makers are obliged to quote on request binding bid and ask prices (quotes) for the series to which they hold a license. The major advantage of the market-maker system is the market liquidity achieved when several market makers actively put quotes into the market for their stock options.

For futures there will be no market-maker system. The assumption is that original interest combined with the advantages of a computerized trading system (transparency, geographical independence, etc.) will generate a liquid market.

Clearing

Clearing involves two key functions:

- **the DTB is the contractual partner for each transaction. Business relations only arise between the clearing house and its members, who are responsible for the settlement of all transactions, and**

- **guaranteeing all obligations assumed at the DTB.**

Clearing participants are:

- **the clearing house**
- **the clearing members**
- **the Landeszentralbank (LZB) Frankfurt as cash-settlement agency**
- **Deutscher Kassenverein (DKV) as custodian**

Clearing Members

There are two kinds of clearing membership:

- **a General Clearing Member (GCM), which can settle its own transactions, customers transactions, as well as transactions of Non-Clearing Members (NCM)**

- **a Direct Clearing Member (DCM), which can settle only its own transactions and those of its customers.**

A NCM must settle its transactions through a GCM.

Collateral System

The collateral system is of major importance for the security of trading and business settlement at the **DTB**. The collateral system ensures that the financial integrity of the clearing system is maintained. Factors making it possible for the clearing house to fulfil its obligations are:

- **capital adequacy requirements for clearing members**
- **a clearing guarantee from a third bank**
- **the margin system**

This means for:

A "GCM"	equity capital DM 250 million + a third bank guarantee of DM 10 million.
A "DCM"	equity capital DM 25 million + a third bank guarantee of DM 2 million.

The **DTB** uses a margin collateral system. Margins are required for:

a) uncovered short positions in options and

b) for both types of positions (long/short) in futures.

The **DTB** accepts as collateral from its clearing-members either cash, a third bank guarantee, or securities eligible as collateral for Bundesbank advances. The margin limits are structured to improve the clearing organization's ability to fulfill its commitments. Margins required are kept as low as possible to prevent a reduction of cost efficiency. The clearing agency calculates the value of each position continuously throughout the day and, in the event of a cover shortfall, immediately demands further collateral from the members.

With the introduction of the German Stock Index and the Bund future contract, the **DTB** will introduce a new risk-based margining system like that of the **OCC**, Chicago. This system will encompass all **DTB** derivatives in one portfolio in order to calculate the margin.

Trading

Brokers and market makers linked via the electronic terminal-based system place bids and offers via their terminals connected to the **DTB** system. When the prices offered by a buyer and seller match via these terminals, the transaction is completed automatically in the **DTB** computer.

Unlike options, there are no plans to introduce a market maker system for trading in futures contracts.

Orders

Order input and monitoring: market participants enter their buy and sell orders and monitor their order book by amending or deleting orders. The system accepts the following types of order:

- market orders
- limit orders

- fill-or-kill and good-till-canceled
- combination orders (i.e. spreads, straddles and strangles)

DTB Transaction Fees

Options	
Opening and closing transactions per contract:	DM 7
Correction of opening and closing transactions:	DM 4
Exercise fees:	
Exercise per contract:	DM 7
a) Bearer share:	additionally 0.25% stock transfer tax on the underlying value
b) Allianz share (cash settlement only):	none
Corrections of exercise (per order):	DM 4
Fees for short positions exercised:	like a) and b) above
Futures	
Opening and closing transactions per contract:	
DAX Future:	DM 4
Bund Future:	DM 1

Early Experience

In the first months the average daily volume of all stock options at the **DTB** was around 23,000 contracts. This was much more than the 10,000 - 15,000 contracts expected in the first year. The volume as not supported by German capital investment companies and German Insurance Companies, who were first allowed to enter the market after March 1, 1990. From March until September 1990, the average daily volume of contracts traded has increased to around 32,000 contracts. During the same period the Put/Call ratio varied between 0.15 and 1.1.

Further Planned Products

Options are planned on the **DAX** cash as well as on the **DAX**-Futures contract. The introduction will probably not be prior to Spring 1991. Other possibilities include:

- **options on the Bund Futures contract**

- **futures contracts on short-term time deposits (e.g. 3 month Eurodeutschemark).**

- **futures contracts on intermediate bonds (e.g. 5 year DM bonds).**

Address

DTB Deutsche Terminbörse GmbH
Grüneburgweg 102
D-6000 FRANKFURT/M1

Tel: (49) 69 15303 0
Fax: (49) 69 557 492

HISTORY of the MARKET

Date	Contract	Trading Vol. (Monthly Ave)
01 July 1988	Creation of **DAX** Index	
26 January 1990	Options on 15 German stocks	
End 1990	Future on **DAX** Index	n/a
End 1990	Future on Notional 6% 8.5 to 10 year German Government Bond	n/a
Spring 1991	Option on **DAX** Index	n/a
Spring 1991	Option on **DAX** Index future	n/a

Spring 1991	Option on Notional 6% 8.5 to 10 year German Government Bond	n/a
Spring 1991	Future on Notional 6% 4 to 5 year German Government Bond	n/a
Spring 1991	Future on 3 Month Deutschemark Interest Rates	n/a

OVERVIEW of PRODUCTS

	Futures	Options
Interest Rates		
Notional 6% 8.5 - 10 year German Government Bonds	§	§
3 Month Deutschemark deposits	§	
Notional 6% 4 - 5 year German Government Bonds	§	
Equities		
Individual stocks		*
DAX Index	§	§
DAX Index Future		§

§ due to launched end 1990/Spring 1991.

DETAILED CONTRACT SPECIFICATION
Interest Rates
Notional 6% 8.5 to 10 Year German Government Bonds (Bund) Futures Contract

The contract, based on German Government bonds with lives of 8.5 to 10 years is expected to trade at the end of 1990.

The **DTB** Bund Future contract is based on a notional 6 per cent German Government Bundes-Anliehen with a residual life of 8.5 to 10 years. The contract is almost identical to that traded on **LIFFE**. The only difference between the **DTB** Bund Future and the **LIFFE** Bund Future is the time to delivery. This is in Frankfurt the last trading day plus two days whereas in London it is last trading day plus three days.

Contract Size:	DM 250,000.
Delivery Months:	Three six and nine months from the March June September and December cycle.
Delivery Day:	The tenth day of the delivery month. If this is not a business day then the delivery date will be the next Frankfurt business day.
Last Trading Day:	Close of trading at 12.30 p.m. two business days before delivery day.
Quotation:	Per DM 100 nominal value to two decimal places.
Minimum Price Movement (Tick Size and Value):	DM 0.01 = DM 25.
Trading Hours:	In discussion although 07.30 a.m. - 18.00 p.m. Frankfurt time is indicated.

Initial Margin:	Risk based margins are charged by the **DTB** for long and short positions is calculated with reference to the projected underlying prices based on daily calculated risk factors. These position values are summed to arrive at a projected liquidation value of a portfolio of positions in the event of an assumed "worse case" change in the price of the underlying instruments. Reduced margin will be applied for spread positions. Margin requirements may be satisfied with cash and/or selected securities.
Price Limit:	No price limit at the moment. However the **DTB** has the right to set limits for the maximum price fluctuations if this should appear necessary due to extreme market conditions.
Position Limits:	These will be implemented however the level will be determined by the Exchange.
Contract Standard:	Physical delivery of any Bundesanliehe with 8.5 to 10 years remaining maturity as at the tenth calendar day of the delivery month. Settlement is two days after delivery day. Delivery takes place through the Deutscher Kassenverein.
Exchange Delivery Settlement Price:	The daily settlement price is the average of the trades in the last minute of trading or of the last five trades whichever is the greater. The **EDSP** is determined using the same method as the daily settlement price except that it is based on 12.30 p.m. Frankfurt time on the last trading day. The Invoice amount will be determined using the **EDSP** and conversion factor formula.
Reuters Pages:	Not known yet.

| Telerate Pages: | not known yet. |

Notional 6% German Government Bond (Bund) Futures Options Contract

The option contract based on the Bund Futures contract is expected in the Spring 1991.

Option Style:	American calls and puts.
Contract Size:	One Bund futures contract.
Delivery Months:	3 6 and 9 months from the March June September and December cycle. No short months will be available.
Delivery Day:	The end of the sixth business day prior to the first day of the delivery month.
Last Trading Day:	Six business days prior to the first day of the delivery month.
Quotation:	Multiples of 0.01.
Minimum Price Movement (Tick Size and Value):	DM 0.01 = DM 25.
Trading Hours:	To be determined. These will be the same as the Bund futures contract.
Initial Margin:	Risk based margins are charged by the **DTB** for long and short positions is calculated with reference to the projected underlying prices based on daily calculated risk factors. These position values are summed to arrive at a projected liquidation value for the margin class. Reduced margin will be applied for spread positions.

Price Limit:	No price limit at the moment. However the **DTB** has the right to set limits for the maximum price fluctuations if this should appear necessary due to extreme market conditions.
Position Limit:	There are no plans for these at present.
Spread Limits:	There can be maximum spreads set by the Exchange. These limits will be flexible and the **DTB** can choose not to implement spread requirements.
Contract Standard:	Physical settlement of a Bund futures contract on the first business day after the exercise day.
Exercise Price:	Nine exercise prices will be listed for each series with exercise intervals of DM 0.50. New prices will be introduced on the business day after the settlement price for the spot month Bund futures contract is within Dm 0.25 of the fourth highest or fourth lowest existing price.
Exchange Delivery Settlement Price:	The price of the last trade if it occurs during the last hour of trading otherwise the average between the best bid and ask prices.
Reuters Pages:	Not known yet.
Telerate Pages:	Not known yet.

3 Month DM Money Market Interest Rates Futures Contracts

This contract, based on a three month DM money market instruments is expected to be launched in Spring 1991.

Contract Size:	DM 1,000,000.
Expiry Months:	Five contract months up to 15 months ahead at three month intervals from the March June September and December cycle.
Expiry Day:	Two business days prior to the third Wednesday of the expiry month.
Last Trading Day:	11.30 a.m. two business days prior to the third Wednesday of the expiry month.
Quotation:	Contract will be quoted to two decimal places as 100.00 minus the rate of interest.
Minimum Price Movement (Tick Size and Value):	DM 0.01 = DM 100.
Trading Hours:	To be determined.
Initial Margin:	Risk based margins are charged by the **DTB** for long and short positions is calculated with reference to the projected underlying prices based on daily calculated risk factors. These position values are summed to arrive at a projected liquidation value for the margin class. Reduced margin will be applied for spread positions.

Price Limit:	No price limit. However the **DTB** has the right to set limits for the maximum price fluctuations if this should appear necessary due to extreme market conditions.
Contract Standard:	Cash settlement on the first business day after the last trading day.
Exchange Delivery Settlement Price:	The daily settlement price will be the average of the last prices paid over the last minute of trading or of the last five trades whichever has the greater number of contracts. Final settlement price is based on the interest rate for three months DM deposits being offered to prime banking names between 11.00 a.m. - 11.30 a.m. on the last trading day stated by a random sample from a list of designated banks. Disregarding the three highest and lowest quotes the settlement price will be 100.00 minus the average of the remaining rates. The procedure for vetting the price will be determined by the **DTB** and the User Approval Group (**UAG** - representatives of the owners of **DTB**).
Reuters Pages:	Not known yet.
Telerate Pages:	Not known yet.

Notional 6% 4 - 5 Year German Government Bond Futures Contract

The contract, based on notional 6% 4 to 5 year German Government Bonds is expected to trade in Spring 1991.

Contract Size:	DM 250,000.
Delivery Months:	Three six and nine months from the March June September and December cycle.
Delivery Day:	The tenth day of the delivery month. If this is not a business day then the delivery date will be the next Frankfurt business day.
Last Trading Day:	Close of trading at 12.30 p.m. two trading days before delivery day.
Quotation:	Per DM 100 nominal value to two decimal places.
Minimum Price Movement (Tick Size and Value):	DM 0.01 = DM 25.
Trading Hours:	In discussion although 07.30 a.m. - 16.00 p.m. Frankfurt time is indicated.
Initial Margin:	Risk based margins are charged by the **DTB** for long and short positions is calculated with reference to the projected underlying prices based on daily calculated risk factors. These position values are summed to arrive at a projected liquidation value for the margin class. Reduced margin will be applied for spread positions. Margin requirements may be satisfied with cash and/or selected securities.

Price Limit:	No price limit is planned at the moment. However the **DTB** has the right to set limits for the maximum price fluctuations if this should appear necessary due to extreme market conditions.
Position Limits:	These are not planned at present.
Contract Standard:	Physical delivery of any Bundesobligationen and Bundesanliehen with 4 to 5 years remaining maturity on the delivery day. Delivery takes place two business days later through the Deutscher Kassenverein (**DKV**).
Exchange Delivery Settlement Price:	The daily settlement price is the average of the trades in the last minute of trading or of the last five trades whichever is the greater. The **EDSP** is determined using the same method as the daily settlement price except that it is based on 12.30 p.m. Frankfurt time on the last trading day. The Invoice amount will be determined using the **EDSP** and conversion factor formula.
Reuters Pages:	Not known yet.
Telerate Pages:	Not known yet.

Equities

Deutscher Aktienindex (DAX) Index Futures Contract

At the end of 1990, an index futures contract will be introduced based on the German stock index - Deutscher Aktienindex (DAX). The DAX was developed jointly by a working group of German Stock Exchanges and the Börsenzeitung. It was introduced on July 1, 1988.

Contract Size:	DM 100 per index point.
Expiry Months:	3 6 and 9 months from the March June September and December cycle.
Expiry Day:	Third Saturday of the expiry month.
Last Trading Day:	12.30 p.m. Frankfurt time on the last business day before the third Saturday of the expiry month.
Quotation:	DM to one decimal place.
Minimum Price Movement (Tick Size and Value):	DM 0.5 per index point = DM 50.
Trading Hours:	Not determined as yet but will depend on the time frame for the calculation of the **DAX**.
Initial Margin:	Risk based margins are charged by the **DTB** for long and short positions is calculated with reference to the projected underlying prices based on daily calculated risk factors. These position values are summed to arrive at a projected liquidation value for the margin class. Reduced margin will be applied for spread positions.

Price Limit:	No price limit. However the **DTB** has the right to set limits for the maximum price fluctuations if this should appear necessary due to extreme market conditions.
Position Limits:	These will be implemented. However
Contract Standard:	Cash settlement the business day following the last trade day.
Exchange Delivery Settlement Price:	The daily settlement price is the average of the trades in the ten minutes of trading. The **EDSP** is determined using the same method as the daily settlement price except that it is based on 12.30 p.m. Frankfurt time on the last trading day.
Reuters Pages:	Not known
Telerate Pages:	Not known

Weighting of the Individual DAX Values

	Prices as of April 30,1990	Factor weight (%)*	% share value
Banks			**16.99**
Deutsche Bank	748.0	5.72578	8.59
Dresdner Bank	407.5	4.44480	3.26
Commerzbank	275.0	3.38185	1.90
Bay. Hypo.-Bank	389.0	2.23717	1.89
Bay. Vereinsbank	363.5	1.66652	1.35

Insurance			**10.40**
Allianz	2,405.0	2.23529	10.40
Engineering			**3.55**
MAN Ordinary	480.0	2.01042	1.60
Linde	947.0	0.86865	1.47
Deutsche Babcock	225.0	1.04314	0.48
Steel/Metalwork			**4.50**
Thyssen	288.0	4.66431	2.39
Mannesmann	354.0	3.79534	2.11
Electricals			**9.04**
Siemens	737.5	7.06034	8.58
Nixdorf Preferred§	340.0	0.83468	0.46
Chemicals/Pharmaceuticals			**20.67**
Bayer	301.0	9.44973	6.16
BASF	299.5	8.49189	5.35
Hoechst	289.5	8.58612	5.29
Schering	834.0	0.96996	1.62
Degussa	525.0	1.08784	1.20
Henkel	620.0	0.86431	1.05
Utilities			**11.17**
Veba	450.0	6.60167	4.92

RWE	469.0	6.59946	4.62
VIAG	402.0	2.32619	1.63
Department Stores			2.85
Kaufhof Ordinary	665.0	1.16010	1.43
Karstadt	648.0	1.07294	1.42
Automobile/Tyres			18.07
Daimler	818.0	6.30548	9.93
Volkswagen Ordinary	556.0	4.47058	4.37
BMW	574.5	2.34706	2.77
Continental	285.5	1.28948	1.00
Paper			1.28
Feldmühle§	530.0	1.04314	1.28
Transportation			1.48
Lufthansa	178.5	3.62415	1.48
TOTAL			100.0

Notes:

* Based on share capital on September 15,1989.

§ On September 1,1990 Nixdorf Preferred and Feldmühle will have been substituted by Preussag and Metallgesellschaft.

Deutscher Aktienindex (DAX) Index Futures Options Contract

This contract, based on the **DAX** futures contract is expected to be launched in the Spring of 1991.

Option Style:	American calls and puts.
Contract Size:	One **DAX** futures contract. DM 100 per **DAX** index point.
Delivery Months:	One two three month contracts with the next two months of the March June September and December cycle .
Delivery Day:	Exercise can be completed by the end of the unrestricted post trading period on any business day up to and including the last trading day.
Last Trading Day:	12.30 p.m. Frankfurt time on third Friday of the delivery month.
Quotation:	Multiples of DM 0.5.
Minimum Price Movement (Tick Size and Value):	DM 0.5 = DM 50.
Trading Hours:	To be determined. It will be similar to the hours of the **DAX** futures contract.

Initial Margin:	Risk based margins are charged by the **DTB** for long and short Index option positions is calculated with reference to the projected index values based on daily published risk factors. These position values are summed to arrive at a projected liquidation value of the margin class. Futures and options on the same index will be in the same margin class.
Price Limit:	There are no plans for these at present. However the **DTB** has the right to set limits for the maximum price fluctuations if this should appear necessary due to extreme market conditions.
Position Limits:	There are no plans for these at present.
Spread Limits:	There will maximum spreads set by the Exchange. Spread limits will be flexible and the **DTB** can choose not to implement spread requirements.
Contract Standard:	Physical delivery of **DAX** futures on the first business day after the delivery day.
Exercise Price:	Five exercise prices will be listed with exercise price intervals of 50 points. New prices will be introduced on the second business day after the settlement price of the spot month **DAX** futures contract exceeds the average of the highest/lowest strike prices.

Exchange Delivery Settlement Price:	The **DAX** settlement price will be based on the average value of the Index over a time interval to be set by the Börsenvorstand. The daily settlement price is the price of the last trade if it occurs during the last hour of trading otherwise the average between the best bid and ask price. The final settlement price will be the value of the of the **DAX** at 12.30 p.m. on the last trade day.
Reuters Pages:	Not known yet.
Telerate Pages:	Not known yet.

Deutscher Aktienindex (DAX) Index Options Contract

This contract, based on the actual **DAX** index is expected to be launched in the Spring of 1991.

Option Style:	European calls and puts.
Contract Size:	DM 10 per **DAX** Index point.
Expiry Months:	One two three month contracts with the next two months of the March June September and December cycle.
Expiry Day:	After the end of the last on-line trading day the exchange will automatically exercise all positions which are in-the-money.
Last Trading Day:	12.30 p.m. Frankfurt time on third Friday of the expiry month.
Quotation:	Multiples of DM 0.1.
Minimum Price Movement (Tick Size and Value):	DM 0.1 = DM 1.

Trading Hours:	To be determined. It will be similar to the hours of the **DAX** futures contract.
Initial Margin:	Risk based margins are charged by the **DTB** for long and short Index option positions is calculated with reference to the projected index values based on daily published risk factors. These position values are summed to arrive at a projected liquidation value of the margin class. Futures and options on the same index will be in the same margin class.
Price Limit:	There are no plans for these at present. However the **DTB** has the right to set limits for the maximum price fluctuations if this should appear necessary due to extreme market conditions.
Position Limits:	There are no plans for these at present.
Spread Limits:	There will maximum spreads set by the Exchange. However spread limits will be flexible. The **DTB** can choose not to implement spread requirements.
Contract Standard:	Cash settlement on the first business day after the last trading day.
Exercise Price:	Five exercise prices will be listed with exercise price intervals of 25 points. New prices will be introduced on the second business day after the settlement price of the spot month **DAX** futures contract exceeds the average of the highest/lowest strike prices.

Exchange Delivery Settlement Price:	The **DAX** settlement price will be based on the average value of the Index over a time interval to be set by the Börsenvorstand. The daily settlement price is the price of the last trade if it occurs during the last hour of trading otherwise the average between the best bid and ask price. The final settlement price will be the value of the of the **DAX** at 12.30 p.m. on the last trade day.
Reuters Pages:	Not known yet.
Telerate Pages:	Not known yet.

Individual Equity Options Contracts on DTB

Trading of stock options for German blue chip equity stocks started on January 26, 1990. The options have been designed in accordance with international standards and can be exercised at any time during their term (American style).

Presently, the underlying stocks are:

	Code
Automobile	
B.M.W.	**BMW**
Daimler	**DAI**
Volkswagen	**VOW**
Banks	
Commerzbank	**CBK**
Deutsche Bank	**DBK**
Dresdner Bank	**DRB**

Chemical Industry	
BASF	BAS
Bayer	BAY
Hoechst	HFA
Electrical Engineering	
Siemens	SIE
Energy and Utilities	
RWE	RWE
VEBA	VEB
Insurance	
Allianz	ALV
Steel and Engineering	
Mannesmann	MMW
Thyssen	THY

Criteria for selected stocks being traded as options are:-

a) Primary criteria:

- continuous trading in the underlying stock (high market liquidity)
- diversified shareholders
- market capitalization over DM 1 billion
- daily turnover over DM 50 million
- no payment defaults in dividends or interest payments

b) Secondary criteria

- minimum stock price DM 150

● regular and accurate information from the company

● stock should be sufficiently volatile

● internationally and domestically recognized stocks.

The selected underlying stocks all represent approximately 50 per cent of the total German equity market capitalization and 65 per cent of the exchange's turnover for 1988. (BMW is selected even though the shareholders are not widely spread. This is because of its high daily turnover and its importance as a large automobile manufacturer.)

Option Style:	American calls and puts.
Contract Size:	50 shares of the underlying stock.
Expiry Months:	One two and three months and the last month of the next quarter from the March June September and December cycle i.e. a maximum of 6 months.
Expiry Day:	The first Friday after the 14th calendar day of the expiry month.
Last Trading Day:	The first Friday after the 14th calendar day of the expiry month.
Quotation:	DM per option to two decimal places irrespective of underlying stock.
Minimum Price Movement (Tick Size and Value):	DM 0.10 = DM 5.
Trading Hours:	07.30 a.m. to 18.00 p.m..
Initial Margin:	Risk based margins are charged by the **DTB** for long and short Index option positions is calculated with reference to the projected stock values based on daily published risk factors. These position values are summed to arrive at a projected liquidation value of the margin class.

Price Limit:	The **DTB** has the right to set limits for maximum price fluctuations if this should appear necessary due to extreme market conditions.
Contract Standard:	Physical delivery of underlying stock two business days after the exercise day **with the exception of Allianz which is cash settled.**
Exercise Price:	At least three strike prices are available for each maturity. When contracts with a new expiry month are introduced they are launched with three series: "at-the-money" "in-the-money" and out-of-the-money" per series based on the closing price of the underlying value on the Frankfurt Stock Exchange. The strike price intervals depend on the price of the equity (see below). New option series are launched as soon as the price of the stock has exceeded or falls below the highest/lowest strike price on two successive trading days.
Exchange Delivery Settlement Price:	
Reuters Pages:	Not known
Telerate Pages:	Not known

Exercise Price Intervals

Price of equity	Exercise Interval
Under DM 100	DM 5
DM 100 - DM 200	DM 10
DM 200 - DM 500	DM 20
DM 500 - DM 1,000	DM 50

Over DM 1,000	DM 100

Total Option Statistics

Daily Volume and Open Interest (Jan 2, 1990 - Jul 31, 1990)

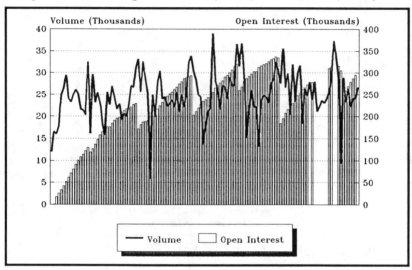

Call and Put Daily Volumes (Jan 2, 1990 - Jul 31, 1990)

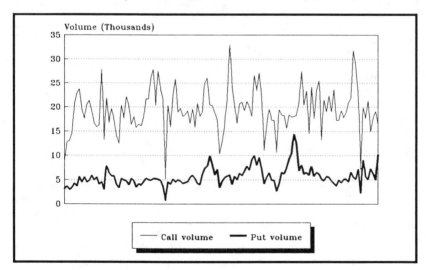

Open Interest and Volume/Open Interest("Liquidity")
(Jan 2, 1990 - Jul 31, 1990)

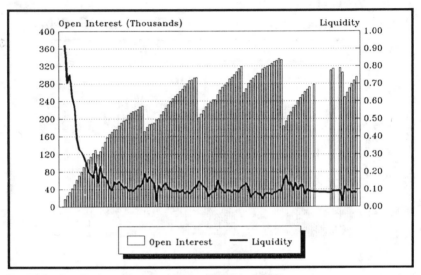

DAX Index Price (Jan 2, 1990 - Jul 31, 1990)

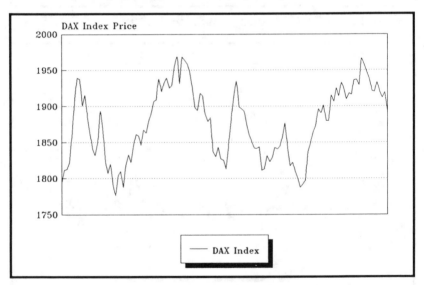

Siemens Shares

Option and Underlying Share Daily Volume (Jan 2, 1990 - Jul 31, 1990)

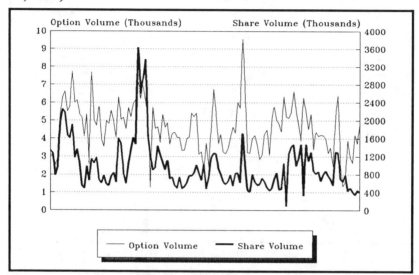

Call and Put Daily Volumes (Jan 2, 1990 - Jul 31, 1990)

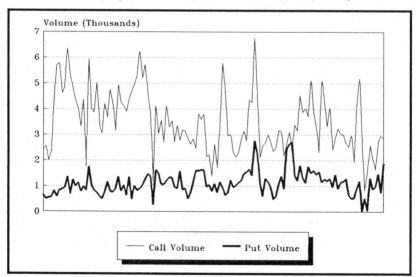

Siemens share price (Jan 2, 1990 - Jul 31, 1990)

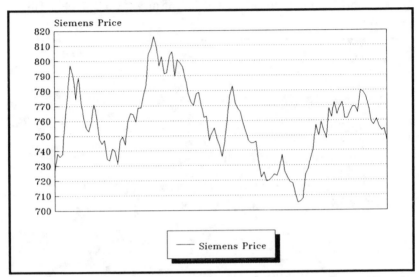

Call and Put Implied Volatilities (Jan 2, 1990 - Jul 31, 1990)

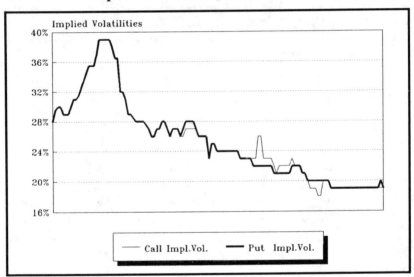

Individual Stock Options Traded on the Stock Exchange

Stock Options Traded at the German Stock Exchange:

The following list of stocks have options traded on the Stock Exchange. Approximately 90 per cent of the total contract volume in stock options at German Stock Exchanges is traded at the Frankfurt Stock Exchange. Yearly contract volume of traded stock options at the Frankfurt Stock Exchange (in average 1.35% of the total

Stock volume between 1970 - 1989): 1 contract = 50 shares

German stocks:	Nixdorf Computer
AEG	Porsche
AGIV	PREUSSAG
Bayerische Hypothekenbank	Rheinmetall Ordinaries
Bayerische Vereinsbank	Rheinmetall Preffered
Bewag	RWE Ordinaries
BHF-Bank	RWE Preffered
Continental	Rütgers
Degussa	Schering
Deutsche Babcock Ordinaries	VARTA
Deutsche Babcock Preffered	VEW
Didier-Werke	VIAG
Feldmühle	Volkswagen Preffered
Harpener	Wella
Henkel	Foreign stocks:

Hoesch	Alcan
Kali und Salz	Chrysler
Karstadt	Elf Aquitaine
Kaufhof	GMC
KHD	IBM
Klöckner Werke	Litton
Linde	Norsk Hydro
Lufthansa Ordinaries	Philips
Lufthansa Preffered	Royal Dutch
MAN Ordinaries	Sony
MAN Preffered	Unilever
Mercedes Holding	Xerox
Metallgesellschaft	

Stock Options' Turnover Volumes on Stock Exchange

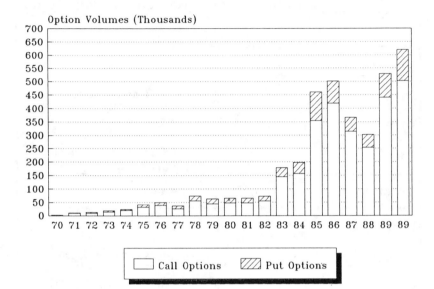

TAXATION

Turnover Taxes

Financial futures and options are not subject to stock exchange turnover taxes or value-added taxes (VAT).

Direct taxes

At present financial futures contracts are not subject to any income taxes on capital gains, since there is no intention to fulfil obligations with the underlying cash instrument.

Income taxes on capital gains made from options are still being discussed by the tax authorities.

a) Private Investors   Presently, profits generated by exchange traded options business, as far as they have been realized within 6 months, are subject to income taxes.

b) Entities   Profits and losses on options are regularly accounted in the P & L statement and thereby subject to taxes on capital gains.

QUOTE VENDORS

Information about the **DTB** can be accessed on the following sources:

Reuters	
DTNA-Z	**DTB option prices**
DTOA-Z	**DTB option prices**
DTBI	**DTB News Board**
TBFA	**DTB OTC (over-the-counter trading for system errors)**
Telekurs	
BH21 (Return)	
for Calls:	**4,_Stock code (i.e. 4,_DAI)**
for Puts:	**5,_Stock code (i.e.5,_DAI)**
VWD (Volkswirtschaftlicher Dienst):	
1235 and following pages.	

Note For Telekurs 4,_DAI should be entered as 4, DAI

RESOURCES

The DTB is providing seminars and PC based programs, as well as publications covering:

the various contracts
rules and regulations
and monthly statistics

Global Fixed Income Research

Currency relationships. Capital flows. Yield curve anomalies. Blips and pips. Let's face it: your performance in global fixed income markets depends on how much you know. On data.

Deutsche Bank's global fixed income research gives you the data. To trade. To succeed.

It's clear, concise and action-oriented. It's a matter of interest.

Deutsche Bank

The spirit of commitment knows no limits.

When doing business in Germany, you'll need a bank whose expertise extends beyond the German market. A truly international bank that is nevertheless at home in the Federal Republic.

A bank that is able to bring the realities of the German marketplace into clear focus for you.

A bank that knows first-hand all the ins and outs of doing business in Germany, Europe's biggest national market. But also a bank that can take maximum advantage of international business opportunities.

In other words, a bank big enough to provide you with a complete range of financial services, yet flexible enough to design tailormade solutions to your specific business problems.

Dresdner Bank is one of Germany's major banks with more than 1,300 domestic branches within the group as well as international offices in over 50 countries. With a century of experience in international banking, Dresdner Bank today serves more than 100,000 firms worldwide.

Dresdner Bank: offering you everything you need to do business in Germany – and much more.

The Futures Market in Ireland

Daniel McLaughlin
Riada & Co.

&

Diarmuid Bradley
Irish Futures & Options
Exchange (IFOX)

INTRODUCTION

A futures' market in Ireland is a recent phenomenon; the Irish Futures and Options Exchange (**IFOX**) opened for trading in May 1989. The slow pace of development in comparison with the major markets only partly reflects the small size of the economy; of more importance was the nature of financial markets in Dublin and in particular, the nature of the market for Irish Government Bonds (Gilts). Fundamental changes in these cash markets over the last few years were the catalyst for the creation of a futures' market in Ireland.

A key development was the Irish pound's break with sterling in 1979, following the former's entry into the Exchange Rate Mechanism of the EMS (the currency had been linked at par with sterling). This proved a significant stimulus to the indigenous financial community and encouraged the creation of a market independent from London. The level of market sophistication and expertise grew as Irish institutions became accustomed to dealing with a plethora of risk management instruments and so, by the mid 1980's, proposals for a formal futures market proved readily acceptable to the bulk of the financial community.

Another important factor in the genesis of **IFOX** was changes in the Gilt market. Traditionally, the Irish Government Broker had dominated the market, quoting two way prices in stocks, with brokers acting as intermediaries between the Government and financial institutions. But, the Government's appetite for borrowing diminished dramatically in the latter years of the 1980's (the borrowing requirement fell to 2.4 per cent of GNP in 1989 from 12.9 per cent in 1986) and activity shifted decisively to the secondary market, with brokers acting as agents in matching buyers and sellers. Liquidity in the market was further enhanced by the upsurge in foreign interest in the Irish market (nonresident holdings of Gilts rose to 30 per cent of the market in 1989 from less than half this level in 1987). Against this background, the desire for a hedging instrument was a natural development.

So, when a working party was set up in 1987 to examine seriously the possibility of a futures Exchange, a cross section of leading Irish financial institutions were represented, including brokers, banks and fund managers. Agreement was quickly reached on the desirability of futures instruments covering Gilts, interest rates and the foreign exchange market, and twenty four members subscribed capital via a private placing in August 1988. Simulated trading commenced in March 1989, and the market went live at the end of May.

ORGANIZATION of the MARKET

IFOX is a domestic (Irish pound based) Exchange. Members trade from their own offices through a computerized network, entering orders and prices via screens which are linked to the central IFOX computer. There is no Exchange floor. International Commodities Clearing House (ICCH) provides the software for the Automated Trading System. IFOX itself developed an on-line clearing/settlement system, which links to the Automated Trading System.

IFOX is a self-regulating body, although under the ultimate supervision of the Central Bank of Ireland. The Board of Exchange is responsible for the organization and operation of IFOX and represents the different interest groups among the membership. Thus, three of the nine member board represent banks, two represent stockbrokers, two are employed by Fund managers and two are IFOX staff members. The latter includes the Chief Executive, who is responsible for the day-to-day running of the Exchange and is backed by eight other staff members. The staff of the Exchange are also available to discuss the operation of the system and an education package is available.

The closing/settlement prices of the IFOX contracts are set by the Exchange after trading ceases (4.15 p.m.). These prices are input to the Clearing System. The Clearing System is on line to the twenty four Members and details of margin call is available at 4.45 p.m. The IFOX margins are collected via the IFOX Settlement Bank (i.e., a specific bank where IFOX and all Members hold accounts through which the daily margin collection system is operated) before 10.30 a.m. each day.

Address

IFOX
Seagrave House
Earlsfort Terrace
DUBLIN 2

Tel: 767413
Fax: 614645

Board of Directors

D.Desmond	(Chairman)
D.Bradley	(Managing)
J.Corrigan	(AIB Investment Managers)

J.Kearney	(AIB Bank)
K.Luddy	(IFOX)
C.Lydon	(Bank of Ireland)
B.O'Loughlin	(Irish Life)
F.Shanley	(Riada & Co.)
M.Wilson	(Ulster Bank)

Membership

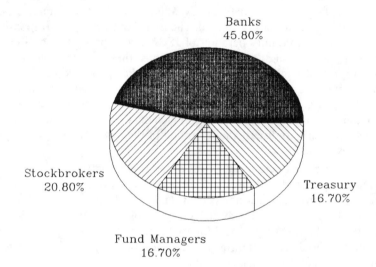

Banks
45.80%

Stockbrokers
20.80%

Treasury
16.70%

Fund Managers
16.70%

The **IFOX** membership has twenty four shareholders. These Members were drawn from the leading Irish banks, stockbrokers, fund managers and treasury operations.

The seat-holders are:

Banks

Agricultural Credit Corporation
AIB Bank
Algemene Bank Nederland
Anglo Irish Bank
Bank of Ireland
Banque Nationale de Paris
Citibank

Gandon Securities
Industrial Credit Corporation
National Irish Bank
Ulster Bank
Woodchester Investment Bank

Fund Managers
AIB Investment Managers
Investment Bank of Ireland
Irish Life Assurance plc.
Shield Insurance (Eagle Star)

Treasury Operations
Bord Bainne
Hibernian Insurance
Irish Telecommunications Investments plc

Stock Brokers
Riada
J & E Davy
Goodbody Stockbrokers
National & City Brokers
Bloxham Maguire

The Exchange is dominated numerically by the banks which is a reflection of the bias of the initial products and so **IFOX** was seen as a natural hedging mechanism for such institutions. In contrast, stockbrokers in Ireland are legally bound to act as agents only, and so the only market maker in Government bonds, the Government broker, is not represented on the Exchange.

In practice, the number of active players on the market is below twenty four. This partly reflects the fact that the natural traders, the brokers, have little incentive to participate very actively as most of the major financial institutions are members. In the gestation period of the Exchange, the brokers advocated "cross transactions" i.e., deals could be matched outside the Automated Trading System, because this would enhance liquidity in the early stages of the market's development. In the event, the majority view prevailed that this facility would weaken the role of the Automated Trading System.

The membership has remained unchanged since the initial placing and there are no current plans to expand the number. Consequently, the Exchange remains an overwhelmingly domestic institution.

Transaction Costs: Members and nonmembers

Members

For members, the charges involve a combination of fixed and variable, with the former relating to the work-stations linked to the Automated Trading System and the latter to the volume of trading. The current schedule is as follows:

Trading Stations

Rental: IR£ 6,000 pa + IR£ 3,000 per additional screen.

Maintenance: IR£ 875 pa per work-station.

Per Contract Traded

Contract	Exchange Fee IR£	Clearing Fee IR£
20 year Gilt	1.00	1.50
3 Month DIBOR	0.50	0.50
Irish Pound/U.S.Dollar	0.50	0.50
ISEQ Index	1.00	1.50

Delivery/Settlement

A delivery fee of IR£10.00 per contract lot per side applies to Long Gilt contracts which run to delivery.

Non-Members

Non-members cannot deal directly as they have no access to the Automated System. Consequently, they have to transact via existing members which would, in practice, mean the brokers. A minimum brokerage charge is in operation which must be levied when a member operates on behalf of a non-member. However, clearing fees are not charged when a position is closed within the same working day.

The minimum brokerage charges are:

20 Year Gilt	IR£5.00 per contract
3 Month **DIBOR**	IR£1.00 per contract
Irish pound/U.S.Dollar	IR£1.00 per contract
ISEQ Index	IR£30.00 per contract (Institutional Clients)
	IR£75.00 per contract (Private Clients)

Brokers commissions are fixed in the cash market and a futures transaction would be cheaper. For example, buying 20 contracts in the Long Gilt future (equivalent to IR£1 million in the cash market, the standard size) would cost IR£150 against around IR£700 commission in the cash market.

OVERVIEW of PRODUCTS

The following four contracts are currently listed on **IFOX**:-

- ●Future on 20 year Irish Gilt
- ●Future on 3 month Inter-Bank Offer Rate in Dublin (**DIBOR**)
- ●Future on Irish Pound/U.S. Dollar Exchange rate
- ●Future in Irish Equity Index (**ISEQ**)

IFOX Gilt Future Contract

The **IFOX** Gilt Contract is based on a IR£50,000 notional 20 year Irish government stock with an 8 per cent coupon. This contract runs to delivery i.e. holders who hold to maturity are obliged to either deliver (seller) or take delivery (buyer) of a long dated Irish government stock. The seller chooses one of a range of Gilts in the 15-25 year maturity area. It is economically sensible for the seller to select only one such stock (known as the "cheapest to deliver").

Three Month DIBOR Future Contract

The **IFOX DIBOR** contract is based on a IR£100,000 deposit at the three-month Dublin Interbank Offer Rate. A cash settlement system operates, i.e. at maturity those holding outstanding contracts either pay or receive the difference between the final settlement amount specified by the

Exchange and the value as of the previous margin call. The Exchange settlement price uses the same formula as that used to settle forward rate agreements (FRAs).

Irish Pound/U.S. Dollar Future Contract

The Irish Pound/U.S. Dollar contract is denominated in units of US$50,000. Quotation uses the Direct method, i.e. in Irish Pounds per U.S.Dollar to the fourth decimal place. This is the inversion of the Indirect Quotation method which is the normal convention in the Irish market i.e. Dollars per Irish Pound (this difference is necessary to facilitate a tick system).

Settlement operates via cash settlement. This contract is scheduled to be discontinued in September 1990.

ISEQ Index Future Contract

The ISEQ contract is valued at IR£10 per full index point. ISEQ is the Irish Stock Exchange index, and includes all official list and USM equities (76 in total). The Exchange Delivery Settlement Price is calculated using an average of the index on the last trading day and the previous business day.

New Products

At present IFOX are listing futures products only, although it is intended that options will be added to the range of products at a later date. The list of futures is constantly under review and a new five year gilt contract is scheduled for inclusion in September.

HISTORY of the FUTURES MARKET

Date of Launch	Type of Contract	Trading Volume (Monthly Average)
29 May 1989	Notional 20 Year Gilt Bond	800
29 May 1989	3 Month DIBOR	3,500
29 May 1989	Irish Pound/U.S. Dollar Rate	122
4 Jan 1990	Irish Stock Exchange Index	36

DETAILED CONTRACT SPECIFICATIONS
Interest Rates
IFOX Long Gilt Futures Contract

After a rather disappointing start, the volume of contracts in the Gilt future picked up in the latter part of 1989. This sluggish activity was a direct reflection of the cash market. The Irish yield curve became steeply inverted in 1989, and long yields were over 3 per cent below short rates. The lower yield at the long end reflected a scarcity premium on long stock as the authorities have not issued long dated bonds for around two years. Consequently, Irish institutions holding such stock were reluctant to sell and volatility at this end of the market fell. Not surprisingly the futures market was adversely affected. However, interest rates in Ireland began to decline in the second quarter of 1990 and the Gilts market experienced a major rally, which stimulated a significant pickup in futures activity.

The stability of the Irish pound within the EMS since the 1987 realignment has led to the Irish bond market closely tracking the German market. As the chart shows, gilt prices fell steeply in the early part of 1990 following the announcement of plans for German unity. However, the second quarter saw a significant recovery and yield spreads against Germany narrowed. The ten year spread declined to a low of 110 basis points against 200 basis points at the start of the year.

Contract Size:	IR£50,000 nominal of a notional 8 per cent 20 year Irish government bond.
Delivery Months:	March June September December.
Delivery Day:	Third Wednesday in Delivery Month (date to be published at least 3 months in advance by the Exchange).
Last Trading Day:	11.00 a.m. two business days before delivery day.
Quotation:	per IR£100 nominal
Minimum Price Movement (Tick size and value):	IR£0.01 & IR£5.00.

Trading Hours:	8.30 a.m. - 16.15 p.m.
Initial Margin:	5 per cent of the nominal value of the contract = IR£ 2,500.
Price Limit:	2 per cent
Contract Standard:	Delivery may be made of any "deliverable" Irish government security with 15-25 years to maturity at the sellers discretion. The initial listing of "deliverable" securities quoted below.
Deliverable Parcel:	The nominal amount of deliverable stock whose value at the delivery date is IR£50,000 on a semi-annual gross redemption yield equal to the notional coupon (i.e. 8 per cent). Exchange delivery is at 11.00 a.m..
Exchange Delivery Settlement Price:	The IFOX Market Price at 11.00 a.m. on the second business day prior to delivery.
Reuters Page:	IFOX

Initial list of deliverable stocks:

- Irish government stocks with 15 - 25 years to maturity.
- No variable rate, index-linked, convertible dual date or partly paid Gilt may be delivered.
- Interest must be payable half yearly.

Initial List*

- 9 per cent Capital 2006
- 8 1/4 per cent Capital 2008
- 8 1/2 per cent Capital 2010
- 8 3/4 per cent Capital 2012

The Exchange reserves the right to exclude any particular stock from the list of deliverable Gilts. In that context, a stock with a low amount in issue (12.5 per cent capital 2005) is excluded from the list of deliverable Gilts.

Daily Volume and Open Interest (Jan 1,1990 - Jun 30,1990)

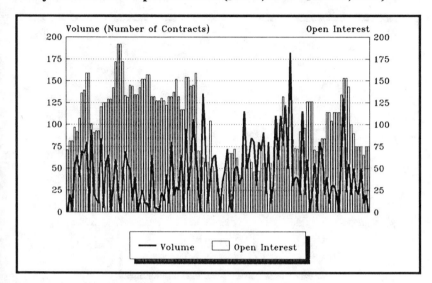

Open Interest and Volume/Open Interest("Liquidity")
(Jan 1,1990 - Jun 30,1990)

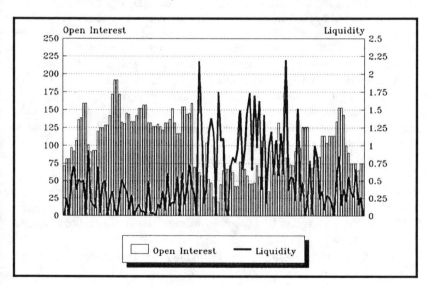

Price/Yield History (Jan 1,1990 - Jun 30,1990)

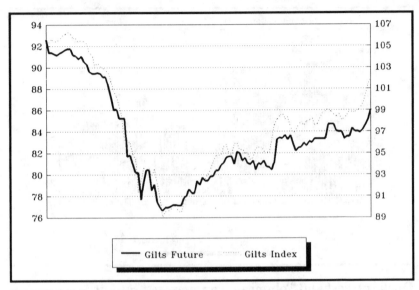

IFOX 3 Month DIBOR Future Contract

This is the most actively traded of the existing futures contract being extensively used by the banks, who account for 50 per cent of **IFOX** membership. Irish short rates moved up over the course of 1990 as the Authorities responded to higher rates within the EMS and to domestic outflows; 3 month money in Dublin rose by 4 per cent. In March 1990, the Central Bank announced further easing of Ireland's Exchange Controls, the effect of which was to make it easier for non-residents to deposit large funds in the Dublin Interbank market. As a result large inflows occurred, taking advantage of the high differential which had opened up between Irish and German rates. Activity in the futures market reflected differing views as to the extent of anticipated fall in rates.

Activity in the **DIBOR** contract now averages 200 lots per day which is well ahead of expectations for this stage of its development and it is now regarded as a key benchmark of short term rates. The two leading Irish banks, AIB and Bank of Ireland, now act as market-makers in the contract, so boosting liquidity.

Money rates in Dublin tumbled in the second quarter of 1990 following moves to ease exchange controls as from 1 April. Up to that time it was difficult for non-residents to place large sums on short term deposit in Ireland, but all such restrictions have now been removed. As a result strong inflows occurred and the 3 month differential between Dublin and Frankfurt fell from 450 basis points to 200 basis points. It is interesting to note that the futures market was not convinced about the downward trend and on several occasions pointed to higher rates.

Contract Size:	IR£100,000 3 month deposit.
Settlement Months:	March June September December.
Settlement Day:	Third Wednesday of Settlement Month.
Last Trading Day:	11.00 a.m. two business days before Settlement Day.
Quotation:	100.00 minus rate of interest (to two decimal places).
Minimum Price Movement (Tick size and value):	IR£0.01 = IR£2.50.
Trading Hours:	8.30 a.m. - 16.15 p.m.
Initial Margin:	0.09 per cent of nominal value of contract = IR£90.
Price Limit:	120 Basis Points.
Contract Standard:	Cash Settlement based on the Exchange Settlement Price.
Settlement:	Cash Settlement only (no delivery).

Exchange Settlement Price:	The "Interest Settlement Rate" on the last trading day is computed in accordance with Clause 5 "Terms and Conditions for the Operations of Forward Rate Agreements in the Dublin Interbank Money Market" (see Appendix). The Interest Settlement Rate for the purposes of calculating the Cash Settlement Amount is rounded to two decimal places.
Reuters Page:	IFOZ.

Daily Volume and Open Interest (Jan 1,1990 - Jun 30,1990)

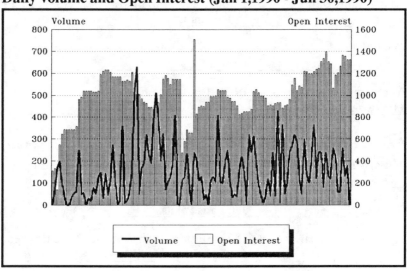

Open Interest and Volume/Open Interest("Liquidity")
(Jan 1,1990 - Jun 30,1990)

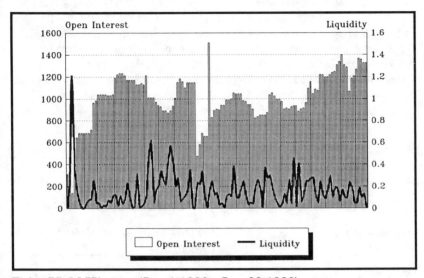

Price/Yield History (Jan 1,1990 - Jun 30,1990)

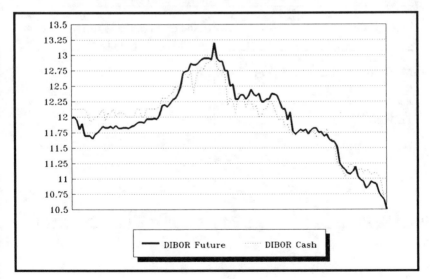

Currencies
IRISH Pound/U.S. Dollar Futures Contract

This contract has seen the least interest on **IFOX** and is scheduled to be wound up in September 1990. Banks and institutions presumably find the existing foreign exchange hedging instruments adequate e.g. the forward market in Dublin. Moreover, trading in the cash market is dominated by Irish Pound/Sterling dealing. This reflects the importance of the United Kingdom in terms of Irish trade; one third of Irish exports go the UK and almost 40 per cent of imports are sourced from Britain.

As the charts show, this contract never established itself as a viable method for hedging foreign exchange exposure.

Contract Size:	US$50,000.
Settlement Months:	March June September December
Settlement Day:	Third Wednesday of Settlement Month.
Last Trading Day:	3.00 p.m. two business days before Settlement Day.
Quotation:	Irish Pound per US$ (up to 4 decimal places e.g. 0.6314 (1.5838).
Minimum Price Movement (Tick size and value):	US$0.0001 = US$5.0.
Trading Hours:	8.30 a.m. - 16.15 p.m.
Initial Margin:	2.5 per cent of nominal value = IR£1,250.
Price Limits:	2 per cent
Settlement:	Cash settlement only (no delivery).

Exchange settlement Price:	The Central Bank's official closing Irish Pound/U.S.Dollar rate (to 4 decimal places) at 15.00 p.m. on the last trading day.
Reuters Page:	IFPA.

Daily Volume and Open Interest (Jan 1,1990 - Jun 30,1990)

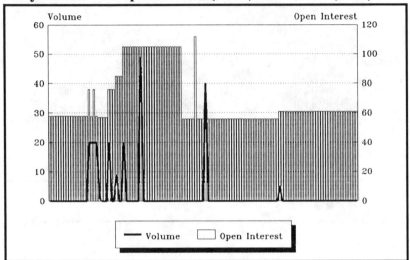

Open Interest and Volume/Open Interest("Liquidity")
(Jan 1,1990 - Jun 30,1990)

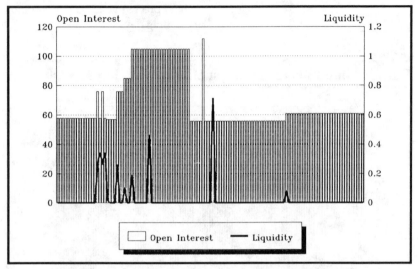

Price/Yield History (Jan 1,1990 - Jun 30,1990)

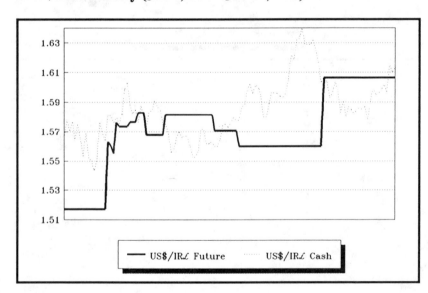

Equities

ISEQ Stock Index Futures Contract

The Irish Stock market is capitalised at IR£9 billion, equivalent to 45 per cent of Ireland's GNP. The market is dominated by Ireland's two quoted domestic banks, which account for 25 per cent of the **ISEQ** Index. Furthermore, another 25 per cent of the Index is accounted for by another two stocks, CRH, a building materials group and Smurfit, a U.S. paper and packaging group.

Irish equity prices rose 8 per cent in the first three weeks of 1990 but then proceeded to fall by 17 per cent in the period to end April. The proximate cause was a series of disappointing results, pointing to a slowdown in economic growth at home and in the United Kingdom, to which a number of Irish companies have exposure. The futures market pointed to a rally in March but this failed to materialize, although the equity market did begin to rally in May on the back of a pickup on Wall Street and in London.

Unit of Trading:	Valued at IR£10 per full index point (e.g. value IR£15,000 at 1,500.00).
Settlement Months:	March June September December.
Settlement Day:	Third Thursday of Settlement Month.
Last Trading Day:	16.15 p.m. one business day prior to Settlement Day.
Quotation:	**ISEQ** index divided by 10.
Minimum Price Movement (Tick size and value):	IR£0.01 & IR£1.00.
Trading Hours:	8.30 a.m.- 16.15 p.m.
Initial Margin:	IR£1,300.
Price Limits:	A 50 point movement in the Index.

| Settlement Price: | The **ISEQ** Index is calculated by the Stock Exchange 4 times a day based on the last dealt prices at 11.00 a.m. 13.00 p.m. 15.30 p.m. and 17.30 p.m.. The Exchange Delivery Settlement Price is calculated using a simple average of these quotations on the last trading day (excluding the 17.30 p.m. quotation) and the previous business day. |

Composition of Index

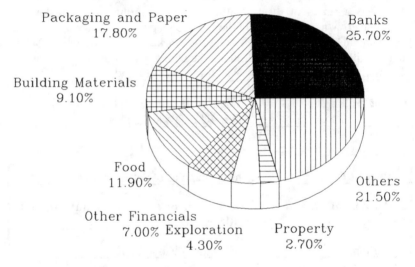

Packaging and Paper
17.80%

Banks
25.70%

Building Materials
9.10%

Food
11.90%

Others
21.50%

Other Financials
7.00%
Exploration
4.30%

Property
2.70%

The Index is calculated as a weighted average of its component parts, with the weights determined by market capitalization. Consequently, a shares' weight in the Index would change if its price moved relative to other equity prices or if the total shares in issue altered

Stock	Per cent	Stock	Per cent
Official List		Norish	0.15
Abbey plc	0.45	Power	2.23

Allied Irish Bank	17.22	Readymix	0.44
Anglo Irish Bank	0.56	Ryan	0.43
Aran Energy	2.03	Seafield	0.59
Ardagh	0.43	Silvermines	0.41
Arnotts plc	0.47	Smurfit Jefferson	16.15
Avonmore	0.45	Unidare plc	0.46
Bank of Ireland	9.09	Waterford Glass	2.94
Barlo	0.09	Woodchester	3.65
Carroll Industries	1.06	Cambridge group	0.51
C R H plc	9.27	Youghal	0.09
CLF Yeoman	0.53	Flogas	0.54
Clondalkin	1.40	Golden Vale	1.16
Countyglen	0.03	U.S.M.	
Crean (James) plc	2.77	Atlantic	0.28
Dunloe House	0.09	Bula	0.29
Dwyer plc	0.26	Cahill May	0.00
Euro'Leisure	0.95	Capital Leasing	0.11
Fitzwilton	1.29	Castletown Press	0.03
FII plc	3.84	Conroy	0.49
Food Industries	0.98	Dakota	0.12
Grafton Group	0.47	Elan	2.33

Green Property	0.26	Emmet R & J	0.19
Hall R & H	0.45	Ennex International	0.11
Heiton Holdings	0.26	F.B.D.	0.46
Hibernian Group	0.98	IAWS	0.34
Independent	1.29	Impshire	0.09
ICC	0.14	Kenmare	0.21
Inistech	1.13	Kingspan	0.34
I.R.G.	0.36	Oliver Resources	0.20
I.W.P.	0.49	Printech	0.27
Jacob	0.35	Reflex	0.36
Jones	0.61	Tullow	0.28
Jurys	0.51	Tuskar	0.70
Kerry Group	1.32	United Drug	0.20
Lyons	0.60	Wardell	0.20
McInerney	0.20	Waterford Foods	0.34
New Ireland	0.34	Xtra-Vision	0.34
Official List	91.64	U.S.M.	8.36

Daily Volume and Open Interest (Jan 1,1990 - Jun 30,1990)

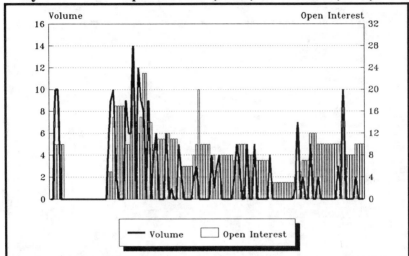

Open Interest and Volume/Open Interest("Liquidity") (Jan 1,1990 - Jun 30,1990)

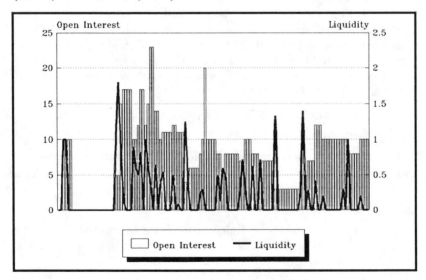

Price/Yield History (Jan 1,1990 - Jun 30,1990)

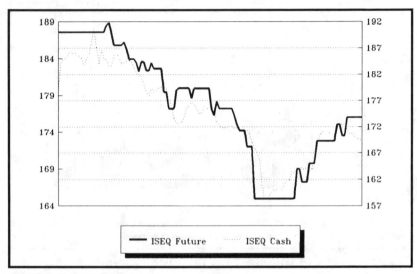

REGULATION

IFOX is a self regulatory body, under the formal supervision of the Central Bank of Ireland. The task of supervising the risk management system is handled internally by the **IFOX** Guarantee and Compliance Officer. He reports directly to the Board of the Exchange. His main duties include the setting of position limits, the monitoring of Members exposures and the supervision of all the rules of the Exchange.

The main aspects of the **IFOX** Risk Management System are as follows:

Initial Margin

Initial margins are a fixed sum for each contract e.g. for the Gilt contract it is equivalent to 5 per cent of the nominal value of the contract i.e. IR£2,500. This is conservative by international standards.

Variation Margin

Variation margin is equivalent to the price difference between one day's closing price and the next. Thus the margin for each contract is equivalent to the change in market value of the contract.

By paying the above two margins, each contract is thus "marked to market" on a daily basis. As a result there is an initial deposit at all times with the **IFOX** Clearing System to guarantee the performance of the contract by the Member involved.

The **IFOX** margins are collected at the **IFOX** Settlement Bank. This is a specific bank where **IFOX** and all Members hold accounts through which the daily margin collection system is operated.

Minimum Capital Requirement

The quality of Exchange Membership is a key to the quality of the **IFOX** Clearing System. As a means of ensuring an acceptable standard of membership, each Member is required to meet a minimum net worth requirement, currently set at IR£1.5 million. This is monitored on a quarterly basis.

Limit on Total Open Interest

To reduce the exposure of the Exchange to adverse market movements, an upper limit of IR£500 million is set for the net open interest on the Exchange (expressed in Gilts or Gilt equivalents). This upper limit on net open interest is based on a guarantee system of IR£6.4 million which is in place. This limit on open interest will be reviewed by the Board from time to time.

Position Limits

A system of position limits set at individual Member level operate on **IFOX**. These are allocated and supervised by the Guarantee & Compliance Officer. Under this system, an upper limit is put on the total level of open interest which the Member may hold with the Exchange. The position limits are set at individual Member level and are based on criteria set by the Board.

IFOX Guarantee System

A default on **IFOX** will occur when a Member is unable to meet his daily margin call under the margining system. If the level of default is sufficiently large, **IFOX** itself may not be in a position to meet its commitments to those Members who are entitled to receive a payment at that day's margin call. To provide security to the Exchange Clearing System, Members of **IFOX** are required to provide a guarantee of IR£265,000 to the Exchange Guarantee System. Thus with its existing twenty four Members, a total guarantee pool in excess of IR£6 million is available to the **IFOX** Clearing System. This provides additional security to the other Members of the Exchange against a default by one or more of the Members.

Price Limit System

IFOX operates a price limit (or "circuit breaker") system. This provides for a suspension of trading in that contract for 90 minutes, if trading prices moves outside limits set relative to the previous day's closing price. During the period of suspension the Exchange may impose an additional margin call. Following the period of suspension, trading in that contract will resume with new price limits.

TAXATION

Income Tax and Capital Gains

A number of changes were made to the Irish taxation legislation to facilitate trading of futures and options. Specifically two changes were introduced to clarify the position of pension funds and to provide taxation exemption to trading on Gilt edged futures.

In the 1988 Finance Act, there is a provision that financial futures and traded options which are quoted on an Exchange within the state are regarded as exempt and thus free of Income and Corporation Tax for pension funds. This brings financial futures and traded options into line with underlying cash market instruments.

In the 1989 Finance Act, an amendment to legislation was introduced which ensures that capital gains on futures linked to Irish government securities carry the same taxation treatment as the equivalent cash market instruments. The effect of this change is that futures linked to currently quoted Irish government securities carry exemption from capital gains tax on any capital gains accrued.

It is likely that further amendments to legislation will be required in the future to facilitate the listing of traded options.

Stamp Duty

There is no stamp duty or turnover tax on the Futures Market.

Withholding Tax

Ireland has no withholding taxes on financial instruments, either futures or cash based.

QUOTE VENDORS

The international Reuters services carries live information on all the **IFOX** contracts. The Reuters **IFOX** page is an index to the services. Reuters now has the following pages:

IFOX	Index
IFOY	Gilts
IFOZ	3 Month Dublin Inter Bank Offer Rate **DIBOR**
IFPA	Irish Pound/U.S. Dollar
IFPB	Irish Stock Exchange Index

Each of these pages shows the current bid and offer prices, the last traded prices, the days high and low traded prices and the day's volume. After the markets close at 16.15 p.m. the days closing and settlement prices and open interest figures are displayed.Plans are at an advanced stage for the listing of **IFOX** prices on Telerate.

EXCHANGE CONTROLS

The capacity of non-residents to invest or disinvest from the Irish securities market is not restricted in any way by Exchange control regulations.

SOURCES of INFORMATION

Central Bank of Ireland (Quarterly Bulletin)

Wide range of general and historical information relevant to the Government securities market, including data on the term structure of outstanding paper and the distribution of holdings across institutions. Data on interest rates and Irish Pound Exchange rates. Detailed money and banking data.

CSO Statistical Bulletin (Quarterly)

General economic data on Ireland; GNP, prices, balance of payments etc.

Budget Booklet (published at budget time in January). General government forecasts, statement of fiscal policy etc.

Irish Press Covering IR£ Markets

The Irish Times

The Irish Independent

The Irish Press

The Sunday Tribune

The Sunday Business post

Finance Magazine

Business & Finance Magazine

Reuters Pages
Riada & Co

RIDA - RIDB	Bond prices in the cash market
RIDC	provides a daily comment on the economy and implications for Irish capital markets.
RIDF	Equity prices in the cash market

J + E Davy

DAVA - DAVQ	Economic commentary, bond and equity prices in the cash market.

NCB Stockbrokers

NCSG - NCSI	Economic commentary, bond and equity prices in the cash market.

APPENDIX

Clause 5 of "Terms and Conditions for the Operations of Forward Rate Agreements in the Dublin Interbank Money Market" reads as follows:

The Interest Settlement Rate is calculated on the following basis: On the settlement date the rates quoted for the contract period by the 10 banks on the Reuter's page **DIBO** at 11.00 a.m. are obtained. The highest and lowest rates are omitted and the average of the remaining 8 rates is rounded to the nearest 4 places of decimals to calculate the relevant interest settlement rate.
Examples:

$$8.56487 \text{ becomes } 8.5649$$

$$8.56484 \text{ becomes } 8.5648$$

$$8.56485 \text{ becomes } 8.5649$$

If no quotations are available on the Reuter's page **DIBO,** the settlement rate will be calculated as above, on the basis of quotations obtained by phone from those banks contributing to the above pages.

In the event of a contract period being used which is not quoted on the Reuter's page **DIBO,** the two parties should refer by telephone to some/all of the contributors to the **DIBO** page. They should obtain a quotation from these banks for the relevant term. The Interest Settlement Rate can then be calculated in the same way as above.

The Futures and Options Markets in Italy

Wilma Vergi
Cassa di Risparmio delle Provincie Lombarde
CARIPLO
Marco Manara
Profilo

INTRODUCTION

Up to the 1980's, Italy did not have a real financial market such as a long term bond market. In those years, the Government issued massive amounts of variable rate bonds - Certificati di Credito del Tesoro and bullet bonds Buoni del Tesoro Poliennali (**BTP**) which created the bond market of today. As inflation fell, the yields on securities was sufficient to cover the interest rate risk without the need for options.

In the last three years, because of the instability of inflation rates, investors discovered the attractions of this market. Only recently has research been initiated about the management of risk and the importance of the options market. With nearly IL 1,000,000 billion of Government bonds outstanding, the conditions are now developing for a modern and efficient capital market, although there is no official market for futures and options is available in Italy at the present for bonds. However, a rapidly developing Over-the-Counter market ("OTC") does exist and has become so active that the Italian financial authorities will feel obliged to control it by means of new legislation.

Interest Rate Futures and Options

Futures and options are currently offered for some securities issued by the Treasury such as Certificati di Credito del Tesoro ("CCT") and Buoni del Tesoro Poliennali ("BTP"). Prices for these products are quoted mainly on Reuters by some brokers and settlement is strictly by delivery.

There is no standard contract form but each is for a specific single bond with terms determined on an individual basis between the counterparties. The price may be considered as a forward rate agreement calculated considers the repo rate. Option contracts (both puts and calls) are of the European type with the expiration date is five days before settlement. The premium has to be paid to the writer within three days of the agreement.

No clearing houses are in place to reduce counterparty risk. Therefore, each contract must consider this risk.

Marketability is gradually increasing due to the growth in the number of players. The volume of futures and option transactions can be estimated at IL 30,000 billion (face value) per year. The contracts are aimed at either speculative transactions or hedging activities. The contracts have a face value of IL 5 billion with mainly banks, security houses, industrial companies and brokers involved.

Soft Commodities Futures and Options

The Italian soft commodity markets have not yet organized official futures or options contracts. The only commodity exchange to quote a future was that in Milan, which specializes in silk and some cereals, in 1962. The exchange did not last too long due to a lack of business and expertise.

While the Italian commodity exchanges had been developed since the beginning of the century with the main goal of improving domestic and overseas trade. Currently, there is no unified exchange but two associations. One is a private organization and the other is responsible to the Chamber of Commerce which establishs the market rules, controls and clearing house. Unfortunately, the public commission responsible for bringing the markets upto date with the introduction of new innovative contracts failed and left the markets in a static and ineffective position. At the moment, the Italian commodity market may only be considered as a barely efficient cash market.

Currencies

There is no official market for currencies and the Over-the-Counter ("OTC") market is extremely weak. Only a few banks offer currency options and quote prices for the most important european currencies U.S.Dollar/Italian Lira and Japanese Yen/Italian Lira. It is possible that in the future, the Government will regulate this branch of the option's market, but, currently there are only intended bills.

Currency options are used mainly by mutual funds, banks and import/export firms to reduce exchange risk for short periods. (Mutual funds were regulated in 1983.) Before April 1986, the Bank of Italy allowed only companies who could supply import/export papers to use currency options, but generally the Italian investor rarely uses options because it is common to buy and sell currencies for fixed periods instead. Still, it is important to note that the Government has only allowed Italian investors to deal in foreign bonds and equities since July 1987. Nowadays the Bank of Italy needs to receive from any bank a written notice of any transactions in foreign currencies.

Generally the contracts on the OTC are constructed in this general format:

Option style:	American calls and puts.
Contract size:	US$ 1 million.

Expiry Months:	One two three six and twelve months.
Quotation:	Per cent of par to two decimal places.
Minimum Price Movement (Tick size and Value):	US$0.01 per cent = US$100.
Contract Standard:	Cash settlement.
Reuters Pages:	None.
Telerate Pages:	None.

SOURCES of INFORMATION

Bank of Italy   Monthly financial & general economic statistics

Italian Press   24 Ore

                   Italian Oggi

                   Milano Finanza

Reuters Pages

MITA - MITZ   Bonds

ATIA - ATIP   Money Markets

BITA - BITI   Bank of Italy Data

PROFILO

Promozioni Finanziarie Lombarde

- Advice on the full range of application of **ITALIAN** bond options and futures

- Comprehensive portfolio analysis of:

Equites - Options

- Experienced brokers to ensure efficent order execution

- Extensive historical online data also available

- Reuters page: **polo**

For further information on our range of services conctact **Marco Manara**, **Arnaldo Grimaldi** at Profilo S.P.A. - Corso Italia, 50 - 20122 Milano - Italy - Tel. 02/ 58308401

The Futures and Options Markets in the Netherlands

Koos 't Hart
Pierson Heldring & Pierson N.V.

Peter van der Linde
Philips Pensioenfondsen

Baldwin Ottervanger
Ottervanger Effectenkantoor B.V.

Peter Versloot
Amsterdam-Rotterdam Bank N.V.

André Wolters
Ottervanger Effectenkantoor B.V.

Willem Zwager

with our thanks to:
Amsterdam Stock Exchange "ASE"
European Option Exchange "EOE"
Financial Futures Exchange Amsterdam "FTA"
Agricultural Futures Market Amsterdam "NLK KAS"
Rotterdam Energy Futures Exchange "ROEFEX"
for their contributions in this respect.

INTRODUCTION

By 1450 A.D., the city of Bruges in The Netherlands (Holland, Belgium and the northern part of France) was regarded as the center of "bond" trading for civilized Europe. Later, after 1500, the city of Antwerp as the largest port and trading center became more important in this respect. Charles V of Spain was in 1523 the first issuers of the "modern" type of bond loan with annuities.

The eighty years' war with Spain, especially the Spanish occupation of Antwerp in 1580, made Amsterdam the most important economic, cultural and financial center of The Netherlands.

At the foundation in 1602 of the "Vereenigde Oost-Indische Compagnie" (United East India Company), the Board decided to go public, starting in that way the first limited liability company -"Actiën Compagnie"- in history. From the start a spontaneous and vivid trading in shares -"Actiën"- and future contracts on shares -"Optiën"- took place, apart from the already existing spot and future trading in goods. The famous Amsterdam architect Hendrik de Keyser was instructed to build a Merchant and Stock Exchange, which opened in 1611.

With the real trade came also speculative activities. The scandal around 1636 regarding spot and future trading in tulip bulbs is an outstanding negative example. On the other side a ban by the States of Holland in 1610 on stock-jobbing in United East India Company shares lacked effect. Stock traders even deemed pleading this ban as a defense to be a breach of honour. The first crash took place winter 1720. The Scot John Law, who had started, in Paris, a bank that issued paper money successfully, started speculating on a large scale in 1717 and found many followers. The end came with a crash in Paris also in London and Amsterdam, at least equal to the well known crash of 1929/1931. Lesser ones followed in 1763 and 1772.

In 1787, 1833 and 1857 traders tried to establish an Exchange Association to regulate the trade. In 1845 a new exchange building, designed by J.D. Zocher was opened. The actual Amsterdam Stock Exchange Association (Vereeniging voor den Effectenhandel) was established on May 17, 1876, followed by the establishment on May 1, 1888 of the Amsterdamsche Liquidatiekas (now: "**NLK KAS**"), who regulated the spot and future Commodities Exchange. Exchange products such as coffee, sugar, tin and cloves were traded then. Nowadays in Amsterdam only potatoes and live hogs are traded on the Commodities Exchange held in the still existing Merchant's Exchange Building, opened in 1903, designed by H.P. Berlage, with a separate floor for the Amsterdam Stock Exchange.

The Amsterdam Stock Exchange got its own still functioning Exchange building, designed by J.Th. Cuypers in 1913. The same Amsterdam Stock Exchange Association initiates the establishment of the association European Option Exchange ("EOE") who starts on April 4, 1978 with trading in call options at the official opening in the Merchant's Exchange Building. In March 1979 put options are introduced, followed by gold options in April 1981. Bond options were introduced in November 1981 and a year later currency options. In April 1983 silver options joined the gold options. With the option trade flourishing a new modern Option Exchange Building was opened in April 1986. In October/November 1986 long term options came in the market.

The European Option Exchange "EOE" initiates the establishment of the Financial FutureS Exchange (Financiële Termijnmarkt) Amsterdam "FTA". At the official opening of the "FTA" in the Options Exchange Building on June 19, 1987 the market started with a future on the "EOE/FTA" bond index. In May and August of the same year the European Option Exchange "EOE" introduced Stock Index Options.

During 1988 the "FTA" introduced an interest rate future ("FTB") on the so called "FTA" Bullet index in May. In August, the "EOE" introduced Bond Index Options and in October the "FTA" again presented a future on the "EOE" stock index ("FTI"). In June 1989 the "FTA" came with a Guilder bond future ("FTO"). The latest development on the modern option and future exchanges in the Netherlands has been the official opening on 31 October 1989 of "ROEFEX", the Rotterdam Energy Futures Exchange N.V. in the World Trade Center at Rotterdam.

ORGANIZATION of the MARKETS

The Vereniging European Options Exchange ("EOE") was formed to regulate the trade in options. The "EOE" owns 100 per cent of the shares of Financiële Termijnmarkt Amsterdam N.V. ("FTA"). This company was formed to establish a regular trade in financial futures. The "EOE" and "FTA" together own 99 per cent of the shares of Goudtermijnmarkt Amsterdam B.V., which company carried out the trade in gold futures. After 1988, this company is inactive. The "EOE" also owns 49 per cent of the Rotterdam Energy Futures Exchange which opened on 31 October 1989.

The commercial activities are carried out by the wholly-owned Optiebeurs N.V. which owns 100 per cent of the European Options Certificates B.V. ("EOC") and of the "EOE" Service B.V.. The last one renders services such as selling information regarding option quotations and leasing of trading equipment. The "EOC" issues bearer certificates on options traded on the "EOE".

The clearing activities are carried out by the fully owned Holding-maatschappij European Options Clearing Corporation B.V. ("EOCC") through the 44.2 per cent owned subsidiary International Options Clearing Corporation B.V. ("IOCC"), the 100 per cent owned subsidiary of European Stock Options Clearing Corporation B.V. ("ESCC"), Associated Clearing House Amsterdam B.V. ("ACHA"), International Petroleum Clearing Corporation B.V. ("IPCC") and 70 per cent owned European Futures Clearing Corporation B.V. ("EFCC"), which is 30 per cent owned by N.V. Nederlandse Liquidatiekas ("NLK KAS") who by itself clears futures on live-hogs and potatoes. The EOCC owns 60 per cent of the "NLK KAS".

European Options Exchange's Membership Division

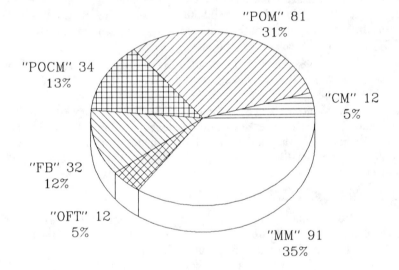

European Options Exchange's Source of Contracts

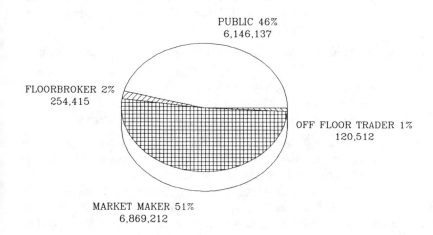

PUBLIC 46%
6,146,137

FLOORBROKER 2%
254,415

OFF FLOOR TRADER 1%
120,512

MARKET MAKER 51%
6,869,212

The "EOE" recognizes the following membership categories:

- **Public Order Member ("POM")**, a bank or broker who may accept orders from private and institutional investors and who ensures that the orders are executed on the exchange floor by a Floor broker.

- **Public Order Correspondent Member ("POCM")**, a bank or broker who may accept orders from private or institutional investors. These are carried out through the intermediary of a Public Order Member.

- **Floor Broker ("FB")**, a trader who has the right to transact business for his own account or for other members. A distinction is made between independent Floor brokers and Floor brokers who are employed by a Public Order Member.

- **Off-Floor Trader ("OFT")**, an options' trader who transact business for his own account via a Floor broker.

- **Market Maker ("MM")**, who trades for his own account and is obligated to maintain a market by providing continuous bid and ask prices in the options' series to which he is assigned. Several Market

Makers are assigned to each class, to ensure competitive price formation.

- **Clearing Member ("CM")**, handles the administrative and financial settlement of the transaction and guarantees that all obligations are met.

Besides the members mentioned above, the following market participants are recognized too:

- **Remisier A (Agent)**, who's sole activity is to bring clients into contact with a Public Order (Correspondent) Member. This agent is not allowed to place orders for the clients he introduces.

- **Remisier B (Agent)**, who are not restricted to introducing clients but can be authorized by the client to give orders on their account to a Public Order (Correspondent) Member.

In 1987, at the initiative of the European Options Exchange in view of the demand by investors for a suitable hedge instrument, the Financial Futures Market ("FTA") was established. Only futures are being traded on this exchange, who by publishing brochures and computer programs that are specifically geared to the professional market, tries to familiarize the Dutch investor with the products.

The products of the "FTA" are traded on the floor of the "EOE". Trading is conducted on the open outcry system, under the supervision of market governors. The "FTA" ensures that prices are concluded on the floor of the exchange in full view of all parties, and that they are solely the result of supply and demand. An extensive network of rules and monitoring procedures prevent price manipulation and guarantee the integrity of the market. Margins and position limits are also governed by the regulations.

Financial Futures Market's Membership Division

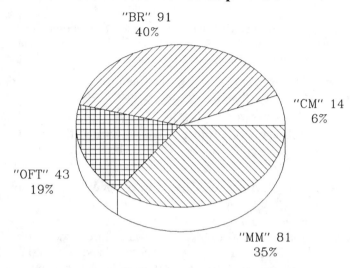

"BR" 91
40%

"CM" 14
6%

"OFT" 43
19%

"MM" 81
35%

Financial Futures Market's Sources of Contracts

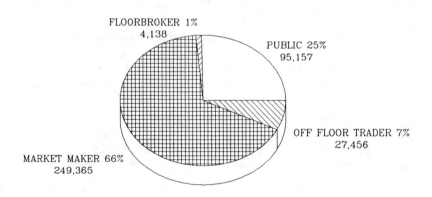

FLOORBROKER 1%
4,138

PUBLIC 25%
95,157

OFF FLOOR TRADER 7%
27,456

MARKET MAKER 66%
249,365

To become seat-holder of the **"FTA"**, one must purchase a subordinated transferable bond, of which 250 have been issued with a nominal value of Dfl. 25,000. One bond entitles the holder to one seat and only one capacity can be exercised per seat. The membership categories are:

- **Market Maker ("MM")**, can conclude transactions for his own account on the floor of the exchange and must be present on the exchange floor during the whole business day.

- **Off-Floor Trader ("OFT")**, who can instruct brokers to conduct futures transactions for his own account.

- **Floor broker ("FB")**, a broker, who can conclude transactions on the exchange floor, or instruct others to conduct these transactions for him, as well for his own (firm's) account or for the off-floor traders, the (floor) brokers, the clearing members and the public.

- **Clearing Member ("CM")**, who are allowed to instruct brokers to conduct futures transactions for firm account.

The Authorized Representative of a Broker is employed to conduct transactions either for the Broker's own account (Firm orders), or for the account of others (Public orders). A Broker who handles both public and firm orders, must own at least two seats and have a minimum of two Authorized Representatives. The two may not substitute for one another. All Market Makers, Off-floor Traders and Brokers must give the "FTA" the name of their Clearing Member before they may become active members. All contracts concluded on the exchange floor must be cleared by a Clearing Member.

In 1990, a fifth category of members - known as locals - may be added. Locals are now a common phenomenon in the futures' markets. Because they have come to play such an important role on both the "LIFFE" and the "MATIF" , the "FTA" has also decided to admit locals to the exchange floor. They are expected to improve the liquidity of the market.

The clearing house for the "FTA" is the European Futures Clearing Corporation ("EFCC"). The responsibilities of the "EFCC" include registering all futures transactions and daily calculation and settlement of profits and losses resulting from futures transactions. The main participants in the futures' market are banks, pension funds,

insurance companies, brokers and market makers. The exact ratio in which the first three parties act as clients is not known. Still client orders account for roughly 40 per cent of the total number of futures traded.

The Rotterdam Energy Futures Exchange ("ROEFEX"), established in 1989, is an official Netherlands exchange, where only futures are traded.

The "**ROEFEX**" will, from the outset, enjoy a character unique in the world. "**ROEFEX**" of course bids the opportunity of keeping price risks in oil controllable by means of futures, but on this futures' market in Rotterdam, the world's most important trading centre for physical oil, contracts that on expiry of the term can be settled for physical delivery of oil, also will be traded.

Transactions are effected on the floor of the exchange by brokers and traders who call aloud the number of futures they want to buy and sell. After this the price is negotiated in open competition. This is known as the open outcry system. Buy and sell orders may only be carried out by brokers who are authorized by the "**ROEFEX**". Profits and losses on outstanding futures positions are settled daily by an independent guarantee and clearing institution, the International Petroleum Clearing Corporation ("**IPCC**").

Rotterdam Energy Futures Exchange's Membership Division

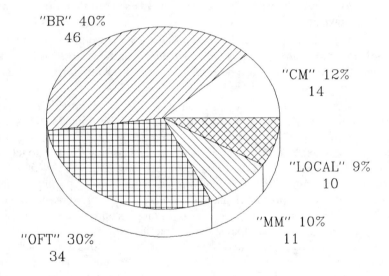

On "**ROEFEX**" the following members are active:

● **Broker ("BR"),** a person or legal entity (Seat-holder) authorized by the **ROEFEX** to conclude on the floor futures contracts for the account of other Brokers, Off Floor Traders, Clearing Members and Principals.

- Clearing Member, a legal entity (Seat-holder) authorized by the IPCC and the **ROEFEX**, who may act as a contracting counterpart for Brokers, Market Makers, Off Floor Traders and Locals.

- **Local**, a person or legal entity (Seat-holder), who may conclude futures contracts on the floor solely for his own account and whom after a Trading Day may not have an open position unless authorized by the market Governor in special circumstances.

- **Market Maker ("MM")**, a person or legal entity (Seat-holder) who may conclude futures contracts on the market floor solely for his own account, and who must be present on the market floor every Trading Day.

- **Off Floor Trader ("OFT")**, a person or legal entity (Seat-holder) who may instruct a Broker to conclude a futures' contract for his own account.

Potential market participants on **ROEFEX** are producers, refineries, consumers, distributors, traders, arbitrage agents and investors. As the exchange just started, there are no detailed figures available regarding these participants and their activities.

The actual Dutch Futures Exchange for Commodities/Edible Goods has a Potato Terminal Market since 1958 and a Porker Terminal Market since 1980. The first one is organized and regulated by the N.V. Nederlandse Liquidatiekas "**NLK KAS**" (Amsterdam Futures Clearing House) together with the Potato Terminal Market Foundation, the last one by the "**NLK KAS**" with the Cattle and Meat Terminal Market Foundation. Trading on the market can only take place with the intermediation of the brokers, authorized by "**NLK KAS**". On the exchange floor trading is conducted on the open outcry system under the supervision of market governors. Market participants are mainly growers and traders of the actual goods although investors can participate as well. All Dutch exchanges are under the supervision of the Securities Board of the Netherlands, the Stichting Toezicht Effectenverkeer "**STE**". This Board has been established by and reports directly to the Ministry of Finance.

OVERVIEW of PRODUCTS

Contracts	Options	Futures
Interest Rates		
Long term bonds	*	
Bond index	*	*
Currencies		
Forex	*	
Equities		
Individual Stocks	*	
Stock Index	*	*
Commodities		
Precious Metals	*	
Crude Oil		*
Gas Oil		*
Heavy Fuel (Energy)		*
Potatoes		*
Live Hogs		*

European Option Exchange - "EOE"

DETAILED CONTRACT SPECIFICATION
Interest Rates
Individual Bond Option Contract

Option Style	American calls and puts.
Contract Size:	Dfl. 10,000.
Delivery Months:	For all bond options - initial lifetimes of 3 6 and 9 months with a cycle of February May August and November. For NLW NLY and NLZ options only initial lifetimes are available for 1 2 and 3 years with a November cycle.
Delivery Day:	Ten days after the last trading day.
Last Trading Day:	Until 16.00 p.m. Amsterdam time on the third Friday of the contract month provided this is a business day.
Quotation:	Per cent of Par to two decimal places.
Minimum Price Movement (Tick Size and Value):	Dfl. 0.05 = Dfl. 500.
Trading Hours:	10.30 a.m. - 16.30 p.m. Amsterdam time until 16.00 p.m. on the last day of trading.
Initial Margin:	Margin for short call/put = (options price + P per cent (2 x the price of the underlying value - exercise price)) x the unit of trading. Consult the Daily Official List for daily margin percentages (P).

Price Limit:	Last traded price adjusted for any net move of plus or minus 1.0 percent in the price of the underlying value.
Position Limits:	See table below.
Contract Standard:	Physical delivery via Giro.
Exercise Price:	Three contracts at one time with exercise intervals of Dfl. 2.50.
Reuters Pages:	EOEI
Telerate Pages:	39455
Commissions & Fees:	Negotiable.

With the permission of the Supervisory Committee, The European Options Exchange has raised the position limit for certain institutional investors in the bond options classes from 1 to 2 percent of the nominal value of the underlying Dutch government bond. As a result, the position limit now equals the position limit for Market Makers. Institutional investors who wish to qualify for this dispensation must meet the following conditions and criteria:

1. **The institutional investor must be recognized as such by the European Options Exchange.**

2. **The institutional investor must submit a written request which shows that the investor has in his portfolio fixed interest securities valued at no less than Dfl. 1 billion.**

3. **For written positions, the margin requirements prescribed by the "EOE" shall apply. For written positions in bond call options, the following rule shall apply: The limit cannot be exceeded unless the position is fully covered.**

Individual Bond Options

Bond Option	"EOE" Symbol
12.75 per cent Nederland 1986/1992-1996	NLA
7.50 per cent Nederland 1989 per 1999	NLD
7.50 per cent Nederland 1985/1991-1995	NLX
7.00 per cent Nederland 1987 per 1993	NLV
7.00 per cent Nederland 1989 I/II per 1999	NLP
6.75 per cent Nederland 1988 per 1998	NLW
6.50 per cent Nederland 1986 per 1996	NLY
6.25 per cent Nederland 1986 per 1995	NLZ
6.50 per cent Nederland 1988 per 1994	NLQ

Position Limits

Bond	Investor	Market Maker
NLA	2,500	25,000
NLD	13,000	65,000
NLX	4,500	45,000
NLV	4,000	40,000
NLP	5,000	40,000
NLW	5,800	44,000
NLY	5,000	40,000
NLZ	7,000	35,000
NLQ	7,200	72,000

General Bond Options Data (based on 21 August 1989)

Bond	Hist.Vol.	Exercise Intervals			Contracts Traded 1989 (Jan - June)
		Nov 89	Feb 90	May 90	
NLA	3.32	120-130	120-127.50	120-125	14,556
NLD	5.03	97.50-105	97.50-105	100-105	16,515
NLX	3.21	97.50-105	97.50-105	100-105	10,230
NLV	3.92	95-102.50	95-102.50	97.50-102.50	6,280
NLP	5.34	95-102.50	95-102.50	n/a	44,538
NLW	5.34	92.50-100	92.50-100	n/a	76,493
NLY	4.61	92.50-100	92.50-100	95-100	77,257
NLZ	4.44	92.50-100	92.50-100	95-100	20,010
NLQ	4.13	92.50-100	92.50-100	95-100	14,908

Total Individual Bond Option Statistics

Daily Volume and Open Interest (Jul 1,1989 - Dec 31,1989)

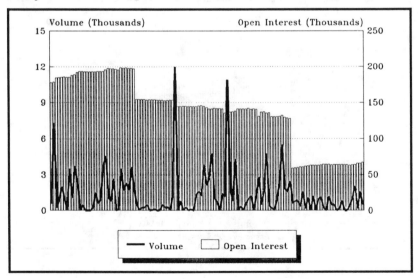

Open Interest and Volume/Open Interest("Liquidity")
(Jul 1,1989 - Dec 31,1989)

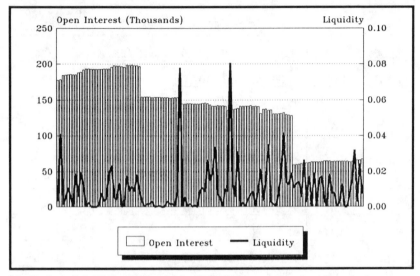

Nederland 6.50% 1986-1996 - "NLY" Bond Option Statistics

Daily Volume and Open Interest (Jul 1,1989 - Dec 31,1989)

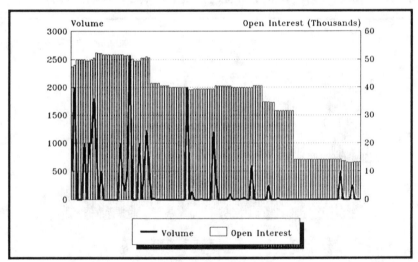

Open Interest and Volume/Open Interest("Liquidity")
(Jul 1,1989 - Dec 31,1989)

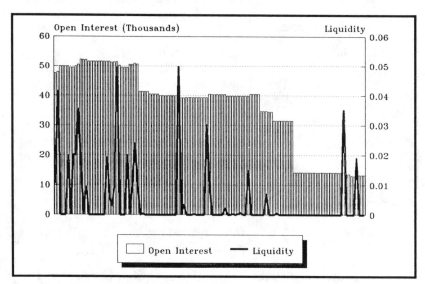

Bond Index Option Contract
"EOE" Symbol - "OBL"

Option Style	European.
Contract Size:	100 x "FTA" Bullet Index.
Expiry Months:	Initial lifetimes of 3 6 and 9 months with a cycle of February May August and November.
Expiry Day:	Three days after last trade day.
Last Trading Day:	Until 16.30 p.m. Amsterdam time on the third Friday of the contract month provided this is a business day.
Quotation:	Dfl. per Index unit.

Minimum Price Movement (Tick Size and Value):	Dfl. 0.05 = Dfl. 5 x "**FTA**" Bullet Index.
Trading Hours:	10.30 a.m. - 16.30 p.m. Amsterdam time.
Initial Margin:	Margin for short call/put = (options price + P per cent (2 x the price of the underlying value - exercise price)) x the unit of trading. Consult the Daily Official List for daily margin percentages (P).
Price Limit:	Last traded price adjusted for any net move in the underlying value of plus or minus 1.00 per cent.
Contract Standard:	Cash settlement.
Exercise Price:	Three contracts at one time with exercise intervals of Dfl. 2.50.
Exchange Delivery Settlement Price:	The settlement price is calculated as follows: For each bond in the index an average is taken of all prices between 09.30 a.m. and 16.30 p.m. on the last day of trading.
Reuters Pages:	**EOEI**.
Telerate Pages:	39455.
Commissions & Fees:	Negotiable.

The first futures contract quoted on the **FTA** was the Guilder Bond Future, a contract based on an index of 8 Netherlands government bonds. The index included both bonds that could be paid off in installments and bullet bonds. In 1988, it became clear that there was a demand for an index made up of bullet bonds only, because all of the bonds being issued by the Dutch Government were bullet bonds. The existing **EOE-FTA** Bond Index was in danger of becoming outdated and in May 1988 the **FTA** Bullet Index was introduced, an index of ten bullet bonds. The future traded on the index has the same name as its predecessor, the guilder bond future.

The old guilder bond future was delisted on 1 June 1989; total volume in this product had reached 102,000 contracts.

The "**FTA**" Bullet Index is the sum, divided by 10, of the last price of the following Dutch government bonds:

Bond	Code Daily Official List
6.00 per cent Netherlands 1987 per 1994	00157
6.00 per cent Netherlands 1988 per 1995	00165
6.25 per cent Netherlands 1988 per 1994	00163
6.25 per cent Netherlands 1987I per 1995	00153
6.25 per cent Netherlands 1987III per 1995	00162
6.25 per cent Netherlands 1987 per 1997	00150
6.25 per cent Netherlands 1986 per 1995	00149
6.25 per cent Netherlands 1986 per 1996	00147
6.50 per cent Netherlands 1986 per 1996	00143
7.00 per cent Netherlands 1987 per 1993	00160

Daily Volume and Open Interest (Jul 1,1989 - Dec 31,1989)

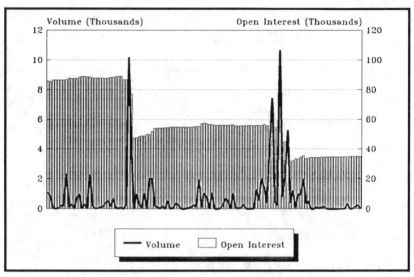

Open Interest and Volume/Open Interest("Liquidity")
(Jul 1,1989 - Dec 31,1989)

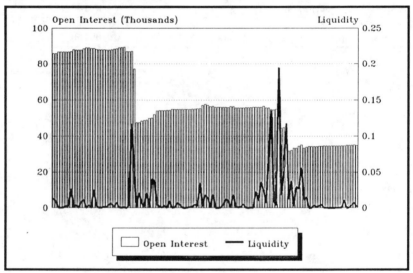

Currencies

U.S. Dollar/Guilder Options Contract
"EOE" Symbol"DGX"

Option Style	American.
Contract Size:	Dfl. 10,000.
Delivery Months:	1 2 and 3 month contracts plus 6 9 and 12 month contracts with March June September December delivery months.
Delivery Day:	Three days after the last trading day.
Last Trading Day:	The third Friday of the contract month provided this is a business day.
Quotation:	Dfl. per 100.
Minimum Price Movement (Tick Size and Value):	Dfl. 0.05 = Dfl. 500.
Trading Hours:	10.30 a.m. - 16.30 p.m. Amsterdam time and until 16.00 p.m. on the last trading day.
Initial Margin:	Margin for short call/put = (options price + P per cent (2 x the price of the underlying value - exercise price)) x the unit of trading. Consult the Daily Official List for daily margin percentages (P).
Price Limit:	The last traded price adjusted for the net move in the underlying value plus or minus 1.00 per cent.
Contract Standard:	Physical (giro) delivery.
Exercise Price:	Three contracts are available at one time with exercise intervals of Dfl. 5.00.

Reuters Pages:	EOEI
Telerate Pages:	39455
Commissions & Fees:	Negotiable.

Daily Volume and Open Interest (Jul 1,1989 - Dec 31,1989)

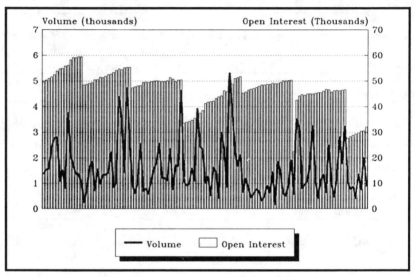

Open Interest and Volume/Open Interest("Liquidity")
(Jul 1,1989 - Dec 31,1989)

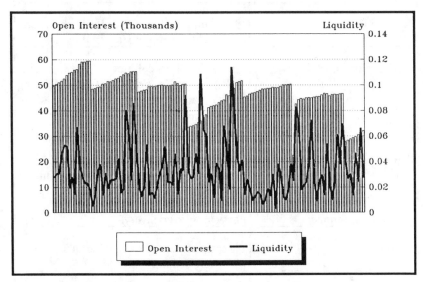

U.S. Dollar/Guilder (Jumbo) Options Contract
"EOE" Symbol"DXJ"

Option Style	European.
Contract Size:	Dfl. 100,000.
Delivery Months:	1 2 and 3 month contracts plus 6 9 and 12 month contracts with March June September December delivery months.
Delivery Day:	Three days after the last trading day.
Last Trading Day:	The third Friday of the contract month provided this is a business day.
Quotation:	Dfl. per 100.

Minimum Price Movement (Tick Size and Value):	Dfl. 0.01 = Dfl. 1,000.
Trading Hours:	10.30 a.m. - 16.30 p.m. Amsterdam time and until 13.00 p.m. on the last trading day.
Initial Margin:	Margin for short call/put = (options price + P per cent (2 x the price of the underlying value - exercise price)) x the unit of trading. Consult the Daily Official List for daily margin percentages (P).
Price Limit:	The last traded price adjusted for the net move in the underlying value plus or minus 1.00 per cent.
Contract Standard:	Physical (giro) delivery.
Exercise Price:	Three contracts are available at one time with exercise intervals of Dfl. 2.50.
Reuters Pages:	EOEI
Telerate Pages:	39455
Commissions & Fees:	Negotiable.

Daily Volume and Open Interest (Jul 1,1989 - Dec 31,1989)

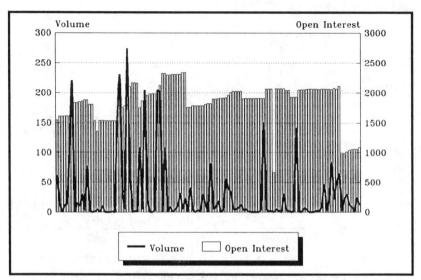

Open Interest and Volume/Open Interest("Liquidity")
(Jul 1,1989 - Dec 31,1989)

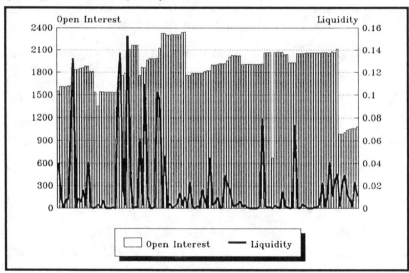

Sterling/Guilder Options Contract
"EOE" Symbol"DGS"

Option Style	American.
Contract Size:	Dfl. 10,000.
Delivery Months:	1 2 and 3 month contracts plus 6 9 and 12 month contracts with March June September December delivery months.
Delivery Day:	Three days after the last trading day.
Last Trading Day:	The third Friday of the contract month provided this is a business day.
Quotation:	Dfl. per 100.
Minimum Price Movement (Tick Size and Value):	Dfl. 0.05 = Dfl. 500.
Trading Hours:	10.30 a.m. - 16.30 p.m. Amsterdam time and until 16.00 p.m. on the last trading day.
Initial Margin:	Margin for short call/put = (options price + P per cent (2 x the price of the underlying value - exercise price)) x the unit of trading. Consult the Daily Official List for daily margin percentages (P).
Price Limit:	The last traded price adjusted for the net move in the underlying value plus or minus 1.00 per cent.
Contract Standard:	Physical (giro) delivery.
Exercise Price:	Three contracts are available at one time with exercise intervals of Dfl. 5.00.
Reuters Pages:	EOEI

Telerate Pages:	39455
Commissions & Fees:	Negotiable.

Daily Volume and Open Interest (Jul 1,1989 - Dec 31,1989)

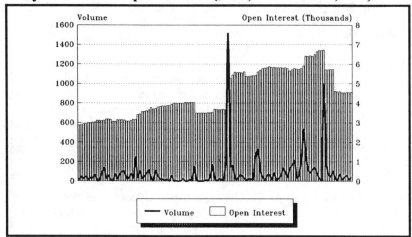

Open Interest and Volume/Open Interest("Liquidity") (Jul 1,1989 - Dec 31,1989)

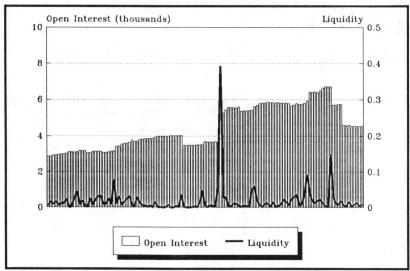

Equities
Individual Stock Option Contracts

Option Style	American.
Contract Size:	100 shares.
Delivery Months:	For all stock options initial lifetimes of 3 6 and 9 months with January April July and October delivery months. For AKZ KLM PHI RD and UNI options are also available with initial lives of three four and five years at October.
Expiry Day:	Ten days after the last trading day.
Last Trading Day:	Until 16.00 p.m. Amsterdam time on the third Friday of the contract month provided this is a business day.
Quotation:	Dfl. per share.
Minimum Price Movement (Tick Size and Value):	Dfl. 0.10 = Dfl. 10.
Trading Hours:	10.00 a.m. - 16.30 p.m. Amsterdam time or until 16.00 p.m. on the last day of trading.
Initial Margin:	Margin for short call/put = (options price + P per cent (2 x the price of the underlying value - exercise price)) x the unit of trading. Consult the Daily Official List for daily margin percentages (P).
Price Limit:	The last traded price adjusted for the net move in the underlying value plus or minus 1.00 per cent.
Contract Standard:	Physical delivery by giro.

Exercise Price:	Three contracts are available at one time with the following exercise intervals depending on the underlying stock price. For stock prices of 0 - 50 (Dfl. 2.50) 50 - 150 (Dfl. 5.00) 150 - 500 (Dfl. 10.00) over 500 (Dfl. 20.00).
Reuters Pages:	EOEI
Telerate Pages:	39455
Commissions & Fees:	Negotiable.

Stock Options	"EOE" Symbol	Hist.Vol.	Contracts Traded
		Jan 1989 - Jun 1989	
Algemene Bank Nederland	ABN	14.5	193,939
Aegon	AGN	13.4	95,158
Ahold	AH	16.3	42,968
Akzo	AKZ	13.4	341,610
AMEV	AMV	21.5	91,465
Amsterdam-Rotterdam Bank	ARB	13.5	108,357
Bührmann-Tetterode	BT	18.7	108,357
DAF	DAF	n/a	5,149
DSM	DSM	14.6	117,448
Elsevier	ELS	18.1	57,618
Gist Brocades	GIS	19.8	121,820

Heineken	HEI	15.2	57,582
Kon. Ned. Hoogovens en Staalfabr.	HO	26.6	742,901
Kon. Luchtvaart Mij.	KLM	20.2	326,047
Kon. Ned. Papierfabriek	KNP	21.5	217,964
Kon. Ned. Petroleum Mij.	RD	14.1	788,663
Nationale Nederlanden	NN	14.3	227,785
NMB Postbank Groep	NMB	n/a	n/a
Nedlloyd Groep	NED	28.6	144,779
Philips	PHI	18.7	618,966
Unilever	UNI	13.1	331,087
Van Ommeren Ceteco	VOC	29.9	187,246
Wessanen	WES	18.7	28,316

Total Individual Equity Option Statistics
Daily Volume and Open Interest (Jul 1,1989 - Dec 31,1989)

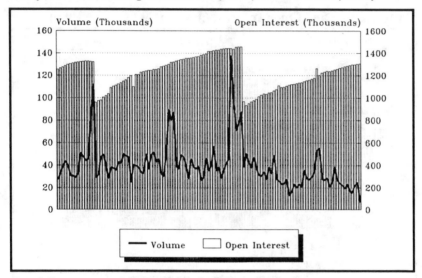

Open Interest and Volume/Open Interest("Liquidity")
(Jul 1,1989 - Dec 31,1989)

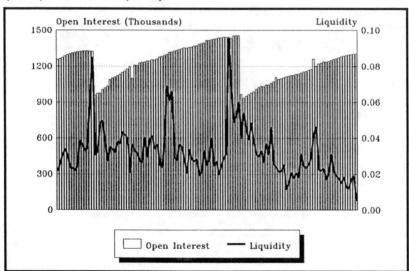

Kon.Ned.Hoogovens en Staalfabr. Equity Option Statistics

Daily Volume and Open Interest (Jul 1,1989 - Dec 31,1989)

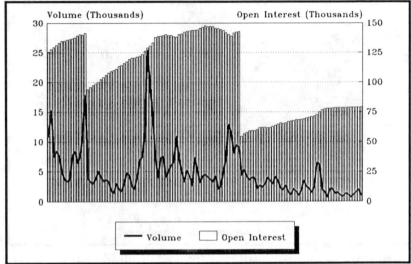

Open Interest and Volume/Open Interest("Liquidity") (Jul 1,1989 - Dec 31,1989)

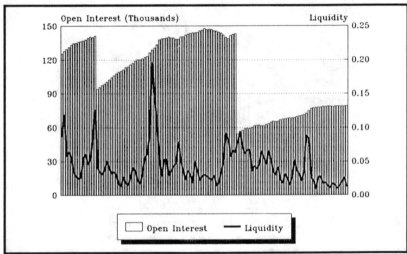

Kon.Ned.Petroleum Mij. Equity Option Statistics
Daily Volume and Open Interest (Jul 1,1989 - Dec 31,1989)

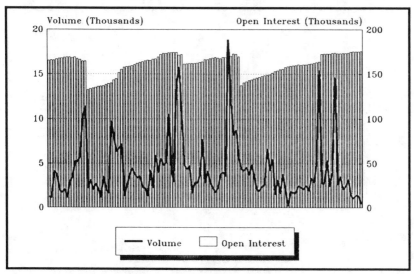

Open Interest and Volume/Open Interest("Liquidity")
(Jul 1,1989 - Dec 31,1989)

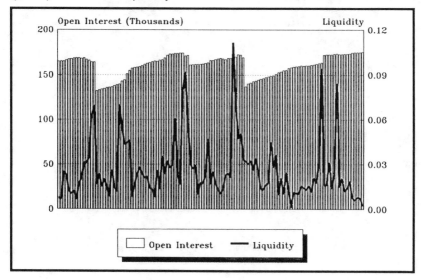

Philips Equity Option Statistics
Daily Volume and Open Interest (Jul 1,1989 - Dec 31,1989)

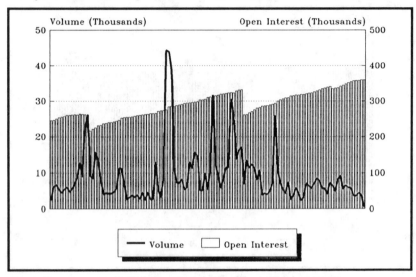

Open Interest and Volume/Open Interest("Liquidity")
(Jul 1,1989 - Dec 31,1989)

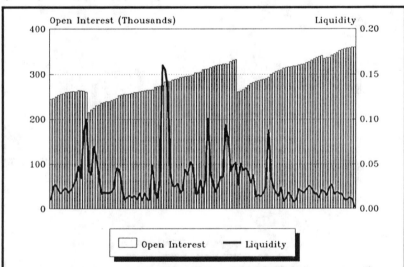

Dutch Stock Index Options Contract
EOE Symbol - "EOE"

Option Style	European.
Contract Size:	100 x the "EOE" Dutch Stock Index.
Expiry Months:	Initial lifetimes of 1 2 and 3 months and 6 9 and 12 months with January April July and October expiry months.
Expiry Day:	Three days after the last trading day.
Last Trading Day:	Until 16.00 p.m. Amsterdam time on the third Friday of the contract month provided this is a business day.
Quotation:	Dfl. per index unit.
Minimum Price Movement (Tick Size and Value):	Dfl. 0.10 = Dfl. 10 x index value.
Trading Hours:	10.30 a.m. - 16.30 p.m. Amsterdam time and until 16.00 p.m. on the last day of trading.
Initial Margin:	Margin for short call/put = (options price + P per cent (2 x the price of the underlying value - exercise price)) x the unit of trading. Consult the Daily Official List for daily margin percentages (P).
Price Limit:	The last traded price adjusted for any net move in the underlying value plus or minus 1.00 per cent.
Contract Standard:	Cash settlement.

Exercise Price:	Three contracts at any one time with intervals for 1 2 and 3 months of Dfl. 5 and for 6 9 and 12 months at Dfl. 10.
Exchange Delivery Settlement Price:	See below.
Reuters Pages:	EOEI
Telerate Pages:	39455.
Commissions & Fees:	Negotiable.

Composition of the EOE Dutch Stock Index as per 31 October 1989:

On October 5 1989, options began trading on a revised EOE Dutch Stock Index. the decision to revise the EOE Index was prompted by the fact that during the period since the introduction of the EOE Index, some stocks had become either too heavily or undervalued.

The composition of the (new) EOE Stock Index is based on prices quoted on the Amsterdam Stock Exchange for 25 leading Dutch stocks (shares or certificates of shares) on which EOE options are traded with the exception of Robeco and with the addition of Fokker and VNU. The (new) EOE Stock Index is based on a basket of the shares of these 25 companies. At the time of introduction, composition was based on two levels of approximately equal investment (roughly 5 per cent and 3.3 per cent respectively) in each stock. The revised EOE index corresponds as far as possible to the old index. The weighing factor shall be revised if the weight of any stock in the index over a period of six consecutive months is more than 1,5 times the base percentage.

The EOE Dutch Stock Index may be revised to take account of stock dividends and bonus payments if the difference between the opening price ex-dividend and the closing price cum dividend is greater than 2 per cent of the closing price cum dividend of the relevant stock. revision occurs on the basis of the number of shares contained in the portfolio. The same procedure may be followed in the event that one of the issuing institutions of the stocks included in the (new) EOE Dutch Stock Index issues a claim, the value of

which (the opening price of the claim) amounts to more than 2 per cent or
Dfl, 1.00 of the closing price cum claim of the pertinent stock.

The settlement value of the (new) **EOE** Stock Index shall be calculated on the last trading day in the expiration month on the basis of the average
of prices quoted for the **EOE** Index at five minute intervals between 15.30 p.m.
and 26.00 p.m..

"EOE" Symbol	No. of shares	Price at 31-10-89	Value at 31-10-89 Dfl.
ABN	36	41.30	1,486.50
AGN	9	106.40	957.60
AH	8	119.90	959.20
AKZ	11	130.80	1,438.80
AMV	19	58.10	1,103.90
ARB	19	78.70	1,495.30
BT	14	66.70	933.80
DAF	20	48.00	960.00
DSM	8	114.80	918.40
ELS	20	72.40	1,448.00
FOK	21	40.00	840.00
GIS	29	33.70	977.30
HEI	11	122.00	1,342.00
HO	11	84.10	925.10
KLM	30	46.40	1,392.00
KNP	20	47.90	958.00

NED	11	89.20	981.20
NMB	20	46.70	934.00
NN	22	65.30	1,436.60
PHI	32	47.80	1,529.60
RD	11	136.80	1,504.80
UNI	11	149.80	1,647.80
VNU	9	106.00	954.00
VOC	29	32.30	936.70
WES	13	73.80	959.40
Total:	444		29,020.30

"EOE" Dutch Stock Index: 29,020.30 / 100 = 290.20

Daily Volume and Open Interest (Jul 1,1989 - Dec 31,1989)

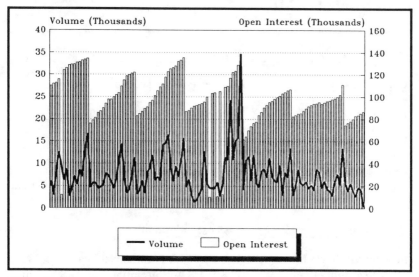

Open Interest and Volume/Open Interest("Liquidity")
(Jul 1,1989 - Dec 31,1989)

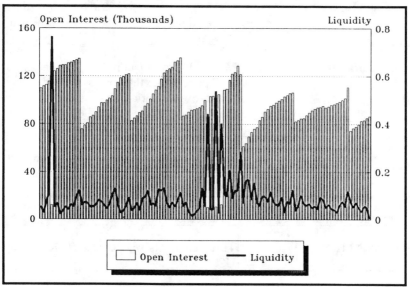

Major Market Index Option Contract
EOE Symbol "XMI"

Option Style	European.
Contract Size:	100 x Major Market Index.
Expiry Months:	3 month contract every month.
Expiry Day:	Three days after the last trading day.
Last Trading Day:	Until 16.30 p.m. Amsterdam time on the third Friday of the contract month provided this is a business day.
Quotation:	US$ per index unit.
Minimum Price Movement (Tick Size and Value):	U.S.$ 1/16 for premiums under U.S.$ 3 and U.S.$ 1/8 for premiums of U.S.$ 3 and higher.
Trading Hours:	"EOE" 12.00 a.m. - 16.30 p.m. Amsterdam time and on AMEX: 9.30 a.m. - 16.10 p.m. New York time.
Initial Margin:	Margin for short call/put = (options price + P per cent (2 x the price of the underlying value - exercise price)) x the unit of trading. Consult the Daily Official List for daily margin percentages (P).
Price Limit:	The last traded price adjusted for any net move in the underlying value plus or minus 1.00 per cent.
Contract Standard:	Cash settlement.
Exercise Price:	Three contracts with exercise intervals of US$ 5.00.

Clearing Organization:	"ACHA" in cooperation with the Options Clearing Corporation ("OCC").
Reuters Pages:	EOEI
Telerate Pages:	39455
Commissions & Fees:	Negotiable.

This contract is traded on the European Options Exchange Amsterdam ("EOE") and the American Stock Exchange ("AMEX"). Transactions conducted in the United States shall be subject to U.S. law and the exchange regulations of the "AMEX", transactions conducted in Amsterdam to Dutch law and the regulations of the "EOE".

Composition of the Major Market Index

The **XMI** Major Market Index is a price index based on equal weighting factors. A given change in the price of any of the twenty components has the same effect on the index.

Composition of the Major Market Index	
American Express	IBM
A T & T	International Paper
Chevron	Johnson & Johnson
Coca-Cola	Merck & Co.
Dow Chemical	Minnesota Mining & Mfg.
Du Pont	Mobil
Eastman Kodak	Philips Morris
Exxon	Proctor & Gamble
General Electric	Sears Roebuck
General Motors	USX

Daily Volume and Open Interest (Jul 1,1989 - Dec 31,1989)

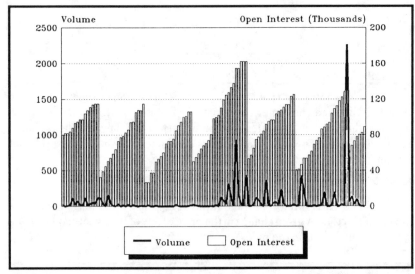

Open Interest and Volume/Open Interest("Liquidity") (Jul 1,1989 - Dec 31,1989)

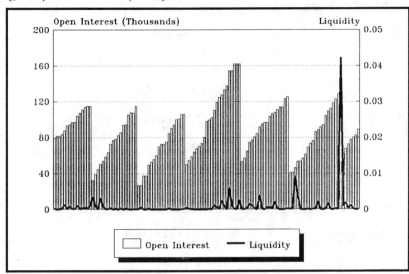

Commodities
Gold Option Contract - "EOE" Symbol - "GD"

Option Style	American.
Contract Size:	10 oz.
Delivery Months:	Initial lifetimes of 4 6 and 9 months with delivery months of February May August and November.
Delivery Day:	Three days after the last trading day.
Last Trading Day:	Until 16.00 p.m. Amsterdam time on the third Friday of the contract month provided this is a business day.
Quotation:	U.S.$ per oz.
Minimum Price Movement (Tick Size and Value):	U.S.$ 0.10 = U.S.$ 1.0.
Trading Hours:	10.30 a.m. - 16.30 p.m. Amsterdam time until 16.00 p.m. on the last day of trading.
Initial Margin:	Margin for short call/put = (options price + P per cent (2 x the price of the underlying value - exercise price)) x the unit of trading. Consult the Daily Official List for daily margin percentages (P).
Price Limit:	Last traded price adjusted for any net move in the underlying plus or minus 2.00 per cent.
Contract Standard:	Physical delivery.

Exercise Price:	Three contracts available at one time with exercise intervals of U.S.$ 10 (gold price less than U.S.$ 600) U.S.$ 20 (gold price over U.S.$ 600).
Reuters Pages:	EOEI
Telerate Pages:	39455
Commissions & Fees:	Negotiable.

Daily Volume and Open Interest (Jul 1,1989 - Dec 31,1989)

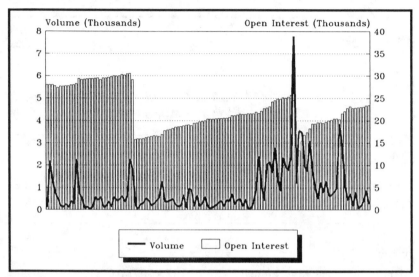

Open Interest and Volume/Open Interest("Liquidity")
(Jul 1,1989 - Dec 31,1989)

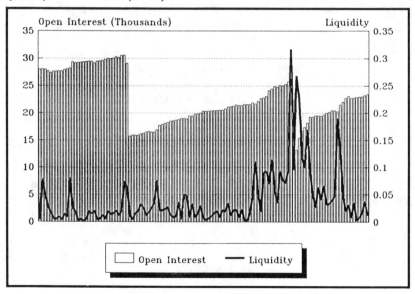

Silver Option Contract - "EOE" Symbol - "SL"

Option Style	American.
Contract Size:	1,000 oz.
Delivery Months:	Initial lifetimes of 4 6 and 9 months with delivery months of March June September and December.
Delivery Day:	Three days after the last trading day.
Last Trading Day:	Until 16.00 p.m. Amsterdam time on the third Friday of the contract month provided this is a business day.
Quotation:	U.S.$ per oz.
Minimum Price Movement (Tick Size and Value):	U.S.$ 1.0 = U.S.$ 1,000.0.
Trading Hours:	10.30 a.m. - 16.30 p.m. Amsterdam time until 16.00 p.m. on the last day of trading.
Initial Margin:	Margin for short call/put = (options price + P per cent (2 x the price of the underlying value - exercise price)) x the unit of trading. Consult the Daily Official List for daily margin percentages (P).
Price Limit:	Last traded price adjusted for any net move in the underlying plus or minus 2.00 per cent.
Contract Standard:	Physical delivery.

Exercise Price:	Three contracts available at one time with exercise intervals of U.S.$ 25 (silver price less than U.S.$ 800) U.S.$ 50 (silver price U.S.$ 800 - U.S.$ 1,500) and U.S.$ 100 (silver price over U.S.$ 1,500).
Reuters Pages:	**EOEI**
Telerate Pages:	39455
Commissions & Fees:	Negotiable.

Daily Volume and Open Interest (Jul 1,1989 - Dec 31,1989)

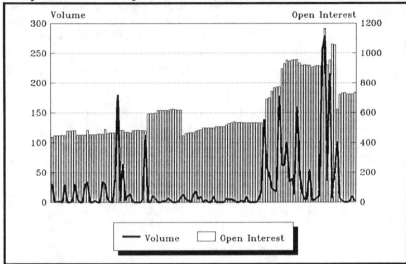

Open Interest and Volume/Open Interest("Liquidity") (Jul 1,1989 - Dec 31,1989)

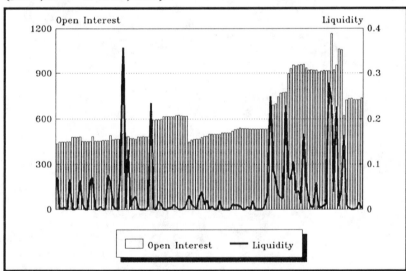

Financial Future Exchange
(Financiële Termijnmarkt) - FTA

DETAILED CONTRACT SPECIFICATION
Interest Rates
Bond Index Futures Contract - FTA Symbol FTB

Contract Size:	1000 x the FTA Bullet Index.
Expiry Months:	The maximum term of a contract is one year. The settlement months are February May August and November.
Expiry Day:	Three days after the last trade date.
Last Trading Day:	The third Friday of the expiry month.
Quotation:	In points. One point is Dfl. 1000 per contract.
Minimum Price Movement (Tick Size and Value):	Dfl. 0.01 per point = Dfl. 10 per contract.
Trading Hours:	9.00 a.m. to 17.00 p.m. Amsterdam time.
Initial Margin:	Dfl 4,000 per contract.
Price Limit:	If the price of the **FTB** Future changes more than 1.50 points relative to the closing quote on the previous business day trading in all contracts except for contracts due to be settled in the current month shall cease for 30 minutes. When trading has resumed there shall be no further break in that day.

Contract Standard:	Cash settlement. The value of the index is equal to the average of the quotes for the selected government loans.
Exchange Delivery Settlement Price:	For each bond in the index the average is calculated from all prices quoted on the last day of business. The index is then recalculated from these averages. The settlement price is equal to the index so calculated.
Reuters Pages:	FTAA
Telekurs Pages:	AF

For details of the FTA Bond Index see the Bond Index Option under the European Options Exchange subchapter.

Daily Volume and Open Interest (Jul 1,1989 - Dec 31,1989)

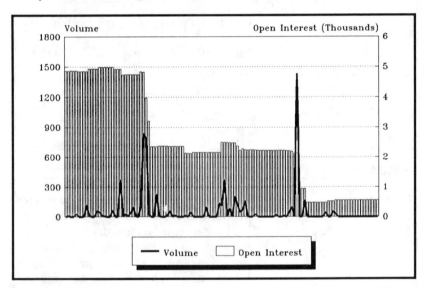

Open Interest and Volume/Open Interest(Liquidity)
(Jul 1,1989 - Dec 31,1989)

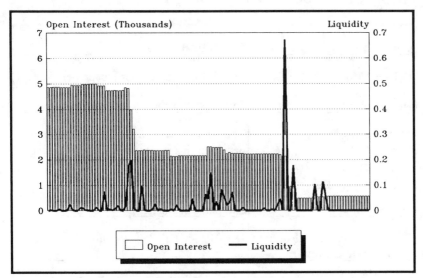

Price/Yield History (Jul 1,1989 - Dec 31,1989)

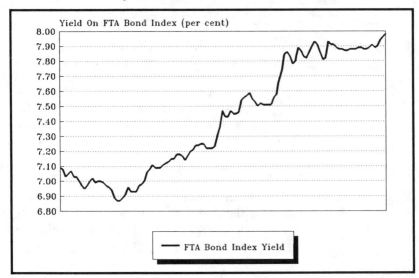

Notional 7.00 per cent Dutch Government Bond Futures Contract - FTA Symbol FTO

Contract Size:	Dfl. 250,000.
Delivery Months:	March June September December.
Delivery Day:	Ten days after the last trading date.
Last Trading Day:	The 7th calendar day of the delivery month provided this is a business day. Trading in the expiring contract will end after a special closing call starting at 16.00 p.m..
Quotation:	Dfl. per Dfl. 100 nominal.
Minimum Price Movement (Tick Size and Value):	Dfl. 0.01 = Dfl. 25 per contract.
Trading Hours:	9.00 a.m. to 17.00 p.m. Amsterdam time.
Initial Margin:	Dfl. 4,000 per contract.
Price Limit:	If the price of the FTO Future changes more than 1 point relative to the closing price on the previous business day trading in all contracts except for contracts due to be settled in the current month shall cease for 30 minutes. When trading has resumed there shall be no further break in that day.
Contract Standard:	Physical delivery. See note below.
Exchange Delivery Settlement Price:	The delivery price of the bonds is equal to the closing price on the last day of trading multiplied by the conversion factor for the particular bonds delivered.
Reuters Pages:	FTAA

Telekurs Pages:	AF

The price of the FTO future depends on the price and conversion factor of the cheapest-to-deliver bond, the life of the contract and the difference between short-term interest and the coupon interest of the cheapest-to-deliver bond and is calculated as follows:

Futures price = (the price of the cheapest-to-deliver bond + the cost of financing - coupon receipts) / the conversion factor. The conversion factor is the theoretical price of the bond on the last day of trading if yield-to-maturity is 7 per cent divided by 100. The **FTA** has published a brochure that contains all conversion factors, so that investors do not have to make these calculations themselves. The **FTA** has also developed a computer program that deals with this product.

Physical delivery shall be made solely based on positions that remain open after the last day of trading. For each open contract delivery is required of nominal Dfl. 250,000 of Dutch government bonds. The seller specifies which bonds will be delivered. These must be Dutch government bonds selected from public issues with an outstanding amount of at least Dfl. 1 billion a single redemption date and having on the first day of the delivery month a remaining life of at least 8 and not more than 10 years. The delivery obligation arising from a single contract must be satisfied by the delivery of a single issue. Bonds allowing early redemption are not acceptable for delivery.

Deliverable Bonds as at July 1, 1990

Bond	Coupon Date	Code	Conversion Factor
Nederland 7.50% 1989 per 1999	15-6	176	1.034025
Nederland 7.25% 1989 per 1999	15-7	177	1.017015
Nederland 7.00% 1989I II per 1999	15-3	173	0.999408
Nederland 7.00% 1989III per 1999	15-5	175	0.999476
Nederland 6.75% 1988 per 1999	1-10	170	0.983427
Nederland 6.75% 1989 per 1999	15-2	172	0.982616
Nederland 6.50% 1988 per 1998	15-7	168	0.967561

| Nederland 6.50% 1989 per 1999 | 15-1 | 171 | 0.966067 |
| Nederland 6.375% 1987 per 1997 | 15-2 | 161 | 0.961401 |

Daily Volume and Open Interest (Jul 1,1989 - Dec 31,1989)

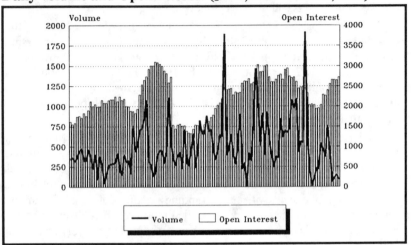

Open Interest and Volume/Open Interest(Liquidity)
(Jul 1,1989 - Dec 31,1989)

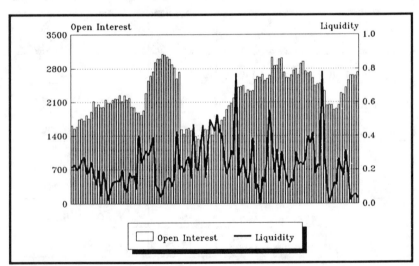

Price/Yield History (Jul 1,1989 - Dec 31,1989)

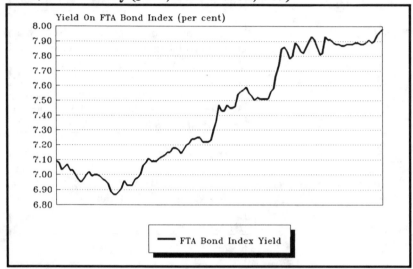

Yield On FTA Bond Index (per cent)

FTA Bond Index Yield

Equities
Dutch Stock Index Futures Contract
FTA Symbol - FTI

Contract Size:	200 x the **EOE** Dutch Stock Index.
Expiry Months:	The first 3 consecutive months and also every 3 months a 6-month future will be introduced with a January
Expiry Day:	Three days after last trading day.
Last Trading Day:	The third Friday of the settlement month
Quotation:	Dfl. per Index Point.
Minimum Price Movement (Tick Size and Value):	Dfl. 0.05 = Dfl. 10.
Trading Hours:	10:15 a.m. to 16:30 p.m. Amsterdam time .

Initial Margin:	Dfl. 400 per contract.
Price Limit:	If the price of contract changes more than 10 points relative to the closing quote on the previous business day trading in all contracts except for contracts due to be settled in the current month shall cease for 30 minutes. When trading has resumed there shall be no further break in that day.
Contract Standard:	Cash settlement.
Exchange Delivery Settlement Price:	Equal to the settlement price of options on the **EOE** Dutch Stock Index
Reuters Pages:	FTAA
Telekurs Pages:	AF2

The **FTA** has published a brochure on the **FTI** contract, and has developed a computer program explaining the many uses of this product. In March 1990, a future will be introduced on a stock index of 5 Dutch Internationals; the **FTA** has plans also for a 3-month deposit future. For further details, see section on index in the European Options Exchange section.

Daily Volume and Open Interest (Jul 1,1989 - Dec 31,1989)

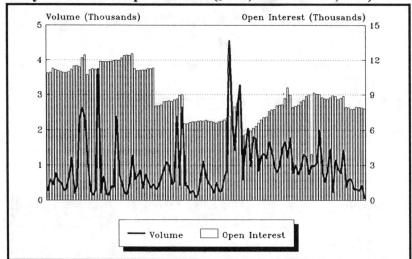

Open Interest and Volume/Open Interest(Liquidity)
(Jul 1,1989 - Dec 31,1989)

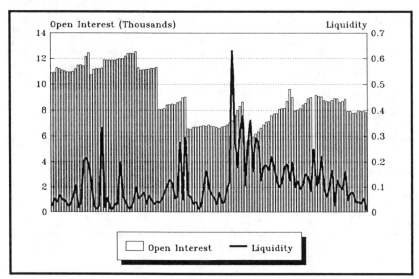

Rotterdam Energy Futures Exchange "ROEFEX"

DETAILED CONTRACT SPECIFICATION

Brent Crude Oil Futures Contract
"ROEFEX" Symbol - "OIL"

Contract Size:	One lot of 1,000 U.S. barrel Brent Blend Crude (42,000 U.S. gallons)
Delivery Months:	Maximum of 9 consecutive months starting with the first tradable delivery month.
Delivery Day:	See below.
Last Trading Day:	Until 18.30 p.m. Rotterdam time on the third business day prior to the 25th calendar day of the month preceding the delivery month provided this is a business day.
Quotation:	U.S.$ to two decimal places per barrel.
Minimum Price Movement (Tick Size and Value):	U.S.$ 0.01 = U.S.$ 10.00.
Trading Hours:	10.00 a.m. - 18.30 p.m. Rotterdam Time.
Initial Margin:	See below.
Price Limit:	See note below.

Contract Standard:	Physical delivery shall be made F.O.B. Paktank through its Europak Tank-terminal at Rotterdam Europoort in accordance with the delivery rules of the "IPCC".
Exchange Delivery Settlement Price:	Open contracts on contract term (see note below).
Reuters Pages:	PPRD
Telekurs Pages:	RE

MARGINS

ROEFEX operates a margining system that depends on the term to delivery. The following table gives details of the requirements:

	Crude Oil	Gas Oil	Heavy Fuel
Initial Margin	US$ 1,000	US$ 1,000	US$ 1,000
Month preceding the delivery month	US$ 2,000	US$ 2,000	US$ 2,000
Last five days of the life of the contract	US$ 4,000	US$ 4,000	US$ 4,000
Straddle margins	US$ 300 per cent		

Crude Oil Definition

A mixture of hydrocarbons that exists in a liquid phase in natural underground reservoirs and remains liquid at atmospheric pressure after passing through surface separating facilities. Crude oil refers to the direct liquid hydrocarbon production from oil wells, or a blend of such, in its natural form, not having been enhanced or altered in any manner or by any process that would result in misrepresentation of its true value for adaptability to refining as such. Condensates are excluded from the definition of Crude oil.

Delivery types   A current export pipeline quality Brent Blend
                              Crude at ongoing quality conforming with the
                              above definition, as well as: FORTIES (at a dis-
                              count of US$ 0.20/barrel), NINIAN (discount of
                              US$ 0.15/barrel), OSEBERG, STATFJORD and
                              BONNY LIGHT (at par). Blends of these are not
                              deliverable in a single contract.

Quality Specification

a) Gravity   not less than 33.5$API, nor more than 40$API by
                              A.S.T.M. Standard D-287 or its latest revision

b) Sulphur   0.50 per cent or less by weight, determined by
                              A.S.T.M. Standard D-129 or latest revision

c) Viscosity   maximum 325 seconds Saybolt Universal,
                              measured by A.S.T.M. Standard D-445 and calcu-
                              lated for Saybolt Seconds by A.S.T.M. Standard
                              D-2161

d) Reid vapor pressure   less than 9.5 pounds per square inch at 100$F,
                              determined by A.S.T.M. Standard D-323 or its
                              latest revision

e) Basic Sediment, water less than 1 per cent as determined by A.S.T.M.
and other impurities   Standard D-473 or its latest revision

f) Pour Point   not to exceed 50$F as determined by A.S.T.M.
                              Standard D-97

Price Limit

The basic maximum price move permitted in any one day: US$ 1 per
barrel above or below the preceding day's closing price. If the closing price
for contracts in any delivery month shall move by the basic maximum in either
direction, the maximum move in either direction for contracts in all delivery
months during the next business day shall be increased to 50 per cent above
the basic maximum move. If no closing price for contracts in any delivery
month for a business day for which the maximum move is 50 per cent above
the basic maximum move, moves by the increased maximum move in either
direction, the maximum move in either direction for contracts in all delivery
months during the next business day shall be the basic maximum move. If the
closing price for contracts in any delivery month for a business day for which
the maximum move is 50 per cent above the basic maximum move, shall move
by the increased maximum move in either direction, the maximum move in

either direction for contracts in all delivery months during the next business day shall be twice the basic maximum move. The increased maximum move established as above shall remain in effect for all subsequent business days up to and including the first day on which no closing price for contracts in any delivery month has moved by the increased maximum move in either direction. For the next business day the maximum move in either direction for contracts in all delivery months shall be 50 per cent above the basic maximum move. Notwithstanding the foregoing, there shall be no maximum price move prescribed for contracts in the month preceding the delivery month.

Delivery Requirements

Delivery of crude oils may be effected as follows:

a) By in tank transfer of title to the buyer, without physical movement of product.

b) By pump over from one tank to another tank (Intertank transfers) at Europak with a minimum quantity of 1,000 barrels per pump over.

c) By delivery ex Europak into a designated pipeline connected to Europak and with prior approval and consent of the owner of the pipeline and with a minimum quantity of 120,000 barrels per batch. Deliveries into pipeline shall be determined by pipeline scheduling.

d) By seagoing vessel with a maximum draft of 68 feet and with a minimum quantity of 120,000 barrels per seagoing vessel.

e) By river barge with a minimum of 1,000 barrels per barge.

f) The price shall be inclusive all costs of delivery of the product.

g) All deliveries made in accordance with these rules shall be final and not subject to appeal.

Delivery

All deliveries must be initiated after the first calendar day and completed before the end of the last calendar day of the delivery month.

Alternate Delivery Procedure ("ADP")   An alternative delivery procedure is available to buyer and seller who have been matched by the Clearing Corporation after the last day of trading. If buyer and seller agree to effect delivery on terms different from those prescribed in the contract specifications, they may proceed on that basis after submitting a notice of their intention to the Clearing Corporation.

Exchange for Physicals ("EFP")   The "ROEFEX" provides for exchange for physicals to take place up to cessation of trading or for such other period as notified from time to time, in accordance with the "EFP" rules as mentioned in the General Rules article 7b. The "ROEFEX" will ask for evidence of the implementation of the transaction.

Daily Volume and Open Interest (Nov 2,1989 - Dec 31,1989)

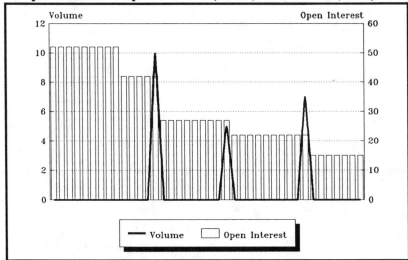

Open Interest and Volume/Open Interest("Liquidity") (Nov 2,1989 - Dec 31,1989)

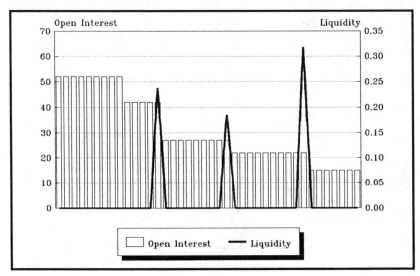

Gas Oil Futures Contract
"ROEFEX" Symbol - "GAS"

Contract Size:	One lot of 100 metric tons
Delivery Months:	Maximum of 9 consecutive months starting with the first tradable delivery month.
Delivery Day:	See below - delivery period.
Last Trading Day:	Until 18.30 p.m. Rotterdam time on the last business day of the month preceding the delivery month.
Quotation:	Prices in U.S.$ and cents per metric ton - E.E.C. duty paid & F.O.B. Antwerp/ Flushing/ Rotterdam/ Europoort/ Amsterdam.
Minimum Price Movement (Tick Size and Value):	U.S.$ 0.05 per metric ton = U.S.$ 5.00.
Trading Hours:	10.00 a.m. - 18.30 p.m. Rotterdam time.
Initial Margin:	See note above on margins.
Price Limit:	See note below.
Contract Standard:	See note below.
Exchange Delivery Settlement Price:	The closing price of the open contract on the last trading day.
Reuters Pages:	PPRD
Telekurs Pages:	RE1

Contract Standard

Physical delivery F.O.B. storage installation/refinery in the Antwerp/ Flushing/ Rotterdam/ Europoort/ Amsterdam range at sellers option in accordance with the delivery rules of the "**IPCC**". Loading will be by barges coasters or tankers or where the sellers facility permits by pumpover or in tank transfer. Product ex refinery can be delivered dyed/undyed in buyers choice (except Esso undyed) ex storage; costs of dyeing are for buyers account and are to be paid direct to the storage company.

-The price shall be inclusive all costs of delivery of the product.

-Additional costs for deliveries of below 5 contracts are for the account of the buyer.

Quality   Basis Din. 51603 + amendments. Gas oil must be of merchantable quality, not containing inorganic acids or halogenated hydrocarbons and conforming to the following specification:

Test	Unit	Limit	Test method
Density at 15$C	kg/l	min. 0.820	ASTM D-1298
		max. 0.860	ASTM D-1298
Cloud point Summer	$C	max. +5	ASTM D-2500
Cloud point Winter	$C	max. +1	ASTM D-2500
Pour Point	$C	max. -6	ASTM D-97
C.F.P.P. Summer	$C	max. -4	IP 309
C.F.P.P. Winter	$C	max. -11	IP 309
Sulphur	mass %	max. 0.20	ASTM D-4294
			ASTM D-2622
Flash point PM	$C	min. 57	ASTM D-93
Colour		max. 2	ASTM D-1500

ASTM			
Appearance	bright & clear	Visual	
Cetane index	min. 45	ASTM D-976	
Distillation at 250$C	v/v per cent	max. 65	ASTM D-86
Distillation at 350$C	v/v per cent	max. 85	ASTM D-86
Viscosity at 20$C	mm2/s	max. 6	ASTM D-445
Oxidation Stability	mg/100/ml	max. 3	ASTM D-2274
Water content	v/v per cent	max. 0.05	ASTM D-1744
Sediments	mass %	max. 0.05	ASTM D-473
Conradson carbon residue	mass %	max. 0.10	ASTM D-189
Calorific value	mj/kg	min. 42.0	ASTM D-240
Ash	mass %	max. 0.01	ASTM D-482
Strong acid number	mg/KOH/g	0	ASTM D-974

Note:

Test methods as indicated or equivalent standardized methods.

Summer: from March 1st. up till September 30th.

Winter: from October 1st. up till February 28/29th.

Settlement basis   A density at 15$C kg/l of 0.845 is par. The contract price will escalate/de-escalate according to actual density loaded. The product must be of E.E.C. origin or E.E.C. qualified.

Price Limit

The basic maximum price move permitted in any one day: US$6 per metric ton above or below the preceding day's closing price. If the closing price for contracts in any delivery month shall move by the basic maximum in either direction, the maximum move in either direction for contracts in all delivery months during the next business day shall be increased to 50 per cent above the basic maximum move. If no closing price for contracts in any delivery month for a business day for which the maximum move is 50 per cent above the basic maximum move moves by the increased maximum move in either direction, the maximum move in either direction for contracts in all delivery months during the next business day shall be the basic maximum move. If the closing price for contracts in any delivery month for a business day for which the maximum move is 50 per cent above the basic maximum move shall move by the increased maximum move in either direction, the maximum move in either direction for contracts in all delivery months during the next business day shall be twice the basic maximum move. The increased maximum move established in accordance with 3 d. shall remain in effect for all subsequent business days up to and including the first day on which no closing price for contracts in any delivery month has moved by the increased maximum move in either direction. For the next business day the maximum move in either direction for contracts in all delivery months shall be 50 per cent above the basic maximum move. Notwithstanding the foregoing, there shall be no maximum price move prescribed for contracts in the month preceding the delivery month.

Delivery Period

All deliveries must be initiated after the fifth business day and completed before the end of the last calendar day of the delivery month.

"ADP"   Available to buyer and seller who have been matched by the Clearing Corporation after the last day of trading. If buyer and seller agree to effect delivery on terms different from those prescribed in the contract specifications, they may proceed on that basis after submitting a notice of their intention to the Clearing Corporation.

"EFP"   the" ROEFEX" provides for exchange for physicals to take place up to cessation of trading or for such other period as notified from time to time, in accordance with the "EFP" rules as mentioned in the

General Rules article 7b. The "**ROEFEX**" will ask
for evidence of the implementation of the transaction.

Daily Volume and Open Interest (Nov 2,1989 - Dec 31,1989)

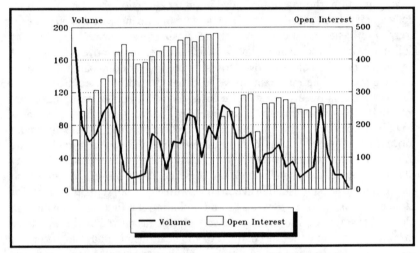

Open Interest and Volume/Open Interest("Liquidity") (Nov 2,1989 - Dec 31,1989)

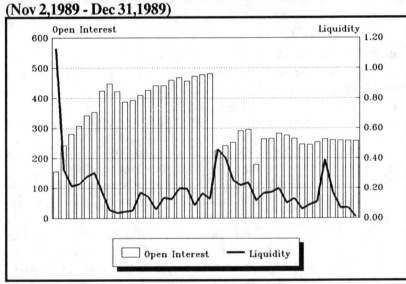

Heavy Fuel Oil Futures Contract
"ROEFEX" Symbol - "FUEL"

Contract Size:	One lot of 100 metric tons
Delivery Months:	Maximum of 9 consecutive months starting with the first tradable delivery month.
Delivery Day:	See below - delivery period.
Last Trading Day:	Until 18.30 p.m. Rotterdam time on the last business day of the month preceding the delivery month.
Quotation:	Prices in U.S.$ and cents per metric ton E.E.C. duty paid & F.O.B. Antwerp/ Flushing/ Rotterdam/ Europoort/ Amsterdam.
Minimum Price Movement (Tick Size and Value):	U.S.$ 0.05 per metric ton = U.S.$ 5.00.
Trading Hours:	10.00 a.m. - 18.30 p.m. Rotterdam time.
Initial Margin:	See note above on margins.
Price Limit:	See note below.
Contract Standard:	See note below.
Exchange Delivery Settlement Price:	The closing price of the open contract.
Reuters Pages:	PPRD
Telekurs Pages:	RE 2

Contract Standard

All contracts still open after closure of the last business day of the delivery month shall be settled via delivery F.O.B. storage installation/refinery in the Antwerp/ Flushing/ Rotterdam/ Europoort/ Amsterdam range at sellers option in accordance with the delivery rules of the "IPCC". Loading will be by barges coasters or tankers or where the sellers facility permits by pumpover or in tank transfer.

-The price shall be inclusive all costs of delivery of the product.

-Additional costs for deliveries of below 5 contracts are for the account of the buyer

Quality

The fuel must be homogeneous and must not contain used lubricating, transformer, or other functional oil (treated or otherwise), fuel oil slops or any similar materials (treated or otherwise), nor contain any coal derivates, chemicals, or any other substance harmful to marine engines and associated equipment and conforming to the following specification:

Test	Unit	Limit	Test method
Density at 15$C	kg/l	max. 0.992	ASTM D-1298
Viscosity at 50$C	mm2/s	max. 420	ASTM D-445
		min. 75	ASTM D-445
Sulphur	mass %	max. 4	ASTM D-4294
		min. 2	ASTM D-4294
Flash point	$C	min. 60	
Ash	mass %	max. 0.15	ASTM D-482
Pour point upper	$C	max. 27	ASTM D-97
Water content	v/v %	max. 0.5	ASTM D-95
Sediment by extraction	mass per cent	max. 0.10	ASTM D-473
Conradson carbon residue	mass per cent	max. 18	ASTM D-189

Vanadium content	mg/kg	max. 425	AAS
Aluminum content	mg/kg	max. 30	AAS
Sodium content	mg/kg	max.1/3 Vanad.cont.	AAS
Hot filtration test existent	mass %	max. 0.10	IP 375
Poly Chlorin.Biphen .(P.C.B.)	mg/l	0	DIN 51527
Total acid number	mg KOH/g	max. 3	ASTM D-664

Note:test methods as indicated or equivalent standardized methods.

Settlement basis The density at 15$C kg/l is 0.992 max. The product must be of E.E.C. origin or E.E.C. qualified.

Price Limit

The basic maximum price move permitted in any one day shall be US$ 6 per metric ton above or below the preceding day's closing price. If the closing price for contracts in any delivery month shall move by the basic maximum in either direction, the maximum move in either direction for contracts in all delivery months during the next business day shall be increased to 50 per cent above the basic maximum move. If no closing price for contracts in any delivery month for a business day for which the maximum move is 50 per cent above the basic maximum move, moves by the increased maximum move in either direction, the maximum move in either direction for contracts in all delivery months during the next business day shall be the basic maximum move. If the closing price for contracts in any delivery month for a business day for which the maximum move is 50 per cent above the basic maximum move, shall move by the increased maximum move in either direction, the maximum move in either direction for contracts in all delivery months during the next business day shall be twice the basic maximum move. The increased maximum move established in accordance with 3 d. shall remain in effect for all subsequent business days up to and including the first day on which no closing price for contracts in any delivery month has moved by the increased maximum move in either direction. For the next business day the maximum move in either direction for contracts in all delivery months shall be 50 per cent above the basic maximum move. Notwithstanding the foregoing, there shall be no maximum price move prescribed for contracts in the month preceding the delivery month.

Delivery Period

All deliveries must be initiated after the fifth business day and completed before the end of the last calendar day of the delivery month.

"ADP"   Available to buyer and seller who have been matched by the Clearing Corporation after the last day of trading. If buyer and seller agree to effect delivery on terms different from those prescribed in the contract specifications, they may proceed so after submitting a notice of their intention to the Clearing Corporation.

"EFP"   The "ROEFEX" provides for exchange for physicals to take place up to cessation of trading or for such other period as notified from time to time, in accordance with the E.F.P. rules as mentioned in the General Rules article 7b. The "ROEFEX" will ask for evidence of the implementation of the transaction.

Daily Volume and Open Interest (Nov 2,1989 - Dec 31,1989)

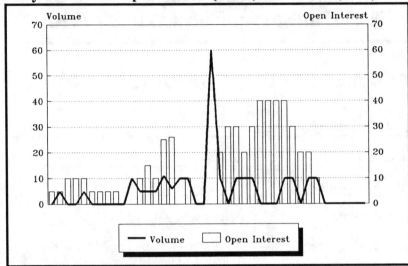

Open Interest and Volume/Open Interest("Liquidity")
(Nov 2,1989 - Dec 31,1989)

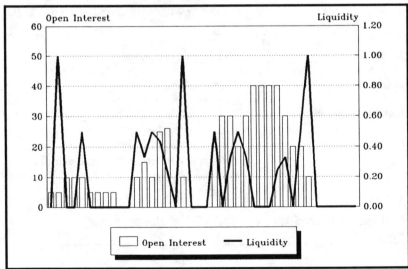

Agricultural Futures Market Amsterdam (Nederlandse Liquidatiekas) - "NLK KAS"

DETAILED CONTRACT SPECIFICATION

Potato Futures Contract

Contract Size:	25,000 kg.
Delivery Months:	April May and November.
Delivery Day:	Each business day of a delivery month.
Last Trading Day:	Until 16.00 p.m. on the Friday of the third full week of the delivery month.
Quotation:	Dfl. per 100 kg.
Trading Hours:	10.45 a.m. - 12.45 p.m. and 14.00 p.m. - 16.00 p.m.
Initial Margin:	15 per cent of contract value.
Price Limit:	No price limit.
Contract Standard:	Physical delivery of the open position on the last business day of the delivery month in accordance with the specifications as determined in article 7 of the General Rules and Regulations of the Potato Terminal Market.
Exchange Delivery Settlement Price:	The previous closing price.

Daily Volume and Open Interest (Jul 1,1989 - Dec 31,1989)

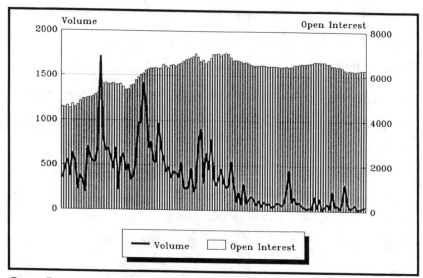

Open Interest and Volume/Open Interest("Liquidity")
(Jul 1,1989 - Dec 31,1989)

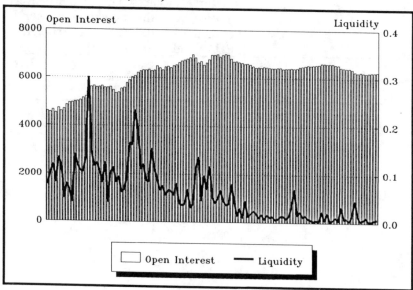

Live Hog Futures Contract

Contract Size:	10,000 kg.
Delivery Months:	All months.
Delivery Day:	Each business day in the delivery month.
Last Trading Day:	Until 16.15 p.m. five calendar days before the first delivery day.
Quotation:	Dfl. per 1 kg.
Trading Hours:	10.30 a.m. - 11.30 a.m. and 13.30 p.m. - 16.15 p.m.
Initial Margin:	15 per cent of contract value.
Price Limit:	No price limit.
Contract Standard:	Physical delivery of the open position on the last three business days of the delivery month where the weight of porker is between 85 and 120 kg - classification SEUAA and/or SEUA.
Exchange Delivery Settlement Price:	The previous closing price.

Daily Volume and Open Interest (Jul 1,1989 - Dec 31,1989)

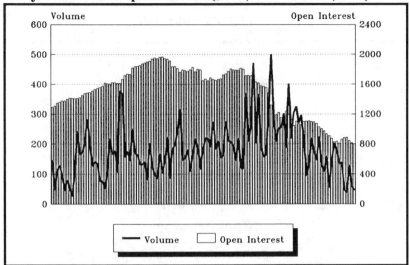

Open Interest and Volume/Open Interest("Liquidity")
(Jul 1,1989 - Dec 31,1989)

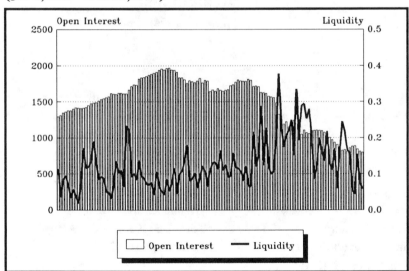

PIERSON, HELDRING & PIERSON
Merchant Bankers

Specialized in:
New Issues
Corporate Finance
Investment Management
Stockbroking
International Custody
Trust Management
Private Banking
Treasury

Head Office: London Representative Office:
Pierson, Heldring & Pierson N.V.   Pierson, Heldring & Pierson (UK)
                                      Limited
Rokin 55   99, Gresham Street
1012 KK AMSTERDAM   LONDON EC2V 7PH
P.O.Box 243   United Kingdom
1000 AE AMSTERDAM   Telephone: (071) 696 0500
The Netherlands   Telex: 885119 and 928095
Telephone: (20) 521 1188   Fax: (071) 600 1927
Telex: 13054 & 12116
Fax: (20) 521 1966

The Futures and Options Markets in Norway

Lars Traberg

&

Widar Kirkeby
Pre Fonds a.s

INTRODUCTION
Equity Options

The history of equity options in Norway has been volatile. Options on equities were traded on an OTC basis until the Ministry of Finance in May 1989 put heavy restrictions on the market in order to promote a listed market at the Oslo Stock Exchange. The listed market was supposed to open in 1987, but various problems delayed the market for two and a half years. The problems were mainly of a political sort. The Parliament was not able to make the necessary legal adjustments until 1989, because of a dispute as to whether there should be competition among different exchanges and different clearing houses. Eventually, they decided to allow competition among clearing houses but not among the exchanges. The result was that all options now are traded at the Oslo Stock Exchange and that clearing is taken care of by two different companies, **NOM** (Norsk Opsjons Marked) and **NCC** (Norsk Clearing Central). All options have to be registered at the Norwegian Registry of Securities. Investors have their own separate accounts in which deposits of stocks for margin purposes are registered in addition to the options.

Equity options on five different stocks. The stocks, listed below under contract specifications were introduced at the Oslo Stock Exchange in May 1990. Since then the market has enjoyed rapid development. In June 1990, options on a market value weighted index was introduced. The index is called **OBX**. The trading in index options has been limited until recently. This has mainly been due to general lack of knowledge among investors and strict margin rules. Knowledge has now increased thanks to information activities from the exchange. The margin requirements are also being adjusted and this will probably mean a lot to the market. Total volumes in both equity and index options have been rising and is currently about 4,000 contracts per day. This represents an underlying share value of about NOK 60 million.

The Oslo Stock Exchange is considering introducing an index futures contract. A possible futures contract will probably be based on the **OBX**-index. If the Exchange decide to start trading, this unlikely to happen before 1991.

Interest Rate Futures and Options

The Norwegian futures and option market on interest rates has so far been limited to an Over-the-Counter(OTC) market on Forward Rate Agreements "**FRA**". The market which is partly standardized has been a success. Options on **FRA**'s are quoted on request by some of the major market makers. Volume is difficult to estimate because of lack of information from the market.

Forwards and options on government and mortgage company bonds are traded on an OTC basis. The market is not liquid and has attracted few brokerage companies. Contact your broker for further information on this market.

The Oslo Stock Exchange are considering launching a futures and option contract on mortgage bonds. A committee is currently discussing various solutions and it seems that the futures contract will be based on an index. A basket of Mortgage company bonds will probably be the underlying asset for the index .

ORGANIZATION OF THE MARKET

The Option Exchange

Trading System at the Exchange

The market is divided into two different order books. One is electronic and takes care of orders not exceeding ten contracts. The other, which attracts almost all the liquidity is the manual block order desk.

The block order desk is a closed order book and handles blocks of ten contracts or multiples thereof. Independent brokers, working for the Exchange, quote prices on behalf of the member firms. The block order officials can also handle spreads and combinations. The best bid and offer price, the highest and lowest prices paid during the day, the volume traded, open interest and other information are distributed on-line through Oslo Borsinformasjon and Reuters. All telephone conversations to and from the block order desk are taped and stored to allow for an objective investigation of any complaints.

Shareholders and Board of Directors

The Option Exchange is a part the Oslo Stock Exchange, which is a self owned non profit based foundation. The Stock Exchange regulations are given by the Ministry of Finance. The Stock Exchange Council is appointed by the Ministry of Finance. Both the member firms, the Parliament and the public are represented on the Board. The Stock Exchange Council in turn appoint members of the Board.

Member Firms

The options exchange has 25 member firms of whom four are market makers. The market makers are required to quote prices with certain maximum spreads in the series they are responsible. A market maker is responsible for continuous quotation of two way prices in the at-the-money and the first in-the-money and out-of-the-money series. During the last 30 minutes of trading a market maker must quote two way prices in all option series of the underlying securities for which he is responsible.

Major member firms are:

> **Alfred Berg Norge a.s**
>
> **Carl Kierulf a.s (Market maker & broker)**
>
> **Den norske Bank**
>
> **Moorgate Options a.s (Market maker)**
>
> **Oslo Securities a.s**
>
> **Platou Securities a.s**
>
> **Pre Fonds a.s (Market maker & broker)**
>
> **SR-Fonds**
>
> **Sundal Collier Montague a.s (Market maker & broker)**

Each firm has to put forward a bank guarantee of NOK 15 million to the securities control to become a member. This requirement is set high to ensure safe trading in a newly established market.

Address

	The Oslo Stock Exchange
	P.O. Box 460 Sentrum
	N-0105 OSLO 1
Tel:	**(+ 47 2) 34 17 00**
Fax:	**(+ 47 2) 41 65 90**
General Manager:	**Roger Kristiansen**

NRS (The Norwegian Registry of Securities)

The **NRS** is a computerized registration system in which all transactions related to Norwegian traded securities must be recorded. The securities registery is owned by the government and is a non profit organization.

All options have to be registered at a separate client account at the electronic registry of securities. Margins in the form of securities are registered on the same account. Brokers are linked to the **NRS**-system and receive on-line information regarding customers positions in options and other securities.

Address

The Norwegian Registry of Securities
P.O. Box 6570 Rodelokka
N-0501 OSLO 5

Tel: **(+ 47 2) 64 61 60**
Fax: **(+ 47 2) 65 24 56**
VP Systems: **Karl O. Kristiansen**

Clearing Houses

The clearing function is taken care of by two competing companies, **NCC** (Norsk Clearing Central) and **NOM** (Norsk Opsjons Marked). Both companies are owned by major Norwegian investors. So far, guarantee funds have not been able to built up, but to ensure safe clearing each house is supervised by and has put forward a bank guarantee of NOK 45 million to the Banking, Insurance & Securities Commission.

Transaction Cost

The Oslo Stock Exchange and the clearing houses currently charge the Exchange and Clearing fees for option transactions, and the broker, in turn, charges his customer. All trading fees are collected by the clearing house chosen to clear the option trade.

	NCC	NOM
Clearing fees:	0.75% (min NOK 6/max NOK12)	0.75%(min. NOK 6/max NOK 12)
Exercise fees:	0.10%	0.10%
Exchange fees:	0.40% (min NOK 2.5 - max NOK 8)	

Margin Rules

For both index and stock options investors have to deposit 30 per cent of the strike price in cash. For out of the money options the difference between the strike price and the stock price is deducted. For in the money options the difference is added to the initial margin. The margin can not be less than 7 per cent of the strike price. Margins are calculated daily. Margin requirements are subject to rapid adjustments to market conditions. Therefore, investors are recommended to contact their broker for uptodate information.

Only cash deposited on a bank account is accepted as collateral for issued put options. For issued call options the underlying stock can be deposited on the client account in the NSR (The Norwegian Registry of Securities).

Address

	Norks Opsjons Marked A/S
	P.O. Box 1494 Vika
	N-0116 OLSO 1
Tel:	(+ 47 2) 3315 50
Fax:	(+ 47 2) 33 27 93
General Manager:	Jan Ketil Paulsen
Address:	Norks Clearing Central A/S
	P.O. Box 278
	N-1322 HOVIK
Tel:	(+ 47 2) 54 61 00
Fax:	(+ 47 2) 54 72 30
General Manager:	Bjorn Oiulfstad

OVERVIEW of PRODUCTS

Name	Brief description
Equity Options	Available on the Oslo Stock Exchange. American style put and call options. 100 shares per contract. Physical delivery. Reuters page OLUA (index)
Stock Index Futures	Not Available but under study.
Stock Index Options	Available on the Oslo Stock Exchange. Based on the **OBX** index
Bond Futures	Available to a limited extent in an OTC - market. Very illiquid and no regular price quotations.
Bond Options	Available to a limited extent in an OTC - market. Very illiquid and no regular price quotations.
Euro NOK Forwards	Available in the OTC - market. Based on **NIBOR** (Norwegian Inter Bank Offered Rate). Standardized to a certain extent with 3 6 and 12 months. Regular quotations by major banks. Cash settlement. Reuter pages FRRU FRRV and FRRW
Currency Options	Available in the OTC - market. Option prices on NOK against major currencies are quoted on request by major banks.

Page 400 The European
Options and Futures Markets

HISTORY of the MARKET

1985	FRA's (OTC - market)
May 22 1990	Stock Options (Oslo Stock Exchange)
June 27 1990	Stock index options (Oslo Stock Exchange)

DETAILED CONTRACT SPECIFICATION
Equities
Individual Stock Options Contracts

The option contract has been designed by the Oslo Stock Exchange and approved by the Ministry of Finance.

The list of options contains options on both restricted and unrestricted classes of shares. Options on unrestricted shares can bee traded freely by foreign investors. On the restricted shares foreigners are allowed to open a position by buying, but not by issuing options. These options can not be exercised by foreign investors and therefore have to be sold before expiry.

Options are traded on following stocks:

Saga Ordinaries (Restricted)
Den norske Bank (Restricted)
Norsk Hydro (Restricted)
Bergesen B
Hafslund Nycomed B

Unrestricted shares in Saga and Den norske Bank are trading at substantial premiums. Through the option market foreign investors can to a limited extent take part in the trading of the restricted classes of shares. OM London also trades options on Norwegian stocks.

Option Style:	American call and put options.
Contract Size:	100 shares per contract.
Delivery Months:	March June September and December.
Delivery Day:	Third Thursday at 2 p.m. in Delivery month.
Last Trading Day:	First Business day before expiration.
Settlement Day:	Fourth Business day after expiration.
Quotation:	NOK per share
Minimum Price Movement (Tick Size and Value):	NOK 0.05 = NOK 5.0 per contract.
Trading Hours:	10.00 a.m. - 15.00 p.m. Oslo Time.
Initial Deposit:	Margins must be paid by 11 a.m. on the day following the transaction day.
Price Limit:	No price limit.
Exercise and Position Limits:	Exercise = max 5% of underlying share capital per day. Position = Not allowed to hold more than 10% of underlying share capital.
Contract Standard:	Physical delivery of stocks.
Exercise Price:	Minimum three
Reuter Pages:	OLUA (Index)
Telerate Pages:	None

Strike prices are fixed with the following increments:

Underlying Stock Price	Increments between Strike Prices
less than 40	2.5
40 - 80	5.0
80 - 200	10.0
200 - 400	20.0
400 - 700	30.0
700 - 1,500	50.0
greater than 1,500	100.0

OBX Stock Index Options Contracts

The index option contract has been designed by the Oslo Stock Exchange and approved by the Ministry of Finance. The option contract is based on the **OBX** index, which is a capital weighted index of the 25 largest companies on the Oslo Stock Exchange. The composition of the index is updated on the 30th of June and 31th of December. Dividends are added to the index value the day the individual stock is traded ex. dividend. This rule is under revision and new rules are expected before dividends are paid (late spring). See below in table for further information about composition.

There is no regulations concerning foreign investors ability to trade Norwegian index options.

Option Style:	European call and put options.
Contract Size:	100 index shares per contract.
Delivery Months:	Every month.
Delivery Day:	Third Thursday in Delivery month.
Last Trading Day:	First Business day before Expiration.
Settlement Day:	Fourth Business day after Expiration.
Quotation:	NOK per index value excluding fees.

Minimum Price Movement (Tick Size and Value):	NOK 0.05 = NOK 5.0 per contract.
Trading Hours:	10.00 a.m. - 15.00 p.m.
Initial Deposit:	Margins must be paid by 11 a.m. on the day following the transaction day.
Price Limit:	No price limits.
Contract Standard:	Cash Settlement.
Exercise Price:	Minimum of five contracts.
Reuter Pages:	OLUX OLUY OLSB
Telerate Pages:	None
Fees:	Exchange: 0.40% - min. NOK2.5 max. NOK 8 Clearing: 0.75% - min. NOK 6.0 max. NOK 16 Brokerage: 1.50 - 2.00%

Strike price increments are the same as for equity options.

Composition of the OBX Index

Composition of index as of 25th of September 1990:

Stock	Price	Weight in Index	Market Cap NOK mil
Norsk Hydro	239.0	27,04%	24,545
Bergesen A	145.0	6.36%	5,775
Bergesen B	144.0	2.70%	2,448
Hafslund A	144.0	4.78%	4,340
Hafslund F	151.0	2.21%	2,004
Hafslund B	147.0	2.43%	2,206

Orkla Borregaard	199.0	4.05%	3,676
Orkla Borregaard F	201.0	1.76%	1,596
Saga A ord.	107.0	7.66%	6,954
Saga B	177.0	6.09%	5,530
Christiania Bank	79.0	2.42%	2,196
Christiania Bank Free	127.0	1.29%	1,171
Kvaerner Ind.	221.0	3.74%	3,397
Kvaerner Ind. B	226.0	1.96%	1,782
Den norske Bank	95.0	3.06%	2,773
Storebrand	83.0	2.94%	2,665
Aker A	79.0	3.74%	2,092
Aker B	77.0	1.96%	676
Elektrisk Beureau	239.0	3.06%	2,779
Elkem	235.0	2.46%	2,235
Norske Skog Ind.	142.0	2.28%	2,066
Bohneur	207.5	2.63%	2,384
Ganger Rolf	205.0	2.07%	1,876
Vard	92.5	2.74%	2,483
Nora Free	310.0	1.23%	1,113
Total market value			90,761

History of the OBX Index (Jan 2,1990 - Oct 1,1990)

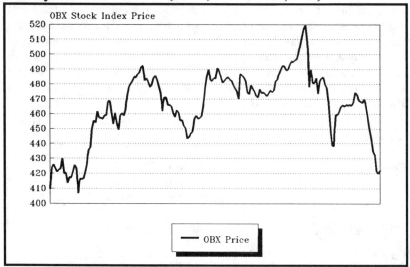

The chart shows the history of the OBX-index. The Index was introduced on the 27th. of June. History before this day is made on the basis of the existing index composition and the current stock prices. The **OBX** duplicates the Olso Stock Exchange Composite Index very good. The correlation factor is very high. After the rapid growth in oil prices recently, the two oil related stocks Norsk Hydro and Saga Petroleum has increased their weight in the Index. The two companies now counts for 40.79% of the Index value.

Interest Rates

Euro NOK Forward Rate Agreements

There is no listed market for short term interest rate futures, but in 1986 the **FRA** (Forward Rate Agreement) market emerged. In the beginning the market resembled the international type of **FRA** market with maturities like 3/6 months and 6/12 months. In 1987 the market was standardized with fixed expirations on the third Wednesday in March, June, September and December. Terms and conditions were made and accepted by all the market makers. The trading volume has shown considerable growth since standardization and today the market is very liquid. The market makers quote satisfying spreads, and prices are normally good for more than the standard contract size. The **FRA**'s can be traded directly with the market makers or through independent interbank foreign exchange brokers.

Investors trading in the **FRA** market will be subject to credit lines valuations. Since there are no clearing companies guaranteeing the fulfillment of the contract, this is an important part of market practices. When making a trade, the investor has to sign an **FRA** agreement with the counterparty, presumably a market maker or an independent broker. When the trade is closed out, a new agreement has to be signed. Cash settlement of the two agreements are carried out on the basis of **NIBOR** (Norwegian Inter Bank Offered Rate) fixing rate on the official fixing day.

There is no regulations concerning foreign investors ability to trade Norwegian **FRA**'s.

Contract Size:	3 months NOK 50,000,000 6 months NOK 50,000,000 12 months NOK 25,000,000
Settlement Months:	March June September and December.
Last Trading Day:	Three Business days before delivery.
Fixing day:	Two Business days before delivery.
Settlement Day:	Third wednesday in Delivery month.
Quotation:	0.01 per cent.
Minimum Price Movement (Tick Size and Value):	0.01 per cent = NOK 1,250 for 3 month contract = NOK 2,500 for 6 month contract = NOK 2,500 for 12 month contract.
Trading Hours:	10.00 a.m. - 15.00 p.m.
Initial Deposit:	None.
Price Limit:	No price limits.
Contract standard	Cash Settlement.
Reuter Pages:	FRRU FRRV FRRW
Telerate Pages:	Not known

FRA Marketmakers:

Christiania Bank & Kreditkasse	CBKU
Den norske Bank	DNOA DNOR
Finansbanken	FBNA
Fokus Bank	FOBR
Sparebanken Vest	SPVT
Sparebanken NOR	UBNF
Midland Montagu	MMOS

Euro Norwegian Krones Forward Rate Agreement Options Contracts

Options on NOK are quoted on request by some of the **FRA** market makers. Options are normally European style with automatic exercise. They expire on the same dates as the underlying **FRA's**, and are normally traded on the basis of the 6 month **FRA** contract. There is no standardized contract size. For further information please call the author of this document or one of the **FRA** market makers. The market is very illiquid.

Currency Options Contracts on Norwegian Krones

Currency options on NOK against major currencies are quoted on request by the major Norwegian based foreign exchange banks. Options are normally European style with physical delivery. There is no standardized contract size. Call your interbank broker or local bank for further information.

Commodities, Metals and Shipping

Norway does not have a commodity exchange and there is no official fixing for metals and commodity prices. An organized market for trading in options and futures does not exist either. Some brokerage houses quote option prices on interest in ships for those vessels in which the house carries out active trading. The market is very illiquid. Call your local broker for further information.

REGULATION

Rules and Regulations at the Oslo Stock Exchange

The Norwegian Ministry of Finance has established a set of rules to maintain a fair and orderly market. These rules are referred to as the General Conditions, and give an in-depth description of the options market. Trading in stock option products at the Oslo Stock Exchange is governed by the General Conditions, by Norwegian laws and other regulations related to securities in general. Rules and Regulations can be obtained through your Norwegian broker or from the Oslo Stock Exchange.

TAXATION

There is no withholding tax for foreign investors. Taxation rules for domestic investors are currently being worked out by the Ministry of Finance. Rules are expected to be effective from the tax year 1991.

Fondsfinans a.s

SECURITIES

Domestic equities	Knut Ellingsberg	
	Tore Elstad Forbrigd	
	Erik Must	
	Kjell Rannug	
	Erik Schultz	
	Kim Tangen	
	Kjell Ulrichsen	
Bonds and money markets		Harald Grimsrud
		Lasse Halvorsen
		Bengt Kirkøen
		Håkon Persen
Economist		Erik Bjørland
Financial advice		Åge Korsvold
		Nils Erling Ødegaard
Research		Jens Vig Jr.
Foreign securities	Tore Elstad Forbrigd	
	Erik Schultz	
	Kim Tangen	

SETTLEMENT

Domestic equities	Ragnar Nyhagen	
	Rudulf Nyhuus	
Foreign securities		Rolf Bunæs
New issues		Kjell Håve
Bonds and moneymarkets	Hilde Utne	
	Kjell Håve	
Transfer agent VPS		Hilde Utne

Haakon VII's gt. 2 - Postboks 1782 Vika, 0122 Oslo 1, Norway
Tel: +47-2-83 66 90 - Fax: +47-2-83 16 20 - Telex: 19159 fonds n
Bankgiro: 8630.06.00141

The Forwards, Futures and Options Markets in Spain

Rodrigo Sousa Suárez
Analistas Financieros Internacionales, SA
Grupo Ahorro Corporación

Introduction

The recent developments in the financial markets in Spain have not yet led to fully implemented futures and options trading. Still, the growth in the bond markets and the adoption of new financial techniques (in the larger sense) opened the market to new trading practices and hedging activity. In March 1988, two years before the establishment of the futures and options markets, the bond market underwent major changes to provide greater liquidity and depth, through the integration of Government securities into a book entry system. In less than one year the basic legal framework of forwards trading had been approved. The main differences between the forwards market and a futures' market are not in settlement and delivery practices, that contracts are not standardized and are bilateral among market participants. There is no clearing house but an office of the Bank of Spain manages the cash and book entry accounts of market participants.

Volume & Yield Histories of 2-3 Year Bonds in Cash Market January 2, 1989 - June 29, 1990

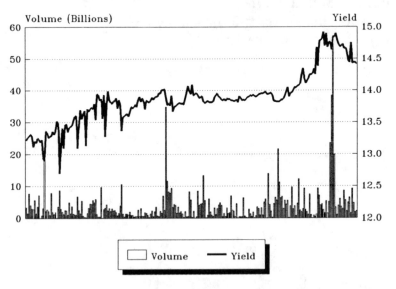

The creation of a book entry market for Government Securities in March 1988 has been followed by a dramatic increase in trading volumes and liquidity. Simultaneously, the high levels of Treasury stocks present in market makers' portfolios, encouraged the development of hedging financial instruments. A short time after the implementation of the book entry market, the first forwards contracts and options on securities started to be traded, more as "gentleman's agreement". The central authorities showed a high level of sensitivity to the problem and quickly established a legal framework for these operations. The forwards' market started operating in March 1989 to provide not only the opportunity to trade regularly certain financial instruments, but also as the first step to building a futures and options market for a wider variety of assets.

During the fourth quarter of 1989, the first options and futures clearing house was created in Spain. This private company, OM Iberia SA, owned initially by Optionsmarknad AB "OM" and three brokerage firms (Cofisa, Fortuny and CIMD) and joined by Banco Bilbao-Vizcaya "BBV" in April 1990, is trying to widen its capital base by attracting other companies. It is developing the first futures and options market in Spain, although the first contracts traded have only been options. The contracts traded and the underlying securities will be both real and notional Treasury bonds available in the book entry market. However this market will work independently from the book entry market, which is devoted to forwards contracts. Trading started in November 1989, in options on one issue of a Government bond (Bonos del Estado 12.50% October 1992). By the beginning of March 1990, the major part of OTC options had been transferred to OM. This has increased market liquidity and depth, with a trading volume over Pts 4 billion. While this is a good start, it is thought that the trading system must be further improved.

A second futures market based in Barcelona started operations in March 1990, run by Mercado de Futuros Financieros sa "MEFF" with more than 44 shareholders. The first contract traded was a notional bond with a 10% coupon and a three year life.

The Forward Market

ORGANIZATION of the MARKET

The only official market to trade forwards contracts is at present in the book entry market, managed by the Bank of Spain through the "Central de Anotaciones". Regulation and monitoring of trades is the responsibility of the monetary authorities, yet the market is largely decentralized.

Forward trading is restricted to medium and long term bonds ("Bonos del Estado" and "Obligaciones del Estado") in the book entry market, but only one or two securities are negotiated in forwards contracts. It is also possible to trade options on these securities but this segment of the market is irrelevant nowadays.

Capital Requirements

Financial institutions with a minimum capital base of Pts 200 million can take part in the book entry market (they are called "titulares de cuentas") for cash trades as well as forwards contracts, but only for their account. Credit institutions and financial brokers or dealers with a capital base of more than Pts 750 million at the beginning, and more than Pts 1 billion two years later, also can trade on their client's account. Such companies are called "entidades gestoras" and also must keep in the book entry accounts they manage an amount of at least Pts 7 billion of short, medium and long term Treasuries (Bonos del Estado, Obligaciones del Estado, Letras del Tesoro and Pagarés del Tesoro) belonging to their clients. When they hold at least one per cent of the outstanding invested by non financial institutions and resident individuals (nearly Pts 155 billion currently), "entidades gestoras" are considered "aspirantes a creadores" (security dealers), and when this proportion reaches 2.5 per cent (around Pts 310 billion), "creadores de mercado" (market makers). Market makers are the most important banks and savings banks. They must keep solvency requirements, provide liquidity to the market and attend regularly to primary markets. In exchange, the Bank of Spain undertakes certain open market operations through them and they can access the inter-dealer brokers network.

Trading is made directly among the institutions accepted in the book entry market, or by the interdealer brokers. The interdealer brokers (usually called in Spain "ciegos", or blind brokers) receive both bids and offers from market makers and "aspirantes" that can be automatically matched, maintaining the anonymity of trader. All contracts traded through the interdealer brokers expire the third Wednesday of each month (previously contracts expired the last Wednesday of each month until March 1990). Trades matched directly among "entidades gestoras" can expire on other dates but most of the contracts adjust their expiry dates to those traded through interdealer brokers.

Market Practices

The traders can wait until the day before their contract expires to decide how to settle their position. Most usually it is agreed from the beginning if there will be delivery of the bond or not at the contract end. The interdealer brokers show on their screens separately bids and offers for contracts with delivery or with cash settlement, although prices are just the same. Brokerage commissions charged are however different: 0.0125 per cent for contracts with cash settlement and 0.015 per cent for contracts with bond delivery (exactly the same commission charged on as cash contracts).

Interdealer brokers maintain a computer network to match automatically bids and offers. But they also can act as "normal" brokers when they are addressed directly by their customers.

Market Makers

Creadores de Mercado

Banco Bilbao Vizcaya
Banco Central
Banco Hispano Americano
Banco Exterior de España
Banco Natwest March
Banco Popular Español
Banco de Santander
Banesto
Bank of America
Bankinter
BNP España
Caixa de Pensions "La Caixa"
Caja de Madrid
Caja Postal
Citibank España
CECA

JP Morgan SVB, SA
Siaf

Aspirantes a Creadores

Banco Atlántico
Banco Pastor
Banco de Sabadell
Banco Urquijo
Bankers Trust
Barclays
Chase Manhattan Bank
Caixa de Barcelona
Credipas
Crédit Lyonais
Descontiber
Dresdner Bank, AG Sucursal en España
BBV Interactivos SVB, SA
Ibercaja
Samedi
SMB

Types of Contracts

In the forwards market it is possible to trade contracts on any of the securities admitted to the book entry market (between 30 and 35 medium and long term issues). However, only 3 or 4 issues with an outstanding over Pts 450 billion are regularly traded as they are the most liquid in the market.

Contract Size:	Pts 100,000,000.
Delivery Months:	Each month of the year.
Expiry Date:	The third Wednesday of each month. But only trades agreed with a settlement date at least 5 days forward are considered forward contracts.
Last Trading Day:	Five business days before the third Wednesday of the month.
Quotation:	Per cent of Par.

Minimum Price Movement (Tick Size and Value):	Pts 0.125 per cent = Pts 125,000.
Trading Hours:	09.00 a.m. - 17.00 p.m. Trades closed after 12.30 p.m. carry the following day's date.
Contract Standards:	Cash and physical delivery. The traders ("titlares de cuentas") or the interdealer brokers have to tell the "Central de Anotaciones (CA)" the terms of each contract to be registered in the accounts held in the Bank of Spain. Contracts are marked to market and the gains or losses charged daily to these accounts. Before the end of the contract the traders tell the "CA" if they prefer to deliver the bonds in the contract or effect cash settlement. The traders also can agree the cash settlement of their contracts at any moment - they only have to notify the CA.
Exchange Delivery Settlement Price:	See note below.
Reuters Pages:	**DPKA - DPKQ & DPJA - DPJZ.**
Telerate Pages:	

Exchange Delivery Settlement Price

There are two systems of price fixing i) for daily marking and ii) for closing contracts for delivery or cash settlement. Both systems are carried market interdealer brokers (different ones each month) and not by an official institution.

i) The daily marking is computed as a weighted average of the weighted average price of the day and the bid and offered prices given by a wide set of dealers at closing time (12.30 p.m.). The spread between bid and offer prices must be less than 15 basis points.

ii) monthly closing prices for contracts with cash settlement is computed by a different method. On the closing date one business day before the contract date between 12.30 p.m. and 12.45 p.m. every dealer must send the broker in charge of the fixing - one bid and one offer for Pts 100 million. The spread must be at most 15 basis points. Bids and offers that would not automatically be matched are shown on the terminals of the book entry market network between 12.45 p.m. and 13.00 p.m.. After that dealers match directly their trades. At 13.00 p.m. the broker's computer gives the weighted average price of the trades that have been taking place since 12.45 p.m. and this is the closing price.

For contracts with bond delivery there is no specific closing price. By the contract end trades executed the previous days are cancelled and the accounts in the CA are settled on the price agreed when the contract closed.

Bonds traded in the market

> 11.70 per cent 3 year bond, April 1991 (until summer 1989)
>
> 12.00 per cent 3 year bond, April 1992 (until winter 1989)
>
> 12.50 per cent 3 year bond, October 1992
>
> 13.75 per cent 3 year bond, May 1993
>
> 13.80 per cent 3 year bond, September 1993

Market Trading

It is possible to compare, with the help of the following graphics, the increasing liquidity of the forwards market, compared to the cash market. The last shows an extremely irregular path in traded volumes with a high volatility in yields. The highest liquid market instruments are the longest forwards contracts. In these graphics the longest contracts traded had the redemption date September 1990, and a few December 1990.

Yield & Volume Histories of 1 Month Forward Contracts

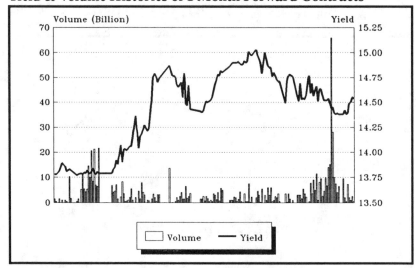

on 2-3 Year Bonds (January 1, 1990 - June 29, 1990)

Yield & Volume Histories of 2 Month Forward Contracts
on 2-3 Year Bonds (January 1, 1990 - June 29, 1990)

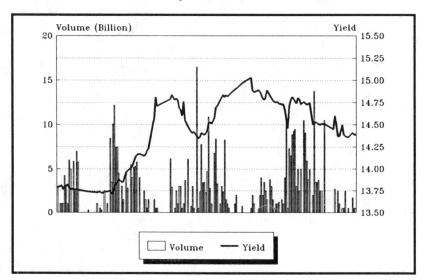

Yield & Volume Histories of 3 Month Forward Contracts on 2-3 Year Bonds (January 1, 1990 - June 29, 1990)

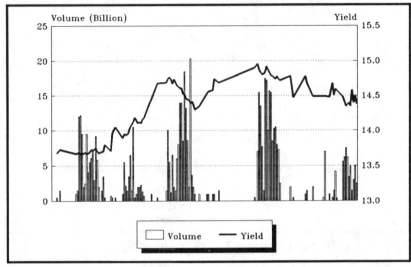

Yield & Volume Histories of Over 3 Month Forward Contracts on 2-3 Year Bonds (January 1, 1990 - June 29, 1990)

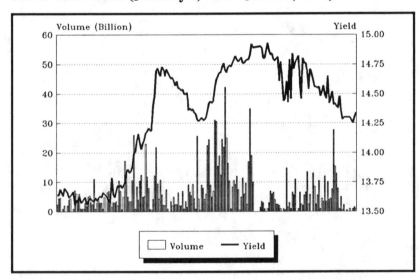

The Futures Market - The Mercado de Futuros Financieros "MEFF"

ORGANIZATION of the MARKET

In March 1990 the first futures contracts started trading in Spain, operated by MEFF, a clearing house based in Barcelona (independent of the Stock Exchange). MEFF is owned by over 44 market members with share capital of Pts 1.5 billion. Trades are based on a notional bond with several underlying physical securities that consist of Government Bonds with a maturity longer than one year and less than five. The next contract to be traded in the futures market will be a three-month deposit in Pesetas. This contract called MIBOR-90 probably will be traded by **OM** Ibérica and "**MEFF**" by the end of August 1990.

Trading is established by a computer network through market members. Market members must always be members of the book-entry market system. They can be shareholders of "**MEFF**" or not, but in the later case, the charges to be admitted to the market and general guaranties asked are higher.

Settling members "miembros liquidadores" deposit margins for open positions in their account or in their customers'accounts and settle with "**MEFF**" their gains and losses (daily marking to market), and deliveries when contracts expire. Settling members also provide to "**MEFF**" general guarantees of their own (the shareholders of "**MEFF**" are exempted). Settling members with capital of over Pts 20 billion and listed as "entidades gestoras" are called "full settling members" ("miembros liquidadores plenos"), and provide settling facilities to "non settling members" of the market ("miembros no liquidadores"). It is not necessary to be a "entidad gestora" to become a settling member of the market, although if the institution has only the degree of "titular de cuentas" its trades are limited to own account ("miembros liquidadores propios").

Market Members

Shareholders　　　　　Banca Catalana
　　　　　　　　　　　　　Bancapital
　　　　　　　　　　　　　Banco Bilbao-Vizcaya
　　　　　　　　　　　　　Banco Central

Banco Comercial Transatlántico
Banco de Crédito Industrial
Banco de la Pequeña y Mediana Empresa
Banco de Sabadell
Banco de Santander
Banco Español de Crédito
Banco Exterior de España
Banco Hispano Americano
Banco Ibercorp
Banco Natwest March
Banco Pastor
Banco Popular Español
Banco del Progreso
Banco Urquijo
Bankinter
BNP España
Caixa de Barcelona
Caixa de Catalunya
Caixa de Pensions "La Caixa"
Caixa Galicia
Caixa Penedés
Caja de Ahorros Municipal de Burgos
Caja de Ahorros Municipal de San Sebastián
Caja Madrid
Caja Postal
CECA
Citibank España
Dresdner Bank, AG Sucursal en España
Ibercaja
JP Morgan SVB, SA

Other members
Banco Santander de Negocios
Banesto, Lombardía y Lacaci SVB, SA
Banque Paribas Sucursal en España
BBV Interactivos SVB, SA
Bolsa 8 AVB, SA
Capital Market Equities AVB
Finacor Futuros AV, SA
Inverbrokers SVB, SA
Lloyds Bank
Manufacturers Hanover Trust Co.

Address

"MEFF"

Vía Layetana, 60 - 61

08003 BARCELONA

Tel: 34-3-412 11 28

Fax: 34-3-412 48 26

Types of Orders

Market

No price limit. Volume limited. None executed part of the order is cancelled.

Limited

To be executed at a specified price or better. Remains in the system until execution or cancellation.

Limited Intermediate

To be executed at a specified price or better. None executed part of the order is cancelled.

Stop

Limited price. Limited Volume. The computer keeps this order until execution or cancellation and presents it as a market order when the price conditions of the order are reached.

Limited stop

Limited price. Limited volume. The computer keeps this order till execution or cancellation and presents it as a limited order when price conditions of the order are reached.

Fill or Kill

Must be executed fully. This order is similar to a limited intermediate order but must be executed fully.

Attack

At a specified price or better. This order is similar to a limited intermediate order but must be the best present in the market.

Market maker

Two limited orders, one short and one long with different prices and volumes over the same contract and with the same expiry.

Straddle

Two limited intermediate orders, one long and one short over different contracts or over the same contract with different expiry dates. The volumes of both sides must be the same. The system executes simultaneously the two orders and always for the same amount. Any volumes not executed are cancelled.

DETAILED CONTRACT SPECIFICATION
Interest Rates
Notional 10% Three Year Bond Futures Contract

Contract Size:	Pts. 10,000,000 nominal.
Delivery Months:	March June September December.
Delivery Day:	The third Wednesday of the contract month.
Last Trading Day:	12.30 p.m. two business days before the delivery day.
Quotation:	Per cent of Par.
Minimum Price Movement (Tick Size and Value):	Pts 0.01 per cent = Pts 1,000.
Trading Hours:	09.00 a.m. - 15.00 p.m.
Initial Margin:	4 per cent = Pts 400,000.
Price Limit:	2 per cent above or below the last settlement price.
Contract Standard:	Physical settlement. The market members maintaining long positions must send written notice to the clearing house before 16.00 p.m. on the last trade day of the contract specifying the nominal value and technical references of the deliverables. The day after MEFF should confirm before 10.00 a.m. the delivery terms to allow settlement. In default of notice MEFF will rule cash settlement.

Exchange Delivery Settlement Price:	After every session the clearing house will publish the settlement price for all notional bond contracts traded for each period. The nearest redemption contract price is calculated through the average price and turnover of the 12 last trades. Other contract prices are computed as the average of the price and turnover of the 6 last trades. In case there are not enough trades to calculate those averages all trades are considered.
Reuters Pages:	MEFF
Telerate Pages:	
Commissions and fees:	The fees charged by MEFF to settling members are Pts 625 for every simple trade and Pts 625 for every straddle. Market makers pay only Pts 100 for every trade.

Delivery period

The delivery period starts on the delivery day and ends six days later and therefore lasts seven days.

Final price = (Last contract price) x (conversion factor) + accrued interest

Underlying securities

The following deliverable Government fixed coupon bullet bonds maturing between one and five years after delivery. In those cases where the bonds are callable or puttable, the exercise date will be taken as the redemption dates.

- 12.00 per cent April 1992
- 12.50 per cent October 1992
- 12.40 per cent January 1993
- 13.75 per cent May 1993
- 13.80 per cent September 1993

Conversion factors

These are computed according to the formula:

$$F = (\ F_i (\ 1 + r\ )^{(-t_i/365)} - ac\ ) / N$$

r = semiannual annual yield corresponding to annual yield in the notional bond (10 per cent yield in the notional corresponds to r = 10.25 per cent)

F_i = Cashflow in period i

n = number of future coupons

t_i = number of days through delivery and coupon payments

N = nominal value of the deliverable

ac = accrued interest of the deliverable

Market Makers

These market members give continuously bid and offer prices for at least 50 per cent of the contracts traded (currently 3 different contracts), within a maximum spread of 20 basis points.

Market Practices

Transactions in this market have started too recently to establish traditional market practices. Common ways of trading are defined by practices from other markets (essentially the book entry market) and the legal procedures.

Legal practices have been implemented to protect investors' and hedgers' interests in market trading. To promote market efficiency and integrity, prices must be public and positions remain anonymous. Market members are forbidden to open their positions at the same or on better terms than their clients. They can never cause artificial prices movements or any practice harmful to their clients. The clients have always priority over market member's own positions. An order must be executed when accepted and confirmed when the computer matches the positions.

The nonstandard orders are based on several standard types of transactions and must be completed when accepted by the market member. Orders implying an increase in a client's risk position can be rejected by the market members, but these dealers must always accept orders trying to diminish risk in an investor's position. Information about the execution of the orders is sent to investors after a five days delay.

Daily Volume and Open Interest (Mar 3, 1990 - May 30, 1990)

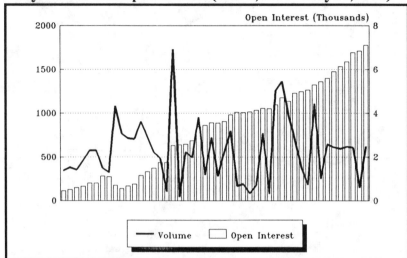

Open Interest and Volume/Open Interest("Liquidity")
(Mar 3, 1990 - May 30, 1990)

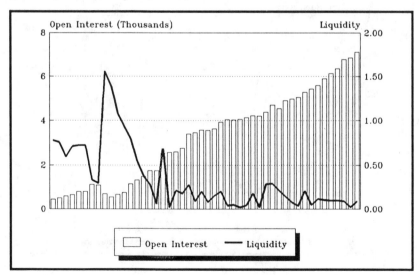

Price/Yield History (Mar 3, 1990 - May 30, 1990)

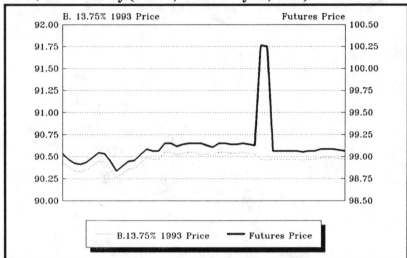

Implied Repo Rate (Mar 3, 1990 - May 30, 1990)

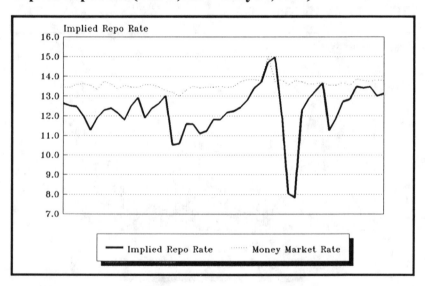

The Options Market - OM Ibérica.

ORGANIZATION of the MARKET

OM Ibérica is the clearing house who established in Spain the first options trading and settlement network on book entry Government bonds. The clearing house is the institution responsible for fixing prices, the settlement methods and to monitor information flows to the market to provide equal opportunities to all members. These general topics come in tangible terms through the market regulations that define

- **the market structure**

- **the way to access or exit the market**

- **trading, pricing and settlement methods**

- **resolve conflicts**

- **margins computation**

- **the specific terms of each negotiable contract**

- **and the contract between OM Ibérica and the market members.**

OM also will provide the markets' members with the necessary know-how to trade its financial instruments.

OM Ibérica guarantees (with its own capital and resources if necessary) every contract traded, even then where margins given by the market members would not cover the risks evolved. The clearing house would ask the members to provide additional funds to cover exceptional implicit risk in their accounts.

Every market member must provide **OM** with enough margin always to cover the risk of any trade closed (although it usually does not ask for margin deposits before 11.00 a.m. the following working day). This sum will be delivered to a deposit institution ("depositarío") and is called margin deposit ("depósito en garantía"). **OM** computes daily the total margin needs of each participant and the necessary adjustments of funds required and sends this information to the market makers ("creadores de mercado"), the brokers ("intermediarios") and the deposit institutions ("depositarios"). Finally, the brokers must get in touch with their clients. The margins can be sent to deposit institutions, directly by the final investors, or through the broker closing the trade.

OM can exceptionally ask for an initial deposit (less than Pts 50 million) to accept one market member. No participants' margin for their positions could exceed the financial solvency of the institution. Taken with the customers' margins, the total margin amount can never be larger than three times the financial solvency of the market member.

Membership

There are three sorts of market member:

- **the market makers (who act only for their account, and provide prices for long and short positions at any time for every financial instrument in the market)**

- **the dealers (who act for their account and for their customers')**

- **and the clients (whose names are kept secret from OM).**

It is possible to become both market maker and dealer, whenever the administrative requirements are fulfilled and this is the most common situation. In fact, market makers must be "titulares de cuentas" and dealers, "entidades gestroras". Customers can open several accounts with a dealer if accepted by the latter and accounts with several brokers. The number of every client account ("identidad comercial") is the only feature controlled by OM about the final investors.

Two other institutions act in the market differently from other market members, as they do not play an active role in trading. These are the deposit institutions (they keep members' margins) and the account keepers ("tenedores de cuentas"). If a client maintains several opened accounts, they can ask an account keeper to open a global account that centralizes the transactions of every separate account.

Members

Shareholders   Ahorro Corporación Financiera
A.B. Asesores Bursátiles
Banco Bilbao-Vizcaya
Banco Exterior de España
Banesto
Caja de Navarra
CIMD
Cofisa

Fortuny
OM Internacional

Market Members

Ahorro Corporación Financiera
A.B. Asesores Bursátiles
BBV Interactivos
Banca Catalana
Bancapital
Banco Bilbao-Vizcaya
Banco Central
Banco Europeo de Finanzas
Banco Exterior de España
Banco Hispano Americano
Banco Pastor
Banco de Santander
Banco Santander de Negocios
Banco Urquijo
Bancotrans
Banesto
Banesto Lombardía Lacaci
Bankers Trust
Banque Bruxeles Lambert
Banque Parisbas
Barclays Bank
Bestinver
Caja de Ahorros de Gerona
Caja de Pensiones "La Caixa"
Caja Postal
Descontíber
Dresdner Bank, AG Sucursal en España
Ibercaja
Iberdealer
Renta 4
Safei - Samedi
Siaf
SMB
Saudesbank

Address

OM Ibérica
Plaza P.Ruiz Picasso

Torre Picasso, planta 26
28020 MADRID
Tel: 34-1-585 08 00
Fax: 34-1-571 95 42

DETAILED CONTRACT SPECIFICATION

In this section we describe the most relevant features concerning the first contract traded in the **OM** Ibérica market. This contract was based on the existing 12.5 per cent Government bond October 1992. This contract has since been abandoned. However, it was established that the underlying security could also be a notional bond, and negotiations evolving this started officially in the second half of May 1990. New contracts based on short term assets are expected to be traded in the coming months.

Interest Rates

12.5% October 1992 Options Contract

Option Style	European.
Contract Size:	Pts 20,000,000 or 10,000,000.
Delivery Months:	Six month contracts with the expiry cycle of March June September December.
Delivery Day:	The third Wednesday in Contract month.
Last Trading Day:	12.00 p.m. two days before expiry date.
Quotation:	Per cent of par.
Minimum Price Movement (Tick Size and Value):	Pts 0.0005 per cent = Pts 1,000 or 500.
Trading Hours:	09.00 a.m. - 18.00 p.m..
Initial Margin:	Computed to the **OM** model based on a Black 76 model. See later.

Price Limit:	NO price limit. However trading can be interrupted if additional margins are necessary.
Contract Standard:	Physical or cash settlement. Settlement will be always executed the 3rd Wednesday of the contract month or the working day immediately after in case of holiday. Before 17.00 p.m. on the expiry date market participants must give notice of which options are going to be exercised and **OM** Ibérica must publish settlement prices. The day following the expiry date **OM** Ibérica tells market members the number of the exercised options. Before 17.00 p.m. every market member is told the settlement procedures for his contracts. Only net positions are settled. If the number of exercised options is less than total number of contracts **OM** decides by drawings which participants must sell or buy bonds. Cash or physical settlement is directly executed for exercised options on real bonds if the settlement price matches the strike price.
Exercise Price:	After every contract date **OM** lauches five options series expiring in six months time with different prices. One of this series is struck at the nearest rounded price to the last exercise price two are struck above that price and two below. If the cash market price of the underlying falls below the lowest series price a new series are launched immediately the cash price is higher or lower than the current series.
Reuters Pages:	**OIMB - OIMK and ESOI - ESOK.**
Telerate Pages:	

Spanish Notional 10% Three Year Bond Options Contract

Option Style	European.
Contract Size:	Pts 20,000,000 or 10,000,000.
Delivery Months:	March June September December.
Delivery Day:	The third Wednesday in the contract month.
Last Trading Day:	Two business days before expiry date.
Quotation:	Per cent of par.
Minimum Price Movement (Tick Size and Value):	Pts 0.0005 per cent = Pts 1,000 or 500.
Trading Hours:	09.00 a.m. - 18.00 p.m.
Initial Margin:	Computed to the **OM** model based on a Black 76 model. See later.
Price Limit:	NO price limit. However trading can be interrupted if additional margins are necessary.
Contract Standard:	See below.
Exercise Price:	After every contract date **OM** launches five options series expiring in six months time with different prices. One of this series is struck at the nearest rounded price to the last exercise price two are struck above that price and two below. If the cash market price of the underlying falls below the lowest series price a new series are launched immediately the cash price is higher or lower than the current series.

Reuters Pages:	OIMB - OIMK and ESOI - ESOK.
Telerate Pages:	

Contract Standard

Physical or cash settlement. Settlement will be always executed the 3rd Wednesday of the contract month or the working day immediately after in case of holiday. Before 17.00 p.m. on the expiry date market participants must give notice of which options are going to be exercised and **OM** Ibérica must publish settlement prices. The day following the expiry date **OM** Ibérica tells market members the number of the exercised options. **OM** plans to know which government bonds will be sold when options are based on a notional bond. Before 17.00 p.m. every market member is told the settlement procedures for his contracts. Only net positions are settled. If the number of exercised options is less than total number of contracts **OM** decides by drawings which participants must sell or buy bonds. Cash or physical settlement is directly executed for exercised options on real bonds as the settlement price matches the strike price. However for options on notional bonds it is necessary to consider both settlement and delivery prices. Delivery prices for the notional are computed on the average yield to maturity of the cheapest to deliver bond (at present 13.75 per cent October 1992) at noon on the last day of trading. Delivery prices can also be produced by the means of conversion factors which are computed in the same way than for futures contracts on the price of the notional bond. The difference between deliver and settlement prices is covered by cash and the difference between settlement price and strike can be settled by cash or by physical.

Underlying Securities

The deliverable bond for options on notionals is presently the 13.75 per cent three years bond, maturing in May 1993 as notified by **OM**. This bond is actually the cheapest to deliver in the cash market.

Margins

Margins for short positions are calculated before 11.00 a.m. the following day for each trade, but **OM** gives notice to market members before 9.00 a.m. of total margins required. To compute margins, **OM** simulates daily with a modified Black & Scholes model every contract value for the difference through the expiry date and the reaction period (period of time necessary to offset the risk effects of a certain contract) for a range of 31 values, whose center is the forward or future price of the underlying security and whose width depends on parameters published by **OM** for each contract.

The pricing method is based on a Black & Scholes model with several changes to compute margins:

- options bought are "undervalued", and sold options negative value is "overvalued".

- every sold option has a minimum negative value, although the model may indicate a better result.

- in margins computation, the time expected to hedge the position of a market participant uncovered, is offset from term to expiry date.

- three volatilities are used to compute options prices in every point of the values interval: the implicit historic, one over and another below. By this method, it is possible to produce three different prices. In margin computation, the worst of these is chosen to assume effective coverage. Net margin for an option is the least computed value through any standard deviation at any point of the values interval.

Margins (cash or physical) can be send directly to a deposit institution by a customer or given to a market member.

Market Practices

The Exchange is as for the futures market a very new one and it is not possible to discuss in depth the market practices and market historic volatility compared to other markets. However the basic features of trading are described below.

There are two trading methods for market members: by telephone (for contracts of 10 or more) or by an electronic network, from 09.00 a.m. to 18.00 p.m. In the electronic network the best prices orders carry the highest priority; the market makers's orders carry a lesser priority than other members. The first order to arrive will be always the first to be executed. Apart from these priorities, in the trading by telephone, the highest priority is given to conditioned orders. Orders intiated by the electronic network can have a date restriction on execution. If no date restriction is indicated, the order is presumed limited to the closing of the sesssion. Orders given by telephone are always limited to the closing of the session. Orders by market makers are also limited to the end of the session.

The control and supervision of the market is managed by **OM** and in a second step by the Bank of Spain, as in the futures market.

It is finally possible to transfer to **OM** market options negotiated directly between two institutions if there exists a firm agreement on contract terms, and both institutions agree to **OM** as a counterpart to their contracts and to accept general conditions on margins and solvency carried by usual options trading.

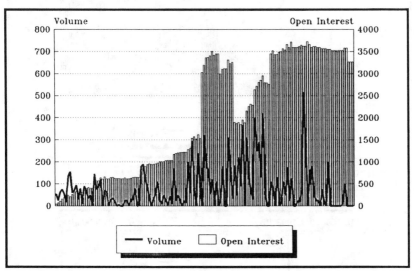

Daily Volume and Open Interest (Jan 2, 1990 - Jun 29, 1990)

Open Interest and Volume/Open Interest("Liquidity")
(Jan 2, 1990 - Jun 29, 1990)

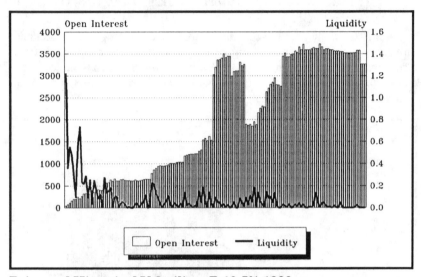

Price and Historical Volatility - B.12.5% 1992
(Jan 2, 1990 - Jun 29, 1990)

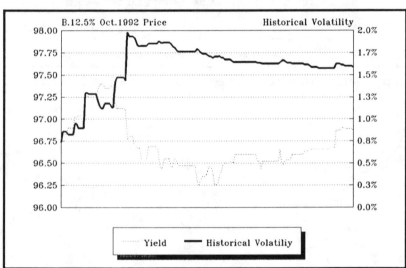

Price and Historical Volatility - B.10.0% May 1993
(Mar 21, 1990 - Jun 29, 1990)

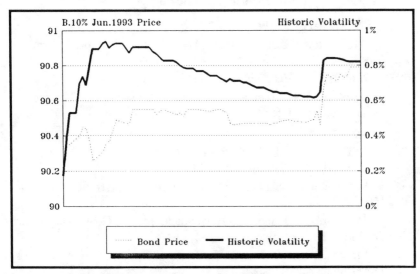

Price and Historical Volatility - B.10.0% Sep.1993
(Mar 21, 1990 - Jun 29, 1990)

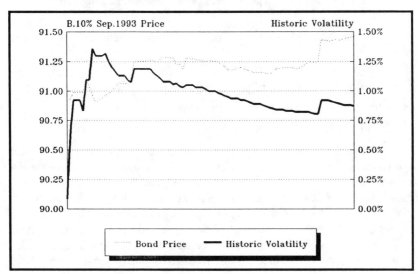

REGULATION

The following regulatory papers may be studied.

Real Decreto 505/1987

April 3, 1987: Regulation of the Book-entry System for Government Securities.

Ministerio de Economia y Hacienda. Orden.

April 19, 1987: Regulation of book-entry securities, "titulares de cuentas" and "entidades gestoras".

Ley 24/1988.

July 28, 1988: Regulation of capital markets.

Banco de España. Circular 12/1988.

September 8, 1988: Forwards book-entry market, trading and members.

Ministerio de Economia y Hacienda. Direccion General del Tesoro y Politica Financiera. Resolucion.

March 21, 1989: Forwards, Futures and Options markets on book-entry Government securities.

Real Decreto 276/1989.

March 22, 1989: Regulation of brokerage and dealing companies.

Real Decreto 717/1989.

June 23, 1989: Regulation of Stock Management and Stock Members.

Ley 4/1990.

June 29, 1990: Public Bedget. Some changes in the Capital Markets law concerning information and administrative controls.

TAXATION

Bonds traded in the Spanish forwards market are considered in tax regulation as financial assets yielding explicit interest. In such circumstances, capital earnings (in this case they are called "incrementos patrimoniales") carry no withholding tax. Financial corporations (the only institutions which can be accepted in the book entry market system) compute capital earnings through the difference between the selling price and the net accounted value. Tax rate on the profits is 35 per cent. As there are no contracts to be settled more than 6 months forward, it is not necessary to introduce time weightings on those earnings in income taxes. Capital losses can be compensated with capital earnings for 5 years.

The tax rate on capital earnings for non residents (corporations and individuals) is 35 per cent.

Tax regulation on futures and options, as well as on another financial assets, is still to be resolved. An important factor which will probably be introduced is a different tax treatment for hedgers and for speculating positions.

SOURCES of REFERENCE

Mercado de Futuros Financieros

Monthly reports   Informe de Actividades - "**MEFF**"

OM Ibérica

Daily report   OM Informa

Other information and simulation systems

OF 3000 by OM Ibérica

Ahorro Corporación is unique in the spanish financial system. The group is involved in all non banking financial activities. We are members of the Madrid and Barcelona stock exchanges, broker deales in the money and public debt markets, members of the Options and Futures market, investment managers, pension fund consultants, as well as administrators of life insurance companies. More over, we are an important participant in all Corporate Finance activities such as the underwriting of debt and equity securities and mergers and acquisitions.

We think that our competitive advantage lies in the quality of our research and our capacity to develop in-house software products and services.

Furthermore, the group enjoys the financial backing of the majority of Spanish Savings banks, who are our only shareholders. The above mentioned guarantees our independence and stability of our project.

Activities

- Stock-Broking.
- Money Market and Public Debt Broking.
- Underwriting (private and public placements).
- Mergers and Acquisitions.
- Asset Management.
- Actuarial and Pension Consulting.

- Life Insurance Administration.
- Fixed Income, Equity and International Markets Research.

Ahorro Corporación Helps you participate in and to understand the spanish futures and options markets

In October of 1989 the Spanish Options Market was created with a contract on a three year "notional" note. Today, there are contracts on 90 days MIBOR and treasury bills. Options on stock indexes has already been created. Ahorro Corporación is a member of O. M. Ibérica as well as an active participant.

Ahorro Corporación is also en active participant in the Barcelona financial Futures market (M.E.F.F.S.A.) created in the beginning of 1990 and where futures on 3 years "notional" and MIBOR '90 days are traded.

The above represent new markets, new opportunities and a bright future that you can share with us.

Address:
Cedaceros, 10
28014 Madrid (SPAIN)

Telephone:
(34-1) 586 93 00,
429 26 60 and 429 29 55

Fax:
(34-1) 429 69 81 and 429 91 84

Contact persons:
Jorge Virgili and Ignacio Cepeda

MUCH MORE
THAN JUST FINANCIAL
INTERMEDIARIES

Ahorro Corporación

OM

SPANISH OPTIONS AND FUTURES MARKET

AHORRO CORPORACION
FINANCIERA
Mr. Domingo Fernández
Tf: 34-1-4297287

ALGEMENE BANK
NEDERLANDEN,NV
Mr. Ignacio Andino
Tf: 34-1-5776044

ASESORES BURSATILES
Mr. Fernando de la Vega
Tel: 34-1-5801120

BANCAPITAL
Mr. Javier Novack
Tel: 34-1-3086050

BANESTO
Mr. Rafael Vidal Medero
Tel: 34-1-3194653

BANKERS TRUST
Mr. Crispin Wilson
Tf: 34-1-4105109

BARCLAYS BANK
Mrs. Nathalie Nicol
Tel: 34-1-3191254

BESTINVER
Mr. Juan Manuel Mazo
Tel: 34-1-3198162

BANCO BILBAO VIZCAYA
Mr. Benito Vivo
Tel: 34-1-3361447

BANQUE BRUXELLES
LAMBERT
Mr. Iñigo Barrera
Tel: 34 -1-5974818

CAIXA DE PENSIONS
"LA CAIXA"
Mrs. Francisco Romero
Tel: 34-1-5865100

CAIXA GIRONA
Mr. Isidre Blanch
Tf: 34-72-204729

CAJA POSTAL
Mr. Ignacio Plaza
Tel: 34-1-5219398

BANCA CATALANA
Mr. Monserrat Jiménez
Tel: 34-3-4043837

BANCO CENTRAL
Mr. José Luis Moreno
Tel: 34-1-3904140

DESCONTIBER
Mr. Andrés Villena
Tel: 34-1-4100114

DRESDNER BANK
Mr. Luis Bononato
Tel: 34-1-2625943

BANCO EUROPEO DE
FINANZAS
Mr. Francisco Martín
Tel: 34-1-5869700

BANCO EXTERIOR DE
ESPAÑA
Mr. Angel González
Tel: 34-1-5427504

BANCO HISPANO
AMERICANO
Mr. Ramón Barajas
Tel: 34-1-5227080

IBERCAJA
Mr. Carlos Fuentes
Tel: 34-76-232821

IBERDEALER
Mrs. María Pintado
Tel: 34-1-4352013

BBV INTERACTIVOS
Mr. Ignacio Fuertes
Tel: 34-1-5827893

BANCO PASTOR
Mr. Javier Barbolla
Tel: 34-1-5329904

BANCO POPULAR
Mr. Carlos Ramos
Tf: 34-1-5779763

RENTA 4
Mrs. Sara Marqués España
Tel: 34-1-5636238

SAFEI-SAMEDI
Mr. Jesús Bedmar
Tel: 34-1-4316159

BANCO SANTANDER
Mr. Emilio Osuna
Tel: 34-1-5972578

BANCO SANTANDER DE
NEGOCIOS
Mr. Lorenzo Goldberg
Tel: 34-1-4314286

SAUDESBANK
Mr. José Manuel Almira
Tel: 34-1-5760103

SERVICIOS MONETARIOS
Y BURSATILES
Mr. José Ramón Núñez
Tel: 34-1-5754440

S.I.A.F.
Mrs. Consuelo Díaz
Tel: 34-1-4103156

BANCO URQUIJO
Mrs. Consuelo Curiá
Tel: 34-1-3372326

OUR MEMBERS CHALLENGING THE FUTURE

OM IBERICA, Torre Picasso, Pta. 26
Pza. Pablo Ruíz Picasso, s/n
28020 MADRID (SPAIN)
Telephone: 34-1-5850800
Telefax: 34-1-5719542

The Futures & Options Markets in Sweden

Per E. Larsson
Stockholms Optionsmarknad
OM Fondcommission AB

INTRODUCTION

Option trading in Sweden was introduced on the initiative of the Stockholm Options Market, **OM**. Operations started on June 12, 1985 through the trading of standardized call options on six Swedish stocks listed on the Stockholm Stock Exchange. Sweden thereby became the sixth country to offer options trading of this type. The timing of organizing a futures and options exchange was perfect. In 1985, different OTC forwards contracts were introduced which put pressure on the level of understanding such derivative products. At the same time the Swedish capital market witnessed a volatile bond market and a bullish stock market which made the futures and options markets interesting for a variety of investors.

Options and futures trading in Sweden has grown at a spectacular rate. As against an anticipated daily trading volume of between 200 and 300 options contracts by the end of 1985, the actual average daily volume in that period was about 5,000 contracts. Today's market totals around 40,000 transactions a day. **OM** now lists options and futures related to stocks, a stock index, bonds and foreign currencies.

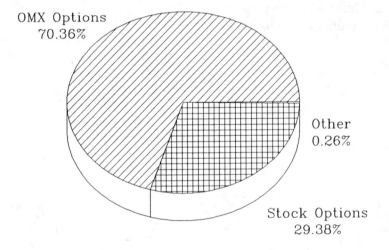

In March 1987, a second index options contract, the **SX16** options, was introduced at the Swedish Options and Futures Exchange, **SOFE**. The Exchange, in competition with the existing **OM**, was based on the open outcry concept with a separate clearing function, the Stockholm Clearing House

(SCH). SOFE and SCH ceased operations on January 1, 1989, mainly due to low volumes after the introduction of the Swedish securities sales tax.

Consequently, **OM** is now the only futures and options Exchange in Sweden. The Exchange operates independently from the Stockholm Stock Exchange and is based on a concept which contains integration of the marketplace and clearing functions.

ORGANIZATION of the MARKET

The marketplace is based on an electronic system combined with a block-order market handled by neutral block order officials at **OM**. The block-order market is a telephone market and is created to absorb the different kinds of complex demands occurring in the marketplace, such as conditional orders or complex strategies involving several contract parties.

OM has no members, in the traditional sense of the word. Never-the-less all transactions are agency transactions, and hence, the clients must use an intermediary when forwarding an order to the marketplace. Swedish banks, brokerage firms and a number of independent market makers are linked to the **OM** system, in which the former two act as intermediaries.

In order to absorb the demand for Swedish products in financial centers such as London, **OM** has established an Exchange on British soil, **OM London Ltd, OML**. As a Recognized Investment Exchange under the Securities and Investment Board **OML** will market Swedish options and futures to the UK investment community. Initially, **OML** offers trading and clearing in **OMX**-options and individual stock options. Other products, Swedish as well as international are planned to be introduced as the market develops. Through a trading link between **OML** and **OM**, participants in the **OML** market will have direct access to Swedish liquidity and vice versa, whereby important liquidity will be added to participants in the Swedish market, and liquidity in the joint marketplace will be guaranteed.

Investors residing outside Sweden may trade all products except those related to Swedish bank shares. However, foreigners may not exercise options on restricted shares.

Supervision and Control

OM, and the products traded thereon, operates under the super-vision of the Swedish Bank Inspection Board. In addition, **OM**, has voluntarily established routines for the monitoring of its own and its members activities, through a special control entity - Clearing Control. Trading at the Exchange is also supervised by trading controllers, designated by the Swedish Stock Brokers Association.

Ownership

OM has the following ownership structure; Swedish banks and brokerage firms that are active in the options market:

- **AB Investor**
- **AB Providentia**
- **Nobel Industries**
- **Volvo (Group Finance Sweden AB)**
- **Olof Stenhammar**
- **Skandia**
- **Trygg-Hansa**
- **and a number of additional companies and individuals.**

In total, **OM** has approximately 1,500 shareholders.

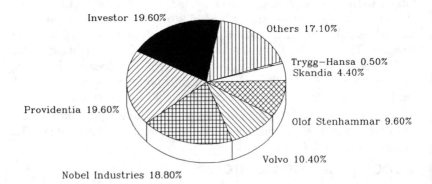

Investor 19.60%

Others 17.10%

Trygg-Hansa 0.50%
Skandia 4.40%

Providentia 19.60%

Olof Stenhammar 9.60%

Volvo 10.40%

Nobel Industries 18.80%

Board of Directors

Hans Werthén	Born: 1919. Chairman. Chairman of the Boards of AB Electrolux, Telefon AB LM Ericsson. Member of the Boards of Förvaltnings AB Providentia, AB Investor and Skandigen AB Board member since 1984.
Lars-Erik Forsgårdh	Born: 1942. President of the National Swedish Association of Shareholders. Chairman of the Board of Best Western Hotels, Sweden. Member of the Boards of Aktiefrämjandet and Aktievisionen. Deputy member of the Board of the Stockholm Stock Exchange. Board member since 1984.
Claes Dahlbåck	Born: 1947. President of AB Investor. Chairman of the Board of Skandigen AB. Member of the Boards or deputy member of ASEA AB, AB Astra, AB Electrolux, Fastighets AB Bevåringen, AB Papyrus and Åkermans Verkstad AB. Board member since 1984.
Björn Kårfalk	Born: 1944. President of Volvo Group Finance Sweden AB. Member of the Board of Argonaut AB. Member of the Board since 1989.
Thomas Nicolin	Born: 1954. President of E. Öhman J:or Fondkommission AB. Board member since 1987.
Olof Stenhammar	Born: 1941. President and CEO. Board member since 1984. Member of the Board of Export-Invest.

Address and Chief Executives

Olof Stenhammar
> President and CEO of the OM Group

Dag Sehlin
> Executive Vice President of the OM Group

Address:	The OM Group
	P.O.Box 16305
	S-103 26 STOCKHOLM
	Sweden
Tel:	(46) 8 700 06 00
Fax:	(46) 8 723 10 92

Telex:

15394 OPTION S

Per E. Larsson

President of Stockholm Options Market

Per-Jonas Carlsson

Executive Vice President of Stockholm Options Market

Address:	Stockholm Options Market
	P.O.Box 16305
	S-103 26 STOCKHOLM
	Sweden
Tel:	(46) 8 700 06 00
Fax:	(46) 8 723 10 92
Telex:	15394 OPTION S

Anders Nyrén

President of OM International

Sören Olausson

Executive Vice President of OM International

Address:	OM International
	P.O.Box 16305
	S-103 26 STOCKHOLM
	Sweden
Tel:	(46) 8 700 06 00
Fax:	(46) 8 21 62 59
Telex:	15394 OPTION S

Members

Aragon

Arapt Partners AB

Aros

Arbitech

B & B

Bank Societe Generale

Bergs

Bohusbanken

Cabanco
Carnegie
Consensus
DnC
Farel
Föreningsbanken
Första Aktiekontoret
Gotabanken
Göteberg
Hagströmer
Handelsbanken
Hägglöf & Ponsbach
JP Bank
Merchant
Montagu
Nordbanken
Opulencia
Partners
P Facklam
PK-Banken
Research & Trade
S-E Banken
Skaraborgsbanken
Skänska Banken
Stockholm AB
Stortorget AB
Swedebank
United Securities
Wermlandsbanken
Öhmans
Östgöta Enskilda Bank

OM London Ltd

OM established **OM** London to provide a marketplace and clearing function for options and futures based on Swedish stock and equity indices outside Sweden. Customers trading Swedish stock and equity indices at **OML** are quoted a combined price i.e. a price which reflects all bids and offers made through both **OM** and **OML**. However, trades ordered through the **OML** office are registered with **OML** as the counterparty. **OML** has been granted status as a Recognized Investments exchange by the Securities and Investment Board **SIB**. **OML** is one of a group of various Exchanges based on the **OM** concept - the concept upon which **OM** has established the Swedish derivative market. The **OM** subsidiary, **OM** International AB, has organized, in cooperation with local partners, options and futures Exchanges in France, Spain, Finland, a derivative clearinghouse in Norway and is in the process of transferring the **OM** system to an options and futures exchange in Austria (ÖTOB).In the future, common links will provide the various **OM** Group Exchanges with the possibility of trading each other's products.

As mentioned above, **OM** operates in an electronic marketplace, complemented by a block-order marketplace.

Electronic Market

All participants with direct access to the marketplace are connected by terminal and such participants place bid and ask orders via such terminals. Orders entered into the computer system are ranked in accordance with the following three criteria:

● **Price**

● **Market Maker order or Customer order**

● **Time**

Orders are primarily ranked on price. The time criteria ranks an earlier placed order ahead of an order placed later. On an identical price, a customer order will be ranked ahead of a Market Maker order regardless of the time the order was entered. When two orders match in the computer system a transaction is executed automatically by the computer. Clearing is effected by a simultaneous recording of the transaction in the accounts of the parties involved.

Block-Order Marketplace

OM provides a block-order marketplace where participants with direct access can enter into transactions by telephone with OM representatives who always act impartially in accordance with the trading rules. Ultimately, the block-order marketplace is intended to be more of a supplement to the electronic marketplace, to enable execution of large orders or orders involving combinations or conditions.

Telephone orders to the block-order marketplace are ranked according to price and the time the order is entered. OM personnel will not reveal the identity of a broker or Market Maker who places an order or who takes part in a transaction. For the purposes of price transparency, the best bid and ask price of the orders given will immediately be entered into the computer system, thereby providing for equal accessibility to block-order information in relation to electronic order-book information.

Participants in the OM marketplace can place orders in the block-order marketplace or the electronic marketplace. As described earlier, the types of order that can be accepted for each marketplace differ. To ensure price transparency between these two order books, there are price dissemination rules, which give parallel information from both marketplaces. Temporary differences in the prices offered are effectively arbitraged away by the Market Makers. Experience shows that the telephone based block-order system plays an important role in creating a center of liquidity with large blocks in the market.

OM has an electronically based block-order system, making it easy to link Exchanges. OM has a direct link with its subsidiary OML, providing trading and clearing on the same liquidity and open interest. Orders placed separately at one of these Exchanges are matched within the same block-order system.

Registration of Transactions

Trades made off the Exchange may be registered on the Exchange provided that they are contracts made in accordance with the General Conditions of OM and satisfy certain other criteria with respect to volume and price. If such contracts are accepted for registration they cease to be direct principal-to-principal contracts and become matching contracts between each contracting party and OM.

Clearing Function

By providing integrated marketplace and clearing functions, **OM** acts as both an Exchange and a clearing house. Through the clearing function, **OM** provides two important services, a clearing and guaranty function and an administrative function.

The administrative function includes registering of transactions concluded, calculating collateral requirements and ensuring the provision of collateral, delivery and payment routines. Only specially selected clearing members are granted the right to register transactions with the clearing organization. The transactions registered are either the clearing member's own transactions or transactions conclude on behalf of a customer.

Registration and the calculation of collateral are done at end-customer level. With respect to end-customer clearing, special accounts are opened for clearing member's customers. Nothing prevents the customer from having more than one account. The clearing member reports the customer account in which to register the transaction. Collateral is calculated separately for each customer's account, which is thereby individualized for each customer.

The system with end-customer clearing provided the possibility for the end-customer to provide collateral to the clearing member (and by the clearing member to the clearing organization, **OM**) or directly to the clearing organization. In the latter case, the clearing member does not have to provide collateral to the clearing organization for the customer's account.

The account structure concerning clearing of interest rate related options and futures contracts differs somewhat from that of the other products. In order for end-customers to act through several different banks and brokerage firms, while their total risk is calculated in one account. **OM** links several trading accounts to a single clearing account. The bank or brokerage firm that administers the customer's clearing account is referred to as the Clearing Account Holder.

This means that the end-customer can open a position via one bank or broker and then close it through another bank or brokerage firm. The customer's total position is registered in the clearing account. As a result, the net position in the clearing account is used to calculate margins, deliveries and payments.

Clearing and Guaranty Function

The guaranty function is fulfilled by OM entering as a legal party into all contracts traded in the marketplace, whereby OM acts as a guarantor for the fulfillment of every contract. Accordingly the counterparty risk on the derivative market is reduced to a credit rating of OM only. OM guarantees each contract by always offsetting the number of contracts written/sold with a number of contracts held/bought at the same transaction price and by requiring each participant to provide collateral corresponding to the risk associated with all accounts held by such participant.

Current Clearing Fees

Swedish Stock Options	
Trades	
Customer Transactions:	Variable clearing fee 0.5% of premium and a fixed clearing fee 1% of premium (minimum of SEK 6 and maximum SEK 14 - applicable to fixed fee).
Market Maker Transactions:	Fixed clearing fee 0.6% of premium (minimum SEK 1 and maximum SEK 8).
Exercise	
Customer Transactions:	0.45% less than 500,000 0.30% over 500,000 (50% Broker discount).
Market Maker Transactions:	0.45% less than 500,000 0.30% over 500,000 (80% Broker discount).

Swedish Stock Futures	
Exercise	
Customer Transactions:	Clearing fee 0.10% (minimum SEK 17)
Market Maker Transactions:	Clearing fee SEK 10.
OMX Index Options	
Trades	
Customer Transactions:	Variable clearing fee 0.5% of premium and a fixed clearing fee 1% of premium (minimum of SEK 6 and maximum SEK 14 - applicable to fixed fee).
Market Maker Transactions:	Fixed clearing fee 0.6% of premium (minimum SEK 1 and maximum SEK 8).
Exercise and Cash settlement	
Customer Transactions:	Variable clearing fee 0.5% of premium and a fixed clearing fee 1% of premium (minimum of SEK 6 and maximum SEK 14 - applicable to fixed fee).
Market Maker Transactions:	Fixed clearing fee 0.6% of premium (minimum SEK 1 and maximum SEK 8).

OMX Index Futures	
Trades	
Customer Transactions:	Clearing fee SEK 25.
Market Maker Transaction:	Clearing fee SEK 10.
Exercise	
Customer Transactions:	Clearing fee SEK 25.
Market Maker Transactions:	Clearing fee SEK 10.

Collateral

The collateral requirement is calculated according to the collateral calculation system (the **OMS** system). According to the **OMS** collateral calculation system, the collateral requirement calculated is sufficient to permit the termination of a customer's positions not later than two days from the time non-fulfillment occurred. The collateral requirement is established by applying historical statistical data to determine a valuation interval for the price of the underlying security. The positions registered in the account are then valued in a number of points within the valuation interval. The collateral requirement is based on the lowest value of the positions registered in the account within the valuation interval.

OMS is a collateral system based on the risks undertaken by each customer. As a result, the collateral each customer must provide reflects the total financial risk to which the customer is exposed when trading in options and futures contracts. In calculating collateral requirements, options held as well as purchased and sold futures contracts in which the customer has unrealized gains reduce the collateral requirements for the customers account. This is known as cross clearing.

The **OMS** provides the brokers with different kinds of information concerning risk management. In addition, a sensitivity analysis can be performed, using a PC-programme available from **OM**.In concluding a transaction with **OM**, a customer must himself, or through a broker, provide collateral for options written and for purchased or sold futures contracts.

Collateral for transactions concluded by a customer through a broker can be provided to **OM** directly, by the customer, or through a broker. The provision of collateral is regulated in the General Conditions. Collateral provided by the customer may take the form of a bank guarantee, a pledge and deposit of Treasury Bills or other negotiable instruments represented by physical certificates or other collateral approved by **OM**, which may include taking a fixed charge over a deposit account. If collateral is provided by the broker the preferred form is a bank guarantee, although a pledge on negotiable instruments or other collateral approved by **OM** may be acceptable. Collateral may be held by a Custodian Bank on the customer's account. Collateral may be provided by the customer in favour of the broker, to support a guarantee obligation which the broker has entered into on behalf of the customer. Such collateral is held by the broker on the customer's account with the broker, which is pledged to the broker. In such cases, the broker, in turn, provides collateral to **OM**, aggregated for the obligations of all such customers as well as for its own transactions. This collateral may be held by a Custodian Bank on the broker's account.

Administrative Services and Settlement

Trades executed via the electronic marketplace are cleared immediately and booked in the respective account. When a trade is executed over the telephone, and thereby a legal relationship between **OM** and the customer has been established, **OM**'s order officials will write a slip and immediately register the trade in **OM**'s clearing system through a terminal. After this, the clearing system takes over the trade. This means that all accounts are updated in real time and brokers with terminals can find all information about the trade in the terminal or through an **OM** ticker (a printer where information of all trades, or just the trades executed by the broker, is printed in real time), where the same information is available.

When the trading day is over, the night batch-clearing program (**NBCP**) becomes effective, operated by **OM**'s overnight personnel. The **NBCP** calculates, in accordance with procedures prescribed by **OM**, all payments for trades and the collateral balance for each account at customer level. In addition, it also performs the random selection, in case of exercise, and registers all exercises.

When all **NBCP** calculations are completed, all lists concerning **OMI** are printed. Such information contained may also be transmitted via electronic computer communication. The brokers, in turn, prepare notes for their customers.

The collateral lists are faxed each morning to the custodian banks. Before 11.00 a.m., they confirm by telefax to **OM**, that participants have provided sufficient collateral. Collateral must always be provided not later than the day after the trade is effected. **OM** also notifies its clearing bank concerning payments to be made, i.e. settlement payments and payments to customers resulting from exercise.

A participant who wants to cancel a trade must send a cancellation form to **OM**. Cancellations are implement by **OM** personnel, in accordance with the General Conditions.

Lists produced by the system consist of:

Settlement notes:	All trades effected by each customer during that day. This item contains information about broker, customer number, instrument, number of contracts, price and clearing fees.
Payment note:	The net of each customer's payments at a certain payment day with respect to all kinds of payments, i.e. settlement, exercise, cancellations etc.
Customer and Collateral list:	Account and collateral balance for all customers.
Exercise/delivery notes	All exercises effected during that day. Contains information about customer number, instrument, number of contracts, exercise price, fees and counterpart.
Confirmation of cancellation:	All cancellations effected during that day for a specific customer number.

The Associated Brokers, Banks, Market Makers and End-Customers

OM's end customers cannot deal directly with **OM**. A broker such as a Swedish bank or a brokerage firm, acts as an intermediary. The broker guarantees to **OM** that the end customer can fulfil his/her obligations in accordance with the terms of an option. The role of the broker is regulated in Swedish law and each broker is subject to supervision by the Swedish Bank Inspection Board.

To create liquidity in each series of options, **OM** has established a system of market makers. They have the obligation to quote bid and ask prices, with certain maximum spreads and minimum volumes, for the series of options for which they have market maker responsibilities. With this system, participants in the market are always able to buy or sell options in each series. The market maker may be a bank, a broker or another party approved by **OM**. To ensure efficient price quoting, **OM** engages a number of market makers for each series of options. Accordingly, the market makers and the brokers are the only parties who deal directly with **OM**. All other trades are agency transactions.

At present, approximately 50,000 end customer accounts are registered at **OM**, with a monthly average of 13,000 end customer accounts engaged in trading. The end customer is designated by a specific customer number, representing the customer's options account at **OM**. Accordingly, **OM** does not know the identity of the end customer.

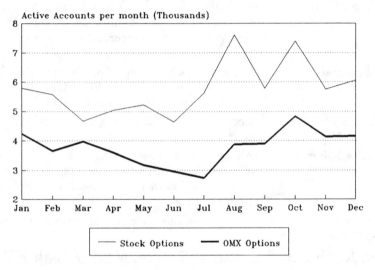

Education

The **OM** Exchange offers education through its subsidiary the **OM** Institute. Different levels of courses and seminars are provided ranging from beginner level to advanced market maker training. The **OM** Institute also provides tailor made taxation and rules and regulation seminars for different customer categories.

OVERVIEW of PRODUCTS

	Futures	Options
Interest Rates		
Notional Long Term Bonds	*	*
Notional Medium Term Bonds		
Notional Short Term Bonds		
Notional Treasury Note	*	
Bond Index		
Currencies		
US Dollar/Deutschemark	*	*
US Dollar/Swedish Krone	*	*
Equities		
Individual Stocks	*	*
OM Stock Index	*	*
Metals		
Commodities		

Comments: The list covers Exchange traded futures and options. The OTC market offers a variety of derivative instruments on bonds, Norwegian Krones, Foreign Exchange, metals and commodities.

HISTORY of the FUTURES & OPTIONS MARKET

Date of Launch	Type of Contract	Trading Volume (Monthly Average)
12 June 1985	Stock Options	227,928
16 March 1986	Interest Rate Options	0
18 December 1986	OMX (Index) Options	389,343
April 1987	OMX(Index) Forwards	317
7 October 1987	Stock Forwards	373
February 1989	Currency Options (US$/DM)	100
February 1989	Currency Futures (US$/DM)	0
April 1989	OMR2 Interest Rate Options	83
August 1989	Currency Options (US$/SEK)	636
August 1989	Currency Futures (US$/SEK)	37
17 April 1990	OMR7 Notional Bond Options	469
17 April 1990	OMR7 Notional Bond Futures	4,706

DETAILED CONTRACT SPECIFICATIONS
Interest Rates

On March 18, 1986, **OM** introduced standardized call and put options related to Swedish five-year Government bonds. Between 1986 and 1988, trading in these options was substantial. During 1987, **OM** recorded an average daily volume of approximately 3,500 options contracts, with a record of 10,000 contracts. Due to the introduction of securities sales taxes on Swedish options and forwards trading in January 1989, **OM** was forced to delist its highly successful interest-rate options. However, in response to market demand, **OM** introduced interest-rate options on five-year Government bonds in April 1989. An interbank forwards based on the same Government bond was introduced in April 1989 and averaged approximately 2-3 billion SEK during 1989.

In mid April 1990 the options and futures contracts based on a 7 year, 11 per cent notional bond were introduced as a bench market product on the market, also open for foreign investors.

Long Term 11.00% 7 Year Notional Bond OMR7 Futures Contract

Contract Size:	SEK 1,000,000.
Delivery Months:	March June September December.
Delivery Day:	
Last Trading Day:	At 12.00 noon six banking days before the settlement day.
Quotation:	Yield to maturity with two decimals eg 13.32%.
Minimum Price Movement (Tick Size and Value):	0.01 of the yield.
Trading Hours:	09.30 a.m. - 15.30 p.m. Stockholm time.
Initial Margin:	see OM's margin system.
Price Limit:	No price limit.

Contract Standard:	Physical delivery of government bonds with a duration not differing more than approximately half a year from the fixing using a conversion factor.
Reuters Pages:	OMOM onwards.
Telerate Pages:	

Treasury Bill Futures Contract- OMVX 180

Contract Size:	SEK 1,000,000 nominal value.
Expiry Months:	Six month contract from the March June September and December cycle.
Expiry Day:	IMM standars normally the third Wednesday in expiry month. If this is not a bank day the delivery day will be the following bank day.
Last Trading Day:	11.00 a.m. Stockholm time three bank days prior to expiration settlement day.
Quotation:	Six month rate.
Minimum Price Movement (Tick Size and Value):	
Trading Hours:	08.30 a.m. - 16.15 p.m. However om expiration day 08.30 a.m. - 13.00 p.m. Stockholm time.
Initial Margin:	see OMS system with valuation intervals of 1.5 percentage points.
Price Limit:	No price limit.

Contract Standard:	Cash settlement of all futures contracts against yield. Thereafter delivery of treasury bills at fixing of net position of all futures contracts. Treasury bills with maturity during the fifth sixth or seventh month after the futures expiration day are deliverable instruments.
Exchange Delivery Settlement Price:	The fixing yield determined in Statsfix at 11.00 a.m. (Stockholm time) on the expiration day of the futures contract which is derived from treasury bills with six months to maturity.
Reuters Pages:	
Telerate Pages:	

Currencies

Following the liberalization of Swedish foreign currency regulations, effectively July 1st 1989. **OM** began to list two currency contracts: options and futures in U.S.Dollar/Deutschemark and U.S.Dollar/Swedish Krona. Contract sizes are U.S.$ 50,000. The Deutschemark contract is notated **OMDM** and the Swedish Krona contract is notated as **OMDS**.

OMDM U.S.Dollar/Deutschemark Futures Contract

Contract Size:	US$ 50,000.
Delivery Months:	March June September December.
Delivery Day:	Two days before the third Wednesday in the expiration month.
Last Trading Day:	Expiration day.
Quotation:	DM 0.0001 per US$.
Minimum Price Movement (Tick Size and Value):	DM 0.0001 = DM 5.

Trading Hours:	09.30 a.m. - 16.00 p.m.
Initial Margin:	see OM's margin system (OMS).
Price Limit:	No price limit.
Contract Standard:	Physical delivery of net positions.
Reuters Pages:	
Telerate Pages:	

OMDM U.S.Dollar/Deutschemark Option

Option Style	European Calls & Puts.
Contract Size:	US$ 50,000.
Delivery Months:	March,June,September,December.
Delivery Day:	Two days before the third Wednesday in the Delivery month.
Last Trading Day:	Expiration day.
Quotation:	DM 0.001 per US$.
Minimum Price Movement (Tick Size and Value):	DM 0.0001 = DM 5.
Trading Hours:	09.30 a.m. - 16.00 p.m.
Initial Deposit:	see OM's margin system (OMS).
Price Limit:	No price limit.
Contract Standard:	Physical delivery with automatic exercise of all in-the-money options on expiration day.
Exercise Price:	2.5 pfennings per US$ intervals.
Reuters Pages:	

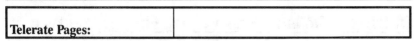

Telerate Pages:

Total Currency Option Statistics
Daily Volume and Open Interest (Jul 1,1989 - Dec 29,1989)

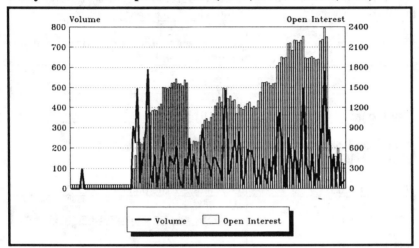

Open Interest and Volume/Open Interest(Liquidity) (Jul 1,1989 - Dec 29,1989)

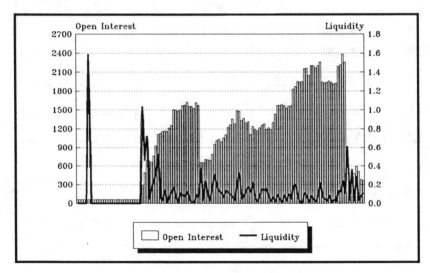

OMDS U.S.Dollar/Swedish Krone Futures Contract

Contract Size:	US$ 50,000.
Delivery Months:	Three and six month contracts. March June September December.
Delivery Day:	Two days before the third Wednesday in the expiration month.
Last Trading Day:	Expiration day.
Quotation:	SEK 0.01 per US$.
Minimum Price Movement (Tick Size and Value):	SEK 0.0001 = SEK 5.
Trading Hours:	09.30 a.m. - 16.00 p.m.
Initial Deposit:	see OM's margin collateral system (OMS).
Price Limit:	
Contract Standard:	Net physical delivery of expiration day positions.
Exchange Delivery Settlement Price:	
Reuters Pages:	
Telerate Pages:	

OMDS U.S.Dollar/Swedish Krone Options

Option Style	European Calls & Puts.
Contract Size:	US$ 50,000.
Delivery Months:	Three and six month options. March June September December.

Delivery Day:	Two days before the third Wednesday in the expiration month.
Last Trading Day:	Expiration day.
Quotation:	SEK 0.10 per US$.
Minimum Price Movement (Tick Size and Value):	SEK 0.0001 = SEK 5.
Trading Hours:	09.30 a.m. - 16.00 p.m.
Initial Deposit:	see OM's margin collateral system (OMS).
Price Limit:	
Contract Standard:	Physical delivery.
Exercise Price:	SEK 0.10 per US$ intervals.
Reuters Pages:	
Telerate Pages:	

Equities

In December 1986, **OM** introduced its **OMX** stock-index options, which are calls and puts related to the **OMX 30** stock market index. The **OMX** option is one of the most liquid index options outside the United States, with a daily average trading volume of 17,000 contracts between January and August 1989, and a record of close to 122,000 contracts during a single day.OM's index instruments were completed in April 1987, with the introduction of futures contracts based on the **OMX** index.The **OMX** index is based on the thirty most heavily traded stocks on the Stockholm Stock Exchange during the preceding quarter. It is designed to measure the market performance of the Exchange. The thirty stocks included in **OMX** account for approximately 65% of the total trading volume and 45% of the total market capitalization of the Stockholm Stock Exchange. **OMX** is a capital-weighted index.The **OMX** index was set at 500 on September 30th 1986, and since the trading start the index has been computed by Findata, an independent firm of indexers. **OMX** shows a high degree of correlation with all broad-based market indices in Sweden.OM also lists **OMX** futures. However, due to the high rate of securities sales taxes, virtually no trading is effected in theses futures.

Individual Stock Futures Contracts

OM lists stock futures for six stocks:-

- S-E-Banken
- Volvo B
- Skandia unrestricted
- Trelleborg B.
- Ericsson
- Elextrolux

However, due to the high rate of securities sales taxes, trading is almost nil. Stock forwards for unrestricted shares are available for both Swedish and non-Swedish citizens. Stock forwards for restricted shares are available for Swedish citizens only.

Contract Size:	100 shares.
Delivery Months:	Three and six month contracts. Two cycles are operated Volvo & Skandia (February,May,August,November-FMAN) and S-E-Banken & Trelleborg (January,April,July,October-JAJO).
Delivery Day:	Third Friday of the expiration month.
Last Trading Day:	The business day before expiration day.
Quotation:	SEK per share.
Minimum Price Movement (Tick Size and Value):	SEK 0.01 = SEK 1.
Trading Hours:	10 a.m. - 16.00 p.m.
Initial Deposit:	See **OM**'s Margin system (**OMS**).
Price Limit:	No price limits.

Contract Standard:	Cash settlement five days after expiration date.
Exchange Delivery Settlement Price:	
Reuters Pages:	
Telerate Pages:	

Individual Stock Options

Trading volumes have continued to increase ever since OM's inception in 1985. Between January and August 1990, daily trading volumes amounted to about 11,000 stock options related to sixteen underlying stocks.

Put options on seven stocks were introduced in June 1987. Due to the regulatory body's requirement regarding the fulfillment of delivery capacity in long put positions, stock put options were experiencing low trading volumes. these restrictions were lifted in May, 1990. Since then the volume of puts has increased.

Stock options are available for trading for both Swedish and non-Swedish citizens. With regard to stock options for restricted shares, they are, however, available for non-Swedish citizens only through Swedish brokers. In exercise situations concerning restricted shares, the Swedish broker will buy or sell the shares on behalf of the non-Swedish customer.

The following stock options are registered at OM.

Underlying Stock	Calls	Puts	Expiry Cycle
Asea A	*		FMAN
Astra A	*		FMAN
Atlas Copco A unrestricted	*		FMAN
Electrolux B unrestricted	*	*	JAJO
Ericsson B unrestricted	*	*	JAJO
Munksjö A	*		MJSD

Pharmacia B	*	*	JAJO
SAAB A	*		MJSD
SCA B	*	*	FMAN
S-E Banken	*	*	JAJO
Skandia unrestricted	*	*	FMAN
Skanska B	*	*	JAJO
SKF B unrestricted	*		MJSD
Svenska Handelsbanken	*		MJSD
Trelleborg B	*	*	JAJO
Trygg Hansa B	*	*	JAJO
Volvo B	*	*	FMAN

Option Style:	American calls and puts.
Contract Size:	100 shares.
Delivery Months:	3 and 6 month contracts with the following three expiry cycles 1. Jan Apr Jul Oct 2. Feb May Aug Nov 3. Mar Jun Sep Dec.
Delivery Day:	Third Friday in the expiration month.
Last Trading Day:	The day prior to expiration day.
Quotation:	Price per share.
Minimum Price Movement (Tick Size and Value):	SEK 0.01 = SEK 1.00.

Trading Hours:	10.00 a.m. - 16.00 p.m.
Initial Margin:	See OMS - OML's margin system.
Price Limit:	No price limit.
Contract Standard:	Physical delivery of shares.
Exercise Price:	Three contracts with exercise intervals of SEK 20.
Reuters Pages:	See Quote Vendors later.
Telerate Pages:	

Total Stock Option Volumes
Daily Volume and Open Interest (Jul 3, 1989 - Dec 29,1989)

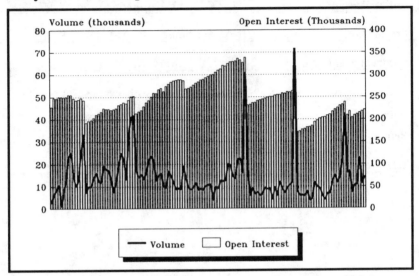

Open Interest and Volume/Open Interest(Liquidity) (Jul 3, 1989 - Dec 29,1989)

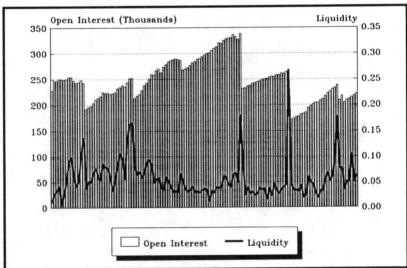

Astra B Free Shares
Price of Share History (Jul 3, 1989 - Dec 29,1989)

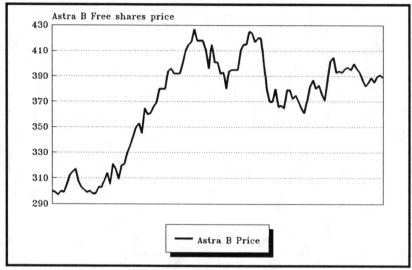

Implied and Historical Volatility (Jul 3, 1989 - Dec 29,1989)

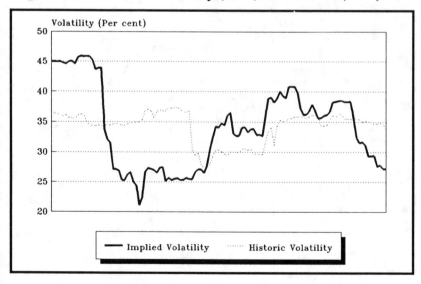

Electrolux B Free Shares
Price of Share History (Jul 3, 1989 - Dec 29,1989)

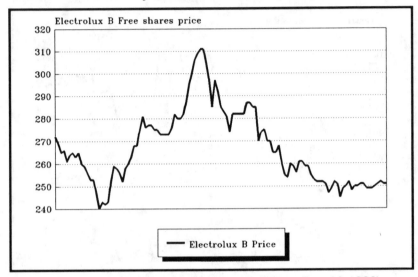

Electrolux B Free shares price

Electrolux B Price

Implied and Historical Volatility (Jul 3, 1989 - Dec 29,1989)

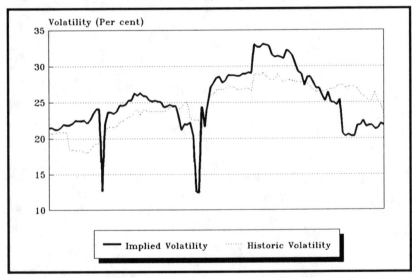

Volatility (Per cent)

Implied Volatility ..... Historic Volatility

Ericsson B Free Shares
Price of Share History (Jul 3, 1989 - Dec 29,1989)

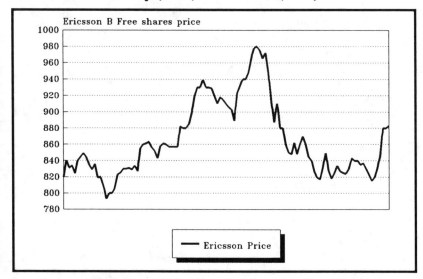

Ericsson B Free shares price

Implied and Historical Volatility (Jul 3, 1989 - Dec 29,1989)

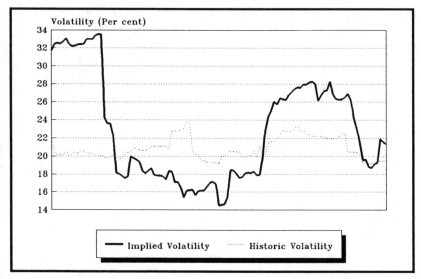

Volatility (Per cent)

Volvo B Free Shares
Price of Share History (Jul 3, 1989 - Dec 29,1989)

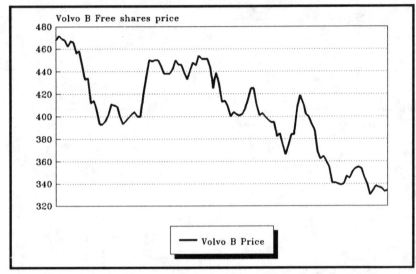

Implied and Historical Volatility (Jul 3, 1989 - Dec 29,1989)

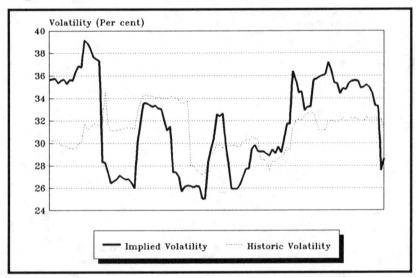

OMX (Stock Index) Option

In December 1986, OM introduced its **OMX** stock-index options, which are calls and puts related to the **OMX 30** Stock market index. The **OMX** option is one of the most liquid index options outside the United States, with a daily average trading volume of 17,000 contracts between January and August 1989, and a record of close to 122,000 contracts during a single day.

OM's index instruments were completed in April 1987, with the introduction of futures contracts based on the **OMX** Index.

The **OMX** Index is based on the thirty most heavily traded stocks on the Stockholm Stock Exchange during the preceding quarter. It is designed to measure the market performance of the Exchange. The thirty stocks included in **OMX** account for approximately 65 per cent of the total trading volume and 45 per cent of the total market capitalization of the Stockholm Stock Exchange. **OMX** is a capital weighted index.

The **OMX** Index was set at 500 on September 30th, 1986, and since the trading start the index has been computed by Findata, an independent firm of indexers. **OMX** shows a high degree of correlation with all broad-based market indices in Sweden.

Option Style	European Calls & Puts.
Contract Size:	Index values times 100.
Delivery Months:	All calendar months with contract lives of one,two and four months.
Delivery Day:	Fourth friday of the Delivery month.
Last Trading Day:	The business day prior to expiration day.
Quotation:	0.01 per cent of an option.
Minimum Price Movement (Tick Size and Value):	SEK 0.01 = SEK 1.
Trading Hours:	10.00 a.m. - 16.00 p.m.
Initial Deposit:	See OM's margin system (OMS).
Price Limit:	No price limit.

Contract Standard:	Cash settlement or physical delivery.
Exercise Price:	In units of 20 index point intervals.
Reuters Pages:	
Telerate Pages:	

OMX Index, based on the 30 stocks (Al-list) with the heaviest volume of trading on the Stockholm Stock Exchange. The Index is updated semi-annually. The Index value times the index multiplier equals currently 85,000.

Composition of OMX Index at 19 December 1989.

Aga	A restricted	Sandvik	B unrestricted
Aga	B unrestricted	SCA	B restricted
Alfa-Laval	B unrestricted	SCA	B unrestricted
Asea	A restricted	S-E-Banken	A restricted
Asea	B unrestricted	SHB	restricted
Astra	A restricted	Skandia	unrestricted
Atlas Copco	A unrestricted	Skansa	B restricted
Avesta	restricted	SKF	B unrestricted
Electrolux	B unrestricted	SSAB	A restricted
Ericsson	unrestricted	Stora	A restricted
Nobel Industries	restricted	Sydkraft	C restricted
Pharmacia	B unrestricted	Trelleborg	B restricted
Saab-Scania	A restricted	Volvo	B restricted
Saab-Scania	B unrestricted	Volvo	unrestricted

Daily Volume and Open Interest (Jul 3,1989 - Dec 29,1989)

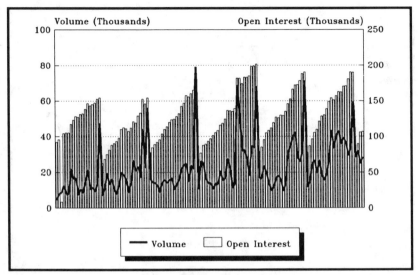

Open Interest and Volume/Open Interest(Liquidity) (Jul 3,1989 - Dec 29,1989)

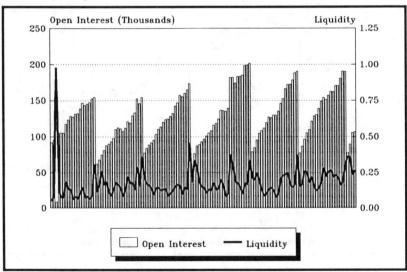

Price History (Jul 3, 1989 - Dec 29, 1989)

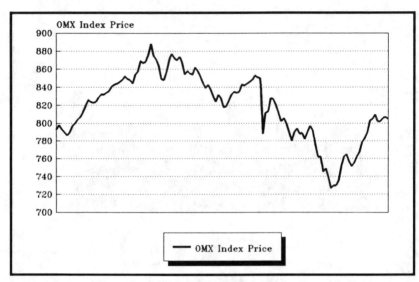

Implied and Historical Volatility (Jul 3, 1989 - Dec 29, 1989)

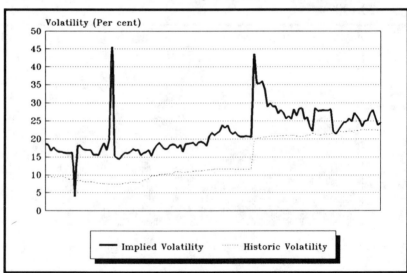

OMX (Stock Index) Futures Contract

Due to the high rate of securities dales taxes, virtually no trading is effected in these futures.

Contract Size:	Index times 100.
Delivery Months:	All calendar months with contracts lives of one,two and four months.
Delivery Day:	Fourth Friday in the Delivery month.
Last Trading Day:	The business day prior to expiration date.
Quotation:	0.01 per cent.
Minimum Price Movement (Tick Size and Value):	SEK 0.01 = SEK 1.
Trading Hours:	10.00 a.m. - 16.00 p.m.
Initial Deposit:	See OM's margin system (OMS).
Price Limit:	No price limit.
Contract Standard:	Cash settlement.
Exchange Delivery Settlement Price:	
Reuters Pages:	
Telerate Pages:	

OTC Products

Various OTC currency and interest-rate products are traded in Sweden. An interest-rate forward contract is traded OTC on the same underlying bond as the standardized OM interest-rate options. Such trading is basically carried out interbank and has also been negatively hit by the new securities sales tax.

REGULATION

The Securities Market Committee was set up by the Swedish Government on behalf of Parliament in the spring of 1987. The tasks of the Committee amounted to a complete reappraisal of Swedish legislation on securities markets. More specifically, the terms of reference covered such matters as stock exchange activities, market for the futures and options, stockbroking and other mediation of securities, insider transactions, market ethics and self-regulation, public supervision and corporate law issues relating to security transactions.

The work of the Committee will probably result in a new law governing Swedish securities markets that will be in effect by July 1, 1991.

TAXATION

On January 1, 1989, the Swedish government raised the sales tax on financial instruments. The increase comprised tax levies on proprietary trading by banks and brokers as well as a quadrupling of the tax rate on options trading for end-customers.In accordance with the new rules, futures trading is subject to tax on the transaction amount and not on the settlement amount. Due to the political motives behind the tax amendments, the government and the financial community engaged in a fierce debate on the subject.

The new taxes were introduced, and today taxes on stock and indices are levied at a rate of 2 percent on the premium for options and on the transaction amount for futures for both buyer and seller. Proprietary trading by brokers and market makers is subject to a 50 percent reduction on this level.

The Ministry of Finance declared in January 1990 that the tax would be abolished April 15,1990 on proprietary trading by Swedish banks and brokers (concerning stocks and indices) and on interest-rate products.

The tax on trading equity products for investors will be reduced with 50 per cent from January 1, 1991 according to the Ministry of Finance.

QUOTE VENDORS

Reuters and Telerate Pages

Reuters	
Information page	OMCA
Stock Options	OMCB - OMCE
Electronic trading Stock Options	OMCF -OMEU
Block-orders Stock	OMHH - OMIS
OMX Index Options	OMGL - OMGM
Electronic trading OMX Index Options	OMGN - OMGZ
Block-orders OMX options & forwards	OMHA - OMHC
Daily volume stock OMX currency interest rate options	OMHD - OMHE
Telerate	
Information page	20879

Providers of Data

Reuters
Telerate
Pont
SIX
Findata Dextel
Aktievision
Esselte Information
Front

The Futures and Options Markets in Switzerland

Philippe Bollag
Arthur Bänziger
Swiss Volksbank, Zurich

INTRODUCTION

Early in 1986, the three major Swiss Stock Exchanges, under the umbrella of Association Tripartite Bourses (**ATB**), together with the five big Swiss banks launched a joint-project - Traded Options & Financial Futures (**TO&FF**). This was done under the project management of the international consulting firm Arthur Andersen. The **TO&FF** project's task was the initiation of a Swiss Options and Futures Exchange that would allow risk management in the Swiss securities market. Switzerland has had a long tradition in OTC-markets such as foreign currencies, precious metals and covered warrants. In late 1986, **SOFFEX** Swiss Options and Financial Futures Ltd. was founded in Zurich as a public limited company. With a share capital of SFr. 5 million, the young TO&FF-project turned into a financially sound venture. **SOFFEX**'s purpose is the operation of a fully electronic exchange with an integrated clearing system (the first worldwide) for traded options and financial futures. On 19 May 1988,it successfully started trading calls and puts on eleven Swiss stocks. New contracts were introduced such as the index option on the Swiss Market Index (**SMI**) on 7 December, 1988 .This **SMI**-contract proved to be an attractive and volume-generating hedging and trading instrument. **SOFFEX**'s software for electronic options trading and clearing set new international standards. The Deutsche Terminboerse (DTB) has acquired the license for the **SOFFEX** software package which offers a sophisticated foundation for Germany's first electronic options exchange.

ORGANIZATION of the MARKET

When **SOFFEX** started trading on May 19, 1988, it was the world's first completely electronic exchange. For this achievement, **SOFFEX** has won the 1990 Computerworld Smithsonian Award. All trades at **SOFFEX** are being matched electronically, bid and ask prices may be hit directly on the computer's screen. The **SOFFEX** workstations are spread all over Switzerland with most of the market participants being located in Switzerland's financial canters of Zurich, Geneva and Lugano. The customer usually places his orders by telephone with a bank acting as broker; the bank in turn executes the order directly through **SOFFEX**'s computers. Trading hours are in the morning between 10.00 a.m. and 13.00 p.m. and in the afternoon between 14.00 p.m. and 16.00 p.m., in line with the cash market.

Shareholders

Association Tripartite Bourses	40 per cent
Credit Suisse	17 per cent
Swiss Bank Corporation	17 per cent
Union Bank of Switzerland	17 per cent
Swiss Volksbank	6 per cent
Bank Leu	3 per cent

Board of Directors

E. Mollet, Chairman	Senior Vice President of the Swiss Bank Corporation, Basle
Dr. G.P. Rossetti	Director of Union Bank of Switzerland, Zurich
P. Odier	Lombard, Odier & Cie, Geneva
Dr. J. Fischer	Bank J. Vontobel & Co.AG, Zurich
Prof.Dr. H. Zimmermann	University of St. Gallen (HSG), St. Gallen
W.M. Ochsner	First Vice President of Credit Suisse, Zurich

Membership

SOFFEX exchange membership is open to all Swiss banks, licensed securities traders and international brokers with offices in Switzerland. For new exchange members, the entry fee is SFr.120,000. **SOFFEX** offers its exchange members three different types of trading accounts:

Market Maker Account

A member running a market maker account takes on the obligation to provide the market with bid and ask quotes. The Rules and Regulations specify the detailed market maker obligations. Market maker transactions profit from considerable lower transaction costs.

Principal Account

Exchange members trading on their own account without holding a market maker license clear their exchange transactions through a principal account. The regular exchange fees are applicable.

Agent Account

All customer business is cleared by the agent account of the exchange member. The regular exchange fees are applicable.

SOFFEX Clearing Functions

SOFFEX offers its exchange members an integrated and fully electronic clearing organisation. Once a trade is matched in the exchange system, it is automatically routed to the clearing system. There, it is administratively processed and notice is given to the respective clearing members' back-offices. Only Swiss banks can apply for SOFFEX clearing membership. High standing and strict clearing membership requirements, as well as a daily margining on uncovered positions maintains the financial integrity of the SOFFEX clearing system. Three different categories of participants are distinguished in the SOFFEX clearing system:

General Clearing Membership (GCM)

The General Clearing Member (GCM) at SOFFEX are mainly identical with the shareholders:

> Union Bank of Switzerland (UBS)
>
> Swiss Bank Corporation (SBC)
>
> Credit Suisse (CS)
>
> Bank Leu
>
> Cantonalbank of Zurich
>
> Banca della Svizzera Italiana.

Swiss banks with a share capital of more than SFr. 500 million can apply for clearing membership whereby a guarantee of SFr. 5 million has to be deposited with SOFFEX Ltd. GCMs can clear their own trades, trades of their customers and trades generated by a Non-Clearing-Member (NCM) that have signed a GCM-NCM-contract.

Direct Clearing Membership (DCM)

Swiss banks with a share capital of more than SFr. 50 million can apply for clearing membership whereby a guarantee of SFr. 1 million is deposited with SOFFEX Ltd. DCMs can clear their own trades and trades of their customers.

Non Clearing Member (NCM)

A NCM is defined as a SOFFEX exchange member who is not member of the SOFFEX clearing system. To clear its transactions, a NCM has to establish a clearing relationship with a GCM.

SOFFEX is the counterparty to every transaction conducted. The commitments of SOFFEX are guaranteed by a pool of funds and/or guarantees which General Clearing Members (GCM) as well as Direct Clearing members (DCM) have to put up. In addition, the shareholders of SOFFEX (UBS, SBC, CS, SVB, Bank Leu) are liable to the extent of their respective holdings.

The Market Makers

The following provides an overview of the SOFFEX-Market Makers, indicating their commitment to quote in underlying shares and indices.

Bank	Committed to Quote
Bank Julius Bär	BBC ROG
Bank Hofmann	NES
Bank Leu	ALU BBC CSH NES ROG SBG
Bank Sogenal	RUKP
Bank J.Vontobel	ALU SANP SMI
BMP AG	BBC CSH JAC NES ROG SBG SBV SMI
Cantonal Bank Zurich	NES
Credit Suisse	ALU BBC CIG CSH NES ROG RUKP SANP SBG SBV ZUR SMI
Handels Bank	BBC
QT Optec AG	ALU CIG CSH JAC ROG SANP SBG SBV SMI
Swiss Bank Corporation	BBC CIG CSH JAC NES ROG SANP ALU SBG SBV RUKP ZUR SMI
Swiss Volksbank	ALU BBC CIG SBG SVB SMI
Union Bank of Switzerland	ALU BBC CIG CSH JAC NES ROG RUKP SANP SBG SBV SVB ZUR SMI

Types of Orders

Order	Characteristics	Transaction
Market	Without price limit	Immediate
Limited	At specified price or better	Immediate or within given period

Date Restrictions

Order	Characteristics	Transaction
Good for the day (GFD)	Daily order	Before closing of Exchange
Good till Canceled (GTC)	Standing order	Anytime until order canceled
Good till Date (GTD)	Valid until close of Exchange on a specified day or option expiration day	Anytime within given period

Execution Restrictions

Order	Characteristics	Transaction
Fill or Kill (FOK)	Must be executed fully	Immediate or it will be canceled
Immediate or Canceled (IOC)	Market or limit order	Immediate (whole or partial parts of the order which are not executed will be canceled)

Transaction Costs (as per December 31, 1989)

SOFFEX Exchange Fees in SFr.(payable to SOFFEX)

Options price		Fee per contract
From 00.10	to 4.99	0.25
From 05.00	to 9.99	0.25
From 10.00	to 19.99	0.75
From 20.00	to 39.99	1.50
From 40.00	to 59.99	2.50
From 60.00	to 79.99	3.50
From 80.00	to 99.99	5.00
From 100.00	to 149.99	7.00
From 150.00	to 249.99	8.00
From 250.00	to 499.99	11.00
Over 500.00		14.00

SOFFEX Commission in SFr.(payable to the broker)

Contract value		Commission (in %)		Cumulative	
				Value	Commission
until	2'000		80	2'000	80
next	2'000	1.00	20	4'000	100
next	3'000	0.9	27	7'000	127
next	3'000	0.8	24	10'000	151
next	10'000	0.7	70	20'000	221
next	10'000	0.6	60	30'000	281

next	20'000	0.5	100	50'000	381
next	50'000	0.4	200	100'000	581
over	100'000	0.3	581 plus 0.3% of excess over SFr100'000		

Reductions for securities dealers & brokers

Margins

Margin payments are claimed when short option transactions are not covered by respective underlying positions. SOFFEX has set a minimum margin requirement. Banks and brokers are free to claim higher margin payments. The following represents a brief overview of the margining process:

	Stock Options	Index Options
In-the-money & At-the-money	Option price plus 10 per cent of underlying stock's settlement price	Option price plus 5 per cent of underlying stock's settlement price
Out-of-money	Option price plus 5 per cent of underlying stock's settlement price	Option price plus 2.5 per cent of underlying stock's settlement price

SOFFEX System Engineering

The SOFFEX system solution for trading and clearing is implemented on computer hardware and system software from Digital Equipment Corporation (DEC). DEC's VAX system architecture and VMS operating system provide a range of compatible computer equipment to support the SOFFEX central trading and clearing system, communication network and user device. A two processor VAX 8700 Cluster performs transaction processing and data base updates for SOFFEX's central trading and clearing system. Depending on the anticipated amount of use, members may choose user devices ranging from a VAX station 2000 to a cluster of large scale VAX processors. The SOFFEX network for on-line trading and clearing functions consists of a backbone network of Communications Servers connected via dedicated lines to the central processors and Members' user devices. Micro VAX II processors are used for the Communications Servers. Multiple Communications Servers are located in Zurich, Geneva and Basle. Exchange members are able to receive back-office and report data via **TKNetz**. **TKNetz** is used to send and receive data from **SEGA** (Swiss securities clearing organisation).

Back Office

Operation of a sophisticated back office system is required from each **SOFFEX** exchange member. The members' auditors have to report to **SOF-FEX** on a regular basis that the high back office standards set by **SOFFEX** are met. As **SOFFEX** is providing electronic data feed to the members' back offices automated data processors are required. In a detailed study, **SOFFEX** has evaluated the various back office solutions and makes recommendations which are available at **SOFFEX**.

SOFFEX Educational Support

For basic training purposes, **SOFFEX** offers the PC-assisted Guided Auto-training Program (**GAP**) which gives a broad introduction into options and futures trading at **SOFFEX** in English, German, French and Italian. The **GAP**-Course can be publicly attended. For larger institutions, it is worthwhile to acquire the **GAP**-license for in-house training.

It has already become a tradition that the Swiss Options and Financial Futures International Conference **SOFFIC** is annually held in the skiing resort of Interlaken where specialists from theory and practice in the derivative markets meet.

Management

Mr. Otto E. Nägeli, Chief Executive Officer
Address: **SOFFEX** Swiss Options and Financial
          Futures Exchange AG
          Neumattstrasse 7
          CH-8953 Dietikon
Telephone: 0041-1-740.3020
Telefax: 0041-1-740.1007
Telex: 828 393

Auditors

KPMG Fides Peat, Zurich

OVERVIEW of PRODUCTS

	Futures	Options
Swiss Interest Rates	(1)	
Swiss Market Equity Index (SMI)	(1)	*
Individual Equities		*

(1) Contracts in planning.

DETAILED CONTRACT SPECIFICATIONS

Interest Rate Contracts

Swiss Franc Interest Rate Futures Contract (in Planning)

A futures contract on Swiss Franc Interest Rates is currently being developed by SOFFEX. So far, it is unclear whether this contract will be based on the short or the long end of the yield curve; the underlying instrument is also still in discussion. Most probably, such a contract will not be introduced prior to early 1991.

Equity Index

Swiss Market Index ("SMI") Options Contract

SMI is a new Swiss Index developed for the trade of a stock index option at SOFFEX. Currently, SMI comprises twenty four bearer shares or participation certificates of the twenty largest Swiss companies. The securities are weighted according to their capitalization on the Stock Exchange. The diversification of securities in SMI guarantees a well-balanced reproduction of the Swiss stock market. Sale and purchase of SMI options are similar to sale and purchase of other SOFFEX stock options. The only difference in the two options is their settlement method. For stock options, contractual fulfillment is via physical delivery of securities and for index options via cash settlement.

SMI options volume averaged well above 10,000 contracts a day during the first quarter of 1990, a period when the Swiss stock markets were well under pressure. During the second quarter of 1990, in a much more favourable stock market environment, daily trading volume amounted on average to above 20,000 contracts per day. Open Interest reached a peak of nearly 110,000 contracts in May 1990. These figures compare very well with other European Options Markets and illustrate the liquidity of the SMI-Options.

Option Style	European Calls and Puts.
Contract Size:	SFr5.0 per index point i.e. SFr7,500 at an SMI of 1,500 points.
Expiry Months:	1,2 & 3 months plus January April July October.
Expiry Day:	Saturday after the third Friday of the expiry month.
Last Trading Day:	Third Friday in the expiry month. If that day is not a business day the first business prior to the third Friday.
Quotation:	Per cent of par.
Minimum Price Movement (Tick Size and Value):	SFr0.10 = SFr0.50 per index point.
Trading Hours:	10.00 a.m. - 16.00 p.m.
Initial Margin:	Minimal margins are fixed by SOFFEX. The bank retains the right to collect higher margins.
Price Limit:	No price limit on the option. However
Contract Standard:	Cash settlement of the difference between index and contract value.
Exercise Price:	Three contracts are traded with exercise intervals of 50 index points.
Exchange Delivery Settlement Price:	The index value at 11.00 a.m. on the third Friday of the expiry month.

Reuters Pages:	SSMI
Telerate Pages:	None

Composition of the Swiss Market Index (SMI)

Listed below are the stocks which make up the SMI, along with their correlation to the SMI as expressed by the two year Beta-Factor (as per September 30, 1989).

	2 year Beta
Transportation sector	
Swissair	1.0
Bank sector	
Union bank of Switzerland (bearer)	1.0
Union bank of Switzerland (part.cert)	0.9
Swiss bank Corporation (bearer)	0.8
Swiss bank Corporation (part.cert.)	0.8
Credit Suisse Holding (bearer)	0.9
Credit Suisse Holding (part.cert.)	0.9
Swiss Volksbank (co-op.cert.)	0.7
Insurance sector	
Swiss Reinsurance (part.cert.)	1.2
Winterhur Insurance (bearer)	1.1
Zurich Insurance (bearer)	1.2

Industrial sector	
Adia (bearer)	1.0
Asea Brown Boveri (bearer)	1.0
Oerlikon-Buehrle (bearer)	1.3
Ciba-Geigy (bearer)	1.1
Ciba-Geigy (part.cert.)	1.2
Electrowatt (bearer)	0.7
Holderbank (bearer)	0.8
Jacobs-Suchard(bearer)	0.9
Nestle (bearer)	1.0
Pargesa (bearer)	0.6
Pirelli (bearer)	0.7
Roche Holding (depot cert.)	0.8
Sandoz (part.cert.)	1.2

SMI Index Specifications

Index:	Swiss Market Index
Symbol:	SMI
Index shares:	Comprised of 24 shares of the 20 most important Swiss companies.
Capitalization:	Approx. 40 per cent of the total market as of June 30,1989.

Calculation:	Continuous after every price paid at the stock exchanges in Basle.
Index basis:	1'500 index points as of June 30,1989.
Weighting:	The number of the actual shares issued.
Dividends:	No dividend adjustments.

Daily Volume and Open Interest (Jan 2,1990 - Jun 29,1990)

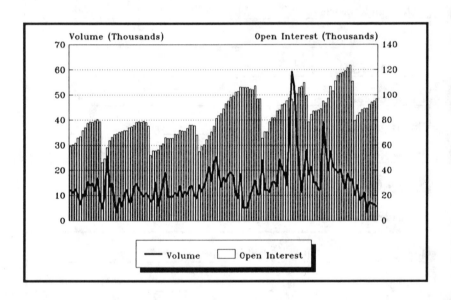

Open Interest and Volume/Open Interest("Liquidity")
(Jan 2,1990 - Jun 29,1990)

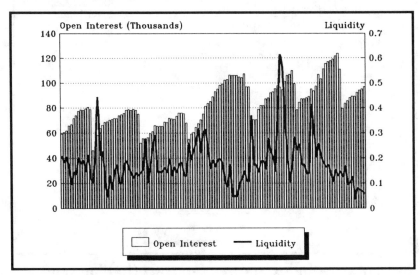

Price of the Swiss Market Index

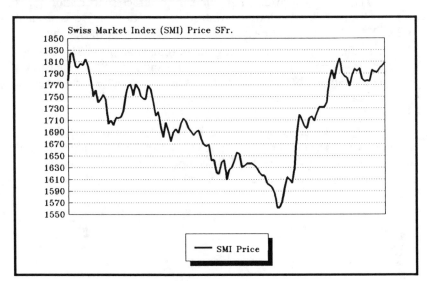

Implied Volatility (Jan 2,1990 - Jun 29,1990)

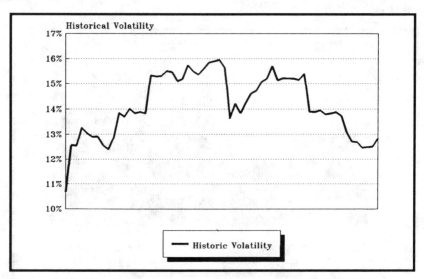

Swiss Market Index Futures Contract (in Planning)

This section provides a preliminary contract specification for a future on the Swiss Market Index; the introduction of this contract is planned for late 1990. The specification is included for reference purposes only.

Preliminary work concerning the introduction of the SMI-Futures Contract was completed in mid-1989. Programming the SMI-applications began in the fall of 1989; software test runs are foreseen for October 1990. Given satisfactory test results, the SMI-Futures may start trading in November 1990.

SOFFEX's exchange role will not change with the addition of a futures product. The primary role of SOFFEX is to provide a competitive and liquid marketplace, by means of a fully computerized exchange system. The Clearing House functions of SOFFEX will also not change with the new futures contract.

Contract Size:	SMI level times trading unit (e.g. 1550 x SFr.50 = SFr. 77,500).
Expiry Months:	The three months closest to the current date plus one month from the January April July October cycle.
Expiry Day:	Saturday after the third Friday of the month.
Last Trading Day:	Third Friday of the delivery month. If the third Friday is not a business day the previous business day.
Quotation:	SFr0.1.
Minimum Price Movement (Tick Size and Value):	SFr0.1 = SFr5.00.
Trading Hours:	Opening will begin shortly after the start (10.00 a.m.) of continuous trading of the Zurich Stock Exchange. Trading will stop fifteen minutes after continuous trading has stopped (16.00 p.m.) at the Zurich Stock Exchange. (These are the same as for SMI options.)
Initial Margin:	SFr.5,000.
Price Limit:	No price limit. But if trading in the underlying assets stop trading in the future ceases to trade - see SMI option.
Contract Standard:	Cash settlement of difference between index and contract value.
Exchange Delivery Settlement Price:	The index value at 11.00 a.m. on the third Friday of the expiry month.
Reuters Pages:	SSMI
Telerate Pages:	None

Individual Stock Options Contracts

The composition of the 13 underlying shares will change during late 1990. First of all, with the takeover of Jacob Suchard AG this stock will be delisted by **SOFFEX**, most likely by end September. With October 1990 maturity, the options contract on Swiss Volksbank will also disappear, due to lack of interest and volume. As an addition to the remaining eleven shares, an options contract on Swissair bearer shares will be added during the course of November 1990.

The **SOFFEX** options on individual shares are offering a varying degree of liquidity, the series on Union Bank of Switzerland, Swiss Bank Corporation, Roche Holding as well Swiss Aluminium offer the best liquidity and relatively tight bid/ask. Even though the liquidity may at times be somewhat limited, especially in the insurance sector, the **SOFFEX** Rules & Regulations guarantee the quoting of a two way price on all the options traded on the exchange.

At **SOFFEX**, the options investor may choose among 13 different underlying shares, which are:

Stock	Ticker Symbol	
	Investdata	Reuters
Financial Sector		
Union Bank of Switzerland (UBS) - bearer	UBS	SBGZ
Swiss Bank Corporation (SBC) - bearer	SBV	SBVZ
Credit Suisse Holding (CSH) - bearer	CSH	CSHZ
Swiss Volksbank (SVB) - co-operative share	SVB	SVBZ
Insurance Sector		
Swiss Re-Insurance - participation cert.	RUKP	RUKP
Zurich Insurance - bearer	ZUR	ZURZ
Industrial Sector		

Roche Holding - Genussscheine	ROG	ROCZ
Ciba Geigy -bearer	CIG	CIGZ
Sandoz - participation cert.	SANP	SANZ
Asea Brown Boveri - bearer	BBC	BBCZ
Swiss Aluminum - bearer	ALU	ALUS
Food Manufacturing Sector		
Nestle - bearer	NES	NESZ
Jacobs-Suchard - bearer	JAC	JACZ

The following contract specifications apply to stock options traded on the above underlying shares:

Option Style	American Calls and Puts.
Contract Size:	5 stocks per contract.
Position limits:	Fixed by **SOFFEX** (see below).
Expiry Months:	1,2 & 3 months plus January April July or October settlement dates (Third Friday in month of expiry).
Expiry Day:	Saturday after the third Friday in the expiry month.
Last Trading Day:	Third friday in the expiry month. If that day is not a business day the previous business day.
Quotation:	SFr to two decimal places.
Minimum Price Movement (Tick Size and Value):	SFr1 = SF5.

Trading Hours:	10.00 a.m. - 16.00 p.m.
Initial Margin:	Minimal margins are fixed by **SOFFEX**. The bank can collect higher margins.
Price Limit:	No price limit in the option. However trading in the underlying equity will cease trading if the price changes by more than 10 per cent (although this is in the control of the Exchanges). This will result in option ceasing to trade.
Contract Standard:	Physical delivery of underlying stock.
Exercise Price:	At least three exercise prices in the region of the share price are fixed by **SOFFEX**.
Reuters Pages:	See following table.
Telerate Pages:	None

Position Limits

SOFFEX has imposed the following position limits on the individual stocks (expressed in **SOFFEX**-contracts, per market participant):

Underlying Stock	Position limit
Swiss Bank Corporation	30,000
Credit Suisse Holding	7,500
Roche Holding	7,500
Swiss Reinsurance	7,500
Union Bank of Switzerland	7,500
Sandoz	5,000
Swiss Aluminum	5,000

Swiss Volksbank	2,500
Asea Brown Boveri	2,500
Ciba Geigy	2,500
Nestle	2,500
Jacobs-Suchard	1,000
Zurich Insurance	1,000

Swiss Aluminium
Daily Volume and Open Interest (Jan 2,1990 - Jun 29,1990)

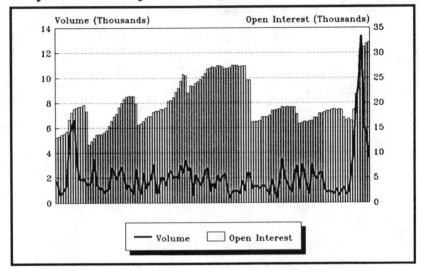

Open Interest and Volume/Open Interest("Liquidity")
(Jan 2,1990 - Jun 29,1990)

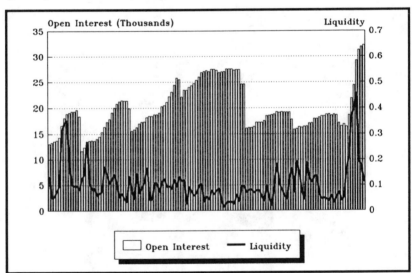

Price of Swiss Aluminium Stock

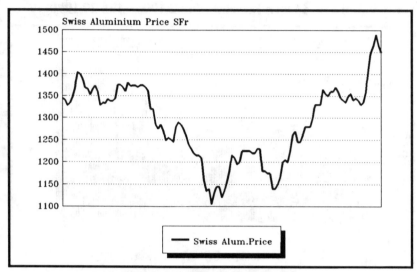

Historical Volatility (Jan 2,1990 - Jun 29,1990)

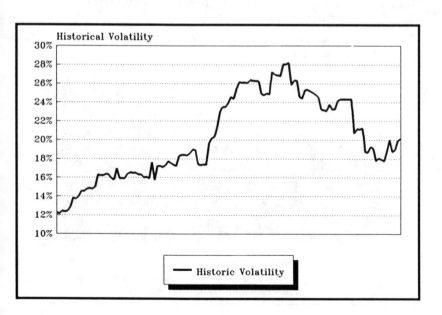

Roche Holding
Daily Volume and Open Interest (Jan 2,1990 - Jun 29,1990)

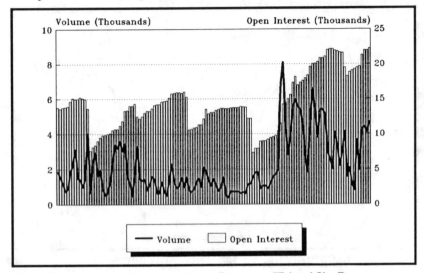

Open Interest and Volume/Open Interest("Liquidity")
(Jan 2,1990 - Jun 29,1990)

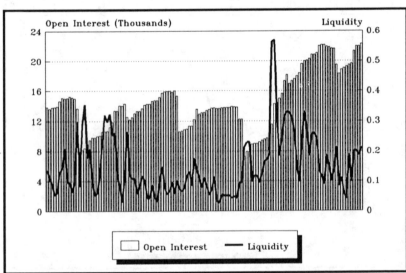

Price of Roche Holdings Stock (SFr)

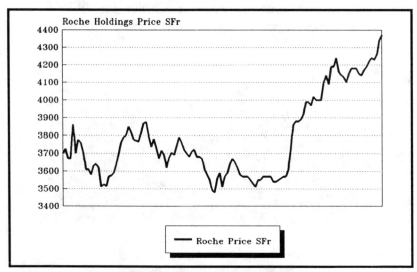

Historical Volatility (Jan 2,1990 - Jun 29,1990)

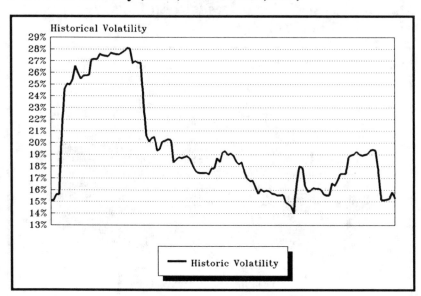

Union Bank of Switzerland
Daily Volume and Open Interest (Jan 2,1990 - Jun 29,1990)

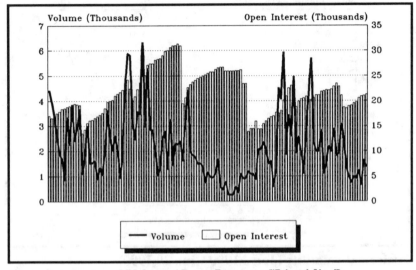

Open Interest and Volume/Open Interest("Liquidity")
(Jan 2,1990 - Jun 29,1990)

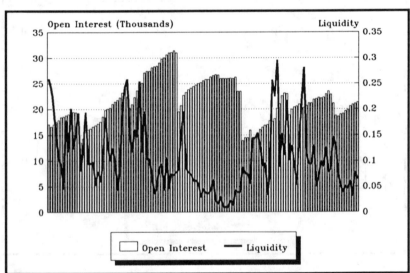

Price of Union Bank of Switzerland Stock (SFr)

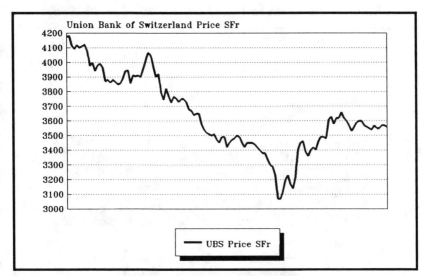

Historical Volatility (Jan 2,1990 - Jun 29,1990)

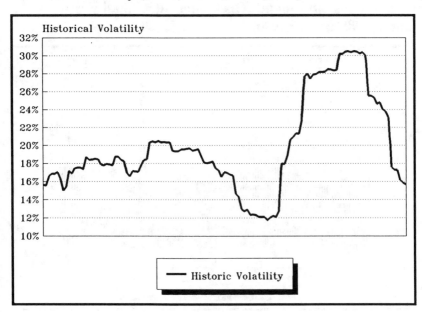

Swiss Bank Corporation
Daily Volume and Open Interest (Jan 2,1990 - Jun 29,1990)

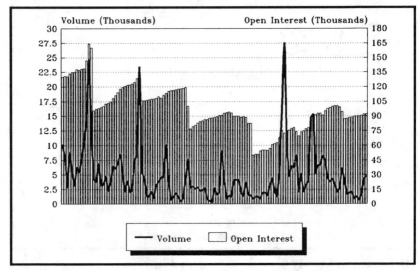

Open Interest and Volume/Open Interest("Liquidity")
(Jan 2,1990 - Jun 29,1990)

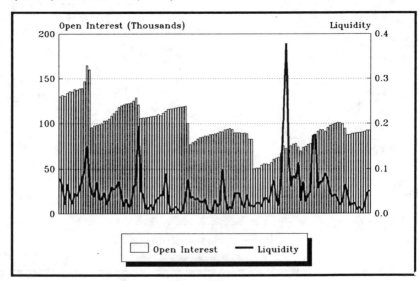

Price of Swiss Bank Corporation Stock (SFr)

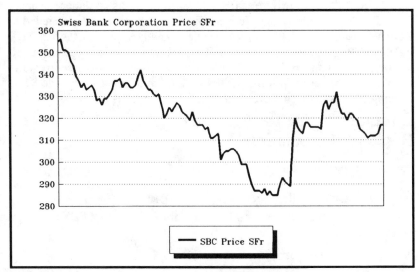

Historical Volatility (Jan 2,1990 - Jun 29,1990)

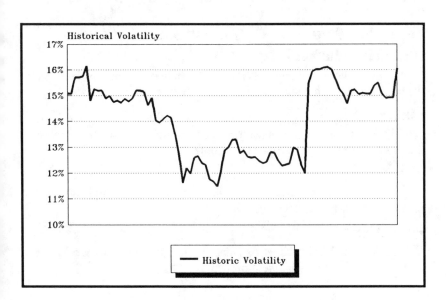

REGULATION

SOFFEX is a private share-holding company listed under the name **SOFFEX** Swiss Options and Financial Futures Exchange Ltd. domiciled in Zurich, Switzerland. **SOFFEX**'s self-regulatory body is based on the **SOFFEX** Rules and Regulations which are similar to Anglo-American exchange and clearing house constitutions. An authorized auditing company controls the member's compliance with the **SOFFEX** Rules and Regulations. The Swiss banking secrecy laws can nevertheless be fully respected.

Circular no. 807 Dated April 8, 1988 by the Swiss Bankers Association

Following topics are regulated:

Compulsory Exchange Trading Rule

SOFFEX contracts must be traded through the **SOFFEX** exchange clearing system.

Managed Accounts

The use of options and futures in managed accounts is limited for hedging transactions. However, the client can explicitly specify extended transactions.

Terms for Trading in Options on Securities and Financial Market Instruments

The client confirms with the signing of above-mentioned terms that the bank or broker has submitted the risk disclosure statement.

Position Limits

The signing of the same terms is committing the client to comply with the position limits stipulated for each contract.

Margining

On uncovered positions, the client is debited with margins calculated on a daily mark-to-market valuation.

Executions

The bank or broker is assigning executions to its customers based on an adequate random assignment procedure.

Basic and Advanced Education

It is the bank's or broker's obligation to adequately train its staff involved in options trading.

Organization and Control

The bank or broker is committed to an adequate front- and back-office organisation as well as setting up an internal control.

This circular had been ratified before the introduction of financial futures contracts at **SOFFEX**.

TAXATION
Stamp Duties (turnover taxes)

Trading with traded options and financial futures is not subject to stamp duties. Stamp duties are only owed in case of delivery of the underlying security.

Withholding taxes

Capital gains originated from trading in traded options and financial futures are not subject to withholding taxes.

Direct Taxes

Private persons are principally not subject neither to direct federal taxes nor to direct cantonal taxes (except the Cantons of Grisons, Jura and City of Basle).

Profits and losses with legal entities (companies) are regularly accounted in the P&L-statement and are taxes are levied accordingly.

Capital taxes

No capital taxes are levied on private persons holding positions in traded options and financial futures. For legal entities, specified capital accounting and tax regulations are to be applied.For further tax information, please contact a Swiss local tax lawyer.

EXCHANGE CONTROLS

Unlike most of the world's other financial centers, Switzerland's stock exchanges are to a large degree self-regulated. The rules and regulations laid down by the exchange members need to be approved by the cantonal authorities and a cantonal commissioner supervises this framework at the exchange. Switzerland knows no formal government agency regulating the exchanges. Legislation on insider dealing has been changed recently and makes such transactions a criminal act.

QUOTE VENDORS

SOFFEX call and put prices are being distributed under the following Reuters page codes:

Swiss Market Index	SWI*.Z (Chain)
Union Bank of Switzerland	SBGZ*.Z (Chain)
Swiss Bank Corporation	SBVZ*.Z (Chain)
Credit Suisse	CSHZ*.Z (Chain)
Swiss Volksbank	SVBZ*.Z (Chain)
Swiss Re-Insurance	RUKZ*.Z (Chain)
Zurich Insurance	ZURZ*.Z (Chain)
Roche Holding	ROCZ*.Z (Chain)
Ciba Geigy	CIGZ*.Z (Chain)
Sandoz	SANZ*.Z (Chain)
Asea Brown Boveri	BBCZ*.Z (Chain)
Swiss Aluminium	ALUS*.Z (Chain)
Nestlé	NESZ*.Z (Chain)
Jacobs-Suchard	JACZ*.Z (Chain)

In addition to reuters, the Investdata System also distributes the **SOFFEX** price information.

SOURCES of REFERENCE

Press coverage, including price and volume information, of **SOFFEX** activities may be found primarily in the "Neue Zurcher Zeitlung" and the "Finanz & Wirtschaft". In addition, **SOFFEX** publishes its own newsletter on a quarterly basis. Various publications concerning **SOFFEX**-products may be ordered directly from **SOFFEX** in Dietikon/Zurich.

Price Information

SOFFEX quotes and prices are being distributed on-line through the Investdata-System offered by Telekurs AG, Reuters and a number of smaller data vendors such as Pont Data. In addition to the straight price and quote information, Telekurs offers along with Ecofin Ltd. theoretical values as well as a number of other relevant option data.

GENERAL SOURCES of INFORMATION

For brochures and general information on **SOFFEX** and its products please contact **SOFFEX** directly. The **SOFFEX**-Member banks may also be contacted either locally or in Switzerland for any queries.

The Futures and Options Markets in the United Kingdom

Stuart K. McLean

The Authors for each Exchange are named at the beginning of the section on the Exchange

Introduction

The United Kingdom has been a major trading nation and as such
has developed London into one of the leading financial centres, not only in
Europe but also in the world. Indeed, the commodity Exchanges can be traced
back to the 16th century. The 1980s has seen a concerted effort to make
London one of the leading centres for financial derivative products. With the
advantage of its position in the world time zone, it is hoped that it will, with
the United States and Tokyo, become one of the major three. Therefore,
several new Exchanges have been formed:

London Traded Options Market - LTOM	1978
International Petroleum Exchange - IPE	1980
London International Financial Futures Exchange - LIFFE	1981
London Futures & Options Exchange - LondonFOX	1987
Baltic Futures Exchange - BFE	1987
OM London - OML	1989

While the growth in futures and options trading has in the past been relatively slow, it is now beginning to grow. One of the main reasons for this
slow start has been the problems for investors concerning taxation of these
products. This is discussed more fully later. The 1988 and 1990 Budgets
have cleared up any confusion. It is expected that trading volumes will ac-
celerate. This is reflected in the figures for the first half of 1990 when compared with those of the first half of 1989, which show LIFFE growing by 48
per cent, LME by 18.6 per cent, London FOX by 23 per cent and IPE by
36 per cent (LTOM's volume fell by nearly 12 per cent) against a world
wide trend showing a fall of 3 per cent. London's main European rivals,
such as MATIF grew by 14 per cent, SOFFEX by nearly 31 per cent while
EOE fell by over 21 per cent and OM by 9 per cent.

Average Daily Trade Volumes of London Exchange (First Half 1990)

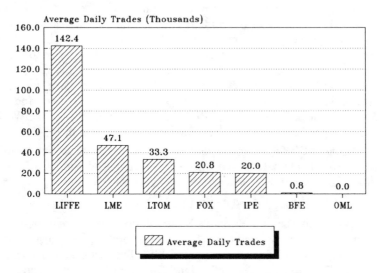

Average Daily Trade Volumes of London Exchange (First Half 1990)

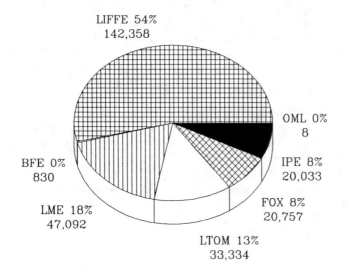

London Futures & Options Exchange (LondonFOX)

The earliest exchanges were the commodity markets. The London Futures & Options Exchange (**LondonFOX**) can trace its origins back to the Royal Exchange where corn was traded and which received its charter from Queen Elizabeth I in 1570. The need to ensure future prices for goods being delivered from overseas after shipping provoked the creation of forward (future) contracts. Over time the Exchange has evolved to cover the major overseas commodities traded such coffee, sugar, cocoa and rubber. Indeed, the Exchange moved to the London Rubber Exchange after the Second World War after its premise were destroyed and remained there until 1954.

LondonFOX is expanding its contracts further by the introduction in 1990 of a MGMI Index (a base metals index) futures and options. It is also looking at a range of other contracts including a property future.

London Metal Exchange (LME)

The second oldest exchange is the London Metal Exchange **LME**, although it may be considered the oldest as it has remained unchanged since 1877. It originally traded tin and copper in 1882. To this was added lead and copper in 1920. Aluminium was added in 1978 and nickel in 1979. The **LME** underwent it toughest test with the "Tin Crisis" when the Tin Council collapsed. However, such has been the strength of the market and its acceptance as the leading base metals exchange that tin trading was resumed recently. Today the aluminium contract lacks a rival in the world. Currently, the Exchange is looking at longer term contracts, out to 39 months and has allowed the settlement of the contracts in both sterling and U.S.dollars. It is considering settlement in other currencies such as the Deutschemark.

Baltic Futures Exchange (BFE)

The Baltic Futures Exchange was only created in its present form in 1987 but can trace several of its contracts to the individual exchanges that existed in the Baltic, such as the London Grain Futures Market (1929), Soyabean Meal Futures Market (1975) and so on. Today, it is the leading agricultural futures exchange in Europe, well ahead of its rivals. Its contracts include grain, live pigs, soyabean meal and freight rates. It recently introduced a new High Protein Soyabean Meal contract in 1990.

London Traded Options Market (LTOM)

In 1978, the London Stock Exchange introduced the trading of options on individual U.K. equities. This later became the London Traded Options Market **LTOM**. It also trades options on the **FTSE100** Index, with American and European exercise types. In 1991, it will amalgamate with **LIFFE** to form the London Derivatives Market.

International Petroleum Exchange (IPE)

The International Petroleum Exchange **IPE** was created in 1980 and has quickly become the major energy futures exchange in Europe. Although the recently formed Rotterdam Energy Futures Exchange **ROEFEX** has opened in November 1989, at present **IPE** is still by far the major exchange. In 1990, the exchange widened its range of products to include a contract on Dubai crude oil. It is looking to further widen its products and is canvassing users.

London International Financial Futures Exchange (LIFFE)

In 1981, the London International Financial Futures Exchange **LIFFE** opened. It originally offered interest rate contracts. The range of contracts was widened to include the **FTSE100** Index future and currencies, although the latter have not been very successful and are being withdrawn. **LIFFE** was the sixth largest futures exchange in the world in the first half of 1990 and saw a growth of 48 per cent over the first half of 1989. This eclipsed its main European rival **MATIF**. The rivalry between these two exchanges has been intense as each vies for the title of Number One European Exchange.

LIFFE has introduced new contracts for German and Japanese Government bonds which have been very successful. The former was so successful that many German banks use it and this has had an effect on the introduction of a similar contract on the **DTB** in Frankfurt. The launching of the Euro-Deutschemark contract in February 1990 was countered with a similar contract by **MATIF**. Many different contracts have been evaluated including one for Eurobonds. However, the Exchange will only create contracts once it has been established that there is demand and that the format is correct.

OM London (OML)

The latest Exchange to open in London has been OM London **OML** in November 1989. This exchange offers the many international fund managers in London an opportunity to participate in the Swedish and Norwegian equity markets. The growth has been pleasing. It is expected that with time the full range of products traded on Sweden's **OM** exchange will become available.

The Position of the London Exchanges

LIFFE has become the sixth largest exchange in the world, the only London exchange in the top ten, ahead of **MATIF** with 6 per cent of world

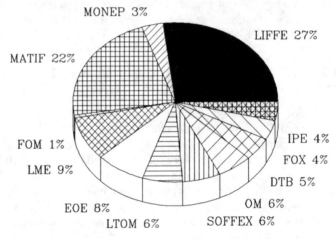

volume. However, **LME** lies 15th., **LTOM** 18th., **LondonFOX** 23rd. and **IPE** 25th.. This belies the fact that there are so many exchanges in London and that the U.K. is relatively a small country. Once **LIFFE** and **LTOM** amalgamate the joint exchange would have been rated fourth (175,692), behind the Chicago Mercantile Exchange (402,054) and ahead of the American Exchange (167,142).

Average Traded Volumes - All European Exchanges (First Half 1990)

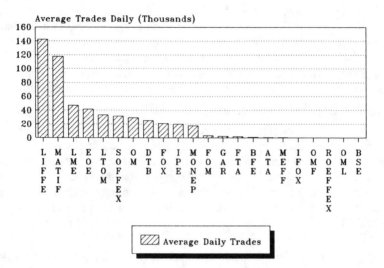

Average Traded Volumes - Top 10 European Exchanges (First Half 1990)

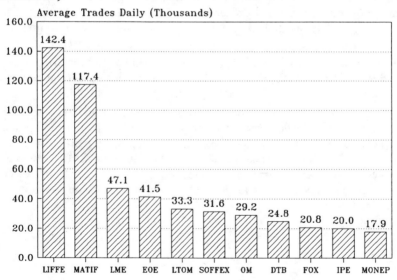

The London Exchanges are well aware of the tremendous competition that is derived from the United States exchanges and those of Europe. All the time, contracts are being refined, trading systems upgraded and settlement procedures evolved. New products are being brought to market as the table below testifies. How will the future develop? Well, already we have seen the amalgamation of **LIFFE** and **LTOM**. It would appear that more consolidation could occur. Yet, already all the exchanges co-operate with each other, sharing the same clearing system (see later). With London's role as a major financial centre, their continued strength should be assured.

The Financial Services Act 1987

As the result of pressure from the Government, the City underwent a major change - the so called "Big Bang". This opened up the exchanges to membership by overseas companies and removed many of the restrictive practices evident before. This increased competition dramatically and saw an increase in turnover levels. However, it was also coupled with legislation to protect the investor and to introduce a high level of integrity in trading methods. It also required that the exchanges and their members were financially viable.

The Financial Services Act required the exchanges to meet strict requirements on financial provisions, trading methods, compliance supervision and transparency. In response to these, several of the London Exchanges had to reform. The Baltic Futures Exchange resulted from the amalgamation of five small exchanges housed in the Baltic building. The London Metal Exchange had to make major revisions to its constitution.

The exchanges were also required to created Self Regulatory Organizations to police their activities. The Association of Futures Brokers and Dealers (AFBD) was thus formed. The costs of meeting these requirements have escalated dramatically putting pressure on their profitability.

The result has been to assure investors as to the high level of security that the United Kingdom exchanges provide. With the futures and options markets being amongst the most volatile markets in the world, it is most important that all contracts are honoured. There is no doubt that the U.K. markets offer investors amongst the most honest and financially protected exchanges in the world. For further details see the section on the London Clearing House.

The Over the Counter and Warrant Markets

Several security houses in London offer OTC contracts on a wide range of products from currencies to equity index products. They are able to provide investors with the type of derivative products that they require. However, they are one to one contracts and are rarely transferrable. To overcome this problem, the Euromarkets have issued a wide range of warrants, the most recent being the covered equity warrants. Warrants are bearer securities that are freely transferrable and are traded by several market makers. Unfortunately, liquidity on some warrants can disappear after a short time.

Warrants are available on bonds, equities (both U.K. and International), worldwide equity indices and currencies. Both put and call warrants are issued. They prove very profitable to the issuing houses such as Bankers Trust and Salomon Brothers, exploiting the differences in valuation of these securities by investors. For those investors denied access to the traditional futures and option markets and the lack of maintenance margin requirements, these securities are very attractive. On occasions, the valuation of these warrants has been excessive in the secondary market, resulting in further issuance and erosion of the premium. Investors should always make their own valuation of these securities using modern option theory or ask for advice from their financial advisors.

HISTORY of the MARKETS

Date	Exchange
1570	Royal Exchange (forerunner of LCE)
1877	London Metal Exchange
1929	London Grain Futures Market (became BFE)
1954	London Commodity Exchange (became London FOX)
1975	Soyabean Meal Futures Market (became BFE)
1978	London Traded Options Market
1980	International Petroleum Exchange
1980	London Potato Futures Market (became BFE)
1981	London International Financial Futures Exchange
1984	London Meat Futures Market (became BFE)
1985	Baltic International Freight Futures Market (became BFE)
1987	London Futures & Options Exchange
1989	OM London
1991	London Derivative Exchange

HISTORY of the CONTRACTS
ALL CONTRACTS by Date of Launch

Date	Contract	Exchange
1899	Tin Future	LME
1899	Copper Future	LME
1920	Lead Future	LME
1920	Zinc Future	LME
1929	EEC Barley	BFE
1929	EEC Wheat	BFE
1929	EEC Wheat	BFE
1929	EEC Barley	BFE
1929	Cocoa No.7	LonFOX
1958	White Sugar No.5	LonFOX
1958	Raw Sugar No.6	LonFOX
1958	Robusta Coffee	LonFOX
1975	Soyabean Meal	BFE
1975	Soyabean Meal	BFE
1978	Aluminium Future	LME
1978	U.K. Individual Equity Options	LTOM
1979	Nickel Future	LME
1980	Potatoes	BFE

1980	Potatoes	BFE
23-May-80	Rubber	LonFOX
06-Apr-81	Gas Oil Future	IPE
1982	U.K. Long Gilt Future	LIFFE
1982	3 Month Euro-Dollar Future	LIFFE
1982	3 Month Euro-Sterling Future	LIFFE
1984	Live Pigs	BFE
1984	FT-SE 100 Stock Index Future	LIFFE
1984	U.S. Treasury Bond Future	LIFFE
1984	FT-SE 100 Stock Index Option (Amer)	LTOM
1985	BIFFEX	BFE
1985	3 Month Euro-Dollar Option	LIFFE
Mar-86	U.S. Treasury Bond Option	LIFFE
Mar-86	U.K. Long Gilt Option	LIFFE
Jul-87	Japanese Government Bond Future	LIFFE
20-Jul-87	Gas Oil Option	IPE
Nov-87	3 Month Euro-Sterling Option	LIFFE
23-Jun-88	Brent Oil Future	IPE
Sep-88	German Government Bond Future	LIFFE
Apr-89	German Government Bond Option	LIFFE
Apr-89	3 Month Euro-Deutschemark Future	LIFFE

11-May-89	Brent Oil Option	IPE
05-Sep-89	Heavy Fuel Oil Future	IPE
Oct-89	3 Month ECU Future	LIFFE
Dec-89	OMX Stock Index Future	OML
Dec-89	OMX Stock Index Option	OML
1990	FT-SE 100 Stock Index Option (Euro)	LTOM
Feb-90	3 Month Euro-Deutschemark Option	LIFFE
Mar-90	Swedish Individual Stock Option	OML
Mar-90	Swedish Individual Stock Future	OML
May-90	Norwegian Individual Stock Option	OML
21-Jun-90	MGMI Index Future	LonFOX
21-Jun-90	MGMI Index Option	LonFOX
19-Jul-90	Dubai Crude Future	IPE
18-Oct-90	Soyabean Meal (Hi Pro) Future	BFE
18-Oct-90	Soyabean Meal (Hi Pro) Option	BFE

Futures Contracts by Launch Date

1899	Tin	LME
1899	Copper	LME
1920	Lead	LME
1920	Zinc	LME
1929	EEC Barley	BFE

1929	EEC Wheat	BFE
1929	Cocoa No.7	LonFOX
1958	Raw Sugar No.6	LonFOX
1958	Robusta Coffee	LonFOX
1958	White Sugar No.5	LonFOX
1975	Soyabean Meal	BFE
1978	Aluminium	LME
1979	Nickel	LME
1980	Potatoes	BFE
23-May-80	Rubber	LonFOX
06-Apr-81	Gas Oil	IPE
1982	3 Month Euro-Dollar	LIFFE
1982	U.K. Long Gilt	LIFFE
1982	3 Month Euro-Sterling	LIFFE
1984	U.S. Treasury Bond	LIFFE
1984	FT-SE 100 Stock Index	LIFFE
1984	Live Pigs	BFE
1985	BIFFEX	BFE
Jul-87	Japanese Government Bond	LIFFE
23-Jun-88	Brent Oil	IPE
Sep-88	German Government Bond	LIFFE

Apr-89	3 Month Euro-Deutschemark	LIFFE
05-Sep-89	Heavy Fuel Oil	IPE
Oct-89	3 Month ECU	LIFFE
Dec-89	OMX Stock Index	OML
Mar-90	Swedish Individual Stock	OML
21-Jun-90	MGMI Index	LonFOX
19-Jul-90	Dubai Crude	IPE
18-Oct-90	Soyabean Meal (Hi Pro)	BFE

Option Contracts by Launch Date

1929	EEC Wheat	BFE
1929	EEC Barley	BFE
1975	Soyabean Meal	BFE
1978	U.K. Individual Equities	LTOM
1980	Potatoes	BFE
1984	FT-SE 100 Stock Index (American)	LTOM
1985	3 Month Euro-Dollar	LIFFE
Mar-86	U.S. Treasury Bond	LIFFE
Mar-86	U.K. Long Gilt	LIFFE
20-Jul-87	Gas Oil	IPE
Nov-87	3 Month Euro-Sterling	LIFFE
Apr-89	German Government Bond	LIFFE

11-May-89	Brent Oil	IPE
Dec-89	OMX Stock Index	OML
1990	FT-SE 100 Stock Index (European)	LTOM
Feb-90	3 Month Euro-Deutschemark	LIFFE
Mar-90	Swedish Individual Stocks	OML
May-90	Norwegian Individual Stocks	OML
18-Oct-90	Soyabean Meal (Hi Pro)	BFE

OVERVIEW of the PRODUCTS

Date	Contract	Exchange	Future	Option
Freight Rates				
1985	BIFFEX	BFE	*	
Livestock				
1984	Live Pigs	BFE	*	*
Soft Commodities				
1929	Cocoa No.7	LonFOX	*	*
1929	EEC Barley	BFE	*	*
1929	EEC Wheat	BFE	*	*
1980	Potatoes	BFE	*	*
1958	Raw Sugar No.6	LonFOX	*	*
1958	Robusta Coffee	LonFOX	*	

23-May-80	Rubber	LonFOX	*	*
1975	Soyabean Meal	BFE	*	
18-Oct-90	Soyabean Meal (Hi Pro)	BFE	*	*
1958	White Sugar No.5	LonFOX	*	*
Oil				
23-Jun-88	Brent Oil	IPE	*	*
19-Jul-90	Dubai Crude	IPE	*	*
06-Apr-81	Gas Oil	IPE	*	*
05-Sep-89	Heavy Fuel Oil	IPE	*	*
Interest Rates				
Oct-89	3 Month ECU	LIFFE	*	*
Apr-89	3 Month Euro-Deutschemark	LIFFE	*	*
1982	3 Month Euro-Dollar	LIFFE	*	*
1982	3 Month Euro-Sterling	LIFFE	*	*
Sep-88	German Government Bonds	LIFFE	*	*
Jul-87	Japanese Government Bonds	LIFFE	*	
1982	U.K. Long Gilts	LIFFE	*	
1984	U.S. Treasury Bonds	LIFFE	*	*
Metals				
1978	Aluminium	LME	*	
1899	Copper	LME	*	*

1920	Lead	LME	*	*
1979	Nickel	LME	*	*
1899	Tin	LME	*	
1920	Zinc	LME	*	*
21-Jun-90	MGMI Index	LonFOX	*	
Equity Index				
1984	FT-SE 100 Stock Index	LIFFE	*	
1984	FT-SE 100 Stock Index (American Type)	LTOM		*
1990	FT-SE 100 Stock Index (European Type)	LTOM		
Dec-89	OMX Stock Index	OML	*	*
Individual Equities				
May-90	Norwegian Individual Stocks	OML		*
Mar-90	Swedish Individual Stocks	OML	*	*
1978	U.K. Individual Stocks	LTOM		*

The Baltic Futures Exchange ("BFE")

James Gray
GNI Limited

with assistance from
Stuart K. McLean

and
Jeremy Wall
The Baltic Futures Exchange ("BFE")

INTRODUCTION

The Baltic Futures Exchange is the smallest of the London Futures Exchanges, indeed it is one of the smaller futures exchanges in the world. But it is the only main agricultural futures exchange outside of the United States and Tokyo. It may also be interesting from the point of view of those who find the structure and organization of exchanges fascinating. For a number of events in the recent history of the Baltic may point the way for other exchanges around the world.

Baltic Futures Exchange Open Interest
(April 1990 - September 1990)

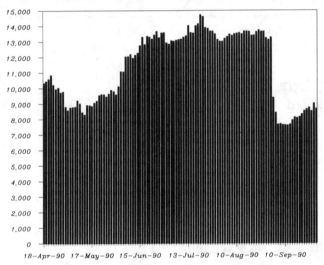

The Baltic Futures Exchange is a new creation having been in existence for a matter of two or three years and created in reaction to the Financial Services Act (1987). This act established what are known as Recognised Investment Exchanges and applied a number of capital and organizational requirements on the exchanges as well as their members with the very good and proper aim of safeguarding clients' funds. Prior to the act, The Baltic Exchange had been the geographic home to five separate, small futures exchanges: The Potato Futures Market, The London Meat Futures Association, The London Soyabean Meal Futures Association, The Grain and Feed Trade Association and The Baltic International Freight Futures Exchange (BIFFEX).

However, faced with the regulatory requirements of the Financial Services Act, it was obvious that five small independent futures exchanges could not continue on their own. They could not satisfy the Bank of England that they were proper investment exchanges. so, in an historic move, the five markets amalgamated into one, the shareholding of each was transferred to a larger parent body, which adopted the name The Baltic Futures Exchange. It now has one board governing all five markets, each of the five market committees continuing to have a direct responsibility for their own contracts, but nonetheless under the overall supervision of the **BFE** Board.

By achieving this amalgamation it has actually been rather more successful than any other futures exchange in london. London FOX (the old London Commodities Exchange) is indeed an amalgamation of the three or four London terminal market Associations, but despite recent organizational changes at London FOX, the individual market committees still exercise a large degree of power and control over their own contracts. The physical arrangements on London FOX maintain the stark independence of the cocoa, coffee and sugar floors, whereas on the Baltic the organizational amalgamation has been taken further into a physical sense as well on one floor.

In doing so the Baltic may have shown the way for the futures markets in London in general. For the independent existence of six separate London Futures Exchanges (LIFFE, LTOM, LME, London FOX, IPE and BFE) in a time of increasing globalization and increasing competition from Europe may well be an anomaly. It is hoped that eventually there would be one London Commodities Exchange offering contracts in such products as diverse as crude oil, soyabean meal, electricity and aluminium. One organization, one regulatory framework, one clearing house, one marketing effort. Not necessarily physical collocation, although there may well be arguments in favour of that as well. But, certainly an combination of all of the London markets in these other functions. It may be that the legal and organizational changes that were put in place in joining the five old markets into the Baltic Futures Exchange may lead the way in that wider London co-operation.

It may just be worth clarifying one point on the name - The Baltic Futures Exchange. It is so called because its physical location in the Baltic Exchange. The Baltic Exchange is the world's only physical shipping exchange, established some hundreds of years ago as a coffee house and now occupying a most splendid marble building in St. Mary's Axe. At the Baltic, ship owners and charterers meet daily to arrange the charter of ships and cargoes and because of the size of its free-hold buildings, the Baltic also acts as host to a number of other functions: The Corn Exchange, for example, where corn traders, physical buyers and sellers of corn, meet every Monday morning, the London Maritime Arbitrators Association, the Air Chartering Organisation, the Grain and Feed Trade Association and so on, all have a physical presence on the Baltic Exchange. But the relationship between the Baltic Futures Exchange and the Baltic is purely one of landlord and tenant.

ORGANIZATION of the MARKET

Membership

In June 1990, there were 106 members of the Exchange of whom 50 held Floor Membership. the membership covers a diverse range of commodity broking, shipping and agricultural merchant companies. The Floor Members of the **BFE** may possess Floor seats for one or more of the five markets which constitute the Exchange. Possession of each seat not only controls the contracts on which a member may execute business but also limit the number of staff which a member may have on the Floor at any one time (three to each Floor Membership owned).

Floor Members who are not members of all **BFE** markets may obtain the right to trade markets for which they do not hold a Floor Membership by the purchase of a limited trading license. This license is renewable annually at the discretion of the Board. Members holding a limited trading license remain restricted to a trading presence in relation to their Floor Memberships.

All Floor Members must be members of a Clearing House, either the International Commodities Clearing House **ICCH** (for details see later) for the clearing of Potatoes, Meat, Soya and Freight Markets, or the GAFTA Clearing Hose **GCH** for the clearing of grain contracts or have a clearing agreement with a Clearing Member.

Associate and General Members may clear business for themselves and their clients, which having been traded on the Floor by a Floor Member, is then given to their account provided membership of the relative Clearing House is held.

Floor Members

	Pots	Meat	BIFFE X	Soya	Grain
Balfour Maclaine (UK) Ltd			X		
Barnes & Co c/o LIT America Inc	X	X			
BDF Commodities Ltd	X				
Cargill Investor Services Ltd	X	X	X	X	X
H Clarkson & Co Ltd			X		
Coley and Harper Ltd c/o Goode Durrant Ltd	X	X	X	X	X
Continental UK Ltd			X		
Credit Lyonnais Rouse Ltd		X			
Czarnikow Futures Ltd	X			X	
Dawkins of Congerstone Limited		X			X
Doimedes Maritime Corporation c/o Embiricos Shipping Agency Ltd			X		
Eggar-Bailey Futures Ltd c/o Eggar Forrester (Holdings) Ltd			X		
Elders IXL Ltd			X		
European Grain & Shipping Limited				X	
F Fehr & Co Ltd				X	
L M Fischel & Co Ltd	X				
J W Gaskell (Commodities) Ltd	X				

Gerald Ltd			X		
Gilbert J McCaul (Overseas) Ltd	X		X		X
Giles W Pritchard-Gordon (Futures) Ltd			X		
Gill & Duffus London Ltd	X				
GNI Limited	X			X	X
GNI Freight Futures Ltd			X		
GNI Wallace Ltd		X			
Goldstock Commodity (Investment) Ltd			X		
Harley Mullion & Co Ltd c/o Czarnikow Futures Ltd			X		
Lambert Bros Shipping Ltd			X		
Lewis & Peat (Futures) Ltd	X	X	X	X	
LIT Futures Ltd	X	X		X	X
E D & F Man International Ltd	X	X	X	X	X
Mardorf Peach & Co Ltd					X
Maritime & General Trading Ltd			X		
Merrill Lynch Pierce Fenner & Smith (Brokers & Dealers Ltd			X		
Muirpace Ltd	X	X	X	X	X
The Produce Brokers Co Ltd				X	
Prudential-Bache (Futures) Limited**		X	X	X	X

J H Rayner (Futures) Ltd		X	X		
Refco Overseas Ltd**		X	X	X	
A Reinstein & Sons Ltd				X	
Rothol Wilet & Glyn Ltd	X				
Rudloff Wolff & Co Ltd	X		X		
Shearson Lehman Hutton Inc			X	X	
SSM Shipping Ltd			X		
Sucden (UK) Ltd	X		X		
Trader Navigation (UK) Limited			X		
Usborne Grain Ltd					X
Vogt & Maguire Ltd			X		
Woodhouse Drake & Carry (Commodities) Ltd		X			

** Limited Trading License Holder

HISTORY of the MARKET

Date	Contract
1929	Barley
1929	Wheat
1975	Soyabean Meal
1980	Potatoes
1984	Live pigs
1985	BIFFEX Freight Index
1990	Soyabean Meal (Hi Pro)

OVERVIEW of the CONTRACTS

	Future	Option
EEC Barley	*	*
EEC Wheat	*	*
Live Pigs (Meat)	*	
Potatoes	*	*
Soyabean Meal	*	*
Soyabean Meal ("Hi Pro")	*	*
"BIFFEX"	*	

DETAILED CONTRACT SPECIFICATION
The London Grain Futures Market

Established in 1929 in its present home -The Baltic Exchange, the London Grain Futures Market now trades in EEC Grain, EEC Barley and EEC Wheat. Although its operations are geared to the U.K. market, almost one-fifth of U.K. production is exported and the buyers of those exports have other sources of supply available to them. the London Grain Futures Market is therefore of interest to those trading outside the U.K..

The London Grain Futures Market has evolved over many years in response to the Grain industry's need to minimize their trading risks. The wheat and barley contracts are traded in an open outcry manner which permits the buying and selling of 100 tonne lots of EEC quality wheat and barley for certain specified months in the future.

An additional advantage of the Grain Futures Market is that when a futures contract becomes spot, there is an active tendering system where a purchase (if wished) will become physical grain, delivered in any one of 80 **BFE** registered stores; all within the U.K. or in reverse one may deliver physical grain against a futures sales into any registered store during the allotted tendering period.

A good example of the risks involved in the grain market occurred this crop year 1990/91 when the EEC increased grain support prices by £5.00 per tonne over night. users of grain in compound feed and flour milling were, in general, caught out by this aggressive stance taken by the EEC. The futures immediately gave them an opportunity to buy as a hedge, and although prices rose £2.00 per tonne overnight, increases of £5.00 were seen over the next four weeks. A later feature for this season was a lack of export demand for EEC grains, as most countries had exportable surpluses. Prices moved back down the £5.00 tonne they had made three months earlier, being caused by both consumer and shipper longs (who had bought aggressively during the harvest time) hedge selling futures against physical grain positions.

Warrant of Entitlement

Transactions on the Exchange are based on Warrants of Entitlement which is the document of title to the delivered grain. A storekeeper who signs a Warrant undertakes to produce on demand the specific quantity and quality of Grain. Once a seller has presented a valid Warrant to the Clearing House his contractual duties have been completed and the buyer, who is now the holder of the Warrant has received what he contracted to buy.

Clearing House

Trading on the London Grain Futures Market is regulated by the Grain and Feed Trade Association ("**GAFTA**") Clearing House. All contracts traded on the market floor are registered with the Clearing House which processes the business and thereafter takes the matter out of the hands of the original buyer and seller becoming itself the buyer to the selling member and seller to the original buying member. In this way, the market is protected from the consequences of a defaulted trader. The Clearing House also processes deliveries against futures contracts, matching physical buyers and sellers and passing warrants of entitlement to buyers forwarding payment for these to the respective sellers.

EEC Barley Futures Contract

Contract Size:	100 tonnes
Delivery Months:	January March May September November.
Delivery Day:	From eight days prior to delivery month up to 22nd/23rd of the delivery month.
Last Trading Day:	23rd day of delivery month.
Quotation:	£ per tonne.
Minimum Price Movement (Tick Size and Value):	£0.05 per tonne = £5.00.
Trading Hours:	10.30 a.m. - 12.30 p.m. 14.30 p.m. - 16.00 p.m.
Initial Margin:	By arrangement with the broker.
Price Limit:	No price limit.
Contract Standard:	Physical delivery - see quality specification below.

Exchange Delivery Settlement Price:	The closing price of the business day prior to delivery day.
Reuters Pages:	BRLE

Quality Specification

a)   Barley to be sound and sweet and in good condition and to contain not more than 3 per cent heat damage

b)   Natural weight to be not less than 62.50 kgs. per hecolitre

c)   Moisture content not to exceed 16 per cent

d)   Admixture:-

     seeds and/or total admixture of farinaceous grain (including wild oats) and dirt not to exceed 2 per cent, of which the dirt content not to exceed 1 per cent

e)   Sprouted grains not to exceed 8 per cent

All the above tests to be calculated on a weight basis. Grain shall be delivered from a registered futures store in mainland Great Britain.

Procedure for Delivery

1)   The deliver must first find a store registered with the Clearing House ("GAFTA").

2)   The storekeeper must agree to take the Grain and sign the Grain and Feed Trade Association's Warrant of Entitlement.

3)   The "Warrant" requires that the storekeeper will maintain the delivered Grain at the required standard and confirms that the tonnage mentioned has been received into store. The warrant is thus "title" to the goods and as such is negotiable and transferable.

4)   In order to "tender" (initiate delivery) against a futures contract, the Grain must be in the store by the "Notice Day".

5)   First notice day for each futures quoted position is eight days before the beginning of the delivery month. To deliver against a contract the Grain must be store and the warrant signed by the storekeeper between this date and the

22nd/23rd of the contract month. (7th July in respect of the wheat contract only.)

6) The deliverer of the Grain must then inform the futures broker of his intentions to deliver. the broker completes and presents a "tender for," to the Clearing House of GAFTA by 11.00 a.m. on the day prior to the tender day.

7) Cash payment is due seven days from the date of tender.

8) The warrant of entitlement which has been signed by the storekeeper and returned to the deliverer of the Grain is sent to the Futures broker.

9) The futures broker is unable to obtain payment for the Grain from the Clearing House until the warrant has been lodged for 24 hours.

10) Within the terms of the contract, the delivered Grain is entitled to remain in store for fourteen days rent free to buyer. This means that the deliverer pays for fourteen days after tendering. Provided that rent is paid, the Grain may remain in store until the following dates:

Barley - 30th June

Wheat - 31st July.

Barley Futures Price (Sept 22, 1989 - Sept 24, 1990)

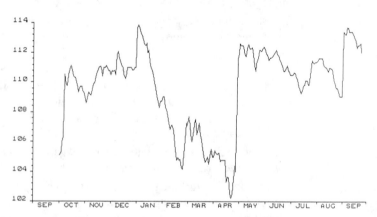

HIGH 113.85   3/ 1/90 LOW 102.25 24/ 4/90 LAST 112.00
Source : Datastream

EEC Barley Options Contract

Option Style	American calls and puts.
Contract Size:	One futures contract.
Expiry Months:	January March May September November.
Expiry Day:	10.30 a.m. on the market day following the last trading day.
Last Trading Day:	Second Thursday of the month prior to the relevant delivery month.
Quotation:	£ per contract to two decimal places.
Minimum Price Movement (Tick Size and Value):	£0.05 per tonne = £5.00.
Trading Hours:	10.30 a.m. - 12.30 p.m. 14.30 p.m. - 16.00 p.m.
Initial Margin:	By arrangement with the broker.
Price Limit:	No price limit.
Contract Standard:	Physical delivery of futures contract.
Exercise Price:	Three contracts are available per price with exercise intervals of £1.00.
Exchange Delivery Settlement Price:	The closing price of the business day before expiry day.
Reuters Pages:	BRLE

EEC Wheat Futures Contract

Contract Size:	100 tonnes
Delivery Months:	January March May June September November.
Delivery Day:	From eight days prior to delivery month up to 22nd/23rd of the delivery month plus the 7th of July.
Last Trading Day:	23rd day of delivery month (22nd day of June).
Quotation:	£ per tonne.
Minimum Price Movement (Tick Size and Value):	£0.05 per tonne = £5.00.
Trading Hours:	10.30 a.m. - 12.30 p.m. 14.30 p.m. - 16.00 p.m.
Initial Margin:	By arrangement with the broker.
Price Limit:	No price limit.
Contract Standard:	Physical delivery - see quality specification below.
Exchange Delivery Settlement Price:	The closing price for the business day prior to the delivery day.
Reuters Pages:	WHLE

Quality Specification

a)   Wheat to be sound and sweet and in good condition and to
              contain not more than 3 per cent heat damage
b)   Natural weight to be not less than 72.50 kgs. per hecolitre
c)   Moisture content not to exceed 16 per cent
d)
Admixture:-   i) seeds and/or total admixture of farinaceous grain (includ-
              ing wild oats) and dirt not to exceed 2 per cent, of which the
              dirt content not to exceed 1 per cent
              ii) ergot or garlic not to exceed 0.001 per cent
e)   Sprouted grains not to exceed 8 per cent

**All the above tests to be calculated on a weight basis. Grain shall be
delivered from a registered futures store in mainland Great Britain.**

Procedure for Delivery

see Barley Futures Contract
Wheat Futures Price (Sept 22, 1989 - Sept 24, 1990)

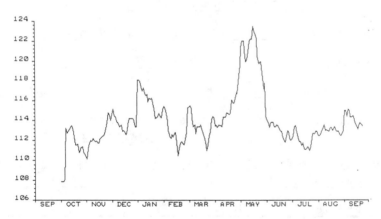

                HIGH 123.45 17/ 5/90 LOW 107.90 3/10/89 LAST 113.45
Source : Datastream

EEC Wheat Options Contract

Option Style	American calls and puts.
Contract Size:	One future contract.
Expiry Months:	January March May July September November.
Expiry Day:	First market day following last trading day.
Last Trading Day:	Second Thursday of the month prior to delivery month.
Quotation:	£ per contract to two decimal places.
Minimum Price Movement (Tick Size and Value):	£0.01 per tonne = £1.00.
Trading Hours:	10.30 a.m. - 12.30 p.m. 14.30 p.m. - 16.00 p.m.
Initial Margin:	By arrangement with the broker.
Price Limit:	No price limit.
Contract Standard:	Physical delivery of one futures contract.
Exercise Price:	Three contracts are available for each price with exercise intervals of £1.00.
Exchange Delivery Settlement Price:	The closing price of the business day before the expiry day.
Reuters Pages:	

The London Meat Futures Market
Live Pigs (Meat) Futures Contract

Futures trading on the London Meat Futures Exchange began in 1984 with the introduction of a Pigmeat Futures Contract. The original contract was a physical delivery contract. In 1987 with the growing popularity in cash settled contracts especially suitable for this kind of contract as an accepted and well-known index already existed for British pig prices in the Average All Pigs Price (AAPP).

The contract is for 3,250 kg settled against the AAPP released on the Wednesday following the last Tuesday of the month. Dealing is for up to ten months forward in all settlement months except December. Trading is by open outcry with buyers and sellers matching bids with offers on the floor of the market.

The physical pig trade has for many years followed a cycle of fluctuating profitability related inversely to fluctuations in herd numbers. The amplitude and frequency of the cycle varies considerably, with large price volatility occurring within the cycle at times creating the need for a futures market to help protect producers and industrial users against the uncertainty in price movements.

Market movements during the first half of 1990, demonstrate the volatility which may be seen in this market. During January the AAPP fell to a level of 101.90 p/kg, with futures trading at 112.00 p/kg basis June futures. The depressed market was in part due to seasonal factors, coupled with Meat and Livestock Commission (MLC) estimates of a growth in the national herd. However, as the year progressed a revision downwards by MLC of the herd size and a fall in imports from the Continent saw AAPP rise to 138.94 p/kg at the beginning of June with futures trading at 137.00 p/kg basis June. Following this, price began to drift lower reaching a level of 105.80 p/kg for AAPP at the end of August.

Contract Size:	3,250 kgs.
Delivery Months:	The current month and the succeeding nine months (but excepting December).
Delivery Day:	

Last Trading Day:	
Quotation:	£0.01 per kilogramme.
Minimum Price Movement (Tick Size and Value):	0.1 pence per kilogramme = £3.25.
Trading Hours:	10.45 a.m. - 12.00 p.m. 14.30 p.m. - 16.30 p.m.
Initial Margin:	By arrangement with the broker.
Price Limit:	10 pence.
Contract Standard:	Cash settlement. No delivery of live pigs.
Exchange Delivery Settlement Price:	The United Kingdom Average All Pigs Price - see below.
Reuters Pages:	
Telerate Pages:	

Average All Pigs Price ("AAPP")

The **AAPP** is the weighted average price paid for all types of pigs sold for slaughter (other than those used for breeding) in the United Kingdom each week. The price, expressed in pence per kg. deadweight, is published each Wednesday afternoon and relates to pigs slaughtered in the previous Monday to Saturday week.

While the sample of abattoirs is chosen to match as closely as possible the national pattern of slaughterings, greater accuracy is ensured by using a set of coefficients to combine the various prices into a single **AAPP**. These coefficients reflect the proportion of the various types of pig in national slaughterings. Because the proportion of the various types of pigs in the national herd gradually changes, the coefficients are reviewed annually. The Meat and Livestock Commission ("**MLC**") classification data are used for the purpose of updating the deadweight coefficients. In addition, data from **MLC** auction market price surveys are used to update the liveweight shares of the total. the coefficients used to calculate the **AAPP** are listed below.

Coefficients Used to Calculate the United Kingdom AAPP

	E&W	Scot	NI	UK	Ctry Coeff. %	
Porkers liveweight (40-67kgs)	1.7	0.1		1.8	Eng. & Wales	95.4
Cutters liveweight (68-82kgs)	4.5	0.1		4.6	Scotland	4.6
Baconers liveweight (83-101kg)	1.5	0.1		1.6	G.Britain	100.0
Method 1 up to 49.5 kg dw	5.1	0.2		5.3	G.Britain	92.4
Method 1 up to 64.5 kg dw	20.8	0.8		21.6	N.Ireland	7.6
Method 1 up to 79.5 kg dw	10.5	0.5		11.0	Un.Kingdom	100.0
Method 1 over 80 kg dw						
Method 2 over 80 kg dw	4.0	0.2		4.2		
Method 2 up to 79.5 kg dw	40.1	2.2	7.6	49.9		
All Pigs	88.2	4.2	7.6	100.0		

Note: When the calculations are carried out more detailed coefficients, to further decimal places are used.

Open Interest (Apr 18, 1990 - Sept 10, 1990)

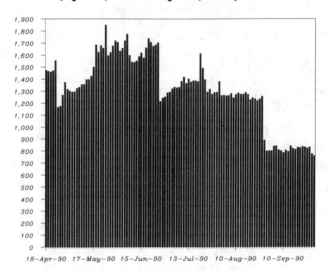

BFE Pigs Futures Price (Sept 22, 1989 - Sept 24, 1990)

HIGH 137.40 31/ 5/90 LOW 102.00 17/ 1/90 LAST 107.90
Source : Datastream

The London Potato Futures Market

The London Potato Futures Market opened at the Baltic Exchange on 16th June 1980. This was the result of two years of discussion and activity by members of the trade, initiated by the Grain and Feed Trade Association Limited and the National Federation of Fruit and Potato Trades Limited.

The London Potato Futures Market is cleared by the International Commodities Clearing House ("ICCH"), one of the largest in the world.

Potato Futures Contract

From its introduction in 1980, market volume steadily grew over the first two years as farmers and merchants learnt the advantages of fixing forwards prices by using the futures market. The 1983/84 season saw a dramatic increase in volume as delayed plantings were followed by a long dry spell giving rise to a large crop deficit. The situation was further aggravated by equally poor crops throughout Europe. Prices for November futures reached an all-time high of £200 per tonne during this time and for the May contract over £300.

The 1983/84 season established the Potato Futures Market as a useful trading tool within the potato trade with traded volumes increasing in the following year.

The contract is for 40 tonnes of potatoes dressed to a Potato Marketing Board specification with the delivery standard being under 5 per cent faults. Samples of between 5 per cent and 20 per cent faults attract a sliding scale of allowance to the buyer. Deliveries over 10 per cent are outright failures which are invoiced back at a price set by an invoicing back panel. Delivery is made in registered stores throughout the U.K. for the months of November, February, April and May with trading taking place by open outcry on the floor of the **BFE**.

The market is opened and closed by the Call Chairman at 11.00 a.m. and 16.00 p.m. respectively with a mid-day break between 12.30 a.m. and 14.30 p.m.. Traded options are available with increments of £10.00.

With U.K. main crop production meeting the vast majority of U.K. demand and with planted area controlled by the PMB quota system, supply is affected by variation on yields due to variable weather conditions. Coupled with the fact that demand is very inelastic, huge fluctuations in price can result giving the market the reputation for being the most volatile in the world.

During 1990, from a relatively high start of £140, basis April 1991, the market rallied on severe drought conditions to values over £200. The rain during June caused prices to fall back to £103. However, a return of prolonged dry conditions during the latter part of the summer and a belief in some quarters that the Spring drought had damaged the drop more severely than first thought, brought a rally back to the £130s. from this level the progress of liftings through the autumn, together with the condition of the crop would decide the direction in which the market would breakout.

Contract Size:	40 tonnes.
Delivery Months:	February April May November.
Delivery Day:	Any day in the delivery month.
Last Trading Day:	Tenth calendar day of the delivery month or the next business day.
Quotation:	£ per tonne.
Minimum Price Movement (Tick Size and Value):	£0.10 per tonne = £4.00.
Trading Hours:	11.00 a.m. - 12.30 a.m. 14.30 p.m. - 16.00 p.m.
Initial Margin:	By arrangement with the broker.
Price Limit:	£15.00.
Contract Standard:	Physical delivery - see quality specification below.
Exchange Delivery Settlement Price:	The closing price on the business day prior to the delivery day.
Reuters Pages:	PTLE

Quality Specification

Potatoes shall be delivered from a registered store, in closed 25 kgs. bags on standard pallets. The potatoes shall be unwashed and of EEC origin. Each delivery shall be from one of the following varieties:

Desiree, Pentland Dell, King Edward VII, Pentland Hawk, Maris Piper, Pentland Squire, Bintje, Romano, Pentland Crown, Cara, Wilja, Estima, Red King.

The potatoes shall be such standard quality and condition as to satisfy the Ware Standard Prescription of the Potato Marketing Board in force at the time of delivery.

Tuber count minimum 90 - maximum 200. Potatoes determined by the Inspector to be inferior to the quality and condition specified in the contract will make an allowance to the buyer as follows:

Up to and including 5% faults	NIL
Over 5% and up to and including 8% faults	NIL
Over 8% and up to and including 9% faults	2%
Over 9% and up to and including 10% faults	3%
Over 10% faults	No allowance and the buyer shall have the right of rejection.

In addition, a single allowance of £10 per tonne will be payable by the seller on all lots inspected and found to contain over 5% and up to 10% faults.

Potato Open Interest (Apr 18, 1990 - Sept 10, 1990)

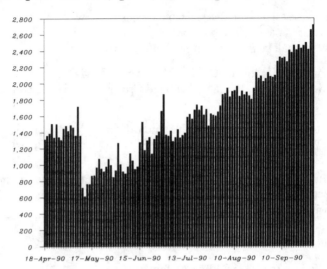

Potato Futures Weekly Price (Sept 22, 1980 - Sept 24, 1990)

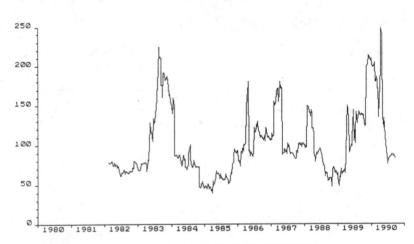

HIGH 249.00 16/ 4/90 LOW 39.90 25/ 3/85 LAST 84.00
Source : Datastream

Potato Futures Price (Sept 22, 1989 - Sept 24, 1990)

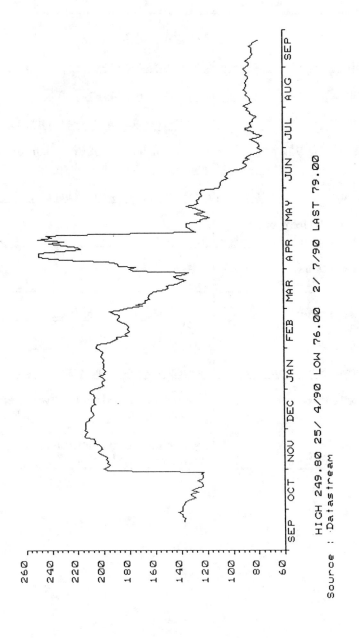

HIGH 249.80 25/ 4/90 LOW 76.00 2/ 7/90 LAST 79.00

Source : Datastream

Potatoes Options Contract

Option Style	American calls and puts.
Contract Size:	One futures contract.
Expiry Months:	February April May and November.
Expiry Day:	Next business day after last trading day.
Last Trading Day:	Second Wednesday of the month prior to delivery month of the underlying contract.
Quotation:	£ per contract to two decimal places.
Minimum Price Movement (Tick Size and Value):	£0.10 per contract = £4.00.
Trading Hours:	11.00 a.m. - 12.30 p.m. 14.30 p.m. - 16.00 p.m..
Initial Margin:	By arrangement with the broker.
Price Limit:	No price limit.
Contract Standard:	Physical delivery of futures contract.
Exercise Price:	Contracts are traded per price with exercise intervals of £5.00.
Exchange Delivery Settlement Price:	The closing price on the business day prior to the expiry day.

The Soyabean Meal Futures Market

The Soyabean Meal Futures Market ("SOMFA") was established by the Grain and Feed Trade Association in 1975, following major disruptions in the world trade of protein meals. it was clear that there was a need for a Futures Market in Europe catering for the needs of one of the largest areas of Soyabean consumption to complement the major market in Chicago. The SOMFA is located in the Baltic Exchange together with the other Agricultural Futures Markets in Grain, Potatoes and Meat. The Baltic Exchange itself owes its origins to the International grain trade in the last century.

Soyabean Meal Futures Contract

The bulk of the world's Soyabeans are grown in North and South America. Since Soyabean Meal is high in protein and energy with the added bonus of being very palatable, it is used to s great extent in the formulation of animal feeds and because of the higher costs in comparison with the cereal ingredients of feed, the proportion od protein included has an important influence on the price of feed. After the USA and Brazil, the main areas of production are China, Russia, Argentina, mexico and Paraguay. Soyabeans are crushed by oilseed processors, producing Soyabean Meal and Soyabean Oil as value by-products.

The Market trades two contracts in Soyabean Meal, the original contract based on meal with a protein content of 46 per cent and the recently introduced Hi Pro contract for meal with 49 per cent protein content.

Both contracts are for 20 tonnes of meal. The Hi Pro contract is delivery ex-store, whilst the standard contract is for delivery in-store. Trading is for upto a year ahead in the delivery months of February, April, June, August, October and December and conducted by open outcry as in the other Exchanges.

As with all crops, planted area and growing conditions are two major influences upon supply. Both factors have been prominent in effecting price movements within the market in 1990.

A reduction in planted area for this season ensured a relatively firm market for the early part of the year with futures trading at £138.00 per tonne basis December 1990, in January and May. Good growing conditions through the summer saw a general drift in prices and together with reduced demand from the USSR, this autumn the market saw a summer low of £112 per tonne, basis December, in August.

Contract Size:	20 tonnes.
Delivery Months:	February April June August October December.
Delivery Day:	Seventh calendar day before the contract month of delivery.
Last Trading Day:	22nd day of the delivery month.
Quotation:	£ per tonne.
Minimum Price Movement (Tick Size and Value):	£0.10 per tonne = £2.00.
Trading Hours:	10.30 a.m. - 12.00 p.m. 14.30 p.m. - 16.45 p.m.
Initial Margin:	By arrangement with the broker approx. 10 per cent.
Price Limit:	£5.00.
Contract Standard:	Physical delivery - see quality specification below.
Exchange Delivery Settlement Price:	The closing price on the business day prior to the delivery day.
Reuters Pages:	SZLE

Quality Specification
Toasted Extracted Soyabean Meal/Pellets

Quality "A"

The quality of the Toasted Soyabean Meal/Pellets to be warranted by the Storekeeper shall be in accordance with the following specification:

Minimum Protein	46%
Maximum fibre	7%
Maximum Sand/Silica	2.5%
Maximum Moisture	12.5%

Quality "B"

Sellers shall have the option of delivering Toasted Soyabean Meal/Pellets warranted by the Storekeeper to be in accordance with the following specification, at a discount of 1.5 per cent to **Quality "A"** above:

Minimum Protein	43.5%
Maximum Fibre	7%
Maximum Sand/Silica	2.5%
Maximum Moisture	13.5%

Quality "C"

Sellers have the option of delivering Toasted Soyabean Meal/Pellets warranted by the Storekeeper to be in accordance with the following specification, at a discount of 3 per cent to **Quality "A"** above:

Minimum Protein	42%
Maximum Fibre	8.5%
Maximum Sand/Silica	2.5%
Maximum Moisture	13.5%

Tenderable Origins

Europe, United States, Canada, Brazil, Argentina, Paraguay and Uruguay.

Tender Points

Federal Republic of Germany, Belgium, Netherlands and the United Kingdom.

Soyabean Meal Open Interest (Apr 18,1990 - Sept 10,1990)

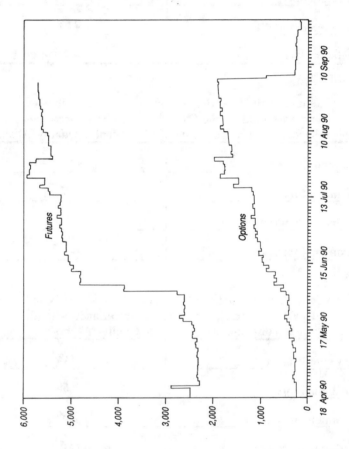

Soyabean Meal Futures Weekly Price (Sept 22,1980 - Sept 24,1990)

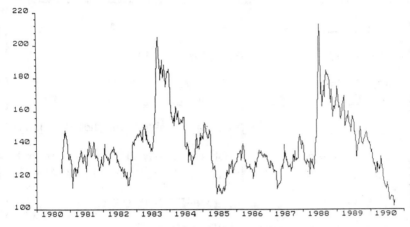

HIGH 213.00 27/ 6/88 LOW 102.00 10/ 9/90 LAST 105.80
Source : Datastream

Soyabean Meal Futures Price (Sept 22,1989 - Sept 24,1990)

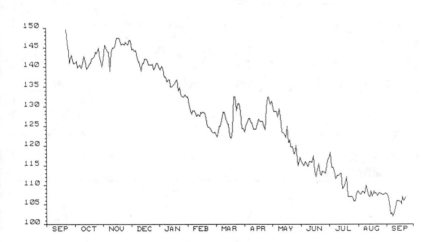

HIGH 149.50 22/ 9/89 LOW 102.00 10/ 9/90 LAST 106.80
Source : Datastream

Soyabean Meal Options Contract

Option Style	American calls and puts.
Contract Size:	One futures contract.
Expiry Months:	February April June August October December.
Expiry Day:	First market day following the last trade day.
Last Trading Day:	First market day of the month prior to delivery month of the underlying contract.
Quotation:	£ per contract to two decimal places.
Minimum Price Movement (Tick Size and Value):	£0.01 per contract = £0.20p.
Trading Hours:	10.30 a.m. - 12.00 p.m. 14.30 p.m. - 16.45 p.m.
Initial Margin:	By arrangement with the broker.
Price Limit:	No price limit.
Contract Standard:	Physical delivery of the futures contract.
Exercise Price:	Contracts are traded per price with exercise intervals of £1.00.
Exchange Delivery Settlement Price:	The closing price on the business day prior to the expiry day.

Soyabean Meal "Hi Pro" Futures Contract

The Soyabean Meal Futures Market, with the authority of the Board, will introduce a new futures contract for "Hi Pro" Soyabean Meal on October 18, 1990.

Hi Pro Soya is known in the trade as such because of its high protein and oil content and is used substantially in the United Kingdom and also throughout Continental Europe. It is used by most good processors as a major ingredient in their animal feed produce. For this Hi Pro contract, only goods the produce of Europe or the United States, may be delivered under the contract.

Contract Size:	20 tonnes.
Delivery Months:	February April June August October December.
Delivery Day:	Sixteenth calendar day of month of delivery month.
Last Trading Day:	At 12.00 p.m. on the business day which is two business days prior to the 16th calendar day of the delivery month.
Quotation:	£ per tonne.
Minimum Price Movement (Tick Size and Value):	£0.10 per tonne = £2.00.
Trading Hours:	10.30 a.m. - 12.00 p.m. 14.30 p.m. - 16.45 p.m.
Initial Margin:	By arrangement with the broker.
Price Limit:	£5.00.
Contract Standard:	Physical delivery - see quality specification below.

Exchange Delivery Settlement Price:	The closing price on the business day prior to the delivery day.

Quality Specification

The quality of the Toasted Soyabean Meal/Pellets to be warranted by the Storekeeper shall be in accordance with the following specification:

Minimum Protein and Oil combined	49%
Maximum Fibre **	3.5%
Maximum Sand/Silica	2.5%
Maximum Moisture	13.5%

* denotes that the seller may deliver to an absolute minimum of 47.5% with payment of an allowance

** denotes that the seller may deliver to an absolute maximum of 4.5% with payment to the buyers of an allowance of 1% for 1% of the contract price.

The contract has not traded at time of writing. Therefore, there are no graphs.

Soyabean Meal "Hi Pro" Options Contract

Option Style	American calls and puts.
Contract Size:	One futures contract.
Expiry Months:	February April June August October December.
Expiry Day:	First market day following last trading day.
Last Trading Day:	First market day of the month prior to delivery month of underlying contract.
Quotation:	£ per contract to two decimal places.
Minimum Price Movement (Tick Size and Value):	£0.01 per contract = £0.20p.
Trading Hours:	10.30 a.m. - 12.00 p.m. 14.30 p.m. - 16.45 p.m.
Initial Margin:	By arrangement with the broker.
Price Limit:	No price limit.
Contract Standard:	Physical delivery of futures contract.
Exercise Price:	Contracts are traded per price with exercise intervals of £1.00.
Exchange Delivery Settlement Price:	The closing price on the business day prior to the expiry day.

The contract has not traded at time of writing. Therefore, there are no graphs.

The Baltic International Freight Futures Market ("BIFFEX")

The lion's share of the world's international trade is transported by sea. A large proportion of it is dry bulk cargo commodities such as grain, iron ore and coal, which are loaded directly into a ship's hold in bulk and without first being packaged. One of the most important elements in the eventual price of those goods is the cost of sea freight. More than US$20 billion is spent annually on dry bulk freight worldwide.

In 1985, the Baltic International Freight Futures Market was established to trade freight futures. Trading from the floor of the Baltic Exchange, the centre of international shipbroking in London for 200 years, **BIFFEX** offers investors the opportunity to take positions on dry bulk rates up to two years ahead.

"BIFFEX" Freight Futures Contract

Contract Size:	Baltic Freight Index valued at US$10 per full Index Point.
Delivery Months:	The current month the following month and January April July October upto 2 years ahead.
Delivery Day:	The first business day after the last Trading Day of the delivery month.
Last Trading Day:	The last business day of the delivery month except December when it will be 20th December or if not a business day then the immediate preceding business day.
Quotation:	US$ per full Index Point.
Minimum Price Movement (Tick Size and Value):	One full Index Point = US$10 per point.
Trading Hours:	10.15 a.m. - 12.30 p.m. 14.30 p.m. - 16.30 p.m..

Initial Margin:	By arrangement with the broker.
Price Limit:	No price limit.
Contract Standard:	Cash settlement - see Index Calculation before.
Exchange Delivery Settlement Price:	The Index figure averaged over the last 5 Trading Days of the Delivery Month.
Reuters Pages:	OFLF - OFLH

"BIFFEX" Freight Index

The underlying commodity of the freight Futures contract is a basket of freight rates as measured by an Index, The Baltic freight Index or **BFI**. The **BFI** represents a weighted average of the rates on 12 major and representative dry bulk cargo trade routes. The Index is computed daily and indicates the overall level and trend of the shipping market.

The Index is compiled by taking a specified number of dry cargo voyages, each voyage weighted according to its importance on the market and historical data. Each day a panel of Baltic Exchange Members submits the spot rate which they consider applicable to each voyage. The secrecy of this information allows known fixture rates to be included; the Panel Members are unaware of each other's contribution and a random sort computer programme ensures total impartiality in assessing the information provided. Thus the daily index accurately and rapidly reflects each day's spot market freight rate movements.

Route No.	Cargo Size		Voyage	Nom Wt.%
1	55,000	Light Grain	US Gulf to North Continent	10.0
1A	64,000 Hitachi Type	Time Charter	trans atlantic Round Voyage	10.0
2	52,000	Heavy Grain	US Gulf to 1 Combo Port South Japan	20.0
3	52,000	Heavy Grain	US North Pacific to 1 Combo Port South Japan	7.5
3A	64,000 Hitachi Type	Time Charter	Trans Pacific Round Voyage	7.5
4	21,000	Heavy Grain	US Gulf to Venezuela	5.0
5	38/42,000 Vessel	Time Charter	Skaw Passero Range/Far East	5.0
6	120,000	Coal	Hampton Roads/Richards Bay or Hampton Roads to South Japan	7.5
7	65,000	Coal	Hampton Roads to North continent	5.0
8	110,000	Coal	Queensland to Rotterdam	5.0
9	55,000	Pet Coke	Vancouver/San Diego to Rotterdam	5.0
10	90,000	Iron Ore	Monrovia to Rotterdam	5.0
11	15/25,000	Phosrock	Casablanca to West Coast India	2.5
12	14,000	Phosrock	Aquaba to West Coat India	5.0
TOTAL				100.0

Definition of Routes

1) One port US Gulf/Antwerp, rotterdam, Amsterdam 55,000 5 per cent, Heavy Soya Sorghum, free in and out. Eleven days Sundays, holidays excepted, laydays ten days forward from date of index, canceling maximum 30 days forward from date of index 3.75% brokerage.

2) One port US Gulf/one port South Japan 52,000 5 per cent Heavy Soya Sorghum free in and out. Eleven days Sundays holidays excepted, laydays 10 days forward from date of index, canceling maximum 30 days forward from date of index. 3.75% brokerage.

3) One port US North Pacific/one port South Japan 52,000 5 per cent Heavy Soya Sorghum free in and out. Eleven days Sundays holidays excepted, laydays 10 days forward from date of index, canceling maximum 30 days forward from date of index, 3.75% brokerage.

4) One port US Gulf/Venezuela 21,000 5 per cent Heavy Soya Sorghum 4 days/1,000 free in and out. Ten days forward from date of index, canceling 25 days froward from date of index, 3.75% brokerage.

5) Antwerp/Jeddah 35,000 10 per cent Bulk Barley free in and out 4,000 SHEX Load/3,000 FHEX Discharge, laydays 10 days forward from date of index, canceling 25 days forward of date of index, 3.75% brokerage.

6) One port Hamptons Roads and Richards Bay/one port South Japan 120,000 10 per cent Coal 8 days Sundays holidays included 15,000 Richards Bays, laydays 10 days forward from date of index, 3.75% brokerage.

7) One port Hampton Roads excluding Baltimore/one port Antwerp, Rotterdam Amsterdam 65,000 10 per cent Coal 5 days Sundays holidays included/Sundays holidays excepted, laydays 10 days forward from date of index, canceling maximum 30 days forward from date of index, 3.75% brokerage.

8) Queensland/Rotterdam 110,000/10 per cent Coal free in and out 40,000 Sundays holidays included/25,000 Sundays holidays excluded, laydays 15 days forward from date of

index, canceling 25 days forward from date of index, 5%
brokerage.

9)   Vancouver - San Diego Range/Rotterdam 55,000/10 per
          cent Petroleum Coke free in and out 10,000 Sundays
          holidays included/10,000 Sundays holidays excluded,
          laydays 15 days from date of index, canceling 25 days for-
          ward from date of index, 5% brokerage.

10)   Monrovia/Rotterdam 90,000 10 per cent Iron Ore, 5 days
          Sundays holidays included, laydays 15 days forward from
          the date of index, canceling maximum 30 days forward from
          date of index, 3.75% brokerage.

11)   Casablanca/West Coast India (30FT SWAD): 15/25,000
          Phosphate rock scale gross/1000 free laydays 10 days for-
          ward from date of index, canceling 25 days forward from ate
          of index, 5% brokerage.

12)   Aquaba/one port West Coast India 14,000 5 per cent Phos-
          phate rock free in and out 3,500/1,000 laydays 10 days
          forward from date of index, canceling 25 days forward from
          date of index, 5% brokerage.

BIFFEX Open Interest (Apr 18, 1990 - Sep 10, 1990)

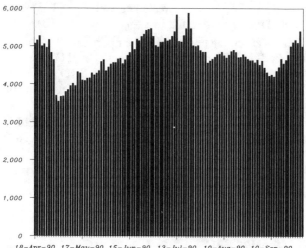

BIFFEX Futures Weekly Price (Jan 1, 1985 - Aug 29, 1990)

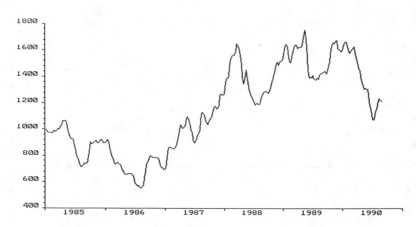

HIGH 1751.00 16/ 5/89 LOW 554.00 5/ 8/86 LAST 1215.00
Source : Datastream

REGULATION

The BFE is a Recognised Investment Exchange (RIE) coming under the supervision of the Securities and Investment Board (SIB).

Members executing business for their parties will be authorised by a self-regulatory body (SRO), of which the Association of Futures Brokers and Dealers (AFBD), is the primary body. The five SRO's come under the umbrella of the SIB and are responsible for the authorization and monitoring of members.

Trading on the Floor is monitored by Exchange staff under the supervision of the Exchange's Compliance Officer who is responsible for ensuring that the Exchange and its member companies comply with all the relevant regulations.

TAXATION

For further information, the section on Taxation later.

QUOTE VENDORS

Contract	Reuters Page
Barley	BRLE
BIFFEX	OFLK
Pigs	PBLG
Potatoes	PTLE
Soyabean Meal	SZLE
Wheat	WHLE
Market News	
BIFFEX Freight Index	OFLF - OFLH
Open Interest	OFLJ
Wheat/Barley Market Summary	GRLB - GRLB

SOURCES of INFORMATION

The following national press carry BFE prices and volumes:

> The Daily Telegraph
>
> The Financial Times
>
> The Times
>
> The Independent
>
> The Wall Street Journal

The following publications carry BFE prices and volumes:

> The Yorkshire Post
>
> Lloyds List
>
> Public Ledger
>
> Farmers Weekly
>
> Big Farm Weekly
>
> Farming News
>
> Meat Trades Journal

The Exchange produces a variety of publications covering the Exchange's contracts and their uses. These are available from the Exchange upon request.

The International Petroleum Exchange of London Ltd. ("IPE")

Alban Brindle
The International Petroleum Exchange of London Ltd.
("IPE")

INTRODUCTION

As a response to the increased volatility of energy prices, the International Petroleum Exchange of London ("IPE") was incorporated on 17 November 1980, and is Europe's first and largest energy futures exchange. The Gasoil futures contract, with physical delivery by warrant, was the first contract to be launched on the Exchange, early in 1981. In response to demands from the trade, this contract was subsequently changed to a Free on Board ("FOB") physical delivery contract in 1984. The Exchange is committed to introducing a range of crude oil and oil product contracts to cover the different components of the refined oil barrel to provide the industry with a flexible hedging ability.

In June 1988, a Brent crude oil futures contract was launched on the Exchange, which used cash settlement, and this contract has progressively gained success, particularly over the last year. It is based on the 15-day Brent crude oil forward market, one of the most widely traded forward crude oil markets in the world. Recent developments, particularly in the co-mingling of the Brent and Ninian crude oil production streams, have meant that the physical base for this contract has expanded, and this should further improve the long-term prospects for the IPE's Brent futures contract.

The idea of cash settlement in energy futures, in particular IPE's Brent crude oil, has now been recognized by the industry as a flexible and effective means of settlement, eliminating the complexities associated with physical delivery. This is substantiated by the significantly higher number of contracts settled in Brent, more than two percent of the total volume, compared to much less than one per cent of contracts going to delivery in a physical delivery contract.

The design of contracts based on cash settlement do not exclude users who require the opportunity to make or take delivery of physical oil. This can be achieved through Exchange for Physicals ("EFPs"). EFPs are flexible and have become established as an effective means of price risk management. They also combine the making or taking of delivery of crude oil and petroleum products against a futures' position under terms and conditions that are tailored to meet the needs of industry participants. The success of EFPs proves that industry participants are increasingly using the IPE for pricing oil, and as a differential pricing mechanism enabling them to separate their pricing and physical supply arrangements.

Option contracts have also been introduced on both the Gasoil futures and Brent crude oil futures contracts. These cover the first three months traded on the underlying futures contract. Since their inception, both

Gasoil and Brent crude oil options have progressively increased in volume and liquidity, and it is expected that progress will continue in this area, due to their superior flexibility over futures contracts.

The authorization by the Commodity Futures Trading Commission ("CFTC") to lift the ban of foreign options in respect of IPE's contracts came into effect on 5 January 1990. As a result, U.S. customers can now freely trade **IPE** options.

In September 1989, the Exchange launched its heavy fuel oil contract, followed by a Dubai sour crude oil contract in July 1990. Again, both new contracts are for cash settlement. Although the heavy fuel oil contract does trade daily, as yet it has not gained wide acceptance as a trading tool by the trade. Yet, with the recent demise of the Littlebrook forward heavy fuel oil contract, it is hoped that the **IPE's** contract will gain greater liquidity.

The new Dubai sour crude contract was launched on 19th July 1990. Although it is still far too early to make an assessment of its future success, this contract fulfills an essential role in the marketplace and it is expected that it will eventually become a widely accepted tool for the hedging of sour crude oils. To help this, the Dubai crude oil contract was developed and launched with the Singapore International Monetary Exchange ("SIMEX"), so that identical contracts are traded on both exchanges. Therefore, both contracts are interchangeable, and traders can now hedge their physical commitments across two time zones, up to eighteen hours per day.

The **IPE** also plans to launch a light product futures contract by the end of 1990. This will most probably be for naphtha, a gasoline feedstock. An unleaded gasoline contract is also under consideration. Once this contract is under way, the **IPE** will then be providing a complete hedging facility covering the whole of the barrel.

ORGANIZATION OF THE MARKET

As market globalization becomes reality, twenty four hour trading is no longer a thing of the future and the performance of an Exchange can no longer be evaluated within its own proximity. Extensive studies have been carried out by the Exchange with its members to address the issue of electronic trading. As a result, the **IPE** has commissioned a survey into the evaluation of a viable automated trading system to serve as a cost effective means of trading outside normal business hours.

Technological developments make necessary a continuous review of the Exchange's existing systems. The evaluation of trade registration requirements in line with increased activity pre-empted the appraisal of other systems. Approval was reached by the IPE earlier this year to introduce the Trade Registration System ("TRS"), a common interface to be used with other Mercantile Exchanges. The implementation of TRS will be administered by the London Clearing House ("LCH") bringing uniformity to the processing of futures business.

The London Clearing House (a subsidiary of the ICCH) has recently reached agreement to introduce the Standard Portfolio Analysis of Risk ("SPAN") margining system for IPE and other London Exchanges Futures' and Options' contracts. SPAN was first introduced by the Chicago Mercantile Exchange in June 1989 and has since become the standard margining mechanism for several U.S. Exchanges.

All contracts on the Exchange are designated in United States Dollars. Trading hours were recently reviewed and extended by the Exchange. This measure, which has been particularly effective in Brent crude oil trading, can provide greater arbitrage opportunities and establish the overall growth and liquidity of IPE contracts.

The following hours apply for each contract:

	Open	Close
Brent crude oil	09.31	20.15
Brent crude oil Options	09.31	20.15
Dubai crude oil	09.25	20.15
Gasoil	09.15	17.30
Gasoil Options	09.15	17.30
Heavy fuel oil	09.40	17.18

All contracts on the Exchange are currently traded by open outcry on the Exchange floor.

The IPE is a non-profit making organization owned by its 35 Floor Member companies, the shareholders. The present board of directors of the Exchange is made up as follows:

IPE Member Directors

D.A. Whiting	Sucden UK Ltd - (Chairman)
D. Butters	ICI Chemicals & Polymers Ltd
D. Hands	Gerald Ltd
P.F. Lynch	Shearson Lehman Hutton
R.D.P. Mullion	Czarnikow Futures Ltd
N. Graham	Neste Oil Limited
N. Saperia	Phibro Energy Fut. Ltd
S. Barkhordar	Falcon Brokers & Invest. SA
R. Rose	CRT Europe Inc
S.R. Pettit	BP Oil International Ltd
M.E.T. Davies	GNI Wallace Ltd

Executive Directors

P.Wildblood	Chief Executive
G.Wright	Exchange Secretary

The efforts and achievements of the Exchange are strengthened through the committee system that draws on the talents of a multitude of members and allows them to participate actively in the progress of the IPE in a meaningful way.

Finance Committee Chairman

Mr Phil Lynch, Shearson Lehman Hutton Inc.

Membership Committee Chairman

Mr John Brackley, Prudential Bache (Futures) Ltd

Public Relations Committee Chairman

Mr Peter Gignoux, Shearson Lehman Hutton Inc

Technical Systems Committee Chairman

Mr David Hardy, International Commodities Clearing House Ltd

Exchange Floor Committee Chairman

Mr Stan Kirby, Cargill Investor Services Ltd

Naphtha Contracts Committee Chairman

Dr Derek Butters, ICI Chemicals and Polymers Ltd

Gasoline Working Party Chairman

Mr Nigel Graham, Neste Oil Ltd

Sour Crude Working Party Chairman

Mr Saeed Barkhorder, Sabex Futures Ltd

Sour crude oil Contracts Drafting Committee Chairman

Peter Wildblood, International Petroleum Exchange of London Ltd

Contracts' committees comprising trade and member representation are convened, as required, to review the structure of existing contracts to ensure the developments in the underlying physical markets are reflected, where necessary, in **IPE** futures contracts. Committee recommendations have led to recent changes in IPE's gasoil specification and contract expiry dates for fuel oil, gasoil and Brent crude oil futures contracts.

Membership Structure

The Exchange was formed with a membership structure comprising 35 floor members, the shareholders and voting members of the Exchange. There are also two categories of associate members; Trade and General, neither have voting rights. The fourth category of membership is Locals, members who trade solely for their account.

Encouraging trading results and the growing awareness of changes taking place within the industry has caused an increasing demand for all categories of **IPE** memberships. Eight floor memberships changed hands in the last financial year, resulting in ninety five percent of memberships available becoming fully active. Trade and general associate memberships were purchased by twelve new participants and eleven new Local members were signed up to partake in the promising future the **IPE** has to offer.

So that the **IPE** may continue to provide access to the increasing number of potential members, proposals for introducing a controlled expansion of **IPE** seats have been recommended based on a recent evaluation of the Exchange's membership structure.

Floor Member Companies

AJD FINANCIAL SERVICES LTD	(Contact: Mr. C. Porter)
AMEREX FUTURES LTD	(Contact: Mr. C. Turnbull)
CARGILL INVESTOR SERVICES LTD	(Contact: Mr. A. Lucey)
CREDIT LYONNAIS ROUSE LTD	(Contact: Mr. P. Gamble)
CRT EUROPE INC.	(Contact: Mr. R. Rose)
CZARNIKOW FUTURES LTD	(Contact: Mr. C. Bellew)
DEAN WITTER FUTURES LTD	(Contact: Mr. M. Seccombe)
DREXEL BURNHAM LAMBERT LTD	
(Under suspension w.e.f. 16/2/90)	
ELDERS FUTURES INC	(Contact: Mr. M. Visser)
ENERGY FUTURES LTD	(Contact: Mr. C. Barbey)
FALCON BROKERS & INVESTMENTS SA	
Trading rights leased to:	
SABEX FUTURES LIMITED	(Contact: Mr. S. Barkhordar)
GERALD LIMITED	(Contact: Mr. D. Hands)
GNI WALLACE LIMITED	(Contact: Mr. A. Norton)
GOLDMAN SACHS FUTURES LIMITED	(Contact: Mr. B. Ash)
HOPE COMMODITIES LTD	(Contact: Mr. A. Al-Rahmani)
LIT FUTURES LTD	(Contact: Mr. B. Hicks)
E.D. & F. MAN	(Contact: Mr. P. Richardson)
E.D. & F. MAN INTERNATIONAL LTD	(Contact: Mr. P. Richardson)
MARK PETROTRADE FUTURES LTD	(Contact: Mr. A. J. Baines)
MERRILL LYNCH PIERCE FENNER & SMITH (BROKERS & DEALER) LTD	(Contact: Mr. M. Mills)
MOCATTA COMMERCIAL LTD	(Contact: Mr. R. Legg)
MOUTAFIAN COMMODITIES LTD	(Contact: Mr. A. Moutafian)
MUIRPACE LTD	(Contact: Mr. M. Davis)
PARIBAS FUTURES, INC.	
Trading rights leased to:	
PARIBAS FUTURES LTD	(Contact: Mr. T. Knight)
PHIBRO ENERGY FUTURES LTD	(Contact: Mr. N. Saperia)
PRUDENTIAL-BACHE (FUTURES) LTD	(Contact: Mr. J. Brackley)

J H RAYNER (FUTURES) LTD	(Contact: Mr. W. Smit)
REFCO OVERSEAS LTD	(Contact: Mr. D. Fawn)
RUDOLF WOLFF & CO LTD	(Contact: Mr. D. Robbshaw)
SHEARSON LEHMAN HUTTON INC	(Contact: Mr. P. Gignoux)
SPECTRON FUTURES LTD	(Contact: Mr. M. Levi)
SUCDEN (UK) LTD	(Contact: Ms. A. Hay)
THOMSON McKINNON FUTURES LTD	(Contact: Mr. D. Tregar)
TRAFALGAR COMMODITIES LTD	(Contact: Mr. B. Ager)
WOODHOUSE DRAKE & CAREY (COM-MODITIES) LTD	

Trading rights leased to:

KIDDER, PEABDODY INTL LTD	(Contact: Mr. S. Wells)

Clearing and Security

The International Commodities Clearing House Limited (ICCH) guarantees fulfillment of all **IPE** contracts traded between its Clearing Members. All **IPE** Floor Member Brokers are obliged to be a member of the ICCH bringing to the Exchange the financial security and backing of six leading London Clearing Banks.

Commission Rates and Transaction Costs

Commissions are fully negotiable. Currently, the ICCH levy fee amounts to 13 pence per contract each way, whilst the **IPE**'s levy stands at 35 pence per contract each way. The Exchange and the ICCH have agreed to waive levy fees in respect of the **IPE**'s Dubai sour crude contract until 1st October 1990.

Margins

Margin rates on the **IPE** are established by the International Commodities Clearing House (ICCH) with the Exchange and are geared to reflect the overnight risk and are adjusted accordingly from time to time. Currently, the following rates apply to the contracts traded on the Exchange:

Contract	Outright	Spread	Inter Spread
Brent crude	$600	$400	$600
Dubai crude	$600	$400	$600
Gasoil	$800	$400	$600
Heavy Fuel	$500	$200	$600

(All rates are denominated in United States Dollars per lot)

Services

The **IPE** maintains a firm commitment to the marketing and promotion of the Exchange. To this end, advertising and promotional campaigns are carried out continuously throughout the year in various parts of the world. Besides attending industry-related conferences, the Exchange also plays an active role in providing speakers for relevant courses and brochures and promotional literature on the Exchange.

The recent addition of a research facility has enhanced the capabilities within the Exchange to generate tailor made market analysis essential for the expansion of its existing contracts and the development of new products.

Education has also been recognised as an important medium for communicating the benefits of energy futures and options. The introduction of traded options basic trading techniques has now been expanded to encompass advanced options trading. Educational courses in futures trading also will also be devised to provide both basic and advanced levels of tuition.

Address

Official Name:	International Petroleum Exchange of London Ltd
Address:	International House
	1 St Katharine's Way
	London E1 9UN
	England
Telephone:	(+44) 71 481 0643
Telex:	927479
Fax:	(+44) 71 481 8485

Principal Officers

Chairman:	Derek Whiting
Chief Executive:	Peter Wildblood
Deputy Chief Executive:	Graham Wright
Director of Marketing and Research:	Alastair J Harris
Research Manager:	Alban Brindle
Compliance Manager	Christopher Cook

Overseas Representative Office

Director of Marketing	Leonard Schuman
Address:	11 West 42nd Street
	8th Floor
	New York, NY 10036
	U.S.A.
Telephone:	(+1) 212 764 1748/301 1724
Fax:	(+1) 212 921 1298

OVERVIEW OF PRODUCTS

The following contracts are currently traded on the **IPE**:

	Futures	Options
Brent crude oil	*	*
Gasoil	*	*
Dubai crude oil	*	
Heavy fuel oil	*	

Brent Crude Oil Future

The **IPE**'s Brent crude oil contract is based on one or more lots of 1,000 net barrels (42,000 U.S. gallons) of Brent Blend crude oil. It provides a flexible hedging and trading mechanism for Brent crude oil and other price-related crudes, as well as Exchange for Physicals (**EFPs**) and arbitrage opportunities. The contract is on a cash settlement basis, thereby eliminating the risk of a delivery squeeze.

Brent Crude Oil Option

This contract is based on the underlying futures contract. However, Brent Options trade only on the first three contract months in the underlying futures contract.

Gasoil Future

The **Gasoil** contract is based on one or more lots of 100 metric tonnes of EEC qualified gasoil on a FOB and EEC duty paid basis. Delivery can be made either by barge, coaster or inter-tank transfer in the Amsterdam, Rotterdam, and Antwerp areas (including Vlissingen). The contract provides for exchange for physicals (**EFPs**) to take place up to the cessation of trading in each delivery month.

Gasoil Option

The Gasoil option contract is based on the underlying futures contract, with trading taking place on the first three months of the Gasoil futures contract.

Dubai Crude Oil Future

This contract is based on one or more lots of 1,000 net barrels (42,000 U.S. gallons) of Dubai crude oil FOB at the Fateh terminal, Dubai. Again, the contract is on a cash settlement basis, by which the settlement price for each month on expiration is determined by a pricing panel. All members of the panel must be recognised as participating in the Dubai crude oil market regularly.

Heavy Fuel Oil Future

The Heavy fuel oil contract is based on one or more lots of 100 metric tonnes of heavy fuel oil. The heavy fuel oil shall be high sulphur fuel oil as traded FOB barges in the Amsterdam, Rotterdam and Antwerp area with a typical sulphur level of 3.5% weight and cargoes CIF North West Europe with a maximum sulphur level of 3.5% weight. The contract is on a cash settlement basis against the fuel oil Index as published by the Exchange.

HISTORY OF CONTRACTS

Date of Launch	Type of Contract	Trading Volume (Avg. Monthly)
6th April 1981	Gasoil Future	15,360
20th July 1987	Gasoil Option	517
23rd June 1988	Brent crude oil Future	27,147
11th May 1989	Brent crude oil Option	959
5th September 1989	Heavy fuel oil Future	9
19th July 1990	Dubai crude oil Future	-

DETAILED CONTRACT SPECIFICATIONS
Gasoil Futures Contract

Contract Size:	100 metric tonnes.
Delivery Months:	Nine consecutive months including the current month.
Delivery Day:	Between the 16th and the last day of the delivery month.
Last Trading Day:	At 12.00 p.m. two business days before the 14th calendar day of the delivery month.
Quotation:	U.S.$ to two decimal places per barrel.
Minimum Price Movement (Tick Size and Value):	US$ 0.25 = US$ 25.00.
Trading Hours:	09.15 a.m. - 17.30 p.m.
Initial Margin:	US$ 800.
Price Limit:	No price limit.
Contract Standard:	Physical delivery into barge or coaster or by inter-tank transfer from Customs bonded refinery or storage in Amsterdam Rotterdam or Antwerp.
Exchange Delivery Settlement Price:	The EDSP is the settlement price on the last day of the delivery month.
Reuters Pages:	PPDA - PPDB PPDE PPDG PPLE PPLJ - PPLK
Telerate Pages:	949 8752 8804

Daily Volume and Open Interest (Jan 2, 1990 - Jun 29, 1990)

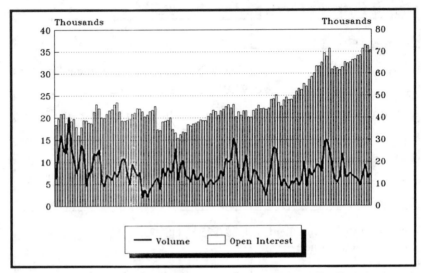

Open Interest and Volume/Open Interest("Liquidity") (Jan 2, 1990 - Jun 29, 1990)

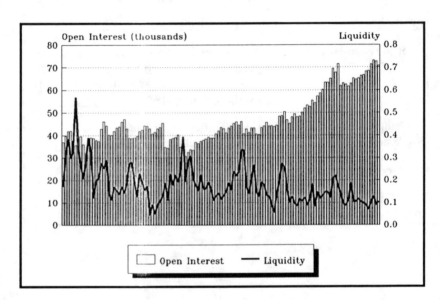

Price History (Jan 2, 1990 - Aug 14, 1990)

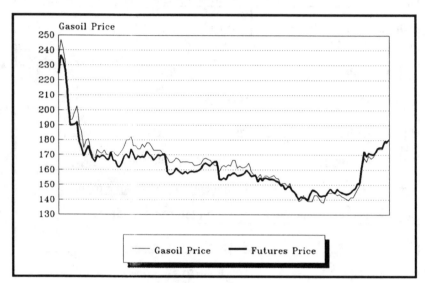

Gasoil Options Contract

Option Style	American calls and puts.
Contract Size:	one lot of IPE's Gasoil Future.
Expiry Months:	The first three months quoted on the underlying gasoil futures contract with a new position being introduced immediately on expiration of the first option month.
Expiry Day:	Close of business on the third Wednesday of the month prior to the month in which notice to deliver is given.
Last Trading Day:	Close of business on the third Wednesday of the month prior to the month in which notice to deliver is given.

Quotation:	US$ to two decimal places per barrel.
Minimum Price Movement (Tick Size and Value):	US$ 0.05 = US$ 5.00.
Trading Hours:	09.15 a.m. - 17.30 p.m.
Initial Margin:	US$ 3,200.
Price Limit:	No price limit.
Contract Standard:	See underlying future.
Exercise Price:	Increments of US$5.00 per tonne.
Reuters Pages:	PPDA PPDB PPDE GQLE - GQLN.
Telerate Pages:	949 8752 15730 - 15740.
Commissions & Fees:	IPE Levy:£0.35 each way. ICCH Levy:£0.13 each way.

Daily Volume and Open Interest (Jan 2, 1990 - Sept 28, 1990)

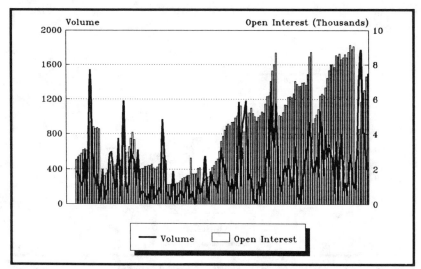

Open Interest and Volume/Open Interest("Liquidity")
(Jan 2, 1990 - Sept 28, 1990)

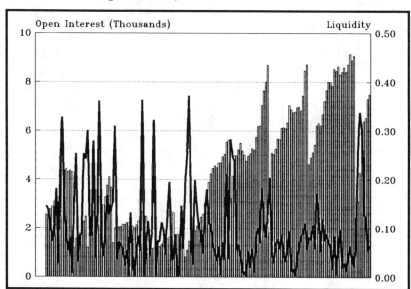

Price History (Jan 2, 1990 - Aug 14, 1990)

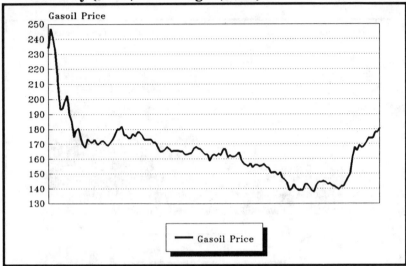

Historical Volatility (Jan 2, 1990 - Aug 14, 1990)

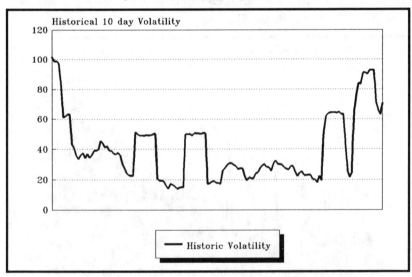

Brent Crude Oil Futures Contract

Contract Size:	1,000 barrels.
Expiry Months:	Six consecutive months following the current month.
Expiry Day:	
Last Trading Day:	Trading shall cease on the business day before the first day of the delivery month becoming "wet" or cargoes dated.
Quotation:	US$ to two decimal places per barrel.
Minimum Price Movement (Tick Size and Value):	US$ 0.01 = US$ 10.00.
Trading Hours:	09.31 a.m. - 20.15 p.m.
Initial Margin:	US$ 4,000.
Price Limit:	No price limit.
Contract Standard:	Cash Settlement against the published settlement price which is the Brent Index price for the last trading day of the futures' contract.
Exchange Delivery Settlement Price:	See Brent crude oil Index below.
Reuters Pages:	PPDA PPDG PPLG PPLB -PPLD.
Telerate Pages:	949 940 28843 8804.

Brent crude oil Index

In cash against the published settlement price, i.e. the Brent Index Price for the last trading day of the futures' contract. As each Brent Index Price refers to the physical market prevailing the day before publication, the price used for settlement is therefore published the day after cessation of trading of the futures contract. Both Index Prices and Settlements are published at 12 noon local time.

The following outlines the procedure **IPE** uses to calculate the **IPE** Brent Index.

1.   The **IPE** receives crude market reports from the following media sources:

> ICIS-LOR
> PETROFAX
> PETROLEUM ARGUS
> PLATTS OILGRAM
> REUTERS PIPELINE
> TELERATE

2.   Each source reports various types of Brent contracts that have been concluded throughout the world wide trading day. In particular there are Dated Brent Contracts, 15-DAY Brent (1st and 2nd month delivery, sometimes more), various inter-month spread trades and book out deals (contracts closing out a chain of Brent contracts).

3.   The contract is designed to reflect the Brent 15-DAY market. The index, and therefore settlement price when it refers to the final day of trading, is calculated on the weighted average of the confirmed 15-DAY Brent deals for the appropriate delivery month. When there are insufficient deals of this nature reported to give a fair and balanced representation of the day's trading, a back-up procedure is used as described in paragraph 7. This also provides a useful cross reference.

4.   Once the listings are completed, based upon the confirmed deals reported by the various media, a summary is prepared (see over).

5.   The summary is a listing of each different price levels reported by the sources with details of multiple deals at any one level, the higher number of which is used in the summary. For example, if ICIS-LOR report 16.05, 16.10 (x3), Argus report 16.08, 16.10 (x2), Telerate report 16.05 (x2), 16.08 and Reuters report 16.05 (x2), 16.10, then the resulting summary will show not only the different levels: 16.05, 16.08 and 16.10, but also the highest number of multiples at each level: 16.05 (x2), 16.08, 16.10 (x3).

6.   From the list above, a weighted average is calculated, i.e.

                16.05
                16.05
                16.08
                16.10
                16.10
                <u>16.10</u>
            96.48 divided by 6 = 16.08

This price is then issued as the daily Index and becomes the settlement price when it refers to the final day's trading in the futures' contract.

7.   If no trades or insufficient trades are reported, then the following procedure is instituted:

            i) **Market Assessments**. Reuters, Telerate and Argus report Brent Assessments throughout the trading day. The mid point of each assessment throughout the day for the appropriate 15 DAY Brent month is used in preparing a specific price that is the average of the assessments for the whole trading day for each of the media reports. These in turn are averaged and a final market assessment prepared.

ii) Each price reporting service reports spread trades on the 15 DAY market and outright deals done on the 2nd -15 DAY Brent month. Calculated individually for each media report the average spread value for the whole trading day is added to or subtracted from the 2nd 15 DAY average price and a "calculated" 1st 15 DAY price is prepared. These calculated prices for each media report are averaged to produce a final calculated Brent price.

The final market assessment and the calculated Brent 15 DAY average price is compared and the average of these is used for the Brent Index.

Daily Volume and Open Interest (Jan 2, 1990 - Jun 29, 1990)

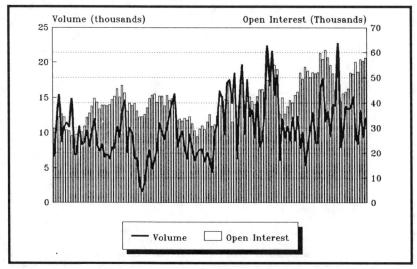

Open Interest and Volume/Open Interest("Liquidity")
(Jan 2, 1990 - Jun 29, 1990)

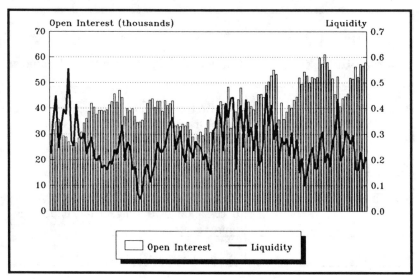

Price History (Jan 2, 1990 - Aug 14, 1990)

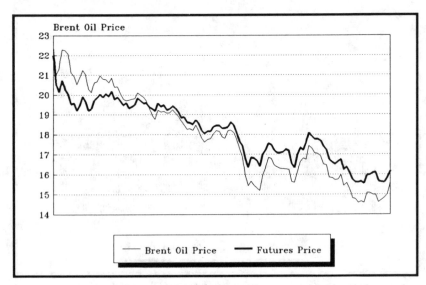

Brent Crude Oil Options Contract

Option Style	American calls and puts.
Contract Size:	One lot of IPE's Brent crude oil Futures contract.
Expiry Months:	The first three months quoted on the underlying Brent crude oil futures contract.
Expiry Day:	
Last Trading Day:	Close of business three business days prior to cessation of trading in the underlying futures contract.
Quotation:	US$ to two decimal places.

Minimum Price Movement (Tick Size and Value):	US$ 0.01 = US$ 10.00.
Trading Hours:	09.31 a.m. - 20.15 p.m.
Initial Margin:	US$ 4,000.
Price Limit:	No price limit.
Contract Standard:	See underlying
Exercise Price:	Increments of 50 cents per barrel.
Reuters Pages:	PPDA PPDG PPLG PPCO - PPCZ
Telerate Pages:	940 8850 - 8852 28843.
Commissions & Fees:	See note.

Daily Volume and Open Interest (Jan 2, 1990 - Sept 28, 1990)

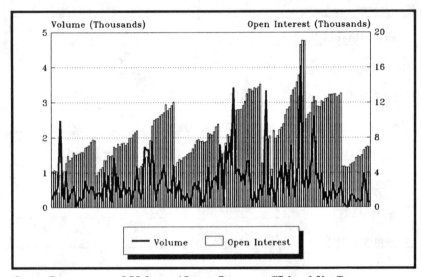

Open Interest and Volume/Open Interest("Liquidity")
(Jan 2, 1990 - Sept 28, 1990)

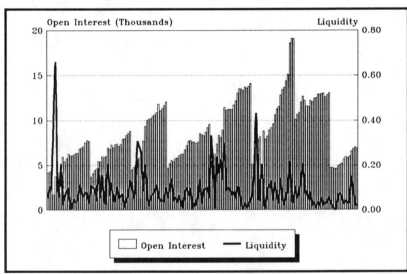

Price History (Jan 2, 1990 - Jul 31, 1990)

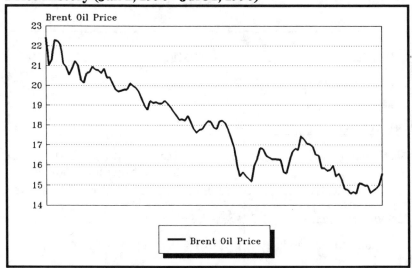

Implied Volatility (Jan 2, 1990 - Jul 31, 1990)

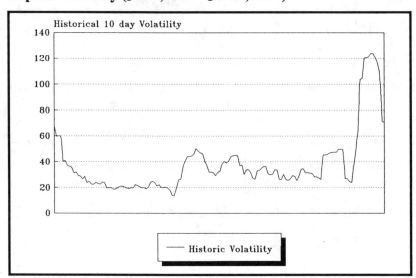

Dubai Crude Oil Futures Contract

Contract Size:	1,000 barrels.
Delivery Months:	Six consecutive months following the current month.
Delivery Day:	
Last Trading Day:	Trading shall cease at 11.00 a.m.GMT on the 15th day of the month preceding the delivery month.
Quotation:	US$ per barrel.
Minimum Price Movement (Tick Size and Value):	US$ 0.01 = US$ 10.00.
Trading Hours:	09.25 a.m. - 20.15 p.m.
Initial Deposit:	US$ 600.
Price Limit:	No price limit.
Contract Standard:	Cash Settlement against the published IPE/SIMEX Dubai crude oil Index. Current export quality Dubai blend crude oil for delivery at Fateh terminal Dubai.
Exchange Delivery Settlement Price:	See Dubai sour crude oil Index below.
Reuters Pages:	PPLS PPDG PPLB - PPLD TECC - TECD.
Telerate Pages:	940 8804.

Dubai Sour Crude Oil Index

A number of participants, active in the Dubai crude oil market, have agreed to form a panel providing two separate prices (the Bid and the Offer) established at 12.00 noon.

The **IPE** uses the following method to calculate the Index:

1.   The average bid-ask spread is calculated

2.   The mid point of each member of the panel's quote is taken and the average of these calculated. (The Dubai Average)

3.   All reported quotes which lie outside the range of the bid/ask average spread either side of the Dubai Average are excluded.

4.   The average of the remaining quotes is then calculated to derive the settlement price.

Example:

1.   10 Quotes are provided:
   a.   15.00-15.10, mid point 15.05
   b.   15.10-15.20, mid point 15.15
   c.   15.20-15.30, mid point 15.25
   d.   14.90-15.00, mid point 14.95
   e.   14.80-14.90, mid point 14.85
   f.   14.95-15.00, mid point 14.975
   g.   14.90-14.95, mid point 14.925
   h.   15.00-15.05, mid point 15.025
   i.   15.00-15.15, mid point 15.075
   j.   14.80-14.95, mid point 14.875

2.   Average bid-ask spread = $0.095

3.   Average of the mid points = 15.0125

4. $15.0125 + $0.095 = $15.1075 = Upper maximum
      $15.0125-$0.095 = $14.9175 = Lower minimum

      Therefore any quotes which lie outside this range are excluded, ie. quotes b,c,e and j.

5.   Average of remaining quotes a,d,f,g,h, and i = $15.00

No graphs are shown for this contract because it is only a very recent contract.

Heavy Fuel Oil Futures Contract

Contract Size:	100 metric tonnes.
Delivery Months:	Six consecutive months including the current month.
Delivery Day:	
Last Trading Day:	Trading shall cease at the close of business two business days prior to the 14th Calendar day of the delivery month.
Quotation:	US$ to two decimal places per tonne.
Minimum Price Movement (Tick Size and Value):	US$0.01 = US$1.00.
Trading Hours:	09.40 a.m. - 17.18 p.m.
Initial Deposit:	US$ 500.
Price Limit:	No price limit.
Contract Standard:	Cash settlement against the fuel oil Index for the last trading day of the futures contract. Heavy Sulphur fuel oil as traded FOB barges in the Amsterdam Rotterdam Antwerp area with a typical sulphur level of 3.5 per cent weight and cargoes CIF North West Europe with a maximum sulphur level of 3.5 per cent weight.

Exchange Delivery Settlement Price:	See Heavy fuel oil Index below.
Reuters Pages:	PPLH PPDG PPLH PPLB - PPLD.
Telerate Pages:	944 8804.

Heavy fuel oil Index

The Exchange will prepare daily a fuel oil Index. This index will be the mean of cash market assessments from the previous day for barges and cargoes for high sulphur fuel oil. The fuel oil Index will be published at 12 noon (local time).

The barge price used will be the average of media quotations for Barges FOB Amsterdam, Rotterdam and Antwerp for prompt high sulphur fuel oil with a typical sulphur content of 3.5% weight, as assessed at close of business London time, and shall be the mean of the high and low assessments.

The cargo price used will be the average of the media quotations for cargoes CIF North West Europe for prompt high sulphur fuel oil and reported as 3.5% weight maximum sulphur assessed at close of business London time, and shall be the mean of the high and low assessments.

Daily Volume and Open Interest (Jan 2, 1990 - Jun 29, 1990)

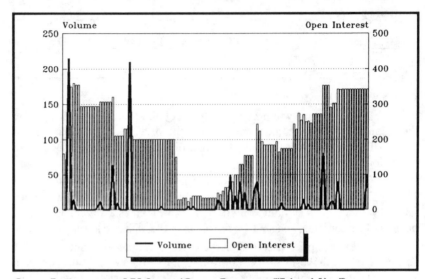

Open Interest and Volume/Open Interest("Liquidity")
(Jan 2, 1990 - Jun 29, 1990)

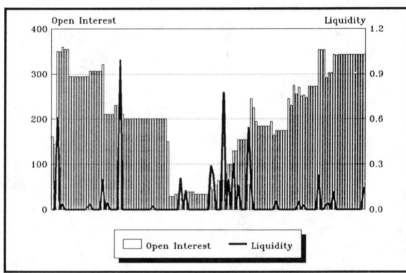

Price/Yield History (Jan 2, 1990 - Sept 28, 1990)

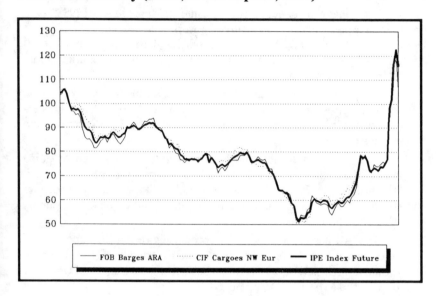

REGULATION

The Financial Services Act 1986 came into force in April 1988. It has created a complex legislative structure of government regulation through the Department of Trade and Industry and self-regulation by the markets. It applies to all participants involved in the futures and options markets, both in the UK and internationally.

The primary self-regulatory body (SRO) for brokers and dealers in futures and options is the Association of Futures Brokers and Dealers (AFBD), which is one of five SROs under the umbrella of the Securities and Investments Board (SIB).

The AFBD is responsible for initial authorization and on-going monitoring of all participants. AFBD rules encompass the conduct of business, the procedures for handling monies, and capital adequacy. The rules allow the SRO to conduct compliance investigations and stipulate disciplinary and arbitration procedures.

The SIB has responsibility for recognising the various options and futures exchanges, as Recognised Investment Exchanges (RIEs). Users of options and futures markets who transact business through an AFBD member are not required to be AFBD authorised.

The **IPE** and its Members operate in accordance with the requirements of the Financial Services Act (FSA) which provides for the observance of the highest standards of service and contract security to the benefit of all users. In accordance with the FSA, all **IPE** Floor Members are also members of the Association of Futures Brokers and Dealers (AFBD).The International Petroleum Exchange is a Recognised Investment Exchange (RIE). The Exchange employs a permanent Compliance Officer, who has responsibility for ensuring that the Exchange and its member companies comply with all the relevant regulations.

TAXATION

Following the release in July 1988 of a Statement of Practice by the Inland Revenue regarding hedging, the grey area that previously existed in respect of the taxation of profits and losses on financial instruments has been much reduced; although considerable uncertainty still exists. The Statement of Practice sets out the criteria by which the Inland Revenue will judge whether profits and losses on financial instruments are hedging transactions.

If a transaction in financial instruments is regarded as hedging then the treatment of gains and losses on the financial instruments will follow that of the underlying transaction. Consequently, if the fund manager can demonstrate that the financial instruments have been used to hedge a capital portfolio, any gains on the financial instruments will be regarded as capital. This is important for certain financial institutions such as unit trusts, investment trusts and pension funds, where capital gains are exempt from capital gains tax.

In March 1990, the Chancellor of the Exchequer announced proposals to exempt from tax trading income from futures and options in the hands of Pension Funds and Authorised Unit Trusts. These changes to the tax treatment are expected to be implemented later this year.

ACCOUNTING

There have been no official pronouncements relating to futures and options. Accounting policies should be designed to reflect the underlying economic consequences of transactions. Where futures and options transactions are of a speculative nature, the mark-to-market method (as employed on the IPE) is considered close to the economic reality. Alternatively, futures positions and purchased options may be stated at the lower of cost or market value, with written options at the higher of proceeds or market value. The mark-to-market method is increasingly accepted for active traders. For hedging transactions the accounting should be consistent with that adopted for the actual or anticipated cash market transaction. To qualify as a hedge the position must satisfy several subjective criteria.

EXCHANGE CONTROLS

Exchange controls do not apply to foreign investors for derivative products.

QUOTE VENDORS

IPE prices and information can be found on the following systems:

Reuters (Monitor System)		
Composite pages		
Gasoil/Brent Index + NYMEX + key currencies	PPDA	
Gasoil/Heating Oil	PPDB	
Market Focus - Gasoil (updated hourly)	PPDE	
Market Focus - crude oil (updated hourly)	PPDF	
Market Focus - Heavy fuel oil	PPLH	
Market Focus - Dubai crude oil	PPLS	
Market Focus - Energy Futures (updated hourly)	PPDG	
IPE News Alert	PPLB	
Futures Pages:	**Delayed Update**	**Fast Update**
Gasoil	PPLE	GO33
Brent crude oil	PPLG	C133
Dubai crude oil	PPLS	DC33
Heavy fuel oil	PPLH	
London Energy Futures	PPLB-D	
Oil and Gas Indices	DEXO	
Dubai crude oil Indices	TECC-D	

Gasoil + crude oil Open Interest	PPLJ-K	
Options Pages		
Gasoil	GQLE-N	IGOA-J
Brent crude oil	PPCO-Z	
Reuters (Energy 2000)		
Gasoil	LGO	
Brent crude oil	LCO	
Dubai crude Oil	LSO	
Heavy fuel oil	:LHO	
Telerate		
Gasoil/Brent crude oil	949	
Brent crude oil	940	
Heavy fuel oil	944	
Dubai crude oil	940	
Gasoil Options	15730/4	
Gasoil Settlements	8752	
Brent crude oil Options	8850/2	
Brent crude oil Settlements	28843	
Volumes & Open Interest	8804	
Composite IPE/NYMEX	8815	
Composite IPE/NYMEX/FOREX/Cash	8805	

IPE News Alert	8769	
Dubai crude oil Index	8904	

SOURCES OF REFERENCE

The following national press carry **IPE** prices and volumes:

> Oil Daily (US Circulation)
> The Daily Telegraph
> The Financial Times
> The Times
> The Independent
> The International Herald Tribune
> The Wall Street Journal

The following publications carry **IPE** prices and volumes:

> Oil Buyer's Guide
> Petroleum Argus
> Petroleum Intelligence Weekly
> Petroleum Times Price Report
> The Barrel

The following is a list of current Exchange publications:

> A guide to the **IPE**'s Brent crude oil Contract.
> A guide to the **IPE**'s Gasoil Contract.
> A guide to the **IPE**'s Heavy fuel oil Contract.
> A guide to the **IPE**'s Brent crude oil Traded Options Contract.
> A guide to the **IPE**'s Gasoil Traded Options contract.
> A guide to the **IPE**'s Dubai sour crude oil Contract.
> **IPE**'s Dubai sour crude oil Contract- your questions answered.
> A guide to Traded Options Strategies.
> A guide to basis trading and EFPs.

London FOX
The Futures and Options Exchange

Veneta Chapple
London FOX,
The Futures & Options Exchange

INTRODUCTION

The history of commodities trading in London dates back almost a thousand years and can be traced back to the activities of the galley men towards the end of the 10th century. They gained this name because they branded their merchandise, consisting chiefly of wines and spices from Genoa, at Galley Quay in Thames Street. The area of Mark Lane and Mincing Lane, around the Tower of London very soon established itself as a centre for commodity traders due to the proximity of a much used river crossing at that point.

In 1570, the Royal Exchange was opened by Queen Elizabeth I, as a centre for trade in the City. The Royal Exchange provided the merchant community of the city with a focus - a news gathering point, a place to find everything and everybody. Although the Royal Exchange building was destroyed in the Great Fire of 1666, commodities trading survived and flourished. During the next four years whilst the Exchange was being rebuilt, the various traders found accommodation in coffee houses. The traders frequented the same coffee houses every day so their customers could find them.

The most famous of these meeting places was a coffee house by the name of Garraways which existed for more than 200 years. In addition to the usual facilities of a coffee house, it had one floor reserved for sales by auction and produce was sold there until as late as 1860 shortly before it was demolished.

As the volume of trade grew and as trading horizons widened with improved communications, merchants buying whole cargoes of goods to arrive many months later, needed a means of insuring themselves against the risk of volatile price movements in a particular commodity between the time of purchase and future sale. The futures markets evolved to enable merchants to hedge their physical purchase or sales by providing a kind of price insurance, thus avoiding running the risk of exposure to volatile movements.

In the early 19th century, trading moved to the London Commercial Sales Rooms. The market remained in this building for more than 100 years until its destruction during the Second World War. Members availed themselves of the hospitality of the London Rubber Exchange in Plantation House and continued to do so until 1954 when the London Commodity Exchange ("LCE") was formed. Within the LCE, commodity traders grouped themselves into terminal market associations, in cocoa, coffee, raw and white sugar.

The LCE was restructured during 1985/86, from a trade association into a commercial company limited by shareholders' capital: the shareholders being the member firms and principal customers. The restructuring of the Exchange was in response to the increasing competition from other worldwide exchanges; the need to rationalize costs and move towards a regulated business environment.

In 1987, the **LCE** moved its markets (cocoa, coffee and raw sugar) under one roof in to a purpose built Exchange at St. Katharine Docks near the Tower of London. In June 1987, the Exchange was relaunched with a new corporate identity, **London FOX**, The Futures and Options Exchange. Traded options were introduced on the underlying futures contracts and "locals" or independent traders were recruited onto the trading floor. **London FOX** is owned by Members of the Exchange which include commodity and broking houses in London with traders based worldwide.

ORGANIZATION of the MARKET

Open Outcry

London FOX employs the traditional form of trading via open outcry in three of its markets - coffee, cocoa and raw sugar as well as the more advanced form - screen trading in its rubber, MGMI and white sugar markets.

Order Processing on the Floor

Once the deal has taken place on the floor both the buyer and the seller fill in trading slips in order to record the details of the trade which has just taken place. The information contained on them is then input from the rostrum on the trading floor into the computer matching system. The system processes these slips; matching sellers with buyers. The information is then transmitted through the International Commodities Clearing House ("ICCH") real-time computer system to both floor members back offices, where the parties involved must then claim the transactions in which they have been involved.

Price Reporting

In the centre of the ring sit the rostrum clerks, who deal with price and trade reporting. They operate one of the most advanced commodity price reporting systems in the world. This gives the traders an instantaneous video price update available to all Members of the Exchange on the floor, and also through the AP Dow Jones, Knight Ridder, Telerate, Reuters and Unicom price reporting systems. The Manifest price reporting system provides information about the last bid and offer in each month, the time it was executed, the high and low of the day and the number of lots traded.

Market Administration

Each of the cocoa, coffee and sugar markets has a Floor Committee. This is responsible for the conduct on the floor for adjudicating disputes during open trading and serves as a link between the Floor and Management Committee. Above the Management Committee is the Futures Market Committee ("FMC") for each market. The people who serve on the FMC are elected by the members of the market. The FMC sets the rules and regulations of its market. A representative of each FMC sits on the main Board of **London FOX**. The board acts as the voice of the commodities futures market to the City, the Bank of England, the Government and to overseas trading associations. It serves to promote the markets competitive success and protect them from any disruptions which may threaten their ability to compete successfully with other commodity markets.

Electronic Trading

London FOX was the first futures exchange in Europe to introduce electronic trading. The first system was introduced in July 1987 when the No 5 white sugar contract was launched. The Exchange's current system, FAST (Fast Automated Screen Trading) corresponds to many of the operations on the trading floor. The system is already in use with the white sugar, rubber and MGMI contracts currently being traded on the screen. More than one million lots have already been traded.

The FAST system also has the ability to incorporate trading both spreads and arbitrage. It can also be programmed to display the volume available at any given price, or not and also either to display the identity of the counterparty or not. The best available bids and offers are always displayed. FAST is able to use international packet switch lines which facilitates the stationing of terminals outside the U.K..

Orders are executed on the screen by responding to a bid or offer that appears on the screen. This is done in real time, with immediate execution. Alternatively, orders are entered into Exchange Members' terminal as strategies. The orders are entered, but not immediately transmitted to the host computer. Once a strategy is released and transmitted to the host computer it becomes an order and the host computer will match an order to buy with the sell order that has the best price and the earliest time of receipt at that price.

FOX Administration

The administration of the markets is undertaken by **London FOX** which provides the actual market place; the necessary secretarial facilities; the staff who provide the back-up support; the writing, printing and distribution of the rules; facilities for grading both coffee and cocoa prior to delivery on the market; upkeep of membership records and arbitration facilities.

The traders on the floor are regulated by the Market Manager or Call Chairman, who supervises the trading and is responsible for making sure that all paperwork relating to a trade matches.

On the cocoa and sugar markets, the Call Chairman starts each trading session by inviting bids and offers in each delivery month. On the coffee market each month is opened by a buzzer signifying that trading can take place.

Membership

In order to work reliably and effectively each futures market is carefully designed. There are two sorts of members on the Exchange - Licensed Traders and Local Members. Licensed Traders must own 20,000 shares in the Exchange to be able to have one trader on the markets or on a screen. Local Members may only trade for their own account and for the account of Licensed Traders.

Members

Authorized Floor Members

A J D Financial Services ltd	(Contact: Mr A J Dickinson)
Arbuthnot Stotler Int. Ltd	(Contact: Mr M J Deneen)
J Aron & Co (UK) Ltd	(Contact: Mr K Ryan)
Balfour Maclaine (Int) UK Ltd	(Contact: Mr J S Kundi)
V. Berg & Sons Ltd	(Contact: Mr M A Culme-Seymour)
Cadbury Ltd	(Contact: Mr I B Taylor)
Cargill Investor Services ltd	(Contact: Mr A Boorman)
Cargill UK Ltd	(Contact: Mr A Thomas)
Credit Lyonnais Rouse Ltd	(Contact: Mr P J Gamble)
CRT Europe Inc	(Contact: Mr J Yuill)
Czarnikow Futures Ltd	(Contact: Mr P Thompson)
Daarnhouwer & Co Ltd	(Contact: Mr M S H Stokes)

Dean Witter Futures Ltd	(Contact: Mr P Burgess)
S Figgis & Co (Broking) Ltd	(Contact: Mr J Proctor)
Frank Fehr & Co Ltd	(Contact: Mr N Fuller)
Geldermann Ltd	(Contact: Ms A Ghosh)
Gerald Ltd	(Contact: Mr D G Over)
Gill & Duffus London Ltd	(Contact: Mr K B Jenkins)
GNI Wallace Ltd	(Contact: Mr J Gray)
GNI Ltd	(Contact: Mr J Gray)
Holco Trading Co Ltd	(Contact: Mr J B G Laing)
Hope Commodities Ltd	(Contact: Mrs E Holder)
Jean Lion (Sugar) Ltd	(Contact: Mrs P L Routledge)
G W Joynson & Co Ltd	(Contact: Mr P W White)
S N Kurkjian (Commodity Brokers) Ltd	(Contact: Mr M Pachaian)
Lewis & Peat (Futures) Ltd	(Contact: Mr C Bloggs)
LIT Futures Ltd	(Contact: Mr S Hicks)
L M Fischel & Co Ltd	(Contact: Mr G V Davies)
Lonconex Ltd	(Contact: Mr G Woodbridge)
E D & F Man Ltd	(Contact: Mr J M Kinder)
E D & F Man Cocoa Brokers Ltd	(Contact: Mr J C Hutchins)
E D & F Man International Ltd	(Contact: Mr A P Rossi)
Marshall French & Lucas Ltd	(Contact: Mr T Everson)
Gilbert J McCaul (Overseas) Ltd	(Contact: Mr M Leseberg)
Merrill Lynch Pierce Fenner & Smith (Brokers & Dealers) Ltd	(Contact: Mrs C A Langham)
Mocatta Commercial Ltd	(Contact: Mr R F Legg)
Moutafian Commodities Ltd	(Contact: Mr K Aslanyan)
Muirpace Ltd	(Contact: Mr M J Davis)
The Nestlé Co Ltd	(Contact: Mr P W Mayes)
B L Oxley & Company Ltd	(Contact: Mr R C L Oxley)
Pacol Futures Ltd	(Contact: Mr K C Jennings)
Paine Webber International Futures Ltd	(Contact: Mr G A Stanley)
Philipp Brothers Futures Ltd	(Contact: Mr B Pink)
Prudential-Bache (Futures) ltd	(Contact: Mr J Brackley)
Rayner Brokerage Ltd	(Contact: Mr C Johnson)

J H Rayner (Futures) Ltd	(Contact: Mr T Truscott)
Refco Overseas Ltd	(Contact: Mr F Spinelli)
Alan J Ridge & Breminer Ltd	(Contact: Mr S T Hubbard)
Rionda Futures Ltd	(Contact: Mr D L Cook)
Rodman & Renshaw Inc	(Contact: Mr J Marney)
Rowntree Mackintosh (Ing.) Ltd	(Contact: Mr J Ross)
Rudolf Wolff & Co Ltd	(Contact: Mr D Robbshaw)
Safic Alcan (Futures) Ltd	(Contact: Mr G P Feraille)
Shearson Lehman Hutton Inc	(Contact: Mrs L Frost)
Sime Darby Commodities Ltd	(Contact: Mr B Clark)
Socomex Futures Ltd	(Contact: Mr A Rapley)
W G Spice & Co Ltd	(Contact: Mr S F Graham)
Henry Stephens & Son (London) Ltd	(Contact: Mr A Babajide)
Sucden (US) Ltd	(Contact: Mr M Overlander)
Tardivat Futures Ltd	(Contact: Mr M S Watson)
Transcontinental Affiliates	(Contact: Mr G Woodbridge)
Truxo Ltd	(Contact: Mr G Herbert)
Unidaf Trading Co Ltd	(Contact: Miss C Watters)
Woodhouse Drake & Carey (Commodities) Ltd	(Contact: Mr J Patterson)

The London Clearing House

The Exchange relies on the support of the London Clearing House, a division of "ICCH" which is a vital element in guaranteeing the financial integrity of the London futures markets.

All futures markets need a clearing house. The **ICCH** is responsible for recording details of all the contracts traded on the markets and ensuring that the obligations entered into by the members are fulfilled. The **ICCH** guarantee is given subject to the regulations of each market and is based on the daily calling of cash or acceptable security equal to a members' liability for deposits and margins. Once a deal has been matched at **London FOX**, the information is fed into the **ICCH** real time computer on line to all members. The parties involved in a deal must then confirm the deal and allocate the trade to either house or client account.

After confirmation and allocation the **ICCH** becomes the counterparty to every trade. Therefore it becomes the buyer to every seller and the seller to every buyer. By providing this substitution of counterparties, the Clearing House eliminates risk for users of the FOX Markets. In order to provide this protection, the **ICCH** clearly requires substantial financial reserves. The **ICCH** is largely owned by the U.K.'s high street or clearing banks which between them provide a discrete tangible backing of £150 million.

Grading

Most of the contracts traded at **London FOX** have the capacity for physical delivery with strict standards of quality closely monitored by the Exchange. The Exchange grades cocoa and coffee. Every lot has a physical sample which is checked to ensure that it is up to standard for delivery. All parcels of cocoa and coffee beans delivered against futures contracts must be to **London FOX** approved warehouses in the port of delivery. Sugar deliveries are made basis free on board "**fob**" at the port of origin again with quality standards strictly adhered to.

Address

London FOX, The Futures and Options Exchange

1 Commodity Quay

St Katharine Docks

LONDON E1 9AX

Tel: 071 481 2080

Fax: 071 702 9923

Telex: 884370

Exchange Management

Chairman	Saxon Tate
Chief Executive	Mark Blundell
Compliance Director	Antony Rucker
Finance and Administration Director	Jim Rodda
Business Development Director	Chris Kennedy

OVERVIEW of PRODUCTS

Contract	Futures	Options
Robusta Coffee	*	*
No 7 Cocoa	*	*
No 6 Raw Sugar	*	*
No 5 White Sugar	*	*
Rubber	*	
MGMI Index	*	*

HISTORY of the FUTURES & OPTIONS MARKET

Date of Launch	Contract	Trading Volume (Avg Monthly)
1929	Cocoa	98,494
1958	Raw Sugar	76,095
1958 Relaunched 27 July 1987	White Sugar	24,575
1958	Robusta Coffee	81,363
23 May 1990	Rubber	1,123
21 June 1990	MGMI	13,326

DETAILED CONTRACT SPECIFICATION
Robusta Coffee Futures Contract

The London FOX Robusta coffee contract has been traded since 1958 and is the largest Robusta coffee futures contract traded in the world. The contract is for 5 tonnes of Uganda unwashed, native grown Robusta coffee and is traded up to 15 months forward with the delivery months being January, March, May, July, September and November.

A devastating frost in Brazilian coffee growing areas in July 1975 set off an unprecedented boom in this commodity. Brazilian production, normally around 25 million bags, fell to 9.3 million bags.

Civil war in Angola and political unrest in Ethiopia and Uganda together with adverse weather conditions in Columbia and other Central American states also caused crops to fall below expectations. The result was that world coffee production fell from 80.5 million bags in 1974-75 to 60.8 million in the 1976-77 season.

The tight supply of the market was exacerbated by a tendency for retailers and households to hoard stocks. The bubble burst when it became apparent that the sharply higher prices had caused a dramatic fall in worldwide consumption. A massive increase in the Brazilian crop exacerbated the imbalance and prices dropped to £750 per tonne in mid 1981 from a peak of £4,000 a tonne in 1977.

A frost in July 1981 once again altered the supply/demand outlook for the following year, but the most dramatic price move occurred in 1985 and 1986 following another poor Brazilian harvest. This time frost was not to blame, but a drought which was responsible for a fall in Brazilian production from 33 million bags in 1985/86 to 13.9 million bags in 1986/87. Global consumption was very strong in 1986/87 at 93.1 million bags, exceeding output by 12 million bags. Evidence of ample inventories, however, caused a swift retracement.

In the year since the International Coffee Agreement collapsed on 4 July 1989 the coffee market has witnessed an extended period of low prices and there still appears little hope of a revival of either prices or an agreement in the near term.

The market remains in oversupply the demand increasing piecemeal with specific interest in better quality milds. During the year we have seen the movement of stocks from the origin countries to the warehouse in consumer countries.

Contract Size:	5 tonnes.
Delivery Months:	January March May July September November. Seven months quoted.
Delivery Day: ·	Last business day of contract month.
Last Trading Day:	Last working day of contract month.
Quotation:	£ per tonne in warehouse London Home Countries Bristol Hull Amsterdam Rotterdam Le Havre Hamburg Bremen Antwerp Barcelona* Trieste* and Felixstowe*.
Minimum Price Movement (Tick Size and Value):	£1.00 = £5.00 per tonne
Trading Hours:	09.45 a.m. - 12.32 p.m. & 14.30 p.m. - 17.00 p.m.
Initial Margin :	£250 per contract.
Price Limit:	No price limit.
Contract Standard:	Cash or physical delivery. For tenderable origins see below.
Exchange Delivery Settlement Price:	Spot price on expiry of contract.
Reuters Pages:	**KQLE -KQLR and LKR**
Telerate Pages:	946

* Effective from June 1, 1990, for July 1991 delivery onwards.

Tenderable Origins

Angola, Brazil, Cameroons, Central African Republic, Ecuador*, Ghana, Guinea, India, Indonesia, Ivory Coast, Liberia, Malagasy Republic, Nigeria, Philippines, Republic of Zaire, Sierra Leone, Thailand*, Tanzania, Togo, Trinidad and Uganda.

Daily Volume (Jan 2, 1990 - Jun 29, 1990)

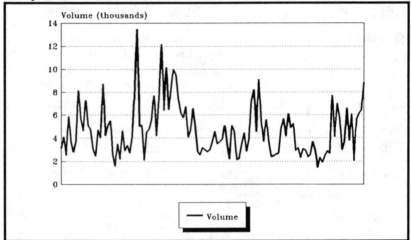

Price History (Jan 2, 1990 - Jun 29, 1990)

Robusta Coffee Options Contract

Option Style	American calls and puts.
Contract Size:	5 tonnes.
Expiry Months:	January March May July September November.
Expiry Day:	The close of business on the third Wednesday in the preceding month. Declaration (or non-declaration) instructions shall be given to the Clearing House not later than one hour after the close of business.
Last Trading Day:	Third Wednesday of the month prior to delivery.
Quotation:	£ per tonnes (see futures contract).
Minimum Price Movement (Tick Size and Value):	£1.00 = £5.00.
Trading Hours:	09.45 a.m. - 12.32 p.m. & 14.30 p.m. - 17.00 p.m.
Initial Margin :	£250 per contract.
Price Limit:	No price limit.
Contract Standard:	Physical delivery.
Exercise Price:	60 contracts of each class are traded with increments of £50 per tonne.
Reuters Pages:	**KQLE - KQLR and LKR**
Telerate Pages:	Not available.

Daily Volume and Open Interest (Jan 2, 1990 - Jun 29, 1990)

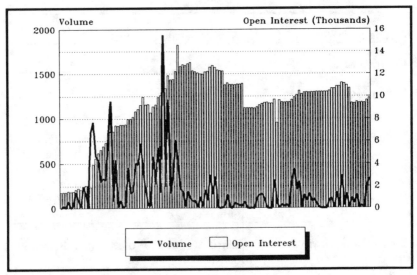

Open Interest and Volume/Open Interest("Liquidity") (Jan 2, 1990 - Jun 29, 1990)

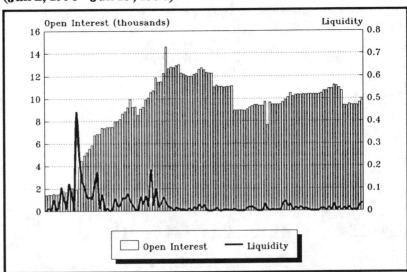

No.7 Cocoa Futures Contract

Futures trading in cocoa began in about 1929 as a result of the sharp increase in trade in the physical commodity during the boom which followed the First World War. Since then volume has grown steadily and today it stands as one of the two largest cocoa markets in the world.

The Cocoa Association of London was formed in 1926, however, it was not until two years later that the London Cocoa Terminal Market was opened. As production grew so did dealers' warehouse stocks and so the need to hedge stocks and commitments was felt by everyone concerned with the industry. There was not the outside speculation that there is today.

From 1940 to 1950 the price of cocoa was controlled by the Ministry of Food, as was its distribution. Futures trading started again in 1951 and the volume of business steadily grew, but gathered momentum in the late 1960s, when shortages in the physical commodity resulted in an increase in the futures market.

The contract is for 10 tonnes of cocoa beans of a growth and quality defined by the rules, delivered at contract price, ex-warehouse or delivered in approved warehouses. Dealing is for up to 15 months forward in the following delivery months: March, May, July, September and December. Trading is done by open outcry with buyers and sellers matching bids with offers on the floor of the cocoa market.

The cocoa market is unique at **London FOX** as it is the only market that trades through a chairman. At any time during the day, the chairman may be called for and business conducted through him should market conditions become hectic.

Market fundamentals altered both suddenly and dramatically in the first half of 1990. Until early March, the markets were remarkable only for their blandness as prices had been confined within narrow trading ranges for more than three months.

After March, the market was extremely volatile and prices surged to eight month highs fuelled by political unrest in the Cote d'Ivoire, a tightening fundamental situation and huge levels of fund buying.

After hitting contract lows of £622 per tonne in mid-February (basis the May 1990 contract), the London market rose more than £250 per tonne to trade at a high of £892 per tonne in mid-April. The market however, has come down from these highs since then and in July 1990 it was trading at £725 per tonne (basis July 1990).

Contract Size:	10 tonnes.
Delivery Months:	March May July September December.
Delivery Day:	Last business day of the month.
Last Trading Day:	Last business day of the month.
Quotation:	£ per tonne ex-warehouse U.K. or in warehouse Amsterdam Antwerp Bremen Hamburg Rotterdam.
Minimum Price Movement (Tick Size and Value):	£1.00 per tonne = £10.00.
Trading Hours:	10.00 a.m. - 12.58 p.m. & 14.30 p.m. - 16.45 p.m. NB The 12.58 p.m. and 16.45 p.m. calls continue until trading interest ceases.
Initial Margin:	£400 per contract.
Price Limit:	No price limits.
Contract Standard:	Cash or physical delivery. For tenderable origins see below.
Exchange Delivery Settlement Price:	Spot price on expiry of contract.
Reuters Pages:	**COKB and LCC**
Telerate Pages:	943

Origins Tenderable

Brazil, Cameroon, Ecuador, Ghana, Grenada, Cote d'Ivoire, Jamaica, Malaysia, Nigeria, Papua New Guinea, Sao Tome, Sierra Leone, Sri Lanka, Trinidad & Tobago, Western Samoa, Zaire and all other growths.

Daily Volume (Jan 2, 1990 - Jun 29, 1990)

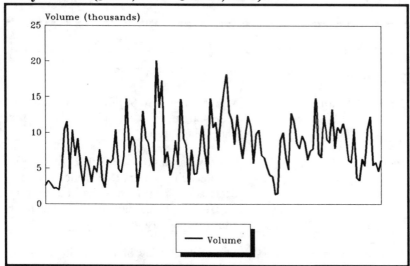

Price History (Jan 2, 1990 - Jun 29, 1990)

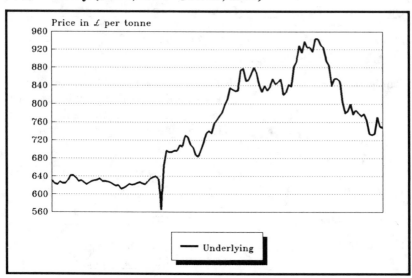

No.7 Cocoa Options Contract

Option Style	American.
Contract Size:	10 tonnes.
Delivery Months:	March May July September December. Identical to the first six months on the underlying futures
Delivery Day:	Close of business on the third Wednesday in the preceding month. Declaration (or non-declaration) instructions shall be given to the Clearing House not later than one hour after close of business.
Last Trading Day:	Third Wednesday of the month prior to delivery.
Quotation:	£ per tonne (see futures contract)
Minimum Price Movement (Tick Size and Value):	£1.00 per tonne = £10.00.
Trading Hours:	10.00 a.m. - 12.59 p.m. & 14.30 p.m. - 16.45 p.m. As for the underlying futures contract - trading continues until trading in the underlying futures contracts has ceased.
Initial Margin:	£400 per contract.
Price Limit:	No price limit.
Contract Standard:	Physical delivery.
Exercise Price:	60 contracts of each class are traded with increments of £50 per tonne.
Reuters Pages:	**CQLE - CQLR and LCC**

Telerate Pages:	not available

Daily Volume and Open Interest (Jan 2, 1990 - Jun 29, 1990)

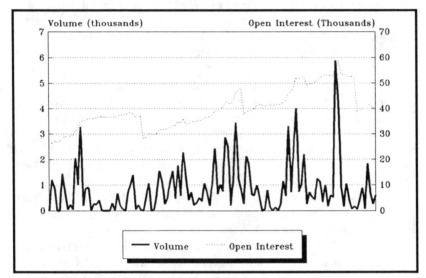

Open Interest and Volume/Open Interest("Liquidity")
(Jan 2, 1990 - Jun 29, 1990)

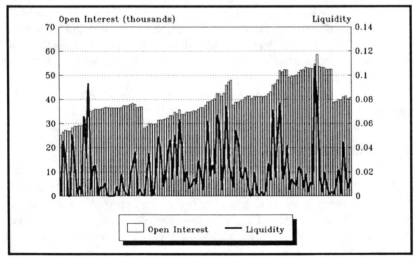

Sugar

The London sugar futures market was established in 1888 with a contract unit of 400 tonnes of raw beet sugar free on board (fob) Hamburg. The market was closed during the First World War and did not reopen until the middle of 1921 when the contract was changed to 50 tons of white sugar exbounded warehouse, London. The change in the tariff structure in 1929 meant that very little refined sugar was imported and as a result a raw sugar contract was developed.

The present No.6 raw sugar contract is for lots of 50 metric tonnes net landed weight, at 96 degrees outturn polarization for delivery free on board at various world ports. The price is quoted in U.S. dollars per tonne, and minimum fluctuations are 20 cents. Delivery can be made on any day of the month in which the contract expires. Trading is in contracts up to 15 months ahead, the delivery months being March, May, August, October and December.

The current raw sugar contract has traded since 1958. In recent years its volume's have fluctuated considerably but are now averaging over 60,000 lots of 50 tonne contracts each month.

The No.5 white sugar contract can be traded on the screen and is also denominated in U.S. dollars with the same delivery months as raw No.6 contract, presenting opportunities for spreading between the two contracts. The Exchange's white sugar contract was launched in July 1983. It reached a milestone on April 11, 1990, when one million lots were traded.

During the first half of 1990, supply and demand prospects for sugar swung round. Carry-over stocks as a percentage of consumption fell back to low levels which were last seen in 1980/81 when production fell below consumption for five seasons. Prices rose sharply on that occasion as widespread crop failures triggered panic buying.

The 1989/90 crop in India continued to improve and closed 1.5 million tonnes higher than first forecasts. Together with a lack of buying from China, this altered the outlook for the important Far East sector of the market.

No 6 Raw Sugar Futures Contract

In March 1990, prompt No.6 London futures peaked at more than US$356 per tonne following concern about tight forward supply prospects.

In the following three months successive falls took prices down to around US$270 per tonne for the prompt position as the factors in India, China and a claimed high crop in Cuba all combined to reduce concern about a possible supply crisis.

Contract Size:	50 tonnes.
Delivery Months:	March May August October December.
Delivery Day:	Last calendar day of the month prior to delivery.
Last Trading Day:	Last working day of the month prior to delivery.
Quotation:	US$ to two decimal places per tonne Free on Board stored (**FOBS**) designated port.
Minimum Price Movement (Tick Size and Value):	US$ 0.20 = US$ 10.00.
Trading Hours:	10.30 a.m. - 12.30 p.m. & 14.30 p.m. - 19.00 p.m.
Initial Margin:	US$600 per contract.
Price Limit:	No price limit.
Contract Standard:	Cash and physical delivery. Raw cane sugar
Exchange Delivery Settlement Price:	Cash spot price on expiry of contract.
Reuters Pages:	**(Raw) SUGB - SULE**
Telerate Pages:	945

Daily Volume (Jan 2, 1990 - Jun 29, 1990)

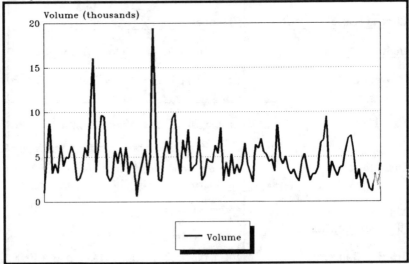

Price History (Jan 2, 1990 - Jun 29, 1990)

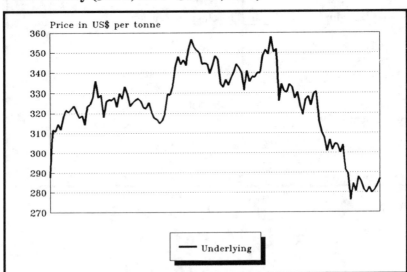

No 6 Raw Sugar Options Contract

Option Style	American calls and puts.
Contract Size:	50 tonnes.
Delivery Months:	March May August October December. Identical to the first six months on the underlying futures
Delivery Day:	Close of business on the third Wednesday in the preceding month. Declaration (or non-declaration) instructions shall be given to the Clearing House not later than one hour after close of business.
Last Trading Day:	Third Wednesday of the month prior to delivery.
Quotation:	US$ to two decimal points per tonne. (see futures contract).
Minimum Price Movement (Tick Size and Value):	US$ 0.05 per tonne = US$ 2.50.
Trading Hours:	10.30 a.m. - 12.30 p.m. & 14.30 p.m. - 19.00 p.m. Trading continues until trading in the underlaying futures contract has ceased.
Initial Margin:	US$600 per contract.
Price Limit:	No price limit.
Contract Standard:	Physical delivery. For tenderable origins see below.
Exercise Price:	60 contracts of each class are traded with price increments of US$ 10 per tonne.
Reuters Pages:	**SQLE - SQLR** or **LSG**

| Telerate Pages: | not available. |

Origins Tenderable

Raw cane sugar, FAQ current crop minimum 96 degrees polarization at time of shipment from the following: Australia, Argentina, Barbados, Belize, Brazil, Colombia, Costa Rica, Cuba*, Dominican Republic, El Salvador, Ecuador, Fiji, French Antilles, Guyana, Guatemala, Honduras, India, Jamaica, Malawi, Mauritius, Mexico, Mozambique, Nicaragua, Peru, Philippine Islands, Reunion, South Africa, Swaziland, Taiwan, Thailand, Trinidad, United States of America and Zimbabwe. * From December 1990.

Daily Volume and Open Interest (Jan 2, 1990 - Jun 29, 1990)

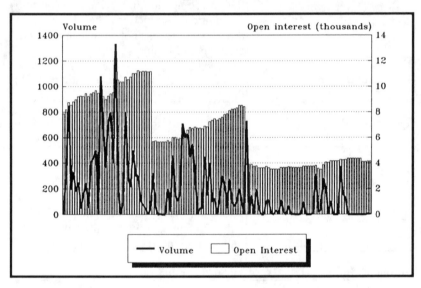

Open Interest and Volume/Open Interest("Liquidity") (Jan 2, 1990 - Jun 29, 1990)

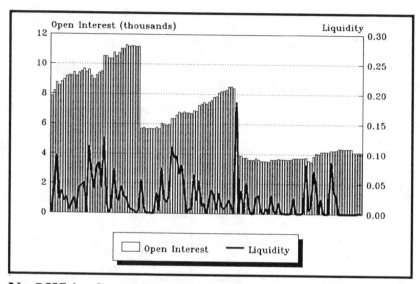

No 5 White Sugar Futures Contract

The first half of 1990 was dominated by a strong upward move led by prospects of a tight statistical outlook, only for most of these gains to be lost again during May and June in a prelude to further falls later in the year. The firm market during the early months was boosted by the severe freeze damage to the Mexican crop at the end of December 1989 and since this increased white sugar demand, the rise was led by the white side of the market, leading to a strong white sugar premium over raws. White sugar prices also led the subsequent fall as crop prospects in India improved significantly.

At the beginning of January prompt March on the London No.5 contract was quoted at US$372 per tonne. Prices increased to peak on 20 March with prompt May on No.5 reaching US$452.90 per tonne. After retreating from these levels, renewed strength returned again in May but whites prices failed to top the March peak with prompt August reaching US$444.50 per tonne. prices fell away rapidly after that with prompt August No.5 touching US$376.50 per tonne by 21 June. Although the August delivery recovered to US$391.00 by the end of that month, there were to be further steep falls in prices in the following months.

Contract Size:	50 tonnes.
Delivery Months:	March May August October December.
Delivery Day:	Sixteen calendar days prior to delivery.
Last Trading Day:	Last business day of the month prior to delivery.
Quotation:	US$ to two decimal places per tonne Free on Board stored (**FOBS**) designated ports of shipment.
Minimum Price Movement (Tick Size and Value):	US$ 0.10 per tonne = US$ 5.00.
Trading Hours:	09.45 a.m. - 19.10 p.m.
Initial Margin:	US$600 per contract.
Price Limit:	No price limit.
Contract Standard:	Cash and physical delivery. White beet or cane crystal sugar or refined sugar of any origin from the current crop (at time of delivery) and subject to certain criteria.
Exchange Delivery Settlement Price:	Cash spot price at expiry of contract.
Reuters Pages:	**SU37 & SULG and LSU**
Telerate Pages:	941

Daily Volume and (Jan 2, 1990 - Jun 29, 1990)

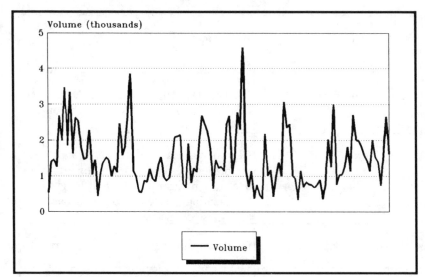

Price History (Jan 2, 1990 - Jun 29, 1990)

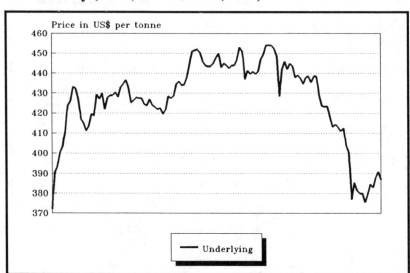

No 5 White Sugar Options Contract

Option Style	American calls and puts.
Contract Size:	50 tonnes.
Delivery Months:	March May August October December. Identical to the first six months on the underlying futures.
Expiry Day:	Close of business on the third Wednesday in the preceding month. Declaration (or non-declaration) instructions shall be given to the Clearing House not later than one hour after close of business.
Last Trading Day:	First business day of the month prior to delivery.
Quotation:	US$ to two decimal places per tonne.
Minimum Price Movement (Tick Size and Value):	US$ 0.05 = US$ 2.50.
Trading Hours:	09.45 a.m. - 19.10 p.m.
Initial Margin:	US$600 per contract.
Price Limit:	No price limit.
Contract Standard:	Physical delivery.
Exercise Price:	60 contracts of each class with price increments of US$ 10 per tonne.
Reuters Pages:	WQLE - WQLR and LSU
Telerate Pages:	not available.

Daily Volume and Open Interest (Jan 2, 1990 - Jun 29, 1990)

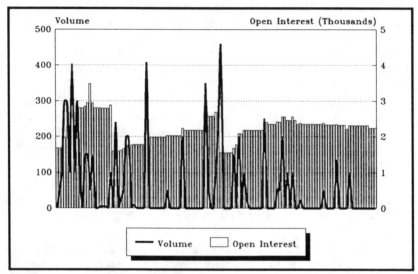

Open Interest and Volume/Open Interest("Liquidity")
(Jan 2, 1990 - Jun 29, 1990)

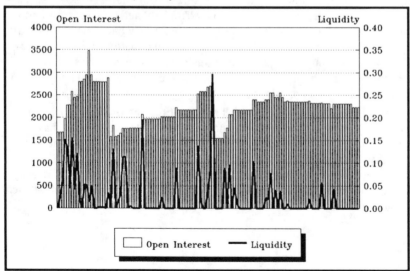

Rubber Futures Contract

London FOX relaunched a rubber futures contract on 23 May 1990. At various times in the past, futures in rubber have traded in London in a number of different forms. However, for a number of reasons all of the contracts failed and trade and industry in Europe and North America were left with no viable hedging medium. This left the market heavily exposed to adverse or unpredictable movements.

The matter came to a head in 1988 when prices both doubled and halved in 12 months. The rubber trade approached **London FOX** and asked it to provide a contract. The Exchange changed the grade of rubber to Technically Specified rubber (**TSR**) which is a semi-manufactured product used extensively in the motor industry.

Delivery was switched from in warehouse Europe to FOB origin to give the contract international appeal. The contract was also introduced onto an electronic system with terminals worldwide to bring overseas traders directly into play.

Rubber is being electronically traded from London, New York and Singapore. The feature of the contract for people such as investment managers is the grade of rubber. **TSR** rubbers are used almost exclusively for the manufacture of car and truck tyres. Vehicle sales correlate to world economies. Thus a downturn leads to a slowdown in new vehicle sales. This in turn means a fall in manufacture demand for **TSR** and thus a corresponding fall in prices. Conversely, an upturn in the economy and demand for **TSR** causes futures prices to rise. The supply/demand equation continues to have a major impact, but perhaps for the investment manager who is able to take a broad view of the market and world economic situation, making money trading rubber becomes a possibility.

June 1990 saw the first full month of trading on the rubber futures market and despite the fact that the underlying physical market has been exceptionally flat, the contract traded well. The contract is showing good liquidity with tight bid/ask spreads regularly quoted on all positions. The open interest has been building and once the physical market starts to move again the benefits of trading a cleared and guaranteed contract will certainly attract hedgers and traders from the business worldwide.

Contract Size:	10.08 metric tonnes (22,222.36 lbs).
Delivery Months:	March June September and December quarters as well as the immediate next three months.
Delivery Day:	Fifteenth day of the calendar month.
Last Trading Day:	First calendar day of the delivery month.
Quotation:	US$ to two decimal places. Free on Board (FOB) Padang Palembang Belawan.
Minimum Price Movement (Tick Size and Value):	US$ 0.125 per pound = US$ 2,778.
Trading Hours:	08.30 a.m. - 11.30 a.m. & 14.00 p.m. - 19.00 p.m. or as decided by the Market Committee.
Initial Margin:	US$300 per contract.
Price Limit:	No price limit.
Contract Standard:	Cash or physical delivery. Tenderable specification is Standard Indonesian Rubber Type 20 (SIR 20).
Exchange Delivery Settlement Price:	Cash spot price at expiry of contract.
Reuters Pages:	LRU
Telerate Pages:	942

MGMI Futures Contract

London FOX launched its MGMI futures market on 21 June 1990. the MGMI is a cash-settled base metal index comprising six non-ferrous metals (aluminum, copper, zinc, lead, nickel and tin) traded on the **London Metal Exchange (LME).** Each metal is weighted according to its share of the six metals' total consumption in the western world and reflects general price movements in the non-ferrous metal markets.

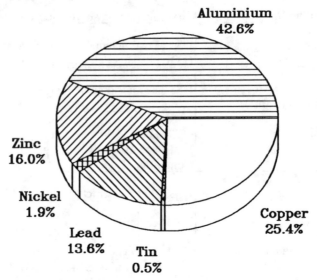

The MGMI is calculated using the official settlement prices published by the Quotations Committee of the **LME**. Prices quoted in sterling (ie copper and lead) are converted to US$ using the average panel of banks' spot US dollar/sterling mid-rates. The formula is a base-weighted aggregative expressed in relative terms with the value for the base year, 1985, set equal to 100.

$$MGMI_t = \frac{Spot\ Value\ of\ Base\ at\ Time\ t}{Current\ Base\ Value} \times 100$$

$$= \frac{\sum_{i=1}^{N} w_i P_{it}}{Current\ Base\ Value} \times 100$$

N = number of metals in the current base; w_i = weight of metal i; P_{it} = spot price of metal i at time t.

Example of Calculation

Metal	Price/Tonne	US$/£	Weight	Product
Aluminum	US$1,580.00	-	0.426	673.08
Copper	£1,512.00	US$1.6610	0.254	637.90
Zinc	US$1,344.00	-	0.160	215.04
Lead	£445.00	US$1.6610	0.136	100.52
Nickel	US$7,700.00	-	0.019	146.30
Tin	US$6,930.00	-	0.005	34.65
Total				1,807.49
Current Base Value				1,110.8003
Index				162.72

(The panel of banks providing the spot US dollar/sterling mid-rates for the final MGMI Settlement Price is:

Barclays Global Treasury Services

Chemical Bank

Citibank, N.A.

Commerzbank AG

Hill Samuel Bank Ltd

Midland Montagu Treasury

The Mitsubishi Bank Ltd

The Royal Bank of Scotland plc

The daily **MGMI** is calculated using spot US dollar/sterling mid-rates provided by Barclays Global Treasury Services.)

The contract has enabled professional investment managers to participate in broad movements of the base metal markets without any involvement in the delivery process. It has also allowed industrial hedgers (traders, producers and consumers) to have new opportunities for managing risk.

Profitable trading thus depends on taking a correct view of the overall direction of non-ferrous metal prices rather than specific metal prices. The **MGMI** has periodically exhibited a higher reward-variability ratio and annualized average daily return than many common components of managed portfolios, making it an attractive investment in its own right and a complement or substitute to direct holdings. The lower volatility of the **MGMI**, compared to that of its components, qualifies it as a relatively stable investment vehicle which could enhance the risk/return profile of an investment portfolio.

The market value of mining companies and non-ferrous metal industries is largely dependent on base metal prices. **MGMI** futures can thus be used by portfolio managers, either singularly or in conjunction with stock index futures, to hedge earnings, share and direct holdings in mining companies and non-ferrous metals industries.

Returns on the **MGMI** and those on equities and bonds do not move in tandem, so incorporating **MGMI** futures into a general fund provides a valuable and flexible form of portfolio diversification across a full economic cycle. Judicious use of **MGMI** futures in combination with the existing range of anti-inflation hedgers can be used by investment managers to hedge the value of equity/bond portfolios against the effects of rising inflation.

The **MGMI** market is electronically traded by 15 brokers and commission houses in London, Germany and the U.S.A.. The volume of contracts traded since June 1990 has seen continuing growth and widespread interest from both the investment and metals community. The **MGMI** itself has become increasingly volatile, ranging from a July low of 171.24 to a high of 184.38. Since its launch, historical volatility measured on a standard basis has risen by more than 5 per cent.

On 13 July 1990, a daily volume record was set for **MGMI** futures at 1,130 contracts. By the end of trading on 18 July, total volume reached 10,051 contracts. In the month of July, 13,306 contracts had been traded, an average of 605 contracts per day. Total turnover up to end of July was 16,126 lots. Open interest has been increasing steadily, indicating a genuine commercial interest in the contract. The maximum open interest in July was close to 800 contracts.

Contract Size:	US$ 100 per full MGMI Index Point. The value of a futures contract is determined by multiplying the index by US$ 100 eg if MGMI @ 165.20 then one contract = US$ 16,520.
Expiry Months:	see Matrix.
Expiry Day:	Monday prior to third Wednesday of expiry month.
Last Trading Day:	Monday prior to third Wednesday of expiry month.
Quotation:	US$ per index point.
Minimum Price Movement (Tick Size and Value):	US$ 10 per 10 MGMI basis points.
Trading Hours:	08.00 a.m. - 19.05 p.m. or as decided by the Market Committee.
Initial Margin:	US$ 500 per contract.
Price Limit:	No price limits.
Contract Standard:	Cash settlement based on the final MGMI settlement price.
Exchange Delivery Settlement Price:	Cash price at expiry of contract.
Reuters Pages:	**IMGM and .MGMI**
Telerate Pages:	947

MGMI Weightings

Each metal in the MGMI is weighted according to the share of the six metal's total consumption in the western world. These shares have been relatively stable over the past 20 years - 1985 is the base year.

MGMI Expiry Month Matrix

	J	F	M	A	M	J	J	A	S	O	N	D	J	F	M	A	M	J	J	A	S	O	N	D	J	F	M
J	A	X	X	B		X			X			X			X												
F		A	X	X	B		X			X			X			X											
M			A	X	X	B		X			X			X			B										
A				A	X	X	B		X			X			X			X									
M					A	X	X	B		X			X			X			X								
J						A	X	X	X		X			X			X			B							
J							A	X	X	B		X			X			X			X						
A								A	X	X	B		X			X			X			X					
S									A	X	X	X		X			X			X			B				
O										A	X	X	B		X			X			X			X			
N											A	X	X	B		X			X			X			X		
D												A	X	X	X		X			X			X			B	

MGMI Options Contract

Option Style	American.
Contract Size:	US$ 100 per full MGMI index point.
Expiry Months:	First three months & March June September December and March (2).
Expiry Day:	Monday prior to the third Wednesday of expiry month.
Last Trading Day:	Monday prior to the third Wednesday of expiry month.
Quotation:	US$ to two decimal places.
Minimum Price Movement (Tick Size and Value):	US$ 5 per 5 basis points.
Trading Hours:	08.00 a.m. - 19.05 p.m. or as decided by the Market Committee.
Initial Margin:	US$500 per contract.
Price Limit:	No price limit.
Contract Standard:	Cash settlement based on the final MGMI futures settlement price.
Exercise Price:	60 contracts with exercise intervals of US$5 per contract.
Reuters Pages:	to be agreed.
Telerate Pages:	to be agreed.

New Developments

London FOX intends launching up to four property futures contracts
by the turn of 1990. Draft contracts have been produced and two committees
drawn from the property industry are now in place advising the Exchange on
final contract specification. An index-based contract designed for the
electricity industry is also being looked into. Producers, distributors and large
users need to hedge this important energy supply. The contract may be
launched in the first quarter of 1991.

Other probable contracts include washed aribica coffee, Brazilian
coffee, rice and possibly naphtha. Contracts under further consideration
include edible oils and re-insurance.

REGULATION

All users of London FOX can take comfort from the fact that the
London futures markets are well regulated by an Act of Parliament which lays
down minimum standards as well as insisting that brokers should be adequately capitalised for the business they transact on behalf of their customers.
London FOX is authorized to operate as a Recognized Investment Exchange
under the Financial Services Act 1986.

All Floor Members of London FOX have to be authorized members
of the Association of Futures Brokers and Dealers (AFBD) which exists to
provide protection to all users of the market. The participation by investors
in the commodity market among others prompted the government to ensure
that the investor is properly looked after by those to whom they entrust their
money. This was accomplished by the introduction of the Financial Services
Act 1986.

The Act aims to enhance and promote London as the international
financial centre and to protect clients through:

- Licensing investment brokers
- Segregation of client funds
- Compensation fund
- Code of conduct and compliance procedures.

The Securities and Investments Board has overall responsibility for
the regulation of financial services. It's powers include the authority to
recognize self-regulatory organizations, exchanges, clearing houses and
professional bodies. Rules, practices and codes of conduct for each body is
determined by the SIB which will monitor and approve any future changes.

TAXATION

The Financial Bill 1990 gives details of the proposed new law on the taxation treatment of futures and options contracts. The new law demonstrates that the Inland Revenue in the United Kingdom is becoming supportive of the key financial markets in this country.

The important changes announced on March 20, 1990 were as follows:

- **Pension schemes and unit trusts will be allowed to use futures and options without fear of a tax charge and there will be an exemption from tax on trading income from futures and options transactions.**

- **Futures and options funds set up as authorized unit trusts will be exempt from tax on futures and options transactions.**

This new law will be particularly appealing to U.K. fund managers in that it will now be an advantage to set up futures and options funds in the U.K. under the new authorized regime.

This is because the tax exemption for futures and options transactions will apply only to those new funds set up as authorized unit trusts. The Government has recognized the need for a broader futures and options market place in the U.K. with more investment risk capital, more practitioners and more customers. The tax change could increase the volume of transactions from abroad and on a domestic base for the futures and options industry in London.

QUOTE VENDORS

Reuters Monitor		
Market	Futures	Options
Robusta coffee	KQLE - KQLR	
Cocoa	COKB	CQLE - CQLR
Raw sugar	SUGB - SULE	SQLE -SQLR
White sugar	SU37/SULG	WQLE -WQLR
MGMI Index	IMGM	
Reuters 2000		
Robusta coffee	LKR	LKR
Cocoa	LCC	LCC
Raw sugar	LSG	LSG
White sugar	LSU	LSU
Rubber	LRU	
MGMI Index	.MGMI	
Telerate		
Robusta coffee	946	
Cocoa	943	
Raw sugar	945	
White Sugar	941	
Rubber	942	

| MGMI Index | 947 | |

      Several quote providers can supply prices from **London FOX**. These include:

ADP	**Bloomberg**
Bridge	**CMA**
CQGI	**Fides**
Futuresource	**ICV**
Knight-Ridder	**Newtime**
Pont	**Quotron**
Reuters	**Telekurs**
Telerate	**Track**

SOURCES of INFORMATION

The following national press carry London FOX prices and volumes:

      The Daily Telegraph

      The Financial Times

      The Times

      The Independent

      The International Herald Tribune

      The Wall Street Journal

The following publications carry London FOX prices and volumes:

      The Public Ledger

      Futures & Options World

      Futures Magazine

      Metal Bulletin

The following is a list of current Exchange publications:

      Futures Trading Now

FOX Options - Trading for Tomorrow

London FOX - Historical Paper

Business Bulletin

London FOX Statistical Yearbook

The London International Financial Futures Exchange ("LIFFE")

Alex Carpenter
Claudio Capozzi
The London International Financial Futures Exchange
(LIFFE)

INTRODUCTION

LIFFE was the first Exchange to trade financial futures in Europe. The Exchange was established in 1981, independently from the existing London Stock Exchange and commodity futures Exchanges and began trading on 30th September 1982, in the Royal Exchange building opposite the Bank of England. The first contracts to be traded on **LIFFE** were currency futures, Three Month Eurodollar and Sterling Interest Rate futures and a long term U.K. Government Bond ("Long Gilt") future. In 1984, **LIFFE** introduced U.S. Treasury Bond and the Financial Times - Stock Exchange (FT-SE) 100 Stock Index future. Options were introduced in 1985.

In 1987, **LIFFE** expanded its range of interest rate contracts to include contracts denominated in currencies other than sterling or U.S. dollars. A Japanese Government Bond ("JGB") future was introduced in 1987, followed by a German Government Bond ("Bund") future in 1988. The latter contract has subsequently grown to be **LIFFE**'s second most active contract in 1989.

In 1989, **LIFFE** launched a Three Month Euromark Interest Rate future which was followed by a Three Month ECU contract later in the year - the first ECU interest rate future to be traded anywhere in the world.

The bulk of volume on **LIFFE** is concentrated in interest rate contracts. **LIFFE** now has the widest and most international range of such contracts of any Exchange in the world, with short term interest rate contracts in four major currencies - £, $, DM and ECU - and long term interest rate contracts on the four largest government bond markets - U.S. Treasuries, Japanese Government Bonds, UK Gilt and German Bunds.

Since the beginning in 1982, volumes on **LIFFE** have grown steadily. In 1989, **LIFFE** traded a record year of 23.9 million futures and options contracts, representing a 53 per cent increase over the previous year. In addition, open interest continued to set record levels throughout the year, ending with 356,000 futures and options contracts, 61 per cent up on the previous year.

This growth was maintained in the first half of 1990 when **LIFFE** traded 17.6 million contracts, making it Europe's largest futures and options exchange.

Business on **LIFFE** is cleared by an independent clearing house - the London Clearing House or **LCH**. The **LCH** is owned by six U.K. clearing banks Barclays, Lloyds, Midland, National Westminster, Royal Bank of Scotland and Standard Chartered. Like the Chicago Exchanges, **LIFFE** is principally a floor-based "open outcry" market with trading continuous between the hours of 08.00 a.m. and 16.15 p.m.. However, in November 1989, **LIFFE** successfully introduced its Automated Pit Trading System (**APT**) for an evening trading session between 16.30 p.m. and 18.00 p.m. in the Euromark and Bund futures contract. In January 1990, forty five of the 191 members had **APT** capability. Other **LIFFE** contracts joined the system early in 1990.

ORGANIZATION of the MARKET
Membership
Geographical Distribution of Membership

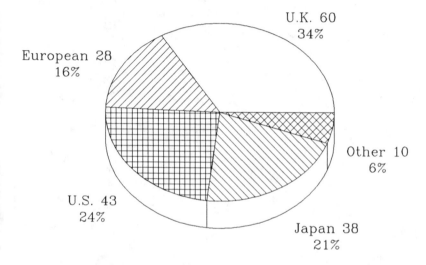

At the end of 1989, there were 192 members of the Exchange, since which Drexel Burnham Lambert Ltd has withdrawn. The membership of **LIFFE** has a very international mix with UK firms representing 31 per cent of the total. The remainder is comprised of U.S. (23 per cent), Japan (20 per cent), Continental Europe (18 per cent) and other (8 per cent) firms.

Types of Shares

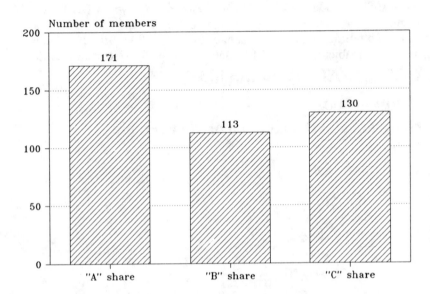

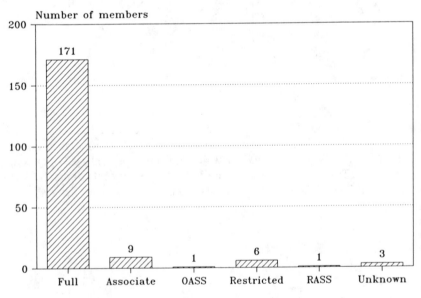

Members of **LIFFE** may own one or more types of share in the
Exchange:

- **A shares (Futures Member) with trading rights in all LIFFE
  futures contracts.**

- **B shares (Options Member) with trading rights in all LIFFE
  options contracts. An options member cannot become a clearing
  member and may not act only as a non public order member.**

- **C shares (Restricted Member) with trading rights in all LIFFE
  futures contracts except Long Gilt, Short Sterling, U.S. Treasury
  Bond and Eurodollar.**

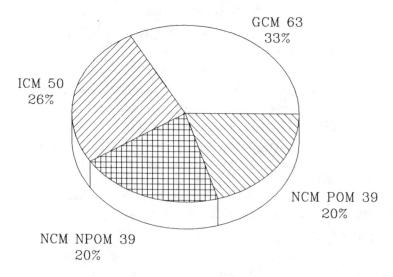

Futures and Options Members must also hold a clearing arrangements registration or exemption certificate. These are issued by the Exchange.
A **Restricted Member** cannot become a clearing member and may act only as
a **Non Public Order Member**. An **Associate Member** will be the lessee of a
futures, options or restricted futures trading permit. An **Associate Member**
does not have voting rights, cannot become a clearing member and may act
only as a **Non Public Order Member. Non Public Order Members are not
permitted to deal with, or for, or advise clients who are not members of the
Exchange.** No member may trade on the market floor or participate in the
Automated Pit Trading system administered by the Exchange unless he holds

or leases in a permit. The permit must be of a kind authorizing trading in the Exchange Contract in which the member wishes to trade. A member may apply to the Exchange for a trading permit on a share owned by the member, or to lease a trading permit from the holder of a permit. A **Restricted Associate Member ("RASS")** of LIFFE leases in one or more restricted futures trading permits. An **Options Associate Member ("OASS")** leases in one or more options trading permits.

Membership Categories

There are four categories of membership defined according to ability of the member to clear and execute business on the Exchange.

- **General Clearing Members ("GCM") may clear their own and other members' business directly with the clearing house.**

- **Individual Clearing Members ("ICM") may clear their own but not other members' business.**

All clearing members may execute public (i.e non-member) orders.

- **Non Clearing Members ("NCM") are divided into two types:**

Public Order Members ("POM") may deal for his own account, for other members, and for clients who are not members of the Exchange.

Non Public Order Members ("NPOM") may only trade **LIFFE** contracts for their own account or on behalf of other members of the Exchange in a pit broking capacity.

Both must clear their business through a General Clearing Member. The latter category include the 31 locals on the Exchange.

General Clearing Members

With 191 members of LIFFE, to give some impression of those institutions present in the Exchange, the General Clearing Members "GCM" in January 1990 only have been listed below.

A I B Capital Markets plc
Australia & New Zealand Banking Group Ltd
Riggs A P Bank Limited
Argus Corporation
Baring Securities Ltd
Banque Nationale de Paris Plc
B A Futures Incorporated
B T Futures Corp
Barclays de Zoete Wedd Futures Ltd

Citifutures Ltd
Continental Bank N.A.
Cargill Investor Services Ltd
Credit Lyonnais Rouse Ltd
James Capel C M & M (UK) Ltd
Czarnikow Futures Ltd
Discount Corporation of New York Futures
Daiwa Europe Ltd
The Dai-Ichi Kangyo Bank Ltd
(Drexel Burnham Lambert Ltd)
Dean Witter Futures Ltd
Elders Futures Inc
Elders Finance Group UK Ltd
First Chicago Futures Inc
First Options of Chicago Ltd
Fulton Prebon Futures Ltd
Geldermann Limited
Gerald Limited
GNI Wallace Ltd
GNI Ltd
Goldman Sachs Futures Ltd
Hill Samuel Bank Ltd
International Clearing Services Ltd
J P Morgan Futures Inc
Kas Clearing Agent Ltd
Kleinwort Benson Ltd
L C F Limited
LIT Futures Limited
Lloyds Bank Financial Futures Ltd
E D & F Man International Ltd
Midland Montagu Futures/Div Midland Bank Plc
The Mitsui Bank Ltd
The Mitsui Trust & Banking Company Ltd
Merrill Lynch Pierce Fenner & Smith (B & D) Ltd
The Mitsubishi Bank Ltd
Nomura International plc
National Westminster Financial Futures Ltd
Prudential-Bache (Futures) Ltd
The Royal Bank of Scotland Plc
Refco Incorporated

Rudolf Wolff & Co Ltd
SUCDEN (UK) Ltd
Shearson Lehman Hutton Inc
Salomon Brothers International Ltd
Standard Chartered Bank
Tokai International Ltd
The Tokai Bank Ltd
Tullett & Tokyo (Futures & Traded Options) Ltd
The United Bank of Kuwait Plc
UBS Phillips & Drew Futures Ltd
Union Discount Futures Ltd
S G Warburg Futures & Options Ltd
Wallace Smith Interfutures/Div Br Trusts Assoc Ltd
Westpac Banking Corporation
Yamaichi International (Europe) Ltd

Board of Directors @ 31/12/1989

A D Burton, Chairman	S G Warburg Futures & Options Ltd
N G Ackerman	LIT Futures Ltd
R R St J Barkshire	ICCH Futures Ltd
P C Barnett	P C Barnett
A J Dickinson	A J D Financial Services Ltd
N J Durlacher, Deputy Chairman	Barclays de Zoete Wedd Futures Ltd
C J Edwards, Deputy Chairman	First Continental Trading Inc
R M Eynon	S G Warburg Futures & Options Ltd
Mrs S S Hanbury-Brown	J P Morgan Futures Inc
C Henry	Baring Brothers & Co Ltd
M N H Jenkins, Chief Executive	LIFFE
D J Keegan	Salomon Brothers International Ltd
B J Lind	Midland Montagu Futures/Div Midland Bank plc
E R Porter	National Westminster Financial Futures Ltd
S J Sanders	Lloyds Bank Financial Futures Ltd
M J Stiller	Tullett & Tokyo (Futures & Traded Options Ltd)
J Wigglesworth	Henderson Administration Ltd
R B Williamson	Gerrard & National Ltd
Mrs R S Wilton	Drexel Burham Lambert Ltd

Management

M N H Jenkins, Chief Executive Officer

Address:	LIFFE The London International Financial Futures Exchange Limited
	Royal Exchange
	LONDON EC3V 3PJ
Telephone:	(44) 71-623 0444
Telefax:	(44) 71-588 3624
Telex:	893893 LIFFE G

Regulation

Until 1988, **LIFFE** was supervised by the Bank of England. Since 1988, it has been supervised by the Securities and Investment Board ("**SIB**"). The day-to-day task of regulating trading on **LIFFE** is handled by the Market-supervision department ("**MSD**") of the exchange. This department has responsibility for the following areas:

1. **Market Supervision**
    MSD supervise the delivery and settlement of futures' contracts and the exercise or abandonment of options' contracts. Members must provide to **MSD** each morning reports of their trades undertaken during the previous day and of their current options positions. However, these are not stated positions limits on **LIFFE**.

2. **Trading Surveillance**
    MSD ensures that trading is properly executed according to the rules of **LIFFE** and investigates complaints and refunds from the Trading Operations department.

3. **Financial Surveillance**
    MSD receives reports of member's net worth quarterly and independently audited accounts yearly. **MSD** have the right to visit member offices and inspect audit trails.

Price Limits

There are no price limits on **LIFFE** contracts with the exception of the Japanese Government Bond Future.

LIFFE Exchange Fees (as at June 30, 1990)

Futures	90p per round trip
Options	60p per round trip

Education (Publications and Courses)

LIFFE offers a variety of publications free of charge covering its contracts and their uses.

Contact: Tel (44) 71 623 0444 ext. 2259

In addition, **LIFFE** offers one and two day courses both in London and the continent.

Contact: Tel (44) 71 623 0444 ext. 2136

Sources of Information
Price and volume information for **LIFFE** products is available in all major daily quality newspapers.

OVERVIEW of PRODUCTS

	Futures	Options
Interest Rates		
U.K. Long Gilt	*	*
U.S. Treasury Bond	*	*
Japanese Government Bond	*	
German Government Bond	*	*
3 month Sterling	*	*
3 month Eurodollar	*	*
3 month Euromark	*	*
3 month E.C.U.	*	
Equities		
FT-SE 100 Stock Index	*	

HISTORY of the FUTURES & OPTIONS MARKET

1982	LIFFE Opening.
1982	3 Month Eurosterling Future.
1982	3 Month Eurodollar Future.
1982	U.K. Long Gilt Future.
1984	FT-SE 100 Stock Index Future
1984	U.S Treasury Bond Future.
1985	3 Month Eurodollar Option.
March 1986	U.S. Treasury bond Option.
March 1986	U.K. Long Gilt Option.
July 1987	Japanese Government Bond Future.
November 1987	3 Month Sterling Option.
September 1988	German Government Bond Future.
April 1989	German Government Bond Option.
April 1989	3 Month Eurodeutschemark Future.
October 1989	3 month ECU Future.
February 1990	3 Month Eurodeutschemark Option.

DETAILED CONTRACT SPECIFICATION
(Correct at April 1990)
Interest Rate Futures and Options

U.K. Government Long Bond ("Long Gilt") Future

The Long Gilt future was the first government bond future to be launched on **LIFFE** and by 1987 was the most active contract on the Exchange. The early success of the contract stemmed in the main from the size of the Gilt market (the world's third largest after U.S. Treasuries and Japanese Government Bonds) and from the spectacular increase in turnover following London's "Big-Bang" in 1986, when the number of market makers was increased from a handful of small British firms to 27 large international houses. Since 1988 the UK government has began to buy back Gilt from the market, reducing both turnover and volatility. As a result, volume in 1989 declined by some 27 per cent to 4.1 million contracts, making it the third most active contract on the Exchange in 1989. However, market conditions improved in 1990 when volumes in the first half reached 3.1 million contracts against 2.2 million contracts in the same period in 1989.

The contract itself was designed on conventional lines as a deliverable contract allowing the seller to choose which Gilt to deliver with an adjustment being made to the invoice amount by means of a price factor. Originally, delivery could be made of any Gilt, as listed by **LIFFE**, with a maturity of between 15 and 25 years. However, because of the lack of new issues in this area, the contract was redesigned in 1989 to allow delivery of Gilts with redemption dates between 1st January 2003 and 31st December 2009. Thus, from the 1st January 1990 for example, Gilt with maturities of between 12 and 19 years can be delivered. **LIFFE** also introduced a Short Gilt future in 1985 and a Medium Gilt future in 1988. However, these contracts were delisted in January 1990.

Contract Size:	£50,000 nominal value notional Gilt with 9 per cent coupon.
Delivery Months:	March June September December.
Delivery Day:	Any business day in Delivery Month (at seller's choice).

Last Trading Day:	11.00 a.m. two business days prior to last business day in Delivery Month.
Quotation:	Per £100 nominal.
Minimum Price Movement (Tick Size and Value):	1/32 per cent = £15.625.
Trading Hours:	08.30 a.m. - 16.15 p.m.
Initial Margin:	1.5 per cent = £750.
Price Limit:	No price limit.
Contract Standard:	Physical delivery may be made of any Gilt with maturities of between January 1 2003 and December 31 2009 as listed by LIFFE. Stocks with optional dates will be deliverable only if both earliest and latest dates meet this criterion. No variable rate index-linked convertible or partly paid may be delivered. Stocks are not deliverable within the period of three weeks and one day or on the XD date.
Exchange Delivery Settlement Price:	The LIFFE market price at 11.00 a.m. on the second business day prior to delivery. The invoicing amount in respect of each deliverable stock is to be calculated by the price factor system. These are calculated by the Exchange and announced before trading for the relevant contract month has commenced.
Reuters Pages:	LIEP
Telerate Pages:	1994

Deliverable Gilt Edged Bonds

Long Gilt Contract (9% Coupon) - Price Factors & Accrued Interest			
Contract Month (June 1990)			
Stock	Price Factor	Daily Accrued	Initial Accrued
Treasury 11.75% 22 Jan 2003/07	1.2055878	16.0959	-836.99
Treasury 11.00% 8 Sep 2003	1.0758839	13.6986	1150.68
Treasury 12.50% 21 Nov 2003/05	1.2695449	17.1233	171.23
Treasury 13.50% 26 May 2004/08	1.3509974	18.4932	1220.55
Treasury 10.00% 18 May 2004	1.0781358	13.6986	178.08
Conversion 9.50% 25 Oct 2004	1.0396210	13.0137	468.49
Conversion 9.50% 18 Apr 2005	1.0402466	13.0137	559.59
Exchequer 10.50% 20 Sep 2005	1.1226358	14.3836	1035.62
Treasury 8.50% 16 Jul 2007	0.9570332	11.6438	-535.62
Treasury 9.00% 13 Oct 2008	0.9996841	12.3288	591.78
Treasury 8.00% 25 Sep 2009	0.9086422	10.9589	734.25

Key:

Daily Accrued	accrued interest per day on £50,000 face value
Price Factor	price factor expressed as a fraction of par
Initial Accrued	accrued interest on £50,000 face value as of the last day of the month prior to the delivery month
Invoicing Amount	(500 x EDSP x Price factor) + Initial Accrued + (Daily Accrued x Delivery day in month)
Issue date	2 January 1990

Daily Volume and Open Interest (Jan 2,1990 - Jun 29,1990)

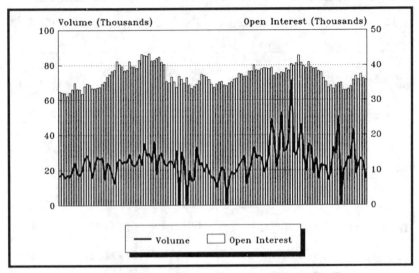

Open Interest and Volume/Open Interest("Liquidity")
(Jan 2,1990 - Jun 29,1990)

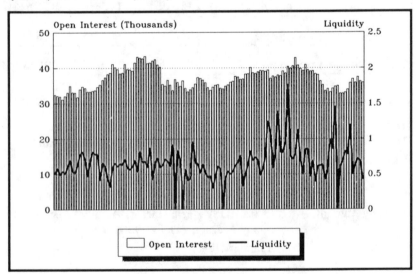

Price/Yield History (Jan 2,1990 - Jun 29,1990)

Implied Repo Rate (Jan 2,1990 - Jun 29,1990)

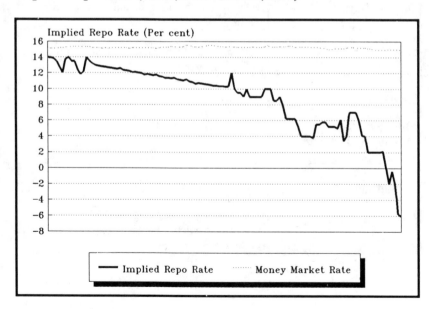

U.K.Government Long Bond ("Long Gilt") Option

The Long Gilt Option was launched on **LIFFE** in March 1986 and grew quickly to become **LIFFE**'s most active options contract in 1988. However, for the same reasons that caused the decline in the Long Gilt future, volumes in the Long Gilt option declined in 1989 by 36 per cent to 727,000 contracts, making it the third most active options contract on the Exchange. As is common for Exchange traded interest rate options, the Long Gilt option is an option on the futures contract with the same face value and expiry cycle as the futures contract. However, the Long Gilt option expires before trading ceases in the futures contract and has a minimum price movement of 1/64 i.e. half the minimum price movement of the futures contract. Long Gilt options may be exercised on any business day prior to expiry (American style), early exercise resulting in the assignment of a futures position.

Option Type:	American.
Unit of Trading:	One Long Gilt futures contract.
Delivery Months:	March June September December.
Delivery Day:	Delivery on the first business day after the exercise day.
Last Trading Day:	16.15 p.m. six business days prior to the first Delivery Day of the Long Gilt futures contract.
Quotation:	Multiples of 1/64.
Minimum Price Movement (Tick Size and Value):	1/64 per cent = £7.8125.
Trading Hours:	08.32 a.m. - 16.15 p.m.
Initial Margin:	Initial margin for long and short options positions is calculated with reference to daily published risk factors.

Exercise Prices:	£1.00 intervals. 13 Exercise Prices are listed for each series. Additional prices will be introduced on the business day after the Long Gilt future contract settlement price is within £ 16/32 of the sixth highest.
Reuters Pages:	LIGU.
Telerate Pages:	15990 - 15993.

Daily Volume and Open Interest (Jan 2,1990 - Jun 29,1990)

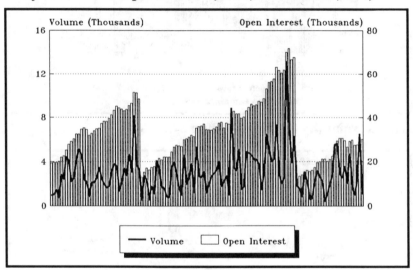

Open Interest and Volume/Open Interest("Liquidity")
(Jan 2,1990 - Jun 29,1990)

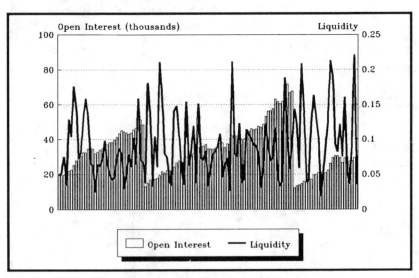

Implied Volatility (Jan 2,1990 - Jun 29,1990)

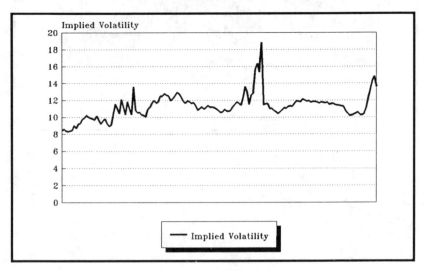

U.S. Treasury Bond ("T-Bond") Future

The U.S. Treasury Bond ("T-Bond") future was launched on **LIFFE** in 1984 and until 1988 was one of the four most active contracts on the Exchange. However, volume in 1989 declined by 50 per cent to 967,000 contracts due in part to the Chicago Board of Trade ("CBOT") opening their contract 40 minutes earlier at 07.20 a.m. Chicago time and to a decline in volatility in the underlying cash market.

The **LIFFE** contract was modelled on the successful U.S. Treasury Bond future trade on the CBOT - a deliverable contract allowing delivery of U.S. Treasury bonds with maturities of 15 years or more. **However, the LIFFE and CBOT are not fungible.**

Like the Long Gilt future, delivery may be made of a range of bonds at the choice of the seller with an adjustment being made to the invoice amount by means of a price or conversion factor.

Contract Size:	$ 100,000 nominal value notional U.S. Treasury bond with a coupon of 8 per cent.
Delivery Months:	March June September December.
Delivery Day:	Any business day in Delivery Month (at seller's choice).
Last Trading Day:	16.10 p.m. seven CBOT business days prior to last business day in Delivery Month.
Quotation:	Per $ 100 nominal.
Minimum Price Movement (Tick Size and Value):	1/32 per cent = $ 31.625.
Trading Hours:	08.15 a.m. - 16.10 p.m.
Initial Margin:	1.25 per cent = $ 1,250.
Price Limit:	No price limit.

Contract Standard:	Delivery may be made of any U.S. Treasury bond in multiples of $ 100,000 with maturities of 15 years or more if not callable
Exchange Delivery Settlement Price:	The LIFFE EDSP shall be that settlement price established on the same day on the Chicago Board of Trade for deliveries into the CBOT US Treasury bond futures contract.
Reuters Pages:	LFDA.
Telerate Pages:	994.

Daily Volume and Open Interest (Jan 2,1990 - Jun 29,1990)

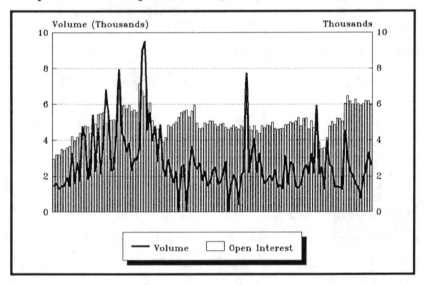

Open Interest and Volume/Open Interest("Liquidity")
(Jan 2,1990 - Jun 29,1990)

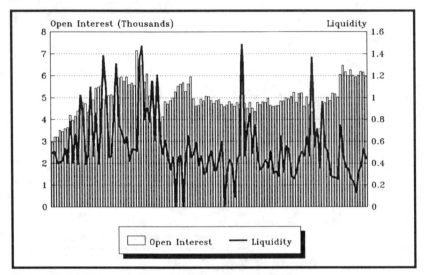

Price/Yield History (Jan 2,1990 - Jun 29,1990)

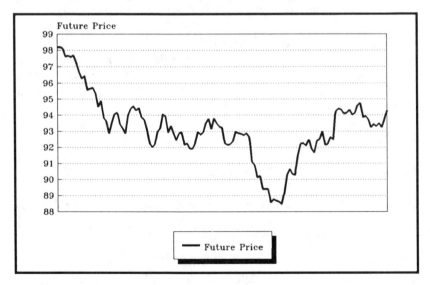

Implied Repo Rate (Jan 2,1990 - Jun 29,1990)

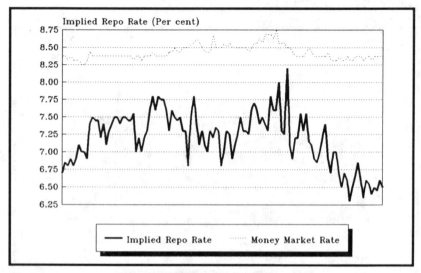

U.S. Treasury Bond ("T-Bond") Option

The U.S. Treasury Bond ("T-Bond") option was launched on **LIFFE** in March 1986. Volume in 1989 was 76,000 contracts, a decline of 10 per cent on the previous year.

Like the Long Gilt option, the U.S. Treasury Bond option is an option on the futures contract - with the same face value and expiry cycle as the futures contract. In the same way, the U.S. Treasury Bond option expires before trading ceases in the futures contract and has a minimum price movement of 1/64 per cent.

Like all **LIFFE** options, U.S. Treasury Bond options are American style. Exercise results in the assignment of a futures position.

Option Type:	American.
Unit of Trading:	One U.S. Treasury Bond futures contract.
Delivery Months:	March June September December.
Delivery Day:	Delivery on the first business day after the exercise day.

Last Trading Day:	16.10 p.m. First Friday preceding by at least six CBOT business days the first Delivery Day of the U.S. Treasury Bond futures contract.
Quotation:	Multiples of 1/64.
Minimum Price Movement (Tick Size and Value):	1/64 per cent = £15.625.
Trading Hours:	08.15 a.m. - 16.10 p.m.
Initial Margin:	Initial margin for the long and short options positions is calculated with reference to daily published risk factors.
Price Limit:	No price limit.
Exercise Prices:	$ 1.00 intervals. 13 exercise prices are listed 6 above and 6 below the current level. New prices will be introduced on the business day after the US Treasury bond futures contract settlement price is within $ 16/32 of the sixth highest or lowest existing exercise price.
Reuters Pages:	**LFDB - LFDM LFVN - LFVV.**
Telerate Pages;	15996 - 15997.

Daily Volume and Open Interest (Jan 2,1990 - Jun 29,1990)

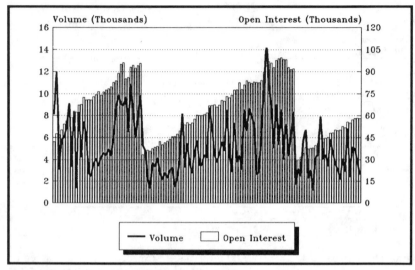

Open Interest and Volume/Open Interest("Liquidity") (Jan 2,1990 - Jun 29,1990)

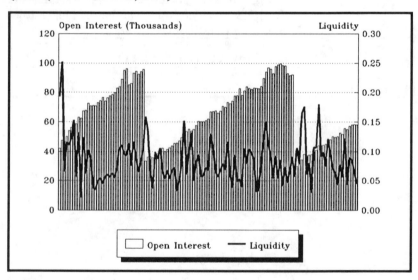

Implied Volatility (Jan 2,1990 - Jun 29,1990)

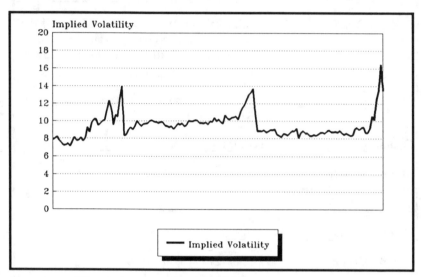

German Government Bond ("Bund")

The German Government Bond ("Bund") future was launched on
LIFFE in September 1988 and grew rapidly to become the Exchange's second
most active contract in 1989 when volume was 5.6 million contracts. This
success was due to the size of the Bund market (the world's fourth largest),
the increased volatility in yields during 1989 and to the lack of a competitive
product elsewhere. Volumes increased further in the first half of 1990 when
5.3 million contracts were traded against 2.0 million in the same period in
1989.

The contract was designed conventionally as a deliverable contract
allowing the seller to choose which Bund to deliver with a price factor
adjustment being made to the invoice amount. Delivery may be made of any
Bund, as listed by **LIFFE**, with a maturity of between 8.5 and 10 years so that
it is a medium term contract like the MATIF bond future. Unlike, the U.S.
Treasury Bond and Gilt futures, however, delivery takes place on a single day
rather than any business day in the Delivery Month.

Contract Size:	DM250,000 nominal value notional German Government Bond with a 6 per cent coupon.

Delivery Months:	March June September December.
Delivery Day:	Tenth calendar day of Delivery Month. If that day is not a business day in Frankfurt then the Delivery Day shall be the next following Frankfurt business day.
Last Trading Day:	11.00 a.m. Three Frankfurt business days prior to Delivery Day.
Quotation:	Per DM100 nominal.
Minimum Price Movement (Tick Size and Value):	0.01 per cent = DM25.
Trading Hours:	08.05 a.m. - 16.00 p.m.
Initial Margin:	2.0 per cent = DM 5,000.
Price Limit:	No price limit.
Contract Standard:	Delivery may be made of any German Government Bond with maturities of between 8.5 and 10 years.
Exchange Delivery Settlement Price:	The LIFFE market price at 11.00 a.m. Frankfurt time on the last trading day.
Reuters Pages:	LFJC
Telerate Pages:	994.

Daily Volume and Open Interest (Jan 2,1990 - Jun 29,1990)

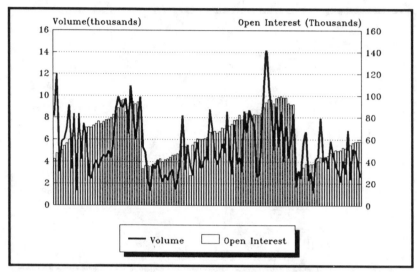

Open Interest and Volume/Open Interest("Liquidity")
(Jan 2,1990 - Jun 29,1990)

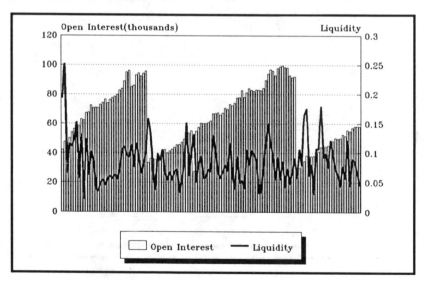

Price/Yield History (Jan 2,1990 - Jun 29,1990)

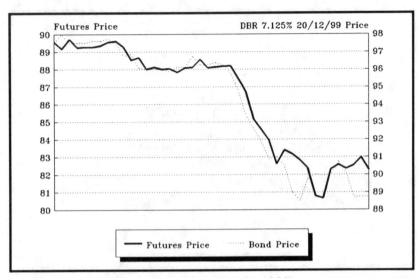

Implied Repo Rate (Jan 2,1990 - Jun 29,1990)

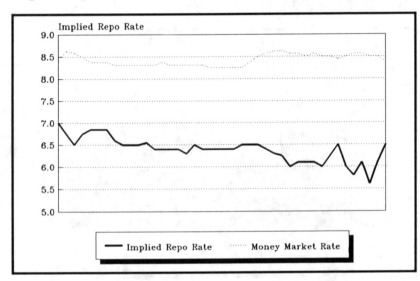

German Government Bond ("Bund") Option

The Bund option was launched on **LIFFE** in April 1989 and has grown to become **LIFFE**'s second most active options contract in 1989 when volume was 469,000 contracts. In the first half of 1990 volumes increased further to 670,000 contracts.

Like the Long Gilt and U.S. Treasury Bond options, the Bund option is an option on the futures contract - with the same face, value expiry and minimum price movement as the futures contract. In the same way, the Bund option expires before trading ceases in the futures contract.

Like all **LIFFE** options, Bund options are American style Exercise of the option results in the assignment of a futures position.

Option Type:	American.
Unit of Trading:	One Bund futures contract.
Delivery Months:	March June September December.
Delivery Day:	Delivery on the first business day after the exercise day.
Last Trading Day:	16.00 p.m. Six business days prior to first day of the Delivery Month.
Quotation:	Multiples of DM 0.01.
Minimum Price Movement (Tick Size and Value):	0.01 per cent = DM25.
Trading Hours:	08.07 a.m. - 16.00 p.m.
Initial Margin:	Initial margin for the long and short options positions is calculated with reference to daily published risk factors.

Exercise Prices:	DM 0.50 intervals. 9 exercise prices are listed 4 above and 4 below the current price. Additional prices are introduced the day after the Bund futures contract settlement price is within DM 0.25 of the fourth highest or lowest price.
Reuters Pages:	**LFJD - LFJM LFVN - LFVV.**
Telerate Pages:	15990 - 15994.

Daily Volume and Open Interest (Jan 2,1990 - Jun 29,1990)

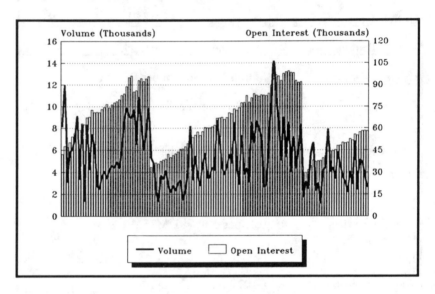

Open Interest and Volume/Open Interest("Liquidity")
(Jan 2,1990 - Jun 29,1990)

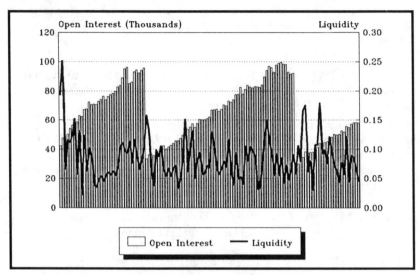

Implied Volatility (Jan 2,1990 - Jun 29,1990)

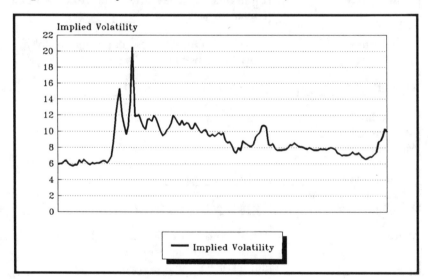

Japanese Government Bond ("JGB") Future

The Japanese Government Bond ("JGB") future was launched on **LIFFE** in July 1987 with the co-operation of the Tokyo Stock Exchange which had already been trading such a contract since late 1985. Volumes have, however, remained fairly stable with 1989 recording a volume of 117,000 contracts (a decline of 3 per cent on 1988).

The **LIFFE** contract is "cash-settled" as opposed to the conventual deliverable format so that it should have the same economic value as the Tokyo Stock Exchange JGB futures contract.

A second departure from the normal contract is that there exist price limits for this contract that do not exist on other **LIFFE** contracts. The limits are ¥1.00 above or below the Tokyo Stock Exchange closing price. If the limit is hit, price limits are removed one hour later for the remainder of the trading day. There are no limits during the last hour of trading on each day.

Contract Size:	¥100,000,000 nominal value notional long term JGB with 6 per cent coupon.
Delivery Months:	March June September December.
Delivery Day:	First business day after the Tokyo Stock Exchange last trading day.
Last Trading Day:	16.05 p.m. One business day prior to Tokyo Stock Exchange last trading day.
Quotation:	Per ¥100 nominal.
Minimum Price Movement (Tick Size and Value):	0.01 per cent = ¥10,000.
Trading Hours:	08.10 a.m. -16.05 p.m.
Initial Margin:	1.0 per cent = ¥1,000,000.
Price Limit:	¥1.00 above or below the Tokyo Stock Exchange closing price. There are no limits during the last hour of trading each day.

Contract Standard:	Cash settlement.
Exchange Delivery Settlement Price:	
Reuters Pages:	LFJB
Telerate Pages:	994

Daily Volume and Open Interest (Jan 2,1990 - Jun 29,1990)

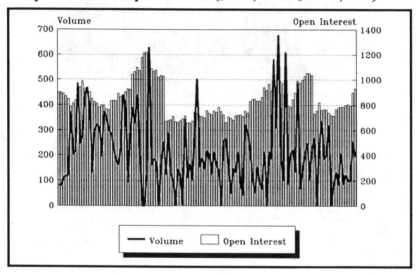

Open Interest and Volume/Open Interest("Liquidity")
(Jan 2,1990 - Jun 29,1990)

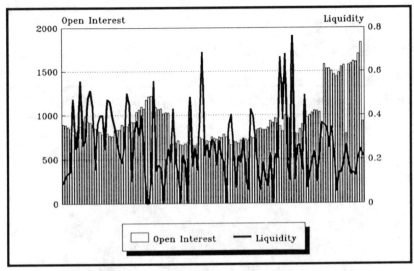

Price/Yield History (Jan 2,1990 - Jun 29,1990)

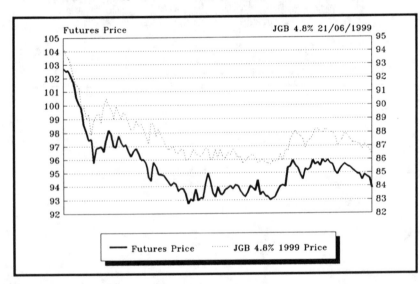

Implied Repo Rate (Jan 2,1990 - Jun 29,1990)

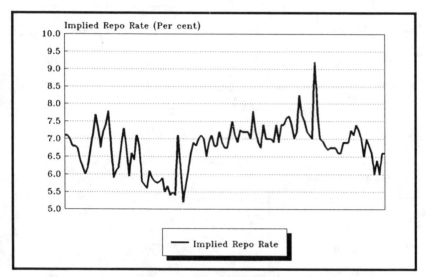

Three Month Sterling Interest Rate ("Short Sterling") Future

The Three Month Sterling Interest Rate or "Short Sterling" future was launched in 1982 and has grown to be **LIFFE**'s most active contract in 1989 when volumes rose by 102 per cent to 7.1 million contracts. This increase has been due mainly to the sharp increase in short term sterling interest rate volatility since mid 1988. In the first half of 1990, volumes increased to 4.2 million contracts against 3.3 million contracts in the same period in 1989.

The Short Sterling future is "cash-settled" i.e. there is no Exchange of the underlying unit of trading on the Delivery Day. Instead, all positions are closed out against the Exchange Delivery Settlement Price or **EDSP**. This price is set by **LIFFE** in the following way. Quotes for 3 month London Inter Bank Offer Rate ("LIBOR") are taken from sixteen banks between 9.30 a.m. and 11.00 a.m. on the last trading day. The three highest and three lowest quotes are excluded and an average is taken of the remaining ten. The **EDSP** is then 100.00 less this average, eg. a price of 90.00 reflects a rate of interest of 10.00 per cent.

Contract Size:	£500,000.
Delivery Months:	March June September December.
Delivery Day:	First business day after the last trading day.
Last Trading Day:	11.00 a.m. third Wednesday of the Delivery Month.
Quotation:	100.00 minus rate of interest.
Minimum Price Movement (Tick Size and Value):	0.01 per cent = £12.50.
Trading Hours:	08.20 a.m. -16.02 p.m.
Initial Margin:	0.75 per cent = £3,750.
Price Limit:	No price limit.
Contract Standard:	Cash settlement.
Exchange Delivery Settlement Price:	Based on LIBOR sampled between 09.30 and 11.00 on the last trading day from a random sample of 16 banks from a list of designated banks. Having disregarded the three highest and three lowest quotes the settlement price will be 100 .00 minus the average of the remaining 10 rates.
Reuters Pages:	LIIA
Telerate Pages:	995.

Daily Volume and Open Interest (Jan 2,1990 - Jun 29,1990)

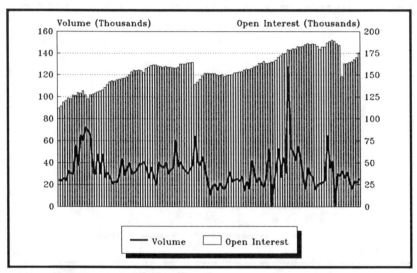

Open Interest and Volume/Open Interest("Liquidity")
(Jan 2,1990 - Jun 29,1990)

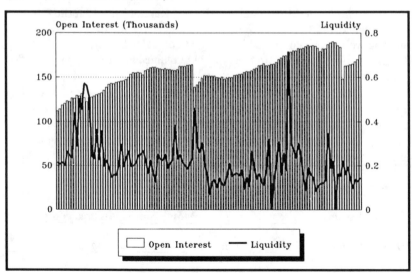

Price/Yield History (Jan 2,1990 - Jun 29,1990)

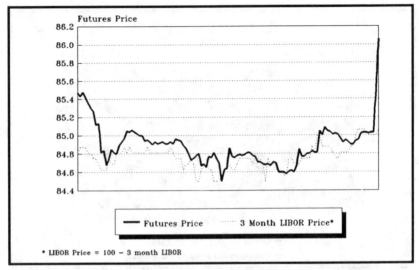

* LIBOR Price = 100 − 3 month LIBOR

Three Month Sterling Interest Rate ("Short Sterling") Option

The Three Month Sterling Interest Rate or "Short Sterling" option was launched on **LIFFE** in November 1987 and has grown to become **LIFFE**'s most active options contract with a volume of 824,000 contracts in 1989, up 85 per cent on 1988. In the first half of 1990, volume increased again to 542,000 contracts against 366,000 in the same period in 1989.

Like other **LIFFE** interest rate options, the Three Month Sterling option is an option on the futures contract with the same contract features, e.g. face value, expiry cycle months, minimum price movement and last trading day. Like all **LIFFE** options, Three Month Sterling options may be exercised on any business day prior in a futures position.

Option Type:	American.
Unit of Trading:	One Three Month Sterling futures contract.
Delivery Months:	March June September December.
Delivery Day:	First business day after the exercise day.

Last Trading Day:	11.00 a.m. last trading day of the Three Month Sterling futures contract.
Quotation:	Multiples of 0.01.
Minimum Price Movement (Tick Size and Value):	0.01 per cent = £12.50.
Trading Hours:	08.22 a.m. - 16.02 p.m.
Initial Margin:	Initial margin for the long and short options positions is calculated with reference to daily published risk factors.
Price Limit:	
Exercise Prices:	Intervals are set of 25 basis points.
Reuters Pages:	**LIIB LFXP - LFXU.**
Telerate Pages:	15742 - 15745.

Daily Volume and Open Interest (Jan 2,1990 - Jun 29,1990)

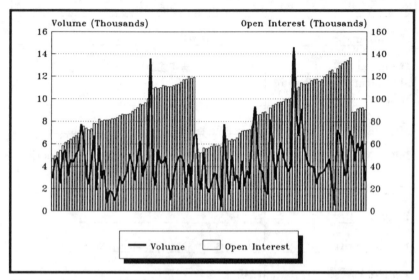

Open Interest and Volume/Open Interest("Liquidity") (Jan 2,1990 - Jun 29,1990)

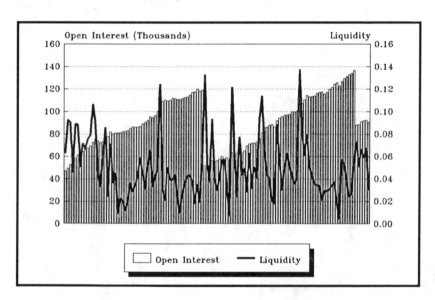

Price/Yield History (Jan 2,1990 - Jun 29,1990)

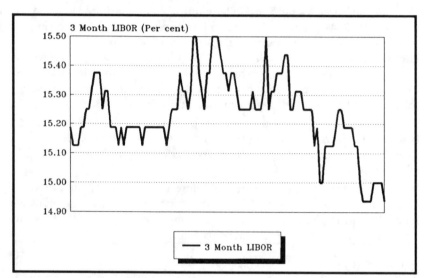

Implied Volatility (Jan 2,1990 - Jun 29,1990)

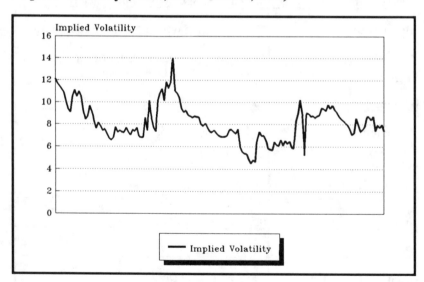

Three Month Eurodollar Interest Rate Future

The Three Month Eurodollar interest Rate future was launched on **LIFFE** in 1982. Although the contract enjoyed early success, it faces competition from the Chicago Mercantile Exchange (**CME**) and the Singapore International Mercantile Exchange ("**SIMEX**") volumes have not grown as rapidly as for other **LIFFE** contracts. However, the increase in short term Eurodollar interest rate volatility during 1989 resulted in an increase in volume over 1988 of some 25 per cent to 2.1 million contracts.

and volumes have not grown as rapidly as for other **LIFFE** contracts. However, the increase in short term Eurodollar interest rate volatility during 1989 resulted in an increase in volume over 1988 of some 25 per cent to 2.1 million contracts.

Like the Three Month Sterling Interest Rate contract, the Eurodollar futures are cash-settled at delivery and prices are quoted as an index of 100.00 less the implied rate of interest. The unit of trading is $1,000,000 with the value of a 0.01 price movement being $25.

Contract Size:	$1,000,000.
Delivery Months:	March June September December.
Delivery Day:	First business day after the last trading day.
Last Trading Day:	11.00 a.m. two business days prior to the Third Wednesday of the Delivery Month.
Quotation:	100.00 minus rate of interest.
Minimum Price Movement (Tick Size and Value):	0.01 per cent = $25.
Trading Hours:	08.30 a.m. -16.00 p.m.
Initial Margin:	0.5 per cent = $500.
Price Limit:	No price limit.
Contract Standard:	Cash settlement.

Exchange Delivery Settlement Price:	Based on the interest rate for 3 month Eurodollar deposits being offered to prime banking names between 09.30 and 11.00 on the last trading day
Reuters Pages:	LIGA.
Telerate Pages:	995.

Daily Volume and Open Interest (Jan 2,1990 - Jun 29,1990)

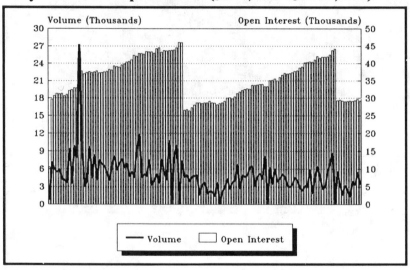

Open Interest and Volume/Open Interest("Liquidity")
(Jan 2,1990 - Jun 29,1990)

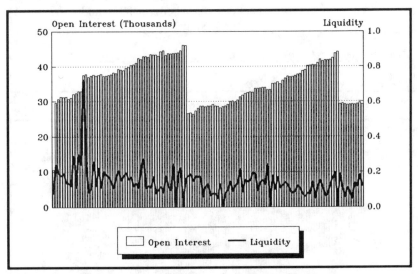

Price/Yield History (Jan 2,1990 - Jun 29,1990)

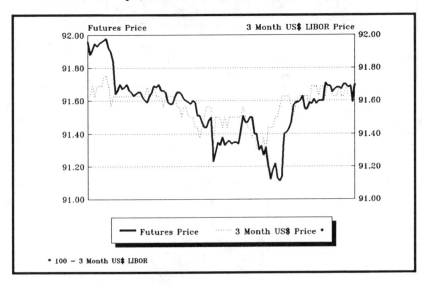

Three Month Eurodollar Interest Rate Option

The Three Month Eurodollar option was launched on **LIFFE** in 1985. Volume in 1989 was 81,000 contracts, an increase of 7 per cent on the previous year.

Like the Three Month Sterling option, the Three Month Eurodollar option is an option on the futures contract with the same contract features as the futures contract, e.g. face value, expiry cycle months, minimum price movement and last trading day. Like all **LIFFE** options, Three Month Eurodollar options may be exercised on any business day prior to expiry (American style), early exercise resulting in a futures position.

Options Type:	American.
Unit of Trading:	One Eurodollar futures contract.
Delivery Months:	March June September December.
Delivery Day:	Delivery on the first business day after the exercise day.
Last Trading Day:	11.00 a.m. last trading day of the Eurodollar futures contract.
Quotation:	Multiples of 0.01.
Minimum Price Movement (Tick Size and Value):	0.01 per cent = $25.
Trading Hours:	08.32 a.m. - 16.02 p.m.
Initial Margin:	Initial margin for the long and short options positions is calculated with reference to daily published risk factors.

Exercise Prices:	0.25 basis points intervals. 13 exercise prices are listed 6 above and 6 below the current price. Additional prices will be introduced on the business day after the Eurodollar futures contract settlement price is within 0.12 of the sixth highest or lowest existing exercise price.
Reuters Pages:	LIGB - LIGW LFXA - LFX0.
Telerate Pages:	981 - 982.

Daily Volume and Open Interest (Jan 2,1990 - Jun 29,1990)

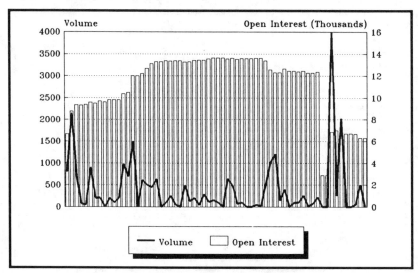

Open Interest and Volume/Open Interest("Liquidity") (Jan 2,1990 - Jun 29,1990)

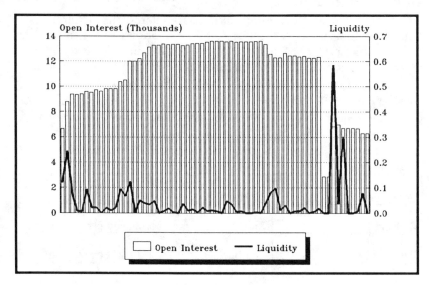

Implied Volatility (Jan 2,1990 - Jun 29,1990)

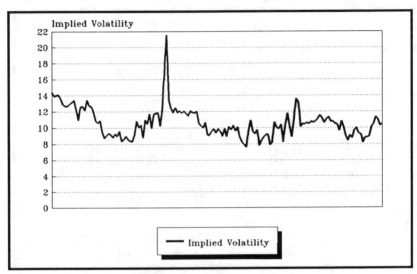

Three Month Eurodeutschemark ("Euromark")
Interest Rate Future

The Three Month Eurodeutschemark Interest Rate ("Euromark") future was launched on **LIFFE** in April 1989 and has grown to become **LIFFE**'s fifth most active futures contract with a volume of 952,000 contracts in 1989. In the first half of 1990 volume increased again to 1.5 million contracts.

The **LIFFE** contract was launched at the same time as an identical contract on MATIF. In November 1989, **LIFFE** accounted for about 60 per cent of the combined volume and 80 per cent of the combined open interest.

Like the "Short Sterling" contract, the Euromark future is cash settled at delivery and prices are quoted as an index of 100.00 less the implied rate of interest.

Contract Size:	DM 1,000,000.
Delivery Months:	March June September December.
Delivery Day:	First business day after the last trading day.

Last Trading Day:	11.00 a.m. two business days prior to the Third Wednesday of the Delivery Month.
Quotation:	100.00 minus rate of interest.
Minimum Price Movement (Tick Size and Value):	0.01 per cent = DM25.
Trading Hours:	08.00 a.m. - 16.10 p.m.
Initial Margin:	0.5 per cent = DM500.
Price Limit:	No price limit.
Contract Standard:	Cash settlement.
Exchange Delivery Settlement Price:	Based on the interest rates for three-month Eurodeutschemark deposits being offered to prime banking names between 09.30 and 11.00 on the last trading day
Reuters Pages:	LFEA.
Telerate Pages:	997.

Daily Volume and Open Interest (Mar 2,1990 - Jun 29,1990)

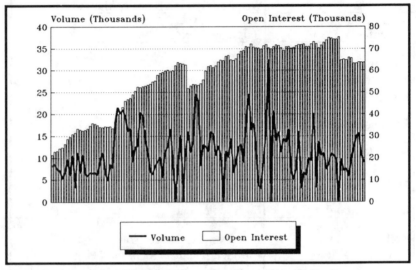

Open Interest and Volume/Open Interest("Liquidity")
(Mar 2,1990 - Jun 29,1990)

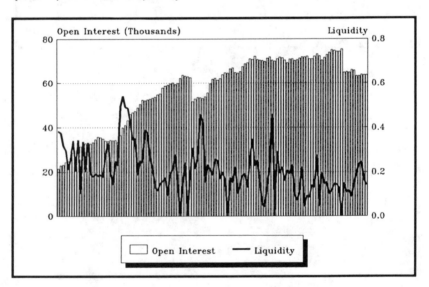

Price/Yield History (Jan 2,1990 - Jun 29,1990)

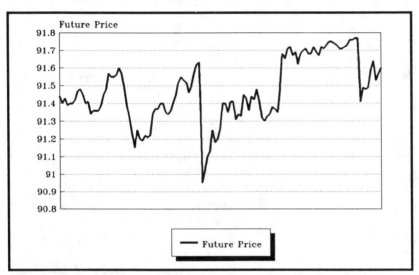

Three Month Eurodeutschemark Interest Rate Option

The Euromark option was launched on the 1st March 1990. Volume in the period up to the end of June 1990 was 94,000 contracts.

Option Style	American.
Contract Size:	One 3 Month Eurodeutschemark futures contract.
Delivery Months:	March June September December.
Delivery Day:	17.00 p.m. on the last trade day.
Last Trading Day:	11.00 a.m. of the last trading day of the Futures contract.
Quotation:	Multiples of DM 0.01.

Minimum Price Movement (Tick Size and Value):	0.01 per cent = DM 25.
Trading Hours:	08.02 a.m. - 16.10 p.m.
Initial Margin:	Initial margin charged by the clearing house for long and short options positions is calculated by reference to daily published risk factors.
Price Limit:	No price limit.
Contract Standard:	Physical delivery of future contract.
Exercise Price:	DM 0.25 intervals. 9 exercise prices will be listed 4 above and 4 below current level. Additional prices will be introduced on the business day after the 3 Month Eurodeutschemark futures contract settlement price is within 0.12 of the fourth highest and lowest existing exercise price.
Reuters Pages:	**LFEB - LFEG.**
Telerate Pages:	15992 - 3.

Daily Volume and Open Interest (Mar 1,1990 - Jun 29,1990)

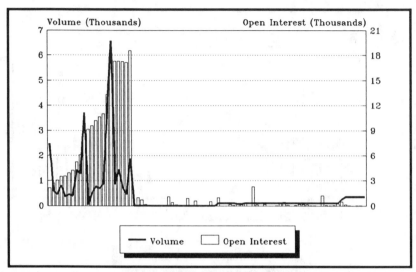

Open Interest and Volume/Open Interest("Liquidity")
(Mar 1,1990 - Jun 29,1990)

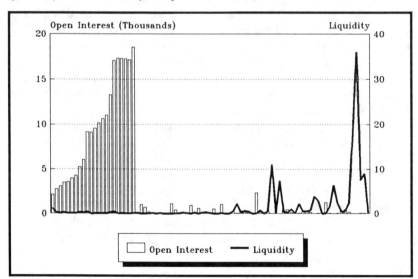

Implied Volatility (Mar 1,1990 - Jun 29,1990)

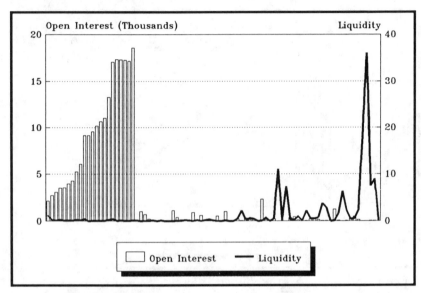

Three Month ECU Interest Rate Future

The Three Month ECU Interest Rate future was launched on **LIFFE** in October 1989 and was the first ECU interest rate future to be traded anywhere in the world. The total volume in 1989 was 16,000 contracts.

Like **LIFFE**'s other Three Month Interest Rate contracts, the ECU future is cash settled at delivery and is quoted as an index of 100.00 less the implied rate of interest. The unit of trading is ECU 1,000,000 with the value of a 0.01 price movement being ECU 25.

The ECU future was unique on **LIFFE** in being supported by a Market Maker scheme during the first six months of trading. There are three Designated Market makers; Generale Bank, Kredietbank N.V. and Istituto Bancario San Paolo di Torino. Each market maker was committed to quote prices within a maximum bid/offer spread of 0.03 per cent for the near month and 0.05 per cent for the far month. In aggregate, the market makers were committed for a minimum of 25 contracts in each contract month.

Contract Size:	ECU 1,000,000.
Delivery Months:	March June September December.
Delivery Day:	First business day after the last trading day.
Last Trading Day:	11.00 a.m. two business days prior to the Third Wednesday of the Delivery Month.
Quotation:	100.00 minus rate of interest.
Minimum Price Movement (Tick Size and Value):	0.01 per cent = ECU 25.
Trading Hours:	08.05 a.m. - 16.05 p.m.
Initial Margin:	0.5 per cent = ECU 500.
Price Limit:	No price limit.
Contract Standard:	Cash settlement.
Exchange Delivery Settlement Price:	The EDSP is based on the British Bankers' Association Interest Rate Settlement Rate ("BBAISR") for 3 Month ECU deposits at 11.00 on the last trading day. The price equals 100.00 minus this rate.
Reuters Pages:	LFCA.
Telerate Pages:	997.

Daily Volume and Open Interest (Jan 2,1990 - Jun 29,1990)

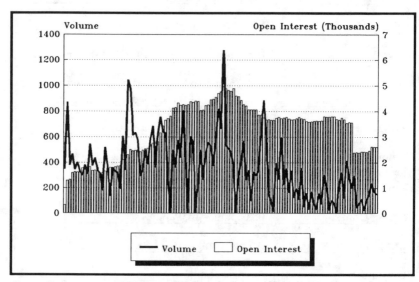

Open Interest and Volume/Open Interest("Liquidity")
(Jan 2,1990 - Jun 29,1990)

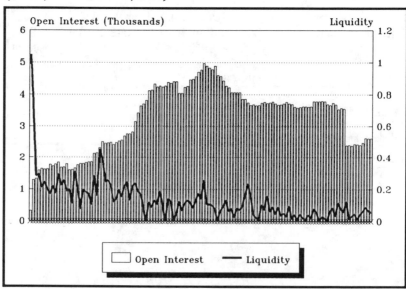

Price/Yield History (Jan 2,1990 - Jun 29,1990)

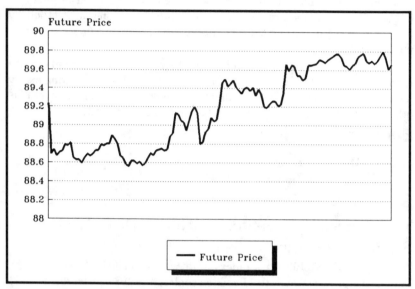

Currency Futures & Options

LIFFE's first currency future, the Sterling - U.S. Dollar contract, was launched in 1982. It was followed by the launches of Deutschemark - U.S. Dollar, Yen - U.S. Dollar, Swiss Franc - U.S. Dollar and U.S. Dollar - Mark contracts.

Although these contracts experienced reasonable volumes initially, volumes have subsequently declined due to the liquidity of the currency forward markets in London. Total volume on **LIFFE**'s currency futures in 1989 was 11,000 contracts, a decline of 31 per cent on 1988.

With the exception of the U.S. Dollar - Mark future prices for **LIFFE** currency futures are quoted in U.S. Dollars, i.e. U.S. Dollars per £. The minimum price movement is 0.01 cents. Prices for the U.S. Dollar - Mark future are quoted in DM per U.S. Dollar with a minimum price movement of 0.01 pfennigs. **LIFFE**'s currency futures are settled by physical delivery of the currency on the Delivery Day.

LIFFE launched the Sterling - U.S. Dollar currency option in 1985 followed by the U.S. Dollar - Mark currency option in 1986. However, volume in **LIFFE** currency options has declined for the same reasons that have affected currency futures to only 1,200 contracts in 1989.

Prices for the Sterling - U.S. Dollar currency option are quoted in U.S. cents, while those for the U.S. Dollar - Mark are quoted in pfennigs. **LIFFE**'s currency options are "Options on cash", i.e. they are settled by physical delivery of the currency, as opposed to delivery of a futures contract on the Delivery Day.

Expiry months are March, June, September and December with three nearby months. For example, in early November, the following expiry months would be available for trading: November, December, January plus other months of March, June, September and December cycle.

Equities

Individual Equities

see London Options Market

Stock Indexes

The Financial Times-Stock Exchange ("FT-SE") 100 Stock Index Future

The **FT-SE 100** Stock Index Future was launched on **LIFFE** in 1984. Volume has grown steadily to 1.0 million contracts in 1989, an increase of 121 per cent over 1988, making it the sixth most active futures contract on **LIFFE**.

Like most stock index contracts, the **FT-SE 100** future is cash settled, i.e. there is no delivery of the underlying shares.

Cash settlement is made against the average of the FT-SE 100 index levels between 11.10 a.m. and 11.20 a.m. on the last trading day, excluding the highest and lowest levels.

The **FT-SE** Index itself represents the average share prices, weighted by capitalization of the top 100 companies listed on London's International Stock Exchange ("ISE"). The index is updated each minute taking the mean of the bid and offer prices quoted by market-makers on **TOPIC**.

Each index point has a value of £25, so that at an index level of 2,000.0 the contract has a notional value £50,000.

Contract Size:	Valued at £25 per index point.
Delivery Months:	March June September December.
Delivery Day:	First business day after the last trading day.

Last Trading Day:	11.20 a.m. the last business day of the Delivery Month.
Quotation:	Index points.
Minimum Price Movement (Tick Size and Value):	0.5 points = £12.50.
Trading Hours:	09.05 a.m. - 16.05 p.m.
Initial Margin:	£2,500.
Price Limit:	No price limit.
Contract Standard:	Cash settlement.
Exchange Delivery Settlement Price:	
Reuters Pages:	LIJA.
Telerate Pages:	996.

Composition of Index

A list of the FT-SE 100 constituents @ 21 March 1990 is displayed below.

Stock	Per Cent
British Telecom	5.44
British Petroleum	5.11
Pearson	5.09
Shell	4.67
Glaxo Holdings	3.73
B.A.T.Industries	3.68

Hanson	3.27
British Gas	2.77
I.C.I	2.41
B.T.R	2.31
SmithKline Beecham	2.00
Barclays Bank	1.96
Guinness	1.78
Cable & Wireless	1.76
Wellcome	1.76
Grand Metropolitan	1.71
G.E.C.	1.68
National Westminster Bank	1.66
R.T.Z.	1.63
Unilever	1.61
Marks & Spencer	1.59
Prudential	1.42
Lloyds Bank	1.20
Allied Lyons	1.01
Bass	0.98
Tesco	0.94
British Steel	0.88

Enterprise Oil	0.84
Racal Electronic	0.83
Midland Bank	0.81
Boots	0.80
BOC Group	0.77
Ladbroke Group	0.76
Abbey National	0.76
G.U.S.	0.75
P & O	0.74
Land Securities	0.73
Sun Alliance	0.70
Royal Insurance	0.69
Fisons	0.69
Cadbury Schweppes	0.68
General Accident	0.67
Reed International	0.66
Rank Organisation	0.65
Thorn EMI	0.63
Trusthouse Forte	0.63
TSB Group	0.61
Commercial Union	0.61

B.A.A.	0.60
Argyll Group	0.59
Rothmans	0.58
G.R.E.	0.57
Legal & General	0.55
Rolls-Royce	0.54
A.B.Foods	0.54
Tarmac	0.51
Trafalgar House	0.51
B.E.T.	0.51
Reckitt & Colman	0.51
Whitbread	0.50
Pilkington	0.49
Lonhro	0.48
British Airways	0.47
M.E.P.C.	0.46
Redland	0.46
Sears	0.45
LASMO	0.45
S.T.C.	0.45
Polly Peck	0.44

United Biscuit	0.43
Royal Bank of Scotland	0.42
Ultramar	0.41
Carlton Communications	0.41
R.H.M.	0.41
Hillsdown Holdings	0.39
ASDA Group	0.39
Stanadard Chartered Bank	0.39
Hawker Siddley	0.39
British Aerospace	0.39
Courtaulds	0.38
Kingfisher	0.38
R.M.C. Group	0.38
Smith & Nephew	0.37
B.I.C.C.	0.37
Maxwell Communications	0.37
Hammersons	0.36
Blue Circle	0.36
Scottish & Newcastle	0.35
Thames Water	0.34
Burmah Oil	0.33

Lucas Industries	0.32
G.K.N.	0.32
(Globe Investment Trust**)	0.28
B.P.B. Industries	0.28
Burton Group	0.28
Taylor Woodrow	0.27
Cookson Group	0.26
English China Clay	0.24

** Globe Investment Trust has since been taken over by the Coal Board
Pension Fund

Daily Volume and Open Interest (Jan 2,1990 - Jun 29,1990)

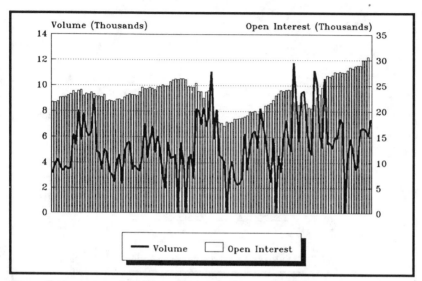

Open Interest and Volume/Open Interest("Liquidity") (Jan 2,1990 - Jun 29,1990)

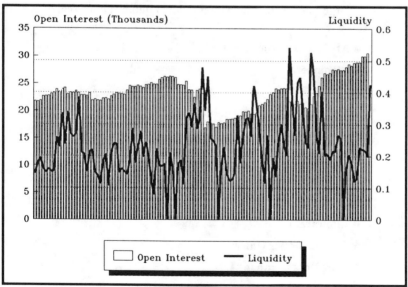

Price/Yield History (Jan 2,1990 - Jun 29,1990)

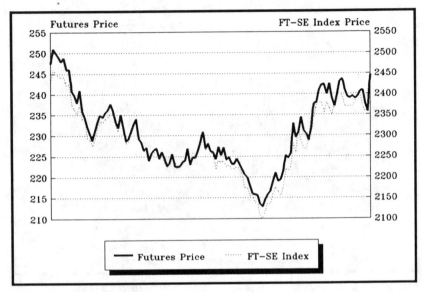

Quote Vendors

A large number of major international quote vendors carry LIFFE prices. These are:

- **ADP Information Services**
- **Bloomberg**
- **CMS**
- **Commodity Quote Graphics**
- **Datastream**
- **Futrend**
- **ICV Citiservices**
- **Newtime**
- **Infowave**
- **Knight Ridder Unicom**
- **Pont Data Company Ltd**

- ● Quick
- ● Quotron
- ● Reuters Ltd
- ● Telerate
- ● TOG Europe
- ● TOPIC

For information on additional quote vending, one should contact:-

Peter Askew
Technical Liason Manager
LIFFE

Tel:

(44) 71-623-0444 Ext 2173.

Reuters Pages	
LFCA	3 Month E.C.U. Future
LFDA	US Treasury Bond Future
LFDB - LFDM	US Treasury Bond Option
LFEA	3 Month Eurodeutschemark Future
LFJB	Japanese Government Bond Future
LFJC	German Government Bond Future
LFJD - LFJK	3 Month Eurodeutschemark Option
LFJD - LFJM	German Government Bond Option
LFVN - LFVV	Bund & US Treasury Bond Options
LFXA - LFXO	3 Month Eurodollar Option
LFXP - LFXU	3 Month Sterling Option

LIEP	UK Long Gilt Future
LIGA	3 Month Eurodollar Future
LIGB - LIGW	3 Month Eurodollar Option
LIGV	UK Long Gilt Option
LIIA	3 Month Sterling Future
LIIB	3 Month Sterling Option
LIJA	FT-SE Stock Future
Telerate Pages	
981 - 982	3 Month Eurodollar Option
994	Bund
995	3 Month Eurodollar & Sterling Future
996	FT-SE Stock Future
997	3 Month Eurodeutschemark & ECU Futures
1994	UK Long Gilt Future
15742 - 15745	3 Month Sterling Option
15980 - 15984	3 Month Eurodeutschemark Option
15990 - 15993	UK Long Gilt & Bund Option
15996 - 15997	US Treasury Bond Option

SOURCES of REFERENCE

The Exchange produces a wide range of publications that are available free of charge from the Publications Department on request. They cover the contracts in detail and on how to use them.

The London Metal Exchange ("LME")

Stuart McLean

with assistance from
R.C. Perry
The London Metal Exchange
R.G.Sampson
Brian Reidy & Associates Ltd
and

INTRODUCTION

The London Metal Exchange ("LME") was formally established in 1877 when Britain's industrial development had given rise to large metal imports, mainly of Chile copper, Straits tin and (then) pig iron. Premises were acquired above a hatter's shop in Lombard Court and telegraph links set up. The first telephone for the use of members was installed in 1880 and in the same year the first company secretary was appointed with the princely salary of £150 per year. The period of contracts was three months, approximately equal to the sailing times from Santiago and Singapore to the U.K..

Differences of opinion developed between the Board and the Members concerning methods of price reporting and the practice of open dealing standing round a ring. So in 1881 the members formed a committee which set up a new company, the Metal Market & Exchange Company Ltd. and took over the assets of the existing company. In 1882 they moved the Exchange to premises in Whittington Avenue, where it remained for 98 years before moving in 1980 to its current location in Plantation House.

In 1899 the present arrangement of dealing in two periods each morning and afternoon was introduced for copper and tin. Dealings in pig iron, lead and zinc were conducted standing around a small secondary ring with no set times and no standard contracts. It was not until 1920 (by which time pig-iron dealings had ceased on the Exchange) that the latter two metals were traded in the main ring. Attempts to prevent business in the Exchange outside official trading times gave rise to dealings taking place outside the building in the street. These became so rowdy that the police intervened and thereafter unofficial dealings were allowed to continue inside the Exchange. The term "kerb dealing" is still in use today.

Except during wartime closures, the exchange has flourished throughout the century. In the years after World War II, trading copper, tin, lead and zinc, and for some years silver, resumed. In 1978 aluminium was introduced and in 1979 nickel. The market moved in 1980 to its present modern premises after 100 years at the older building. Its tin market was suspended after the international default of October 1985, but has since resumed. Today, the **LME**'s aluminium market lacks rival in the world. The **LME** acts as a barometer of supply and demand for metals worldwide and its official prices for aluminium, copper, lead, nickel, tin and zinc are used by producers and consumers for their long-term contracts. These prices can be hedged on the Exchange through a variety of futures and options contracts.

The Exchange operated as a principals' market for the first 111 years of its existence and had a two-tier management system comprising a Board and Committee. In 1986, to meet the requirements of the Financial Services Act, the members voted to form a new company with a full-time chief executive and one-tier management structure to take over the running of the Exchange.

The new company, called The London Metal Exchange Limited, was formed in July 1987. It has a new constitution and a managing board composed of ten representatives drawn from the membership, one appointee (the chief executive) and four invited directors, two of whom are chosen from the metals industry.

The **LME** and its activities now fall under the Financial Services Act (**FSA**) and accordingly under the regulation of the Securities & Investment Board (**SIB**). In April 1988, the exchange was approved as a Recognized Investment Exchange (**RIE**). To qualify, the exchange had to conform with the requirements of the **SIB**, the most important of which was the introduction of a clearing house system and, with it, price transparency and audit trails. Because of its unique and proven trading practices that involve both floor and interoffice trading, a non-cash clearing system operating on bank guarantees was devised so that the **LME**'s predominantly international trade did not suffer through domestic legislation.

With the adoption of a clearing-system the **LME**'s board took the opportunity to introduce further far-reaching changes. The most significant of these was the extension of the trading-period from three-months to 15-months forward. Cash to three months is still dealt on a daily prompt basis and dealings beyond three months have a single prompt date (the third Wednesday of each month). Prompt dates remain subject to review and may be changed to meet the best interests of the metal trade. In 1987, traded options were introduced as official **LME** contracts. In 1989, the **LME** discontinued its silver contract and reintroduced its tin futures contract. While copper and lead continue to be officially priced in sterling, the major currency for aluminum, nickel, tin and zinc is now the U.S dollar - in which medium all the metals may now be cleared, and there are plans to approve further currencies for clearing purposes. All these additional features have greatly broadened the trading facilities offered by the exchange.

Expansion of the international warehouse system has also been a priority. The first warehouses to be registered outside Europe were in Singapore, in 1987. This port is now second to Rotterdam in turnover of **LME** metals. Further expansion took place in July 1989 when, after years of negotiation, Japan opened its doors to allow **LME**-listed warehouses for the storage of high-grade aluminium and delivery points have now been established for this metal at Yokohama, Nagoya, Osaka, Hakata, Moji and Kobe. Plans are also well advanced to open similar facilities in the USA, in particular for aluminium, nickel and special high-grade zinc.

Total Monthly Average Daily Futures Volume (June 1987 - July 1990)

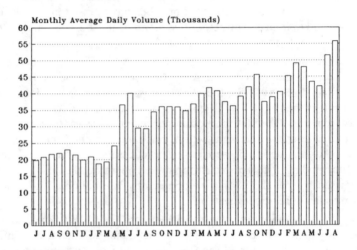

Monthly Average Daily Volume (Thousands)

Total Monthly Average Daily Options Volume (June 1987 - July 1990)

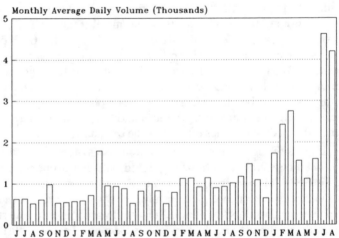

Monthly Average Daily Volume (Thousands)

The London's Metal Exchange's performance in 1989 was its best ever. Its turnover figures were over 100 million lots, representing 250 million tonnes of metal, valued at around £450 billion. The invisible earnings generated by the **LME** should considerably exceed those of 1988, which were £77 million according to the Bank of England.

About 85 per cent of **LME** clearing members firms are owned by overseas companies and approximately 97 per cent of the **LME**'s business comes from abroad, making it the world's only truly global hard commodity market. The **LME** share (by weight) of the world terminal market trading non-ferrous metals in 80 percent of all copper, 99.9 per cent of aluminium and 100 per cent of lead, nickel and zinc. Meanwhile, the recently reintroduced tin contract is also gathering momentum.

ORGANIZATION of the MARKET

The London Metal Exchange, the world's chief base-metals exchange, has a membership of over 70 major firms. Of these, 18 take part in Ring-dealing in the open-outcry sessions occurring four times a day, while others join them in the continual trading of futures and options between offices that nowadays accounts for the greater part of **LME** business. The exchange is highly international in its membership, with 90 per cent of the Ring-dealing firms owned or partly owned by overseas companies, so that now more than ever it is well constituted to reflect changes in supply and demand of the metals worldwide, while allowing various interests in the trade to establish prices and to protect themselves for price transparency and audit trails.

Both floor and interoffice trading are covered by a matching system run by a division of the International Commodities Clearing House. Another advanced electronic system keeps watch over prices bid, offered and traded, to provide up-to-the-minute data on market activity to the world.

All sales due for delivery are backed by warrants relating to metal stored in listed warehouses in several European countries, in Singapore and Japan. The **LME** has had delivery points abroad since 1962 when it established one at Rotterdam.

Structure

The Exchange is run by a cooperative board elected by its members and run by an administrative body led a Chairman and Chief Executive.

Most categories of membership may engage in interoffice trading throughout the day.

Members

The categories comprise some 18 Ring-Dealing Members, 18 Associate Broker Clearing Members, three Associate Trade Clearing Members, two Associate Broker Members, 42 Associate Trade Members, 19 Individual members and 18 Honorary members*§.

LME Membership Requirements

	Ring	Clearing Associates	Other Associates
Corporate entity	X	X	X
Incorporated in the U.K.	X		
Properly established office in London	X		
Commercial interest in the business of the Exchange	X	X	X
Meet the financial requirements as periodically specified by the Managing Board	X	X	X

* Individual members must be persons not currently employed by either a member company or by a company which, while outside the Exchange, could qualify for membership.

§ Honorary membership status may be granted by the Managing Board to individuals who have given conspicuous service to the Exchange over the years but are no longer LME members.

Ring Dealing Members

Amalgamated Metal Trading Limited

Anglo Chemical Metals Limited

Barclays Metals Limited

Billiton-Enthoven Metals Limited

Brandeis (Brokers) Limited

Cerro Metals (UK) Limited

Charles Davis (Metal Brokers) Limited

Gerald Limited

Lazmet Limited

Metallgesellschaft Limited

Metdist Trading Limited

Mocatta Commercial Limited

Refco Overseas Ltd.

Sharps Pixley Limited

Lehman Brothers Commodities Ltd

Sogemin (Metals) Ltd.

Triland Metals Limited

Rudolf Wolff & Co.Ltd.

Associate Broker Clearing Members

Balfour Maclaine International (UK) Limited

C.A. & L. Bell Commodities Corporation Pty Ltd.

Credit Lyonnaise Rouse Limited

CRT Europe Inc.

Dean Witter Futures Limited

Geldermann Ltd.

GNI Limited

Gourlay Wolff Futures Ltd.

LIT Futures Limited

E.D. & F. Man International Ltd.

MG Futures Limited

Merrill Lynch Pierce Fenner & Smith (Brokers &
Dealers) Limited

F. Murphy (Metals) Limited

Paine Webber International Futures Ltd.

Prudential-Bache (Futures) Limited

J.H.Rayner (Futures) Limited

Sucden (U.K.) Limited

Shearson Lehman Hutton Inc.

Associate Trade Clearing Members

Hydro Aluminium a.s.

Marc Rich & Co. Ltd

Toyota Tsusho Corporation

Trading System

Trading is in warrants that apply to physical material in listed warehouses. All members' deals subject to the rules of the Exchange are evidenced by an exchange contract input into the matching and clearing system. The central spectacle of the Exchange is its open-outcry market attended by representatives of 19 Ring-dealing firms, yet the bulk of trading is transacted through interoffice dealing.

The terminal network matching system employed for the clearing of **LME** contracts facilitates the unique system of trading. A large volume of trading is done interoffice, allowing **LME** to operate as a 24 hour market. Trading on the floor takes place in two sessions daily from 11.50 a.m. - 13.25 p.m. and from 15.20 p.m. - 17.00 p.m..

The two sessions are each broken down into two rings made up of five minutes trading in each contract. Each session is followed by a short period of open-outcry trading, in all metals simultaneously, known as "kerb trading". After the second ring of the first session the official prices for the day are announced. These prices, confirmed by the "quotations committee", made up of three members and a **LME** official are used as benchmark prices by the international metals trade.

Market Calls		
First Session		
Tin	11.50 to 11.55	
Aluminium	11.55 to 12.00	
Copper	12.00 to 12.05	
Lead	12.05 to 12.10	
Zinc	12.10 to 12.15	
Nickel	12.15 to 12.20	
Interval		
Copper	12.30 to 12.35	Official
Tin	12.35 to 12.40	Official
Lead	12.40 to 12.45	Official
Zinc	12.45 to 12.50	Official
Aluminium	12.50 to 12.55	Official
Nickel	12.55 to 13.00	Official
Kerb trading follows official prices until 13.25		
Second Session		
Lead	15.20 to 15.25	
Zinc	15.25 to 15.30	

Copper	15.30 to 15.35	
Aluminium	15.35 to 15.40	
Tin	15.40 to 15.45	
Nickel	15.45 to 15.50	
Interval		
Lead	16.00 to 16.05	
Zinc	16.05 to 16.10	
Copper	16.10 to 16.15	
Aluminium	16.15 to 16.20	
Tin	16.20 to 16.25	
Nickel	16.25 to 16.30	
Kerb trading until 17.00		

Price Reporting System

The London Metal Exchange operates a quotation vending system which offers a direct real-time price feed to financial information vendors for distribution worldwide.

The price feed provides a comprehensive report of market activity from the floor during morning and afternoon Ring and Kerb trading sessions. In addition 12 Ring Dealing firms and one Associate Broker Clearing member have been authorised by the Exchange to contribute indicative 3 months bid and offer prices throughout the day. To avoid confusion, **LME** market staff are solely responsible for reporting each individual metal during the 5 minute period when it is being traded on the Ring. A Reuter monitor network is used as the data collection mechanism, feeding quotations from members' offices to the **LME** central computer. The system ensures that all quote vendors, including Reuters, receive the off-floor prices simultaneously. In time it is planned to include option prices, daily turnovers and weekly stock figures in the price feed and it is anticipated that the number of member firms contributing to the system will increase.

Settlement

Contracts are settled by offset or physical delivery.

Delivery Points

The standard **LME** contract always calls for receipt or delivery of a registered **LME** brand on the due date from or into an **LME** approved warehouse. There is no force majeure clause in an **LME** contract. The warehouse are situated at delivery points in the U.K., Europe and the Far East as follows:

United Kingdom   Avonmouth, Felixstowe, Glasgow, Goole, Hull, Liverpool and Newcastle.

Continental Europe Antwerp, Gothenburg, Helsingborg, Rotterdam, Genoa, Leghorn, Trieste, Bremen, Hamburg and Dunkirk.

Far East*   Singapore, Hakata, Kobe, Moji, Nagoya, Osaka and Yokohama.

*Japanese warehouses are registered for High Grade Primary Aluminium Storage only.

The Clearing System

The clearing system on the **LME** is operated by the International Commodities Clearing House Limited ("ICCH") who in collaboration with the management of the **LME** developed the unique matching system which covers both floor and inter office trading. The system is based on electronic data input and capture terminals located in each members' office which are linked with the central terminal at **ICCH**. members are responsible for inputting all trades made with other clearing members. Each trade is recorded twice - once by the seller and once by the buyer - so that a balanced position is arrived at each day at 17.00 p.m.. Trades made after this time are entered into the next day's clearing. In fact each business day is divided into a number of matching periods so that any mismatches are resolved as soon as possible.

This matching system ensures that the clearing-house is always "square" against the market. However, one member may have a loss making position and the other a profitable position. Should a member be unable to meet his obligations the clearing-house guarantees to perform that member's obligations to the Market. In order to support its guarantee the **ICCH** operate a margin system. Initial margins are required on all futures contracts entered into and variation margin calls are made daily on all open positions if the market price moves unfavourably against them.

To reduce costs and capital outlay the clearing system operated on the **LME** allows for all margin requirements to be covered by bank guarantees.

Commission Rates
These are established by member firms with their clients.

Investor protection
The London Metal Exchange is a Recognized Investment Exchange (**RIE**) under the U.K.'s Financial Services Act.

Prospective Developments
The London Metal Exchange is considering futures contracts that stretch to 39 months compared with the current 15 months. The Exchange is also considering contracts being denominated in currencies other than U.S. dollars and sterling.

The London Metal Exchange's turnover in 1989 was 10 million lots and promises to be as high during 1990. The London Metal Exchange's policy of expanding its use of warehouses now numbering in excess of 160 in Europe and the Far East - continues with U.S. depots under consideration.

Address   The London Metal Exchange (run by the London Metal Exchange Limited)
Plantation House
Fenchurch Street
London EC3M 3AP

Telephone: (44) 71 626 3311
Telex: 8951367
Fax: (44) 71 626 1703

Principal Officers
Chairman   Mr J Wolff
Chief Executive   Mr D E King
President   Mr J K Lion OBE
Marketing Director   Mr M Abbott
Company Secretary   Mr N D Banks
Director of Operations   Mr B S Dorking

HISTORY of the MARKET

1899	Copper trades in main ring
1899	Tin trades in main ring
1920	Lead trades in main ring
1920	Zinc trades in main ring
1978	Aluminium traded
1979	Nickel traded
1987	Traded options introduced

OVERVIEW of PRODUCTS

Contract	Future	Option
Aluminium	*	*
Copper	*	*
Lead	*	*
Nickel	*	*
Tin	*	
Zinc	*	*

DETAILED CONTRACT SPECIFICATION
Aluminium Futures Contract

Contract Size:	25 tonnes.
Delivery Months:	Each monthly for next 15 months.
Delivery Day:	Daily for three months forward then the third Wednesday of the month for the next 12 months.
Last Trading Day:	Two business days before prompt day (delivery day).
Quotation:	US$ per tonne.
Minimum Price Movement (Tick Size and Value):	US$ 1 per tonne = US$25.
Trading Hours:	11.55 a.m. -12.00 p.m. 12.50 p.m. - 12.55 p.m. (official) 15.35 p.m. - 15.40 p.m. 16.15 p.m. - 16.20 p.m.
Initial Margin:	By arrangement with the broker.
Price Limit:	No price limit.
Contract Standard:	Physical delivery of high grade primary aluminium of minimum 99.70% purity in the form of ingots T-bars or sows. Ingot weights range from 12 kgs to 26 kgs each - the maximum permitted T-bar weight is approx. 675 kgs and the maximum permitted weight of each sow is approx. 750 kgs. All aluminium delivered must be of brands listed in the **LME**-approved list.
Exchange Delivery Settlement Price:	Official seller's cash price on delivery day.

Daily Volume (Jan 2, 1990 - Jun 29, 1990)

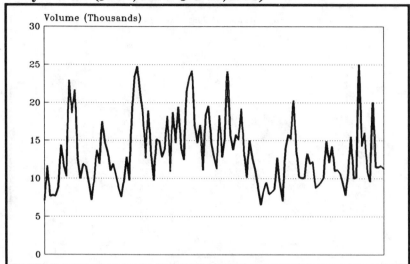

Monthly Average Daily Volumes (Jun, 1987 - Jul, 1990)

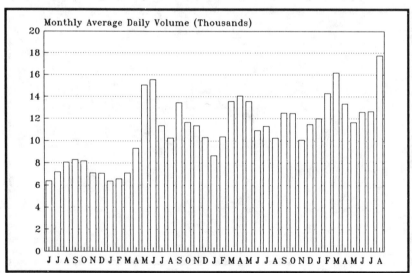

Month-end Open Interest (Jan, 1990 - Jul, 1990)

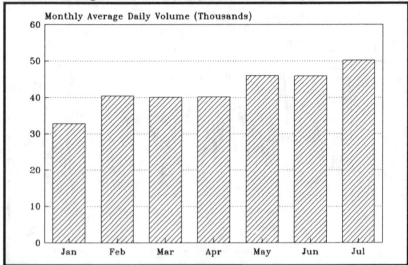

Price Histories (Jan 2, 1990 - Jun 29, 1990)

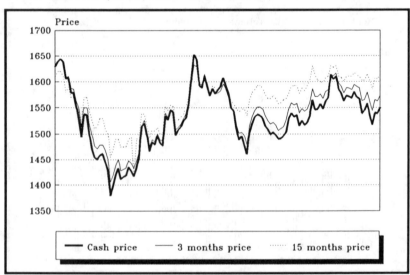

Weekly Stock Levels in tonnes (Jan 5, 1990 - Aug 23, 1990)

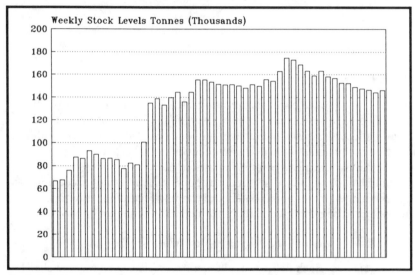

Special Contract Rules for High Grade Primary Aluminium

Quality

Aluminium deliverable under this contract shall be:

a) Primary aluminium of minimum 99.70 per cent purity with maximum permissible iron constant 0.20 per cent and maximum permissible silicon content 0.10 per cent, or

b) Primary aluminium with impurities no greater than in the registered designation P1020A in the Registration record of Aluminium Association Designations and Chemical Composition Limits for Unalloyed Aluminium of the Aluminium Association Inc., U.S.A. (May 15th, 1982)

c) Brands listed in the LME-approved list of aluminium brands

Shapes and Weights

Aluminium deliveries may be in the form of ingots, T-bars or sows and ingots shall be securely strapped in bundles suitable for stacking. Ingot weight shall be within the permitted range 12 kgs to 26 kgs each. T-bar weight shall not exceed 5 per cent more than 675 kgs each, and the weight of each sow shall not exceed 5 per cent more than 750 kg.

Size of Lots

25 tonnes

Warrants

Each parcel particularized in each Warrant shall comprise either ingots, T-bars or sows, shall lie at one warehouse, be the production of one country and shall consist of aluminium of one brand shape and size subject, in the case of ingots, to the necessity of including different shapes and sizes at the bottom of each parcel for palletisation. Each parcel of ingots placed on warrant shall be delivered securely strapped in bundles not exceeding two tonnes each. Warrants must contain the warning regarding entrapped moisture referred to in the Special Rules for Placing Aluminium on Warrant.

Special Rules Governing the Placing of Aluminium on Warrant

1) Each delivery of aluminium for placing on warrant shall be accompanied by a Certificate of Origin and a producer's Certificate of Analysis both of which must be lodged with the warehouseman. The Certificate of Analysis shall be within the quality specification set out in Special Rule 1 for the relevant grade of aluminium as above set out. A Bulk Analysis Certificate or a copy thereof is acceptable but if a producer's Certificate is not available an Analysis certificate must be prepared and signed by an assayer on the list of approved assayers. All analysis certificates must show each heat number.

2) The party intending to place on warrant aluminium for delivery in satisfaction of any Contract must advise the warehouseman of the name of a Ring dealing or a Clearing Associate member of the London Metal Exchange who will accept responsibility for the initial placing of the Warrants on the market. Such Warrant(s) must be issued to the order of the said member who, prior to its or their endorsement,

must be satisfied that the documentation is evidence of good delivery.

3)   Each Warrant shall be made up from the production of one country and shall consist of one brand which is listed as being a good delivery. Each Warrant shall state the total weight of the parcel particularized thereon, its country of origin, brand and the date(s) and reference number(s) of the Certificates of Origin and of Analysis lodged with the warehouseman. Each Warrant shall be of 25 tonnes (2% either more or less) and shall state the number of bundles or T-bars or sows and in the case of bundles the number of ingots making up each bundle. In the case of either T-bars or sows the Warrant shall state the piece weight of each.

4)   The warning clause set out below must appear on the Warrant:

WARNING The buyer is advised that this metal may contain crevices and hidden recesses holding entrapped moisture. The metal should be handled and processed with this possibility in mind. Entrapped moisture may cause an explosion if the metal is introduced into a melting-furnace without proper drying.

5)   On request, the warehouseman is obliged to submit to the holder of the warrant Certificates of Origin/Analysis or copies thereof if the 25 tonnes parcel forms a part of a larger delivery covered by Bulk Analysis.

Aluminium Options Contract

Option Style	American calls and puts.
Contract Size:	25 tonnes.
Expiry Months:	
Expiry Day:	The first Wednesday of each month. If the Wednesday is not a business day - the next business day.

Quotation:	The nearest 12 months only are tradeable in US$ per tonne and the nearest 6 months only are tradeable in £ per tonne.
Minimum Price Movement (Tick Size and Value):	
Trading Hours:	
Initial Margin:	By arrangement with the broker.
Price Limit:	No price limit.
Contract Standard:	Physical delivery - see futures contract.
Exercise Price:	Contracts are available with exercise price intervals of US$50 per tonne/£25 when the aluminium price is between US$1,750 and US$2,950 and rises to US$100/£50 when over US$3,000.
Exchange Delivery Settlement Price:	Official seller's cash price on expiry day.

Daily Volume (Jan 2, 1990 - May 31, 1990)

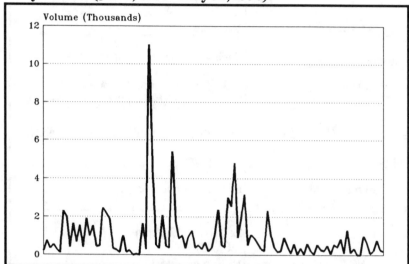

Monthly Average Daily Volumes (Jun, 1987 - Aug, 1990)

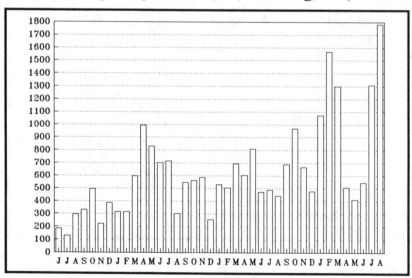

Copper Futures Contract

Contract Size:	25 tonnes.
Delivery Months:	Each month for the next 15 months.
Delivery Day:	Daily for three months forward then third Wednesday of the month for next 12 months.
Last Trading Day:	Two business days before prompt day.
Quotation:	£ per tonne.
Minimum Price Movement (Tick Size and Value):	£0.50 per tonne = £12.50.
Trading Hours:	12.00 p.m. - 12.05 p.m. 12.30 p.m. - 12.35 p.m. (official) 15.30 p.m. - 15.35 p.m. 16.10 p.m. - 16.15 p.m.
Initial Margin:	By arrangement with the broker.
Price Limit:	No price limit.
Contract Standard:	Physical delivery of grade A - electrolytic copper in the form of either grade A cathodes or grade A wirebars of standard dimensions in the weight range of 110 kgs to 125 kgs in seller's option. All copper delivered must be brands listed in the **LME**-approved list and conform with the appropriate British Standard.
Exchange Delivery Settlement Price:	Official seller's cash price on delivery day.

Daily Volume (Jan 2, 1990 - Jun 29, 1990)

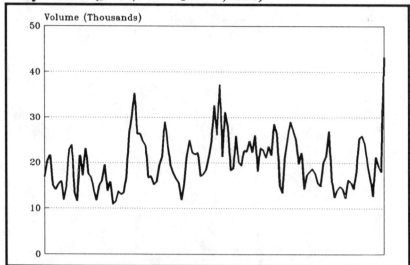

Monthly Average Daily Volumes (Jun, 1987 - Jul, 1990)

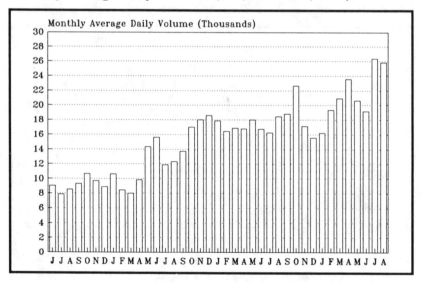

Month-end Open Interest (Jan, 1990 - Jul, 1990)

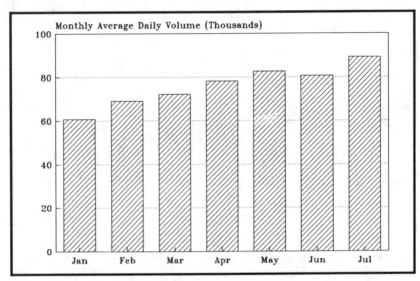

Price Histories (Jan 2, 1990 - Jun 29, 1990)

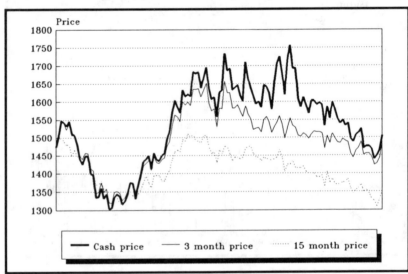

Weekly Stock Levels in tonnes (Jan 5, 1990 - Aug 23, 1990)

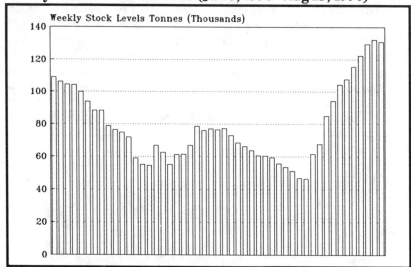

Special Contract Rules for Copper -Grade A Quality

The copper delivered under this contract must be electrolytic copper in the form of either

a)   Cathodes Grade A, or

b)   Wirebars - Grade A of standard dimensions in the weight range of 110 kgs to 125 kg

in the seller's option.

With effect from October 31, 1990 the option to deliver wirebars may, subject to at least three months' notice being given, be officially withdrawn at any time after January 31, 1991.

All copper delivered must be if brands listed in the **LME**-approved list of Copper -Grade A brands and must conform with BS 6017-1981 including Amendment 5725 (cathode grade designation Cu CATHH-1, wirebar designation Cu-ETP-2)

Shapes and Weights

Each parcel of 25 tonnes shall lie at one warehouse and be of one brand, shape and size, but, in the case of cathodes, shall be of full or cut plates subject to the necessity of including different shapes and sizes at the bottom of each parcel for the purpose of palletisation. Cut plates shall not be less than quarter size. Each parcel of copper cathodes placed on warrant shall be not less than quarter size. Each parcel of copper cathodes placed on warrant shall be delivered securely strapped in bundles not exceeding 4 tonnes and with the brand shown on the strapping. In the case of wirebars each parcel shall consist of wirebars of uniform piece weight subject to the usual tolerances. On or after June 1, 1985 each parcel of wirebars placed on warrant shall be delivered securely strapped, in bundles not exceeding 2.5 tonnes. Warrants issued prior to June 1, 1985 for unstrapped wirebars shall constitute a good delivery.

Size of Lot

25 tonnes

Warrants

Warrants shall be of 25 tonnes each (2% either more or less)

Each cathode warrant must state the total weight of the parcel, the brand, the name of the producer, and the number of plates making up each parcel. Warrants for cathodes issued on and after September 1, 1981 also must state the number of bundles making up each parcel.

Each wirebar warrant must state the total weight of the parcel, the brand, the wirebar piece weight and the number of wirebars making up each parcel. Warrants for wirebars issued on or after June 1, 1985 also must state the number of bundles making up each parcel.

Each warrant must be identified as Copper - Grade A.

Copper Options Contract

Option Style	American calls and puts.
Contract Size:	25 tonnes.
Expiry Months:	See Futures contract.
Expiry Day:	The first Wednesday of each month if the Wednesday is not a business day the next business day.
Quotation:	The nearest 12 months are tradeable only in US$ per tonne and the nearest 6 months in £ per tonne.
Minimum Price Movement (Tick Size and Value):	
Trading Hours:	See Futures contract.
Initial Margin:	By arrangement with the broker.
Price Limit:	No price limit.
Contract Standard:	Physical delivery - see futures contract.
Exercise Price:	Contracts are traded with exercise intervals of US$50 per tonne/£25 when the copper price is between US$1,750 and US$2,950 and rises to US$100/£50 when over US$3,000.
Exchange Delivery Settlement Price:	Official seller's cash price.

Daily Volume (Jan 2, 1990 - May 31, 1990)

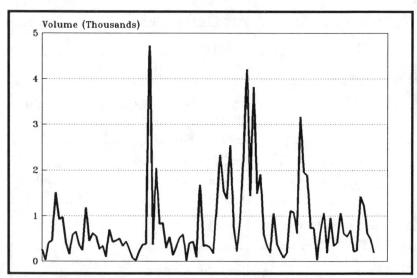

Monthly Average Daily Volumes (Jun, 1987 - Aug, 1990)

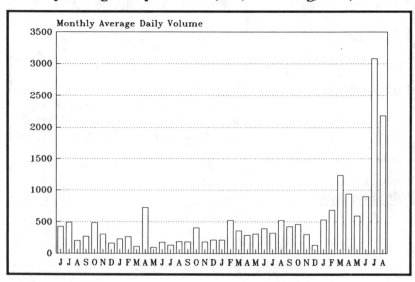

Lead Futures Contract

Contract Size:	25 tonnes.
Delivery Months:	Each month for the next 15 months.
Delivery Day:	Daily for three months forward then the third Wednesday of the month for the next 12 months.
Last Trading Day:	Two business days before delivery day.
Quotation:	£ per tonne.
Minimum Price Movement (Tick Size and Value):	£0.25 per tonne = £6.25.
Trading Hours:	12.05 p.m. - 12.10 p.m. 12.40 p.m. - 12.45 p.m.(official) 15.20 p.m. - 15.25 p.m. 16.00 p.m. - 16.05 p.m.
Initial Margin:	By arrangement with the brokers.
Price Limit:	No price limit.
Contract Standard:	Physical delivery of refined pig lead assaying not less than 99.97% purity in pigs weighing not more than 55 kgs each. All lead delivered must be of brands listed in the LME-approved list.
Exchange Delivery Settlement Price:	Official seller's cash price.

Daily Volume (Jan 2, 1990 - Jun 29, 1990)

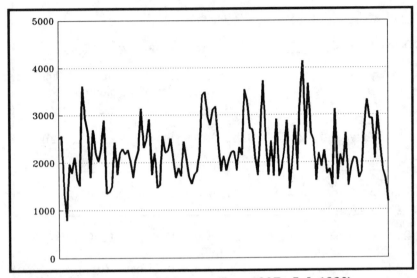

Monthly Average Daily Volumes (Jun, 1987 - Jul, 1990)

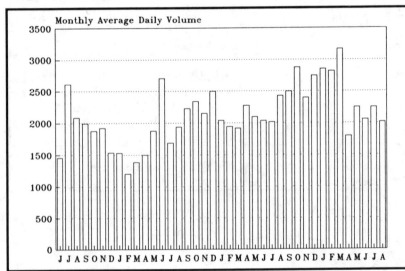

Month-end Open Interest (Jan, 1990 - Jul, 1990)

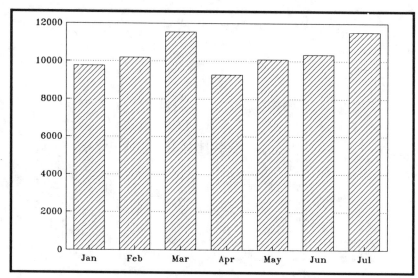

Price Histories (Jan 2, 1990 - Jun 29, 1990)

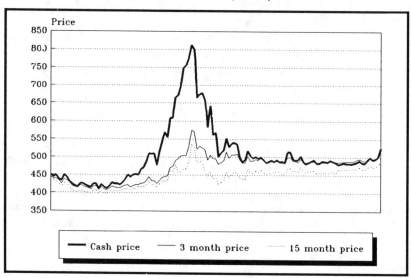

Weekly Stock Levels in tonnes (Jan 5, 1990 - Aug 23, 1990)

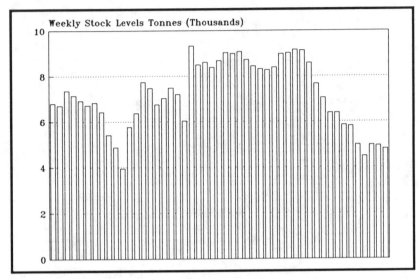

Special Contract Rules for Standard Lead

Quality

The lead delivered under this contract must be refined pig lead (minimum 99,97% purity). All lead delivered must be:

    a)   Of brands listed in the **LME**-approved list of lead brands

    b)   In pigs weighing not more than 55 kgs each.

Shapes and Weights

Each parcel of 25 tonnes shall lie at one warehouse and be of one brand and shall consist of pigs of one size, subject to the necessity of including different shapes and sizes at the bottom of each parcel for the purpose of palletisation. On and after June 1, 1985 each parcel placed on warrant shall be delivered securely strapped, in bundles not exceeding 1.2 tonnes. Warrants issued prior to June 1, 1985 for unstrapped pigs shall constitute a good delivery.

Size of lots

25 tonnes

Warrants

Warrants shall be for 25 tonnes each (2% either more or less). Each warrant must state the total weight of the parcel, the brand and the number of pigs making up each parcel. Warrants issued on or after June 1, 1985 also must state the number of bundles making up each parcel.

Lead Options Contract

Option Style	American calls and puts.
Contract Size:	25 tonnes.
Expiry Months:	see futures contract.
Expiry Day:	The first Wednesday of each month if the Wednesday is not a business day - the next business day.
Quotation:	The nearest 3 months only are tradeable in US$ and £ per tonne.
Minimum Price Movement (Tick Size and Value):	
Trading Hours:	See futures contract.
Initial Margin:	By arrangement with the broker.
Price Limit:	No price limit.
Contract Standard:	Physical delivery - see futures contract.
Exercise Price:	Contracts are traded with exercise intervals of US$50 per tonne/£25.
Exchange Delivery Settlement Price:	Official seller's cash price.

Daily Volume (Jan 2, 1990 - May 31, 1990)

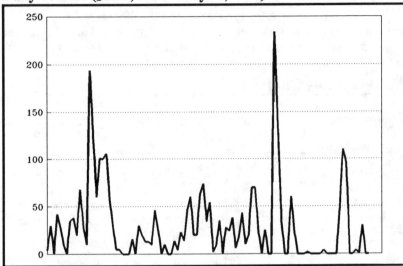

Monthly Average Daily Volumes (Jun, 1987 - Aug, 1990)

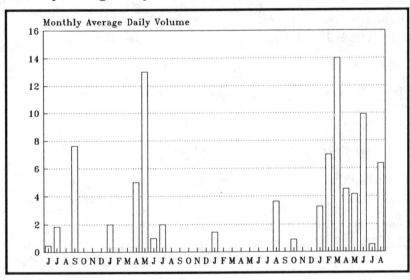

Nickel Futures Contract

Contract Size:	25 tonnes.
Delivery Months:	Each month for the next 15 months.
Delivery Day:	Daily for three months forward then the third Wednesday of the month for the next 12 months.
Last Trading Day:	Two business days before delivery day.
Quotation:	US$ per tonne.
Minimum Price Movement (Tick Size and Value):	US$ 1 per tonne = US$25.
Trading Hours:	12.15 p.m. - 12.20 p.m. 12.55 p.m. - 13.00 p.m. (official) 15.45 p.m. - 15.50 p.m. 16.25 p.m. - 16.30 p.m.
Initial Margin:	By arrangement with the broker.
Price Limit:	No price limit.
Contract Standard:	Physical delivery of primary nickel of minimum 99.80% purity with chemical analysis conforming to the current ASTM specification in the form of cathodes pellets or briquettes. All nickel delivered must be of the production of producers in the LME-approved nickel list.
Exchange Delivery Settlement Price:	Official seller's cash price.

Daily Volume (Jan 2, 1990 - Jun 29, 1990)

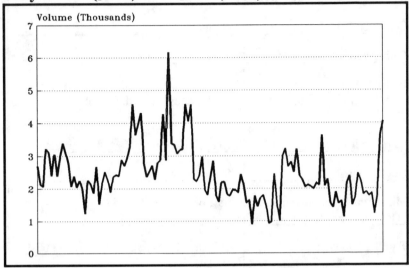

Monthly Average Daily Volumes (Jun, 1987 - Jul, 1990)

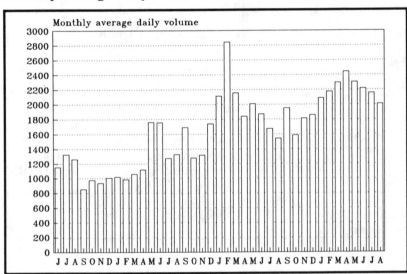

Month-end Open Interest (Jan, 1990 - Jul, 1990)

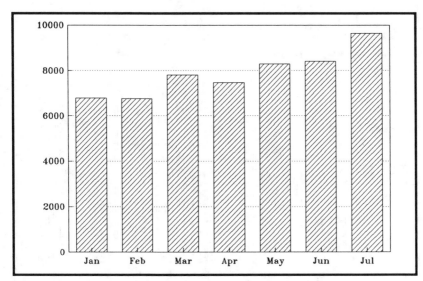

Price Histories (Jan 2, 1990 - Jun 29, 1990)

Weekly Stock Levels in tonnes (Jan 5, 1990 - Aug 23, 1990)

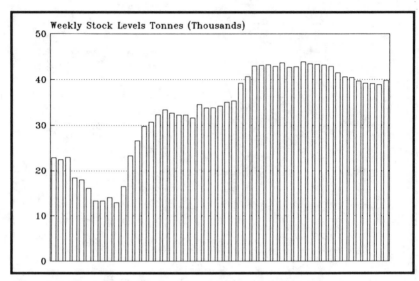

Special Contract Rules for Primary Nickel
Quality

The nickel delivered under this contract must be Primary nickel of minimum 99.80% purity with chemical analysis conforming to the current ASTM specification.

Shapes and Weights

All nickel delivered must be:

a)   Of the production of those producers named in the LME-approved list

b)   In the form of either cathodes or pellets or briquettes.

In the case of cathodes deliveries shall be made in the form of sizes cut to either 100 mm. x 100 mm. (4"x4"), 50 mm. x 50 mm. (2"x2") or 25 mm. x 25 mm. (1"x1"), size tolerances in accordance with internationally accepted trade practice. Each warrant shall consist of only one size.

All nickel delivered shall be packed in sound steel drums with a nett weight of minimum 150 kgs and maximum 500 kgs Each warrant shall consist of drums of uniform size and weight. The gross and nett weights must be clearly marked/stamped on each individual drum together with the producer's or brand name.

All drums delivered under this contract must be opened and emptied on arrival by the receiving **LME**-listed warehouse and the nickel inspected and repacked in original drums where possible. The warehouse will be responsible for resealing all inspected drums using their own numbered seals. All costs incurred will be accounted of the party instructing the warehouse to place the material on warrant.

Size of Lots

6 tonnes

Warrants

Warrants shall be for 6 tonnes each (2% either more or less). Each parcel of 6 tonnes shall be the product of one producer in one country and shall consist of one shape and size and shall lie in one warehouse. Each warrant must state the name of the producer, the shape, the dimensions of cathodes where applicable, the gross and nett weights and the numbers of the drum seals making up each parcel.

Special Note on Placing Nickel on Warrant

The party intending to place nickel on warrant for delivery to the Market must advise the warehouseman of the name of a Ring Dealing Member or Associate Clearing Member who will be responsible for the initial placing of the warrant(s) on the Market and such warrant(s) must be issued to the order of that Ring Dealing Member or Associate Clearing member.

Nickel Options Contract

Option Style	American calls and puts.
Contract Size:	6 tonnes.
Expiry Months:	See futures contract.
Expiry Day:	The first Wednesday of each month if the Wednesday is not a business day then the next business day.
Quotation:	Nearest 6 months are tradeable only in US$ per tonne and the nearest 3 months only are tradeable in £ per tonne.
Trading Hours:	See futures contract.
Initial Margin:	By arrangement with the broker.
Price Limit:	No price limit.
Contract Standard:	Physical delivery - see futures contract.
Exercise Price:	Contracts are traded with exercise intervals of US$100 per tonne.
Exchange Delivery Settlement Price:	Official seller's cash price.

Daily Volume (Jan 2, 1990 - May 31, 1990)

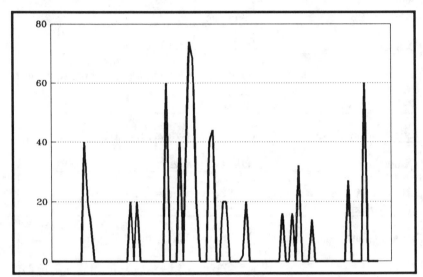

Monthly Average Daily Volumes (Jun, 1987 - Aug, 1990)

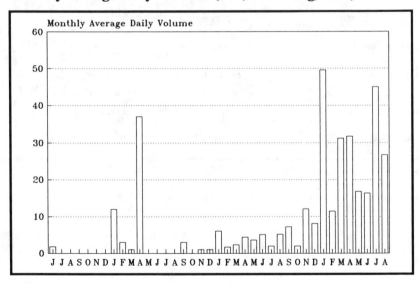

Tin Futures Contract

Contract Size:	5 tonnes.
Delivery Months:	Each month for the next 15 months.
Delivery Day:	Daily for three months forwards then the third Wednesday of the month for the next 12 months.
Last Trading Day:	Two business days prior to the delivery day.
Quotation:	US$ per tonne.
Minimum Price Movement (Tick Size and Value):	US$1 per tonne = US$5.
Trading Hours:	11.50 a.m. - 11.55 a.m. 12.35 p.m. - 12.40 p.m. (official) 15.40 p.m. - 15.45 p.m. 16.20 p.m. - 16.25 p.m.
Initial Margin:	By arrangement with the broker.
Price Limit:	No price limit.
Contract Standard:	Physical delivery of special high grade tin of minimum 99.85% purity subject to BSI restrictions on impurities.
Exchange Delivery Settlement Price:	Official seller's cash price.

Daily Volume (Jan 2, 1990 - Jun 29, 1990)

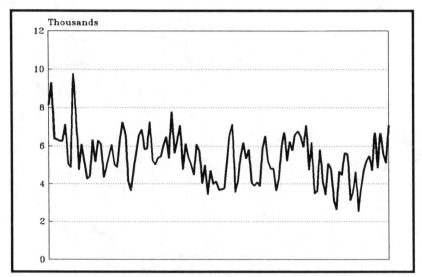

Monthly Average Daily Volumes (Jun, 1987 - Jul, 1990)

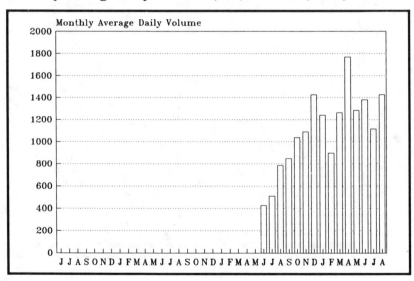

Month-end Open Interest (Jan, 1990 - Jul, 1990)

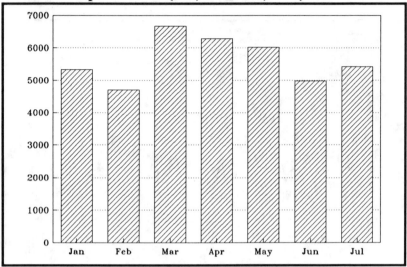

Price Histories (Jan 2, 1990 - Jun 29, 1990)

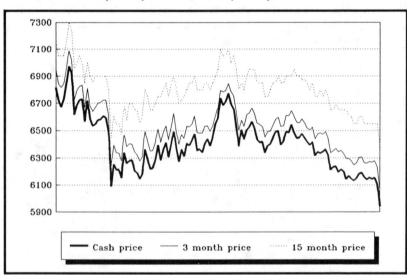

Weekly Stock Levels in tonnes (Jan 5, 1990 - Aug 23, 1990)

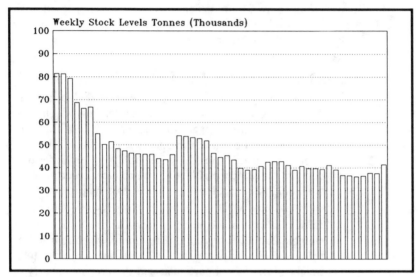

Special Contract Rules for Tin
Quality

The tin delivered under this contract must be refined tin of minimum 99.58% purity and conforming to BS3252:1986. All tin delivered must be:

a)   Of brands listed in the **LME**-approved list of tin brands;

b)   Either in ingots or slabs each weighing not less than 12 kgs or more than about 50 kgs

Shapes and Weights

Each parcel of 5 tonnes shall lie at one warehouse and be of one brand, shape and size, subject to the necessity of including different shapes and sizes at the bottom of each parcel for the purpose of palletisation. Each parcel placed on warrant shall be delivered securely strapped, in bundles not exceeding 1.2 tonnes.

Size of Lot

5 tonnes

Warrants

Warrants shall be for 5 tonnes each (2% either more or less). Each warrant must state the total weight of the parcel, the brand and the number of ingots or slab making up each parcel and also must state the number of bundles making up each parcel.

Special Rules Governing the Placing of Tin on Warrant

1) Each delivery of tin for placing on warrant shall be accompanied by a producer's Certificate of Analysis which must be lodged with the warehouseman. The Certificate of Analysis shall be within the quality specification set out in Special Contract Rule 1. A Bulk Analysis Certificate or a copy thereof is acceptable, but if a producer's Certificate is not available an analysis certificate must be prepared and signed by an assayer on the list of approved assayers.

2) Each warrant shall be made up from the production of one country and shall consist of one brand which is listed as being a good delivery. Each warrant shall state the total weight of the parcel particularized thereon, its country of origin, brand and the date(s) and reference number(s) of the Certificate of Analysis lodged with the warehouseman.

3) On request, the warehouseman is obliged to submit to the holder of the warrant Certificates of Analysis or copies thereof if the 5 tonnes parcel forms a part of a larger delivery covered by Bulk Analysis.

Zinc Futures Contract

Contract Size:	25 tonnes.
Delivery Months:	Each month for the next 15 months.
Delivery Day:	Daily for three months forward then the third Wednesday of the month for the next 12 months.
Last Trading Day:	Two business days before delivery day.
Quotation:	US$ per tonne.
Minimum Price Movement (Tick Size and Value):	US$0.50 per tonne = US$12.50.
Trading Hours:	12.10 p.m. - 12.15 p.m. 12.45 p.m. - 12.50 p.m. (official) 15.25 p.m. - 15.30 p.m. 16.05 p.m. - 16.10 p.m.
Initial Margin:	By arrangement with the broker.
Price Limit:	No price limit.
Contract Standard:	Physical delivery of special high grade zinc of minimum 99.995% purity produced in the form of slabs plates or ingots weighing not more than 55 kgs each. All zinc delivered must of brands listed in the **LME**-approved list.
Exchange Delivery Settlement Price:	Official seller's cash price.

Daily Volume (Jan 2, 1990 - Jun 29, 1990)

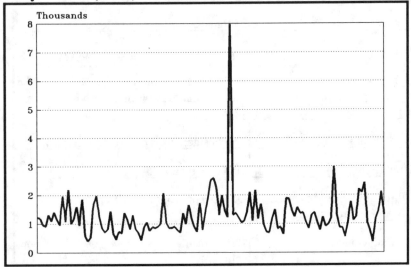

Monthly Average Daily Volumes (Jun, 1987 - Jul, 1990)

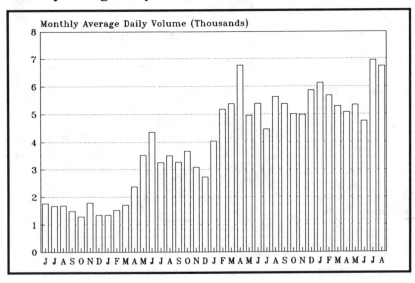

Month-end Open Interest (Jan, 1990 - Jul, 1990)

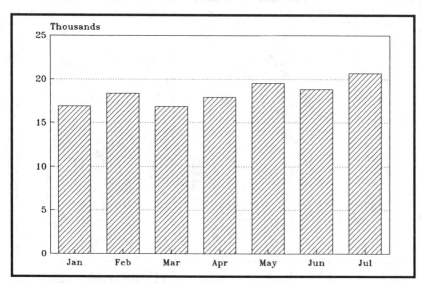

Price Histories (Jan 2, 1990 - Jun 29, 1990)

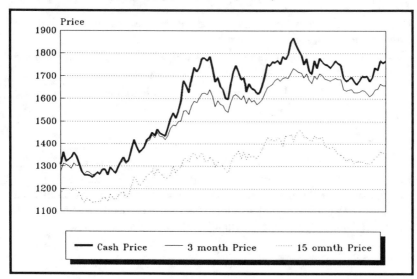

Weekly Stock Levels in tonnes (Jan 5, 1990 - Aug 23, 1990)

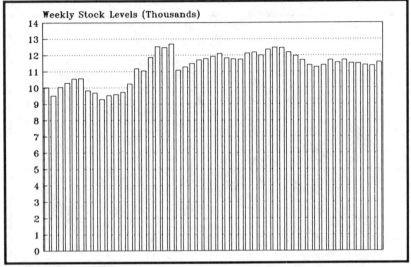

Special Contract Rules for Special High Grade Zinc

Quality

The zinc delivered under this contract must be zinc of minimum 99.995% purity. All zinc delivered must be:

a)   Of brands in the **LME**-approved list of special high-grade zinc brands;

b)   Either in slabs or in plates or in ingots weighing not more than 55 kgs each.

Shapes and Weights

Each parcel of 25 tonnes shall lie at one warehouse and be of one brand and shall consist of either slabs, plates or ingots of one size subject to the necessity of including different shapes and sizes at the bottom of each parcel for the purpose of palletisation. Each parcel placed on warrant shall be delivered securely strapped in bundles not exceeding 1.2 tonnes.

Size of Lot

25 tonnes

Warrants

Warrants shall be for 25 tonnes each (2% either more or less). Each warrant must state the total weight of the parcel, the brand and the number of slabs, plates or ingots making up each parcel. Warrants issued on or after June 1, 1985 also must state the number of bundles making up each parcel.

Zinc Options Contracts

Option Style	American calls and puts.
Contract Size:	25 tonnes.
Expiry Months:	See futures contract.
Expiry Day:	The first Wednesday of each month if the Wednesday is not a business day then the next business day.
Quotation:	The nearest 6 months are tradeable in both US$ and £ per tonne.
Minimum Price Movement (Tick Size and Value):	
Trading Hours:	See futures contract.
Initial Margin:	By arrangement with the broker.
Price Limit:	No price limit.
Contract Standard:	Physical delivery - see futures contract.
Exercise Price:	Contracts are trade with exercise intervals of US$20 per tonne/£20 and rises to US$50 when the zinc price rises over US$2,000.
Exchange Delivery Settlement Price:	Official seller's cash price.

Daily Volume (Jan 2, 1990 - May 31, 1990)

There were NO trades in this contract.

Monthly Average Daily Volumes (Jun, 1987 - Aug, 1990)

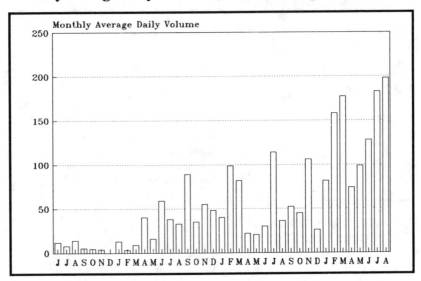

REGULATION

The London Metal Exchange is a Recognised Investment Exchange
and therefore comes under the supervision of the Securities and Investments
Board. Its Self Regulatory Organisation is the Association of Futures brokers
and Dealers.

QUOTE VENDORS

Reuters and Telerate provide a large number of pages covering the physical metal and futures exchanges. Further information is also provided by:

ADP	Bloomberg
Bridge	CMA
CQGI	Futurescope
ICV	Knight-Ridder
Newtime	Pont
Quotron	Reuters
Telerate	

SOURCES of REFERENCE

The following national press carry London Metal exchange prices and volumes:

> The Daily Telegraph
> The Financial Times
> The Times
> The Independent
> The International Herald Tribune
> The Wall Street Journal

The following publications carry London Metal exchange prices and volumes:

> Futures & Options World
> Futures Magazine
> Metal Bulletin

The Exchange also produces a range of publications that can be obtained at the Exchange or via:

> Brian Reidy & Associates Ltd
> Plantation House
> Fenchurch Street
> LONDON
> EC3M 3AP

Tel:	**(44) 71 283 3617**
Fax:	**(44) 71 895 0198**

The London Traded Options Market

David Rodan
Barclays de Zoete Wedd

INTRODUCTION

Traded options were introduced onto the London Stock Exchange in April 1978, initially trading call options on a limited number of underlying equities. Put options were introduced in 1981 and options on the FT-SE 100 share index in 1984. Turnover in the market was initially very low, with trading volume averaging less than 1000 contracts per day for the first two years. There were two major reasons for this slow start. UK institutional and private investors needed to be educated in the use and advantages of traded options; and from the start of the market the regulations governing the use of traded options by institutions and uncertainty surrounding the taxation of option profits restricted the number of active users of the market. The tax treatment of Traded Options was only finally resolved in the Budget of 1990, twelve years after the market opened.

Currently the London Traded Options Market (LTOM) trades option contracts on 68 UK equities together with options on Vaal Reefs and American and European style options on the FT-SE 100 Share Index. Call and put options are available in all contracts. LTOM has in the past listed options on French equities, UK Gilts and on currencies. However, none of these contracts proved successful and all have now been withdrawn. Trading in LTOM is by open outcry on the floor of the International Stock Exchange (ISE).

Turnover in LTOM is heavily weighted towards options on the FT-SE 100 Share Index (both American and European style options are available) and ten to fifteen of the equity options listed. Turnover in the least traded equity options is sporadic. Options on equities, when exercised or assigned are settled by delivery of the underlying security in normal International Stock Exchange account. However options on the FT-SE-100 Share Index and on the Euro FT-SE 100 Share Index are cash settled.

ORGANIZATION of the MARKET
Trading

Dealing in traded options is by open outcry on the floor of the International Stock Exchange (**ISE**) between 08.35 a.m. and 16.10 p.m.. No off floor or out of hours dealings are permitted.

Any member of the **ISE** can operate in the **LTOM** on behalf of its clients, but individuals working for member firms must qualify, by examination as a Registered Option Trader (**ROT**) before being allowed access to the floor.

In addition to the dealers executing orders, there are 22 member firms registered as market-makers in options, who deal as principals and have obligations to make a market in those classes of options in which they have registered as market makers. In return for the obligations which market making entails, market makers in **LTOM** receive certain privileges. They have some rights of priority of dealing at their price, and have the ability to borrow stock and exemption to stamp duty on stock purchased when their dealings in shares forms part of their option market making activity. A member firm executing a client order must show the order to the floor of the market, but is able to deal with either a market maker, or a non market maker or with the public limit order board (**PLOB**). Market makers are not allowed direct access to clients and other off floor participants in the market; they can only deal with traders or brokers on the floor.

Membership of LTOM

At the time of writing **LTOM** is wholly owned by the International Stock Exchange **ISE**. However it is expected that early in 1991 **LTOM** will merge with the London International Financial Futures Exchange **LIFFE** to form the London Derivatives Exchange **LDE**.

In its current structure, all members firms of the **ISE** have the right to operate in **LTOM**. However, before an individual employed by a member firm can gain access to the trading floor he must qualify by examination as a Registered Option Trader (**ROT**). Only **ROT**'s are allowed to trade in the market. A member firm that does not have any **ROT**'s, or which does not have a presence on the floor of **LTOM** can deal through a floor broker. Only member firms of the **ISE** can receive orders or execute trades in the market.

Clearing

All bargains in **LTOM** are registered and settled at the London Options Clearing House (**LOCH**), a wholly owned subsidiary of the **ISE**.

The clearing structure is one of "client to principal" in which each clients position with the clearing house and his margin lodged are separately identified at Clearing House as well as broker level. This contracts with the "principal to principal" system which is used in most other derivative exchanges; in which a clients positions are identified only at broker level; with the clearing house margining its members net exposure without identifying individual clients positions or margin. Changes in the clearing structure which would ease the administrative burden on **LOCH**, while retaining protection of clients margin lodged, have been under discussion within **LTOM** for some time. The merger of **LIFFE** and **LTOM** will inevitably involve some changes to the existing clearing structure. Members of the **ISE** who are not clearing members of **LOCH**, can open an account with a clearing agent (A clearing member of **LOCH** who is able to clear for other **ISE** members).

Clearing Members of the London Options Clearing House (LOCH)

S G Warburg Securities

Credit Suisse Buckmaster & Moore Ltd

James Capel & Co

Citioptions Limited

County Natwest Traded Options

CRT UK Ltd

Barclays de Zoete Wedd (Agency)

Barclays de Zoete Wedd (Market Makers)

Elders Finance Group UK Ltd

Hoare Govett Securities Ltd (HGO)

Hoare Govett Securities Ltd (HOA)

International Clearing Services Ltd

KAS Clearing Agent Ltd

Kitcat and Aitken

Kleinwort Benson Securities Ltd

CL-Alexanders Laing & Cruikshank

ED & F Man International

Natwest Stockbrokers
UBS Phillips & Drew
Robert Fleming & Co Ltd
SBC Stockbroking
Security Settlements Options Limited
Seligman Harris & Co
Sheppards
Smith Newcourt Securities plc
Smith New Court (Agency)
S G Warburg Futures and Options Limited

Address

	London Traded Options Market
	The International Stock Exchange
	London EC2N 1HP
Tel:	(+44) 71 588 2355
Telex:	886557
Fax:	(+44) 71 374 0451

Management
Principal Officer

Managing Director	A P de Guingand

Other Officers

Risk Management	Vincent Mercer

Services
Education and Literature

LTOM runs a number of educational courses, more information available from Nicola Child (071) 588 2355 Ext 29981.

LTOM staff regularly visit both ISE Member Firms and institutions and in house presentations at a variety of levels can be arranged. More details from Giles Marshall/Patrick Thompson on (071) 588 2355 Ext 29977/26760.

LTOM publications include a "Guide to Traded Options" which outlines the basic features of options and "Risk Management" which looks at how options can be used to manage risks inherent in holding an equity based portfolio.

Booklets are available from The Options Market Department, the International Stock Exchange, London EC2N 1HP.

The Management of LTOM

LTOM is a wholly owned subsidiary of the International Stock Exchange. In March 1989 the Council of the ISE agreed to the creation of :. irate strategic business units, reflecting the distinct business functions of the Exchange. One of these business units is the London Traded Options Market. The Council has delegated comprehensive powers and responsibilities, coupled with full accountability for the London Traded Options Market to the LTOM Divisional Board.

The LTOM Divisional Board have established four sub-committees to monitor specific functions of the market:

The Clearing Members Committee

The Floor Committee

The Rules and Supervision Sub-Committee

and the Regional Brokers Users Group.

These Committees act in an advisory capacity and are intended to bring together representatives from the Divisional Board and practitioners with expertise in particular aspects of the market.

Committee Members

LTOM Divisional Board

June Wright	Secretary
G H Chamberlain*	Chairman
	London Investment Trust (L.I.T.)
D W Parry	Deputy Chairman
	Independent Options Member
G D Freedman	Smith New Court Securities
D Watkins*	Goldman Sachs
M Freyd	UBS Phillips & Drew Securities Ltd
D L N Heron	James Capel & Co Securities
D H Roden	Barclays de Zoete Wedd
S Boswell **	Warburg Securities
C A Williamson	Sheppards

S Hills	Hills Independent Traders
A de Guingand	(Managing Director)
	LTOM
K B Sinclair*	Barclays de Zoete Wedd
A Haynes	Bankers Trust (Traded Options)
B Bird**	Independent Options Member

* Counc'l Member

** Sub-Committee Chairman

IN ATTENDANCE - CHAIRMAN OF:

Regional Brokers User Group

Institutional User Group

ICCH Representative

Clearing Members Committee

Bridget Watts	Committee Secretary
B Bird (D.B.M.)	Chairman
D H Roden (D.B.M.)	Barclays de Zoete Wedd
H W van Arem	KAS Clearing Agents Ltd
R Bennett	Security Settlement Options Ltd
C Cullum	Robert Fleming Securities
T Freeburn	Kleinwort Benson Securities
S Grimwood	International Clearing Services Ltd
D Loader	Warburg Futures & Options
G Green	NatWest Stockbrokers
M Parker	UBS Phillips & Drew Securities Ltd
M Weeks	Citioptions
S Lamont	Kitcat & Aitken
A J MacFarlane	James Capel & Co Ltd
K Ferris	Alexanders. Laing & Cruickshank

D.B.M. = Divisional Board Member

Floor Committee

Yvonne Nichols	Committee Secretary
D W Parry (D.B.M.)	Chairman
W C Leask	Smith New Court plc

D Hodges	Barclays de Zoete Wedd Securities
D Rowley	Warburg Securities
C Coates	Citioptions
J P Thwaytes	Barings Securities Ltd
P Sheridan	Sheppards
I Thurgood	Societe Generale Strauss Turnball
A Weaver	MGA (UK) Ltd
D McNeil	Kleinwort Benson Securities
K Harvey	Hoare Govett

D.B.M. = Divisional Board Member

Rules & Supervision Sub-Committee

Declan Ward	Committee Secretary
C A Williamson	(Chairman) (D.B.M.)
	Sheppards
M Parker	(CS-CM)
	UBS Phillips & Drew Securities Ltd
A MacFarlane	(CS-CM)
	James Capel & Co Ltd
K T Agyare	O'Connor Securities Ltd
Mrs L Powell	
I Thurgood (FS-CM)	Societe Generale Strauss Turnball Secs Ltd
D Hodges	Barclays de Zoete Wedd Securities
G D Freedman (D.B.M.)	Smith New Court Securities plc

D.B.M. = Divisional Board Member
CS-CM = Clearing Sub-Committee Member
FS-CM = Floor Sub-Committee Member

Regional Brokers User Group

Nick Maggs	Secretary
P Hepworth	(Acting Chairman)
	National Investment Group plc (North)
J Sreeves	Albert E Sharp
D Farrington	(all correspondence via N Maggs)
M McEnearney	Henry Cooke Lumsden

I Rankine	Anglo Pierson Options Ltd
C Runacre	Stock Beech & Co Ltd
Q Burrows	NatWest Stockbrokers Ltd
L Baxter	Northern Stockbrokers
P Dyson	Brown Shipley
A Kitching	Allied Provincial

The Merger of LIFFE & LTOM

By the end of the 1980's practitioners in **LTOM** had become increasingly convinced that the growth of the Traded Options market was being constrained by the lack of independence of **LTOM**. Work was started on proposals which would lead to the separation of **LTOM** from the **ISE** creating an independent Traded Options market. Progress in this direction was slow and in April 1990 a Joint Action Group, Chaired by Pen Kent of the Bank of England, was established to consider ways in which **LTOM** could be integrated with **LIFFE** in a form likely to be acceptable to:

a)   **LIFFE** Members and

b)   **ISE** Members particularly those who are participants in **LTOM**.

In June 1990 the Action Group made its report. Its main recommendations were:-

1.   That **LIFFE** and **LTOM** merge to form a single exchange to be called the London Derivatives Exchange (LDE).

2.   That the LDE should adopt with certain modifications the existing membership structure of **LIFFE**, under which membership, and trading and voting rights attach to share ownership or leasing.

3.   That recognizing the existing entry rights of all **ISE** members to **LTOM** and the value of **ISE** brokers to the new market, that **ISE** members not wishing to apply for shares in the LDE should be able to apply for affiliate membership of the LDE.

4.   That the structure of the Board of the LDE should, with certain modifications, follow the existing **LIFFE**

structure which blends widespread representation
with flexibility.

5. That a member of the **ISE** Council should be appointed to the LDE Board ex-officio and that the **ISE** Council should make reciprocal arrangements.

6. That there should be a single clearing house for all LDE contracts. The clearing relationship should be one of "principal to principal", and the underlying guarantee should be of the highest quality and backed by sound risk management and first rate systems.

The LDE will be located in Cannonbridge with a single trading floor. At the time of writing it is expected that the two markets merge early in 1991 and will move into Cannonbridge at the beginning of 1991.

Clearing and Security

The London Options Clearing House (**LOCH**) a subsidiary of the International Stock Exchange, guarantees all **LTOM** contracts.

Commission Rates and Transaction Costs

Commissions are fully negotiable. Each contract carries an exchange fee of 70p each way.

Margins

Margin is required for each short option position.

Margin on short equity options is calculated daily as:

20 per cent of the underlying security price plus or minus the in or out-of-the-money element of the option.

Margin on index options is:

12.5 per cent of the index level plus or minus the in or out-of-the-money element of the option.

Margin can be in the form of UK alpha securities, or any optionable security, or UK gilts or a range of other fixed interest securities or as cash. Each security lodged is subject to a level of discounting from its market value, depending on the volatility of the price of the class of security. The level of discount is greatest for equities and lowest for short dated gilts.

Clients lodging securities as margin continue to receive all dividends or coupons paid on those securities.

Margin concessions are available for cross positions involving more than one option series on the same underlying security.

HISTORY of OPTIONS CONTRACTS

Date of Launch	Type of Contract	Trading Value (Daily Average) Jan-June 1990
1978	Options & UK Equities	22,450
1984	Options & FT-SE 100 Index	10,000
1990	European style Options on FT-SE 100 Index	1,056

DETAILED CONTRACT SPECIFICATIONS
Equities
FT-SE 100 Index Options Contract

Option Style:	American calls and puts.
Contract Size:	£10 x Index.
Expiry Months:	Nearby four consecutive months plus up to two additional months up to 12 months maximum.
Expiry Day:	Last business day of the contract month.
Last Trading Day:	Last business day of the contract month.
Quotation:	£ to one decimal point.
Minimum Price Movement:	0.50 per index point = £5.00.
Trading Hours:	08.35 a.m. - 16.10 p.m.
Initial Margin:	12.5 per cent of index.
Price Limit:	No price limit.
Position Limit:	50,000 contracts per class.
Contract Standard:	Cash Settlement on the business day following exercise.
Exercise Price:	Five contracts with exercise intervals of 50 points. The prices used are the even ones ie 100 and 150 etc.. It is in contract to the Euro **FT-SE 100** Index which is also 50 point intervals but set at 125 and 175 etc..

TOPIC Pages:	*510#.
Reuters Pages:	LKRU - LKSE.

Top 10 Constituents in FT-SE 100 Index

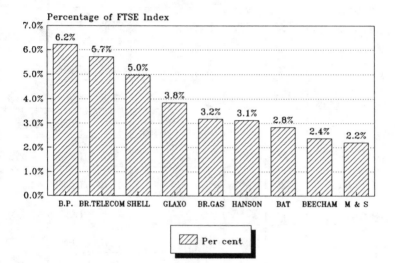

Composition of the FT-SE 100 Index

In Alphabetic Order			In Descending Percentage Order			
Stock	Shares Ms	Weight %	Stock	Shares Ms	Weight %	Total Weight
Abbey Nat.	1310	0.96%	Brit.Petroleum	5362	6.20%	6.20%
All.Lyons	781	1.23%	Brit.Telecom	6139	5.71%	11.91%
Anglia Water	295	0.22%	Shell	3315	4.97%	16.88%
Argyll	947	0.76%	Glaxo	1493	3.85%	20.72%
ASDA	1173	0.48%	Brit.Gas	4261	3.17%	23.89%

Ass.Brit.Foods	448	0.59%	Hanson	4798	3.12%	27.01%
B.A.A.	501	0.66%	BAT Industries	1473	2.84%	29.85%
Bk.of Scotland	759	0.28%	Smithkline Beecham	1326	2.37%	32.21%
Barclays Bank	1583	1.95%	Marks & Spencers	2709	2.20%	34.41%
Bass	354	1.20%	Guinness	900	2.17%	36.58%
BAT Industries	1473	2.84%	ICI	708	1.95%	38.54%
BET	743	0.53%	Barclays Bank	1583	1.95%	40.48%
BICC	273	0.33%	Grand Met.	992	1.87%	42.35%
Blue Circle	548	0.39%	BTR	1740	1.82%	44.18%
BOC GROUP	469	0.75%	GEC	2699	1.69%	45.87%
Boots Co.	983	1.02%	Unilever	798	1.66%	47.52%
Brit.Petroleum	5362	6.20%	Sainsbury	1517	1.56%	49.08%
BPB Industries	413	0.26%	Cable & Wireless	1070	1.51%	50.59%
Brit.Aerospace	259	0.46%	Nat.West.Bank	1613	1.48%	52.07%
Brit.Airways	721	0.33%	Prudential	1857	1.36%	53.42%
Brit.Gas	4261	3.17%	Wellcome	849	1.33%	54.76%
Brit.Steel	2000	0.83%	RTZ	987	1.31%	56.06%
Brit.Telecom	6139	5.71%	Tesco	1629	1.26%	57.32%
BTR	1740	1.82%	All.Lyons	781	1.23%	58.55%
Burmah Oil	182	0.30%	Bass	354	1.20%	59.74%

Cable & Wireless	1070	1.51%	Lloyds Bank	1239	1.13%	60.87%
Cadbury Schweppes	697	0.71%	Boots Co.	983	1.02%	61.89%
Commercial Union	428	0.68%	Reuters	434	0.98%	62.87%
Courtaulds	396	0.41%	Abbey Nat.	1310	0.96%	63.84%
Dalgety	224	0.27%	Enterprise Oil	456	0.96%	64.79%
Enterprise Oil	456	0.96%	G.U.S.	247	0.85%	65.64%
Fisons	687	0.83%	Sun Alliance	793	0.83%	66.48%
GEC	2699	1.69%	Brit.Steel	2000	0.83%	67.31%
General Accident	432	0.68%	Fisons	687	0.83%	68.13%
GKN	258	0.25%	Land Sec.	504	0.82%	68.95%
Glaxo	1493	3.85%	Ladbroke	860	0.81%	69.75%
Grand Met.	992	1.87%	Argyll	947	0.76%	70.52%
G.U.S.	247	0.85%	BOC GROUP	469	0.75%	71.26%
G.R.E.	861	0.57%	P & O	416	0.73%	72.00%
Guinness	900	2.17%	Cadbury Schweppes	697	0.71%	72.70%
Hammerson	166	0.29%	Rothmans Intl.	300	0.70%	73.40%
Hanson	4798	3.12%	Racal Elecs.	1300	0.69%	74.09%
Harr.& Crosfield	685	0.33%	General Accident	432	0.68%	74.77%

Hawker Sidderley	198	0.27%	Commercial Union	428	0.68%	75.45%
Hillsdown	530	0.49%	T.H.F.	786	0.68%	76.13%
ICI	708	1.95%	B.A.A.	501	0.66%	76.79%
Kingfisher	453	0.57%	TSB Group	1503	0.66%	77.45%
Ladbroke	860	0.81%	Reed Intl.	554	0.66%	78.11%
Land Sec.	504	0.82%	Royal Ins.	484	0.66%	78.76%
LASMO	358	0.51%	Whitbread A	444	0.65%	79.41%
Legal & General	482	0.65%	Legal & General	482	0.65%	80.06%
Lloyds Bank	1239	1.13%	Reckitt & Colman	149	0.61%	80.67%
LONRHO	642	0.45%	Rank Org.	308	0.61%	81.28%
Lucas Industries	690	0.27%	Thorn EMI	290	0.59%	81.87%
Marks & Spencers	2709	2.20%	Tarmac	726	0.59%	82.46%
Maxwell Comm.	647	0.30%	Ass.Brit.Foods	448	0.59%	83.05%
MEPC	322	0.49%	Pearson	271	0.59%	83.63%
Midland Bank	782	0.56%	Kingfisher	453	0.57%	84.20%
Nat.West.Bank	1613	1.48%	G.R.E.	861	0.57%	84.78%
North West Water	356	0.26%	Rolls Royce	961	0.57%	85.35%
P & O	416	0.73%	Midland Bank	782	0.56%	85.90%

Pearson	271	0.59%	BET	743	0.53%	86.43%
Pilkington	746	0.40%	LASMO	358	0.51%	86.94%
Prudential	1857	1.36%	Redland	276	0.51%	87.45%
Racal Elecs.	1300	0.69%	S.T.C.	560	0.50%	87.95%
R.H.M.	355	0.35%	Hillsdown	530	0.49%	88.44%
Rank Org.	308	0.61%	MEPC	322	0.49%	88.93%
Reckitt & Colman	149	0.61%	ASDA	1173	0.48%	89.40%
Redland	276	0.51%	United Biscuits	444	0.46%	89.87%
Reed Intl.	554	0.66%	Brit.Aerospace	259	0.46%	90.33%
Reuters	434	0.98%	Scot.& Newcastle	393	0.46%	90.79%
RMC Group	194	0.40%	LONRHO	642	0.45%	91.24%
Rolls Royce	961	0.57%	Courtaulds	396	0.41%	91.66%
Rothmans Intl.	300	0.70%	Ultramar	369	0.41%	92.07%
Royal Bk of Scot.	755	0.37%	Pilkington	746	0.40%	92.47%
Royal Ins.	484	0.66%	Sears	1505	0.40%	92.87%
RTZ	987	1.31%	RMC Group	194	0.40%	93.27%
Sainsbury	1517	1.56%	Blue Circle	548	0.39%	93.66%
Scot.& Newcastle	393	0.46%	Royal Bk of Scot.	755	0.37%	94.03%
Sears	1505	0.40%	R.H.M.	355	0.35%	94.37%

Severn Trent Water	354	0.23%	Trafalgar House	503	0.33%	94.71%
Shell	3315	4.97%	Brit.Airways	721	0.33%	95.04%
Smith & Nephew	994	0.33%	Harr.& Crosfield	685	0.33%	95.37%
Smithkline Beecham	1326	2.37%	Smith & Nephew	994	0.33%	95.70%
Standard Chartered	234	0.22%	BICC	273	0.33%	96.03%
S.T.C.	560	0.50%	Burmah Oil	182	0.30%	96.33%
Sun Alliance	793	0.83%	Maxwell Comm.	647	0.30%	96.63%
Tarmac	726	0.59%	Hammerson	166	0.29%	96.92%
Tesco	1629	1.26%	Thames Water	384	0.28%	97.20%
Thames Water	384	0.28%	Bk.of Scotland	759	0.28%	97.48%
Thorn EMI	290	0.59%	Lucas Industries	690	0.27%	97.75%
T.H.F.	786	0.68%	Hawker Sidderley	198	0.27%	98.01%
Trafalgar House	503	0.33%	Dalgety	224	0.27%	98.28%
TSB Group	1503	0.66%	North West Water	356	0.26%	98.54%
Ultramar	369	0.41%	Wiggins Teape	493	0.26%	98.81%
Unilever	798	1.66%	BPB Industries	413	0.26%	99.07%
United Biscuits	444	0.46%	GKN	258	0.25%	99.32%

Wellcome	849	1.33%	Severn Trent Water	354	0.23%	99.56%
Whitbread A	444	0.65%	Standard Chartered	234	0.22%	99.78%
Wiggins Teape	493	0.26%	Anglia Water	295	0.22%	100.00%

FT-SE Option Volume Statistics
Daily Volume and Open Interest (Jan 2,1990 - Jul 31,1990)

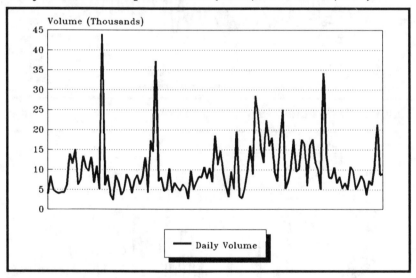

Call and Put Volumes (Jan 2,1990 - Jul 31,1990)

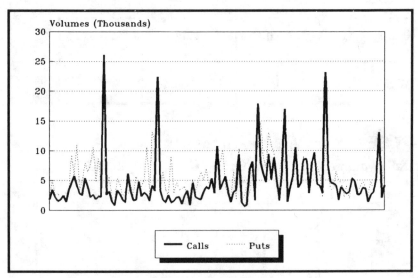

Call/Put Ratio (Jan 2,1990 - Jul 31,1990)

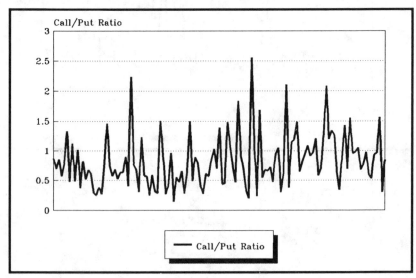

FT-SE 100 Index Price (Jan 2,1990 - Jul 31,1990)

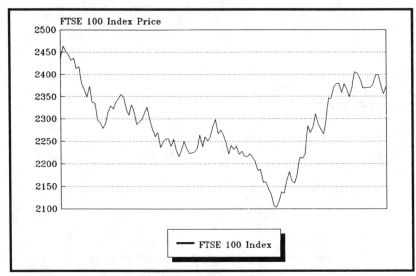

Implied Volatility (Jan 2,1990 - Jul 31,1990)

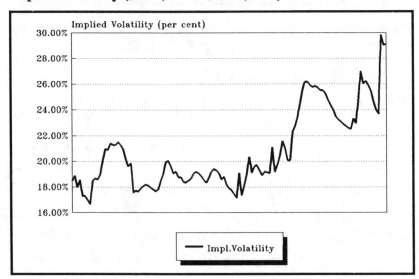

Historical Volatilities (Jan 2,1990 - Jul 31,1990)

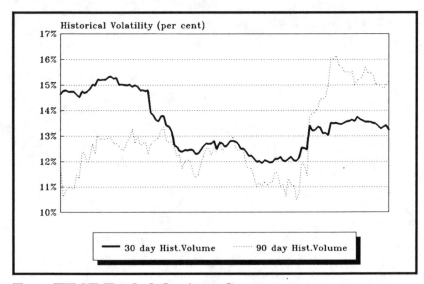

Euro FT-SE Traded Options Contract

Option Style:	European Exercise. Exercise is only possible at expiry.
Contract Size:	£10 x Index point.
Expiry Months:	Three consecutive months together with five months on the March June September and December cycle (one of which will be included in the first three consecutive months).
Expiry Day:	The last business day of the contract month.
Last Trading Day:	The last business day of the contract month.
Quotation:	£ to one decimal point.

Minimum Price Movement;	0.5 index point = £5.00.
Trading Hours:	08.35 a.m. - 16.10 p.m.
Initial Margin:	12.5 per cent of index.
Price Limit:	No price limit.
Positions Limits:	50,000 contracts per class.
Contract Standard:	Cash settlement on the business day following exercise.
Exercise Price:	Five contracts with exercise intervals of 50 points. The prices used are the odd ones ie 125 and 175 etc.. It is in contract to the **FT-SE** 100 Index which is also 50 point intervals but set at 100 and 150 etc.
Exchange Delivery Settlement Price:	Expiry is at 11.20 a.m. on the last trading day in the contract month. The **FT-SE** Index is calculated at one minute intervals between 11.10 a.m. and 11.20 a.m.. The highest and lowest levels are rejected and the settlement price is the average of the remaining nine readings rounded to the nearest 0.5 index point.
TOPIC Pages:	*680#.
Reuters Pages:	LKSH - LKSO.

Euro - FT-SE Options Statistics
Daily Volume and Open Interest (Jan 24,1990 - Jul 31,1990)

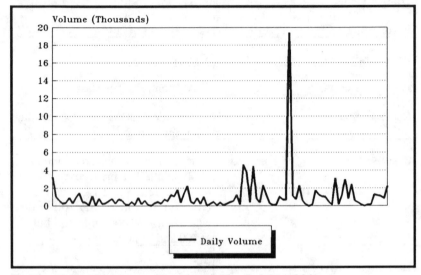

Call and Put Volumes (Jan 24,1990 - Jul 31,1990)

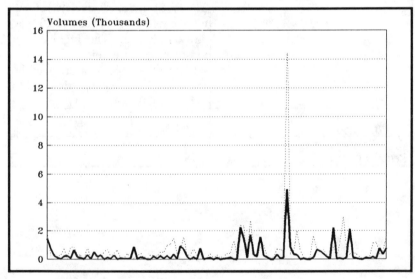

Call/Put Ratio (Jan 24,1990 - Jul 31,1990)

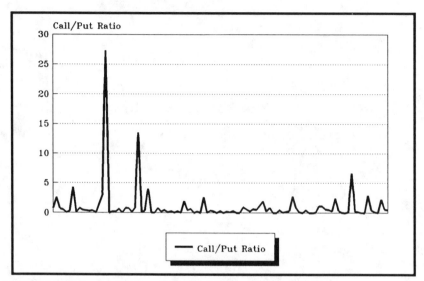

FT-SE 100 Index Price (Jan 24,1990 - Jul 31,1990)

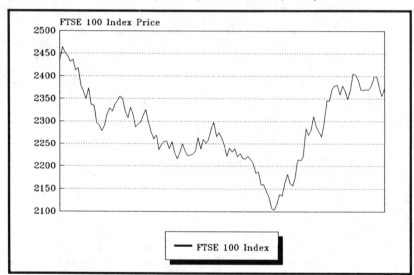

Implied Volatility (Jan 24,1990 - Jul 31,1990)

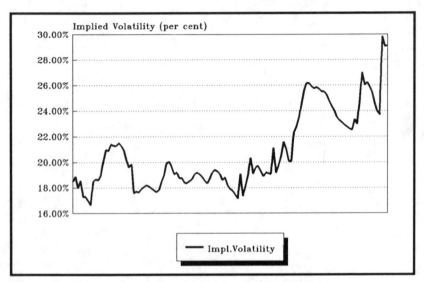

Historical Volatilities (Jan 24,1990 - Jul 31,1990)

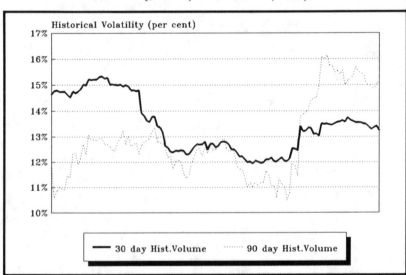

Individual UK Equity Traded Options Contract

Option Style:	American calls and puts - on any day with the exception of the last day of any stock exchange account.
Contract Size:	1,000 shares.
Delivery Months:	Three month contracts from a quarterly expiry cycle. See below.
Delivery Day:	The last Wednesday in the last complete Stock Exchange Account in the expiry month.
Last Trading Day:	The last Wednesday in the last complete Stock Exchange Account in the expiry month.
Minimum Price Movement:	£0.0025 per share = £2.50.
Trading Hours:	08.35 a.m. - 16.10 p.m.
Initial Margin:	20 per cent of the underlying security's price.
Price Limit:	No price limit.
Position Limits:	Maximum positions limits depending on the market capitalization of the Equity.
Contract Standard:	Exercise or assignment of an option results in a bargain in the underlying equity which will fall for settlement as a bargain for standard **ISE** account settlement.
Exercise Price:	Three contracts are available. See table below for exercise intervals based on price of underlying share.

| TOPIC Pages: | see table below. |
| Reuters Page: | see table below. |

Total Options Statistics
Daily Volume and Open Interest (Jan 2,1990 - Jul 31,1990)

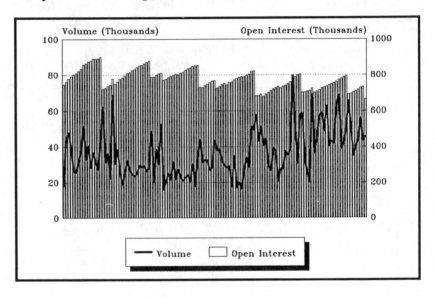

Open Interest and Volume Open Interest ("Liquidity") (Jan 2, 1990 - Jul 31, 1990)

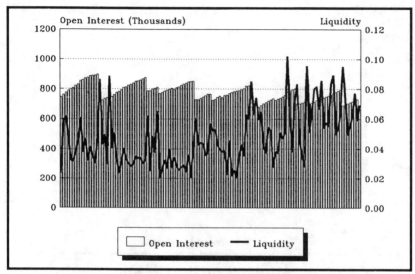

Call and Put Volumes (Jan 2, 1990 - Jul 31, 1990)

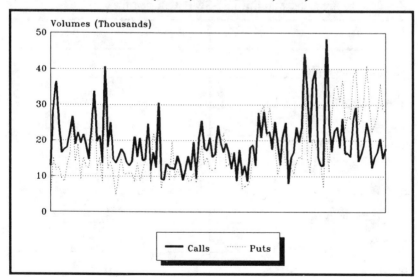

CallPut Ratio (Jan 2,1990 - Jul 31,1990)

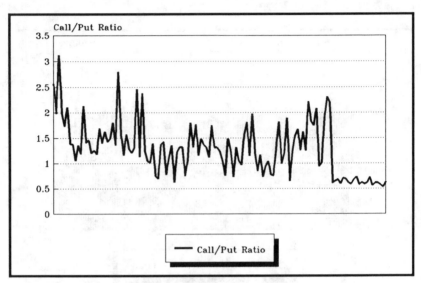

Traded Options Available on the LTOM

FT-SE 100 Share Index and Euro FT-SE 100 Share Index

	Expiry Cycle
Abbey National plc	III
Allied Lyons plc	I
Amstrad plc	III
Asda Group plc	I
BAA plc	II
BAT Industries plc	II
BTR plc	II
Barclays plc	III

Bass plc	I
Blue Circle plc	III
Boots Co plc	I
British Aerospace plc	II
British Airways plc	I
British Gas plc	III
British Petroleum plc	I
British Steel plc	I
British Telecom plc	II
Cable & Wireless plc	I
Cadbury Schwepps plc	II
Commercial Union Ass Co plc	I
Courtaulds plc	I
Dixons Group plc	III
Ferranti International Signal plc	(RLO) Nov Jan
Fisons plc	(RLO) Feb Oct Dec
General Electric Co plc	II
GKN plc	I
Glaxco Holdings plc	III
Grand Metropolitan plc	I
Guinness plc	II

Hanson plc	II
Hawker Sidderley Group plc	III
Hillsdown Holdings plc	III
Imperial Chemical Industries plc	I
Kingfisher plc	I
Ladbroke Group plc	I
Land Securities plc	I
LASMO plc	II
Lonrho plc	III
Lucas Industries plc	II
Marks and Spencers plc	I
Midland Bank plc	III
Peninsular and Oriental Steam Nav Co	II
Pilkington plc	II
Polly Peck International plc	II
Prudential Corp plc	II
Racal Electronics plc	II
Reuters Holdings plc	III
Rolls Royce plc	III
RTZ Corporation plc	II
STC plc	I

Sainsbury plc	I
Scottish and Newcastle Brewery plc	II
Sears plc	III
Shell Transport and Trading Co plc	I
Smith Kline Beecham plc	I
Storehouse plc	I
TSB Group plc	III
Tesco plc	II
Thames Water plc	II
Thorn EMI plc	III
Trafalgar House plc	I
Trusthouse Forte plc	III
Ultramar plc	I
Unilever plc	I
United Biscuits (Holdings) plc	I
Vaal Reefs Exploration and Mining Co Ltd	III
Water Package	II
Wellcome plc	III

There are three expiry cycles:

I	January April July and October
II	February May August and November
III	March June September and December
	(excluding FT-SE 100 Index)

Each stock is allocated to one of the three expiry cycles, normally chosen so that expiry dates do not coincide with announcement of the companies results or with an ex-dividend on the shares. Contracts expire on the last Wednesday of the last complete Stock Exchange account in the month.

At any time there will be three contract months traded.

Restricted life options (**RLO's**) are on a two monthly cycle. When the options are introduced, three contract months are available. When the near month series expires, a further series may be introduced, or alternatively there may be no additional series. If no additional series are introduced the option contracts in that stock will have all expired within four months, and there will no longer be options available on that stock. At the time of writing traded options on Ferranti are **RLO's** which are not being replaced on expiry. The expiry date for **RLO** options within a given contract month is the same as for full traded option classes ie the last Wednesday on the last full Stock Exchange Account in the month.

Exercise Intervals

Share price	Exercise Interval
0 - 140	10
160 - 300	20
330 - 420	30
460 - 500	40
Over 500	50

Liquidity Based on Turnover (Jan - June, 1990)

Stock	Turnover	Per cent
FT-SE	1,253,425	29.89
Hanson	158,762	3.79
Rolls Royce	158,587	3.78
British Gas	136,780	3.26
BP	134,269	3.20
British Steel	123,301	2.94
British Telecom	114,510	2.73
Euro FT-SE	106,555	2.54
ICI	91,348	2.18
Trust House Forte	90,003	21.5
Sears	85,690	2.04
Amstrad	84,902	2.02
GEC	78,879	1.88
Cable & Wireless	58,424	1.39
Water Package	57,697	1.38
Grand Metropolitan	53,725	1.28
STC	51,756	1.23
Ladbroke	49,401	1.18
British Aerospace	48,597	1.16

United Biscuits	47,464	1.13
Asda	45,435	1.08
Cadbury Schwepps	45,229	1.08
BTR	39,400	0.94
Ferranti	38,882	0.93
Blue Circle Industries	38,308	0.91
Boots Co	37,632	0.90
Dixons	35,582	0.85
Marks & Spencers	37,559	0.90
British Airways	36,795	0.88
Guinness	35,272	0.84
Storehouse	34,220	0.82
Pilkington	34,165	0.81
TSB	34,058	0.81
Allied Lyons	34,004	0.81
Smith Kline Beecham	33,841	0.81
BAT Industries	32,470	0.77
Polly Peck	32,093	0.77
Racal Electronics	31,665	0.76
Thames Water	31,630	0.75
RTZ	30,645	0.73

Glaxo	30,041	0.72
Lonrho	27,763	0.66
Barclays	26,064	0.62
Shell	25,697	0.61
Scottish & Newcastle	22,331	0.53
Prudential	21,429	0.51
Wellcome	20,852	0.50
Land Securities	20,471	0.49
Abbey National	19,684	0.47
Reuters	19,217	0.46
GKN	19,100	0.46
Tesco	18,418	0.44
Midland Bank	18,179	0.46
Kingfisher	17,574	0.42
Trafalgar House	17,548	0.42
Commercial Union	17,516	0.42
BAA	15,924	0.38
P&O	15,127	0.36
Hillsdown	14,687	0.35
Thorn EMI	13,075	0.31
Unilever	12,634	0.30

Courtaulds	9,695	0.23
LASMO	9,256	0.22
Bass	8,577	0.20
Ultramar	7,265	0.17
Sainsbury	6,500	0.16
Hawker Sidderley	6,332	0.15
Lucas	4,396	0.10
Total	4,193,387	100.00

Turnover in **LTOM** is heavily weighted towards a few of the most heavily traded classes. In the first half of 1990 turnover in the **FT-SE** 100 Index Options accounted for nearly 30% of the total market volume. The **FT-SE** and 23 other stocks provided 75% of volume, with the remaining 25% of turnover spread over forty five of the least traded classes. However liquidity is deeper than these raw statistics suggest; only a handful of classes are illiquid. It is normally possible to deal with market makers in the majority of option classes.

Price Information

	TOPIC	Reuters
Index Pages	*501#	IDLL-P
FT-SE 100	*510#	LKSH-O
Euro FT-SE	*680#	LKSH-O
Abbey Nat	*677#	LKDY-ED
Allied Lyons	*515#	LKAA-F
Amstrad	*516#	LKMC-H
Asda	*675#	LKRK-P

BAA	*518#	LKNG--L
BAT	*519#	LKAS-X
BTR	*521#	LKCI-N
Barclays	*523#	LKAG-L
Bass	*524#	LKAM-R
Blue Circle	*528#	LKBE-J
Boots	*530#	LKBK-P
British Aero.	*532#	LKCC-H
British Airways	*533#	LKLK-P
British Gas	*538#	LKKS-X
BP	*540#	LKBQ-V
British Steel	*544#	LKRE-J
British Telecom	*546#	LKBW-CB
Cable & Wireless	*552#	LKCO-T
Cadbury	*554#	LKCU-Z
Commercial Union	*556#	LKDA-F
Courtaulds	*561#	LKDM-R
Dixons	*565#	LKEE-J
Ferranti	*679#	LKFQ-V
Fisons	*569#	LKHA-F
GEC	*571#	LKES-X

GKN	*573#	LKEY-FD
Glaxo	*575#	LKFE-J
Grand Met	*578#	LKFK-P
Guinness	*580#	LKGC-H
Hanson	*583#	LKGI-N
Hawker Sidderley	*584#	LKPC-H
Hillsdown	*586#	LKQG-L
ICI	*589#	LKGO-T
Kingfisher	*594#	LKKY-LD
Ladbroke	*595#	LKHG-L
LASMO	*601#	LKHS-X
Lonrho	*605#	LKHY-ID
Lucas	*608#	LKDG-L
Marks and Spencers	*610#	LKIE-J
Midland Bank	*612#	LKIK-P
P&O	*615#	LKIQ-V
Pilkington	*617#	LKOK-P
Polly Peck	*618#	LKNM-R
Prudential	*622#	LKMU-Z
Racal Elec	*625#	LKIW-JB
Reuters	*627#	LKMI-N

RTZ	*628#	LKJC-H
STC	*634#	LKDS-X
Sainsbury	*636#	LKOQ-V
Scottish & Newcastle	*638#	LKQY-RD
Sears	*639#	LKLQ-V
Shell T & T	*641#	LKJI-N
S K Beecham	*526#	LKAY-BD
Storehouse	*643#	LKOE-J
TSB	*646#	LKKG
Tesco	*648#	LKJO-T
Thames Water	*651#	LKPI-N
Thorn EMI	*650#	LKJU-Z
Trafalgar House	*652#	LKKA-F
Ultramar	*656#	LKQA-F
Unilever	*658#	LKNS-X
United Biscuits	*659#	LKQS-X
Vaal Reefs	*663#	LKKM-R
Water Package	*665#	LKPO - T
Wellcome	*667#	LKNY-OD

REGULATION

All participants in **LTOM** are members of the International Stock Exchange (**ISE**). The primary regulatory body for brokers and traders in **LTOM** is The Securities Association (**TSA**) which is one of the five self Regulatory bodies controlled by the Securities and Investments Board (**SIB**).

The **ISE** is a Recognised Investment Exchange **RIE** recognised by the **SIB** and as a subsidiary of the **ISE**, **LTOM** and its members are monitored by the **TSA** and the **SIB**.

TAXATION

The uncertainty about the taxation of profits and losses on Traded Options has been one of the greatest impediments to the growth of the market. At the start of the market in 1978 traded options were regarded as wasting assets with the premium paid amortised over the life of the option. This resulted in users of the market who had made a loss on options bought being assessed for capital gains tax on notional 'profits' under the wasting asset rule. This anomaly was rectified in 1980 but the problems surrounding the use of options by pension funds, investment trusts and unit trusts remained. Before the budgets of 1988 and 1990 it was not clear that dealing in Traded Options would be considered by the Inland Revenue to be part of the investment activity of these funds. The 1990 Budget has clarified the situation, and as a rule of thumb profits or losses made on Traded Options by funds that are not deemed to be trading, are of a capital nature and are not subject to tax as income; provided that the option transactions were undertaken as hedging an underlying asset or reducing risk associated with it.

Broadly for institutions transactions in traded options or financial futures that can be regarded as hedging an underlying asset or reducing risk associated with it, will be treated as capital transactions where transactions in the underlying are regarded as capital.

Greater detail of the taxation and regulations applying to transactions in Traded Options, for institutions and private investors are available from **LTOM**.

OM London - OML

Denise Neuhaus
OM London

INTRODUCTION

OM London, OML, began trading in December 1989 with its OMX equity index contract, based on the thirty most actively traded shares on the Stockholm Stock Exchange. OMX is the most liquid index contract in Europe, trading approximately 20,000 contracts daily. OM London is a UK Recognized Investment Exchange and a subsidiary of the Stockholm Options Market, OM.

OML was established to offer trading and clearing in futures and options based on Swedish securities to the U.K. market through a link with the Swedish Options Market. OML has since introduced options on Norwegian stocks and plans to list additional new products.

OM London's Turnover of OMX Options
December 15, 1989 - June 29, 1990.

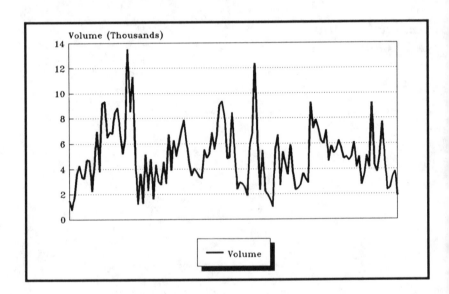

OM London's Turnover of OMX Futures
December 15,1989 - June 29,1990.

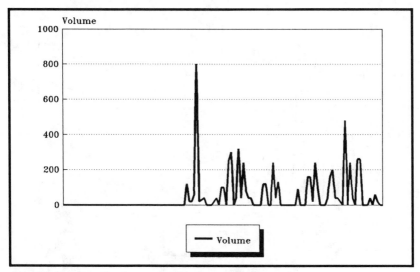

OM London's Turnover of Stock Options
April 2,1990 - June 29,1990.

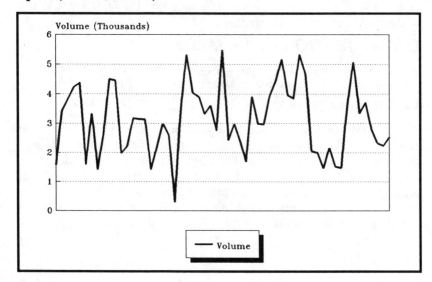

OM London's Turnover of Stock Futures
April 2,1990 - June 29,1990.

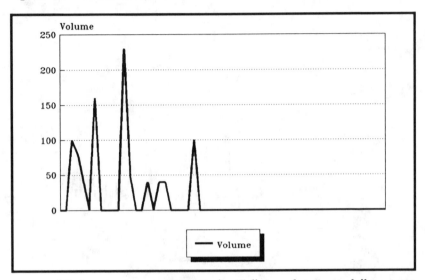

Market response to **OML** was immediate and strong: a daily average of 32,500 OMX contracts traded during OML's first six weeks of trading, 5,500 of which were generated on average daily from London. OML's record daily trading has been over 13,000 contracts.

ORGANIZATION of the MARKET

OML is a profit-orientated exchange and offers the market a commercial orientation responsive to market needs and developments.

Linked Marketplace

OM London is the first European-linked exchange. At present, all of **OML**'s products trade in a linked marketplace with its parent exchange, the Stockholm Options market. This single marketplace combines the liquidity in both Stockholm and London and provides market participants with integrated orders and an identical price profile. Thus, investors trade and clear in their own country while trading in a more liquid market and at the best price, whether that price is quoted in Stockholm or London.

LINKED MARKETPLACE

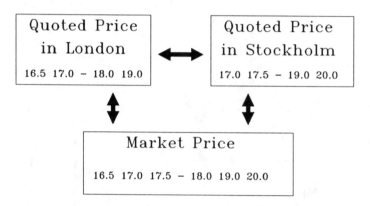

OML has two types of members:

● **broker members**

● **market maker members**

both of which may place bids and offers.

Trading

At present, all trading at **OML** is conducted by telephone through the block order desk. The block order desk handles orders of 10 contracts or multiples of 10 and complex orders such as combinations.

OML plans to introduce in the near future a separate and parallel electronic trading system which will automatically execute orders. At the block order desk, **OML**'s market place officials, who are fully employed by **OML** and do not take positions, match orders according to price and time received. Best prices are distributed to members via Reuters, **OML**'s information system and other electronic information systems. Trading hours depend on the trading hours of the underlying market.

Trading at OM London

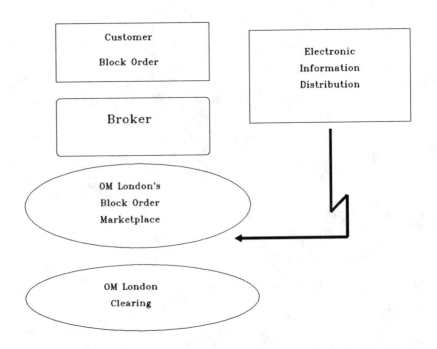

Clearing

OML is an integrated marketplace and clearing house. **OML** is the legal counterparty in all trades - as buyer to sellers and seller to buyers - and guarantees the fulfilment of all contracts through its capital resources and its margin system, **OMS**. Customers trade at **OML** through a member broker. Customers are anonymous to **OML** and designated by their account number. All information is recorded at the customer level: transactions, payments and margins. This reduces member brokers' administrative work. Brokers connected to **OML**'s information system can keep track of changes in customers' positions and margin requirements as well as stay abreast of market information.

Shareholders

OML is a wholly owned subsidiary of **OM**. **OM**'s owners include Swedish banks and brokerage firms - Investor, Providentia, Nobel Industrier, Volvo Group finance Sweden, Skandia, Trygg-Hansa, Olof Stenhammar (founder and president), **OM** staff and members of the public. **OM** has approximately 2,000 shareholders.

Board of Directors

Chairman, President & CEO	Olof Stenhammar, OM Group
Managing Director	Peter Jorgensen, **OML**
Marketing Director	Karin Forseke, **OML**
President OM International	Anders Nyren
President OM Division	Per Larsson
Executive Vice President OM Group	Dag Sehlin

Membership as of July 10, 1990

Geographical Distribution of Members

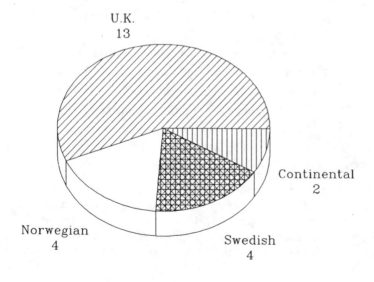

U.K.
13

Continental
2

Norwegian
4

Swedish
4

Market Makers Members

Derivatan Ltd (United Kingdom)

Opulencia APS (Denmark)

Servisen Ltd (United Kingdom)

United Securities Fondkommission Ltd (United Kingdom)

Broker Members

ABB Aros Securities Netherlands BV (Netherlands)

Alfred Berg Norge A/S (Norway)

Arapt Partners Fondkommission AB (Sweden)

Bankers Trust International Ltd (United Kingdom)

BNP Securities Ltd (United Kingdom)

Carl Kierulf & Co (Norway)

Carnegie Fondkommission AB (Sweden)

Consensus Fondkommission AB (Sweden)

DnB Fonds AS (Norway)

E. Ohman J:r Fondkommission AB (Sweden)

Enskilda Securities - Skandinaviska Enskilda Ltd (United Kingdom)

Kansallis Gota Securities Ltd (United Kingdom)

LIT Futures Ltd (United Kingdom)

Morgan Stanley International (United Kingdom)

Oslo Securities AS (Norway)

Robert Fleming Securities Ltd (United Kingdom)

S.G.Warburg Futures and Options Ltd (United Kingdom)

Salomon Brothers International Ltd (United Kingdom)

Svenska International PLC (United Kingdom)

UBS Phillips & Drew Securities Ltd (United Kingdom)

United Securities Fondkommission Ltd (Sweden)

OMS -OML's Margin System

OMS is based on the concept that margins should correspond to the risk associated with a customer's portfolio. By using the same information that the market uses to price options, OMS accurately assesses price and liquidity risk and calculates these for all contracts in a customer account based on the same underlying instrument - both futures and options. This cross-margining across a portfolio reduces collateral requirements to what is needed to cover the account risk as a whole.

Using the Black-Scholes and the Black-76 valuation models, **OMS** calculates the highest possible cost to the exchange of closing all the contracts in an account within a certain range of market prices for the underlying instrument. Margin requirements are calculated daily at closing values. The range of market prices for the underlying instruments is determined by the maximum historical price movements. Because **OMS** uses a portfolio valuation algorithm to calculate margin requirements, the results accurately reflect the risk of an account. All factors influencing the value of the contract are accounted for: the risk-free interest rate, time until expiration, volatility and price of the underlying instrument and the strike price.

Internal studies at the Stockholm Options market have shown the **OMS** system to be highly accurate. The analysis compared **OMS** with two other margins systems used by other exchanges. The historical data used included the 1987 crash. Over the period studied, **OMS** never failed to calculate sufficient margins to close any position. At the same time, **OMS** calculated significantly lower margin requirements than the other margin systems.

Transaction Costs

There are no membership or seat fees at OML. There are no fees for trading. Instead OML charges a clearing fee per trade.

Clearing Fees

Swedish Stock Options	
Trades	
Customer Transactions:	0.5% of premium + 1.0% of premium - the latter a minimum SEK 6 and a maximum SEK 14.
Market Maker Transaction:	0.6% of premium - minimum SEK 1 and maximum SEK 8.
Exercise	

Customer Transactions:	0.45% less than SEK 500,000 0.30% greater than SEK 500,000 (50% Broker discount).
Market Maker Transaction:	0.45% less than SEK 500,000 0.30% greater than SEK 500,000 (80% Market Maker discount).

Swedish Stock Futures

Exercise

Customer Transactions:	0.10% (minimum SEK 17).
Market Maker Transaction:	SEK 10.

OMX Index Options

Trades

Customer Transactions:	0.5% of premium + 1.0% of premium - the latter a minimum SEK 6 and a maximum SEK 14.
Market Maker Transaction:	0.6% of premium - minimum SEK 1 and maximum SEK 8.

Exercise and Cash settlement

Customer Transactions:	0.5% of premium + 1.0% of premium - the latter a minimum SEK 6 and a maximum SEK 14.
Market Maker Transaction:	0.6% of premium - minimum SEK 1 and maximum SEK 8.

OMX Index Futures

Trades

Customer Transactions:	SEK 25.

Market Maker Transaction:	SEK 10.
Exercise	
Customer Transactions:	SEK 25.
Market Maker Transaction:	SEK 10.
Norwegian Stock Options	
Trades	
Customer Transactions:	0.5% of premium + 1.0% of premium - the latter a minimum NOK 6 and a maximum NOK 14.
Market Maker Transaction:	0.6% of premium - minimum NOK 1 and maximum NOK 8.
Exercise	
Customer Transactions:	0.45% less than NOK 500,000 0.30% greater than NOK 500,000 (50% Broker discount).
Market Maker Transaction:	0.45% less than NOK 500,000 0.30% greater than NOK 500,000 (80% Market Maker discount).

Education and Information Services

On-line Information Services

OML offers market participants a direct connection to OML's central system.

The following services are available:

- **Order placement**
- **Security deposit information**
- **Contract information**
- **Price and premium information**

- Open-position balances

- Margin information

- Daily account allocation

OML provides a user handbook explaining how maximum benefit can be obtained from these services. Demonstrations can also be arranged. The computer connection requires a Digital Equipment VT terminal. A direct telephone connection (which can be ordered through OML) must be arranged as well as suitable data-cabling from the telephone connection to the work place.

Contract Ticker

Members using OML terminals may wish to add a Contract Ticker that provides print-outs of transactions executed. Members interested in this service should contact OML for additional information.

Price Feed

OML provides a price feed (the Reuters feed) to all interested members. The feed can constitute a useful tool in an in-house analysis system.

PC-Link

OML plans to offer all members the opportunity to transfer trading information to a local IBM compatible personal computer. Please contact OML for additional information.

Education

OML will provide information on the exchange and its products, as well as educational and training assistance. The OM Group has highly developed training programs and materials for brokers and end-customers in basic options trading and advanced strategies.

For further information, please contact:

Peter Jorgensen, Managing Director
Karin Forseke, Marketing Director
OM London Ltd.
107 Cannon Street
LONDON EC4N 5AD
Tel: (071) 283 - 0678
Fax: (071) 283 - 0504

OVERVIEW of PRODUCTS

	Futures	Options
Swedish stocks		
Astra B free	*	*
Electrolux B free	*	*
Ericsson B free	*	*
Volvo B free	*	*
Norwegian stocks		
Bergesen B unrestricted		*
Norsk Hydro		*
Hafslund-Nycomed B unrestricted		*
Indices		
OMX Index	*	*

OMX is the most liquid index contract in Europe. The Index is based on the thirty most actively traded stocks on the Stockholm Stock exchange and is updated semi-annually. (See **OMX** Index Composition - The Futures & Options Markets in Sweden.)

HISTORY of the MARKET

OM was established in 1985 by Olof Stenhammar, President of OM and was the first derivatives exchange in Sweden. Trading volumes quickly exceeded market expectations and today over 30,000 contracts trade daily at OM. OM's success in the Swedish market led to the establishment of other exchanges based on the OM model in Finland and Spain (see OM Iberica - The Forwards, Futures & Options Markets in Spain). OM also markets its integrated trading/clearing system which is being used by the new Austrian Futures & Options Market.

July 1985	OM established offering contracts on Swedish stocks
December 1986	Futures and options on the OMX index introduced
December 1989	OM London established offering contracts on the OMX
March 1990	Futures and options on Swedish stocks introduced at OML
May 1990	Options on Norwegian stocks introduced at OML

DETAILED CONTRACT SPECIFICATION
Equities (Swedish)
Individual Stock Futures Contract

Contract Type:	American calls and puts.
Contract Size:	100 shares.
Expiry Months:	Three and six months with the following three cycles: 1.Jan Apr Jul Oct 2.Feb May Aug Nov 3.Mar Jun Sep Dec.
Expiry Day:	Third Friday in the expiry month.
Last Trading Day:	The day prior to expiration day.
Quotation:	SEK per share.
Minimum Price Movement (Tick Size and Value):	SEK 0.01 = SEK 1.0.
Trading Hours:	10.00 a.m - 16.00 p.m.(Stockholm time) 09.00 a.m. - 15.00 p.m.
Initial Margin:	See **OMS: OML**'s margin system.
Price Limit:	No price limit.
Contract Standard:	Physical settlement five days after the day of transaction.
Exercise Price:	Dependent on the market value of the underlying share (see OML stock list for detailed information).
Exchange Delivery Settlement Price:	Closing price of previous day.

Reuters Pages:	OMHN OMHP OMHR OMIT - OMIV
Telerate Pages:	20844 onwards

Expiration Cycle

Swedish stocks	
Astra B free	3
Electrolux B free	1
Ericsson B free	1
Volvo B free	3
Norwegian stocks	
Bergesen d.y. B unrestricted	3
Hafslund-Nycomed B unrestricted	2
Norsk Hydro	3

Individual Stock Option Contract

Option Style	American calls and puts.
Contract Size:	100 shares.
Delivery Months:	3 and 6 month contracts with the following three expiry cycles 1.Jan Apr Jul Oct 2.Feb May Aug Nov 3.Mar Jun Sep Dec.
Delivery Day:	Third Friday in the expiration month.
Last Trading Day:	The day prior to expiration day.

Quotation:	Price per share.
Minimum Price Movement (Tick Size and Value):	SEK 0.01 = SEK 1.00.
Trading Hours:	10.00 a.m - 16.00 p.m.(Stockholm time) 09.00 a.m. - 15.00 p.m.(London time).
Initial Margin:	see OMS: OML's margin system.
Price Limit:	No price limit.
Contract Standard:	Physical delivery.
Exercise Price:	3 contracts. see OML stock list for detailed information.
Commissions & Fees:	see OML transaction costs.

Expiration Cycle

Swedish stocks	
Astra B free	3
Electrolux B free	1
Ericsson B free	1
Volvo B free	3

Total Stock Option Turnover

Daily Volume and Open Interest (July 3,1989 - December 29,1989)

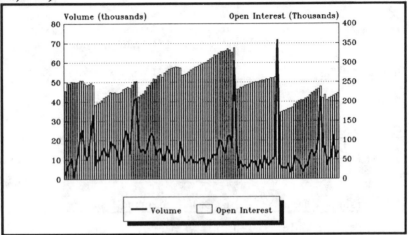

Open Interest and Volume/Open Interest(Liquidity) (July 3,1989 - December 29,1989)

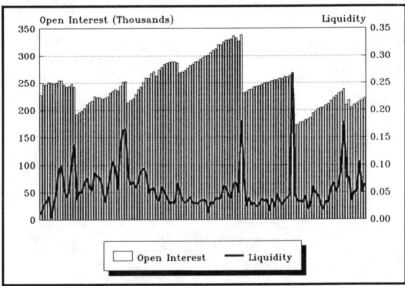

Astra B Free shares

Price/Yield History (November 1,1989 - April 10,1990)

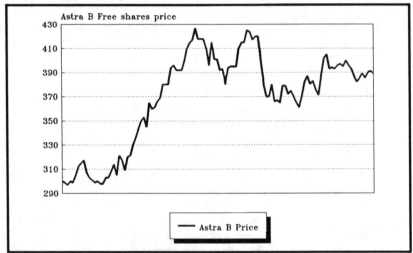

Implied and Historic Volatiltity (November 1,1989 - April 10,1990)

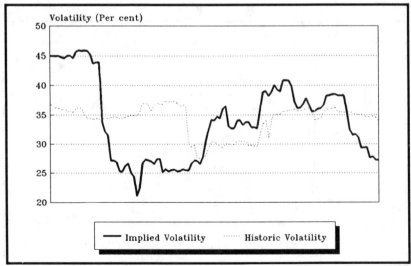

Electrolux B Free shares

Price/Yield History (November 1,1989 - April 10,1990)

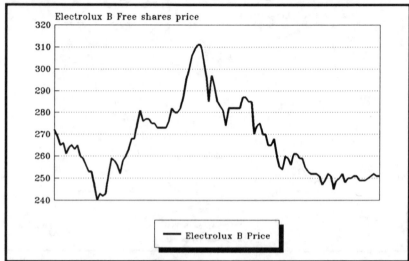

Implied and Historic Volatiltity (November 1,1989 - April 10,1990)

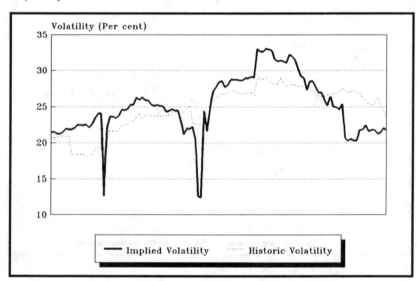

Ericsson B Free shares

Price/Yield History (November 1,1989 - April 10,1990)

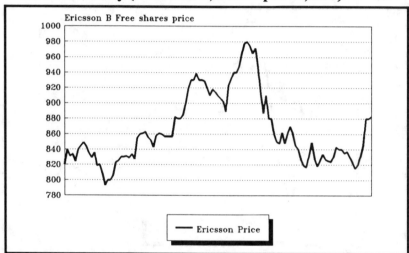

Implied and Historic Volatiltity (November 1,1989 - April 10,1990)

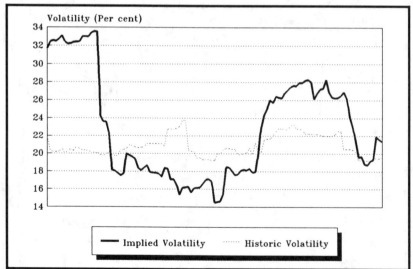

Volvo B Free shares

Price/Yield History (November 1,1989 - April 10,1990)

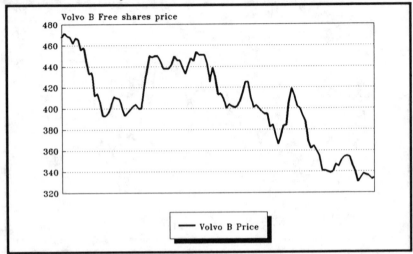

Implied and Historic Volatiltity (November 1,1989 - April 10,1990)

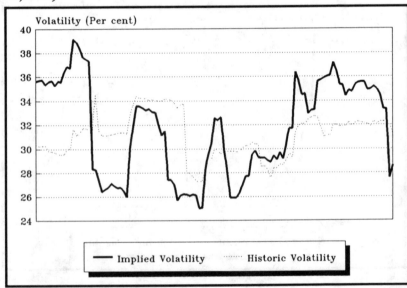

OMX Index Futures Contract

Contract Size:	Index value X index multiplier (SEK 100). (Currently approximately SEK 90,000).
Expiry Months:	One two and four month contracts for every month.
Expiry Day:	Fourth Friday in the expiration month.
Last Trading Day:	The day prior to expiration day.
Quotation:	Prices quoted 0.01 of **OMX** index value.
Minimum Price Movement (Tick Size and Value):	SEK 0.01 = SEK 1.00 X Index value.
Trading Hours:	10.00 a.m - 16.00 p.m.(Stockholm time) 09.00 a.m. - 15.00 p.m.(London time).
Initial Margin:	See **OMS: OML**'s margin system.
Price Limit:	No price limit.
Contract Standard:	Cash delivery.
exchange Delivery Settlement Price:	Average index value for the trading day prior to expiration day.
Reuters Pages:	
Telerate Pages:	

Composition of Index

The **OMX** Index, based on the 30 stocks (A1 list) with the heaviest volume of trading on the Stockholm Stock exchange. The index is updated semi-annually. For more detail see **OMX** Index composition in The Futures & Options Markets in Sweden chapter.

OMX Index Option Contract

Option Style	European calls and puts.
Contract Size:	Index value X index multiplier (SEK 100). (Currently approximately SEK 90,000).
Expiry Months:	One two and four contracts for each month.
Expiry Day:	Fourth Friday in the expiration month.
Last Trading Day:	The day prior to expiration day.
Quotation:	SEK 0.01 of the option price.
Minimum Price Movement (Tick Size and Value):	SEK 0.01 = SEK 1.00 X Index value.
Trading Hours:	09.00 a.m. - 15.00 p.m.
Initial Margin:	See **OMS: OML**'s margin system.
Price Limit:	No price limit.
Contract Standard:	Cash settlement.
Exchange Delivery Settlement Price:	Average index value for the trading day prior to expiration day.
Exercise Price:	Three contracts with exercise intervals of 20 points.
Reuters Pages:	**OMIH**
Telerate Pages:	20844 onwards
Commissions & Fees:	See transaction costs.

Daily Volume and Open Interest
(July 3,1989 - December 29,1989)

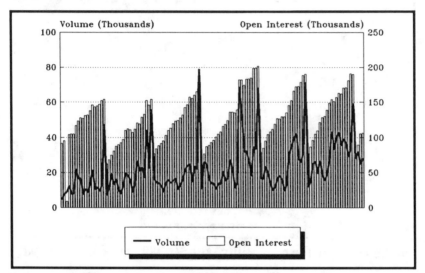

Open Interest and Volume/Open Interest(Liquidity)
(July 3,1989 - December 29,1989)

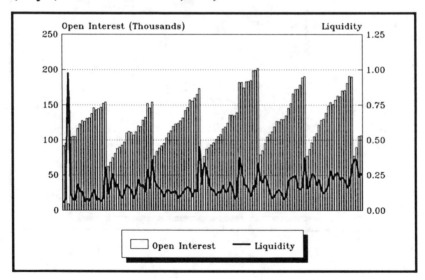

Price/Yield History (July 3,1989 - December 29,1989)

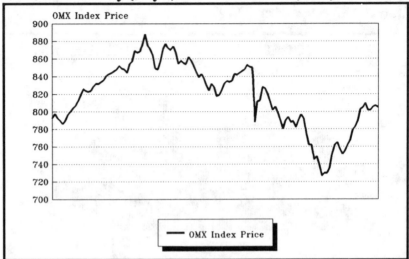

Implied and Historic Volatility (July 3,1989 - December 29,1989)

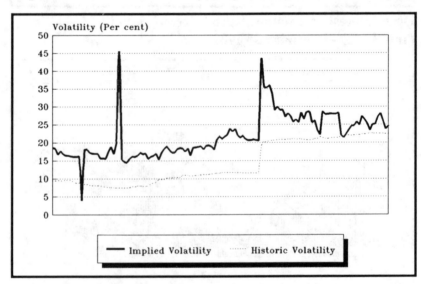

Equities (Norwegian)
Individual Stock Options

Option Style	American calls and puts.
Contract Size:	100 shares.
Expiration Months:	3 and 6 month contracts with the following three expiry cycles 1.Jan Apr Jul Oct 2.Feb May Aug Nov 3.Mar Jun Sep Dec.
Expiry Day:	Third Friday in the expiration month.
Last Trading Day:	The day prior to expiration day.
Quotation:	Price per share.
Minimum Price Movement (Tick Size and Value):	NOK 0.01 = NOK 1.00.
Trading Hours:	10.00 a.m - 16.00 p.m.(Oslo time) 09.00 a.m. - 15.00 p.m.(London time).
Initial Margin:	See **OMS: OML**'s margin system.
Price Limit:	No price limit.
Contract Standard:	Physical delivery.
Exercise Price:	See **OML** stock list for detailed information.
Reuters Pages:	**NOPD NOPE NOPG**
Telerate Pages:	20844 onwards
Commissions & Fees:	See transaction costs.

Expiration Cycle

Norwegian stocks	
Bergesen d.y. B unrestricted	3
Hafslund-Nycomed B unrestricted	2
Norsk Hydro	3

REGULATION

OM London is a UK Recognized Investment exchange operating under the supervision of the Securities and Investment Board. UK members of OM London must be a member of The Securities Association (TSA) or the Association of Futures Brokers and Dealers (AFBD).

OML as a clearing house guarantees fulfillment of all contracts based on its capital resources and its margin system, OMS. OML's capital at present totals £10 million in equity and UK bank guarantees and will be increased as appropriate to trading volumes. There are currently no position limits.

QUOTE VENDORS
Reuters Pages
OMCA onwards   OMX and Swedish stock options & futures.
NOPA onwards   Norwegian stock options.

SOURCES of INFORMATION

OM and OML will provide statistical data upon request. Prices are published in the Swedish Press.

The London Clearing House a division of The International Commodities Clearing House "ICCH"

The London Clearing House

INTRODUCTION

Since it was founded in 1888 as the London Produce Clearing House to clear sugar and coffee trading in London, the International Commodities Clearing House Limited (ICCH) has played a leading part in the development of commodity, financial futures and options trading in London and elsewhere (including the new Belgian Futures and Options Exchange - BELFOX).

A futures contract represents an obligation between two parties to make or take delivery, at an agreed price, of a soft commodity, metal or financial instrument on a pre-determined future date. The primary role of the Clearing House is to guarantee contract performance by becoming the central counterparty to all contracts registered in the names of its clearing members. This removes bilateral obligations from the market and allows certain offsetting trades to be canceled out. ICCH is a totally independent guarantor backed by a group of major U.K. banks.

Through the London Clearing House (LCH) division, ICCH clears both futures and options contracts for the following London exchanges:

The Baltic Futures Exchange	Pigs, Soyabean Meal, Soyabean Meal (Hi-Pro), Potatoes and Baltic Freight Index (**BIFFEX**)
The International Petroleum Exchange	Brent Crude, Dubai Crude, Gas Oil and Heavy Fuel Oil
The London Futures and Options Exchange (LondonFOX)	Cocoa, Coffee (Robusta), MGMI Index, Rubber, Sugar (Raw) and Sugar (White)
The London International Financial Futures Exchange (LIFFE)	U.K.Gilts, U.S. T-Bond, German Bund, Japanese Bond, 3 month Sterling, 3 month Eurodollar, 3 month Euromark, 3 month E.C.U. interest rate and U.K.FT-SE 100 Stock Index.
The London Metal Exchange	Aluminium, Copper, Lead, Nickel, Tin and Zinc

It provides a comprehensive service to members including registration, clearing and settlement, central banking and treasury, the administration of physical deliveries and risk management.

In addition, the London Clearing House provides a facilities management service to the London Options Clearing House for the administration of clearing on the London Traded Options Market (**LTOM**).

ORGANIZATION of the CLEARING HOUSE

As the Clearing House to the London futures exchanges, it is able to provide a centralized service to clearing members across the different contracts and markets with particular regard to banking, systems and delivery administration.

As independent guarantor to five London markets the Clearing House has a wide diversification of risk. The Clearing House's effective internal risk management incorporates data on clearing members' trading across a range of different contracts, providing the Clearing House with an overall view of financial, metal and soft commodity futures and options activity in London. Being independent the Clearing House is able to balance the financial integrity of the markets with the commercial pressures on the exchanges and their members.

While owing no allegiance to any one exchange, the Clearing House is dedicated to the promotion and growth of London's derivative markets both in the U.K. and in the international arena. In providing a centralized service across markets, the Clearing House benefits from significant economies of scale. Clearing members benefit directly from more standardized back-office trade processing procedures across different markets and centralized margin payments and receipt routines.

In funding its own guarantee backing of £150 million, the Clearing House enables clearing members to control their own risk without the additional uncertainty of the risk associated with a mutual guarantee.

Ownership

ICCH Limited is owned by six of London's largest clearing banks:

> **Barclays Bank PLC**
>
> **Lloyds Bank PLC**
>
> **Midland Bank plc**
>
> **National Westminster Bank PLC**
>
> **The Royal Bank of Scotland plc and**
>
> **Standard Chartered Bank PLC.**

As the Clearing House is an independent clearing house there is no mutual guarantee or common bond liability placed on members who are insulated from the effects of a default by another member.

The Clearing House may itself call upon the following resources:

- **the margin deposits of the defaulting firm**

- **surplus capital of the Clearing House**

- **discrete backing of £150 million provided by the consortium banks and insurance market, financed independently by the Clearing House.**

Membership Requirements

The system employed for vetting applicants to membership forms an integral part of counterparty risk management. Membership is open to companies and partnerships who can fulfil certain criteria concerning financial integrity and probity, trading history, net worth, management reputation, parentage, type of business, administrative efficiency and relevant exchange and regulatory body membership.

The financial requirements for clearing members measure both liquidity (in terms of net current assets) and permanent capital base. The level of requirement varies depending on which markets are to be cleared by the member and on the category of membership. The standards required for each market are determined in consultation with the relevant exchange. Each exchange also has its own established membership requirements and application procedures.

In addition to these safeguards, the Clearing House clearing and settlement systems are designed to ensure that reliance is not placed solely on a member's net worth to make good any market losses, as in most circumstances the amount required will already be held as initial margin within the clearing system.

Application for Membership

To be considered for membership of the Clearing House an applicant must provide the following background information and documentation:

- latest audited accounts

- Memorandum and Articles of Association, Certificate of Incorporation

- details of group structure, including the audited accounts of the parent company (if any)

- identity of major shareholders

- names of directors and relevant senior executives.

All clearing members must sign a standard Clearing Member Agreement with the Clearing House which establishes the legal nature of the relationship between the two parties.

Delivery and Banking Administration

A key element of the Clearing House operations is the provision to clearing members of the centralized delivery and banking facilities.

Delivery

As the counterparty to all clearing members' open positions, the Clearing House undertakes a central role in the final settlement of futures and options contracts at maturity, in effect guaranteeing the financial performance of the contract by both parties. The range of products cleared by the Clearing House includes those contracts involving the physical delivery of a soft commodity, metal or financial instrument in addition to a number of cash settlement contracts. In respect of physical deliveries, the Clearing House administers the allocation of sellers to buyers, although in many instances neither party will know of the other's identity. In all cases, to ensure the integrity of the market, the seller must pay the Clearing House prior to receiving delivery. Wherever the underlying cash or physical market allows, same day delivery versus payment is achieved.

Banking

The daily recalculation of margin liabilities generates daily payments and receipts between the Clearing House and each of the clearing members. As far as possible, payments and receipts within the same currency are netted for each clearing member account. This practice considerably reduces the number of monetary transactions for those members trading across several different contracts and exchanges. In addition, the Clearing House allows members the flexibility to cover their initial margin liabilities with cash or collateral of a different denomination. The Clearing House operates a centralized treasury function, enabling it to pay members a reasonable rate of interest on the bulk of their margin deposits. This central system is also utilized by the Clearing House for the collection of exchange and Clearing House fees from clearing members.

Risk Management and Surveillance

The Clearing House's central role in the London markets and the real time systems available (which cover trade matching, allocation, confirmation, clearing, risk management and banking) provide a continuous and progressive monitoring and amalgamation of liabilities. This facilitates overall market monitoring which the Clearing House can undertake either independently or in conjunction with the exchanges and regulatory bodies as the **SIB,AFBD** and **TSA**. The mutual interchange of information on matters of crucial importance to the efficient and orderly functioning of the markets is a requirement of the Financial Services Act.

Further controls exist in the requirement on the members to provide regular balance sheet and other financial information and the carrying out of specific trading reviews if the circumstances require.

The Clearing House makes its own independent assessment of members' resources and monitors the ratio of members' initial margin liabilities to their resources.

The Clearing House maintains comprehensive statistical information to enable its risk analysis team to survey and monitor historical volatilities, implied volatilities, seasonal price movements and correlations between delivery months or different contracts. This statistical information is essential to a full analysis of market conditions, liquidity, positions and deliveries.

The Risk Management Department within the Clearing House has specific responsibility for financial and market surveillance, margin requirements and membership applications and monitoring.

Segregation of Customer Funds

One of the cornerstones of the regime of investor protection under the Financial Service Act (**FSA**) is the requirement placed on brokers to segregate their clients' money into client bank accounts which are held on trust for their clients. At clearing house/exchange level, however, the rules require the members' money paid to the clearing house/exchange to be dealt with according to their own regulations.

Under U.K. legislation private investors' funds must be segregated by their brokers. Other (business and professional) clients may chose in negotiation with their broker whether or not to request segregation. These arrangements are governed by the Client Money Rules of the Securities and Investment Board (**SIB**).

Under its regulations and procedures, the Clearing House has provided facilities for each clearing member to use two separate clearing accounts; one account in respect of the trades and positions of any member's segregated clients and one account in respect of all house and non-segregated client business.

Both clearing accounts are margined separately on a net basis with separate margin calls, payments and receipts. Neither the Clearing House nor the clearing members has any right of offset or netting across these two accounts.

In addition, for certain exchanges, the Clearing House has established further subdivisions of the clearing members' non-segregated business (e.g. a split of house and non-segregated client trading) for position maintenance and regulatory purposes.

Default of a Clearing Member

Under the General regulations of the Clearing House a clearing member is deemed to be in default in a number of circumstances which include the following:

- **where a member is in breach of relevant Clearing House, exchange or regulatory body rules or procedures**

- **where a member fails to make any payment due or fails to perform any tender or delivery obligation**

- **where, in respect of a member, there is a bankruptcy or winding up or where an administrator or receiver is appointed.**

In the event of a member default the Clearing House has the power to act in a variety of ways, including the following:

- **to close out and settle open contracts**

- **to transfer open contracts to another member with the recipient's agreement**

- **to call in any relevant bank guarantees**

- **to realize any relevant securities being held as collateral.**

While seeking to limit its own liability, the Clearing House would keep all the relevant exchanges and regulatory authorities fully informed of the situation regarding a member's default and seek to act in the best interests of the market, the clients and the member involved.

All default procedures must take account of the segregation provisions so that collateral held for a member's segregated client account may only be realized in respect of a default involving a member's segregated client account. In addition there can be no set-off between a member's house and segregated client accounts.

In taking any of the actions described above, the Clearing House has been granted protection by the 1989 Companies Act against challenges under the existing U.K. insolvency rules.

Principal Officers & Address

Board of Directors

K. Albright	London International Financial Futures Exchange
S. Carter	The Baltic Futures Exchange
A. de Guingand	The London Traded Options Market
J.M. Eades	**Chairman**, London Clearing House
M. Liddiard	Czarnikow Futures Ltd
P. Shuman	Entores (Metal Brokers) Ltd
D. Whiting	Sucden (UK) Ltd

Other Principal Officers

J. Martin Eades	Chairman
David Hardy*	Managing Director
James Henry*	Director - Market Services
Trevor Slade*	Director - Finance
David Stuart*	Director - Risk Management

* indicates Executive Member of the Divisional Board

Address	The London Clearing House
	Roman Wall House
	1-2 Crutched Friars
	LONDON EC3N 2AN
Tel:	(44) 71 488 3200
Fax:	(44) 71 481 3462
Telex:	887234

THE SYSTEM of MARGINING

As the ultimate counterparty to every trade and guarantor to the markets the Clearing House is at risk to the default of a clearing member. The extent of this risk is related to the size of each clearing member's net open position in each of the different markets. All open positions are revalued on a daily basis and any profits/losses arising are paid/received by the Clearing House by way of variation margin. To cover its risk exposure the Clearing

House requires collateral or margin deposits on all net open positions held by clearing members; this requirement is referred to as initial margin.

Initial Margin

The Clearing House, in conjunction with the exchanges, set rates of initial margin for all contracts which it clears. These rates are set to cover one day's price risk with reference to the volatility of each contract and hence may vary from time to time. Initial margin is intended to provide the Clearing House with sufficient funds to make good any losses following a forced close-out. Clearing members may impose more stringent requirements on their customers in accordance with the rules of the relevant exchange(s). All clearing members must provide the full initial margin daily: the Clearing House may, at its discretion, require additional margin buffers in special circumstances.

Initial margin requirements are set with primary reference to daily price moves, and are usually set to cover 90-98 per cent of observed daily price movements. Reference is also made to other market data e.g. the spread of open interest and implied (option) volatility. Initial margin deposits are normally set at between 0.1% and 10% of contract value. Rates are set to cover outright positions: separate rates for spreads (straddles) are determined in the same way. Options are margined with reference to the underlying instrument taking account of offsetting risks.

Clearing members' margin liabilities are assessed throughout the day and recalculated at the end of each day. If a member does not have sufficient cover lodged with the Clearing House a Protected Payment System (**PPS**) call is issued to his bank at 08.30 a.m.. Initial margins must be covered in one of the forms of approved collateral which are currently cash (normally sterling, U.S. dollars, Deutschemark, ECU or yen), certain Government Securities or Bank Guarantees from Clearing House approved banks.

Margining is on a "net" basis. Net margining ensures that the margin held is directly proportional to the risk inherent in a member's position. The Clearing House does not monitor its members' relationships with clients but works closely with the exchanges and appropriate regulatory authorities to ensure the financial viability of its members.

Variation Margin

London's financial and commodity futures markets operate on a daily settlement (or mark) to market basis. This means that at the end of each day's trading all open contracts are registered or revalued anew at that day's closing price. This is, in practice, determined by the relevant exchange but the

Clearing House reserves the right to determine its own official quotations, if necessary.

Debits and credits arising from the settlement (or mark) to market process are posted daily to members' account. These procedures are also applied to traded options. If there is any shortfall a call to the member's bank will be made through the **PPS** by 08.30 a.m.. During periods of extreme volatility the Clearing House may call for additional variation margins to be paid during the day but now eroded to the extent of the adverse price move. Additional margins must be paid within an hour of such a call being issued.

The only exception to the daily settlement process is the London Metal Exchange (**LME**). LME futures contracts cannot be settled before the prompt day. However, each open contract is compared with that day's closing price and a contingent variation margin is calculated. If this is a credit (e.g. current market prices are above that when the contract was brought), this may be used to offset contingent debits. Net debits must be covered in the same way as initial margins. These procedures are also applied to contracts that are to be fulfilled by physical tender (of bonds, cocoa, etc).

REGULATION

Under the regulatory regime in London governed by the Financial Services Act 1986 (**FSA**), a Clearing House may only retain recognized status if several stringent criteria are met to the satisfaction of the Securities and Investment Board (**SIB**), the lead regulator in the U.K.. Those criteria are:

- **sufficient financial resources**

- **adequate monitoring and compliance arrangements**

- **the provision to exchanges of the clearing services necessary for their own recognition**

- **the maintenance of high standards of integrity and fair dealings**

- **willingness to co-operate in the sharing of information with the Secretary of State and other relevant regulatory agencies.**

In addition, to meeting these specific requirements of the legislation the Clearing House has developed over many years a system of risk management to handle the counterparty, market price and delivery risks arising.

Customer Protection

In order that a firm may execute and clear trades on behalf of customers in any of London's futures markets it must satisfy the membership requirements of the appropriate Self Regulatory Organisation (**SRO**), the Clearing House and the relevant exchange(s).

Dealings in futures and options contracts are regulated by one of two **SRO**'s: the Association of Futures Brokers and Dealers Ltd (**AFBD**) or The Securities Association (**TSA**), depending on the firm's mix of investment business. Having achieved membership of the appropriate bodies the firm must subsequently ensure its strict compliance with the various rules, regulations and reporting requirements, or risk disciplinary action and possible curtailment of its investment activities.

The Clearing House, exchange and **AFBD/TSA** membership screening procedures form the first line of defence for clients, in conjunction with the rules for the segregation of clients' money, against the event of a default by a member.

The provision of segregated accounts at clearing house level and the prohibition of client/house account set-off provide further safeguards for the client.

A compensation scheme designed specifically for smaller clients in the event of a broker's insolvency is administered by the **SIB**. Under this scheme the **SIB** is empowered to compensate such an investor up to 100 per cent of the first 30,000 loss suffered by the client and up to 90 per cent of the next 20,000 making a maximum sum of 48,000 per claim.

Taxation of Futures and Options in the United Kingdom

Stuart K. McLean
based on a LIFFE publication

As tax law and practice are still developing in this area, this section should be regarded only as a general guide. The tax position will depend upon individual circumstances; readers are therefore recommended to obtain specific independent professional advice.

Introduction

The taxation of commodity futures has never been a problem as the use of futures was seen as a means to guarantee future prices for the commodity. Therefore the profits/losses were evaluated as part of the trading profit/losses of that company. Since for such companies the rate of tax is the same for income and capital gains there is no difficulty. However, the same could not be said for the taxation of financial futures when the London International Financial Futures Exchange (**LIFFE**) opened. Indeed, due to the ambiguities that existed, many institutions felt unable to take advantage of the market. This was one of the main reasons for the initial low level of interest from U.K. institutions in the market.

When **LIFFE** opened in 1982, U.K. financial institutions usually operated as distinct companies within a defined market sector. Rarely did an organisation diversify into other areas. For example, building societies were the main source (over 95 per cent) of home finance while banks provided other forms of loans to the public and corporate sectors. These organizations did not compete with each other. This was all to change as the U.K. financial services markets became deregulated. The taxation of these institutions also was differentiated according to the type of business, as the table shows.

	Income Tax	Capital Gains Tax*
Individuals (Top Rate)	60.0%	30.0%
Banks	52.0%	52.0%
Corporates (trading in securities)	52.0%	52.0%
Corporates (not trading in securities)	52.0%	30.0%
Building Societies	40.0%	30.0%
Life Insurance Co.	37.5%	30.0%
Pension Funds	0.0%	0.0%

* Gilt Edge securities are free of capital gains if held for longer than one year and one day. Capital gains are also index linked and the first £5,000 per year are free of tax.

    As can be seen, for many institutions capital gains were levied at a rate of tax lower than income. Therefore, it was essential for U.K. institutions to be able to offset capital gains profits/losses on the underlying asset against the profits/losses on futures assessed as capital and not income when hedging. Unfortunately, at that time few institutions could be certain that this would be the case. A further problem was that it was also unclear whether transactions in the futures market would be considered as "trading" and therefore could threaten the special tax exemptions enjoyed by some funds especially pension funds. The legal framework clarifying the tax treatment of futures and options has been established in the Finance Acts of 1984, 1985, 1987 and 1990. The legislation is further supported by case law.

Tax Treatment of Different Types of Institutions

- Schedule D Case I is levied on trading income
- Schedule D Case VI is levied in the rare cases where income from speculating or other transactions fall outside Schedule D Case I or Capital Gains tax treatment.
- Capital Gains Tax is levied on capital transactions

Institution	Transaction	Taxation Treatment
Banks	Trading	Schedule D Case I
Investment Trusts	Capital	Exempt from Tax on Capital Gains (1)
Authorised Unit Trusts	Capital	Exempt from Tax on Capital Gains (1)
Pension Funds	Capital	Exempt from Tax on Capital Gains (2)
Charities	Capital	Exempt from Tax on Capital Gains

Insurance Companies	Capital/Trading	(a) Schedule D Case I: non-Life non-Pension business (b) Capital Gains Tax: transactions linked to fixed capital (c) Schedule D Case VI: Pension/Annuity business (3)
Building Societies	Trading	Schedule D Case I

Notes:

(1) Capital Gains Tax in respect of Investment and Unit trusts is paid by the individual who holds the shares/units.

(2) For non-trading transactions, pension funds are exempt from tax for financial futures contracts and traded options quoted on a recognized stock exchange or **LIFFE**. Currently options contracts on other exchanges and the over-the-counter market do not fall within this exemption.

(3) In this case Schedule D Case VI treatment is statutory (Section 436 Income and Corporation Taxes Act 1988).

There has always been some difficulty, in the past, in identifying whether a transaction in a derivative product was one pertaining to capital or income. If the transaction was considered to be of a capital nature it would be subject to assessment under Capital Gains Tax, while it was considered to be a trading transaction it would normally be assessed under Schedule D Case I, except for the rare occasions where Schedule D Case VI is applied.

This distinction has lost some meaning since the tax rates for income and capital gains are now the same. However, it is still of crucial importance to some institutions such as pension funds, investment trusts and unit trusts where a capital profit is exempt from tax. For derivative products, such as financial futures this distinct has not always been clear cut.

Important Factors in Determining Trading

When determining whether a transaction should be considered as part of a trade or as capital, a number of factors are considered which have been developed as a result of case law. The question of trading for institutions such as pension funds, unit trusts and investment trusts for whom the capital exemptions is so important.

The question of trading for these institutions has until recently been decided upon tests relating to **activity** and **level of income** which were likely to be as follows:

- **Time scale: the holding period of the derivative contract.**

- **Frequency of transactions.**

- **Profit seeking motive:e.g. purchasing futures or options with a view to selling at a profit rather than to hedge.**

- **Buying futures or options in several markets where this indicates a profit seeking motive.**

- **Amount of money involved.**

- **Number of transactions.**

The last item in particular has caused some concern; futures and options have an inbuilt level of activity because they expire, so requiring the position to be re-established, where this would not be the case in the underlying market.

Finally, an overall income test was applied whereby if the levels of profit from transactions in futures and options was higher than a reasonable level to the total fund, then income treatment would automatically apply. There was real concern at the difficulty in knowing precisely how tax law would be applied.

Current Approach

The current approach is laid out in the Statement of Practice (see later). In this the factors are refined into general principles which determine whether or not a taxpayer is trading futures or options.

The central approach is one of symmetry. The normal tax treatment of the user, or of the underlying instrument, is taken as the starting point. For institutions making a market in derivative products trading treatment, consistent with their normal activities will apply. However, the position for fund managers will depend on certain criteria set out below. Subject to these a fund will receive capital treatment, and as a consequence will gain the appropriate capital exemptions, in the same way that a gilt futures hedge , for example, while capital, will not incur tax as the underlying gilts themselves are exempt.

The most important criterion requires that a transaction in financial futures and options is directly related to an underlying asset or transaction: the tax treatment of the derivative product will then follow that of the underlying.

Where it can be shown that a relationship does exist in such a way that the derivative product can be regarded as hedging an underlying asset or transaction or reducing risk associated with it, then capital treatment will arise where transactions in the underlying are regarded as capital. The appropriate exemptions will then apply. The intention of the fund manager when entering into the transaction is of paramount importance, and the number of transactions is no longer of major significance in itself.

It is important to remember that the guidelines revolve around symmetry of treatment between the derivative products and the underlying instruments. An institution which is normally regarded as trading in equities or gilts will also be regarded as trading in derivative products. However, an institution whose focus is investing will normally be regarded as using futures and options as investment management instruments. So if the institution, or investment itself, also received tax exemptions, these will be mirrored in the tax treatment of the derivatives.

Basic Conditions of Hedging

The basic conditions which have to be met if a transaction is to be regarded as hedging are as follows:

- **The transaction must be economically appropriate to the reduction in risk of the appropriate asset or portfolio.**

- **The price fluctuations of the derivative product must be directly and demonstrably related to the fluctuations in value of the underlying transaction at the time of the hedge is initiated.**

Other Capital Transactions

The Statement also sets out criteria for transactions which are not regarded by the Inland Revenue as falling precisely into the category of hedging, but may still be regarded as "capital". Broadly speaking these are strategies where futures and options are used as a temporary means of effecting a long term investment strategy.

The basic conditions which have to be met are similar to the hedging criteria of risk reduction and correlation, but there is also a stress on the temporary nature of such transactions For example, futures or options may be used to manage or reduce the transaction costs in effecting an asset switch out of one category of asset and into another. However, the Statement stresses the importance of subsequently effecting the same transactions in the underlying assets and unwinding the futures or options positions as this shift takes place, unless the original motive for the reallocation falls away.

Areas Not Covered by the Statement of Practice

The main area which is not covered by the Statement of Practice is that of using futures and options as investments in their own right.

This means that a fund whose main objective is investment which is obtained exclusively through a combination of futures, options and money market deposits, or a fund which uses futures or options to gain additional long term market exposure is not covered by the Statement of Practice.

However, strategies falling outside the guidelines will not automatically be regarded as "trading" strategies, but will be assessed according to the facts and circumstances of each individual case.

Main Practical Points

The main areas that the fund manager will need to consider in order to ensure that capital treatment applies are as follows:

- **Ability to demonstrate that the reason for entering into the derivative product transaction was to hedge, i.e. reduce existing price risk.**

- **Significant correlation between price fluctuation of the derivative product and the underlying asset so that there is effectively a matching of movement in economic terms.**

- **The transaction should substantially reduce risk and not provide additional exposure.**

- **Thorough documentation so that the intention of the fund manager is clear. Such information should always be available for an historic review. Typically this would take the form of notes made by the fund manager at the time of the transaction which may be written at the time of the trade in a diary, or, if there is a more general overall intention of the fund, could be included in minutes of meetings dictating policy. In any case the format of such documentation must be established prior to undertaking the transactions.**

Problem Areas

Problem areas which can arise are as follows:

- It is essential to be able to demonstrate a high degree of correlation. If the transaction in the derivative product is not linked to the underlying then there is a potential that the results from the transaction will not be capital.

- If the fund manager changes his mind so that the original intention of the transaction falls away, the whole of the transaction must be thoroughly documented so that there is no danger that there would be insufficient evidence available to support the hedging stance.

- There is currently an area of uncertainty surrounding long hedges using cash settled or index products. If the fund manager wishes to purchase stock index futures with a view to acquiring a portfolio of securities at a later date in time, there is a danger that such a transaction would still be regarded as trading, unless a clear intention to purchase the underlying equities can be demonstrated. This is because the futures position provides a means of gaining exposure to the market in anticipation of purchasing the underlying equities as opposed to the reduction of risk in an existing portfolio.

The position is much clearer with short-term asset swaps. A fund manager may, for example, be switched out of one market into another. Where the fund is switching asset exposure from U.K. gilts into U.K. equities, this can be achieved by first shorting gilts futures/buying FT_SE futures and then unwinding these positions as the transactions are executed in the underlying market.

In this case the transaction would almost certainly be capital, provided it is followed within a reasonable period of time, by the corresponding transaction in the underlying.

STATEMENT of PRACTICE SP4/88
Issued by the Inland Revenue 22nd July 1988
Tax Treatment of Transactions in Financial Futures and Options

1. This Statement sets out the Inland Revenue's view on the tax treatment of transactions in financial futures and options carried out by investment trusts, unit trusts, pension funds, charities and companies which either do not trade or whose principal trade is outside the financial area. The principles set out apply to all futures and options, whether traded on an exchange or otherwise.

2. Section 72 Finance Act 1985 provides, broadly, that transactions in commodity and financial futures and traded options on recognised exchanges will be treated as capital in nature unless they are regard as profits or losses of a trade. Section 81 Finance Act 1987 extends this treatment to other transactions in futures and options. If, under normal statuory and case law principles, profits or losses fall to be treated as trading in nature then Section 72 and 81 have no application to those profits or losses. It is therefore necessary first to determine whether or not a taxpayer is trading in futures or options without reference to the provisions of Section 72 and 81.

3. Whether or not a taxpayer is trading is a question of fact to be determined by reference to all facts and circumstances of the particular case. Consideration is given to the "badges of trade". Generally, a person will not be regarded as trading if the transactions are infrequent or to hedge specific capital investments. An individual is unlikely to be regarded as trading as a result of purely speculative transactions in options or futures.

4. If the taxpayer in question is a company, which would include an investment trust or authorised unit trust, it is necessary to consider not only the normal case law defining trading but also the case of Lewis Emanuel and Son Ltd v White (42 TC 369). The broad effect of the judgement in this case is that generally a company cannot speculate and that any transactions carried out by a company must either be trading or capital in nature.

5. If a transaction in financial futures or options is clearly related to an underlying asset or transaction, then the tax treatment of the futures or options contract will follow that of the underlying asset or transaction.

In general, the Inland Revenue take the view that this relationship exists where a futures or options contract is entered into in order to hedge an underlying transaction, asset or portfolio by reducing the risk relating to it; and the intention of the taxpayer in entering into the transaction is of considerable importance. Where the underlying transaction is itself treated as giving rise to a capital gain or loss, the related futures or options contract will also be treated as a capital matter and not as trading.

6.   The basic conditions which have to be met if the transaction is to be treated as hedging in this sense are:

(1)   the transaction must be economically appropriate to the reduction in risk of the underlying transaction, asset or portfolio; and

(2)   the price fluctuation of the options and futures must be directly and demonstrably related to the fluctuations in value or composition of the underlying transaction, asset or portfolio at the time the hedging transaction is initiated.

7.   This applies equally to long or short positions, and is not dependent upon the form of the eventual disposition. In other words it will apply whether the futures position is closed out or held to maturity, or in the case of an options position, closed out, exercised or held to final expiry.

Examples

8.   Transactions would be treated as giving rise to capital gains or losses in the following circumstances:-

(1)   A taxpayer who holds gilts sells gilt futures to protect the value of his capital in the event of a fall in the value of gilt-edged securities generally.

(2)   A taxpayer purchases an asset in two stages by purchasing a foreign currency future in advance of the purchase of an asset denominated in that currency, or by purchasing an option in respect of an underling asset as a first step towards the acquisition of the asset itself.

(3)   A taxpayer who holds a broadly based portfolio sells index futures or purchases index put options to protect himself against the risk to the value of the options from a fall in the market, (provided the

fall in the index futures or options is directly and demonstrably correlated to the loss on the portfolio as it was constituted at the date the hedge was initiated).

9.   But even if a transaction is not a hedging transaction in the sense of paragraph 6 above, it may, nevertheless, be regarded as capital in nature, depending on all facts and circumstances. to take two specific examples:-

      (1)   If a taxpayer is committed to making a bond issue in the near future and enters into an interest rate future or option with a view to protecting himself against rises in interest costs before he is able to make the issue, the Revenue will regard the transaction as being of a capital nature.

      (2)   If a taxpayer sells or buys options or futures as an incidental and temporary part of a change in investment strategy, (e.g., changing the ratio of gilts and equities), that transaction is likely to be treated as being of a capital nature, if the transaction in the assets themselves would be a capital matter.

10.   A further uncertainty may arise if a transaction is originally undertaken as a capital hedge but the underlying transaction or motive falls away. If the futures or options transaction is closed out within a reasonably short period after the underlying motive falls away then the transaction will continue to be treated as capital in nature in accordance with the principles outlined above. If however the transaction is not closed out at that time it may be arguable that any profit or loss arising subsequently is of a trading nature. In practice the Revenue would not normally take this point in view of the original intentions of the taxpayer and the practical difficulties of making the necessary calculation.

11.   Where a company enters into these transactions as incidental to its trading activity, for example a manufacturer entering into transactions to hedge the price of his raw materials, then the profits or losses from these transactions would be taken into account as part of the profits and losses of the trade.

         Reproduced by kind permission of the Inland Revenue.

      Further copies of this Statement may be obtained by writing (enclosing a stamped addressed envelope) or by calling personally at the Public Enquiry Room, West Wing, Somerset House, Strand, LONDON WC2R 1LB.

Information and Advice

Further information on tax matters relating to financial futures is available from:

Address: The London International Financial Futures Exchange

                      Royal Exchange

                      LONDON EC3V 3PJ

Tel: (44) 71 623 0444

Contact: Julie Elbourne

                      Nicholas Carew Hunt

                      Victoria Ward

LIFFE also produces an informative publication on this matter.

GLOSSARY

NOTES: This glossary contains a number of terms in the language of the country. The country is indicated by the following abbreviations:

D.	Germany
Fr.	France
Sp.	Spain
Nd.	Netherlands

abandon	to allow an option to expire without exercising it.
accrued interest	interest earned but not yet due and payable.
"ACG"	*see Adherents Compensateurs Generaux.*
"ACHA"	*see Associated Clearing House Amsterdam.*
"ACI"	*see Adherents Compensateurs Individeuls.*
actiën (Nd.)	shares
Actiën Compagnie (Nd.)	limited liability company
actuals	a physical or cash security as distinguished from a *financial futures contract* (*qv*).
Adherents Compensa-teurs Generaux "ACG"	*General Clearing Members* (*qv*) *of MATIF* (*qv*).
Adherents Compensa-teurs Individuels "AGI"	*Independent Clearing Members* (*qv*) *of MATIF* (*qv*).
"ADP"	*see Alternative Delivery Procedure.*
"AFB"	*see Association Française des Banque.*
"AFBD"	*see Association of Futures Brokers and Dealers.*
All or None "AON"	an order that may be executed only in its entirety.
Alternative Delivery Procedure	if the buyer and the seller agree to effect delivery on terms different from those prescribed in the contract specification, they may proceed after submitting a notice of intention to the Clearing House.
American option	a put or call option which may be exercised at any time prior to expiration *cf European option.*
"AMEX"	*see American Stock Exchange.*
American Stock Exchange "AMEX"	the options exchange in New York which trades option contracts in various stock indexes such as the Major Market and International Index as well as options in nearly 200 individual U.S. equities.
Amsterdamsche Liquidatiekas	founded in 1888, this exchange regulates agricultural commodity trading in the Netherlands. It is now known as *NLK KAS* (*qv*).
anticipatory hedge	1. a long anticipatory hedge is initiated by buying futures contracts to protect against a rise in the price of an asset to be purchased at a later date. 2. A short anticipatory hedge is initiated by selling futures contracts to protect against the decline in

	the price of an asset to be sold at a future date, or to protect against a rise in interest rates on the anticipated occurrence of a fixed rate liability or a future repricing on a variable rate liability.
"AOM"	*see Australian Options Market.*
"AON"	*see All or None.*
arbitrage	1. the purchase of a security in one market and the simultaneous sale of that security or its equivalent in the same market or other markets for the purpose of profiting from a temporary aberration prevailing because of conditions peculiar to each market 2. the sale of one security and simultaneous purchase of a similar security to meet the same investment objectives.
ASch	Austrian Schillings
"ASE"	Amsterdam Stock Exchange
aspirantes a creadores (Sp.)	when *entidades gestoras (qv)* hold 1 per cent of client funds, financial institutions become aspirantes a creadores (security dealers). *see creadores de mercado.*
assign	to designate an option *writer (qv)* for fulfillment of his obligation to sell stock (call option writer) or buy stock (put option writer). The writer receives an assignment notice from the *Options Clearing Corporation (qv) cf early exercise.*
assignment note	formal notification from an options exchange to the *writer (qv)* informing him that an option has been exercised by an option holder and he is required to fulfill his contractual obligations.
Associated Clearing House Amsterdam	a clearing house based in Amsterdam mainly known of its settlement of the *Major Market Index option (qv)* traded on the European Option Exchange and the American Stock Exchange.
Association Française des Banque "AFB"	The French Banking Association which amongst its other functions calculates and conforms *the Paris Inter Bank Offered Rate PIBOR (qv).*

Association of Futures Brokers and Dealers "AFBD" — A self regulatory organization set up under the U.K. Financial Services Act to monitor futures and options contracts for commodities and foreign exchange.

at-the-money — describes an option when the value of its underlying security is equal to the option *strike price (qv)* *cf in-the-money* and *out-of-the-money*.

Australian Options Market "AOM" — the options exchange in Sydney which trades option contracts in gold and silver as well as over 1,000 Australian equities.

automated trading systems — a number of computerized systems exist that match bids and offers and complete transactions. *see CATS, FAST, PATS and TRS.*

automatic exercise — a protection procedure whereby the *Options Clearing Corporation* (qv) attempts to protect the holder of an expiring *in-the-money* (qv) option by automatically exercising the option on behalf of the holder.

Baltic Futures Exchange "BFE" — the futures and options exchange in London that trades futures and option contracts for EEC Barley and Wheat, Live Pigs, Potatoes, Soyabean Meal and the Baltic Freight Index.

Baltic Freight Futures Index "BIFFEX" — an index based on twelve shipping routes used as an benchmark for the cost of sea freight.

Banque Centrale de Compensation "BCC" — the commodity clearing house purchased by MATIF SA.

Barrel of oil — equals 42 U.S. gallons.

basis — the price difference between a financial futures contract and its underlying asset.

basis point ("b.p.") — 1/100th of 1 per cent, ie 0.01 per cent, used to express yield spread or differential, not to be confused with a *point (qv)*. Prices (eg of FRNs) are also, expressed in basis points *cf pips*.

basis trade — a transaction to take advantage of any anomaly between the price of the derivative and the underlying security.

basket delivery	the delivery mechanism for futures contracts, such as Treasury bond or note futures, that have several underlying cash instruments.
basket warrant	a warrant that represents a group of underlying securities.
"BBAISR"	the British Bankers' Association Interest Rate Settlement Rate. This rate is used for the settlement of the ECU futures contract on *LIFFE (qv)*.
"BCC"	*see Banque Centrale de Compensation.*
bear spread	an option strategy which makes its maximum profit when the underlying stock declines, and has its maximum loss if the stock rises in price. This strategy can be implemented with either puts or calls. *cf bull spread.*
bearer securities	a system of evidencing ownership by physical possession of share/bond certificates and attached dividend/interest coupons. *cf book entry.*
BEF	Belgian Franc.
"BELFOX"	*see Belgian Futures and Options Exchange.*
Belgian Futures and Options Exchange "BELFOX"	the futures and options exchange due to open in 1991 in Brussels which will be based on the *ICCH (qv)* clearing house system.
bespoke option	an option especially created to meet the requirements of the buyer. *cf traded and traditional option.*
"BFE"	*see Baltic Futures Exchange.*
"BIFFEX"	*see Baltic Freight Futures Index.*
Black and Scholes model	a frequently used option valuation model-different varieties of the method apply to different types of options. *cf Cox-Rubenstein model.*
Board official	an employee of the *International Stock Exchange (qv)* who is responsible for the custody/execution of *public limit orders (qv)* and the orderly conduct of trading in the option classes he is allocated.
Bonos del Estado (Sp.)	medium dated Spanish Government bonds.
Bons du Trésor "BTAN"	French Government Treasury bills with lives out to five years.

book entry	a system of evidencing ownership of securities by entries in a register. *cf bearer securities.*
box spread	a type of option *arbitrage* (**qv**) in which both a *bull spread* (**qv**) and a *bear spread* (**qv**) are established for a risk less profit. One spread is established using *put* (qv) options and the other *calls* (**qv**). The spreads may be both *debit spreads (call bull spread vs put bear spread)* **or** *credit spreads (call bear spread vs put bull spread).*
b.p.	*see basis point.*
"BR"	the abbreviation used for *ROEFEX broker (qv).*
"BRF"	BRFkredit. One the Danish mortgage institutions.
break-even point	the price of an underlying security at which an option buyer recovers the *premium (qv).* For a *call option (qv)*, this is the *exercise price (qv)* plus the premium and for a *put option (qv)*, the exercise price minus the premium.
broker "ROEFEX"	a seat holder on *ROEFEX (qv).*
broker dealer	a member firm or part of a member firm that is not committed to act as market makers (qv) and acts as a representative for clients.
brokerage	a commission charged by a broker.
"BTAN"	*see Bons de Trésor.*
bull spread	an options term for the simultaneous purchase of a nearby delivery month and sale of a deferred delivery month fixed income future in expectation of short term interest rates falling, thereby increasing the relative attractiveness of the front month contract. *see buying the spread cf bear spread and selling the spread.*
Bundesverband Deutscher Banken	The Association of German Banks
business day	1. in the Euromarket, when markets are open for banking business 2. in the domestic markets, any day excluding Saturdays, Sundays and legal holidays on which business can be conducted.

butterfly spread	an option strategy that has both limited risk and limited profit potential, constructed by combining a *bull spread (qv)* and a *bear spread (qv)*. Four strike prices (qv) are involved, with the lower two being used in the bull spread and the higher two in the bear spread. The strategy can be established with either *puts or calls*. There are four different ways of combining options to construct the same basic position.
buy on close	to purchase an option at the end of a trading session at a price within the closing range *cf buying on opening*.
buy on opening	to purchase an option at the start of a trading session at a price within the opening range *cf buy on close*.
buy write	an option strategy which involves writing options against a security which is already held.
buyer	the purchaser of either a call or put option.
buying the spread	for financial instruments, anticipating rising prices by going long the front contract month and selling the deferred contract month. *see bull spread cf bear spread and selling the spread*.
cabinet bid	a closing sale by the holder of a deep *out-of-the-money (qv)* option at a notional price of 1p per contract.
"CAC"	*see the Compagnie des Agents de Change*.
"CAC40"	an index of the 40 major French shares used for futures and option contracts traded on the Paris futures exchange "MATIF" and option exchange "MONEP".
call option	an option to purchase a security at a specific price on a specified date or dates or at any time during a specified period. *cf put option*.
capital gains tax	a tax that is levied on the difference between the purchase and sale prices when an investment is bought and sold. In some countries, a taxable loss amy be off-settable against any taxable gains.

carry	the cost of financial positions (qv); the rate of interest earned from the securities held less the cost of funds borrowed to purchase them. When the interest earned is greater than the cost of funds, there is positive carry; when the cost of funds is greater than the interest earned, there is negative carry.
cash	1. a physical commodity or underlying security as opposed to futures and options contracts. 2. a very short term security.
cash market	the market in the *actual (qv)* financial instrument on which the futures or options is based.
cash settlement	a transaction for immediate settlement. In the futures market; refers to the delivery process where no underlying securities are delivered, but positions are marked to market based on the price of the underlying security. *cf physical delivery.*
CATS	*see Continuous Automated Trading System.*
"CBOE"	*see Chicago Board Options Exchange.*
"CBOT"	*see Chicago Board of Trade.*
"CBV"	*see Conseil des Bourses de Valeurs.*
"CCIFP"	*see Chambre de Compensation des Instruments Financiers de Paris.*
Central de Anotaciones (Sp.)	the book entry office of the Bank of Spain.
"CFTC"	*see Commodity Futures Trading Commission.*
Chambre de Compensation des Instruments Financiers de Paris "CCIFP"	this was the name of the major French Clearing House. it changed its name to MATIF SA
cheapest to deliver	the cash instrument (usually a bond) which generates the maximum profit or minimum loss to a *cash and carry (qv) arbitrage (qv).*
Chicago Board of Trade "CBOT"	the futures and options exchange in Chicago that trades futures contracts in corn, oats, soyabeans, soyabean meal, soyabean oil, wheat, gold, silver, Major Market Index, U.S. T-notes, U.S.T-bonds,

Municipal bond index and 30 day U.S. interest rates. It also trades option contracts in corn, soyabeans, soyabean meal, soyabean oil, wheat, silver, U.S.T-notes, U.S.T-bonds, Municipal bond index and the Japanese TOPIX index (qv).

Chicago Board Options Exchange "CBOE"

the options exchange in Chicago that trades option contracts in S & P 100, S & P 500 stock indexes, U.S.T-notes, U.S.T-bonds and over 200 individual U.S.equities.

Chicago Mercantile Exchange "CME"

the futures and options exchange in Chicago that trades futures contracts in feeder cattle, live cattle, live hogs, pork bellies, random lumber, gold, S & P 500 stock index, eurodollars, U.S.T-bills, Swiss francs, Australian dollars, Deutschemarks, Canadian dollars, Sterling, Japanese yen and French francs. It also trades option contracts in feeder cattle, live cattle, live hogs, pork bellies, random lumber, S & P 500 stock index, eurodollars, Swiss francs, Deutschemarks, Sterling, Japanese yen and Canadian dollars.

ciegos (Sp.)

interdealer brokers (qv) in Spain locally called "blind dealers".

clear or settle

to complete a trade by delivery of securities in proper form to the buyer and by payment to the seller. Trades that are not cleared by the settlement date are said to fail. *cf fail.*

clearing agent

a clearing member authorized to clear business on its own behalf and for other member firms.

clearing house

1.   an organization which registers, monitors, matches and guarantees trades on a futures Exchange and carries out the financial settlement of those transactions. *see Board of Trade Clearing Corporation, International Commodities Clearing House, MATIF SA, Norwegian Clearing Central and Norwegian Options Markets.*

2.   an organization which settles and acts as custodian for bearer securities in the international markets.

clearing member	a member firm of a futures clearing house. Each clearing member must also be a member of an Exchange, but not all members of an Exchange are also members of a clearing house. All trades of a non-clearing member must be registered with, and eventually, settled through, a clearing member. *see General Clearing Member, Individual Clearing Member and Non Clearing Member.*
Clearing Member "FTA"	a member of the *"FTA" (qv)* exchange who handles the administrative and financial settlement of the transactions and guarantees all obligations are met.
Clearing Member "ROEFEX"	contracting counterparty for brokers, market makers, floor traders and *locals (qv)* on *"ROEFEX" (qv).*
close	the period at the end of the trading session. *cf open.*
close out	a transaction which leaves the trade with a zero net commitment to the market.
closing price	the price, or range of prices, at which transactions are made just before the *close (qv)* on a given day. This price is often quoted in the press and is used in the valuation of portfolios and indexes.
closing range	the high and low prices at which transactions take place during the *close (qv).*
closing transaction	the termination of an open position by its corresponding offset. Closing buy transactions reduce *short (qv)* positions and closing sell transactions reduce *long (qv)* positions.
"CME"	*see Chicago Mercantile Exchange.*
"CM-FTA"	*see Clearing Member "FTA".*
"CM-ROEFEX"	*see Clearing Member "ROEFEX".*
"CMATIF"	*see Conseil du Marché a Terme des Instruments Financiers.*
Coffee, Sugar & Cocoa Exchange "CSCE"	the futures and options exchange in New York that trades futures in coffee, cocoa, No.11 , No.14 and white sugar as well as option contracts in coffee, cocoa and No.11 sugar.

combination	a variation of a *straddle (qv)* with the put and call having different terms. Typically, the *strike prices (qv)* differ.
"COMEX"	*see Commodity Exchange.*
Commissaires Agréés	authorized brokers in the French commodity exchanges.
Commission Maystadt	the Commission set up by the Belgian Government to study how to set up a Futures and Options market in Belgium.
Commodity Exchange "COMEX"	the futures and options exchange in New York trading futures contracts in aluminium, copper, gold, silver and corporate bond index as well as option contracts in copper, gold and silver.
Commodity Futures Trading Commission "CFTC"	the Federal agency which regulates futures trading in the United States.
Compagnie des Agents de Change "CAC"	the French Stockbrokers Association after which the *CAC 40 (qv)* stock index has been named
confirmation	a notice a clearing firm sends to its customers to confirm each transaction. The confirmation is mailed daily.
Conseil des Bourses de Valeurs	The French Stock Exchange Council which is responsible for the running and promotion of the exchanges throughout France.
Conseil du Marché a Terme des Instruments Financiers "CMATIF"	the Council governing the operation of "MATIF".
Continuous Automated Trading System"CATS"	the computerized trading system found in Belgium.
contract	a financial futures' binding agreement to make or take delivery at a specified date of a fixed quantity of a specified underlying asset or cash equivalent.
contract grade	in the context of futures; the type of cash instruments and quality of commodities listed in the rules of the Exchange which can be used for delivery in transactions. *see cash.*
contract standard	*see contract grade.*

convergence	the process by which futures prices move towards cash prices over time. In a cash-settled contract, the futures price equals the cash price at settlement.
conversion	an *arbitrage (qv)* strategy involving the purchase of the underlying instrument, offset by the establishment of a *synthetic (qv)* short position in the option (the purchase of a put and sale of a call). The overall position is unaffected by price movements in the underlying instrument. This trade would be established when small price discrepancies open up between the long position in the underlying instrument and the synthetic short position on the option.
conversion factor	*see delivery factor.*
cost of carry	*see carry.*
Council	the governing body of the *"ISE", the International Stock Exchange of Great Britain and the Republic of Ireland (qv).*
covered call	a *short position (qv)* in a call option for which the writer owns sufficient deliverable securities or other eligible collateral to satisfy an exercise of that call by the holder. *cf covered put.*
covered position	a *position (qv)* in a security that is matched with a counter position in another security, thus effectively neutralizing the initial position. *cf naked position.*
covered put	a *short position (qv)* in a *put option (qv)* for which the writer owns sufficient eligible collateral to ensure his ability to take delivery of the underlying security in the event of the put being exercised. *cf covered call.*
covered writing	a setting of a call option covered by an existing long position in the underlying security. This strategy is intended to increase overall returns by earning fee income from the options.
"CRCE"	the Chicago Rice and Cotton Exchange which is an affiliate of the Midamerica Commodity Exchange which only trades rice futures at the present.

creadores de marcado (Sp.)	when *entidades gestoras (qv)* hold 2.5 per cent of client funds, these financial institutions become creadores de marcado (*market makers (qv)*). *see aspirantes a creadores.*
cross clearing	in calculating collateral requirements, options held as well as purchased and sold futures contracts in which the customer has unrealized gains reduce the collateral requirements for the customers account.
crowd	a group of market makers, broker dealers and Board officials.
"CSCE"	*see Coffee, Sugar & Cocoa Exchange.*
"CSE"	Copenhagen Stock Exchange
current delivery	a futures contract that will become deliverable during the coming month. *cf deferred futures.*
daily price limit	the maximum price change, set by the Exchange permitted for a futures contract during a trading period.
"DAX"	*see Deutscher Aktienindex (D).*
day order	a buy or sell order which is automatically canceled if it is not filled during the day it is entered.
declaration date	*see expiry date and prompt date.*
deferred futures	the most distant delivery months in which futures trading is taking place. *cf current delivery.*
deliverable	a security which meets standards of *futures contracts (qv)* as to quality, maturity, principal amount and coupon rate and which may be *physically delivered (qv)* to satisfy the contract (not applicable for municipal futures contract and cash settlement contract).
delivery	1) the tender and receipt of an actual financial instrument or cash in settlement of a futures contract. *see good delivery.* 2) the physical settlement of futures or option contracts. *cf expiry.*
delivery date	the day, or days, during which delivery against a futures contract can be made.

delivery factor	in futures contracts that have *basket delivery (qv)*, the delivery prices of the futures contract is adjusted by a factor to determine the delivery of each cash security. Also known as the *conversion factor.*
delivery mechanism	the procedure used to fulfil futures contract obligations at delivery date, including *basket delivery (qv)*, cash settlement, or simple delivery where only one specific instrument can be delivered.
delivery month	the month during which a futures contract can be fulfilled.
delivery notice	a seller's notice of intention to make delivery against a short futures position on a specified day.
delivery price	*see Exchange Delivery Settlement Price.*
delta	the theoretical change in the value of an option for a small change in the value of the underlying security. The inverse of the delta gives the theoretical *hedge ratio (qv). see gamma.*
delta hedge	a method used by option writers to hedge risk exposure of written options by purchase or sale of the underlying asset in proportion to the delta. For example, a call option writer who has sold an option with a delta of 0.5 may engage in delta hedging by purchasing an amount of the underlying instrument equal to one-half of the amount of the underlying that must be delivered upon exercise. A delta-neutral position is established when the writer strictly delta-hedges so as to leave the combined financial position in options and underlying instruments unaffected by small changes in the price of the underlying security.
DEM or DM	Deutschemark.
derivative	a security whose price is linked to an *underlying security (qv)* such as a future, option, swap or warrant but does not itself have the attributes of that security such as interest payments. This securities usually have a finite life on expiration of which the owner may actual receive or be expected to delivery the underlying security (*physical delivery*

	(qv)) or will receive or pay a cash payment linked to the price of the underlying security on that day *(cash settlement (qv))*.
Deutsche Terminbörse **"DTB"**	the futures and options exchange set up in 1990 in Frankfurt to trade options in 14 German equities as well as futures and option contracts in German Bunds and the DAX index.
Deutscher Aktienindex **(D) "DAX"**	an index of 30 stocks traded on the Frankfurt stock exchange created in 1988.
Deutscher Kassenverein **"DKV"**	the German clearing house for domestic securities.
Dfl	Guilder - Abbreviation derived from Dutch Florin.
"DIBOR"	Dublin Inter Bank Offered Rate.
Differenzeinwand (D)	the German Speculating and Gambling laws.
direct hedge	a futures purchase or sale intended to reduce price level risk for a deliverable financial instrument.
DKK	Danish Krone.
"DKV"	*see Deutscher Kassenverein.*
DM	Deutschemark
"DTB"	*see Deutsche Terminbörse.*
early exercise	the exercise of an option before the *expiration date (qv).*
"EBC"	*see the European Bond Commission.*
"ECU"	*see European Currency Unit.*
"EDSP"	*see Exchange Delivery Settlement Price.*
"EFCC"	*see European Futures Clearing Corporation BV.*
"EFFAS"	*see European Federation of Financial Analysts Societies.*
"EFP"	*see Exchange for Physicals.*
"EKA Stock"	this is a fund of mainly Austrian equity stocks which is traded on the Vienna Stock Exchange. It is currently used as an Index of the Austrian market.
"EMS"	*see European Monetary System.*
entidades gestores (Sp.)	financial institutions who can trade in the Spanish *book entry (qv)* market. They can trade for their

own and client accounts. *see aspirantes a creadores and creadores a mercado.*

"EOC" European Options Certificates BV who issues bearer certificates for options traded on the *"EOE"* (*qv*).

"EOCC" European Options Clearing Corporation (Holding-maatschappij Options Clearing Corporation BV) - a holding company responsible for clearing options traded on the *"EOE"* (*qv*).

"EOE" *see European Options Exchange.*

"EOE" an option traded on the *"EOE"* (*qv*) based on the *"EOE" Stock index* (*qv*).

"EOE" Stock Index a weighted stock index based on 25 major Dutch equities on which a future and option are based.

"EOE/FTA" Bond Index a bond index for the Dutch bond market on which both futures and options are based.

epsilon (eta) the ratio by which the price of an option moves relative to the underlying futures contract or financial instrument.

"ESCC" European Stock Options Clearing Corporation BV.

estoppel a conclusive admission which cannot be denied by the party whom it affects.

European Bond Commission "EBC" a standing commission of *EFFAS* (*qv*) whose aim is the raising of standards of bond analysis and widening the information on European bond markets. Its members are drawn from the major research departments of the major European banks and investment houses in fifteen European countries.

European Currency Unit "ECU" a composite currency, the value of which is determined on the basis of a basket of European currencies (DM, FF, Lira, Dfl, Bfr, Luxfr, DOK, IR£, Ptas and Dr). It is designed as a unit of account for the EMS (*qv*) and is used as an issuing currency by several borrowers including Governments of The United Kingdom, France and Italy.

European Federation of Financial Analysts Societies "EFFAS"	the overall body for the various domestic European investment analysts' societies. It holds a major conference bi-annually and has standing commissions in order to co-ordinate investment analysis standards.
European Futures Clearing Corporation BV	the clearing house for the *"FTA" (qv)*.
European Monetary System "EMS"	a group of European countries (Belgium, Luxembourg, Denmark, Germany, France, Italy, Ireland, the Netherlands and Spain) which agreed in March 1979 to keep their respective currencies within certain defined upper and lower limits in relation to each other. When one of these currencies is devalued, a realignment within the EMS takes place and all the proportions of the currencies are correspondingly adjusted.cf European Currency Unit.
European option	an option that may only be exercised on its expiration date. *cf American option.*
European Options Exchange "EOE"	the exchange in Amsterdam responsible for the trading of options on both individual and indexes for bonds and equities, currencies and precious metals.
Exchange Delivery Settlement Price"EDSP"	a price, fixed by the clearing house, at which deliveries on futures contracts are invoiced.
Exchange for Physicals "EFP"	an exchange between a physical and a future which takes place off Exchange between parties. These transactions are very flexible and can differ in terms. the International Petroleum Exchange on proof will accept them as offsetting positions to future positions.
exercise	to complete a transaction, the terms of which are mentioned in an option, for example, when a call option is exercised the holder buys securities from the option writer.
exercise price	the price at which an option holder may buy or sell the underlying security as defined in the terms of his option contract. It is the price at which the call

holder may buy the underlying security, or the put holder may sell the underlying security. For listed options, the exercise price is the same as the *strike price (qv)*.

expiry
the cash settlement of a futures or options contract. cf *delivery*.

expiry cycle
for options, there are preset expiry dates which are spaced at regular dates. On the "LTOM" (qv) there are three such cycles:
January, April, July and October.
February, May, August, November.
March, June, September, December.

expiry date (expiration date)
the day on which an option (warrant) contract terminates and thereafter becomes null and void, ie the last day on which a warrant holder may either buy from, or sell to, the borrower a given number of securities at specified terms.

factor slippage
refers to the phenomenon that a hedge or arbitrage ratio can be slightly distorted due to the fact that there can be a change in the cheapest to deliver instrument on the futures contract, which will cause the futures market to begin tracking another instrument with a different delivery factor from the one originally used to calculate the hedge or arbitrage ratio.

fair value basis
see theoretical basis.

"FAST"
Fast Automated Screen Trading. The *automated trading system (qv)* used on *London FOX (qv)*.

FF
French Franc.

fill or kill
an order to be executed or canceled immediately.

financial futures contract
a futures contract in the financial markets as opposed to the commodity markets. These cover interest rates, bonds, stocks and stock indices.

Financial Services Act "FSA"
an Act of Parliament in the U.K. in 1987 that was designed to provide greater control and regulation of the financial services in the U.K.. Its main thrust was the protection of investors. It created the *Self Regualtory Organizations "SRO"s (qv), the "RIE"s*

(qv) and imposed strict requirements on all participants in the industry.

Financial Times-Stock Exchange Index "FT-SE"   the Index of the 100 largest capitalizes stocks traded on the London International Stock Exchange.

Financiële Termijn-market Amsterdam (Nd.) "FTA"   the futures exchange in Amsterdam responsible for the trading of futures contracts for both bond and stock indexes.

firm orders   i) orders in the Netherlands for one's own account cf public order
ii) confirmed orders to be transacted.

fixed option hedge   an options hedge where the number of options contracts corresponds to the equivalent futures hedge.

floor   the physical trading floor of an exchange.

floor broker   a trader on an Exchange floor who executes the orders of investors, such as public customers, who do not have physical access to the trading area.

"FMA"   *see France Matif Automatique.*

"FMC"   the Futures Market Committee on *London FOX (qv)* which sets the rules and regulations for each market traded on the exchange.

"FOB"   *see free on board.*

forward contract   a cash transaction in which a buyer and seller agree upon a future trade. As opposed to a futures contract, a forward contract is not transferrable, its terms are not standardized and it is not *market to market (qv) daily.*

Forward Rate Agreement "FRA"   this agreement is similar to an interest rate futures contract in that it is a contract in which two parties agree the interest rate to be paid on a notional deposit of specified maturity on a specific future date. Unlike interest rate futures, the FRA is traded OTC (qv) market and is largely confined to the interbank market.

"FOX"   *see London FOX, the London Futures and Options Exchange.*

"FRA"   *see Forward Rate Agreement.*

France Matif Automatique	the new name of *OMF (qv)* since its takeover by *MATIF (qv)*.
free on board	an indication of the costs of putting the commodity on the transport - delivery, inspections and boarding costs - have all been paid for by the seller. Costs of transporting to ports of destination are not included and are the responsibility of the buyer as are all other risks.
FRF	French Franc.
"FSA"	*see Financial Services Act.*
"FTA"	*see Financiële Termijnmarket Amsterdam.*
"FTA" Bullet bond Index	a bond index based on ten Dutch government bonds with maturities between 1994 and 1997 which is adjusted periodically and is the basis for a number of futures and options contracts such as *"OBL" (qv) option and "FTB" (qv) future.*
"FTB"	a futures contract on the *"FTA" (qv)* based on the *"FTA" Bullet bond (qv)* Dutch government bond index.
"FTI"	a futures contract traded on the *"FTA" (qv)* based on the *"EOE" Stock Index (qv).*
"FTO" Bond future	a future based on a notional Dutch government bond with a 7 per cent coupon with physical delivery of underlying bands.
"FT-SE"	*see Financial Times-Stock Exchange Index.*
"FUTOP"	the **FUT**ures and **OP**tions exchange in Copenhagen which trades futures and option contracts on individual mortgage and Government bullet bonds as well as a bond and equity *"KFX" (qv)* index.
future	a contract to buy or sell a specific amount of securities or commodities for a specific price or yield on a specified future date.
futures contract	*see future.*
futures delivery	the process of meeting an obligation to deliver or receive securities or commodities on a certain date and in a location as specified by terms of the con-

	tract (not applicable for a municipal futures contract, a cash settled contract).
futures market	a market in which contracts for future delivery of commodities or securities are traded.
gamma	the rate at which a delta changes over time.
"GCM"	*see General Clearing Member.*
General Clearing Member "GCM"	members of a futures Exchange who may clear their own and other members' business directly with the *clearing house (qv)*.
Gilt	*see gilt-edged security.*
gilt-edged security "Gilt"	domestic sterling-denominated security backed by the full faith and credit of the United Kingdom and issued by the U.K. Treasury. It derives its name from the gold edge on the original certificates, subsequently replaced by green certificates.
good till canceled "GTC"	an open order to buy or sell securities which remains in effect until the order is executed or canceled. *cf. fill or kill.*
hedge	1. a technique of making offsetting commitments to minimize the impact of contrary movements. 2. a fixed commitment in a futures market which serves as a temporary substitute for an intended purchase or sale of a financial instrument for delivery and payment at a later date at the then current market price.
hedge period	the time interval between the initial transaction (creating an open position) and the offsetting futures transactions.
hedge ratio	the number of futures, options or bonds bought or sold against a position in the underlying security in order to hedge the position. *cf. delta and gamma.*
"HKFE"	*see Hong Kong Futures Exchange.*
Hong Kong Futures Exchange "HKFE"	the futures exchange in Hong Kong that trades futures contracts in gold, soyabeans, sugar and the Hang Seng stock index.
holder	owner of an options contract.
"ICCH"	*see International Commodities Clearing House*

"ICM"	*see Individual Clearing Member.*
"IFOX"	*see Irish Futures and Options Exchange.*
"IFT"	*see Independent Floor Traders.*
imperfect hedge	unequal price changes on the two sides of a hedged position during a hedge period; it may result from a favorable or unfavorable basis change.
implied repo rate	the financing rate at which a long cash short futures arbitrageur would neither gain nor lose on the transaction. The implied repo rate can also be viewed as the rate of return earned on the funds used to purchase the cash security in the cash and carry strategy.
implied volatility	a measure of *volatility (qv)* of the underlying asset determined by using the market prices of traded options.
in-the-money "ITM"	in the context of options; a *call (qv)* option is *in-the-money (qv)* if its *strike price (qv)* is less than the value of the underlying security. A *put option (qv)* is in-the-money if the strike price is greater than the value of the underlying security. *cf. at-the-money and out-of-the-money.*
Independent Floor Traders "IFT"	locals (qv) on the MATIF.
Individual Clearing Member "ICM"	members of a futures Exchange who may clear their own but not other members' business with the *clearing house (qv).*
Initial Deposit	*see Initial Margin*
initial margin	the amount of *margin (qv)* required in order to establish a position in a *futures contract (qv) cf. maintenance margin or variation margin.*
interdealer brokers	dealers in securities who only have access to *market makers (qv)*. They do not carry out transactions for other participants in the market. Their role is to match transactions between market makers and maintain their anonymity.
interest rate futures	futures *contracts (qv)* for securities whose prices are determined by interest rates.

International Commodities Clearing House "ICCH"	an independent central guarantee organisation used by the United Kingdom's six largest clearing banks acting as clearing agent for contracts on *"LIFFE" (qv)*.
International Options Clearing Corporation	a clearing house for the *"EOE" (qv)* Options exchange.
International Petroleum Clearing Corporation	a clearing house for the *"ROEFEX" (qv)* exchange.
International Petroleum Exchange "IPE"	the future and options exchange in London that trades futures and option contracts in Brent crude, Dubai crude, gas oil and heavy fuel oil.
intrinsic value	a call option has intrinsic value if the *exercise price (qv)* is lower than the price of the underlying asset. A *put option (qv)* has intrinsic value if the exercise price of the option is higher than the price of the underlying security. In each case, the intrinsic value is the difference between the exercise price and the price of the underlying security.
invoice amount	the actual cash amount received when delivering a cash bond against a bond futures contract.
"IOCC"	*see International Options Clearing Corporation BV*
"IPCC"	*see International Petroleum Clearing Corporation BV*
"IPE"	*see International Petroleum Exchange.*
Irish Futures and Options Exchange "IFOX"	the futures and options exchange in Dublin that trades futures contracts in Irish Long *Gilts (qv)*, *DIBOR (qv)*, Irish pound/U.S.dollar and *ISEQ (qv)* equity stock index.
"ISE"	*see International Stock Exchange.*
International Stock Exchange of Great Britain and the Republic of Ireland	formerly the London Stock Exchange, the name was changed to reflect the considerable volume of transactions in international stocks and bonds on the Exchange.
"ISEQ"	an weighted index of 76 Irish equities traded on the Dublin exchange.
Kansas City Board of Trade	the futures and options exchange in Kansas that trades futures contracts in No.2 Red Wheat, No.2

Grain sorghum, the Value Line and Mini Value
Line stock indexes and option contracts in No.2
Red Wheat.

"KCBOT" — *see Kansas City Board of Trade.*

"KD" — Kreditforeningen Danmark. One of the major mortgage institutions in Denmark.

kerb trading — the simultaneous trading of all metals after the official trading period of a specific metal at the *LME (qv).*

"KFX" — the equity index for the Copenhagen stock exchange which takes its name from the Danish words for Copenhagen Stock Exchange - Kobenhavns Fondsbörs.

"KLCE" — *see Kuala Lumpur Commodity Exchange.*

Kuala Lumpur Commodity Exchange — the futures exchange in Kuala Lumpur that trades in futures contracts for cocoa, crude palm oil, rubber - SMI 20 and tin.

Landeszentralbank "LZB" — the German cash settlement agency for the Deutscher Terminbörse **DTB (qv).**

"LCH" — *see London Clearing House.*

"LDE" — *see London Derivative Exchange.*

"LIBOR" — *see London Interbank Offered Rate.*

"LIFFE" — *see London International Financial Futures Exchange.*

"LME" — *see London Metal Exchange.*

local — a trader (seat holder) on a options and/or futures exchange who trade solely for their own account.

"LOCH" — *see London Options Clearing House.*

London Clearing House. a division of ICCH that covers the clearance of transactions in LIFFE and IPE.

London Derivative Exchange — the new name of the exchange to be formed by the merger of the *London Traded Options Market (qv)* and the *London International Financial Futures Exchange (qv).*

London FOX — *see London Futures and Options Exchange.*

London Futures and Options Exchange "London FOX"	the futures and options exchange in London which trades in futures and option contracts for cocoa, coffee, raw and white sugar, rubber and the *MGMI (qv)* metals index.
London Interbank Offered Rate "LIBOR"	the rate at which prime banks offer to make Eurocurrency deposits with other prime banks for a given maturity which can range from overnight to five years in London.
London International Financial Futures Exchange "LIFFE"	the futures and options exchange in London that trades futures and option contracts for U.K. long gilt, U.S.T-bond, Japanese T-bond, German Bund, 3 month sterling, 3 month eurodollars, 3 month euromark and the futures contract for the *FT-SE (qv)* equity index.
London Metal Exchange	the futures and options exchange in London that trades futures and option contracts in aluminium, copper, lead, nickel, tin and zinc.
London Options Clearing House "LOCH"	a wholly-owned subsidiary company of the ISE responsible for the registration and settlement of all traded option transactions.
London Traded Options Market	the Exchange responsible for trading stock options in London. It is due to amalgamate with "LIFFE" (qv) in 1990.
long	to buy a futures or options contract. *cf.short.*
long straddle	a *straddle (qv)* in which an investor buys put and call options.
long-term	1. in most bond markets; refers to initial maturities longer than seven years.
	2. under standard accounting practice; often refers to debt with a remaining maturity of greater than one year.
	3. a period of holding securities or releasing an investment strategy of at least one year. *cf. medium-term and short-term.*
"LTOM"	*see London Traded Options market.*
"LZB"	*see Landeszentralbank.*
maintenance margin	the amount by which the *initial margin (qv)* for a futures position may be depleted by adverse price

changes before additional monies are required to restore the initial margin amount. *See margin 2).*

Marché a Terme International de France formerly known as Marché a Terme des Instruments Financiers when it merged with the French commodity exchange MTMP in December 1987. This Exchange was set up in 1986 to trade financial futures in Paris including French T-bonds, French T-bills, 3 month PIBOR, 3 month Eurodeutschemark, long term ECU bonds, CAC40 stock index, cocoa, potatoes, white sugar and soya cattle cake.

Marché des Options Négoiables de Paris the Exchange in Paris dedicated to the trading of individual Stocks and Stock Index options.

margin 1. an adjustment, expressed in basis points, which is added to or subtracted from a reference interest rate (e.g. six month *"LIBOR" (qv)*) to establish the coupon of a floating rate or short-term money market security. *See quoted margin and spread.*
". a measure of return on floating rate notes calculated with reference to some interest rate such as LIBOR. *See discount margin and simple margin.*
3. cash deposits required for each futures contract to serve as a good faith deposit guaranteeing that both parties to the agreement will perform the transaction some time in the future. *cf. initial margin and maintenance margin.*

margin call a call for cash in a margin position. *See margin 3).*

mark to market the revaluing of a security, commodity or futures contract according to

market a forum for the sale and purchase of securities which may be physical, such as an Exchange, or abstract, such as *over-the counter (qv).*

market-maker a dealer who consistently quotes both bid and offered prices for an issue of securities on a firm basis. *see principal 2.*

"MATIF" *see Marché a Terme International de France.*

"MATIF SA" the clearance house for the MATIF.

"MCE" *see Midamerica Commodity Exchange.*

"ME"	*see Montreal Exchange.*
Mercado de Futuros Financieros "MEFF"	the futures exchange in Madrid that trades Spanish Government bond futures. cf OM Ibérica.
"MEFF"	*see Mercado de Futuros Financieros.*
"MGE"	*see Minneapolis Grain Exchange.*
"MGMI" index	an index of six base metals, aluminium, copper, lead, nickel, tin and zinc weighted according to the share of the metals' total consumption in the western world and traded on the *LME (qv).*
Midamerica Commodity Exchange "MCE".	the futures and options exchange based in Chicago that trades futures contracts in corn, oats, soyabeans, soyabean meal, wheat, CRCE cotton, CRCE rice, cattle, hogs, gold, platinum, silver, U.S.T-bonds, U.S.T-bills, Sterling, Deutschemark, Yen, Swiss Francs, Canadian dollars and U.S.T-notes. It also trades options in soyabeans, wheat and gold.
"MIFE"	*see Manila International Futures Exchange.*
Manila International Futures Exchange	the futures exchange in Manila that trades futures contracts in cane sugar, robusta coffee, copra and soyabeans.
Minneapolis Grain Exchange	the futures and options exchange in Minneapolis that trades futures contracts in hard red spring wheat, oats, white wheat and high fructose corn sugar. It also trades an options contract in hard red spring wheat.
"MM" Market Maker (Netherlands)	a trader who trades for their own account and maintain a market by providing continuous bid and ask prices in the series of options to which he has been assigned.
"MONEP"	*see Marché des Options Négoiables de Paris.*
Montreal Exchange	the exchange in Montreal which trades option contracts in Canadian T-bonds, Canadian Bankers Acceptances, gold*, platinum* and over 25 individual equity stocks. *The precious metal options are listed on a mutual offset link with the Vancouver

and Australian stock exchanges and the *"EOE" (qv)* in Amsterdam.

"NBCP"   *see night before clearing program.*

"NCC"   *see Norwegian Clearing Central "NCC".*

"NCM"   *see Non Clearing Member.*

nearby   the nearest active trading month of a financial futures market.

"NEC"   *see Négociateurs Courtiers.*

N.V. Nederlandse   the Agricultural Futures Market Amsterdam
Liquidatiekas (Nd.)   responsible for the trading of futures in potatoes
"NLK KAS"   and live hogs in the Netherlands.

Négociateurs Courtiers   trader brokers on the *MATIF (qv).*

net writer   a market-maker who has written or sold more options tan he has purchased.

negative carry   *see carry.*

Negociateurs Individuels a *local (qv)* on the French futures and options
de Parquet (Fr.)   exchanges.

New York Cotton   the futures and options exchange in New York that
Exchange "NYCE"   trades futures contracts in U.S.dollar index, ECU, U.S. 5 year T-notes, cotton and orange juice. It also trades option contracts in U.S.dollar index, U.S. 5 year T-notes, cotton and orange juice.

New York Futures   the future and options exchange in New York that
Exchange "NYFE"   trades futures contracts in *NYSE (qv)* composite stock index, Russell 3,000 stock index, Russell 2,000 stock index and CRB commodity price index. It also trades option contracts in NYSE composite stock index and CRB commodity index.

New York Mercantile   the futures and options exchange in New York that
Exchange "NYMEX"   trades futures contracts in No2 heating oil, propane, unleaded gasoline, *WTI (qv)* crude oil, platinum and palladium. It also trades option contracts in heating oil, WTI crude oil and unleaded gasoline.

New York Stock   the stock exchange in New York that also trades
Exchange "NYSE"   option contracts in the NYSE composite stock index and nearly 40 individual U.S. stocks.

New Zealand Futures Exchange "NZFE"	the futures and options exchange in Auckland that trades futures contracts in the Barclays stock index, N.Z. 90 bank bills, N.Z. T-notes, 3 month U.S. dollar and 3 month N.Z.dollar. It also trades option contracts in the 3 month N.Z. dollar, Barclays stock index and N.Z. T-notes.
"NIBOR"	Norwegian Inter Bank Offered Rate.
night before clearing program	a system used by *OM (qv)* in Sweden for reconciling futures and options positions and offsetting ALL such positions in order to determine an individual clients margin requirements. This program is run over night.
Nikkei	an index of 225 Japanese stocks. *cf TOPIX.*
"NIPS"	*see Negociateurs Individuels de Parquet (Fr.).*
"NLK KAS"	*see N.V. Nederlandse Liquidatiekas (Nd.)*
NOK	Norwegian Krone.
"NOM"	*see Norwegian Options Market "NOM"*
Non clearing member "NCM"	members of a futures Exchange who amy transact trades for their own or on behalf of other members, but can not clear these transaction.
Norwegian Clearing Central "NCC"	one of two organizations responsible for Futures trading and clearing in Norway. *see Norwegian Options Market "NOM"*.
Norwegian Options Market "NOM"	one of two organizations responsible for Futures trading and clearing in Norway. *see Norwegian Clearing Central "NCC"*.
"NLK KAS"	the agricultural futures exchange in Amsterdam that trades futures contracts in potatoes and live hogs.
"NYCE"	*see New York Cotton Exchange.*
"NYFE"	*see New York Futures Exchange.*
"NYMEX"	*see New York Mercantile Exchange.*
"NYSE"	*see New York Stock Exchange.*
"NZFE"	*see New Zealand Futures Exchange.*

"OAT"	*see Obligation Assimilables du Trésor.*
"OBL"	an option traded on the *"EOE" (qv)* based on the *"FTA" Bond Index (qv).*
Obligaciones del Estado (Sp.)	long term Spanish Government bonds.
Obligation Assimilables du Trésor	French Government bonds that are issued regularly using the *tap (qv)* system.
"OBX"	the Norwegian Stock Index.
"OCC"	*see Options Clearing Corporation.*
Österreichische Termin und Optionsbörse	the new Austrian Futures & Options exchange which expects to open in 1991. It will be based on the *OM (qv)* system.
Off Floor Trader	an options trader who transacts business for his own account via a floor trader on the *"EOE" (qv).*
"OFT"	*see Off Floor Trader.*
"OM"	Optionsmarknad. The futures & options market in Sweden that trades futures contracts in OMX 30 stock index as well as option contracts on the OMX 30 stock index, individual Swedish stocks and currencies such as the US$/Swedish Krone and Sterling/Swedish Krone. As a commercial company, it has extended its operations to France, Spain and the U.K..
OM Ibérica	this the independent futures and options exchange in Spain and is a member of the *"OM" (qv)* group. It trades options contracts on notional 10% Government bonds and the 12.5% government bond 1992.
"OMF"	Organisation des Marché Financiers. This is an independent futures and options exchange in France operated by *"OM" (qv)*. It has been absorbed by *MATIF (qv) and has been renamed "FMA" (qv)*. It trades option contracts on a notional BTAN Government bond and the OMF 50 stock index. *cf MONEP.*
"OMF50"	an index of the most traded 50 French stocks calculated by "OMF" and is the basis of a futures and options contract.

"OML"	OM London. A futures & options exchange in London trading in selected Swedish and Norwegian stocks and *the OMX 30 index (qv)*.
"OMX"	the stock index for the Swedish stock market calculated by OM.
on-the-money	*see at-the-money.*

open contract	futures contracts that have been bought or sold without the transactions having been completed or offset by:
	    a) subsequent sale
	    b) purchase
	    c) actual delivery
	    d) receipt
	of the underlying financial instrument.

open interest	contracts not yet offset by offsetting futures transactions or fulfilled by delivery. Also called open position.
open order	a purchase or sale order at a stated price which is *good until canceled (qv)*.
open outcry	in the context of futures, an auction system used in the trading pits on the floors of futures exchanges. All bids and offers are made openly by public, competitive, outcry and hand signals.
open position	*see open interest.*
opportunity cost	an economic term which defines cost in terms of the value of the alternative or other opportunities which have to be foregone in order to achieve a particular objective. Thus, the returns from a particular course of action are compared with the real cost involved in undertaking it.
Optiën (Nd.)	a futures contracts on shares.
option	a contract giving the holder the right either to buy from or sell to the issuer of such a contract a given number of securities at a fixed price at any time on or before a given date.
option class	all options of the same type pertaining to the same underlying security. Calls and puts comprise separate classes.

option period or life	the lifetime of the option as specified in the contract and within which the buyer must execute.
Options Clearing Corporation "OCC"	a corporation formed by U.S. options Exchanges. It sells and buys options from their holders, thus eliminating the credit risk by coming between them.
Osaka Securities Exchange "OSE"	the stock exchange in Osaka that trades futures contracts in the Nikkei 225 Stock Average and the 50 individual Japanese stock futures.
"OSE"	*see Osaka Securities Exchange.*
"OTC"	*see over-the-Counter.*
out-of-the-money	a *call option (qv)* is out-of-the money if its *strike price (qv)* is greater than the value of the underlying security. A *put option (qv)* is out-of-the money if its strike price is less than the value of the underlying security.*cf.at-the-money and in-the-money.*
outstanding contract	an option contract that has not expired nor been closed out by a closing purchase or sale.
over-the-counter "OTC"	a market, the *Euromarket (qv)*, for example, which is separate from the stock exchanges and where transactions are completed by principals over the telephone, telex or by computer.*cf stock exchanges and unlisted securities market.*
Pacific Stock Exchange	the stock exchange in San Francisco that trades option contracts in the FNCI stock index and over 100 individual U.S. stocks.
"PSE"	*see Pacific Stock Exchange.*
par	1. price; 100 per cent of the principal value of a debt security 2. value: that price assigned by a corporation to its common or preferred stock 3. the principal amount or denomination at which an issuer contracts to redeem the bond at maturity. The par value is stated on the face of the bond.
Partly Assisted Trading System	a computerized trading system operated in Austria for *warrants (qv) and "shorties" (qv).*

"PATS"	*see Partly Assisted Trading System.*
perturbation	measuring the sensitivity of bond prices by determining the cash price change for a specific change in the bond's yield to maturity.
Philadelphia Stock Exchange "PHLX"	the stock exchange in Philadelphia that trades futures contracts in Australian dollars, Sterling, Canadian dollars, Deutschemarks, French Francs, Japanese yen, Swiss francs, ECU and the National OTC stock index. It also trades option contracts in the National OTC stock index, the Value Line composite index, the Gold/Silver stock index, the Utility stock index, Australian dollars, Sterling, Canadian dollars, Deutschemarks, French Francs, Japanese yen, Swiss Francs, ECU and over 100 individual U.S. stocks.
physical delivery	the delivery of a security or the underlying asset for settlement of a transaction or exercise of an option or future.*cf cash delivery.*
physical security	1. a cash security. 2. a security with physical form eg a bearer security.
"PIBOR"	Paris Inter Bank Offered Rate.
pip	*see basis point.*
pit	a trading area on the floor of an exchange where only one kind of security is traded. In futures, it is a trading area on the floor of the exchange where one or more types of *futures contracts (qv)* may be traded. *cf ring.*
"PLOB"	*see Public Limit Order Board.*
"POCM"	*see Public Order Correspondent Market.*
"POM"	*see public order member.*
position	1. to go long (qv) or short (qv) in a security. 2. the amount of securities owned (long position) or owed (short position).
position trading	a type of trading involving the holding of open futures contracts for an extended period of time.

positive carry	*see carry.*
premium	1. in the context of options; the total price of an option contract. The sum of the *intrinsic value (qv)* and the *time value (qv).* 2. in the context of futures; the difference between the futures price and the cash price of the underlying index or commodity. 3. in the context of convertible securities; the difference between a convertible's market price and its conversion value expressed as a percentage over the current equity price.
price factor	the factor used to convert a bond futures price into an equivalent price for the bond actually delivered. It represents the price per unit of nominal at which it yields the notional yield on the first day of the delivery month.
price limit	1. price fluctuation on a *futures contract (qv)* in one trading day allowed by the exchange. 2. the price at which a client is willing to give an order to purchase or sell a security.
prompt date	usually used on *LME (qv). see delivery date.*
"PHLX"	*see Philadelphia Stock Exchange.*
Pts	Peseta.
public limit order	a firm dealing instruction which may be passed to a Board Official (qv) for execution if possible.
Public Limit Order Board "PLOB"	the centre for orders for transactions on *MONEP (qv).*
public order	orders in the Netherlands for other than one's own account *cf firm order ii).*
Public Order Correspondent Market "POCM"	a member of the *"EOE" (qv)* exchange who can accept orders from private clients and institutions which must be transacted by a *"POM" (qv).*
public order member	a broking firm which, being neither a *market maker (qv)* nor a *clearing member (qv),* deals in options or futures on its own behalf as principal or on behalf of its clients as agent. A "POM" may only deal in options or futures if it has appointed a clearing agent to act on its behalf.

put date	the date on which an investor may exercise his right to put a security. *see put option.*
put option	an option to sell a specified amount of securities at a specified price on a specified date or dates (*see European option*) or at any time during a specified period (*see American option*).*cf. call option.*
put price	1. the price at which a put option may be executed. 2. the price, usually par, at which an investor may ask an issuer to purchase a puttable bond on the put date.
regulated futures contract "RFC"	*futures contracts (qv)* traded on or subject to the rules of an exchange designated by the *Commodity Futures Trading Commission (qv)* and which use the *marked to market (qv)* method of determining margin account equity.
ratio hedge	an options hedge where the delta of the option is used to determine the optimum number of options contracts.
Recognized Investment Exchange "RIE"	exchanges authorised under the *FSA (qv)* for the purposes of carrying out financial transactions. Each has its own *SRO (qv)* and is required to meet strict regulations on membership, conduct and practice.
Registered Options Trader "ROT"	a person who is able to trade on *LTOM (qv).*
Remister A (Agent) (Nd.)	an agent whose sole activity is to introduce clients to *"POCM" (qv)* and can not place orders themselves.
Remister B (Agent) (Nd.)	an agent who is not restricted to introducing clients but can give orders.
repo	*see repurchase agreement.*
repurchase agreement "RP" or "repo"	1. two simultaneous transactions: the purchase of securities (the collateral) by an investor from a bank or dealer and the commitment by the bank or dealer to repurchase the securities at the same price at an agreed future date and rate. 2. a method of borrowing by using a security as collateral for a loan. The interest rate and term of

the loan are agreed upon in advance, and upon repayment of the loan the security is returned to the owner. The borrower retains any possession of the security and continues to receive any interest payments during the term of the agreement.
3.   in reference to Federal Reserve actions; a means of temporarily adding to reserves. The Fed buys securities under a contract to sell them back at an agreed price and date. (Generally, repos mature within one to seven days, maximum term being fifteen days). Dealers may repurchase prior to the maturity of the repo if they wish.

Restricted Life Options "RLO"   options on *LTOM (qv)* with lives of only two months.

"RIE"   *see Recognized Investment Exchange.*

ring   the trading pit for trading metals on the *LME (qv)*. *cf pit.*

risk factors   the factors ("deltas") which are published by the Exchange and which indicate the risk of an option position relative to that of the related futures contract. These factors are used as the basis of the option margining system.

"RLO"   *see Restricted Life Options.*

"ROEFFEX"   *see Rotterdam Energy Futures Exchange.*

"ROT"   *see Registered Options Trader.*

rotation   a short period of time during which prices in all series are updated and during which no public limit order may be submitted or withdrawn.

Rotterdam Energy Futures Exchange "ROEFFEX"   the futures exchange in Rotterdam which is responsible for the trading of crude oil, heavy fuel and gas contracts Since writing this book this exchange has closed.*cf the International Petroleum Exchange "IPE".*

round trip   buying and selling a futures or options contract.

"SBF"   *see Société des Bouses Françaises.*

"SBV"   *see Spécialistes en Valeurs du Trésors.*

"SCH"   *see Stockholm Clearing House.*

| "SCMC" | see *Société de Compensation des Marchés Conditionnels.* |

Securities & Investment Board — the major regulatory body under the *FSA (qv)* which devolves responsibility to an number of *SROs (qv).*

security
1. a marketable claim upon, or interest in, assets of a borrower which may be in either bearer or registered form. These instruments are normally evidenced by a certificate, but, for example, in the case of certain U.S. and most U.K. Treasury obligations, ownership is evidenced by a book-entry only.
2. colloquially, the degree of legal protection, right to recourse and degree of a claim on the borrower's assets of a lender in an event of default.

security dealers — organizations that may conduct transactions for their own and their clients behalf. *cf market makers and interdealer brokers.*

SEK — Swedish Krone.

Self Regulatory Organization — an organization responsible for the monitoring and control of a market. It creates the rules and regulations and polices them. eg are the *TSA (qv)* for the securities industry, the *AFBD (qv)* for futures and options trading and *AIBD (qv)* for off-shore markets traded in London.

selling the spread — *see bear spread.*

series — all options of the same class having the same *exercise price (qv) and expiry date* (qv).

settle or settlement — *see clear.*

settlement date — the date a transaction is cleared i.e. payment is effected and securities are delivered. In the Euromarket, the settlement date is usually seven days after the trade date in the case of Eurobonds (including FRNs) and is usually two days after the trade date in the case of CDs. The exact difference between trade and settlement date varies widely from market to market and should always be checked before transacting any business. *cf.trade date.*

settlement price	the price established by the clearing house at the end of a trading session as the closing price that will be used in determining profits and losses for the *mark to market (qv) process for margin accounts.*
"SFE"	*see Sydney Futures Exchange.*
short	selling a futures or options contract. *cf long.*
short term	1. in the Eurobond market; refers to initial maturities shorter than two years. 2. often under standard accounting practice; refers to debt with a remaining maturity of less than one year. 3. period of holding securities or realizing an investment strategy of less than one year. *cf. medium term and long term.*
"shorties"	a warrant traded in the Austrian market with many of the features of orthodox options except that for each date only one strike price is offered.
"SIB"	*see Securities & Investment Board.*
"SIMEX"	*see Singapore International Mercantile Exchange.*
simple basis	this represents the difference between the underlying asset and the future. at maturity of the futures contract the simple basis will converge to zero. *cf theoretical basis and see value basis.*
Singapore International Mercantile Exchange "SIMEX"	the futures and options exchange in Singapore that trades futures contracts in gold, high sulphur fuel oil, the *Nikkei stock index (qv)*, Eurodollars, Sterling, Deutschemarks and Japanese yen. It also trades options contracts in Eurodollars, Deutschemarks and Japanese yen.
"SMI"	*see Swiss Market Index.*
Société des Bourses Françaises "SBF"	the body charged with the administration and promotion of the French stock exchanges.
Société de Compensation des Marchés Conditionnels "SCMC"	the body charged with the surveillance, control and clearing functions of the french exchanges.
"SOFE"	*see Swedish Options and Futures Exchange.*

"SOFFEX"	*see Swiss Options & Financial Futures Exchange "SOFFEX".*
sole trader	a one director company or individual authorized to transact business either as a market maker or floor trader. *see local.*
"SPAN"	*see Standard Portfolio Analysis of Risk.*
Spécialistes en Valeurs du Trésors "SVF"	primary dealers in French Government securities.
spot month	the contract month close to delivery or expiry.
spreading	the simultaneous purchase and sale of different futures contracts.
	"SRO"
	see Self Regulatory Organization.
Standard Portfolio Analysis of Risk	the standard margining mechanism first introduced by the Chicago Mercantile Exchange in June 1989 used by a number of U.S.Exchanges and now being introduced into the U.K..
"STE"	*see Stichting Toezicht Effenctenverkeer (Nd.).*
Stichting Toezicht Effenctenverkeer (Nd.)	the supervision authority for securities in the Netherlands.
stock exchange	a physical location where trading in listed securities is carried out by professional members of the stock exchange.
Stockholm Clearing House	the clearing house that was set up by *SOFE (qv)* in competition to *OM (qv)* in Stockholm that ceased operating in 1989.
straddle	1. an option position that is a combination of a put and a call on the same security at different strike prices for the same expiration date. 2. a futures position that is a combination of both long and short contracts of the same security for different delivery months. *cf.strangle and strap.*
strangle	an option strategy of purchasing a put option with a *strike price (qv)* below that of the underlying instrument, and a call option with a strike price above that of the underlying instrument. If it is believed that the market is overestimating

volatility, a strangle should be sold. *cf straddle and strap.*

strap — an option position which is a combination of two calls and one put on the same security at different strike prices for the same expiration date. *cf. straddle and strangle.*

strike price — the price at which an option may be exercised.

Swedish Options & Futures Exchange — the second futures & options exchange in Sweden that ceased operating in January 1989.

SwF — Swiss franc.

Swiss Market Index "SMI" — an index of the 24 most important Swiss stocks that is used as the basis for the SMI futures and options contracts.

Swiss Options and Financial Futures Exchange "SOFFEX" — the Swiss futures and options exchange based in the three main Swiss stock exchanges in Zurich, Geneva and Basel which trades options in the *SMI (qv)* Swiss Market stock index and almost 20 individual Swiss stocks. It is expected to also trade futures in the SMI and Swiss interest rates.

Sydney Futures Exchange "SFE" — the futures and options exchange in Sydney that trades futures contracts in gold, wool, live cattle, All-Ordinaries stock index, 90 day Australian bank bills, Eurodollars, 10 year Australian Government bonds and U.S. T-bonds. it also trades options contracts in the All-Ordinaries stock index, 90 day Australian bank bills and 10 year Australian Government bonds.

synthetic — an artificial futures or options contract created from a combination of other contracts and/or cash.

"TAM" — *see Taux annuel movitaine.*

Tap — a system of issuing securities by bringing further tranches of the security to market at current rates.

Taux annuel movitaine "TAM" — the average of overnight French money market rates over one year .

"TFE" — *see Toronto Futures Exchange.*

theoretical basis "fair" value basis — this is a calculated number and represents the level the futures should trade at relative to the underlying asset, given net financing costs. At maturity of

the futures contract the theoretical basis will con-
verge to zero. This calculated by:
Theor.basis = Und.Asset x $(1 + (rT)/365)$-(I or D)
where
Und.asset = underlying asset
r = financing rate
T = number of days to expiry of the futures contract
I or D = Interest or Dividends
cf simple basis and see value basis.

theta   the change in the value of an option associated with
                             a specific reduction in time to expiration.

"THS"   *see Transactions Hors Séance.*

time spread   an option position created by selling one call and
                             buying another with a longer expiration date at the
                             same strike price. Also called calendar spread.

time value   the part of an option premium which reflects the
                             remaining life of an option and the interest rate that
                             can be earned. It is often calculated as the value of
                             an option exceeds its intrinsic value.

titulares de cuentas (Sp.) financial institutions who are able to operate in the
                             Spanish book entry (qv) market. However they can
                             only trade for their own account. *cf aspirantes a
                             creadores and creadores de mercado.*

"TOB"   *see Österreichische Termin und Optionsbörse.*

Tokyo Stock Exchange   the stock exchange in Tokyo that trades futures
"TSE"   contracts in 10 year Government bonds, 20 year
                             Japanese Government bonds and *the Tokyo Stock
                             Price Index "TOPIX" (qv).*

"TOPIC"   the information delivery system of the *ISE (qv)* in
                             London that carries prices, news and information.

"TOPIX"   the Tokyo Stock Price Index. *cf Nikkei.*

Toronto Futures   the future and options exchange in Toronto that
Exchange "TFE"   trades futures contracts in Canadian T-bills,
                             Canadian T-bonds and the TSE 35 stock index. It
                             also trades options contracts in Canadian T-bonds,
                             silver, the TSE 35 stock index and over 40 in-
                             dividual Canadian stocks.

Trade Registration System "TRS"	the computerized transaction recording system used by *"IPE" (qv)* in London.
trader	a person whose purpose is to profit from the buying and selling of securities, rather than from holding them for long-term investment purposes. This term usually refers to "professionals" in the bond markets.
transaction	the process of either buying or selling securities. Also known in some markets as a deal or a bargain.
Transactions Hors Séance "THS"	an acronym used in France meaning "Out of Exchange". It means that securities listed THS, means that transactions can only take place before or after official trading hours. If the contract is not listed, THS designated transactions are entered on an OTC basis but officially cleared by the Exchange.
"TRS"	*see Trade Registration System.*
"TSE"	see Tokyo Stock Exchange.
"TSE"	Toronto Stock Exchange.
"TSR"	Technically Specified Rubber - the quality of rubber traded on the *London FOX (qv)*.
underlying asset	the asset that an option or warrant holder has the right to buy or sell.
US $	United States (U.S.) Dollar
value basis	this represents the difference between "fair" value futures price and actual futures price i.e. the difference between *theoretical basis (qv) and simple basis (qv)*. If the difference is large there is an arbitrage opportunity between cash and futures. At maturity of the futures contract value basis will converge to zero.
value date	*see delivery date and expiry date.*
Vancouver Stock Exchange "VSE"	the stock exchange in Vancouver that trades options contracts on gold, silver, platinum and the Canadian dollar.
variation margin	funds which must be posted to bring the equity in an account back up to the *initial margin (qv)* level.

valuation trading	the purchase of undervalued and simultaneous purchase of overvalued options according to an option valuation model.
variation margin	profits or losses on open option positions in futures and options contracts which are paid or collected daily.
Vereeriigde Oost-Indische Compagnie (Nd.)	the United East India Company of the Netherlands.
volume	number of transactions during a trading session.
"VSE"	*see Vancouver Stock Exchange.*
"WCE"	*see Winnipeg Commodity Exchange.*
Winnipeg Commodity Exchange "WCE"	the futures exchange in Winnipeg that trades futures contracts in Alberta barley, domestic barley, flaxseed, domestic oats, rapseed/canola, rye and domestic wheat.
withholding tax	a tax on income deducted at source which a paying agent is legally obliged to deduct from its payments of interest on securities issued by a borrower.
writer	a person who executes an opening sale of an option contract.
"WTI"	West Texas Intermediate. A type of oil traded on the U.S. futures and options exchange. cf with Brent and Dubai sour.

The Futures & Options Markets in Finland

Päivi Härkönen
Startel Inc

with assistance from:
The Finnish Options Market
The Finnish Options Exchange

INTRODUCTION

The Finnish derivative markets have grown up as a consequence of deregulation of the Finnish financial markets and an increase in their efficiency. During the 1980s, the Finnish stock market expanded and share turnover grew considerably. One can say, that before 1986 the liquidity and price information in the stock market would almost certainly have been insufficient to sustain functioning derivative markets.

Trading in standardized options started in November 1987 on the Finnish Options Exchange, **FOE** with basket options including put and call options. In May 1988, the Finnish Options Market, **FOM** started trading in index options and futures. Both the two exchanges act as clearing houses too. Nowadays, the products traded on **FOE** include index options and futures, currency futures and options on currency futures. The underlying currency is US dollar. Standardized currency options were introduced into the Finnish derivative markets in May 1989. In **FOM**, there are traded index options and futures as well as stock futures. The trading in stock futures began in October 1990. **Standardized interest rate options are not traded in Finland.** On the other hand, interest rate options have been traded over-the-counter in the interbank money market since September 1989. **So far, foreign investors have not been able to participate in the Finnish money markets. However, on November 1st, 1990, the Bank of Finland announced that from January 1st, 1991 all remaining foreign exchange restrictions, except those regarding private individuals raising loans abroad, will be rescinded. The most important are those that apply to short term capital movements such as money market instruments, foreign exchange, interest rate derivative instruments and the commercial background for forward currency contracts. It also removed the prohibition on the sale abroad of bonds which were issued prior to February 1st, 1990.**

In Finland, trading has almost entirely focussed on index-related products. Trading in stock options has not been successful stopped in December 1989. The main reason for this was the difficulty in finding interesting underlying stocks. Other reasons were the high cost of the physical delivery of the stocks and settlement as well as the lack of interest by market makers in stock options.

The fact that major Finnish commercial banks own a majority of the shares in **FOM** (Finnish Options Market), it is the leading market place in Finland. It has had most of the trading volume in index products. The strategy of **FOE** is to limit the trading costs to a minimum and to compete for trading commissions with **FOM**. The future development of the derivative market will depend on that of the stock market itself. When the Helsinki Stock Exchange switches to a paperless trading system from the beginning of 1992, it probably will result in increased trading volumes.

In 1990, the Helsinki Stock Exchange has faced a bear market. Stock prices have come down by 30 per cent during January - September, 1990 and turnover has declined. High interest rates, poor corporate earnings and the slowdown in the economy have all affected the stock market. Equities traded on the Helsinki Stock Exchange totalled about FIM 12.1 billion during the first nine months of the year 1990. Free shares, i.e. shares available to non-Finnish investors, accounted for FIM 3.8 billion, 32 per cent of the total. The increased cross-ownership between listed companies in Finland is likely to reduce the liquidity of the stock market and the reliability of prices. Another problem is still the distinction between free and restricted shares.

In spite of the above mentioned defects, the trading in derivative products is expected to increase because the Bank of Finland made a decision in July 1990 to allow foreign investors to trade in the Finnish derivative markets. According to that decision, derivative instruments based on Finnish shares and warrants carrying the right to purchase restricted shares may be sold to non-residents as from September 1st, 1990. However, legislation restricting foreigners' ownership rights prohibits the transfer of restricted shares underlying derivative contracts and warrants to non-residents. This decision applies to all standardized and unstandardized options and futures on Finnish shares and other contracts of similar nature. The sale to non-residents of derivative contracts based on other securities is not allowed.

During the 1990's different types of index options and futures are likely to become the most traded derivative instruments in Finland. The efficiency of the market could be further enhanced by the laying down of clear rules on the short selling of shares. Short selling is not allowed in Finland although there has been some exceptions.

ORGANIZATION of the MARKET

The Finnish derivative markets are organized so that orders can be made by telephone or by computer. On the Finnish Options Market, one can trade by either. However, on the Finnish Options Exchange transactions are completed so far only by telephone, however, they are developing an electronic trading system.

The task of the marketplace is to match buy and sell orders with the minimum of delay. This is done by ranking orders in accordance with two stated criteria:

- price

- and time.

In the electronic system, brokers and market makers place orders in their offices via terminals to the trading system. When the prices match, the transaction is completed automatically. The telephone based trading system is designed for block orders, i.e. orders above a certain lot size. Currently, this is 20 contracts. Contracts are available to all who have access to the exchange's terminals or the major international electronic information systems, like Reuters and Telerate. The options exchanges give information also to the Finnish Startel Inc., which provides electronic information to the domestic financial markets.

Transaction Costs

In **FOM**, the trading cost for index options is 1.6 per cent of the premium and settlement cost is 0.9 per cent. Minimum settlement price is FIM 6.50. To this is added the broker's fee which is usually 2 - 3 per cent of the premium. The settlement cost for index futures is FIM 40 per future in **FOM**. There are no transaction costs for index futures nor stamp duty. When the future is carried out, the client has to pay FIM 40 settlement costs and 1 per cent stamp duty of the nett value.

In **FOE**, the trading cost for index options is 1.5 per cent of the premium, with a minimum of FIM 8 per option. In currency options, the cost is 1.5 per cent, but with a minimum of FIM 4 per option. In index futures the transaction cost is FIM 30 per future. The transaction costs for options on currency futures is FIM 20 per future.

The FOX and SOP 25 Stock Indexes

The two exchanges offer stock index products based on indexes of the 25 most traded stocks on the Helsinki Stock Exchange, **FOX** on **FOM** and **SOP 25** on **FOE**. Both indexes are calculated used the same formula and are reconstructed twice a year on the same date i.e. February 1st and August 1st. The weights of the individual stocks are the same.

However, while the index values are virtually the same for the closing prices, there are variations during the day. This is due to the use of prices of all trades by **FOE**, while **FOM** only uses the prices of round lot trades. The two contracts are not fungible.

HISTORY of the MARKETS

Date		Exchange
November 1987	Introduction of individual stock options	FOE
May 1988	Introduction of Index futures & options	FOM
May 1989	Introduction of currency options	FOE
December 1989	Ceased trading individual stock options	FOE
October 1990	Introduction of individual stock futures	FOM

OVERVIEW of PRODUCTS

	Exchange	Futures	Options
Stock Index			
FOX	FOM	*	*
SOP 25	FOE	*	*
Individual Stocks	FOM	*	
Interest Rates			
3 Month HELIBOR	OTC		*§
Currencies			
US $/Finnish Markka	FOE	*	*

§ Foreign investors can not participate in the Finnish money markets.

Finnish Options Market "FOM"
- Suomen Optiomeklarit Oy

INTRODUCTION

Established in 1987, the Finnish Options Market **FOM** serves as an integrated exchange and clearing house for trading and clearing of standardized derivative instruments. At present, **FOM** offers standardized stock futures and standardized stock index options and futures on the Finnish Options Index - **FOX**. **FOX** is a market value weighted stock price index, which is calculated continuously, based on the 25 most traded shares on the Helsinki Stock Exchange. The structure of **FOX** is changed semi-annually based on the trading activity during the previous six months and is very similar to the **SOP 25** Index on which the Finnish Options Exchange **FOE** bases its contracts.

Trading and clearing is governed by the Rules and General Conditions applying to each product traded and cleared at **FOM**, and by laws and other regulations pertaining to such trading. Applicable rules also include those issued to brokers via announcements as well as Specification of the **FOX** Index. The regulatory authority of **FOM** is the Banking Supervision Board.

ORGANIZATION of the MARKET

Currently, **FOM** has approximately 50 employees. The organization's main sectors are responsible for trading, clearing, product development, information systems development, marketing, training and research, legal affairs and administration.

Shareholders

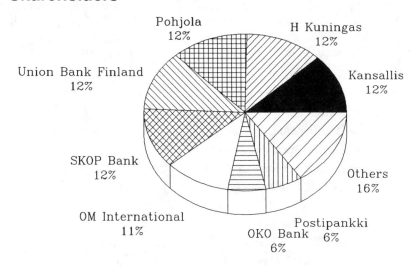

FOM's major shareholders comprise Finnish banks and brokerage companies active in the Finnish capital market. The company's major shareholders are:

Kansallis Banking Group	12.33%
H Kuningas Ltd (brokerage company)	12.33%
Pohjola (insurance company)	12.33%
Union Bank of Finland	12.33%
SKOP-Bank	12.33%
OM International Ltd	10.58%
OKO-Bank	5.97%
Postipankki Oy (bank)	5.97%

Altogether, **FOM** is currently owned by 41 shareholders.

Brokers, Market Makers and End Customers

FOM has authorized 18 brokers and 6 market makers to trade in options and futures. A company can operate both as a broker and a market maker. All brokers and market makers are based in Helsinki. End customers cannot deal directly with the **FOM**. A broker, which may be a Finnish bank or brokerage company, acts as an intermediary. The broker acts as a guarantor to FOM that the end customer can fulfill his obligations in accordance with the terms of an option or a future. In the FOM's computer system, an end customer is designated by a customer code pertaining to the customer's clearing account at FOM. This ensures the anonymity of the end customers.

Members

ABB Aros Securities Oy
Evli-Optiot Oy
Pankkiiriliike Ane Gyllenberg Oy
Helsingfors Sparbank
Interbank Osakepankki Oy Ltd
Kansallis Osaka Pankki
Optiopositio Oy
Opstock Pankkiriliike
Pankkiriliike Erik Selin Oy
Pankkiriliike Protos Oy
Postipankki Oy
Servisen Arctos & Partners Oy
Skandinavian Optio ja Futuurivälittäjät Oy
SKOP Bank
SP-Suomalaisen Optio Oy
Suurhelsingen Osuuspankki
Unitas
United Bankers
Oy United Rahoitus Ab

Market Makers

Kansallis Osaka Pankki
Optiopositio Oy
Opstock Pankkiriliike
Postipankki Oy
Servisen Arctos & Partners Oy
Unitas

Trading

The task of the marketplace is to match buy and sell orders with the minimum of delay. This is done by ranking orders in accordance with two stated criteria:

- Price
- Time

Electronic System

Brokers and market makers using FOM's electronic trading system place orders in their offices via terminals connected directly to the FOM's trading system. When the prices match, the transaction is completed automatically.

Block Order Desk

Parallel with the electronic trading system, the FOM provides a trading function in which FOM's brokers accept and match orders by telephone which is designed for block orders (i.e. orders above a certain lot size, currently 20 contracts). When a transaction is complete, it is documented on a trade slip, which is then time-stamped immediately. The contract is keyed in immediately to the marketplace's computer system and information on the trade becomes available to all who have access to FOM's terminals or to the major international electronic information systems (Reuters, Telerate). In order to be able to resolve conflicting views relating to deal transactions, all telephone conversations involving block orders are recorded.

Clearing

Clearing has several functions:

- **FOM's clearing system guarantees the rights and obligations of all option and future contracts.**
- **Margining.**
- **Cash transactions.**
- **Risk management.**

All transactions update the position on a clearing account of the broker's customer, each of whom has a unique clearing account at the Finnish Options Market. Each customer is designated by an account code and only the broker knows the identity of the party behind the code. A broker who is connected to the electronic system via a terminal can constantly keep track of all changes in a customer's position and keep abreast of trades and quotes and other market information. On the morning following a trading day, every broker receives reports containing trade and position notifications pertaining to the broker's overall account and to the broker's individual customer accounts.

Guarantee Function

FOM is a party to each traded contract, acting as a seller with respect to the buyer and as a buyer with respect to the seller, provided that they agree on the same price and quantity. Through its margin system, and ultimately through its own capital resources, FOM guarantees the rights and obligations of each option and future contract, assuring that every market participant will be able to exercise his rights. Since FOM is a party to each contract, the buyer and seller have no rights or obligations with respect to one another, but only with respect to FOM. FOM may not have a position of its own.

Margin Requirement

FOM specifies daily the amount of margin each customer must provide on a position notice. FOM calculates the amount of margin required based on the position on each account using a risk management model. FOM requires sellers of options and buyers and sellers of futures to deposit the required margin in a custodian bank approved by FOM. Should the custodian bank inform FOM's clearing facility that the margin placed is inadequate, the broker is required to furnish the balance.

The basic principle of FOM's margining system is to be able to close the position on an account with the required margin. The closing value of a position is based on parameters which reflect unfavourable changes in market conditions. In estimating the closing value of a position, FOX index options are priced using the Black-76 option pricing model for a number of different FOX index future values (at the moment 31) within a valuation interval. In addition, at each of these 31 valuation points, the option prices are calculated using 3 different volatility factors. To sum up; in the OPTIVA margin requirement model, options are valued on 93 (3 X 31) different alternative market situations.

In the OPTIVA model, FOX index futures are priced based on their theoretical value at a number of different FOX index points (31) within the valuation interval. The valuation interval, volatility factors and other parameters used in the OPTIVA model are fixed by the managing director of FOM. Currently, the low point of the valuation interval is roughly 18 per cent below the present FOX index and the high point about 13 per cent above.

When calculating the theoretical option and future prices, the OPTIVA model takes into account several other factors, such as whether options are bought or written.

For example, on July 4th the **FOX** index moved within 440 - 442 points (FIM 44,000 - 44,200). Writing a call option **FOXH440** (time to expiration 50 days) would have required a margin of FIM 7,000 (before rounding FIM 7,059) and writing a put with the same expiration date and striking price (**FOXT440**) similarly would have required a margin of FIM 7,000 (before rounding FIM 7,461). Of course, the closing value of a written call is calculated using the high point of the valuation interval and the closing value of a written put using the low point of the valuation interval.

If one had bought a **FOX** index futures (**FOXV**, time to expiration 113 days) at 439.50, one would have had to set up a margin of FIM 6,000. It has to be kept in mind that at **FOM**, **FOX** index futures are not marked to market daily except in margining and the cash flows due to a future transaction takes place on the expiration day.

Fees

FOM charges all fees from the broker and the broker, in turn, charges his clients.

Address

> Finnish Options Market
> Marketing and Information
> P.O. Box 926
> SF-00100 HELSINKI
> Finland

Tel: 358 0 13 12 11

Fax: 358 0 13 12 12 11

HISTORY of the MARKET

Date	
May 1988	Exchange Opens
May 1988	Introduction of FOX Index Futures & Options
October 1990	Introduction of Individual Stock Futures

OVERVIEW of PRODUCTS

	Futures	Options
Stock Index		
FOX 25	*	*
Individual stocks	*	

DETAILED CONTRACT SPECIFICATIONS
Stock Indexes
Finnish Options Index "FOX" Option Contract

The **FOX** Index includes the 25 most traded stocks of the Helsinki Stock Exchange during the past six months. (**FOX** = Finnish Options Index.) The Index is updated continuously and is restructured semiannually.

Option Style:	European calls and puts.
Contract Size:	Strike price X FIM 100.
Expiry Months:	Two and four month contracts with the expiry cycle of February April June August October December.
Expiry Day:	The fourth Friday of the expiry month.
Last Trading Day:	The trading day immediately prior to the expiration day.
Quotation:	Index price to two decimal prices.
Minimum Price Movement (Tick Size and Value):	0.05 index points = FIM 5.
Trading Hours:	Via telephone 10.00 a.m. - 15.30 p.m. and by electronic system 10.00 a.m. - 16.00 p.m. Helsinki time.
Initial Margin:	1.6% plus 0.9% settlement charge.
Price Limit:	No price limit.
Contract Standard:	Cash settlement five days after the expiry date based on the exercise settlement price.
Exercise Price:	Initially three contracts with exercise intervals of 20 index points.

Exchange Delivery Settlement Price:	The index value calculated on the last day of trading at 14.30 p.m..
Reuters Pages:	FOMA to FOMM.
Telerate Pages:	From page 20830.

The Finnish Options Index "FOX"
Introduction

The Finnish Options Index - **FOX** is a market value weighted share price index. It is computed on a continuous basis from the most recent prices of the 25 most traded shares on the Helsinki Stock Exchange. The stock series of the **FOX** index are checked semi-annually and are selected in ranked order from among the previous half year's daily median trades per stock series. This manner of selection ensures that the **FOX** index is composed of the stock exchange's liquid shares. Their share of the total trading on the Helsinki Stock exchange as well as of the market value is approximately 50 per cent. The index is computed by Suomen Optiomeklarit Oy (the Finnish Options Market, **FOM**) which functions as a neutral marketplace and clearing house for the trading of options. The **FOX** index is checked daily by having it computed fully and independently by a subsidiary of Elinkeinoelämän Tutkimuslaitos (The Research Institute of the Finnish Economy).

The base date for the **FOX** index is March 4th 1988. The market price level at the end of that day has given the index a value of 500. The **FOX** index reached its all time high of 697.69 on April 17th 1989. Since then, the index has fallen rapidly.

The **FOX** index shows a strong correlation with the Unitas index depicting the overall trend on the stock exchange and with the new HEX index. The standardized options and futures based on **FOX** are excellent choices for those international investors who wish to protect themselves against Finland's country risk or who wish to get their share of the income potential of Finnish stocks.

The value of the **FOX** index at any given time and the market prices of **FOX** options and futures as well as the statistics compiled on trading are all available on a real-time basis via Reuters (page **FOMA - FOMM**) and Telerate (starting from page 20830) The same information is also disseminated via **FOM**'s own SOMTEL data service system. The historic data on trading in standardized options and futures right from the beginning of trading are also available as microcomputer compatible electronic files.

Computation Rules Applying to FOX

Detailed computation rules for **FOX** are included in the **FOM** Product Specifications, Appendix 4. The following is a presentation of the fundamental principles involved.

Selection of Index Shares

The structure of the index is reformulated semi-annually. A new structure comes into force at the beginning of February and August. The stock series selected to form the index are the top 25 shares on the Helsinki Stock Exchange in terms of daily median trading during the previous half of the calendar year.

The above selection principle means that the **FOX** index is made up of the exchange's most liquid stocks. They are thoses that are traded daily or almost daily and this means that the index is based on the latest possible prices. Moreover, the liquidity of the shares in the **FOX** index basket also facilitates the arbitrage between the stock and derivative markets, thereby invigorating the functioning of the two markets.

Weighting of the Index

The **FOX** index is a market value weighted stock price index. The weight of each stock series is determined by the relative proportion of its market value in the total market value of all **FOX** index stocks. The weights of the stock series vary as the market prices of the shares change and as a result of adjustments to the index stock's numbers of shares.

The number of shares used to compute the market value are determined on a quarterly basis at the beginning of February, May, August and November. The February and August adjustments are carried out in conjunction with the changing of the basket. Nevertheless, the numbers of shares are adjusted in conjunction with subscription issues on the first day of the issues in order to take the resulting discontinuities properly into account. Consequently, the numbers of shares in an index basket is always fixed for three months at a time unless subscription issues are carried out during the period. Thus, with little difficulty, investors themselves are able to calculate and simulate the development of the index since the market price data is readily available. The regularly occurring adjustments to the numbers of shares ensure that the index basket correlates quite well with the structure of the markets. The weighting structure of the index, conforming with the basket, that came into force on August 1st 1990 is shown below.

Index Formula

The **FOX** index is calculated by dividing the market value of the index stocks at the moment t by their market value at moment t-1. When the market value ratio is used to multiply the index number at moment t-1, the result is the index number at moment t.

Subscription issues cause discontinuities in the stock prices, numbers of shares as well as in market values. if the current market value is calculated using the post-issue numbers of shares, then the sum of money invested by the shareholders must be added to the pre-issue market value. By doing this, it eliminates, in the ratio of market values, the increase in market value caused by the increase in the number of shares. What remains is the increase in the market value caused by changes in the prices of the stock series.

The Fox index formula is as follows:

$$l_t = \frac{\sum\limits_{i=1}^{25} P_{it} \times Q_{it}}{\sum\limits_{i=1}^{25} P_{i,t-1} \times Q_{i,t-1} + S_{it}} \times l_{t-1}$$

in which:

$l_t =$	**FOX** index number at moment t
$P_{it} =$	the most recent trading price of stock series i at moment t
$Q_{it} =$	the number of shares in stock series i
$P_{i,t-1} =$	the most recent trading price of stock series i at moment t-1
$Q_{i,t-1} =$	the number of shares in stock series i at moment t-1
$S_{it} =$	adjustment factor by means of which the increase in the market value caused by the stock issue is added to the pre-issue market value
$l_{t-1} =$	**FOX** index point at moment t-1

Example: Computation of the FOX on August 2, 1990 at 17.05.

Stock series (Reuters designation)	Number of shares	Trading Prices 01/08/90 @ 5.05 p.m.	Trading Prices 02/08/90 @ 5.05 p.m.
KOP	164,062,500	34.50	35.00
KOP F	21,875,000	47.90	47.50
UBF A	240,928,000	24.00	24.30
UBF B	50,400,000	13.80	13.80
UBF CF	28,872,110	26.40	26.50
POHJOLA B	12,014,821	54.10	55.00
POHJOLA BF	8,055,179	95.00	95.00
SAMPO A	8,940,000	403.00	402.00
KESKO	90,213,400	49.00	49.00
SPONTEL	48,048,587	30.80	30.50
KONE B	3,859,749	410.00	410.00
KONE BF	1,141,131	655.00	655.00
OUTOKUMPU	62,384,661	44.00	44.00
RAUTARUUKKI	87,281,500	27.30	27.00
ENSO RF	14,706,290	20.50	20.00
KYMMENE	67,083,072	82.00	80.00
KYMMENE F	14,916,928	84.00	83.50
AMER A	12,902,743	98.00	96.00

AMER AF	4,060,568	123.00	123.00
HUHTAMAK K	12,277,134	147.00	150.00
HUHTAM I	5,941,504	67.00	68.00
INSTRU A	5,034,150	270.00	275.00
NOKIA	35,065,488	84.00	83.00
NOKIA PF	6,388,156	92.00	94.00
PARTEK	31,949,341	123.00	127.00
Market Value		52,168,301,015	52,276,690,794
FOX Index		448.80	449.74

The above array shows the market prices of the **FOX** stocks at 17.05
p.m. on August 1st & August 2nd, 1990. The numbers of shares remained
unchanged and the adjustment factor is 0 as none of the index enterprises
issued new subscription rights. The **FOX** index on August 1st was 448.80. The
FOX index on August 2nd, 1990 is obtained by applying the formula:

$$l_t = 449.74 = \frac{52,276,690,794.50}{52,168,301,015.70} \times 448.80$$

Trading of stocks on the Helsinki Stock exchange ends at 17.05 p.m.
and this is the time when the most recent market prices of each stock can be
determined. The independent supervisor of the index computes the **FOX**
index each day on the basis of these market prices and checks that **FOM's**
continuous index has the same value. The computation of the index continues
in the morning of the next trading day on the Helsinki Stock Exchange at 09.00
a.m. from the index number checked in this manner.

Stock Issue Adjustment

In conjunction with subscription issues, a coupon is detached from the share. This coupon entitles the holder to subscribe for new shares either free of charge or at a price below the market price. This is why a market price develops for the subscription coupon and the price of the actual share falls abruptly.

With the FOX index, the first post-issue market value of a stock series is computed according to the post-issue number of shares and the exchange's post-issue market price in which investors have taken into account the effects of the issue. The sum of money invested in the company is added to the pre-issue market value, this sum being denoted by S in the index formula. By doing this, the effect of the additional insertion of capital from the change in market value is eliminated and what remains is the real change in price of the share.

The added number of shares resulting from the issue of stock is obtained by multiplying the former number of shares by a so-called stock issue factor. If the number of shares in a stock series had been, for example, 2,000,000 and the owner of two old shares could purchase one new share, then the post-issue number of shares would be 3,000,000. This is obtained as follows: 2,000,000 + ½*2,000,000.

The amount of money invested into a company in conjunction with a stock issue is calculated by multiplying the subscription price by the added number of shares. If the subscription price were FIM 50, then a total of FIM 50,000,000 would be invested in the company; i.e. FIM ½*2,000,000*50.

The stock issue adjustment is carried out in conjunction with a bonus issue, rights issue and the splitting of stock. The adjustment is made the moment the first post-issue trading price is obtained for the issued stock. In conjunction with the splitting of stock, the new number of shares is arrived at simply by multiply the old number of shares by the ratio of new shares to be obtained for one old share. In this case, the adjustment factor S to be added to the denominator in the index formula is equal to 0, because no subscription price is paid for the new shares.

The additions in the numbers of shares caused by directed stock issues and offer issues and corresponding issues such as warrants and convertible debentures are taken into account in connection with the quarterly checks on the number of shares.

The Effect of Dividends

FOX is a stock price index. The payment of dividends is not taken into account when computing the index. Once dividends begin to be paid out, the market price of the stock usually drops abruptly and this is also reflected in the index. During the spring of 1990, dividends caused a fall of approximately 17 points in the index. The dividends for the FOX stocks were paid out between early March and June, most of them before the expiration of the index options and futures for April.

Computation of the Index under Exceptional Circumstances

The continuous FOX index is computed on the basis of the most recent prices for actual trades. This rule is departed from when computing the index on the expiration date used in the exercising of standardized options and futures and in conjunction with changing the index when computing the most recent market prices of stock series being deleted from the index and the first market prices of those entering the index.

When the value of the index at expiration is being computed, the most recent market price for each stock series is obtained by using the mean market prices if the prices of electronic trading (09.00 a.m. - 14.35 p.m.) weighted by the traded volume. The index at expiration is computed from the market prices preceding the cash settlement of the net value.

In conjunction with the changing of the index, the most recent market price of the new stocks to be deleted from the index and the first market price of the new stocks are both computed during the last day of validity of the old index as mean values of the prices of electronic trading weighted by the traded volume.

The aim of these rules for exceptional situations is to ensure that, even on expiration days and during the changing of the index, the index will reflect only those factors that normally influence the prices of index stocks.

The independent supervisor of the FOX index also checks the changed index and the index at expiration. The index at expiration is checked and confirmed by FOM together with an index ombudsman whose task is to consult the option market in matters connected to the computation and development of the index.

Daily Volume and Open Interest (Jan 2, 1990 - Aug 28, 1990)

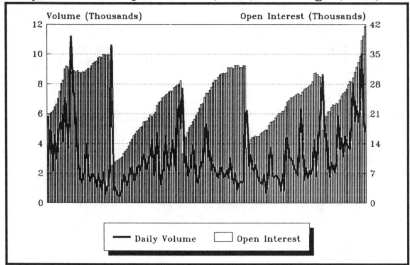

Open Interest and Volume/Open Interest("Liquidity")
(Jan 2, 1990 - Aug 28, 1990)

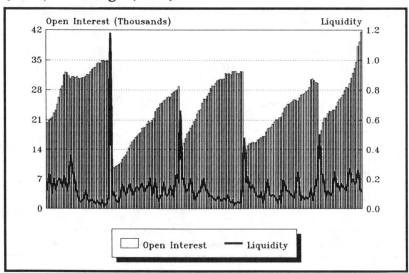

Value of FOX Index (Jan 2, 1990 - Aug 28, 1990)

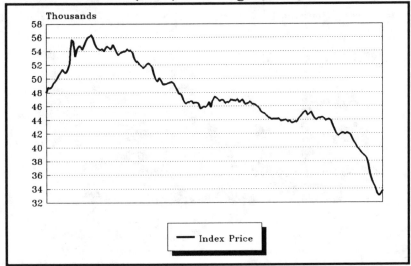

Implied and Historical Volatility (Jan 2, 1990 - Aug 28, 1990)

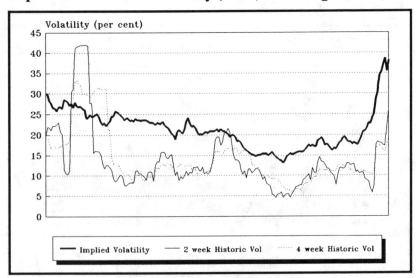

Finnish Options Index "FOX" Futures Contract

Contract Size:	Index value X FIM 100.
Expiry Months:	Two and four month contracts from the expiry cycle of February April June August October and December.
Expiry Day:	The fourth Friday of the expiry month.
Last Trading Day:	The trading day immediately prior to the expiry day.
Quotation:	Index price to two decimal prices.
Minimum Price Movement (Tick Size and Value):	0.05 index points = FIM 5.
Trading Hours:	Via telephone 10.00 a.m. - 15.30 p.m. and by electronic system 10.00 a.m. - 16.00 p.m. Helsinki time.
Initial Margin:	Contact **FOM** for further details.
Price Limit:	No price limit.
Contract Standard:	Cash settlement five days after the expiry date based on the exercise settlement price.
Exchange Delivery Settlement Price:	The index value calculated on the last day of trading at 14.30 p.m..
Reuters Pages:	FOMA to FOMM.
Telerate Pages:	From page 20830.

Daily Volume and Open Interest (Jan 2, 1990 - Aug 28, 1990)

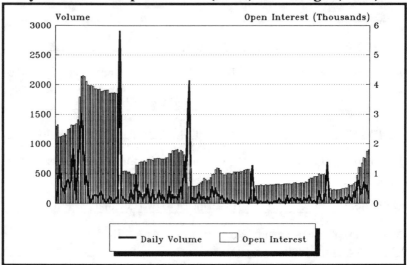

Open Interest and Volume/Open Interest("Liquidity")
(Jan 2, 1990 - Aug 28, 1990)

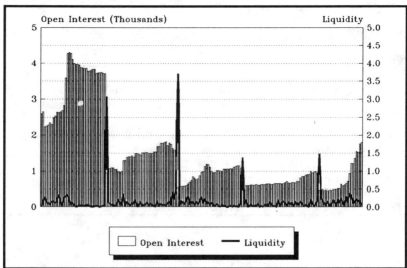

Price History of Contracts and Index
(Jan 2, 1990 - Aug 28, 1990)

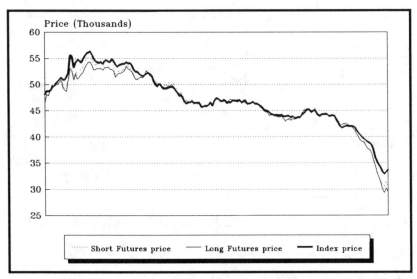

Implied Repo Rate (Jan 2, 1990 - Aug 28, 1990)

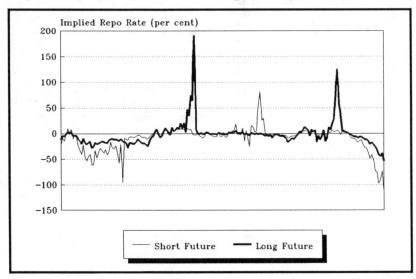

Individual Stocks

These contracts had only just opened for trading in October 1990.

Contract Size:	See list below.
Delivery Months:	The stock futures expire in even months. New series will be opened for trade so that there always will be the series of two four eight and twelve months open for trade.
Delivery Day:	The expiration day is the third Friday of the expiry month. If that day is not a trading day the stock futures will expire on the preceding day.
Last Trading Day:	The trading day prior to the expiration day.
Quotation:	The stock futures are quoted FIM per share.
Minimum Price Movement (Tick Size and Value):	See list below.
Trading Hours:	10.00 a.m. - 14.30 p.m.
Initial Margin:	A margin is required from both the buyer and the seller of stock futures. Security collateral is required from the seller of a stock futures contract. This security collateral shall be deposited before the tenth business day prior to expiry day. Contact **FOM** for further details.
Price Limit:	No price limit.

Position Limit:	The open interest of stock futures on one clearing account must not exceed five per cent of the number of the underlying shares and the open interest of all clearing accounts must not exceed fifteen per cent of the number of the underlying shares.
Contract Standard:	The stock futures will automatically be executed on the expiry date. there will be cash settlement of those stock futures on the clearing account of which there are offsetting amounts. Those in excess amounts will be exercised ny physical delivery of shares. In such cases the buyer of the future will receive the underlying shares in return for paying the agreed contract price. The seller of the future will receive the contract price in return for delivering the underlying shares. The contract price and/or the cash settlement amount shall be paid by the fifth banking day after expiry day.
Reuters Pages:	FOEA - FOEH.
Telerate Pages:	

Individual Stocks and Contract Sizes

Stock	Type	No.of shares
KOP	restricted	1,000
UBF A	restricted	1,000
Kesko Ltd	restricted	1,000
Kymmene Co	restricted	500
Partek Ltd	restricted	200

| Nokia Co | preferred
restricted | 200 |

SOURCES of INFORMATION
Distribution of Information

Brokers and market makers linked to the **FOM**'s computer system receive information on prices, quotes, positions, trading volumes, etc. in real time. Market information is also distributed to the market in real time through a number of other electronic information systems. (Reuters starting from page **FOMA** and Telerate starting from page 20830).

The prices of options and futures traded at Finnish Options Market are also published in leading Finnish newspapers.

Additional information

Additional information may be obtained from Finnish banks and brokerage companies or directly from **FOM**. For further information, please contact:

Address:	Finnish Options Market
	Marketing and Information
	P.O. Box 926
	SF-00100 HELSINKI
	Finland
Tel:	358 0 13 12 11
Fax:	358 0 13 12 12 11
Contact persons:	
Mr. Asko Schrey	President
Mr. Matti Byman	Vice President for Information, Marketing and Product Development

Finnish Options Exchange "FOE" - Oy Suomen Optiopörssi Finlands Optionsbörs AB

INTRODUCTION

The Finnish Options Exchange was established in 1987. It started trading stock index options in November 1987. Nowadays, the products include index options and futures, currency futures and options on currency futures.

ORGANIZATION of the MARKET

Shareholders

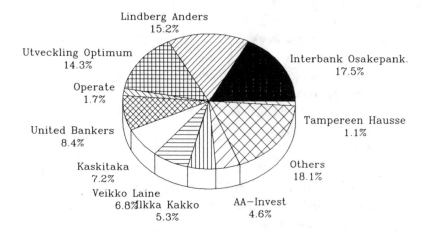

Interbank Osakepankki Oy Ltd	17.47%
Lindberg Anders	15.21%
Utveckling Ab Optimum	14.29%

Oy United Bankers	8.36%
Kastitaka Oy	7.21%
Veikko Laine Oy	6.79%
Ilkka Kakko	5.27%
AA-Invest Oy	4.55%
Operate Oy	1.67%
Tampereen Hausse Oy	1.06%

Principal Officers

Anders Lindeberg	Managing Director
Maija Mela	Company Lawyer
Carla Winkler	Chief Dealer
Barbro Sundholm	Administrative Manager

Members

ABB Aros Securities Oy

Evli-Optiot Oy

Pankkiiriliike Ane Gyllenberg Oy

Helsingfors Sparbank

Interbank Osakepankki Oy Ltd

Kanta-HämeenAluesäästöpankki

Optiopositio Oy

Pankkiriliike Erik Selin Oy

Pankkiriliike Protos Oy

Postipankki Oy

Servisen Arctos & Partners Oy

Skandinavian Optio ja Futuurivälittäjät Oy

SP-Suomalaisen Optio Oy

Oy United Rahoitus Ab

New members have to be approved by the Finnish Options Exchange.

Market Makers

Postipankki Oy

Servisen Arctos & Partners Oy

Skandinavian Optio ja Futuurivälittäjät Oy

Clearing

Structure

Integrated electronic batch system. All completed trades are entered
into the system after the trade has been executed.

Organization

All clearing takes place at the marketplace.

Transaction costs

Stock Index Options	
Options:	1.5% of premium - minimum FIM 8 per option.
	If broker is also market maker or transaction fees are over FIM 50 per month costs are: 0.9% of premium - minimum FIM 8 per option.
Futures:	FIM 30 per future.
Market maker:	FIM 15 per month if quoting 10 options FIM 10 per month if quoting 20 options.
US Dollar/Finnish Markka Currency Options	
Options:	1.5% of premium - minimum FIM 4 per option.
Futures:	FIM 20 per future.

Market maker:	0.5% of option premium FIM 5 per future.

Margining

The Finnish Option Exchange has created its own margin system. The system is based on a calculated market risk makes safe operations possible if all procedures are followed properly. The market risk is primarily estimated by two parameters, maximum movement of underlying in one day and the calculated volatility (standard deviation) of the underlying commodity.

Address

Suomen Optiopörssi Oy
Erottajankatu 11 B
00130 HELSINKI
FINLAND

Tel: 358 0 601499
Fax: 358 0 604442

OVERVIEW of PRODUCTS

The Finnish Option Exchange has index options and futures which based on 25 most traded stocks in the Helsinki Stock Exchange. They are European options and may not be exercised before expiry. FOE also has Finnish Markka/US Dollar currency options and futures which are American options as they can be exercised before expiry. Both index and currency options are trade by telephone at the moment, however, an electronic market is under development.

	Futures	Options
Stock Index		
SOP 25	*	*
Currency		
US Dollar/Finnish Markka	*	*

DETAILED CONTRACT SPECIFICATIONS
Stock Index
Suomen Optiopörssi "SOP" 25 Index Futures Contract

Contract Size:	Index value X 100.
Expiry Months:	Every second month beginning February.
Expiry Day:	Third Friday of the expiry month.
Last Trading Day:	The trading day before the expiry day.
Quotation:	FIM 100 times the price.
Minimum Price Movement (Tick Size and Value):	FIM 0.05 = FIM 5.
Trading Hours:	10.00 a.m. - 16.30 p.m.
Initial Margin:	15 per cent.
Price Limit:	No price limit.
Contract Standard:	Cash settlement.
Exchange Delivery Settlement Price:	
Reuters Pages:	SOPI & SOPJ.
Telerate Pages:	20947 & 20948.

Suomen Optiopörssi "SOP" 25 - Composition of Index

Stocks included during 1/8/1990 - 31/1/1991	Per cent
UBF A	10.99
KOP	10.76
Kymmene	10.59
Kesko	8.40
Partek	7.71
Sampo	6.83
Nokia K	5.60
Outokumpu	5.34
Rautaruukki	4.55
Huhtamäki K	3.50
Kone B	3.07
Spontel	2.82
Instrumentarium A	2.68
Kymmene F	2.41
Amer A	2.40
KOP F	1.99
UBF C F	1.48
Pohjola B F	1.49
Kone B F	1.42

UBF B	1.29
Pohjola B	1.24
Nokia P F	1.12
Amer A F	0.98
Huhtamäki I	0.76
Enso R F	0.55

Index stocks are to be checked the 1st of February and the 1st of August annually.

Daily Volume of Both Options & Futures (Jan 2, 1990 - Oct 19, 1990)

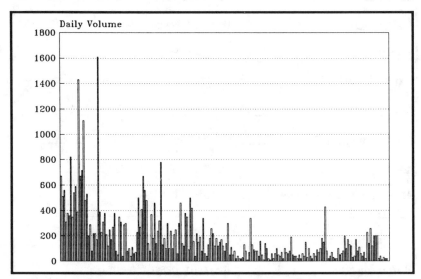

Price History of SOP 25 Index (Jan 2, 1990 - Oct 19, 1990)

Suomen Optiopörssi "SOP" 25 Index Options Contract

Option Style:	European calls and puts.
Contract Size:	Index value X 100.
Expiry Months:	Every second month beginning February.
Expiry Day:	Third friday of the month.
Last Trading Day:	The day before expiry day.
Quotation:	100 times index value.
Minimum Price Movement (Tick Size and Value):	FIM 0.05 = FIM 5.
Trading Hours:	10.00 a.m. = 16.30 p.m.
Initial Margin:	Delta factor based. 15 per cent.
Price Limit:	No price limit.
Contract Standard:	Cash settlement.
Exercise Price:	FIM 20 exercise intervals.
Exchange Delivery Settlement Price:	
Reuters Pages:	SOPI & SOPJ.
Telerate Pages:	20947 & 20948.

Currencies
US Dollar/Finnish Markka Futures Contract

Contract Size:	US$ 40,000.
Delivery Months:	March June September and December.
Delivery Day:	Thursday before third Wednesday of the month at 12.00 p.m. Helsinki time.
Last Trading Day:	Expiry day upto 12.00 p.m..
Quotation:	FIM per US$ to four decimal places.
Minimum Price Movement (Tick Size and Value):	0.05 Pn = FIM 20.
Trading Hours:	10.00 a.m. - 16.30 p.m.
Initial Margin:	7 per cent.
Price Limit:	No price limit.
Contract Standard:	Cash settlement.
Exchange Delivery Settlement Price:	
Reuters Pages:	SOPK SOPL SOPN SOPO.
Telerate Pages:	20949.

Daily Volume of Both Futures & Options
(Jan 2,1990 - Oct 19,1990)

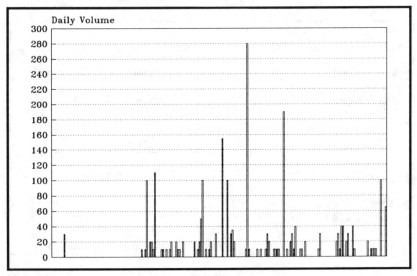

Price History (Jan 2,1990 - Oct 19,1990)

US Dollar/Finnish Markka Option Contract

Option type:	American calls and puts.
Contract Size:	US$ 40,000.
Delivery Months:	March June September and December.
Delivery Day:	Thursday before third Wednesday of the month at 12.00 p.m. Helsinki time.
Last Trading Day:	Expiry day upto 12.00 p.m..
Quotation:	FIM per US$ to four decimal places.
Minimum Price Movement (Tick Size and Value):	0.05 Pn = FIM 20.
Trading Hours:	10.00 a.m. - 16.30 p.m.
Initial Margin:	7 per cent.
Price Limit:	No price limit.
Exercise Prices:	Exercise intervals of FIM 0.10 per US $.
Contract Standard:	Cash settlement.
Exchange Delivery Settlement Price:	
Reuters Pages:	SOPK SOPL SOPN SOPO.
Telerate Pages:	20949.

SOURCES of INFORMATION
Last quotations and number of deals are sent by fax to the major
newspapers and to Startel, every day after trading.

LEGISLATION
The Act On Tarde in Standardized Options and Futures came into
force on November 1st, 1988. It is applied only to standardized derivative
instruments. All standardized instruments are traded on the option exchanges
and the terms of these instruments are defined in the regulations of the
options exchanges. Furthermore, the act is not applied to interbank trade
between banks and major companies or to over-the-counter (OTC) options
and futures agreements.

The Act On Tarde in Standardized Options and Futures lays down
that a license is required for the operation of an exchange serving as a trading
and clearing organization for derivative instruments. The act says also that
option exchanges, brokers and market makers are subject to supervision by
the Banking Supervision Office. Option exchanges are also required to draw
up rules for approval by the Ministry of Finance. The minimum share capital
requirement for a clearing organization is FIM 10.0 million.

Another act, the Securities Markets Act entered into force on August
1989. It also contains some general paragraphs concerning trading in standardized options and futures.

TAXATION
Stamp Duty
Foreign investors, who trade in the Finnish derivative markets, pay
the same stamp duty as the residents. It is 1 per cent of the premium and the
buyer pays it. When the contract is carried out, one must pay another 1 per
cent of the nett value.

Withholding, Income and Capital Gains Taxes for Foreign Investors
Foreign investors, non-residents, do not have to pay withholding tax,
income tax or capital gains tax in Finland. Finland usually has a double
taxation agreement with most countries.

Index

3 Months

90 Day

A

B

Bond Futures

D

E

European Options Exchange

F

France
   See MATIF
   See MONEP
   See OMF/France Matif Automatique
France Matif Automatique
   See OMF/France Matif Automatique
FOX
   See Finnish Options Index

G

H

I

IFOX
See Irish Futures & Options Exchange
Independent Clearing Member
Independent Floor Broker
Independent Floor Trader
Individual Clearing Member
Individual Bond Options
Individual Dutch Bond Options
Individual Dutch Stock Options
Individual Finnish Stock Futures
Individual Finnish Stock Options

Introduction

IPE

See International Petroleum Exchange "IPE"

Ireland

See Irish Futures & Options Exchange

Irish ISEQ Stock Index Future

Irish Pound/U.S. Dollar Future

J

K

M

N

P

Q

R

S

T

U

X

Z